On Writing Research:
The Braddock Essays
1975-1998

EDITORS OF
COLLEGE COMPOSITION AND COMMUNICATION

Charles W. Roberts
March 1950 – May 1952

George S. Wykoff
October 1952 – December 1955

Francis E. Bowman
February 1956 – December 1958

Cecil B. Williams
February 1959 – May 1959

Francis E. Bowman
October 1959 – October 1960

Cecil B. Williams
December 1960 – December 1961

Ken Macrorie
February 1962 – December 1964

William F. Irmscher
February 1965 – December 1973

Edward P. J. Corbett
February 1974 – December 1979

Richard L. Larson
February 1980 – December 1986

Richard C. Gebhardt
February 1987 – December 1993

Joseph Harris
February 1994 – December 1998

CONFERENCE ON COLLEGE COMPOSITION
AND COMMUNICATION CHAIRS

1949	John C. Gerber	1975	Lionel R. Sharp
1950	John C. Gerber	1976	Marianna W. Davis
1951	George S. Wykoff	1977	Richard Lloyd-Jones
1952	Harold B. Allen	1978	Vivian I. Davis
1953	Karl W. Dykema	1979	William F. Irmscher
1954	T. A. Barnhart	1980	Frank D'Angelo
1955	Jerome W. Archer	1981	Lynn Quitman Troyka
1956	Irwin Griggs	1982	James Lee Hill
1957	Francis Shoemaker	1983	Donald C. Stewart
1958	Robert E. Tuttle	1984	Rosentene B. Purnell
1959	Albert R. Kitzhaber	1985	Maxine Hairston
1960	Glen Leggett	1986	Lee Odell
1961	Erwin R. Steinberg	1987	Miriam T. Chaplin
1962	Frances E. Bowman	1988	David Bartholomae
1963	Priscilla Tyler	1989	Andrea A. Lunsford
1964	Robert M. Gorrell	1990	Jane E. Peterson
1965	Richard S. Beal	1991	Donald McQuade
1966	Gordon Wilson	1992	William W. Cook
1967	Richard Braddock	1993	Anne Ruggles Gere
1968	Dudley Bailey	1994	Lillian Bridwell-Bowles
1969	Wallace W. Douglas	1995	Jacqueline Jones Royster
1970	Ronald E. Freeman	1996	Lester Faigley
1971	Edward P. J. Corbett	1997	Nell Ann Pickett
1972	Elisabeth McPherson	1998	Cynthia L. Selfe
1973	James D. Barry	1999	Victor Villanueva
1974	Richard L. Larson		

On Writing Research

The Braddock Essays 1975-1998

edited by

Lisa Ede

OREGON STATE UNIVERSITY

Published in cooperation with the
Conference on College Composition and Communication
National Council of Teachers of English

BEDFORD / ST. MARTIN'S   Boston • New York

For Bedford/St. Martin's
Executive Editor: Marilyn Moller
Editorial Assistant: Eva Peck
Production Editors: Diana Puglisi and Jessica Zorn
Production Supervisor: Joe Ford
Marketing Manager: Karen Melton
Text and Cover Design: Anna George

President: Charles H. Christensen
Editorial Director: Joan E. Feinberg
Editor in Chief: Nancy Perry
Director of Editing, Design, and Production: Marcia Cohen
Managing Editor: Erica T. Appel

NCTE Stock No. 34580

Published in cooperation with the
Conference on College Composition and Communication
National Council of Teachers of English
1111 W. Kenyon Road
Urbana, Illinois 61801-1096
www.ncte.org

Library of Congress Catalog Card Number: 98-89302

Manufactured in the United States of America.

4   3   2   1   0   9
f   e   d   c   b   a

For information, write: Bedford/St. Martin's, 75 Arlington Street, Boston, MA 02116   (617-426-7440)

ISBN: 0-312-20264-4 (paperback)
          0-312-24350-2 (hardcover)

Acknowledgments
The essays in this volume were first published in *College Composition and Communication,* the journal of the Conference on College Composition and Communication. Copyright © 1975–1998 by the National Council of Teachers of English. Reprinted with permission.

Richard Braddock's essay first appeared in *Research in the Teaching of English.* Copyright © 1974 by the National Council of Teachers of English. Reprinted with permission.

FOR

EDWARD P. J. CORBETT
October 19, 1919–June 24, 1998

JIM W. CORDER
September 25, 1929–August 29, 1998

SCHOLARS, MENTORS, FRIENDS

A NOTE FROM
THE PUBLISHER

Bedford/St. Martin's is pleased to join with the National Council of Teachers of English to publish *On Writing Research: The Braddock Essays, 1975–1998* in recognition of the fiftieth anniversary of the Conference on College Composition and Communication. This book celebrates the field of rhetoric and composition by collecting some of the most honored texts of the discipline and providing an occasion for the authors of these texts to reflect upon them. In so doing, it presents the opportunity to revisit some of the important ideas in the field—and to consider where the discipline has been, where it is now, and where it might go in the future.

We are most grateful to Lisa Ede for editing this book, and we think that her thoughtful introduction, "Reading—and Rereading—the Braddock Essays," will help us all to do just that. Indeed, Lisa Ede is the perfect editor for this volume, having been a student of the discipline for some twenty years now and having spent the last several years studying the relationship between theory and practice in our field.

Her introduction, together with new afterwords contributed by the writers, make *On Writing Research* much more than a commemorative volume. We hope that it will be a useful—and even provocative—addition to the ongoing conversations and dialogues that characterize the field of composition and rhetoric. All of us at Bedford/St. Martin's are proud to be a part of this field—and a part of these conversations.

PREFACE

*O**n** Writing Research: The Braddock Essays, 1975–1998* celebrates the fiftieth anniversary of the Conference on College Composition and Communication by reprinting all of the essays honored by the CCCC's Braddock Award. As recipients of this annual award, these essays have been recognized for contributing significantly to research on the teaching of writing. The Braddock essays are of substantial interest, then, for their content—for what they *say* about such topics as the writing process, revision, teacher education, basic writing, etc. They are of interest as well for the methodologies they employ—from historical research to textual, rhetorical, empirical, and multimodal analysis.

On Writing Research includes more than just the Braddock essays. It is enriched first of all by new commentaries written for this collection by the authors of the Braddock essays (or in the case of Richard Braddock and Jim W. Corder, by those who knew them and their work well). It includes as well an introductory essay in which I attempt to look at the Braddock essays not just as exemplary research studies on writing but for what they can reveal about the development of composition studies as a scholarly discipline. *On Writing Research* thus provides an opportunity for readers to consider the costs as well as the benefits of disciplinarity and the relationship between theory and practice in a field committed to pedagogical as well as scholarly action. My hope is that this book will help us all to consider where the field of composition has been and where it might or could be going. *On Writing Research* invites readers—whether experienced teachers or graduate students—to consider the rhetoric, politics, and ethics of the scholarly work of composition.

ACKNOWLEDGMENTS

On Writing Research grows out of—and, I hope, reflects—my years of work in the field of composition studies. Over the years, many persons have encouraged and supported me in this work. I came to composition as an academic field in the mid-1970s, a time when a perceived literacy crisis provided expanded professional opportunities for those interested in studying and teaching writing. As a graduate student at Ohio State University, I worked with a group of teachers and fellow students whose commitment to the teaching of writing both inspired me and demonstrated in the most forceful manner how intellectually challenging and rewarding the work of composition—work at that time generally devalued within English studies—could be. I would like here to acknowledge this support and encouragement.

I never studied with Susan Miller or Edward P. J. Corbett—not formally at least—but I learned with and from them. Susan and Ed were generous and supportive mentors. Others in the Ohio State Ph.D. program also encouraged and inspired me. There are many I could name here, but I want to acknowledge the particularly important role that three close friends—Andrea Lunsford, Suellynn Duffey, and Elizabeth Flynn—have played in my professional and personal life.

As a participant in Richard Young's 1979–80 NEH seminar, I entered another community. When I think of that time, I realize the importance of the intense personal and intellectual friendships I experienced with my colleagues in the seminar: Sharon Bassett, James Berlin, David Fractenberg, Bill Nelson, Robert Inkster, Charles Kneupper, Sam Watson, Victor Vitanza, and Victoria Winkler. These friendships enabled me to take intellectual and professional risks I might not otherwise have ventured. I miss our times together, and I miss the presence of Jim, Bill, and Charles.

Many, many others have played crucial roles in my twenty-five years in the profession. I have taught in two English departments—SUNY Brockport and, since 1980, Oregon State University—with colleagues who have in general endeavored to resist conventional hierarchies of knowledge that privilege literature over writing. In each department, two chairs (Bob Gemmett and Paul Curran at SUNY Brockport, Robert Frank and Robert Schwartz at OSU) have gone out of their way to support my teaching, research, and writing program administration and to value the pedagogical, administrative, and scholarly work of composition. Over the years I have worked with many colleagues in rhetoric and composition—Chris Anderson, Suzanne Clark, Vicki Collins, Moira Dempsey, Cheryl Glenn, Anita Helle, Jon Olson, Lex Runciman, Simon Johnson, Roberta Sager, and Matt Yurdana—who have taught me what it means to collaborate in a supportive, productive fashion.

On Writing Research has brought another opportunity for collaboration. This project would not have been possible without the intellectual and professional support of Marilyn Moller at Bedford/St. Martin's. Marilyn is an editor's editor, and in my work on this project I have benefitted from her experience and advice in countless ways. Marilyn is deeply committed to and knowledgeable about the scholarly work of composition, and it has been a privilege to collaborate with her on this project.

Others at Bedford/St. Martin's have played key roles in making this book possible. I would especially like to acknowledge the work of Eva Peck, who's been a knowledgeable, patient, and supportive editor, and of Diana Puglisi and Jessica Zorn, whose attention to detail and thoughtfulness have made such a difference. I thank Anna George for the beautiful book design.

And for generous support of this project, I thank Chuck Christensen, Joan Feinberg, and Nancy Perry.

The authors of the Braddock essays of course played key roles in making *On Writing Research* possible. Presented with tight deadlines, they responded with professionalism and flexibility, and their afterwords substantially enrich the collection. Equally generous with their time and energy were Keith Miller and Richard Lloyd-Jones, who wrote commentaries to accompany Richard Braddock's and Jim Corder's essays. Composing these afterwords must have been a difficult and emotionally charged task; I am grateful for their effort.

Those who embark upon collections of essays know how time-consuming and demanding such projects can be—and how the encouragement and support of friends and colleagues can make all the difference. I thank Vicki Collins, Cheryl Glenn, Anita Helle, and Andrea Lunsford. Several times as I worked on this project I emailed Robert Connors with a query about the early years of the CCCC; I'd like to thank him for his quick and thorough responses. Peter Caster took time from his busy teaching and writing schedule to do the index and also to respond to a draft of the introduction. And I want to acknowledge the essential role that Saundra Mills, secretary at Oregon State University's Center for Writing and Learning, played from start to finish of this project. With efficiency and flexibility—and most importantly of all cheerfulness and good will—Saundra helped move this project forward.

I would also like to acknowledge the support of my university for *On Writing Research*. A fellowship at OSU's Center for the Humanities provided the time necessary to think long and hard about the professionalization of composition as an academic discipline. OSU's Research Council and Library Travel grants enabled me to travel to the headquarters of the National Council of Teachers of English to do archival research on the early years of the CCCC. A number of staff members at NCTE helped me to research this topic, including Debbie Fox, Cherie Cameron, and Edith Smith.

Finally, I would like to (but cannot adequately) thank my husband, Gregory Pfarr. Greg and I met at just about the same time that I was mulling over the question of whether the commitment I felt to the work of composition might take on a scholarly, as well as a pedagogical, life. My artist friend, and later husband, helped convince me of the power (and multiple meanings) of the word "composition." For twenty-five years we have composed a life together—and for that I am most grateful of all.

On Writing Research is dedicated to the memory of Edward P. J. Corbett and of Jim W. Corder. Both have been role models not only for me but for many, and both gave selflessly to several generations of scholars. They are and will continue to be missed.

I never met Richard Braddock, but those who did know him and worked with him speak compellingly of his commitment to the field of composition, to his power as a person, and to his generosity. The Braddock Award stands as a testimony to his many contributions to research on writing, and to the field.

Lisa Ede
Oregon State University

CONTENTS

On Writing Research:
The Braddock Essays
1975-1998

Conference on College Courses in Communication

February 28 – March 1, 1947 — Stevens Hotel — Chicago

Friday, 9:30 a.m. — *Content and General Method*

Hosts, the cooperating committees of the Speech Association of America and the National Council of Teachers of English

Glowing Ideals and Tough Realities in Communication Skills Courses – LENNOX GREY, Teachers College

Reading, Speaking, and Writing – J. HOOPER WISE, University of Florida

A Basic Communication Course – WILSON B. PAUL, University of Denver

Friday, 2 p.m. — *Selection and Training of Staff*

Chairman, GLEN E. MILLS, Northwestern University

Who Should Teach Communication? – PORTER G. PERRIN, Colgate University

In-Service Training of Teachers – CLYDE W. DOW, Michigan State College

Saturday, 9:30 a.m. — *Testing and Evaluation*

Chairman, EDWARD A. TENNEY, Ripon College

Evaluating a Course in Terms of Students' Needs – WESLEY WIKSELL, Stephens College

A Testing Program – JOHN C. GERBER, State University of Iowa

Practical Principles and Procedures for Testing the Communication Skills – FRANKLIN H. KNOWER, Ohio State University

Saturday, 2 p.m. — *Administration of Courses*

Chairman, PAUL D. BAGWELL, Michigan State College

In a Liberal Arts College – WRIGHT B. THOMAS, Grinnell College

In a University – HAROLD B. ALLEN, University of Minnesota

Time is provided for discussion following the speakers at each session.

COMMITTEE OF THE SAA:	COMMITTEE OF THE NCTE:
Paul D. Bagwell, Chairman	John C. Gerber
Donald C. Bryant	Lennox Grey
Franklin H. Knower	Porter G. Perrin, Chairman
Glen E. Mills	
Wesley A. Wiksell	

READING —
AND REREADING —
THE BRADDOCK ESSAYS

still remember the moment in the summer of 1995 when I encountered the single sheet of paper on the facing page. I was sitting in the small library at the headquarters of the National Council of Teachers of English (NCTE), looking through boxes of archival materials. For what? At the time I didn't quite know. All I knew was that I wanted to gain a richer understanding of the development of composition studies as an academic discipline. I had come to NCTE headquarters interested in—I might even say obsessed with—such issues as the consequences of professionalization for the field and the rhetoric, politics, and ethics of its scholarly practices. For reasons that this essay I hope will clarify, then, as now, I have been concerned with the question of what constitutes disciplinary progress in a field committed to pedagogical, as well as scholarly, action. Before traveling to the NCTE, I had spent a good deal of time reading, thinking, and even upon occasion writing about these issues.[1] But as I did so I was aware of the extent to which my own lived history within the field inevitably influenced my understanding. What I needed, I felt, were different histories, different frameworks and perspectives. The NCTE archives seemed a good place to start.

The sheet of paper before me then, the one-page program for the 1947 Conference on College Courses in Communication—a conference that preceded the formation of the Conference on College Composition and Communication (CCCC) by two years—certainly provided a jolt. The contrast between that program's brevity and singular focus on pedagogy with the elaborate and highly specialized programs of the Conference on College Composition and Communication was a striking reminder of how much our field has changed in five brief decades.

Of course I was already aware that the CCCC, like the field of composition studies, had changed over the years. When I began attending the CCCC in the mid–1970s, for instance, the conference was not only much smaller but less formal as well. Only in 1979 did then–program chair Lynn Quitman Troyka institute a proposal process for those wishing to present at the annual conference. Previous program chairs had relied upon informal communications between those wishing to present papers and the program chair. Those who have entered the field in recent years, and who thus take multipart proposal forms and fierce competition for speaking roles at the conference for granted, may find it hard to imagine that as recently as twenty years ago someone wishing to present at the CCCC could simply drop a line to the program chair indicating a willingness to serve.

The CCCC turned fifty in 1999. As Keith Gilyard, 1999 program chair, observes in his call for program proposals, "At the age of fifty, people ought to be able to give an account of themselves—or at least not be surprised if asked to do so" (1). And so, Gilyard implies, should professional organizations and their membership. The publication of the Braddock essays in *On Writing Research: The Braddock Essays, 1975–1998* provides an opportunity for one such accounting.

To understand the importance of the Braddock Award and the role it has played in the field of composition studies, some background may be helpful. The CCCC was founded in 1949, and from its inception through 1974 it—unlike many similar professional organizations—had no means of recognizing exemplary research. In 1975, the CCCC established the Richard Braddock Award in honor of Richard Braddock, founder of the journal *Research in the Teaching of English*. His essay "The Frequency and Placement of Topic Sentences in Expository Prose" was the first essay honored by the award.[2] The CCCC now grants six annual awards, four of which were instituted in the early 1990s.[3] But from 1975 until 1982, when the CCCC established an award for an outstanding essay published in *Teaching in the Two-Year College*, the Braddock Award represented the sole opportunity for scholarly work in the field of composition studies to be recognized by its major professional association.

Because it was the first award recognizing scholarly work for the field—and because it was the sole award during the years from 1975 to 1982, when the field had the disciplinary equivalent of a growth spurt—the Braddock Award played a central role in representing the scholarly aspirations of those in the field. Readers will find, I believe, that in many ways the essays compiled in *On Writing Research* reflect well upon these aspirations. Anyone familiar with research in the field who scans the list of Braddock Award essays will certainly recognize efforts that in pivotal ways defined or extended the scholarly project of composition. Collectively, the Braddock essays provide important, and at times foundational, explorations of such topics as revision, basic writing, discourse theory, the writing process, teacher education, and rhetorical history. The Braddock essays are of interest as well for the methodologies that various essays employ—from historical research to textual, rhetorical, empirical, and multimodal analysis. In addition, *On Writing Research* includes afterwords by the authors of the Braddock essays (or, in the case of deceased authors, by colleagues who knew them and their work well). Although relatively brief, the afterwords raise a panoply of issues and questions, as the following excerpts from these commentaries suggest:

[T]he recent resurgence of rhetorical studies hasn't so much been a discovery of new rhetorics; it has been a recognition of already/always rhetorical activities, of our new-found ability and willingness to listen to unheard and untold stories: feminist, womanist, activist, religious, medical, African American, Native American, Hispanic, and Asian rhetorics, for example.

– CHERYL GLENN

Specific theories and practices of our discipline will come and go. The one thing that does not change is our obligation to draw on the lived experience of teaching and learning as we test, refine, and sometimes reject the innovations that will continue to come our way.

– LEE ODELL

If I were to write "Responding to Student Writing: Part Two," I would try to write less in the voice of a self-righteous researcher, pointing her finger at her fellow teachers, and more like a fellow teacher. For it is as a teacher that I am curious about the ways in which students read and interpret my comments, why they find some comments useful, others distracting, and how these comments work together with the lessons of the classroom.

– NANCY SOMMERS

Perhaps the field of composition *is* mainly pedagogical? Whatever the case, what is the role of a scholarly component? I think we do not have clear answers to these questions.

– GLEN MATOTT

We need to study the micropolitics of actual classrooms: how new perspectives come into play or get shut down; how student writings repeat, contest, parody, or transform the ideas and phrasings of their books and teachers.

– JOSEPH HARRIS

The past decade has seen a significant shift in composition studies toward social and political analysis, providing much-needed awareness of the broad contexts that inform writing and writing instruction. The concern we have is how to continue to develop ways to fuse social analysis with close examination of language used in complex settings that people inhabit. Such a development could move us beyond the current "theory" vs. "empiricism" divide and into generative paradox: What might a critical empiricism look like? Is a data-driven post-post-structuralist theory possible?

– GLYNDA HULL AND MIKE ROSE

I now see the Braddock Award given to "The Modes" as an early signal of the growth of historical consciousness in the rapidly organizing field of composition studies.

– ROBERT CONNORS

Much has happened in the teaching of writing and literature since 1976 that suggests that our earlier emphasis on structure and sequence may have been misguided and naïve. Yet I see signs as we move beyond postmodernism that we are entering a new era of structural transformations and relationships, convergences, and commonalities in the attention being paid to postcolonial and world literatures, global culture, and cosmopolitanism.

— FRANK D'ANGELO

In their afterwords, the authors of the Braddock essays contextualize and extend their earlier work. Many contributors, particularly those whose essays appeared some time ago, take this opportunity to consider the extent to which their understanding of their subject has evolved in subsequent years. Some comment on research trends in the field. Others situate their essays and the Braddock Award in their personal and professional lives at the time, and since. And still others call attention to the need for a cautious and situated assessment of the significance of the Braddock Award itself. In writing about their 1989 essay, for instance, Christina Haas and Linda Flower observe that:

> . . . one of the dangers inherent in this kind of reflective exercise is a tendency to overlay a developmental narrative, a narrative only available in hindsight, onto one's own work or onto the work of the discipline as a whole. We have tried to avoid the temptation to see the "event" of our Braddock essay as part of a narrative of linear development and thereby avoid the teleology that that kind of narrative implies.

I share Haas and Flower's concern, and I do so for several reasons. It is important, first of all, to acknowledge the element of serendipity in the decision-making process that results in a CCCC appointed committee recognizing one essay (and not another) with the Braddock Award. Equally important is the recognition of the extent to which the Braddock essays are situated in particular disciplinary, cultural, and social contexts. An essay that won the award in the 1990s might literally have been unpublishable in the 1970s, and vice versa.[4] Each Braddock essay narrates a particular moment in the development of composition studies as a discipline—but the significance of that moment is multiple and overdetermined (is intertwined, for instance, in personal, social, and institutional as well as professional contexts) and thus not subject to a single or univocal reading. Nor, I would hasten to add, can the collection of moments that the Braddock essays comprise be similarly read. Though judged exemplary at particular moments in time, the Braddock Award essays do not chart a univocal evolutionary narrative of scholarly progress or any other univocal narrative.

The reprinting of the Braddock essays here is intended not as a paean to progress in the field of composition studies but rather as an opportunity for reflection and inquiry—for asking hard but important questions. In the afterword to our essay, for instance, Andrea Lunsford and I call attention to the extent to which any marking of "success," whether personal or professional, is charged with tensions and competing motives. In the case of the Braddock Award one useful way to begin unpacking these tensions might be to think about the audiences which it, like any award, "not only address and invoke but exclude, ignore, or transform." Such an effort calls for as much attention to absences as well as presences in the Braddock essays, to what is not said or not represented as well as to that which appears on the page.

It also calls for attention to the complexities and tensions inherent in references to the "discipline" or "profession" of composition studies, and to the relationship between theory and practice in the field. For the professionalization of composition studies as an academic discipline has brought higher status and better working conditions to some—but by no means all—of those engaged in the work of composition. Indeed, as Anne Ruggles Gere observes in "The Long Revolution in Composition," many large writing programs today replicate a "hierarchical relationship between tenured and relatively well paid WPAs and the nontenure-track instructors whom they supervise," one that evokes the hierarchy between literature and composition that so many in composition studies have lamented (126).

What *is* the significance of the Braddock Award and the award-winning essays given, for instance, the working conditions of most teachers of writing? In their afterword, Arnetha Ball and Ted Lardner articulate the hope that "the work for which we have won this award might affect the teaching of composition and the lives of real students within composition classrooms." When they think about the material conditions that obtain in many colleges and universities, however, Ball and Lardner see little likelihood of such a consequence:

> Imagine a writing program at a modestly sized midwestern urban university. In a typical semester, sixty-nine sections of various first-year writing courses will be taught by a mix of full-time faculty and part-timers. Among the teachers who will staff these sections, perhaps two subscribe to CCC. No one, no one here has read our article. No one knows what the Braddock Award is. Furthermore, here the prevailing attitude toward first-year writing is the usual: Faculty and administrators love the credit hours it generates but hold their noses when they must teach it.

Ball and Lardner's observations raise additional questions. What can and should count for disciplinary progress in a field committed to pedagogical, as well as scholarly and professional action? To what extent have composition studies' claims for legitimation in the academy depended upon an unproblematized understanding of the relationship between theory and practice, one that assumes that scholars in the field can and will provide authoritative pedagogical knowledge for the practitioners who teach the majority of composition courses?

These are questions generally not posed in the Braddock essays—yet the essays nevertheless provide a rich resource for exploring these and related concerns. For in addition to their considerable significance as explorations of the writing process, revision, basic writing, rhetorical history, and other subjects, the Braddock essays also serve as textual and professional artifacts that can be read for traces of their situatedness in particular times and particular (disciplinary) places. It is such a reading that I propose to undertake in this introduction. I hope in the pages that follow to call attention to the multiple ways that the Braddock essays can be situated within ongoing research, teaching, and writing program administration in the field of composition studies. I will be reading the Braddock essays—but I will be reading them, as Emily Dickinson would say, "slant."

My goal is to situate the essays in contexts that will generate heuristic questions about the disciplinary work of composition. I have found it helpful, for instance, to examine the Braddock essays in light of the aspirations of those who played central roles in the early years of the CCCC. Such an examination calls attention to anxieties and expectations that I believe still circulate within composition studies, though in muted and variant forms. I consider the first five Braddock essays in some detail, looking in particular at the ways in which they reflect these anxieties and expectations, and I discuss some of the debates that circulate in and around later essays. Such discussion necessarily focuses upon the content of various Braddock essays—on the positions they explicitly avow or resist—so I then shift strategies and attempt to read the essays not for what they *say* but for what they *do* or *enact* at the level of discursive practice. Continuing this effort to read the Braddock essays "slant," I next look at the essays in the context of other documents of our field—CCCC resolutions on various subjects, proposal forms for the annual conference, CCCC chairs' addresses, and surveys of the development of Ph.D. programs in composition. In these and other ways I hope to raise questions that those committed to the work of composition can consider as the CCCC embarks on its next fifty years.

I. Anxieties and Expectations: The Early Years of the CCCC

In the first issue of *College Composition and Communication* (March 1950), the quarterly bulletin of the newly formed CCCC, John C. Gerber, who served as the first chair, introduces the association with these words:

> Someone has estimated that there are at least nine thousand of us teaching in college courses in composition and communication. Faced with many of the same problems, concerned certainly with the same general objectives, we have for the most part gone our separate ways, experimenting here and improvising there. Occasionally we have heard that a new kind of course is working well at Upper A. & M. or that a new staff training program has been found successful at Lower T. C. But we rarely get the facts. We have had no systematic way of exchanging views and information quickly. Certainly we have had no means of developing a coordinated research program.
>
> To meet such obvious needs the Conference on College Composition and Communication has been formed. (12)[5]

After describing the organization of the CCCC and its status within NCTE, Gerber closes his discussion by reemphasizing the pragmatic orientation of the association:

> We believe that the activities of this new organization are aimed at prac-
> tical needs in the profession, that the standards of the profession will be
> raised because of them. We hope that you and others from your institu-
> tion will join the CCCC, not because we are after a large membership as
> such but because we want your information and ideas in exchange for
> our own. (12)

As Nancy K. Bird emphasizes in her 1977 dissertation on the development of the CCCC, the post–World War II boom in university enrollments,
which brought not only increased numbers of students to college campuses
but increasingly diverse students as well, lent particular force and urgency to
Gerber's words. As Bird argues, and as more recent work by Richard Lloyd-
Jones, Sharon Crowley, and Robert J. Connors confirms, in response to these
and other educational (and social and cultural) changes, many involved with
the teaching of first-year writing felt a strong need for curricular reform. One
such effort brought the institution of what at the time were called basic communication or communication skills courses—courses that combined instruction in first-year writing and public speaking.

In *Composition in the University: Historical and Polemical Essays*, Sharon
Crowley observes that "it is no accident that the founding of the Conference
on College Composition and Communication followed hard upon the advent
of communication skills programs" (181). According to Crowley, the development of such courses called attention to the unpreparedness of the graduate students and instructors who typically taught required first-year writing
classes. When such teachers taught traditional writing classes, they could
(appropriately or not) draw at least in part upon their literary training. Such
was not the case with communication skills classes. Moreover, "full-time
tenured academics were in charge of designing and administering the required first-year course for the first time since the late nineteenth century"
(182). These new program directors instituted regular staff meetings, which
raised additional questions about and opportunities for first-year writing
programs—and these in turn stimulated a desire on the part of program administrators to talk with others who shared their situation and interests.
"Hence," Crowley observes, "a professional organization was born" (182).

That birth is described by Richard Lloyd-Jones in his 1992 *CCC* essay,
"Who We Were, Who We Should Become":

> The Conference on College Composition and Communication began in
> Chicago in the Fall of 1948 simply as another session for the college
> people at the annual NCTE convention. The folks who came to that
> meeting were pressed by what seemed to be a crisis and wanted to have
> practical talk about how to deal with a flood of new students—many of
> whom were first-generation college students, most somewhat older vet-
> erans. . . . In a single year—1946—college enrollments had doubled. . . .

> Survival under the mob of students required that colleges develop "pro-
> grams" with administrative conveniences, like placement and exemp-
> tion tests. That is, new quasi-administrators had to solve unfamiliar
> problems. They came to their NCTE session in desperate need of help
> and wanted to keep raising problems and solutions indefinitely. They
> were persuaded to quit only when the program chair . . . agreed to orga-
> nize a Spring meeting in Chicago to continue the discussion. These were
> not people trying to get ahead in academic hierarchies; they wanted
> help in dealing with what was often described as a short-term enroll-
> ment problem. Not high theory, but practical need brought them to-
> gether. (487)[6]

Although those involved in the CCCC recognized from the start the need to
develop a scholarly body of research on the teaching of writing, the most urgent concerns of those who worked to establish this association were curricular and administrative.[7]

These concerns are evident in the program of the Conference on College
Freshman Courses in Composition and Communication held on April 1–2,
1949 at the Stevens Hotel in Chicago and attended by over five hundred
people. (Invitations to the meeting had been sent to all two- and four-year
colleges in Minnesota, Wisconsin, Iowa, Missouri, Illinois, Kentucky, Ten-
nessee, Indiana, Michigan, and Ohio.[8]) The conference, which was sponsored
by NCTE, was designed as a series of general sessions. Topics included
"Concepts Basic to Freshman Courses in Composition and Communication,"
"Curriculum: Four Theories of Course Organization," "The Needs and Possibilities for Research," "Integrating High School and College Work," "Instructional Methods," "Business Meeting," and "Obtaining, Training, and Keeping a Competent Staff." On the second day of the conference, during a lunch
meeting of directors of first-year writing programs, this group asked John
Gerber to request permanent status for the conference within NCTE. On November 23, 1949, the NCTE Executive Committee agreed to recognize the
CCCC for three years with certain provisions, such as the requirement that
CCCC members must also be members of NCTE, that the NCTE Executive
Committee must approve the editorial board of the periodical the conference
wished to publish, etc.[9] Two days later, at an organizational lunch for those
involved with writing programs during the NCTE annual conference, the
fifty-five persons present voted to accept the Executive Committee's proposal and elected its first slate of officers: chairman, John C. Gerber, University of Iowa; secretary, George S. Wykoff, Purdue University; and editor,
Charles W. Roberts, University of Illinois.

The first official Conference on College Composition and Communication took place in 1950 at the Stevens Hotel in Chicago. Those attending the
conference appeared to see themselves primarily as sharing an interest in a
particular course, first-year English, and in the professional status and conditions of those who taught this course. This vision is reflected in the conference program. On the facing page is an illustration of a conference advertise-
ment that ran in the very first issue of *CCC*. Although conflicts inevitably

The 1950 Spring Meeting
(Open to anyone interested)

SPONSOR: the Conference on College Composition and Communication.

DATES: March 24–25, 1950.

PLACE: Stevens Hotel, Chicago. Write to hotel for room reservations.

SESSIONS:
1. Three general sessions for everyone . . . nationally known speakers like Rudolf Flesch (*The Art of Readable Writing,* etc.), Kenneth Burke (*The Philosophy of Literary Form,* etc.)

2. Fourteen workshops for those who register in advance. Write to Wallace Douglas, Northwestern University, Evanston, Illinois, indicating first, second, and third choice.

    1. The Function of the Composition Course in General Education

    2. The Function of the Communication Course in General Education

    3. Objectives and Organization of the Composition Course

    4. Objectives and Organization of the Communication Course

    5. Grammar in the Freshman Course

    6. Semantics in the Freshman Course

    7. Reading and Grading Themes

    8. Construction and Use of Objective Tests

    9. Organization and Use of Writing Laboratory

    10. Organization and Use of a Reading Clinic

    11. Freshman English for Engineers

    12. Articulating High School and College Work

    13. Administration of the Composition Course

    14. Administration of the Communication Course

3. Three discussion meetings for those not attending workshops: Individualization of training, the use of audio-visual aids, the application of the principles of group dynamics to the freshman course.

REGISTRATION FEE: one dollar, payable at the time of the conference.

WHO MAY COME: anyone. Membership in the CCCC or NCTE is *not* necessary.

For further information: write George Wykoff, Secretary of the CCCC, Purdue University, Lafayette, Indiana.

occurred, early reports and issues of *CCC* convey a strong sense of optimism and purpose.[10] Here, for instance, is Charles Roberts's introduction to a series of fourteen reports of workshops held during the 1950 CCCC, published in the May issue of the first volume of *CCC*:

> The following reports represent the most extensive and concerted frontal attack ever made on the problems of teaching college freshman English. The rosters of the workshop groups reveal that some of our best minds, representing all types of higher education in all corners of the country, have met to suggest solutions to some of those problems. . . . the reader will note . . . that some ideas run like a refrain through reports from groups working ostensibly on quite different topics. It is in these that we may detect a philosophy of freshman English emerging." (3)

Not addressed in Roberts's optimistic comment is the relationship between the development of a "philosophy of freshman English" and the material conditions of the many teachers who would need—if the "problems of teaching college freshman English" were genuinely to be addressed—to enact that philosophy.

II. Conflicting Desires: The Braddock Essays and the Profession

The CCCC—and the profession it was created to support and foster—has been marked from its inception by a tension between the desire to address "practical needs of the profession," and thus raise its "professional standards," and the equally strong desire to develop "a coordinated research program" (Gerber 12). Those taking on this responsibility in the late 1940s did so in the context of what at the time was experienced as a crisis, "a flood," as Lloyd-Jones termed it, "of new students" (487). Despite the optimism of some, many felt acutely aware that the "problem" of freshman English would not easily be addressed.[11] A 1951 *CCC* article by Robert S. Hunting provides a compelling demonstration of this belief. In "A Training Course for Teachers of Freshman Composition," Hunting follows a description of the problems that characterize typical training courses by arguing that the best way to address such problems is to accommodate them. Since most graduate students don't respect the teaching of writing enough to take a training course seriously, Hunting argues, the training course should be planned so that it doesn't interfere with "regular" graduate courses, should be noncredit, etc. Hunting closes by observing that "when, and if, the freshman composition course acquires the professional respect it deserves, then, and only then, will graduate students entertain a genuine respect for a Training Course for Teachers of Freshman Composition." (6).

The belief that the teaching of writing is not granted the professional and disciplinary respect it deserves within the academy did not die in the 1950s, but has continued—though perhaps in somewhat muted form—to the present.[12] Writing in 1970, Janice Lauer insists that "freshman English will never reach the status of a respectable intellectual discipline until both its theorizers and its practitioners break out of the ghetto" (80). Similarly, James L. Kinneavy introduces his monumental 1971 *A Theory of Discourse* with the following observation:

> The present anarchy of the discipline of what is commonly categorized as "composition," both in high schools and colleges, is so evident as scarcely to require proof.
>
> Composition is so clearly the stepchild of the English department that it is not a legitimate area of concern in graduate studies, it is not even recognized as a subdivision of the discipline of English in a recent manifesto put out by the major professional association (MLA) of college English teachers . . . in some universities is not a valid area of scholarship for advancement in rank, and is generally the teaching province of graduate assistants or fringe members of the department. (1)

More recent comments continue this theme. In his 1988 *Plato, Derrida, and Writing,* for instance, Jasper Neel cautions that "writing must be 'saved' from philosophy before it can receive attention as a legitimate field of study" (xi). And in her 1998 *Composition in the University,* Sharon Crowley also calls attention to the difficulties the field has experienced in achieving "the traditional goals of disciplinarity" (253). In a statement that resonates ironically with the aspirations of those who founded the CCCC, she attributes this difficulty to the field's commitment to the required first-year writing course. She writes:

> I think that the universal requirement in introductory composition, which is the institutional manifestation of composition's service ethic, has kept the traditional goals of disciplinarity—the pursuit of knowledge and the professional advancement of practitioners—beyond the reach of composition studies until very recently. (253)

Service to colleagues, students, and society—or progress as a scholarly discipline? Since the inception of the CCCC, many have believed that it is possible and necessary to achieve both goals. Indeed, many have hoped not only to achieve these goals but also to contribute broadly to progressive values and practices—to function, in other words, as agents of social, political, and economic change. (See Patricia Bizzell's *Academic Discourse and Critical Consciousness* as an example of such a project.) Beliefs such as these have marked the field as transgressive within the academy, even as many in the field have worked to acquire such accouterments of traditional disciplinarity as graduate programs and specialized journals, conferences, and associations (all of which, of course, have had the effect of extending the scholarly and professional enterprise of composition beyond the domains of the CCCC and CCC.)[13]

Awards for outstanding scholarly research are another accouterment of traditional disciplinarity, another mark of disciplinary success, suggesting as they do that a field has a developed body of research and that such research can be evaluated by a group of "objective" experts. Even in traditional disciplines, scholarly awards represent the aspirations that a field holds for itself. But if history and institutional location are any indication, composition studies is not a traditional discipline, just as the CCCC at its inception was not a traditional scholarly association. Most professional associations in the academy were founded primarily to advance research. The CCCC was founded to address the needs of those charged with administering and teaching a required course, one viewed by many colleagues in the academy as a basic skills course without disciplinary content.[14] If those in the field were to persuade their colleagues, both within and without departments of English, that their work merited professional respect, they had a particularly strong need to develop the "coordinated research program" that Gerber called for in his introduction of the CCCC (12). The Braddock Award and the essays it honors bear the mark of that need, and of the desire that need engendered.

III. "OF WHAT DOES SKILL IN WRITING REALLY CONSIST?": THE BRADDOCK ESSAYS 1975–1978

When the Braddock Award was instituted in 1975, for many in the field the title of the award would have evoked not only memories of a much-beloved friend and colleague, but also called to mind Braddock, Lloyd-Jones, and Schoer's 1963 *Research on Written Communication,* their influential review of 504 research studies on the teaching of writing. Many scholars can still recall one of the major conclusions of this study; that "today's research in composition, taken as a whole, may be compared to chemical research as it emerged from the period of alchemy: some terms are being defined usefully, a number of procedures are being refined, but the field as a whole is laced with dreams, prejudices, and makeshift operations" (5).

In 1963, Braddock, Lloyd-Jones, and Schoer looked primarily to the sciences as a model for improving the scholarly work of composition. They note, for instance, that research in composition, "complex though it may be . . . has not frequently been conducted with the knowledge and care that one associates with the physical sciences" (5). The authors thus take for granted that a coordinated research program, to be successful, would have to achieve the kind of reliability, validity, and predictability that researchers in the sciences claim for their work. Such research would necessarily be skeptical of conventional pedagogical practices, of a teacher's insistence that "this assignment or that teaching strategy really works in my class."[15] This skepticism is indeed implicit in the list of questions presented under the heading Unexplored Territory in a chapter titled "The State of Knowledge about Composition." This list of twenty-four questions begins with the following three queries:

1. What kinds of situations and assignments at various levels of schooling stimulate a desire to write well?

2. What do different kinds of students prefer to write about when relieved of the expectations and requirements of teachers and others?

3. What are the sources of fear and resentment in writing? (52)

Closing the list of items is the question:

24. Of what does skill in writing really consist?" (53).

In "'Of What Does Skill in Writing Really Consist?': The Political Life of the Writing Process Movement," James Marshall considers the presence and power of the single word *really* as it appears in this question. Reflecting upon its rhetorical function in the sentence, Marshall observes:

> We might say that it is just there for emphasis, to indicate that the au-thors were interested in the truth, the whole truth, the "real" as opposed to the "unreal" truth. But they might have gotten that job done without the "really." The simpler "Of what does skill in writing consist?" seems cleaner, more empirical, objective, and researcher-like in tone than it does when that "really" intrudes. Let me suggest that the "really" is there for the same reason "really" shows up in everyday conversation— to call into doubt an assertion that has already been made." (46)

Marshall goes on to suggest that scholars in composition studies "have con-sistently positioned ourselves in this way, that is, that we have consistently and insistently represented ourselves as outsiders who doubt the validity, the truth, the value of what has traditionally gone on in writing classrooms" (47).

In certain respects, the earliest Braddock essays support Marshall's ob-servation. For in varying ways, the first five essays—Richard Braddock's "The Frequency and Placement of Topic Sentences in Expository Prose" (1975), Jim W. Corder's "What I Learned at School" (1976), Frank D'Angelo's "The Search for Intelligible Structure in the Teaching of Composition" (1977), Glenn Matott's "In Search of a Philosophical Context for Teaching Composi-tion" (1977), and Richard C. Gebhardt's "Balancing Theory with Practice in the Training of Writing Teachers" (1978)—demonstrate a strong desire to provide a surer and firmer grounding for the field than practitioner knowl-edge. Such aspirations are particularly clear in D'Angelo's essay, which ap-provingly cites an assessment of the state of composition presented in Vir-ginia M. Burke's 1965 CCC essay "The Composition-Rhetoric Pyramid":

> "There is chaos today in the teaching of composition because since the turn of the century, composition has lacked an informing discipline, without which no field can maintain its proper dimensions, the balance and proportion of its various parts, or its very integrity. Consequently, the practice of composition has shrunk, has lost important elements, has become a victim of all manner of distortion." (qtd. in D'Angelo 51*)

D'Angelo closes his essay by arguing, "The vast proliferation of knowledge and the lack of simplifying ideas is a grave embarrassment in the field of composition today" (57*).

There is, furthermore, a systematizing, clearing-the-ground impulse in several of these essays, as evidenced in the nature and scope of their in-quiries. Braddock, for instance, undertakes a systematic textual analysis of a

---

*Note: Page numbers with asterisks refer to page numbers of the present volume.

representative sample of twenty-five professional essays, hoping to answer two questions: "1. What proportion of the paragraphs contain topic sentences? 2. Where in the paragraphs do the topic sentences occur?" (30*). The essays by D'Angelo, Matott, and Gebhardt rely more strongly on theoretical (or, in the case of Matott, philosophical) inquiry—but like Braddock they aspire to establish a firmer, more coherent, more theoretically sophisticated grounding for the field. D'Angelo, for instance, argues that:

> ... composition does have an underlying structure which gives unity and coherence to the field, that that structure can be conceived of in terms of principles and forms (akin to those found in music or painting, for example), and that these principles and forms need to be taught in an orderly sequence. (53*)

In his essay, D'Angelo presents "some tentative concepts" (53*), he argues, that "do not exhaust the principles of discourse that we ought to be concerned with in the study of composition, but ... [that] do suggest that with a little time and effort, we can identify some of the most important principles which are fundamental to the discipline" (55*). Similarly, Gebhardt provides an ambitious conceptual framework to guide courses for future teachers of writing, organizing his essay around "four kinds of theoretical or conceptual information that ... should be included in teaching-of-writing programs" (68*).

Of the first five Braddock essays, Matott's most strongly invokes the general social, cultural, and political milieu of the time in which he wrote, the late seventies. Matott's essay expresses his concern over what he saw as a trend in composition, one "characterized by a desire to assist the student toward self-awareness and self-expression" (60*).

> It strikes me that in recent years, especially during the stressful years of direct American involvement in Viet Nam, we have seen students painfully locked into their own solitariness: students expressing in shouted slogans their awareness of frustration and anger but incapable of coherent argument; students turning to mind-bending drugs to alleviate the pain of isolation within the self (a masturbatory act: *self*-awareness, *self*-expression); students—18 years old—with marble eyes, as if staring inward upon nothingness. (63–64*)

The primary thrust of Matott's essay is philosophical; however: his essay represents a sustained argument that the work of Martin Buber provides a better grounding for pedagogy in composition than does that of Sartre, whose influence Matott saw in pedagogical practices at that time.

Jim Corder's "What I Learned at School" sits uneasily with the other four essays—at least at first glance. For in his essay Corder appears to speak not as a researcher but as a classroom teacher, one who in a moment of "coltish vigor" promised his students "that I would write an essay every time they did and that I would turn my essays over to them as they turned theirs in to me" (43*). Corder also takes a determinedly modest approach to the consequences of his inquiry, observing that "When I try to tally the things I learned while writing essays, the total is not impressive" (43*). He immediately adds the following qualification, however, that "what's there is sufficiently troublesome, perplexing, confusing, instructive, and vexatious to bring me up short and to cast doubt upon certain assumptions about freshman composition" (43*). Corder then proceeds to move from generalizations about his experiences to two larger issues: "Problems in the inventive capacities given by a semester, and problems in establishing occasions for writing" (44*).

Though Corder's essay is certainly strikingly different in tone and method from those of Braddock, D'Angelo, Matott, and Gebhardt, some telling similarities do, I believe, exist. In reflecting on his experience, for instance, Corder at one point comments: "Perhaps what I really learned is that I have not learned enough. Or perhaps what I really learned is that part of what I know *about* writing (though right enough in its way) is not germane or immediate or companionable when one is *doing* the writing" (44*). Though Corder writes as a classroom teacher, in statements such as this he questions his previous pedagogical assumptions and practices and thus calls for inquiry that challenges practitioner knowledge (including, of course, his own). Indeed, in deciding to write in response to the same assignments he gave his students and to submit the resulting essays to his students for response and evaluation, Corder established (though he does not refer to it in this way) an informal experiment, with himself as guinea pig. Undergirding Corder's explicit stance as not just a teacher but a folksy, witty, self-deprecating teacher, then, is the stance of a researcher. It is interesting to observe in this regard that although Corder's essay does not refer to *Research on Written Communication,* his essay in fact addresses the first three questions raised by Braddock, Lloyd-Jones, and Schoer, for it devotes a good deal of attention to the "kinds of situations and assignments . . . [that] stimulate a desire to write well," to the consequences of writing in response to "the expectations and requirements of teachers," and to possible "sources of fear and resentment of writing" (Braddock, Lloyd-Jones, and Schoer 52).

A second look at the essays by Braddock and Matott indicate that just as Corder's essay seems to be firmly situated in the classroom but has traces of a scholarly grounding and project, so too do these essays (though explicitly organized around the authors' research agendas) bear traces of their pedagogical—and in the case of Matott also cultural and political—situations. For though Matott focuses primarily upon elaborating what he characterizes as a "Buberian pedagogy for composition" (66*), he makes it clear that his essay is motivated by very real experiences with very real students. It is motivated as well by broader concerns about the social and cultural consequences of "a disintegrated version of Jean-Paul Sartre's existential view of the human condition," a view which Matott believes "has taken its course through the Beat Generation, the hippie movement, a meadow of flower children, and Charles Manson's family" (62*).

Even Braddock's essay, which of all the essays is the most limited in focus and most clearly modeled on scientific inquiry, ends with a paradoxical twist. In his analysis, Braddock discovered that "only 13% of the expository paragraphs of contemporary professional writers begin with a topic sentence, [and] that only 3% end with a topic sentence" (39*). From this

Braddock concludes that "students should not be told that professional writers usually begin their paragraphs with topic sentences" (39*). He goes on to observe, however, that his findings do *not* suggest to him "that composition teachers should stop showing their students how to develop paragraphs from clear topic sentences. Far from it. In my opinion, often the writing in the 25 essays would have been clearer and more comfortable to read if the paragraphs had presented more explicit topic sentences" (39*). Braddock the researcher thus defers—or so it seems to me—to Braddock the reader, writer, and, especially, teacher.

And what of D'Angelo's and Gebhardt's essays? Perhaps because their essays share a particularly strong systematizing impulse, they seem most firmly situated in the domain of theory and bear the fewest traces of the authors' pedagogical (social, cultural, or other) situations. Even though Gebhardt attempts to address a long-standing pragmatic concern of members of the CCCC (training the teachers who actually work with students in writing classrooms throughout the country), and even though he refers at times to courses he has taught for future writing teachers, the strongest emphasis in his essay is on developing a systematic, theoretically informed framework for instruction. Gebhardt does acknowledge the difference between knowing *that* and knowing *why* and *how*, as well as the need for the "balancing of knowledge with experience" (73*). But his essay creates little space for either his own or his students' experiences in the classroom.

Without wanting to erase the significant differences that exist among the first five Braddock Award essays, I hope I have demonstrated that in an important respect all share similar ambitions for research in composition. For all their differences, each of these essays in effect says something like this: there's a lot of work to be done in the field, we need to do that work now, and in doing that work we can't rely on the mishmash of understandings that we have heretofore entertained about the teaching of writing. Whether we subject our own teaching to scrutiny, analyze the writing of professional essayists, articulate foundational theories or philosophies for the field, or develop a systematic framework for the education of writing teachers, we must look beyond the immediate experiences of teachers and students for valid and useful knowledge. Even while making this point, however, Braddock's, D'Angelo's, and Matott's essays enact a movement back and forth—or a tension between—the domain of the classroom and of the scholar's study.[16] And Gebhardt's essay similarly attempts to respond to the scholarly desire to articulate sophisticated theoretical frameworks to govern practice in the field while also addressing the professional and pragmatic needs of those responsible for training future teachers of writing.

IV. A DISCIPLINE IN THE MAKING: THE BRADDOCK ESSAYS 1979–1998

In this reading of the first five Braddock essays, I have attempted to call attention to the ways in which these essays both embody and enact the desires of a discipline in the making, but to do so without reducing the essays to car-

icatures or mere traces of that desire. A more seamless analysis might well
have emphasized the similarities among Braddock's, D'Angelo's, Matott's,
and Gebhardt's essays and then presented Corder's essay as in effect the odd
man (literally) out. But such an analysis would, I think, tell too neat a story—
not only of the past but also of the present. Because they were written twenty
years ago, it is easy for contemporary readers to distance ourselves from
these essays, to be aware of their otherness in the context of current scholarly
efforts. And, indeed, when several of these authors look back at their essays,
they call attention to limitations of their earlier work or to ways in which the
field has moved on. D'Angelo suggests, for instance, that "our earlier emphasis on structure and sequence may have been misguided and naïve." Similarly, Gebhardt observes, "It now seems clear that testing ideas and teaching
approaches against 'some [i.e., one] theoretical framework' or against 'some
[i.e., any] theoretical framework' (no matter how narrow) is less effective
than working through several 'integrating views' (plural) to understand our
field."

When I read these five essays, however, I am struck by continuities and
connections linking these early Braddock essays to subsequent efforts. From
1975 to the present, for instance, a significant group of researchers has felt
Braddock's urge to ground his inquiry in data that have an intractable material existence and that can be subjected to systematic (and in recent years often
collaborative) investigation. During this same time period, many in the field
have, like Matott, found it productive to turn to the scholarly projects of
those not directly engaged in the work of composition—to Richard Rorty,
Kenneth Burke, Donna Haraway, Michel Foucault, Mikhail Bakhtin, bell
hooks, Gloria Anzaldúa, and many others—for theoretical underpinnings
for current projects. The urge for order and parsimony, for "intelligible structure" in theory and practice that characterizes both Gebhardt's and D'Angelo's essays has also continued—not only in such projects as James L. Kinneavy's theory of discourse but also in the taxonomies developed by Lester
Faigley, Richard Fulkerson, James Berlin, and others, and in teacher guides
such as Erica Lindemann's *A Rhetoric for Writing Teachers*. And, finally, the
impulse evidenced in Corder's essay to ground one's scholarly work in the
daily experience of teaching and writing—and to reflect upon that experience in a personal, rather than academic, voice—has also struck a resonant
chord with many in recent years, particularly feminists, teacher researchers,
and those writing from marginalized positions within the academy or society, as demonstrated in the work of such scholars as Olivia Frey, Lillian
Bridwell-Bowles, Ruth E. Ray, and Jacqueline Jones Royster.

This is not to suggest that research in the field has somehow remained
stable and unchanged in the years from 1975 to the present. Many readers
will need only to glance at the list of Braddock essays to be reminded of
broad trends that have swept through the field in recent decades—from an
early emphasis on establishing theoretical, philosophical, and pedagogical
groundings to cognitive research on the writing process to essays that manifest the impact of feminist, critical pedagogy, cultural, and postcolonial

studies on the academy.[17] Along with these trends have come substantial—indeed, at times fierce—debates among scholars advocating various positions and projects. Most notable, perhaps, have been critiques of cognitive research on writing, which is associated with but by no means limited to the work of Linda Flower and her coauthors. This work seemed to many in the early 1980s poised to fulfill the theoretical and pedagogical promise of the writing process movement, but in recent years cognitive research has been charged with failing to attend sufficiently to the social, political, and cultural contexts in which writing occurs. The grounds for this charge vary. Some scholars, such as Elizabeth Flynn, fault cognitivists' commitment to empiricist methods and epistemologies. Others, including Linda Brodkey and Marilyn Cooper, critique the image of the writer that they believe informs such research. In "The Ecology of Writing," for instance, Marilyn Cooper argues that:

> The ideal writer the cognitive process model projects is isolated from the social world, a writer I will call the solitary author. The solitary author works alone, within the privacy of his own mind. He uses freewriting exercises and heuristics to find out what he knows about a subject and to find something he wants to say to others; he uses his analytic skills to discover a purpose, to imagine an audience, to decide on strategies, to organize content; and he simulates how his text will be read by reading it over himself, making the final revisions necessary to assure its success when he abandons it to the world of which he is not a part. The isolation of the solitary author from the social world leads him to see ideas and goals as originating primarily within himself and directed at an unknown and largely hostile other. Writing becomes a kind of parthenogenesis, the author producing propositional and pragmatic structures, Athena-like, full grown and complete, out of his brow. (365–66)

Finally, in articles such as "Contemporary Composition: The Major Pedagogical Theories" and "Rhetoric and Ideology in the Writing Class" James Berlin charges cognitive researchers with refusing to acknowledge the powerful role that ideology plays in any act of communication. Because cognitive researchers view language "as a system of rational signs that is compatible with the mind and the external world," Berlin argues in "Rhetoric and Ideology in the Writing Class," their "entire scheme can be seen as analogous to the instrumental method of the modern corporation, the place where members of the meritocratic middle class, the twenty percent or so of the work force of certified college graduates, make a handsome living managing a capitalist economy. . . . The pursuit of self-evident and unquestioned goals in the composing process parallels the pursuit of self-evident and unquestioned profit-making goals in the corporate marketplace . . ." (483).

Given the commitment of many in the field to enacting progressive social and cultural (as well as pedagogical) change, Berlin's identification of cognitive research with the conservative forces of American capitalism represents a particularly strong challenge to this project. In recent years, Flower and others have addressed this and other challenges, and they have done so in several ways. Flower now characterizes her work, for instance, as an effort to develop a cognitive theory of writing that acknowledges the social as well as the individual aspects of composing. In her recent book *The Construction of Negotiated Meaning: A Social Cognitive Theory of Writing*, Flower takes care to dissociate empirical research from a naïve positivism and to characterize it instead as "observation-based theory building grounded in the investigation of actual writers in specific contexts . . . [that calls] for a willingness to be surprised and challenged by the unpredicted, by the data of experience" (43). Whereas much of her and her coauthors' early research depended upon think-aloud protocols of individual writers, more recent studies employ such practices as collaborative planning. And in 1989 Flower cofounded Pittsburgh's inner-city Community Literacy Center, a university-community collaboration that intertwines scholarly inquiry with social action. In their CCC essay "Community Literacy," Wayne Campbell Peck, Linda Flower, and Lorraine Higgins describe the center, situating it in the context of both previous community action projects (such as the settlement house movement of the early 1900s) and current research on literacy. They also describe several characteristic programs, such as the "Whas-sup with Suspension" project. This project attempted to address high suspension rates for male African American high school students in Pittsburgh by bringing suspended teenagers, school officials, and others together for inquiry and action. Eventually, the project resulted in a student-written newsletter which "denounced mindless authoritarianism by adults, illustrated feelings of both students and teachers involved in suspension disputes, and gave a series of dramatic scenarios for understanding how suspensions occur" (212).

Other debates circulate within and around many of the Braddock essays. That tensions continue between researchers who espouse empirical inquiry and those who advocate other research methods—especially the collection of scholarly practices that have come to be called *theory*—seems clear. In the afterword to their 1991 Braddock essay, quoted earlier, Glynda Hull and Mike Rose call attention to "the current 'theory' vs. 'empiricism' divide" and ask whether it is not possible to transcend such a divide and move into "generative paradox." Some scholars have certainly attempted to acknowledge the limitations of such a situation and the need for multiple perspectives in research on writing. In "Cognition, Convention, and Certainty: What We Need to Know about Writing," for instance, Patricia Bizzell acknowledges that "[a]nswers to what we need to know about writing will have to come from both the inner-directed and the outer-directed [or cognitive and social constructionist] schools if we wish to have a complete picture of the composing process" (218). More often, however, as Carol Berkenkotter points out in "Paradigm Debates, Turf Wars, and the Conduct of Sociocognitive Inquiry in Composition," research in the field "suggests that we cannot entertain cognitive and social perspectives simultaneously and that to foreground the individual writer/rhetor as an active, constructive agent of meaning is to ignore the myriad of social, historical, and ideological factors that permeate the contexts of writing" (151). As a result, many conducting empirical research feel compelled to defend their project, as Davida Charney does in her recent "Empiricism Is Not a Four-Letter Word."

The question of whether scholars in composition studies can tolerate, and perhaps even encourage, "generative paradox" is relevant to the work of another Braddock Award author, Peter Elbow. For although Elbow's articles and books, particularly *Writing without Teachers* and *Writing with Power: Techniques for Mastering the Writing Process,* have influenced many in the field, his work has in recent years been critiqued as having the limitations of "expressionistic" rhetoric. In "Rhetoric and Ideology in the Writing Class," for instance, James A. Berlin characterizes expressionistic rhetoric, which he associates with Elbow, Ken Macrorie, Donald Murray, and others, as emphasizing the individual and privileging authentic self-expression and creativity, with the result that it is "inherently and debilitatingly divisive of political protest. . . . [and] is easily co-opted by the very capitalist forces it opposes" (487). Elbow, however, resists such categorization. In an exchange with David Bartholomae that took place first at the 1989 and 1991 meetings of the CCCC and later in the pages of *CCC,* Elbow, addressing Bartholomae directly, observes:

> . . . you assume without argument that if I celebrate "independent, self-creative, self-expressive subjectivity," I must be against the notion of people as socially constructed. But I am not.
>
> There is a crucial matter of theory here. You say in passing that I can't have it both ways, that I can't stick up for both perspectives on the human condition. But you never give any reason for this theoretical position. I insist I *can* have it both ways. . . . *Embracing Contraries* is entirely devoted to arguing for "both/and" thinking and trying to show the problems with "either/or" thinking—showing how we can validly maintain opposites in various realms of theory and practice. ("Being a Writer" 88)

Bartholomae did not have an opportunity to respond to Elbow's assertion, for it appears in their final exchange. But his comments in "Writing with Teachers: A Conversation with Peter Elbow," suggest that Bartholomae remains convinced that expressionist rhetoric, which he is careful to observe may or may not represent Elbow's own position and practices, has negative consequences, for it prevents students "from confronting the power politics of discursive practice . . . [and keeps] them from confronting the particular representations of power, tradition and authority reproduced whenever one writes" (64).

As these examples indicate, there has been considerable attention in recent years to the intersections of the political and the pedagogical in composition studies. Not all have been happy with this focus, however. Maxine Hairston, whose 1983 "The Winds of Change: Thomas Kuhn and the Revolution in the Teaching of Writing" helped to authorize the writing process movement, in 1992 published "Diversity, Ideology, and Teaching Writing." In this essay, Hairston levels a series of charges against those who espouse an explicitly social and political agenda for the field: "... I see a new model emerging for freshman writing programs, a model that disturbs me greatly. It's a model that puts dogma before diversity, politics before craft, ideology before critical thinking, and the social goals of the teacher before the educational needs of the student" (180).

Hairston is in the minority, however—at least in published scholarship in the field. From Joseph Harris's "The Idea of Community in the Study of Writing" to Ellen Cushman's "The Rhetorician as an Agent of Social Change" and Arnetha Ball and Ted Lardner's "Dispositions toward Language: Teacher Constructs of Knowledge and the Ann Arbor Black English Case," many recent essays—like much research in the field in general—demonstrate an interest in articulating ways in which, as Ball and Lardner observe, teachers can "re-envision their capacity to function as catalysts of positive growth and development in students" (423*). In a sense, of course, this has always been the goal of researchers and teachers of writing. But whereas Nancy Sommers's 1983 Braddock essay addresses this issue with a careful study of teachers' comments on students' writing, in 1998 Ball and Lardner emphasize the need to "more adequately address questions of language diversity and race in order to affect the climate in the writing classroom" (414*).

V. PRESENCES—AND ABSENCES—IN THE BRADDOCK ESSAYS

And yet, Ball and Lardner ask, how can such questions of language diversity and race adequately be addressed, given differences in the material situations of those engaged in the scholarly work of composition and of the majority of teachers in writing, many of whom have little time and incentive to read, much less engage in, research? That question, along with this brief excursion into debates within the field of composition studies in recent years, serves as a reminder of the tensions between the field's desire to develop its scholarly project (and thus gain disciplinary status and authority) and the desire to address practical needs in the profession. It calls attention, as well, to absences as well as presences in the Braddock essays.

Largely absent, for instance, are the voices of classroom teachers, especially classroom teachers who characterize their efforts—or whose efforts are characterized by those writing about them—as successful and productive.[18] I have already noted the extent to which early Braddock essays accept as commonsensical the need to turn away from practitioner knowledge to inquire more systematically and thoroughly about writing and the teaching of writing. It is in the nature of scholarly work, of course, to identify significant theoretical and pedagogical problems and to attempt to address and, where possible, resolve them. But perhaps scholars in composition studies have not attended sufficiently to potential tensions or contradictions between the desire (one manifested in a good deal of scholarly work in the field) to represent teachers as in some way lacking or in need of the guidance of researchers and the desire to serve as advocates for teachers—for lighter teaching loads and improved working conditions and professional recognition. Perhaps we have not attended sufficiently to the relationship between the will to knowledge and the will to (disciplinary and institutional) power.[19]

I invite readers, then, to read the essays collected in *On Writing Research* not only for what they *say* but also for what they *do* or *enact* at the level of discursive and rhetorical practice. Here are some questions that such a reading might consider.

- To what extent do these essays create a space for the voices of students and teachers? In what contexts and for what purposes do these voices appear? Do students and teachers appear as subjects *in* discourse or as subjects *of* discourse? Are they given opportunities to signify about the research study of which they are a part?

- What images of students and teachers do these essays either assume or portray? To what extent are students and teachers identified with deficiencies, difficulties, or problems? To what extent are they identified with opportunities or with pedagogical successes?

- What scenes of writing are portrayed in or implied by these essays? Classrooms? Writing centers? Offices? Community centers? MUDs? Other spaces?

- What audiences do these essays address and invoke? Is it possible to identify additional audiences? Audiences that are excluded? Ignored? Repressed? Rejected? Denied?

- In what ways do these essays represent or characterize the relationship among researchers, teachers, and students? Is this relationship dynamic? Fixed? Distant? Close? What might a metaphoric reading of these relationships reveal?

- What assumptions about the relationship between theory and practice are evident in these essays? To what extent is this relationship discussed explicitly, and to what extent does it remain implicit? What assumptions seem to undergird this relationship? That theorists will teach and teachers will learn? That theorists and teachers (and students?) will inquire together?

- What exigencies motivate or ground these essays? Theoretical? Pedagogical? Social? Cultural? Political? A combination thereof? To what extent are these exigencies explicitly articulated? To what extent do they remain implicit?

- What scholarly moves are privileged in these essays? Where is proof required? Where is it taken for granted? Indeed, what counts as proof?

- How open are these essays to the possibility of multiple, and even paradoxical, understandings of writing and teaching?

I pose these questions not to devalue the scholarly contributions that the Braddock essays have made and continue to make to the discipline. Rather, the questions I pose here are intended to add another perspective or opportunity for reflection, to encourage attention to what is not said as well as said, to tensions, gaps, and absences as well as to assertions.

VI. Rereading the Braddock Essays with (and against) Other Texts

As I observed earlier, the Braddock essays narrate particular moments in the development of composition studies as a discipline, but the significance of these moments is multiple and overdetermined, not univocal. As a reminder of that multiplicity, I would like to suggest additional ways of reading the Braddock essays, ways that I hope call attention to their situatedness as textual and professional artifacts while also providing opportunities for rereading the development of composition as a discipline. The Braddock essays, it is important to remember, comprise just one of many kinds of documents upon which one might draw in studying composition's development as a discipline. What would happen, for instance, if these essays were read in the context of various efforts within the field to improve the material situations of teachers of writing—against the report on the Wyoming Conference initiatives by the CCCC Committee on Professional Standards for Quality Education, the NCTE's "Guidelines for the Workload of the College English Teacher," or the CCCC's "Statement of Principles and Standards for the Postsecondary Teaching of Writing"? What if the essays were read not in the context of documents such as these but rather of the 1974 CCCC resolution on "Students' Right to Their Own Language" and of current debates over Ebonics? Would readers see congruences? Contradictions? Absences? Tensions?

The Braddock essays were written in particular times and (social, cultural, political, economic) places, so another way of reading them would be to reread them back into the general milieu in which they were written. Just a year after the CCCC ratified "Students' Right to Their Own Language" as official policy, for instance—and the same year the Braddock Award was instituted—*Newsweek* published "Why Johnny Can't Write," an article that fueled the back-to-the-basics movement. As Lester Faigley writes in *Fragments of Rationality*, those committed to the scholarly work of composition stand in complicated and even contradictory relation to what was at the time characterized as an urgent literacy crisis. Concerns about this crisis caused many colleges and universities for the first time to create positions for faculty specializing in composition—and they did so at a time when the job market for Ph.D.s in literature was significantly depressed. So in a very literal sense, many new faculty members with a scholarly interest in composition (including myself) benefited from this crisis. Negotiating the varying expectations of different institutional and civic constituencies—as well as honoring our own understandings of the nature and significance of student writing—was, and continues to be, a difficult task.

What traces of concerns about the material conditions of teachers of writing, about the rights of students, about the expectations placed on directors of writing programs, about the "problem" of student literacy and the need to address that problem without mistaking difference for inability are discernible in the Braddock essays? Conversely, what cultural, political, social, and other presences of previous or contemporary times do not find their way into the Braddock essays, and why not? (For an example of an effort to undertake such a reading, in this case not of the Braddock essays but of research in the field in general, see Geoffrey Sirc's "Never Mind the Tagmemics, Where's the Sex Pistols?")

In what other contexts might the Braddock essays be read? Since 1978, the first year the CCCC chair gave a formal address at the annual conference, CCC has published the chair's address in its February issue. Though not all chairs view the occasion of their address in the same way, many understand the moment as an opportunity to take stock of where CCCC has been—and where it might go. In 1988, for instance, the year that Robert Brooke's "Underlife and Writing Instruction" received the Braddock Award, Miriam T. Chaplin's address, "Issues, Perspectives, and Possibilities," was published. Chaplin begins her address with a letter written by a "distressed composition teacher in Florida." Here is a portion of that letter:

> I am a non-tenured composition teacher in a large university. I teach 4 classes 4 days a week and spend two hours in the writing lab each of the four days. There is no time for me to do any kind of research and yet I will not be tenured without it. Of course I might not be tenured if I had publications because my institution has little respect for publications in composition. (52)

Chaplin's introduction calls attention to a different kind of academic "underlife" than that discussed in Brooke's essay. What other connections or disconnections exist between these two texts, or between other chairs' addresses and Braddock essays? Are these texts in conversation, or do they speak at cross (or simply different) purposes?

Pulling another February CCC off my shelf, I note that in 1994—the year that Gesa E. Kirsch and Peter Mortensen's essay "On Authority in the Study of Writing" received the Braddock Award—Anne Ruggles Gere's chair's address, which focused on "The Extracurriculum of Composition," appeared. Gere focuses not on professional concerns but rather on "the need to enact pedagogies that permit connections and communication with the communities outside classroom walls" (91). Did Gere's 1994 address in some way prepare the ground for Ellen Cushman's 1997 Braddock essay "The Rhetorician as an Agent of Social Change"? What metaphors might best characterize the relationship of CCCC chairs' addresses and the Braddock essays? Conversation? Debate? Cross talk?

A quite different sort of reading would look at the Braddock essays not in the context of formal addresses written to be presented at an epideictic moment but rather at texts designed to further the bureaucratic administrative work of the field—such as the CCCC proposal forms. Each year since 1980 the program chair has determined the categories that appear under the "Area to be emphasized" section of the form. In addition to their literal function—proposers must check the area they feel best characterizes their proposal—these categories serve as artifacts indicating the range of interests and topics that the program chair feels best represent current work in the field. Lynn Quitman Troyka's proposal form, for instance, included the following twelve categories: the composing process, rhetorical theory, invention, language, basic writing, technical writing, ethnic studies, assessment, reading/writing relationships, approaches to teaching, interdisciplinary, and other. In 1981 James L. Hill changed "technical writing" to "technical communication"; in 1982 Donald C. Stewart added invention to "rhetorical theory," so that it read "rhetorical theory/invention." Otherwise, from 1980 to 1982 the categories remained unchanged.

For the 1983 CCCC program proposal form Rosentene Bennett Purnell expanded the categories from twelve to nineteen, adding options such as language learning theories; environments for learning; teaching teachers or tutors of writing; audience analysis; language, ethnicity, and culture; business communication; discourse analysis; cognitive styles; interdisciplinary approaches to language instruction; and cultural literacy. Since that time, the proposal forms have reflected each individual program chair's sense of where the field of CCCC not only is going currently but also might (or should) go.

If the Braddock Award essays convey a particular selection committee's sense of what constituted an exemplary publication in CCC, the proposal forms for the annual conferences convey one particular program chair's vision of the categories that best encompass ongoing scholarly and pedagogical efforts in the field. It is interesting in that regard to review the CCCC proposal forms with an eye to those areas of emphasis that are represented on the forms—but as of yet have not been the focus of Braddock Award essays. Such areas include writing centers, writing across the curriculum, business communication, collaborative writing, computers and composition, technical communication, writing program administration, intellectual property, and portfolio evaluation, among others. What, if anything, should one make of these absences? Do they simply reflect the ongoing specialization of research in composition—and the expectation that the Braddock Award should honor essays that address issues of broad interest and application? Or does this list point to repressed hierarchies of knowledge within the field, hierarchies that would place research on, say, writing centers or writing across the curriculum somehow beneath or below other topics?

That the field of composition studies has—as academic disciplines tend to do—become increasingly specialized is evident. One indication of this specialization is the growth of graduate programs in the past two decades. Here, for instance, is the introduction to Stuart C. Brown, Paul R. Meyer, and Theresa Enos's 1994 study of doctoral programs in rhetoric and composition:

> Growth, consolidation, diversification—these words sum up the evolution of rhetoric and composition doctoral programs since David Chapman and Gary Tate published the first comprehensive survey of the discipline in 1987. Much has happened since then. Chapman and Tate identified 53 doctoral programs in English that offered a specialization in rhetoric and composition, but many of these were only nominal programs. Only "38 [schools] produced written materials describing

comp/rhet specialization, and many flatly admitted that their programs had not been formally recognized or that they did not have the faculty to make the program viable" (125). As of the summer of 1993, 72 were willing to document their programs—21 of these being programs established since 1986. The number of students reported to be pursuing doctoral degrees in rhetoric and related areas has also increased dramatically over the last seven years. In 1985–86, according to the programs listed in the Chapman and Tate survey, 526 students were pursuing doctoral degrees in rhetoric and composition in the United States. In 1993 we estimate that there are approximately 1,174 students pursuing doctorates in rhetoric and composition or closely related areas, an increase of 124 percent. (240)

Has the development of Ph.D. programs influenced the Braddock essays? One sign of their impact is the presence of several collaborative projects, some multimodal, that might well be impossible for an individual working alone to accomplish. In the case of Mary N. Muchiri, Nshindi G. Mulamba, Greg Myers, and Deoscorous B. Ndoloi's "Importing Composition," the presence of three African graduate students, and of their radically different experiences as researchers and teachers, obviously played a key role in catalyzing their project. But might a reading of the Braddock essays in the context of the development of Ph.D. programs reveal absences as well as presences? How might we read the Braddock essays, for instance, in the context of the comments of graduate students and part-time instructors participating in *Rhetoric Review*'s "Burkean Parlor," whose vision of the development of the field includes "Adversaries and Mentors" (by RLV), "MLAise in March" (by Anon.), and "Tales from the Field" (by SM)?

And what about reading the Braddock essays with and against the many, many textbooks that are published each year. After all, though textbooks are written primarily for students, they often educate teachers as well— particularly when those teachers are new teaching assistants or overworked instructors who do not have time to keep up with research in the field. What kind of disjunction or conjunction, I have wondered, would appear if it were possible to identify the best-selling first-year writing textbook in any given year and to place that textbook and the Braddock essays in conversation? Would that textbook reflect the concerns of the current—or of previous—Braddock Award essays? And this question raises other questions. Why, for instance, has it seemed obvious that the CCCC should have an award for an exemplary article in *CCC* (as well as additional awards that have been added over the years) but that exemplary textbooks should not be so recognized? The number of textbooks published in any given year is certainly a practical disincentive for such a reward: the process of reviewing these textbooks would be grueling. But might the absence of an award for an exemplary textbook reflect other assumptions, such as assumptions about the nature, value, and relationship of theory and practice? Might it call attention to the possibility that despite scholars' tendency to announce pedagogical revolutions at the level of theory (as in the case of the writing process, writing as a social process, and postprocess movements) such revolutions do not always make their way into textbooks or classrooms?

Others could, I am sure, suggest additional contexts and questions that would provoke productive readings of the Braddock Award essays—readings that go beyond the words on the page to suggest their situatedness in the work of composition. Readings such as these call attention to tensions and contradictions within—as well as the accomplishments of—the scholarly work of composition. They remind us as well that the scholarly work of the field is itself a form of practice—one that can (and I believe should) itself be theorized. If such theorizing raises complicated, and even at times troubling, questions about just what has and has not been accomplished in the fifty years since the CCCC was founded, it also suggests opportunities for reflection and for dialogue about composition's past, present, and future.

Lisa Ede
Oregon State University

The Frequency and Placement of Topic Sentences in Expository Prose

RICHARD BRADDOCK

ost textbooks on English composition have presented some concerted treatment of topic sentences, long hailed as means of organizing a writer's ideas and clarifying them for the reader. In the most popular composition textbook of the nineteenth century, for example, Alexander Bain recognized that topic sentences may come at the end of a descriptive or introductory paragraph, but he emphasized that expository paragraphs have topic sentences and that they usually come at the beginnings of paragraphs:

> 19. The opening sentence, unless obviously preparatory, is expected to indicate the scope of the paragraph. . . . This rule is most directly applicable to expository style, where, indeed, it is almost essential (Bain, 1890, p. 108).

In one of the more popular composition textbooks of the present, Gorrell and Laird present a similar statement about topic sentences—a statement which is paralleled in many other textbooks these days:

> Topic sentences may appear anywhere, or even be omitted. . . . but most modern, carefully constructed prose rests on standard paragraphs, most of which have topic sentences to open them.

And of 15 items on "Paragraph Patterns" in a commercial test of "writing," three involve the identification of topic sentences in brief paragraphs. In each of the three, the correct answer is the first sentence in the paragraph (*Basic Skills*, 1970).

How much basis is there for us to make such statements to students or to base testing on the truth of them? To clarify the matter, I studied the paragraphs in representative contemporary professional writing, seeking the answers to these two questions:

This essay was first published in *Research in the Teaching of English*, Volume 8, Number 3, Winter 1974.

1. What proportion of the paragraphs contain topic sentences?
2. Where in the paragraphs do the topic sentences occur?

PROCEDURE

As a body of expository material representing contemporary professional writing, I used the corpus of 25 complete essays in American English selected by Margaret Ashida, using random procedures, from 420 articles published from January, 1964, through March, 1965, in *The Atlantic, Harper's, The New Yorker, The Reporter,* and *The Saturday Review.* Ashida indicated possible uses of the corpus:

> ... this corpus could be used for a wealth of investigations by students, teachers, and research scholars—for anything from a relatively superficial examination of controversial matters of usage, to the exploration of the deep (and equally controversial) questions being raised by theoreticians of the new rhetorics. Because the sample has its own built-in validity, it represents a *common* corpus for use by many different scholars—something we desperately need in rhetorical research ... (Ashida, 1968, pp. 14–23).

Paragraphs

Working one-by-one with zerographic copies of the 25 articles,[1] I numbered each paragraph from the first paragraph of the essay to the last. For this study, a paragraph was what we normally take to be one in printed material—a portion of discourse consisting of one or more sentences, the first line of type of which is preceded by more interlinear space than is otherwise found between lines in the text and the first sentence of which begins either with an indentation or with an unindented large initial capital.

Headnotes and footnotes were not counted as parts of the text for this study and hence were not numbered and analyzed. A problem appeared when one article included an insert, consisting of a diagram and some ten sentences of explanation, which was crucial to an understanding of the text proper.[2] This insert arbitrarily was not counted as a paragraph in the article. In those few essays in which dialog was quoted, each separately indented paragraph was counted as a paragraph, even though it consisted in one case merely of one four-word sentence (Taper, p. 138).

T-Units

After numbering the paragraphs in an essay, I proceeded to insert a pencilled slash mark after each T-unit in each paragraph and to write the total number of T-units at the end of each paragraph.

The T-unit, or "minimal terminable unit," is a term devised by Kellogg Hunt to describe the "shortest grammatically allowable sentences into which . . . [writing can] be segmented" (Hunt, 1965, pp. 20–21). In other words, consideration of the T-units of writing permits the researcher to use a rather standard conception of a sentence, setting aside the differences occurring between writers when they use different styles of punctuation. A T-unit, then, "includes one main clause plus all the subordinate clauses attached to or embedded within it . . ." (Hunt, p. 141). Hunt wrote that an independent clause beginning with "and" or "but" is a T-unit, but I also included "or," "for," and "so" to complete what I take to be the coordinating conjunctions in modern usage.

Although in the vast majority of cases, there was no difficulty knowing where to indicate the end of a T-unit, several problems did arise. Take, for instance, the following sentence:

> The Depression destroyed the coalfield's prosperity, but the Second World War revived it, and for a few years the boom returned and the miner was again a useful and honored citizen (Caudill, p. 49).

Obviously, one T-unit ends with "prosperity" and another with "revived it," but is what follows "revived it" one T-unit or two? I made the judgment that "for a few years" was an integral part of both clauses following it and that "and for a few years the boom returned and the miner was again a useful and honored citizen" was one T-unit. Similarly, I counted the following sentence as one T-unit, not two, judging the intent of the first clause in the speech of the Protocol man to be subordinate, as if he had said "If you put an ambassador in prison":

> For another, as a Protocol man said recently, "You put an ambassador in prison and you can't negotiate with him, which is what he's supposed to be here for" (Kahn, p. 75).

In marking off T-units, a person must be prepared for occasional embedding. Sometimes a writer uses parentheses to help accomplish the embedding:

> Gibbs & Cox (Daniel H. Cox was a famous yacht designer who joined the firm in 1929, retired in 1943, and subsequently died) is the largest private ship-designing firm in the world (Sargeant, p. 49).

That sentence, of course, has one T-unit embedded within one other. In the following example, dashes enclose two T-units embedded within another, and the entire sentence consists of four T-units:

> "They're condescending, supercilious bastards, but when the 'United States' broke all the transatlantic records—it still holds them, and it went into service in 1952—they had to come down a peg" (Sargeant, p. 50).

But embedding does not prove to be a problem in determining what is and what is not a T-unit. With the exception of perhaps a dozen other problems in the thousands of sentences considered in the 25 essays, marking off and counting the T-units was a fairly mechanical operation.

Topic Sentences

The next problem was to decide which T-unit, if any, constituted a topic sentence in each paragraph. After several frustrating attempts merely to underline the appropriate T-unit where it occurred, I realized that the notion of what a topic sentence is, is not at all clear.

Consultation of composition textbooks provided no simple solution of the problem. Gorrell and Laird, for example, offered this definition of a topic sentence:

> Most paragraphs focus on a central idea or unifying device expressed in topical material. Occasionally this topical material is complex, involving more than one sentence and some subtopics; sometimes it carries over from a previous paragraph and is assumed to be understood or is referred to briefly; but usually it simply takes the form of a sentence, sometimes amplified or made more specific in a sentence or two following it. This topic sentence may appear at the end of the paragraph as a kind of summary or somewhere within the paragraph, but most frequently it opens the paragraph or follows an opening introduction or transition (Gorrell and Laird, p. 25).

The authors further clarify their definition (pp. 25–26) by stating that a topic sentence has three main functions: (1) to provide transition, (2) to suggest the organization of the paragraph, (3) to present a topic, either by naming or introducing a subject or by presenting a proposition or thesis for discussion. In the next several pages, the authors consider various types of "topic sentences as propositions" (or theses) and the problems in writing them with precision.

From my preliminary attempts to identify topic sentences in paragraphs, I could see the truth of a complex definition like Gorrell and Laird's. But such a comprehensive definition presents problems. Sometimes a paragraph opens with a sentence which we could all agree is transitional but which does not reveal much about the content of the paragraph. The second sentence may name the topic of the paragraph but not make a statement about it. The actual thesis of the paragraph may be stated explicitly in a succeeding sentence or in several sentences, or it may merely be inferred from what follows, even though it is never stated explicitly. In such a paragraph, which is the topic sentence—the first, second, a succeeding sentence, perhaps even all of them? Many of the sentences seem to fit the definition. An all-embracing definition does not seem helpful to me in deciding which sentence can be named the topic sentence.

Furthermore, as Paul Rodgers demonstrated (1966), paragraphing does not always correspond to a reader's perceived organization of ideas. Sometimes a paragraph presents an illustration of the thesis of the preceding paragraph. The second paragraph thus extends the previous paragraph, and the paragraph indentation seems quite arbitrary. Or sometimes a thesis is stated in a one-sentence paragraph and the following paragraph explains that thesis without restating it. In such situations, one cannot simply identify a topic sentence in each paragraph.

It seemed to me that the best test of topic sentences is the test a careful reader might make—the test offered when one constructs a sentence outline of the major points of an essay, drawing the sentences insofar as possible from the sentences the author has written. In constructing a sentence outline, one usually omits transitional and illustrative statements and concentrates on the theses themselves. Consequently, I decided to prepare a sentence outline of each of the 25 essays and then determine which paragraphs had topic sentences and where in the paragraphs they occurred.

Outlines

From the beginning of the first one, I was aware of the serious problems in constructing a sentence outline to study the organization of another person's writing. To what degree would I tend to impose on an essay my own interpretation of what was written? Does it do violence to discursive writing to cast it into the form of a sentence outline, trying to make the outline understandable by itself when the essay includes details of thought and qualities of style omitted in the process? Would the paragraphing and other typographical features of the edited essay distract me from the ideas and structure of the written essay? Of course I would try to preserve the author's intent in all of these matters, but what I actually did would be so much a matter of judgment that I should expose my outlines for the criticism of others, permitting comparison to the original articles. Moreover, the outlines might be helpful to other investigators who would like to use them without going to the extensive effort of preparing their own. Although it is impractical to include the outlines here, I will make them available to others for the cost of the copying.

In outlining an article, I read it through in sections of a number of paragraphs which seemed to be related, underlining topic sentences where I could find them and constructing topic sentences where they were not explicit in the article. In constructing a topic sentence, I tried to include phrases from the original text as much as possible. Whatever sentences, phrases, or key words I did use from the original I was careful to enclose in quotation marks, indicating by ellipsis marks all omissions and by brackets all of my own insertions. Opposite each entry in the outline I indicated the number of the paragraph and T-unit of each quotation used. Thus the notation 20:2,3 and 4 indicates that quoted portions of the outline entry were taken from the second, third, and fourth T-units of the twentieth paragraph in the essay. On a few occasions where I took an idea from a paragraph but it did not seem possible to cast it in the author's original words at all, I put the paragraph number in parentheses to indicate that. But I tried to use the author's words as much as I could, even, in some cases, where it yielded a somewhat unwieldy entry in the outline.

To illustrate the approach, let me offer in Figure 1 the opening paragraphs from the first article in the corpus, indicating the corresponding entries in the outline.

Notice the different types of outline entries necessitated by the various kinds of paragraphs the author writes. Topic Sentence B is an example of what I would call a *simple topic sentence,* one which is quoted entirely or almost entirely from one T-unit in the passage, wherever that T-unit occurs. (Incidentally, the last sentence in Paragraph 2 is not reflected in Topic Sentence B because that last sentence is an early foreshadowing of the main idea of the entire article.)

Topic Sentence C is a fairly common type, one in which the topic sentence seems to begin in one T-unit but is completed in a later T-unit. In Paragraph 3, the first sentence does not make a specific enough statement about the two existing statutes to serve as a complete topic sentence, even though it

FIGURE 1   Sample Paragraphs and Outline Entries

Opening Paragraphs from Drew, p. 33	*Excerpt from Outline*	
1. Among the news items given out to a shocked nation following the assassination of President Kennedy was the fact that Lee Harvey Oswald had purchased his weapon, a 6.5-mm Italian carbine, from a Chicago mail-order house under an assumed name. The rifle was sent, no questions asked, to one "A. Hidell," in care of a post-office box in Dallas. The transaction was routine in the mail-order trade; about one million guns are sold the same way each year.	I. "By the ordinary rules of the game, the events in Dallas should have ensured prompt enactment . . . " of gun control legislation by Congress.	2:2
	A. "President Kennedy" had recently been shot with one of the "one million guns . . . sold . . . each year" through "the mail-order business in guns."	1:1,3,4
2. At the same time, a bill was pending in Congress to tighten regulation of the rapidly expanding mail-order business in guns. By the ordinary rules of the game, the events in Dallas should have ensured prompt enactment, just as the news of Thalidomide-deformed babies had provided the long-needed impetus for passage of stricter drug regulations in 1962. But Congress did not act—a testimonial to the deadly aim of the shooting lobby.	B. "At the same time, a bill was pending in Congress to tighten regulation of the rapidly expanding mail-order business in guns."	2:1
3. Two existing statutes presumably deal with the gun traffic. Both were passed in reaction to the gangsterism of the prohibition era. But because of limited coverage, problems of proof, and various other quirks, they have had a negligible impact on the increasing gun traffic.	C. "Two existing statutes. . . . [had] a negligible impact on the increasing gun traffic."	3:1,3
4. The investigation of the mail-order traffic in guns began in 1961 under the auspices of the Juvenile Delinquency subcommittee. . . .		

reveals the subject of the paragraph. One must go to the third sentence to find the predicate for the topic sentence. Let us term this type a *delayed-completion topic sentence.* Not all delayed-completion topic sentences stem from separated subjects and predicates, though. Sometimes the two sentences present a question and then an answer (Fischer, 18:1,2), a negative followed by a positive (Fischer, 38:1,2), or metaphoric language subsequently explained by straight language (Drucker, 8:1,2). The T-units from which a delayed-completion topic sentence is drawn are not always adjoining. In one instance, I discovered them separated by three T-units (Collado, 29:1,2,6); in another, in adjoining paragraphs (Caudill, 17:2 and 18:1); in still another, nine paragraphs apart (Lear, 1:1,2 and 10:1).

Notice that Topic Sentence A is an example of a statement assembled by quotations from throughout the paragraph. The first sentence in Paragraph 1 cannot properly be considered the topic sentence: it includes such phrases as "the news item" and "a shocked nation" and such details as the name of the assassin, the size and make of the carbine, and the location of the mail order house—such matters as are not essential to the topic sentence; and it omits such a detail as the scope of the problem—"one million guns . . . sold . . . each year"—which helps convey the idea in Statement I. To ease later reference to this type of topic sentence, let us call it an *assembled topic sentence.*

Finally, there is what we might call an *inferred topic sentence,* one which the reader thinks the writer has implied even though the reader cannot construct it by quoting phrases from the original passage. Though the paragraph in Figure 2 comes out of context—from an article on cutting the costs of medical care—it may still be clear why the corresponding topic sentence had to be inferred.

As I was determining what were the topic sentences of an article, I was also keeping an eye out for what we might call the *major topic sentences* of the larger stadia of discourses. That is, a series of topic sentences all added up to a major topic sentence; a group of paragraphs all added up to what William Irmscher (1972) calls a "paragraph bloc" within the entire article. A major topic sentence (designated with a Roman numeral) might head as few as two topic sentences (designated with capital letters) in the outline or as many as 12 topic sentences (in the Kahn outline) or 15 (the most, in the Mumford outline). On the other hand, it was frequently apparent that the main idea of a paragraph was really a subpoint of the main idea of another paragraph. Let us call these *subtopic sentences.* As few as two and as many as seven subtopic sentences (in the Taper outline) were headed by a topic sentence. Sometimes a major topic sentence or a subtopic sentence was simply stated in a single T-unit, but sometimes it had to be assembled, sometimes inferred. Some occurred as delayed-completion topic sentences.

After completing the rest of the outline, I arrived at the main idea (the thesis) or, in the case of the Kahn and Sargeant articles (both *New Yorker* "Profiles"), the purpose. And as with the various types of topic sentences, I drew quoted phrases from the article to construct the statement of the main idea whenever possible, but with one exception—if a term or phrase occurred frequently in the article, I would not enclose it in quotations and note

FIGURE 2   Sample of Paragraph Yielding Inferred Topic Sentence

Paragraph from Sanders, p. 24	*Excerpt from Outline*
Fortunately most ailments do not require such elaborate treatment. Pills cost a good deal less but even they are no small item in the medical bill. From 1929 to 1956 prescription sales climbed from $140 million to $1,466 million a year, and the average price per prescription rose from 85 cents to $2.62. Citing the findings of the Kefauver Committee, Professor Harris makes a strong case for more—and more stringent—regulation of the pharmaceutical industry by the government.	Prescription drug costs have risen.

its location unless it seemed to me to have been put by the author in a particular place or signalled in a particular way to suggest that he was at that time intentionally indicating to readers the nature of his main idea.

After all of the outlines were completed, I went back through each one, classifying each topic sentence as one of the four types and checking the outline against the text of the original essay.

FINDINGS

A tabulation of the frequency of each type of topic sentence for each of the 25 essays is presented in Table 1. It should not escape the reader that the number of topic sentences in an outline does not correspond directly to the number of paragraphs in its essay. Sometimes a major topic sentence and a topic sentence occurred in the same paragraph, and sometimes several paragraphs seemed devoted to the presentation of one topic sentence. (The total number of topic sentences—including the main idea or purpose, major topic sentences, topic sentences, and subtopic sentences, if any—and the total number of paragraphs are given in the two columns at the right of the table.)

One conclusion from Table 1 is that the use made of the different types of topic sentences varies greatly from one writer to the next. Another is that the four articles taken from the *New Yorker* (each one a "Profile") tend to have yielded a higher proportion of assembled topic sentences than most of the other essays.

Frequency of Types of Topic Sentences

Table 2 combines the data for the 25 essays, indicating the distribution of topic sentences of each type. It is clear that less than half of all the topic sen-

TABLE 1   Frequency of Types of Topic Sentences in Each of the 25 Essays

Essay No.	Author	Magazine	Main Idea	Simple			Del-Comp.			Assembled			Inferred			Total TS's	Total Pars.
				MTS	TS	STS	MTS	TS	STS	MTS	TS	STS	MTS	TS	STS		
1	Drew	Reporter	Inf.	3	8	2	0	2	0	2	2	2	0	0	0	22	2
2	Tebbel	Sat. Rev.	D-C	1	5	2	1	2	0	0	5	2	1	2	1	23	25
3	Collado	Sat. Rev.	Sim.	3	8	3	1	1	2	0	4	9	0	1	0	33	50
4	Sargeant	New York.	Inf.	1	3	0	0	0	0	1	13	6	3	3	1	32	26
5	Chamberlain	Atlantic	Inf.	3	5	2	0	2	0	1	7	3	0	0	0	24	24
6	Daniels	Sat. Rev.	Sim.	3	8	0	0	0	0	0	6	0	0	0	0	18	27
7	E. Taylor	Reporter	Ass.	3	8	0	0	2	0	1	2	0	0	0	0	17	19
8	Kaufman	Atlantic	Ass.	2	13	5	1	2	7	1	0	2	0	1	0	35	41
9	Kahn	New York.	Inf.	0	7	0	0	1	0	1	25	0	4	5	0	44	45
10	Handlin	Atlantic	Sim.	4	11	0	0	7	0	1	4	0	0	0	0	28	35
11	Francois	Reporter	Ass.	2	5	0	0	1	0	0	3	0	0	1	0	13	13
12	Sanders	Harper's	Sim.	3	12	0	0	4	0	1	6	0	2	3	0	32	35
13	Lear	Sat. Rev.	Sim.	0	7	0	2	2	0	2	15	0	2	1	0	32	67
14	Lyons	Atlantic	Sim.	4	8	0	1	1	0	1	13	0	0	2	0	31	53
15	Ribman	Harper's	Inf.	5	20	0	0	4	0	1	12	0	1	0	0	44	56
16	Taper	New York.	Inf.	4	14	1	0	3	0	3	16	11	0	0	0	53	53
17	Fischer	Harper's	Inf.	4	11	9	0	1	1	1	9	3	0	1	0	41	42
18	Mumford	New York.	Inf.	2	17	0	0	2	0	3	27	0	2	0	0	54	49
19	Drucker	Harper's	Sim.	5	15	1	0	5	1	0	16	1	0	0	0	45	53
20	Caudill	Atlantic	Sim.	2	10	3	0	7	0	2	6	0	0	0	0	31	39
21	C. Taylor	Atlantic	Sim.	1	11	0	0	1	1	2	7	3	1	1	0	29	29
22	Cousins	Sat. Rev.	Sim.	1	2	0	1	2	0	1	3	0	0	0	0	11	13
23	Clark	Harper's	Sim.	4	8	0	1	1	1	0	4	1	0	0	0	21	26
24	Durrell	Atlantic	Sim.	1	5	0	1	0	0	1	6	0	0	0	0	15	13
25	Rule	Atlantic	Ass.	3	15	0	1	3	0	1	9	0	0	0	0	33	36
Totals			25	64	236	28	10	56	13	27	220	43	16	21	2	761	889

MTS = major topic sentence   TS = topic sentence   STS = subtopic sentence

37

tences (45%) are simple topic sentences and almost as many (39%) are assembled. It is also apparent that—except for the statements of the main idea or purpose—the more of the text that the topic sentence covers, the more likely it is to be a simple topic sentence. That is, of the 117 major topic sentences, 55% were simple; of the 533 topic sentences, 44% were simple; of the 80 subtopic sentences, 33% were simple.

One might well maintain that simple and delayed-completion topic sentences are relatively explicit, that assembled and inferred topic sentences are relatively implicit. Pairing the types of topic sentences in that fashion, Table 2 reveals no great changes in the tendencies of the percentages. Slightly more than half of all the topic sentences (55%) are explicit, slightly less than half (45%) implicit. Again, with the exception of statements of main idea and purpose, the more of the text which the topic sentence covers, the more likely it is to be explicit.

If what the composition textbooks refer to as "the topic sentence" is the same thing as this study terms the simple topic sentence, it is apparent that claims about its frequency should be more cautious. It just is not true that most expository paragraphs have topic sentences in that sense. Even when simple and delayed-completion topic sentences are combined into the category "explicit topic sentences"—a broader conception than many textbook writers seem to have in mind—the frequency reaches only 55% of all the entries in a sentence outline. And when one remembers that only 761 outline topic sentences represent the 889 paragraphs in all 25 essays, he realizes that considerably fewer than half of all the paragraphs in the essays have even explicit topic sentences, to say nothing of simple topic sentences.

Placement of Simple Topic Sentences

How true is the claim that most expository paragraphs open with topic sentences? To find out, I studied the paragraph location of the 264 topic sentences and subtopic sentences in the outline. Gorrell and Laird, like others, had written that the "topic sentence may appear at the end of the paragraph as a kind of summary or somewhere within the paragraph, but most frequently it opens the paragraph or follows an opening introduction or transition" (p. 25). Thus I decided to tabulate the occurrence of each simple topic

TABLE 2   Percentages of Topic Sentences of Various Types

Types of Topic Sentences	No.	Percentages					
		Sim.	D-C	Explicit	Ass.	Inf.	Implicit
Main idea or purpose	25	48	4	52	16	32	48
Major topic sentences	117	55	9	63	23	14	37
Topic sentences	533	44	11	55	41	4	45
Subtopic sentences	86	33	15	48	50	2	52
All types together	761	45	11	55	39	6	45

sentence as it appeared in each of four positions: the first T-unit in the paragraph, the second T-unit, the last, or a T-unit between the second and last. To do that, of course, I could consider only paragraphs of four or more T-units. Consequently, I excluded from consideration paragraphs with three or fewer T-units. The results are presented in Table 3.

More than a fourth (28%) of all those paragraphs presenting simple topic sentences or simple subtopic sentences contained fewer than four T-units. Of the rest, 47% presented a simple topic sentence or simple subtopic sentence in the first T-unit, 15% in the second T-unit, 12% in the last T-unit, and 26% elsewhere. But these figures are based on the 190 paragraphs of four or more T-units which contain simple topic sentences or simple subtopic sentences. There were 355 paragraphs from which other topic sentences or subtopic sentences were drawn—delayed-completion, assembled, and inferred. One cannot say that they "have topic sentences to open them." Consequently, it is obvious that much smaller percentages than the above pertain to expository paragraphs in general. Furthermore, there were at least 128 paragraphs from which no topic sentences at all were drawn. If one adds the 190, 355, and 128, he has a total of 673 from which percentages may be computed, if he wishes to estimate what percentage of *all* of the paragraphs in the 25 essays open with a topic sentence. Using those figures, I estimate that only 13% of the expository paragraphs of contemporary professional writers begin with a topic sentence, that only 3% end with a topic sentence.

IMPLICATIONS FOR TEACHING

Teachers and textbook writers should exercise caution in making statements about the frequency with which contemporary professional writers use simple or even explicit topic sentences in expository paragraphs. It is abundantly clear that students should not be told that professional writers usually begin their paragraphs with topic sentences. Certainly teachers of reading, devisers of reading tests, and authors of reading textbooks should assist students in identifying the kinds of delayed-completion and implicit topic statements which outnumber simple topic sentences in expository paragraphs.

This sample of contemporary professional writing did not support the claims of textbook writers about the frequency and location of topic sentences in professional writing. That does not, of course, necessarily mean the same findings would hold for scientific and technical writing or other types of exposition. Moreover, it does not all mean that composition teachers should stop showing their students how to develop paragraphs from clear topic sentences. Far from it. In my opinion, often the writing in the 25 essays would have been clearer and more comfortable to read if the paragraphs had presented more explicit topic sentences. But what this study does suggest is this: While helping students use clear topic sentences in their writing and identify variously presented topical ideas in their reading, the teacher should not pretend that professional writers largely follow the practices he is advocating.

TABLE 3 Location of Simple Topic Sentences and Simple Subtopic Sentences

											Essay Number																
Location	1	2	3	4	5	6	7	8	9	10	11	12	13	14	15	16	17	18	19	20	21	22	23	24	25	Tot.	%
(Paragraph shorter than 4 T-units)	1	1	4	0	3	2	6	5	0	4	1	7	4	0	9	0	6	1	4	2	0	1	6	1	6	74	(28)
First T-unit	6	2	2	3	3	2	0	2	6	4	2	2	1	2	7	5	7	3	6	5	8	1	0	3	7	89	47
Second T-unit	1	4	2	0	0	1	1	2	0	1	0	1	0	1	1	0	4	5	0	2	2	0	1	0	0	29	15
Last T-unit	0	0	1	0	0	1	0	4	0	0	0	0	2	0	0	1	1	4	3	2	1	0	1	0	1	22	12
Elsewhere	2	0	2	0	1	2	1	5	1	2	2	2	0	5	3	9	2	4	3	2	0	0	0	1	1	50	26
Total no. of TS's and STS's in essay	10	7	11	3	7	8	8	18	7	11	5	12	7	8	20	15	20	17	16	13	11	2	8	5	15	264	
Total no. of paragraphs in essay	20	25	50	26	24	27	19	41	45	35	13	35	67	53	56	53	42	49	53	39	29	13	26	13	36	889	

Dick Braddock was a man of common sense. He believed that the ordinary person doing systematic work could discover important truths. Neither genius nor high theory was required. That made him a genial social democrat who welcomed all comers.

His essay shows off one side of his matter-of-factness. He doubted the accepted lore about topic sentences as presented in most textbooks of the time, so he carefully picked out samples of published prose and tabulated the location of topic sentences. His only theory was that people should not argue ahead of their evidence. Although as an administrator of a large program he had to use mass testing, he offered many strictures on how tests should be interpreted and in Research in the Teaching of English (RTE) *led the battle to reform the testing of writing that resulted in the National Assessment of Educational Progress (NAEP). His students were always allowed several escape routes from the verdict of mass tests.*

Braddock's view of research characterized the organization of the 1963 extended review essay Research in Written Composition, *which Braddock, Lowell Schoer, and I coauthored. It also informed the nature of RTE, the journal that Braddock founded. With his commitment to study the state of knowledge about composition, he intended merely to encourage teaching practices that were in accord with what people actually knew, but he found that the evidence from research was thin indeed. He therefore suggested practical guidelines about how one ought to conduct and report research. Having offered such guidelines, he felt one needed a publication to exhibit that kind of work. He recognized that some theory was essential—Aristotle and Dewey were his guides—but he did not really recognize theoretical studies or even historical studies as research. RTE was narrowly empirical.*

Dick Braddock modified this extreme position when he team-taught a summer National Defense Education Act (NDEA) Institute course designed to improve teaching in the schools. He remained doubtful about stylistic variation for its own sake and the propriety of irony in the classroom, but he conceded that in the right hands such concerns were valid. He recognized that students were enthusiastic about being treated as writers. He was also moved by a colleague in the writing program who made assignments seem optional and yet acquired more writing from students than did instructors who assigned set tasks. Students who cared about their writing wrote more.

For all that, he still saw writing as a basic skill necessary in a free society. He wanted students to define issues, compile evidence, and make careful and fair judgments. His students were not writers, but ordinary people expressing themselves responsibly. He wanted them and their audiences to represent all parts of society. In the early 60s, he urged the CCCC to select an African American for chair (they declined). And when Martin Luther King, Jr., was murdered during the CCCC convention, he turned the second day of the meeting into a seminar on race relations in colleges and in society generally. He was especially energetic in helping two-year colleges develop their programs to serve all students.

Dick deplored over-statement in private and public life. Given the journalistic and political discourse of these later years, we miss his temperate advice.

—Richard Lloyd-Jones
University of Iowa

What I Learned at School

JIM W. CORDER

When fall comes and the school year begins, I'm sometimes plagued by a temporary friskiness that tends to cause me some trouble before it subsides. This friskiness, I think, rises from two sources: part of it is left over from the summer when for a moment or two I'm led to think that I can really be a teacher, chiefly because there are not any committee meetings in the summer; part of it is left over from old times when I thought September 1 was New Year's Day because soon school would start and the Sears Roebuck catalogue would come.

At any rate, I am sometimes troubled by this coltish vigor before it wanes to be replaced by the decrepitude that is my more normal wont. This year, it led me to make a special mess of things. In an excess of zeal during the first meeting of my freshman composition class, I vowed that I would write an essay every time they did and that I would turn my essays over to them as they turned theirs in to me. Once I had said that, I was led by fear, desperation, and a smidgin of honor to do what I had said I would do. Now, nine essays and some short written exercises later, the term has ended, and I am blurred and fuzzy around the edges. Still, I want to do two things: I want to report what I think I learned while I was writing essays with my students, and I want to exhibit the last of these essays as one way of thinking about a composition class.

When I try to tally the things I learned while writing essays, the total is not impressive, but what's there is sufficiently troublesome, perplexing, confusing, instructive, and vexatious to bring me up short and to cast doubt upon certain assumptions about freshman composition.

1. I learned that writing out one's own assignments is a marvelous corrective to any tendency one might have for using merely habitual assignments or for witlessly making thoughtless or stupid assignments.

2. With some of the arguments and assumptions that undergird freshman composition I am familiar. I know that "the ability to write a literate

---

This essay was first published in *CCC*, Volume 26, Number 4, December 1975.

essay is the hallmark of the educated person." I know that "a competent student ought to be able to produce a decent piece of writing on call." But I also learned that to write nine essays in a semester of fourteen weeks (I'm leaving out holiday weeks and the like) is a task very nearly not doable. I thought for a while that I would have to give myself an "I" for the course. I'll return to this item a bit later.

3. I learned that I often did precisely what I urged my students not to do: I hurried; I waited until the last moment, because that was the only moment there was; I accepted available subjects that came easily to mind; I wrote some "nice" essays and some "acceptable" essays; once or twice I turned in rough drafts as if they were finished papers. Perhaps I should add that I did usually get semicolons in the right place.

4. I need to say more about items 2 and 3 in order to tell what I really learned, to tell why writing nine essays is a task very nearly not doable. Perhaps what I really learned is that I have not learned enough. Or perhaps what I really learned is that part of what I know *about* writing (though right enough in its way) is not germane or immediate or companionable when one is *doing* the writing. Perhaps I shall be thought merely naive, but as I was writing the nine essays I found myself being shocked and surprised and stunned. (I'd not want anyone to think I was in a state of heightened sensibilities all of the time—a good part of the time I was simply stuporous.) The things that kept disturbing me can be suggested best, I think, under two headings: problems in the inventive capacities given by a semester, and problems in establishing occasions for writing.

I know some of the hopes and goals associated with invention or "prewriting" and some of the methods developed to foster rich and generative invention. But a term has markedly little time in it. Last semester when I was writing the nine essays, I was busy (and I'd like to stop and sing a sad song or two about that), but that's no great matter: every person's life is usually busy to the level that can be tolerated. Students in the class, who also had to write nine essays, were in this sense as busy as I was. A semester affords precious little time for genuine invention, exploration, and discovery. I found that I frequently was unable to do what I often advised my students to do in searching out subjects and finding ways to be with the subject and an audience in a paper. Actually, in class I was pretty reckless in recommending ways of thinking into subjects: I proposed that my students use journals and write existential sentences; we tackled the topics; I recommended the series of exploratory questions offered by Richard E. Larson (in *College English,* October, 1968); we practiced using problem-solving systems for locating the materials of a paper; we hungered after various heuristic models for discovery; we looked at this, that, and the other thing as particles, waves, and fields. We even tried the TUTO rhythmic method (and I'll be glad to answer letters inquiring after the TUTO mysteries).

But the sorry truth is that, whatever the students were able to do as they were writing, I was almost never able to think a paper out ahead of time; I was never able to write a draft and let it alone awhile before I revised it for final copy; I was never able to try portions of the essays from different perspectives and in different styles. I was never able to take a possible subject, hold it in my hand, look at it in this way and that way, and scout its possibilities. What I actually did was to cash in ideas I *already* had for writing, threshing around among scraps of paper, notebooks, and lists of things to do that were piled on my desk, finding subjects and sketched designs for writing that I wanted to do some time. A dark thought struck me one night: What if I didn't have these notions collected to cash in? That dark thought was followed by another: What if I were not in the habit of writing, of expecting to write, of saving notes against the time when I would write? In other words, I finally thought, what if I were in the same fix that most of the students in my class were in?

But the perturbation I felt went further. I found myself continually troubled by the character of what I'll call the occasions for writing. I remember sitting at my desk one evening when I *had* to get an essay written to give to my students the next morning. I remember the moment clearly. I was sitting there looking at the assignment I had given to my students, when another dark thought came: "I *know* how to write this thing," I remember saying to myself, "but why in hell would anybody *want* to?"

What I am trying to get at here is that the occasion is wrong. The occasion contains no immediacy; it offers no genuine need that must be genuinely answered. I mean to suggest that even some of our best assignments—imaginative and thoughtful as they may be—do not elicit a driving need to write. I mean to suggest that some of our best assignments do not elicit the students' investment of themselves in the work.

Perhaps I should learn not to worry. Perhaps I should learn to accept the freshman composition course as a place for the acquisition of tools and for practice in using them skillfully in finger exercises. There'd be no shame in that—indeed, nothing but good. But I think I won't learn that, because I keep learning something else at school, every term. I can best begin to say what that is, I believe, by exhibiting the last essay I wrote with the students in my class.

HALF THOUGHTS ON A WHOLE SEMESTER

I was ruminating last night over certain features of English 1203, sensing a weight that some of its parts carry. Ruminating, I should say, is an activity, better still a condition, I assign high priority to. Given the choice, I'll ruminate anytime rather than turn the compost pile or paint the dining-room or grade papers or fix the shelf that's been waiting for five and a half years or work on the manuscript that's due March 1. At any rate, I was ruminating, turning the semester's topics this way and that to see how they looked from the under side and what consequence they had.

But I can only speak of consequence in certain ways. I'd not presume to declare that topics of my devising had this, that, or the other specific consequence for students. I'm generally inclined to think that all courses are failures: there's always more to be said than can be said in a given moment, always more reaches of thought to be in than one can be in at a given moment. So if I speak of consequences, I am not speaking of consequences of the course, but of consequences, weights, significances carried by the topics of concern themselves. The topics, the issues, the practices carry meaning, I think, even if it is not presently realized in us. The subject makes its own assertions, to which we're seldom equal.

On the first day of the term, I remember remarking that I wanted to conceive of the work we might do not as the work of a single term, but as the work of a two-term, nine-month period. I said then, I recall, that as I was presently able to understand the work before us, it could be seen in three stages: the practice of *invention,* the shaping of *structure,* and the tuning of *styles.* As I recollect the occasion, I noted that I expected the end of the fall term to come between the second and third of these.

Since that day much has happened, though often without notice. Miss Puckitt has always come early, usually followed by Miss Ramsey. Miss Daniel and Miss Cesarotti have always been punctual—two minutes late. Miss Pugh and Miss FitzSimmon have walked down the hall together. Mr. Ragsdale has written an essay about toothpaste. Mr. White has been quiet in the back, though his essays are not quiet alone but forceful. Miss Steinberg has seen to it that I remembered to be humble. Miss Stamper has found sonata form in Stegner's essay. Miss Westbrook has meditated on epistolary ills. Mr. Spleth from a "Bad Beginning" has surged toward who knows what ending. Miss Fouch has found a way to talk about intravenous tubes and cats in the same essay. Mr. Haney has embarked upon a series of essays that may come at last to seventeen volumes and be studied by freshmen. Miss Bachman has told a strange Thanksgiving narrative in which much depended on a word heard out of context. Mr. Hayes has vowed his distaste for hickory nuts. Mr. Posselt, lately arrived from the north, has encountered a street evangelist. Mr. Sherwood has found in empathy a way of distinguishing among teachers. Miss Lawson has almost learned to be decisive. Mr. Whitney has celebrated his home town's virtues, though we both hope that the actual text of the celebration is not to be published abroad in Tyler. And Mr. Steimel has slept as well as could be reasonably expected, though of late he has taken to staying awake and disturbing the class.

Meanwhile, with various fanfares, flourishes, and fallings-down, I like to imagine that I have been talking about *invention* and *structure.* What I think I said (as distinct from what you may have heard, distracted by 372 pipe lightings) arranged itself in something like this order:

INVENTION (the exploration that precedes and leads to writing)
   —where you find subjects if you don't have one, or what to do with a
      subject that someone else hands you
   —taking a subject over, making it into something of your own
   —seeing the fullness of a subject, learning its potential
   —ways of thinking through subjects

—relationships among writer, subject, and audience, and the distances between them

—using the resources that you need to deal with a subject

—logical development and emotional appeals

—learning to be real with an audience

STRUCTURE (design, organization, shape in writing)

—some practice in describing structures

—some talk about structural transfers from one medium or art form to another

—using structures that others use

—some talk about the relation of structure and meaning

A little earlier, you may recall, I was talking about the consequences such topics have, trying to establish that the consequences I am talking about are not those of the course, but the weights, values, meanings the topics themselves carry. I can illustrate what I mean, I think, by referring to the list just above. For example, we talked at various times about using the resources that are available to you, including research, and about taking over and using a structure that other writers have used. Those two notions, whether I managed to say it fully or not, whether you managed to hear it fully or not, can carry an import in their own right, an import and significance not limited to freshman composition. They give us a way of knowing that we are, after all, together with each other, that we are in community if we wish to be, that others have striven and learned, and that we may learn from them with less strife, that we are not alone, though we can be if we wish. In some way or another, I think each of the items arranged above carries such meaning.

But I have been thinking from the start not about the signification of each topic raised, but about the meaning carried by invention itself, by structure itself, and by the order in which they appeared. Such meaning—and it is of course not complete—stretches out, it seems to me, from English composition to everything, but can at the moment best be expressed in the context and language of a composition class, as I have tried to do below. I herewith advance to you certain propositions intended to suggest what is learnable from composition study and practice (though it's also nice if you learn where to put semicolons). If you find the numbering system below a bit strange, you will understand from it, I think, that there are yet other propositions I have not found.

Ninth law of composition: Everything comes from somewhere and goes some place. You touch other people, and they enter your world, coming from another. You read a book and capture its author into your world. Both come from somewhere and move elsewhere, into your thoughts, giving texture to the universe you live in, becoming finally the words you speak.

Eleventh law of composition: Some things precede other things. Invention precedes structure. Thinking and feeling and being precede writing. Structures made without invention are false or superficial. There probably is a fit sequencing of things, even if we don't always see it.

Eighteenth law of composition: You are always standing somewhere when you say something. You are in a world, you have thoughts, you've made choices (whether or not consciously) any time you say anything. If you are in a position whenever you say anything, it's probably best to know what the position is.

Twenty-fifth law of composition: Invention is an invitation to openness. It asks of you that you open yourself to the ways other people think, to the knowledge that already exists, to the intricacies and whims of your own being. It asks of you that you therefore be tentative a while, consider alternatives a while, be in process a while.

Twenty-sixth law of composition: But structure is a closure. You can't organize an essay or a sonata unless you have ruled out other organizations. When structure begins to be made, you are no longer open: you have made choices.

Twenty-seventh law of composition: Invention and structure, then, represent a way of being in the world. They exert certain demands upon you, and they afford you certain pleasures. Invention invites you to be open to a creation filled with copious wonders, trivialities, sorrows, and amazements. Structure requires that you close. You are asked to be open and always closing.

Thirty-second law of composition: What follows feeds, enlarges, and enriches what precedes. Invention precedes and is open. Structure follows and closes. That may seem a narrowing disappointment, a ruling out of possibilities. It needn't be. Every choice, every decision, every structure has the potential of being another entry in the inventive world you live in, modifying it, punching it in here, pooching it out there, giving color to it yonder. Invention precedes, structure follows, but invention does not cease thereby. The structure we make today may give grace to tomorrow's invention. That means that if today we fail to be wise and generous and good, tomorrow we may succeed, and if not, we may fail at a higher level.

I should report, in closing, that when the students in my class examined my papers, as I examined theirs, they concluded that I was given to rambling.

AFTERWORD . . . .

For Jim Corder, the daily, metaphysical necessities were few: smoking a pipe every minute, drinking gallons of coffee, teaching, and writing. Constantly writing.

When my son Andrew and I visited Jim and Roberta Corder last August, Jim was gravely ill. After our visit, Roberta encouraged me to scan his unpub-

lished manuscripts. His office reeked of pipe smoke, as always. Lying on his desk was a notecard with a typical list of things to do. At the top were two words: "Ede Essay." I assume that this phrase indicated the afterword that he was planning to write for this book. He never got a chance: he died the next day.

You will have to settle for me, his former student.

For decades, Corder was an extremely popular professor at Texas Christian University. He directed many dissertations and served for years as department chair, then as dean. He published ceaselessly: a handbook that went into six editions; one of the best process composition textbooks of the late 1970s; and many essays for CCC, College English, Rhetoric Review, Freshman English News, Rhetoric Society Quarterly, PRE/TEXT, *and scholarly collections. Before large audiences at CCCC conventions, he appeared alongside such luminaries as Richard Young, Wayne Booth, Jim Berlin, and Ross Winterowd.*

In Uses of Rhetoric—*his pioneering, but scandalously neglected work from 1971—Corder notes the strangulation that results from organizing English curricula according to literary genres and periods. And he provocatively and ingeniously applies classical rhetoric to canonical literature and to ephemeral popular "texts," such as magazine ads. He also proposes not Writing across the Curriculum, but Rhetoric across the Curriculum—the entire curriculum. In short, an academic revolution.*

Corder abhorred English curricula that monumentalize poetry, fiction, and drama while ignoring what is now called "creative nonfiction." He especially relished works by Loren Eiseley and John Graves. He loved Samuel Johnson and liked Peter Elbow—a combination I am still trying to fathom.

Corder was paradoxical. A groundbreaking rhetorician, he rarely flat-out argued, either in person or in print. I think he hated argument. "What I Learned at School" is typical Corder: a personal essay about rhetoric that persuades by suggesting rather than insisting.

His best essay, however, is "Argument as Emergence, Rhetoric as Love," which crystallizes his desire for a rhetoric capacious and inclusive rather than antagonistic.

Beginning in 1988, Corder wrote fewer academic pieces, sacrificing part of his audience as he produced creative nonfiction. Lost in West Texas *and* Chronicle of a Small Town *present a hard-scrabble boyhood in tiny Jayton during the Great Depression.* Hunting Lieutenant Chadbourne *treats a young soldier who left a cache of letters before dying in the Mexican War.*

Yonder—*to my mind the best of these books*—*features prose poems in which Corder subjects his later self to severe scrutiny.*

In these works, Corder examines antinomies: the necessity for and unreliability of memory, the obsession with and absurdity of nostalgia, the compulsion to understand one's self and the impossibility of doing so.

Corder wrote three unpublished books of reflections: Making It in Las Vegas, Scrapbook, *and* To the Carolinas. *And he left an unissued* Rhetorics, Remnants, and Regrets, *which Roberta Corder calls "his last word on rhetoric." With any luck, all these books will appear soon and his entire achievement can be measured.*

–KEITH D. MILLER
Arizona State University

1977

The Search for Intelligible Structure in the Teaching of Composition

FRANK J. D'ANGELO

It has been a little over a decade since George B. Leonard, writing in *Look* magazine, contended,

> Writing is the disgrace of American education. Millions of our boys and girls are graduating from high school—and thousands from college—unable to write 500 sensible words on a single subject. Teachers of composition have grown accustomed to working under "impossible" conditions. The best of them do huge labors and get little thanks. The worst of them—probably a majority—know next to nothing about teaching writing and can barely tell good writing from bad.[1]

This point of view has been amply documented by teachers and scholars in the field. For example, George Stade writes that the teaching of composition "is in a bad way. Everyone says so, even people who are responsible for its being as it is . . . it has suddenly become as embarrassing and superfluous as it is difficult to part with."[2] Virginia Burke emphasizes this point even more forcefully: "There is chaos today in the teaching of composition because since the turn of the century, composition has lacked an informing discipline, without which no field can maintain its proper dimensions, the balance and proportion of its various parts, or its very integrity. Consequently, the practice of composition has shrunk, has lost important elements, has become a victim of all manner of distortion."[3]

More recently, Malcolm Scully, in *The Chronicle of Higher Education*, reports that a recent survey of English department chairmen in colleges and universities reveals that students entering college today are just as deficient in basic writing skills as their counterparts in the early 60's and that even the more verbally gifted students can't express their thoughts in writing. Many entering students are in fact "functionally illiterate."[4] As a result, many major state universities are offering remedial composition courses. In view of this latest "crisis" in composition, few teachers today would take seriously

This essay was first published in *CCC*, Volume 27, Number 2, May 1976.

Warner Rice's proposal, made in 1960, that freshman composition be abolished.[5]

Many reasons have been given for our failure to teach writing adequately: heavy class loads; inadequate or nonexistent teacher-preparation programs in composition; the lack of clear goals; the lack of any discernible structure or logical sequence in the composition program; the dearth of good composition texts; the neglect of teaching composition in favor of teaching literature, media, or some other related subject area; poor student motivation; poor teaching; inappropriate course content, and counter-influences in society which are beyond the control of the teacher. But *one* of the most important reasons for our inability to teach composition adequately is that we have failed to identify the most significant principles and concepts in the field which will make intelligible everything we do. As Virginia Burke puts it,

> The power of a discipline to identify and maintain a field and to energize practice in it should be self-evident. *Without a discipline,* arbitrary decisions to add or drop a composition course, to write a theme a week or a theme a month, to use this textbook or that, to feature one kind of writing or one kind of reading over another, to evaluate papers chiefly for content or for organization or for mechanics—all such arbitrary decisions are without rationale; no decision at all may do as well as a decision one way or the other. *With a discipline,* some reasonable sequence, moving *from* something identifiable *toward* something identifiable, is clearly suggested; and the scope of concerns within the discipline must be explicitly taken into account. *Without a discipline,* undergraduate and graduate offerings in advanced composition and rhetoric can continue slight or nonexistent; and the preparation of teachers of high school and college composition can be treated in familiar, cavalier fashion; *with a discipline,* we must confront the peculiarities and gaps in our undergraduate and graduate offerings as well as our whole approach to English studies.[6]

Unfortunately, there have been few attempts by teachers and scholars to try to identify the underlying principles that constitute the discipline in composition. To add to the confusion, there appears to be a semantic muddle in our use of terms in trying to come to grips with the problem. For example, composition has been described as both a content and a content-less subject in the field of English studies. Those who view it as having a content describe that content as variously being literature, the humanities, communication skills, the students' own writing, grammar, linguistics, semantics, logic, and so forth. Those who view it as being content-less argue that there is no specific subject matter that must be covered in order for the teacher to achieve his objectives, that in fact we don't even know the relationship between the wide variety of content found in composition courses and the development of writing skills.

This multiplication and confusion of terms, goals, and means has obscured our ability to see our field of inquiry clearly and to see it whole. According to James Moffett, our approach to composition has been "far too substantive. . . . The failure to distinguish *kinds* and *orders* of knowledge amounts to a crippling epistemological error built into the very heart of the overall curriculum. The classification by 'subject matters' into English, history, math, science, French, etc., implies that they are all merely contents that differ only in what they are about."[7]

My thesis is that composition does have an underlying structure which gives unity and coherence to the field, that that structure can be conceived of in terms of principles and forms (akin to those found in music or painting, for example), and that these principles and forms need to be taught in an orderly sequence.[8] In the remainder of this paper, therefore, I would like to delineate a few of the most important of these principles and forms and to discuss their implications for the teaching of composition.

I would like to begin my exposition of the structure of composition by presenting some tentative concepts in the following diagrammatic form:

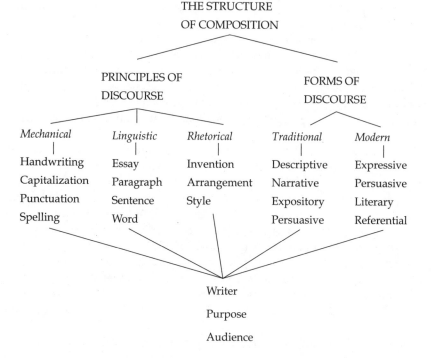

THE STRUCTURE
OF COMPOSITION

PRINCIPLES OF DISCOURSE			FORMS OF DISCOURSE	
Mechanical	*Linguistic*	*Rhetorical*	*Traditional*	*Modern*
Handwriting	Essay	Invention	Descriptive	Expressive
Capitalization	Paragraph	Arrangement	Narrative	Persuasive
Punctuation	Sentence	Style	Expository	Literary
Spelling	Word		Persuasive	Referential

Writer

Purpose

Audience

The principles of discourse pertain to the fundamental laws, rules, and conventions of discourse. These principles are the basic principles determining the intrinsic nature of discourse.[9] They can be found in all forms of discourse; consequently, they can be said to inform the modes of discourse. The forms of discourse refer to the different modes of existence of a discourse. They are concerned with the shape and structure, the overall plan or design or configuration of particular kinds of discourse. These modes are extrinsic in relation to the nature of discourse. Thus, for example, a specific kind of expository writing may be said to be a form of discourse. It in turn may be informed by the linguistic principles of coordination and subordination or by the rhetorical principles of cause and effect. This fundamental distinction between principles and forms should become clearer as we go along. Suffice it to say at this point that writing ability consists in the ability to use these underlying principles and basic forms.

The mechanical principles are basically four: handwriting, capitalization, punctuation, and spelling. The use of the term "mechanical" is not to be taken in a pejorative sense, but it is clear that these principles are not as central to the composition process as are the linguistic principles and the rhetorical principles. One might argue, however, that the principles involved in some of the mechanical skills, punctuation, for example, are inextricably tied in with the other principles, that punctuation is tied in with the linguistic principles of stress, pitch, and juncture, for instance. Nevertheless, it is more useful to consider these principles as being peripheral rather than central to the composition process.

The linguistic principles may be divided into four basic categories: the principles of the essay, the paragraph, the sentence, and the word. The linguistic principles are those that are delineated in the major grammatical texts. These principles are syntactic, morphological, phonological, or graphological, and semantic. They are exemplified by such concepts as coordination and subordination, embedding, negation, relativization, nominalization, compounding, clipping, blending, derivation, functional shift, and the like. These principles may also be found in the major composition texts as well as scattered throughout the journals. There has been so much done with the grammar of the sentence and of the word that extensive discussion of the underlying principles is not necessary. Less familiar perhaps is the work being done with the grammar of the paragraph or of the essay. I might mention as typical examples Alton Becker's tagmemic approach to paragraph analysis, Francis Christensen's generative rhetoric of the paragraph, Paul Rodger's discourse-centered rhetoric of the paragraph, Zellig Harris's discourse analysis, Willis Pitkin's discourse blocs, Michael Grady's conceptual rhetoric of the composition, and my own work with discourse structure. Quite obviously, much more work needs to be done in this important area.

The rhetorical principles are those which are ordinarily found in composition and rhetoric books and those derived from rhetorical theory.[10] I have listed the major principles as being those of invention, arrangement, and style. The principles of invention are exemplified in rhetoric texts by the topics: categories such as analysis, definition, comparison, and cause and effect which suggest questions that a student can use to probe any subject, to discover ideas before he begins to write. The principles of internal arrangement are exemplified by such concepts as analysis, classification, comparison, thesis and support, induction, deduction, and so forth. The schemes and tropes of classical rhetoric are directly concerned with rhetorical principles of style on the sentence level. (Some typical examples of these are parallelism, inversion, various schemes of repetition such as anaphora, metaphor, metonymy, and various kinds of puns.) The principles of diction, as a part of style, are usually approached in terms of paired opposites: general/particular; abstract/concrete; literal/figurative; formal/informal; Anglo-Saxon/Latinate, and so forth.

These concepts do not exhaust the principles of discourse that we ought to be concerned with in the study of composition, but they do suggest that with a little time and effort, we can identify some of the most important principles which are fundamental to the discipline. Clearly, we need to identify and explicate many more.

I had previously mentioned that the principles of discourse are the basic elements that determine the intrinsic nature of discourse. The forms or modes of discourse determine the extrinsic nature of discourse. The modal approach is based on the idea that all writing can be classified on the basis of form. As far as can be determined, Alexander Bain was the first to establish the classification of the four modes of discourse (description, narration, exposition, and argumentation) found in many textbooks today. Bain's categories, however, included poetry as a fifth mode. According to Bain, the forms of discourse are the kinds of composition which relate to the faculties of the mind (the understanding, the will, and feelings), to the aims of discourse (to inform, to persuade, and to please), and more generally to the laws of thought. Thus narration, description, and exposition relate to the faculty of understanding; persuasion relates to the will; and poetry relates to the feelings.

Since Alexander Bain, many other scholars have been interested in the forms-of-discourse approach to writing.[11] One of the most significant of the new approaches to the modes of discourse has been articulated by James L. Kinneavy in his book *A Theory of Discourse*. Following Alexander Bain, Kinneavy contends that each mode of discourse corresponds to a different kind of thinking and to a different view of reality. Furthermore, the reason for the existence of these modes can be found in the human uses of language and the purpose to which this language is put. Thus Kinneavy is as much concerned with the "aims" of discourse as he is with the "modes" of discourse.

Although Kinneavy's theory of mode derives in part from the aims of discourse, it owes part of its theoretical justification to communications theory. The aims of discourse are based on the four elements of the communication triangle: the encoder (the speaker or writer), the decoder (the audience or reader), the reality (the outer world), and the message (the work itself). The following scheme depicts the relationships that obtain among these four modes:

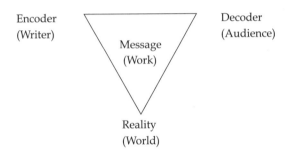

The aims of discourse and the modes of discourse are closely connected. If the writer's aim is self-expression, then the emphasis is on the writer or speaker himself (the encoder), and the result is expressive discourse. If the writer's aim is to convince or persuade, then the stress is on the audience (the decoder), the reader or listener, and the result is persuasive discourse. If the writer's aim is to convey reality, then the emphasis is on that reality (the world), and the result is referential discourse. Finally, if the writer is concerned with the text itself (the message), and the stress is on the internal ordering of the formal characteristics of the text, then the result is literary discourse. These four modes (the expressive, the persuasive, the referential, and the literary) constitute the basic forms of discourse.

Expressive discourse includes such forms as diaries, journals, conversations, protests, gripe sessions, and the like. Referential discourse includes news stories, articles, textbooks, summaries, histories, interviews, theories, taxonomic classifications, descriptive analyses, and so forth. Persuasive discourse comprises advertising, propaganda, oratory, political speeches, sermons, and editorials. Literary discourse embraces the genres of literature, songs, puns, the limerick, jokes, and the T.V. drama.

The reader will notice that an emphasis on the forms of discourse necessarily brings into play a consideration of the writer, his purpose, and his audience. A modal approach to discourse forces us to consider the interrelationships that exist between the writer and his audience, the writer and the text, and the writer and the world, or between the audience and the text, the audience and the world, or the world and the text. Thus the writer, the writer's purpose, the writer's audience, the text, and the rhetorical context (perhaps best exemplified by Kenneth Burke's Pentad: Act, Scene, Agent, Means, Purpose), are principles that are fundamental to the study of composition.

What are the implications of emphasizing the structure of a discipline, of identifying the fundamental principles of a field? The first implication is that a knowledge of the basic ideas of a subject will enable us to use them effectively in developing new curricula. Curricula in composition must be organized around the most fundamental principles of the discipline if they are to be meaningful. Clearly, some sense of progression, some sense of sequence, some kind of connection among various activities is needed in individual courses and from course to course. The second implication is that a knowledge of fundamental principles will help us delineate general goals and specific objectives. How can teachers set up behavioral objectives for composition (as many are increasingly called upon to do) unless they have some basic understanding of the underlying principles of the field? Such objectives can only end up being either idiosyncratic or impressionistic at best. The third implication is that a grasp of basic principles is a necessary precondition for effective teaching. Course "content," teaching techniques, approaches to evaluation, and the choice of the best available texts are just a few things related to effective teaching that depend upon a knowledge of underlying principles and concepts. A fourth implication is that teacher-preparation programs in composition might be substantially improved. If a knowledge of linguistic and rhetorical principles and forms is necessary for good composition teaching, then surely teacher-preparation programs should include some knowledge of linguistics, of new grammars, of semantics, of classical and modern rhetoric, of rhetorical theory, and of new approaches to the teaching of composition. A final implication is that a knowledge of basic principles will help us to identify the gaps in our knowledge and as a consequence encourage us to generate new research. Unfortunately, in some areas, composition does not have the same kind of relevant research to draw upon as other related disciplines.

Identifying the underlying structure or structures of the discipline is not a panacea for all of our composition ills. It is, however, an important first step in bringing a new unity and order to the field. The vast proliferation of knowledge and the lack of simplifying ideas is a grave embarrassment in the field of composition today. The next major advance in composition can come about only as we begin to discover the underlying principles that will inform everything we do. Our task is not merely to identify these fundamental principles and concepts, but to see them as simple. If there exists a simple order in the universe, then clearly the universe of discourse must reflect that order. The call then is for articulate structure in the teaching of composition. As teachers and scholars, we can have no greater goal.

AFTERWORD . . . .

When I wrote "The Search for Intelligible Structure in the Teaching of Composition" in 1976, I was responding to earlier attempts to define composition as a discipline. According to many critics, the composition curriculum was a loose amalgam of separate skills and content which tried to pursue its various objectives in a bewildering variety of ways. Albert Kitzhaber called for agreement on a particular body of content and for basic and applied research. Virginia Burke called for the identification of "an informing discipline" which would make intelligible everything we do.

Scholars knew, more or less, what the structure of classical rhetoric was. But what was the structure of composition? Prior to 1976, the forms of discourse informed many of the most popular textbooks, setting up a sequence of assignments moving from description, to narration, to exposition, to argumentation and persuasion. But James Kinneavy, as early as 1969, in "The Basic Aims of Discourse," questioned the validity of the aims and kinds of discourse prescribed in these textbooks and argued that other aims of discourse ought to be considered.

In a series of articles and conference talks between 1963 and 1975, Wayne Booth, Ed Corbett, James Murphy, Robert Gorrell, and others called for the revival of classical rhetoric in the composition classroom and for the possibility of new rhetorics. Some saw the roots of a new rhetoric in I. A. Richards, Kenneth Burke, the general semanticists, Christensen's generative rhetoric, Young, Becker, and Pike's tagmemic theory, and so forth. Although Gorrell had argued that classical rhetoric deserved more emphasis in the composition classroom, he was also convinced that "there is a subject matter called composition *[which] can be both respectable and profitable" ("Not by Nature" 409).*

Having participated in two NDEA fellowship programs at the University of Illinois and the University of Nebraska between 1966 and 1970, I was familiar with the various attempts to define English as a subject by participants at the Dartmouth Conference and the various Project Englishes. Teachers of composition at the college level, for the most part, rejected the growth model of the Dartmouth Conference and opted for structure and sequence. The dominant influences were Jerome Bruner and Northrop Frye. In The Process of Education, *Bruner had argued that "the foundation of any subject may be taught to anybody in some form" (33). In* Anatomy of Criticism, *Frye contended that literature could be learned progressively and that the structural principles of myth could provide the structural principles of literature.*

In my essay, "The Search for Intelligible Structure in the Teaching of Composition," I tried to identify what was known about the principles and forms of composition at that time. Like Bruner, I reasoned that "grasping the structure of a subject is understanding it in a way that permits many other things to be related to it meaningfully." To be ignorant of what composition is, I concluded, was to be a slave to someone else's course outline, textbook, or point of view. In sum, I believed that identifying the underlying principles and forms of composition would enable teachers and students to be able to put the bits and pieces of

their knowledge about composition into a structured pattern for better understanding and transfer of learning.

Much has happened in the teaching of writing and literature since 1976
that suggests that our earlier emphasis on structure and sequence may have
been misguided and naïve. Yet I see signs as we move beyond postmodernism
that we are entering a new era of structural transformations and relationships,
convergences, and commonalities in the attention being paid to postcolonial and
world literatures, global culture, and cosmopolitanism.

−FRANK J. D'ANGELO
Arizona State University

In Search of a Philosophical Context for Teaching Composition

GLENN MATOTT

will argue these main points: (1) that the most recent (even though, by now, well-established) trend in the teaching of composition entails a radical shift from the traditional focus and methodology; (2) that this trend reflects a view of human experience which is best explained by popularized Sartrean existentialism; (3) that this philosophical orientation is both inappropriate for teachers of communication skills and potentially dangerous for students; and (4) that Martin Buber's thought points the way toward an alternative which is neither a return to the past nor a continuation in the present direction.

1.

The modern trend in teaching composition is characterized by a desire to assist the student toward self-awareness and self-expression. In the abstract, these are admirable goals and ones which are recognized as legitimate even by teachers who do not have the new orientation. However, self-expression—*creativity* is the usual term—is now an end in itself, and this was not previously true. The traditional goal of teaching was not to tap the student's creativity but to shape it.

Different pedagogical goals engender, naturally, different views of where the teacher's responsibility mainly lies. In relation to the student's creativity, for example, it is illuminating to consider the question of responsibility in terms of *person, process,* and *product.*

For a very long time—through most of the history of civilization, I suspect—the teacher's major concern was with product. And this concern was a concern for excellence-of-product; consequently, the act of teaching had to do mainly with the process by which excellence-of-product might be achieved: here is the way to hold the brush, here is the way to strike the chisel, here is the way to turn the phrase.

This essay was first published in *CCC,* Volume 27, Number 1, February 1976.

The inherent shortcomings of this traditional orientation are all too obvious. It easily could, and did, lead to overreliance on models and tradition, insensitivity to individual characteristics, and blindness or indifference to originality. In short, teachers could, and did, "kill" creativity.

Nevertheless, there were virtues in a mode of teaching informed by a vision of excellence-of-product, and typified by the transmission of specific processes by which excellence-of-product might be achieved. After all, the concept of culture is inseparable from the observable facts of tradition and evolution, and the exercise of critical judgment is impossible in the absence of bench-mark achievements. Besides, it can be demonstrated that even the most innovative of conceptions have their roots in something which has gone before. And I suspect that working close to a tradition is the key factor in some fine achievements of less than primary importance—Mendelssohn's, say, or Eudora Welty's. In short, the old mode of teaching which focused on process and product was not all bad.

However, for quite some time now, the focus—especially in the expressive disciplines—has been shifting from *process and product* to *person and process;* and in this shift, process no longer refers to the achieving of an excellent product but, instead, points back to person—that is, to what may be done with or to the individual in order to call forth, or tap, or force out, creative energy. The value of any product which may result tends to be measured not in relation to other products-of-excellence of the same kind but, instead, in terms of the degree to which personhood is presumed to have been self-expressed. This is to say, of course, that product is not evaluated; it is merely valued.

A former student of mine expressed this modern pedagogical orientation with the passionate zeal which so often characterizes it. "I do not believe," she wrote, "that creativity is innate. Even if it were, I think a method must be found whereby this power can be forced out of the individual and harnessed into a precious treasure."

It is encouraging to think that the "harnessed" part of this astonishing credo reflects recognition of the teacher's responsibility to do more than merely "force" the student to a creative act. However, if it really does reflect such recognition, it is an exceptional rather than a typical statement. In the following, the modern viewpoint is more accurately expressed:

> . . . we feel that the writing class should keep the individual student at its center by focusing, more completely than is typical, on writing as a creative process of self-awareness and self-expression. The writing class . . . should not dictate a single writing process.[1]

Certainly there is much here with which to agree. No doubt, writing is, at best, a liberating activity. Surely, too, it is admirable to insist that "the writing class should keep the individual student at its center." And one has no fundamental objection, really, to viewing writing "as a creative process of self-awareness and self-expression." One may insist, however, that the creative process entails a great deal more than self-awareness and self-expression. (To scream is self-expressive, but is it creative?) The creative process—especially if it is to achieve the highest order of self-expressiveness—also demonstrates command of techniques appropriate to the expressive/creative medium: and in the older pedagogy this is where the teacher came in—and not merely to "dictate," either.

What I have referred to as a radical shift from the traditional focus and methodology poses, then, the question of whether the teacher's main function is, as in the new view, to do something to the student to tap his creative resources or, as in the old, to do something with the resources once they have been tapped.

Split by this false dilemma, composition teachers have not seriously addressed the question of a genuine third way. The answer is not to be found on the surface of things—in technological hardware, behavioral objectives, or manifestoes from our professional meetings. Instead, it must emerge from, and reflect with clarifying power, an altered view of human experience.

2.

My argument is, of course, that the conceptual underpinnings of the new pedagogical orientation are very weak.

Whatever the underlying philosophical viewpoint may be, the new pedagogical orientation apparently does not expect the individual to do much more than self-express. It does not require the individual to be measured against any norm, nor to be placed in relationship to any other human being. It is, apparently, a view of the human experience which values the individual in all his uniqueness—or, one might say, his isolation.

I suggest that a disintegrated version of Jean-Paul Sartre's existential view of the human condition makes a close fit with the viewpoint just described. Existentialism—especially Sartrean existentialism—was the popular rage on college campuses immediately after World War II and well into the 1950's. If my memory does not deceive me, Sartre was, indeed, nearly synonymous with existentialism. In the popular mind, he was a sort of intellectual glamor boy, having been active in the underground against the Nazis. Besides, from his fiction and drama one could garner the general character of his thought without taking the trouble to read his philosophy. (In any case, his major philosophical work, *Being and Nothingness,* first published in 1943, did not appear in English until 1956—and that fact alone considerably diminished the potential audience in the earlier years.)

I am unaware of any other view of the human condition which has so grasped the popular imagination in our lifetimes. The original source is by now nearly forgotten, yet in retrospect is it not clear, that, floating the banner of "doing one's own thing," the most polluted stream of Sartreanism has taken its course through the Beat Generation, the hippie movement, a meadow of flower children, and Charles Manson's family? At the same time, a somewhat purer branch has, among other things, floated a whole raft of dreary novels of alienation, produced a wave of interest in situational ethics, and gotten frozen into certain brands of counseling and educational psychology.

These existential manifestations in psychology have in common an emphasis on the individual's freedom—if not, indeed, his duty—to define his own human essence or, in Abraham Maslow's phrase, "to self-actualize." Admirably enough, they extoll the worthiness of human individuality; in the counseling psychology of Carl Rogers, for example, the therapist must maintain an attitude of "unconditional positive regard" toward the client. Obviously, it is also thought that the individual may be assisted toward self-actualization. This implies technique—things that can be done with or to the individual to help him tap his untapped resources.

The corresponding elements in education are obvious. Again, technique is presupposed: the teacher has, or attempts to find, methods for assisting the student toward self-awareness and self-expression. Ironically, these methods (e.g., standing the student before a full-length mirror or requiring the student to make frequent entries in a journal) may be very prescriptive, even while any inclination to "dictate a single writing process" is religiously eschewed. Any writing which emanates from the student's self-awareness and self-expression is likely, too, to be held in reasonably unconditional positive regard—and especially so if, by virtue of some characteristic (e.g., the exposing of private matters or even the wrenching of language from its usual meaning and syntax), it appears to be of a highly personal or innovative nature. Thus it is that one has seen, somewhere, "chicken gravy clouds" praised as a highly creative image; questions of accuracy and effectiveness were not raised.

Quite aside from reservations about what effects such pedagogical maneuvers may have upon the student's ability to write, I wish to raise the more serious issue of the effect upon the student himself.

3.

In 1925, in Heidelberg, Martin Buber addressed an international educational conference whose major theme was the development of the student's creative powers. He contrasted two modes of education and found shortcomings in both. The older mode, he said, was characterized by the habit of authority, while the newer was characterized by the tendency to freedom. "The symbol of the funnel," he remarked, "is in course of being exchanged for that of the pump."[2] And on the specific question of the effect upon the student of the newer mode, he warned: "An education based only on the training of the instinct of origination would prepare a new human solitariness which would be the most painful of all."[3] (For "the instinct of origination" read "self-awareness" or "self-expression" or "creativity.")

It strikes me that in recent years, especially during the stressful years of direct American involvement in Viet Nam, we have seen students painfully locked into their own solitariness: students expressing in shouted slogans their awareness of frustration and anger but incapable of coherent argument;

students turning to mind-bending drugs to alleviate the pain of isolation within the self (a masturbatory act: *self*-awareness, *self*-expression); students—18 year olds—with marble eyes, as if staring inward upon nothingness.

Obviously, education need not take the whole blame; nevertheless, dare I suggest that disturbingly often these same students come out of elite high schools where they have had the very latest training in self-awareness, self-expression, creativity? No. I dare not. I must not. And yet I know for a fact my own growing preference, in my own classes, for small-town kids, farm and ranch kids, black and Chicano kids—kids with their eyeballs turned outward; kids willing to enter into "communion" (Buber's word) with a rotten world which, to be sure, they never made; kids who have (again in Buber's words) "the courage to shoulder life again."[4]

Unlike Sartre, who seeks the essence of the human in the radically isolated individual, Buber insists that this essence is emerging in "dialogue"—that is, in the *relationship* between the individual and the world—including, of course, other individuals. Consequently, he speaks directly of Sartre as follows:

> Sartre regards the walls between the partners in a conversation as simply impassable. For him it is inevitable human destiny that a man has directly to do only with himself and his own affairs. The inner existence of the other is his own concern, not mine; there is no direct relation with the other, nor can there be. This is perhaps the clearest expression of the wretched fatalism of modern man.[5]

The disturbing possibility exists that teachers of composition and other communication skills are unwittingly yet tacitly accepting a view of human experience which effectively eliminates the possibility—or at least the *point*—of the very thing they purport to teach. If man is indeed alone, both as a species and individually, then his powers of communication are rendered trivial in the most fundamental sense. Still, these same abilities retain some significance as vehicles of self-expression; it appears, then, that the modern pedagogy has found intuitively a conclusion which might have been derived logically from the Sartrean premise about the nature of human experience.

4.

Martin Buber made a distinction between individuals and persons, saying that one may become more and more an individual without becoming more and more human; as he said, "I'm *against* individuals and for *persons*."[6] And Maurice Friedman, the foremost American authority on Buber's thought, makes the following distinction:

> [Carl] Rogers emphasizes an unqualified acceptance of the person being helped, whereas Buber emphasizes a confirmation which, while it accepts the other as a person, may also wrestle *with* him against himself.[7]

A psychiatrist, Leslie H. Farber, writes as follows on the importance of Buber's concepts:

> Buber's thought can help us as psychiatrists, I believe, not only in providing a general framework against which to measure the special virtues and limitations of our special craft, but also in revising some of the most technical and specific details of our craft.[8]

The case may be the same for teachers—especially for teachers of communication skills. Whether or not the modern orientation in teaching composition derives specifically from popularized Sartreanism, certain resemblances remain; consequently, what Buber said on Sartrean existentialism and on creativity in education is, I think, highly pertinent to our current situation. (There is the advantage, too, that, since he died in 1965 at the age of 87, he cannot possibly be considered a partisan in an intra-professional tussle.)

Buber takes from the drawing class the example for his own vision of how education should proceed. A teacher of the old school would begin with rules and patterns, with the result that the drawings of all the children are more or less the same. In contrast, a teacher of the new school would elicit from each child a free expression of the subject, with the result that there is great diversity in the drawings.

The second teacher has done, Buber claims, all that *can* be done to tap creativity—he has given it the freedom to emerge. But the releasing of the student's creative instinct, Buber asserts, "should not be any more than a *presupposition* of education."[9]

Obviously, the teacher *could* merely encourage the student—that is, give the student the freedom—to develop his creative instincts in a more and more individualistic way. Indeed, this freedom of development, Buber writes, "is charged with importance as the actuality from which the work of education begins, but," he adds, "as [the] fundamental task [of education] it becomes absurd."[10] Obviously, then, in the Buberian system, the real task of education *begins*—as real education always has, I think—at the moment when creativity has taken a tangible form.

Buber describes the teaching process in the following passage:

> Now the delicate, almost imperceptible and yet important influence begins—that of criticism and instruction. . . . In the former instance the preliminary declaration of what alone was right made for resignation or rebellion; but in the latter, where the pupil gains the realization only after he has ventured far out on the way to his achievement, his heart is drawn to reverence for the form, and [is] educated.[11]

What we see here is, of course, the extension into education of Buber's existential philosophy. To the extent that education is a process whereby the person discovers and refines his unique and essential humanity, it takes place in the dialogue between human and human. It is as simple—and as difficult—as that.

Merely to applaud the creative act is not enough, for the human creative instinct—or "instinct of origination"—is conjoined with an "instinct of communion"—"the longing for the world to become present to us as a person, which goes out to us as we to it, which recognizes us as we do it, which is confirmed in us as we in it;" the instinct of communion is, in short, "what teaches us the saying of Thou."[12]

The central concept of Buber's philosophy is that what is truly human is defined neither by the isolated individual nor by man *en masse,* neither by individuality nor by collectivity, but by the *meeting* of the *I* and the *Thou,* a meeting which establishes the realm of the "between":

> The fundamental fact of human existence is man with man. What is peculiarly characteristic of the human world is above all that something takes place between one being and another the like of which can be found nowhere in nature.[13]

This "something" which takes place is "the saying of Thou."

The meaning of Buber's distinction between *I-It* and *I-Thou* relationships is suggested by—indeed, is contained in—the German familiar second-person pronoun *du.* (Unfortunately, *I and Thou*—*Ich und Du*—is the only one of Buber's works which is at all widely known in America.) For the *I* in the *I-It* relationship, the world is simply an aggregate, a sum of various parts; another human being is but an object among other objects—an "it." The world of *It* can be manipulated but is essentially lacking in meaning in any larger sense. The questions of meaning—of values, responsibilities, choices: all of those things which define the human *as human*—enter fully only in the *I-Thou* relationship. And, obviously, only in the *I-Thou* relationship do the "instinct of origination" and the "instinct of communion" strike a balance and mature.

For composition teachers, Buber's concepts mean, I think, that the teacher's expertise is not in relation to the *person* as creator, nor yet with the *process* of creation; rather, they point the way back to the traditional concern with the created *product*—but with a difference. When, in freedom, the student's creative instinct, operating through highly personal and inscrutable processes, has produced a created product, then the teacher *responds* to the product and thus to the creator. This response must be genuine. It need not —nor will it characteristically—reflect "unconditional positive regard," for the whole aim of the response is to assist the creator in achieving ever greater command over the medium through which the "instinct of origination" *and* "the instinct of communion" are expressed.

Just as Leslie Farber believed that Buber's thought might provide a general framework within which to revise some of the most technical and specific details of psychiatry, so I suspect that a Buberian pedagogy for composition—a pedagogy for composition—a pedagogy which would avoid the perils of either the funnel or the pump—could be defined.

Martin Buber's thought is, of course, neither original nor unique in the strictest sense; he himself identified the Hasidic tradition and the work of

Feuerbach as sources, and certain correspondences in the thought of Gabriel Marcel are readily apparent. But this is as it should be. This is as a proper understanding of the richly creative life should lead us to expect it to be. We may be thankful, indeed, that he is *not* alone. His special importance is that he speaks so specifically to teachers. And beyond that, he represents a tradition which refutes and transcends the reductive tendencies which characterize so much of what is specifically "modern" in education: the vocational reduction, the behavioral reduction, the technological reduction: not unuseful, but in themselves mere *petits culs-de-sac* of the human spirit.

AFTERWORD . . . .

The Braddock Award played a very small part in my professional life. To my amusement, some years after I received it, a young colleague, fresh from CCCC, asked, with an air of suspended disbelief, "Are you the Glenn Matott I saw listed among Braddock Award winners?" I trust it was reassuring to her to learn that that *must be some other Glenn with the same unusual surname!*

Possibly, however, my essay has played or will play a role in the life of the profession. Some years ago, a doctoral candidate at a midwestern university wrote to say she had found therein the topic of her dissertation. The real point, of course, is Martin Buber's thought, not mine.

From the perspective of retirement (hors de combat, so to speak), I can only offer a few musings.

Perhaps the field of composition is mainly pedagogical? Whatever the case, what is the role of a scholarly component? I think we do not have clear answers to these questions. If composition is an emerging discipline, what shaping influences may be brought to bear from other fields? (My essay attempted to shed some light from the direction of philosophy; Robert Zoellner, my colleague at Colorado State University, drew upon the field of behavioral psychology. I personally see no fundamental incompatibility between a Buberian perspective and a Skinnerian technique.) What lessons can we learn from our most successful practitioners? For instance, perhaps the greatest teacher of composition in recent times was Nadia Boulanger—in music. If I were young again and energetic, I would try to ferret out her "secrets."

—GLENN MATOTT
Colorado State University

1978

*Balancing Theory with Practice
in the Training of Writing Teachers*

RICHARD C. GEBHARDT

A title such as mine may sound innocuous—who, after all, would want to split theory from practice completely? It may also sound pretentious—who can explain in a few pages just what a comprehensive balance of theory and practice of composition teaching might be? But "Balancing Theory with Practice in the Training of Writing Teachers" does indicate my thesis: that students preparing to teach writing in public school or college should understand important conceptual underpinnings of composition and the teaching of writing and should test them out in practice. So without being too innocuous or too pretentious, I will try to outline four kinds of theoretical or conceptual information that I think should be included in teaching-of-writing programs, and then I will try to illustrate briefly what I mean by a balance between theory and practice.

Four Kinds of Knowledge for the Writing Teacher

Ideally, the student preparing to teach writing would master a world of knowledge that runs from transactional analysis to neat handwriting, from conventions of the sonnet to the pyramid structure of the news story, from the most venerated ideals of Aristotle to the most voguish ideas of the latest educational trend. But no writing program can do everything, and it seems to me that four kinds of knowledge are especially important for future teachers of writing.

First, writing teachers need to have an understanding of the *structure and history of the English language* sound enough to let them apply their knowledge to the teaching of revision, style, dialect differences, and the like. The program Francis Christensen outlined in his article "The Course in Advanced Composition for Teachers"[1] is a good example of this sort of knowledge. Christensen wrote that the future teacher should move through a sequence of courses beginning with grammar, progressing to language history,

This essay was first published in *CCC*, Volume 28, Number 2, May 1977.

and ending in composition. The goal of this sequential program, Christensen made clear, is thoroughness of preparation: an understanding of grammar complete enough that students can apply it in practical situations; an understanding of language history that reinforces grammatical principles learned in the earlier course; and a sense of usage that rests on a clear understanding of how the language has developed. Something like this language program is essential in the training of writing teachers.

The second kind of knowledge that writing teachers need to have is a solid understanding of *rhetoric*. The range of such knowledge is illustrated in Donald Nemanich's article "Preparing the Composition Teacher." Nemanich writes that he has his students "read such books as Dudley Bailey's *Essays on Rhetoric* or Ross Winterowd's *Rhetoric: A Synthesis* or Edward P. J. Corbett's *Classical Rhetoric for the Modern Student* for some kind of historical perspective." And Nemanich continues this way:

> I expect students in my classes to know something of Aristotle and what he had to say about the art of persuasion. In addition, I want my students to know of recent work in rhetoric and composition, especially Ken Macrorie's "free writing," Francis Christensen's "generative rhetoric," and Robert Zoellner's "talk-write" pedagogy. . . . I hope that some time during the course, we would also talk about the work of Wallace Douglas, Janet Emig, James Moffett, and Edward Jenkinson, and Donald Seybold — among others.[2]

The sheer mass of possible information about rhetoric that is implied by this list of titles and names may suggest that the training of writing teachers must involve considerable technical understanding of rhetoric. A highly technical grounding in rhetoric is not absolutely necessary, as the NCTE book, *What Every English Teacher Should Know*, implies when it distinguishes between "good" and "superior" writing teachers. The latter, the book indicates, should have "a detailed knowledge of theories and history of rhetoric," though the "good" teacher need only be able to recognize "such characteristics of good writing as substantial and relevant content; organization; clarity; appropriateness of tone."[3] Similarly, in an article in *The Journal of Teacher Education*, Richard Larson denies that future writing teachers need "extended study of rhetorical theory" but argues that they should understand fundamentals of rhetoric. And what does Larson mean by fundamentals of rhetoric? This is how he puts it:

> . . . future teachers should recognize that writing is a series of choices among alternatives and that a good writer must shape his discourse carefully to make it reach its intended audience effectively and accomplish its intended purpose. This view of rhetoric . . . encourages teachers to approach their writing and that of their students with such questions as these: Whom am I addressing? On what occasion am I addressing him? What is my purpose in speaking? What is my relationship to him? What tone of voice ought I assume in this discourse? What kinds of

language will best enable me to achieve my purpose in addressing this audience?[4]

An intelligent understanding of—and ability to use—such questions is, I think, the second essential part of the training of writing teachers.

The third kind of knowledge that composition teachers need to master is some *theoretical framework* with which to sort through the ideas, methodologies, and conflicting claims of texts, journal articles, and convention addresses. Writing teachers face a confusing abundance of theories and approaches. They may pick up an essay, such as Wallace Douglas's chapter in *How Porcupines Make Love,* and read that effective writing classes must be flexible and fairly unstructured, since good writing instruction requires freedom, spontaneity, and a lucky combination of events and feelings.[5] But as they read, they may remember this claim from a text on sentence exercises:

> Writing is a skill, and like playing the violin or throwing a discus, it may be learned by observing how others do it—by trying to imitate, carefully and thoughtfully, the way it was done. In writing, we can "observe" by copying sentences and paragraphs written by master stylists. And we can imitate these sentences and paragraphs in our own writing, making them a part of our basic repertoire.[6]

Writing teachers need to be able to make some sense out of the obvious differences in emphasis—if not outright contradictions—between such approaches. Similarly, they need to be able to find their way through the jungle Donald Stewart outlines in *Freshman English Shop Talk:*

> We teach beginnings, middles, and ends; topic sentences and development; the word, the sentence, the paragraph, the theme; narration, description, exposition, and argument; definition, classification, comparison and contrast, analysis, theme indivisible, or strategy unlimited. If we are linguists, we work on their syntax; if we are perceptionists, we improve their powers of observation; if we are pre-writers, we help them get their concepts manipulable before they begin to write; if we are behaviorists, we get them behaving and then proceed to modify that behavior on the spot; if we are rhetoricians, we make them aware of the subject, speaker/writer, and audience triangle and the way they must mediate between these entities.[7]

Part of the preparation of writing teachers, then, is some theoretical framework against which writing teachers can test new materials and ideas in order to find effective and compatible approaches for their classes. Three overlapping frameworks that I suggest are these: *Classical/Existential, Thinking/Writing,* and *Product/Process.*

The first of these three pairs of concepts contrasts assumptions of objective truth, reality, and value that often are called "classical" with the more subjective tendencies of existential thought. The conceptual difference is one that Richard Ohmann implied when he contrasted the older rhetorical assumption "that the speaker or writer knows in advance what is true" with the more contemporary rhetorical "pursuit—and not simply the transmission—of truth and right."[8] When students understand the possibilities of the Classical/Existential framework, they are better able to draw useful and coherent distinctions between teaching approaches as different as Douglas's interest in freedom and flexibility and Weathers and Winchester's system of imitating the work of masterful stylists or approaches as far apart as Lou Kelly's "open" writing class[9] and Elizabeth Oggel's idea that students should be "furnished with a set of standards" so that they can see how their writing "measures up to these standards."[10]

The second pairing of concepts, Thinking/Writing, recognizes that behavioral psychology is making changes in the concept of the writing process but that, at the same time, many teachers and materials follow an older idea of the writing process. Recognizing differences in approaches and materials that stem from basic differences in the psychology of writing lets future teachers find their way to consistent materials through the storm of contradictions suggested by two statements by Ray Kytle and Peter Elbow. First, there is this statement from *Composition: Discovery and Communication:*

> Composition of an essay does not begin when you put pen to paper . . . an essential part of the total process of composition takes place before that first word is written. For before you can begin to write on a subject, you must discover what you want to say about it.[11]

And just as convinced that writing precedes ideas as Kytle is that thought precedes composition, Peter Elbow writes this in *Writing Without Teachers:*

> Instead of a two-step transaction of meaning-into-language, think of writing as an organic, developmental process in which you start writing at the very beginning—before you know your meaning at all—and encourage your words gradually to change and evolve. . . . Meaning is not what you start out with but what you end up with.[12]

The third pair of concepts, Product/Process, lets future teachers decide whether teaching approaches and materials place more emphasis on the written artifact produced by the student or on the process that leads toward this product. Obviously, product and process are both important to the writing teacher, and neither can be put aside without seriously oversimplifying the writing process. But differences in emphasis do result in different methodologies. Product-centered teaching tends to work by applying standards—marking papers, grading, and the like. Process-centered teaching tends to keep instruction in grammar, structure, usage, punctuation, and organization within the highly individualized context of the writer writing. Future writing teachers should understand these distinctions so that they can more intelligently develop their own teaching styles and select compatible teaching materials.

Besides knowledge of the history of the English language, of rhetoric, and of some theoretical frameworks with which to understand the wide range of approaches and materials available to them, future writing teachers need a broad awareness of *reliable, productive methods* to help students learn to write. I think, for instance, that prospective teachers should understand the ideas summarized in the dozen and a half points in the 1974 Position Statement of the NCTE's Commission on Composition.[13] Even more specifically, I think every would-be writing teacher should understand these five ideas:

1. The importance of *writing* in the composition class and the value of what James Moffett calls "Learning to Write by Writing."[14]

2. The importance of *audience* in any writing situation and the pedagogical usefulness of writing for groups of students and for audiences other than the teacher.

3. The importance of seeing writing as a *process* that moves and grows so that initial ideas and sentences become more coherent, complex, and clear. Whether students conceive of this process as starting with thoughts or with physical behavior seems less important than that they know that writing is not a static thing. Indeed, teachers should understand the logic, usefulness, and limitations of pre-writing and behavioral approaches so that they will be able to modify their teaching to fit the individuals they will teach.

4. The importance of *positive instruction by teachers experienced in the agonies of trying to write.*

5. The importance of *helping students take responsibility for their own writing so that they become their own best editors and teachers.*

BALANCED PREPARATION FOR WRITING TEACHERS

Teachers of writing, then, need to know quite a lot about concepts of composition teaching, about rhetoric, about the English language. But they should not just know these subjects, in the sense of being able to pass multiple-choice tests on them. Instead, they need to know information *and* the principles behind the information. They need to know the "what" of composition teaching; but they also need to know the "how" and the "why." In fact, Richard Larson feels that writing teachers have a greater need to know "why" than "how," since the teacher "must be able to reveal to his students the choices that confront them as they write and the possible consequences of those choices, and enough about how words work and thoughts connect so that he can set tasks before his students in the order and against the background that will help them perform at their best" ("A Special Course," p. 172).

Of course, it is one thing to read such words as these and quite another to make good on them. And the question faced by anyone developing a training program for future writing teachers is, essentially, how can the student learn the necessary *what's* and *how's* and *why's*? Courses in grammar, linguistic history, and rhetorical theory, on the one hand, may teach students much useful information (*what*) without helping them internalize the information enough to understand the all-important underlying principles. Advanced composition courses, on the other hand, may emphasize the *how* of writing to such an extent that they do not adequately help students toward *why's* of words, thoughts, and choices so important to the writing teacher.[15] Clearly, what is needed is a synthesis of some sort: a way to guarantee that students do not merely learn facts of grammar, rhetoric, or pedagogy but that they think about what they learn, relate the facts to each other, examine the underlying principles behind the facts, and use the information in the kind of practical context that can give it genuine meaning for the students.

Such a synthesis requires, first of all, the information that comes in courses in The Structure of the English Language, The History of the English Language, and Advanced Composition and Rhetoric. Beyond these courses comes the real balancing of knowledge with experience. The Teaching of Writing program should include a special course in Writing for Teachers of Writing. It should provide practical work in tutoring, editing, and grading, both within the Writing for Teachers of Writing course and in supervised programs within a campus writing-center or writing-laboratory. And it should provide, for students seeking certification as public school teachers, student-teaching placements that emphasize work in writing.

The Writing for Teachers of Writing course should be, first of all, a writing course in which students continue to develop their skills as writers and become more self-consciously familiar with the frustrations, dead-ends, and pitfalls that their students will encounter. In *A Writer Teaches Writing,* Donald Murray writes that "the most inexperienced student writer shares with the most experienced writer the terror of the blank page."[16] The Writing for Teachers of Writing course should exploit this fact and try to help students realize how their writing experiences in the course—especially their frustrating and exhausting ones—are helping them become good teachers. Secondly, the course should press home to students the necessity, as a natural pre-requisite of their chosen profession, of their being writers. In *What Every English Teacher Should Know,* J. N. Hook, Paul Jacobs, and Raymond Crisp make the point that writing teachers must be writers: "Can a golf coach who never swings a club be successful? Can a shop foreman who never operates a machine do a good job? Can a writing teacher who never writes teach writing well? Probably not." They go on to say that this does not mean that every writing teacher must be a professional, but that every writing teacher "should be able to make ideas hang together in prose, should know how to make each sentence express a clear idea clearly, should have a precise knowledge of mechanics." And they say, later, that this writing should be given up to sharp criticism, since the teacher "who has experienced candid, constructive criticism can often become a more constructive critic" (p. 35). This matter of criticism is a third general feature of the Writing for Teachers of Writing course. The course should provide opportunity for students to serve as critics of other students' papers—and, of course, to have their papers examined by sharp-eyed students as well. It should do this in a friendly, constructive, but serious climate. And students should see that such activity is necessary, again as a pre-requisite of their chosen profession.

The Writing for Teachers of Writing course, then, is a writing course informed by the general spirit of Pope's lines from *An Essay on Criticism:*

> Let such teach others who themselves excell,
> And censure freely [well, not *too* freely] who
> have written well.

But in order that students learn specific information—*what, how,* and *why*—about the teaching of composition, the Writing for Teachers of Writing course should ask students to write *about* the teaching of writing. And to provide material about which to write, it should use readings, guest speakers, lectures, and discussions to direct students to a wide range of approaches and materials.

My own approach is to organize readings and materials into these areas:

1. *What is a writing teacher?* Donald Murray has a good deal of intelligent information about this in *A Writer Teaches Writing.* I also direct students to *What Every English Teacher Should Know,* to English methods texts, and to articles in *English Journal, College Composition and Communication, College English,* and other sources.

2. *What's wrong with writing teaching today?* This may sound like a negative topic, but my aim is to focus on problems that students will confront when they start to teach their classes and also to use these problems as springboards to talk about productive solutions. Here, students read Eugene Smith's *Teacher Preparation in Composition* and other materials and hear presentations by a number of classroom teachers.

3. *What are the elements of effective writing instruction?* This huge area is prevented, by the brevity of the academic term, from ever being complete enough. Typically, I ask students to become well versed in four topics:
   a. The "Learning to Write by Writing" Concept in James Moffet's *Teaching the Universe of Discourse.*
   b. Students as Their Own Editors and Teachers—an idea deriving from Moffett and Murray, from Kenneth Bruffee's "Collaborative Learning" (*College English,* Feb. 1973), and from my own forthcoming text, *Teamwork: Collaborative Strategies for the College Writer.*
   c. Evaluating Student Writing. I draw on a wide range of materials here—from the CCCC Language Statement (*CCC,* Fall 1974), to methods texts, to Barrett Mandel's "Teaching Without Judging" (*College English,* Feb. 1973), to R. W. Reising's "Controlling the Bleeding" (*CCC,* Feb. 1973).
   d. Holding Student Conferences. Here, again, I use Murray, as well as Lou Kelly's "Is Competent Copyreading a Violation of the Students' Right to Their Own Language?" (*CCC,* Oct. 1974), and a variety of other materials.

In addition to these four subjects, I have students read material and hear presentations on a range of other topics: Motivating Students, "Publishing" Student Writing, Creating Interesting Assignments, Developing Lesson Plans, Writing Behavioral Objectives, and The Students' Right to Their Own Language.

Since what I am recommending is a *writing* course, readings over such important topics as these cannot be allowed to become ends in themselves. They are grist for the writers' mills; they are substance for papers. To guarantee that students think of their reading as a prelude to writing, I ask them to maintain a looseleaf notebook with sections for "Writing Tips," "Teaching Tips," and "Reactions." I also ask students to write papers—such as an examination of the causes of poor writing instruction, a definition of a "good" writing teacher, and an argument on behalf of some specific approach to writing instruction—that require them to develop their own perspectives on ideas contained in the readings.

And, to help blend theory and practice even further, I have students work on these papers in small writing-workshop groups where they practice the concepts of feedback, diagnosis, and prescription about which they are reading. In these groups, students learn about audience definition and audience response, and about how it feels to have a key point missed by readers interested in little but well-placed commas. In these groups, students come to understand the importance of cooperation, the power of peer pressure, the difficulty of opening up to a critic, the bitterness of a writer under attack. And all of these things reinforce what the students are reading and writing about and thereby help students prepare to be effective writing teachers.

AFTERWORD . . . .

"Balancing Theory with Practice in the Training of Writing Teachers" argued that colleges should offer teaching of writing courses—a fresher idea in the 1970s than it sounds today—and it described a course in which students read and wrote about articles dealing with topics such as What Is a Writing Teacher? and What Are the Elements of Effective Writing Instruction?

Looking at them now, the topics and the materials I listed with them seem awfully dated. Where, one might ask today, are Britton et al.'s The Development of Writing Abilities, *Shaughnessy's* Errors and Expectations, *Emig's "Writing as a Mode of Learning," and writing-process studies by Flower, Perl, Sommers, and others? What about Hairston's "The Winds of Change" (or any mention of current-traditional methods and new paradigms), Bizzell's "Cognition, Convention, and Certainty" (or other research on discourse communities), and Bruffee's "Collaborative Learning and the 'Conversation of Mankind'" (or social constructionism generally)? The fact is, of course, that those works—and many others we now take for granted or consider passé—didn't exist as resources for composition faculty and students in the first half of the 1970s.*

It's also true, of course, that by the mid-1970s many new resources were becoming available. My Findlay College course, ENG 345, Teaching of Writing, changed a bit each year as I tried to incorporate new approaches. By the time I described it in "Training Basic Writing Teachers at a Liberal Arts College," the course had evolved to have ten units—among them, Writing Processes; Rhetorical Forces; Productive Climates for Instruction; Grammar and the Sentence; The Basic College Writer; Reading and Writing; The Paragraph and Coherence; and Making, Responding To and Grading Assignments—and nearly 60 percent of the items in the reading list had been published after 1975.

A few years later, the same ten units still structured my course but the flow of publications in composition research, theory, and pedagogy made "keeping up" frustrating and futile. So when I wrote "Unifying Diversity in the Training of Writing Teachers" for Charles Bridges's Training the New Teacher of College Composition, I focused less on the content students should learn in a teaching of writing course than on another idea from my 1977 CCC article— helping students find "some theoretical framework with which to sort through the ideas, methodologies, and conflicting claims" of our expanding field. As I put it in 1986: "A training program in composition teaching should help its clients develop comprehensive, integrating views of writing and the teaching of writing" ("Unifying" 4).

The contrasts between those two quotations suggest how my perspective has changed as I've watched composition develop, over twenty-five years, toward the sort of diversity I sketched in Academic Advancement in Composition Studies. It now seems clear that testing ideas and teaching approaches against "some [i.e., one] theoretical framework" or against "some [i.e., any] theoretical framework" (no matter how narrow) is less effective than working through several "integrating views" (plural) to understand our field.

–RICHARD C. GEBHARDT
Bowling Green State University

The Feminine Style: Theory and Fact

MARY P. HIATT

*C*ritics often have trouble dealing with style, probably for two reasons. In the first place, stylistic theory itself ranges widely. Some stylisticians hold that style is totally a matter of one individual's writing—that, in effect, there is no such thing as a group or mass style. Others take an opposing view and maintain that it is possible to describe the characteristics of a group of writers or of writers of a certain era. Stylisticians further differ on whether style is the sum total of the characteristics of the writing or whether it describes in what way the writing departs from a norm, roughly defined as a standard or commonplace manner of writing. Some theorists also hold that any style can only be adequately described in the context of another style, whether individual or group. The state of the theory itself is therefore conflicting and confusing.

In the second place, the metalanguage of style often relies on inadequate descriptors. Thus, in considering an individual's writing style, impressionistic adjectives abound: "muscular," "manly," "clear," "hothouse," "lush," "lean," etc. And in considering group style—or types of style—we are confronted with the traditional adjectives such as "plain," "high," and "grand," as well as "Baroque," "Ciceronian," "Attic," "Augustan," and so on. Few of these descriptors, whether of individual or group styles, have been objectively assayed, for upon close evaluation, they might vanish, leaving the critic at an unendurable loss for words.

Castigation of the manifold efforts at stylistic description serves little purpose. Nonetheless, an awareness of some of the pitfalls and complexities involved in the task of such description is essential to any adequate consideration of written style. To some degree, the critic of style is faced with choosing or developing a theory.

As mentioned above, a theory has persisted over the years that common characteristics in the writing of certain groups, perhaps during certain eras, do exist, despite the abjurations of those theorists who claim that style can

---

This essay was first published in *CCC*, Volume 29, Number 3, October 1978.

only be an individual matter. This group-style theory is reflected in the descriptors "masculine" style and "feminine" style. Men and women, it is commonly believed, write differently. The conviction has run strong. Notably absent are any data to support the conviction.

But whereas data are missing, we generally find, once again, a plethora of adjectives being flung about. The "masculine" style is held to be terse, strong, rational, convincing, formidable, and logical. The "feminine" style is thought to be emotional, illogical, hysterical, shrill, sentimental, silly, and vapid. The "masculine" style seems to be described in terms of a male view of *men*—not necessarily of men's style. And the "feminine" style is described in terms, often pejorative, of a male view of *women*—not of women's style. Whether or not the difference exists at all is important to establish, but most certainly the stereotyped descriptors are impressionistic, biased, and consequently less than useful.

Opting for the theory, however, that style need not always be an individual matter and that there do exist types of style consisting of linguistic features shared by groups of writers at particular times, I have studied a large sample of contemporary American prose to see, first, whether there are discernible differences between the way men write and the way women write, and, second, if there are differences, what these differences are.[1] One hundred books, 50 by women and 50 by men, were objectively selected for the study. Objectivity was maintained by *not* choosing books on the basis of literary "merit," for merit is a subjective matter. To have selected books because anyone in particular—I, my friends, critics in general—liked them would have seriously prejudiced the study. In the study, therefore, the books include non-fiction by Albert Ellis, Telford Taylor, Marjorie Holmes, and Frances Fitzgerald, and fiction by Charles Simmons, Bernard Malamud, Andrea Newman, and Joyce Carol Oates.

The two categories (women's books and men's books) were subdivided equally into fiction and non-fiction. From each of the 100 books, four 500-word selections of running text were randomly chosen. Each book, therefore, contributes a 2000-word sample to the study, which finally consists of 200,000 words of contemporary prose.

If one is attempting to discern stylistic differences between two sets of 100,000 words each, one can, of course, try to read all these words and note the occurrence of such stylistic matters as sentence-length and complexity, inserts, types of modification, and so on. One can try to do this, but no one should. The human mind is often an inaccurate perceiver, and errors inevitably occur. A mechanical mind is not inaccurate. Hence, the only objective and accurate way to deal with such a vast amount of text is to use a computer.

The 200,000 words of prose were therefore keypunched onto IBM cards. Each of the 100 samples was scanned by computer for such major aspects of style as sentence-length and complexity, logical sequence of ideas, similes, *-ly* adverbs, parenthetical expressions, structural parallelism, and rhetorical devices.

The findings indicate that contemporary male and female authors do write differently. I can report, with a fair degree of confidence, that there is a feminine style that is not the same as a masculine style. I definitely do not postulate, however, that either style is a "norm," from which the other style varies, although the way men are thought to write tends to be considered the way *to* write, probably because there are so many more male authors and critics than female authors and critics. The emergence of specific differences between the two groups of writers does, however, lend valid support to the theory that types of styles or styles characteristic of groups of writers do exist.

Of greater interest, perhaps, is the discovery that the masculine style and the feminine style do not always differ in the commonly perceived or described ways. A consideration of some specific results bears out this conclusion.

For example, close study of sentence-lengths[2] and average sentence-lengths of all the authors reveals that the men are not terse and that the women are not verbose. Of the non-fiction authors, the men's average sentence-length is 23 words; the women's, 21 words. The gross averages are not significantly different. All that can be said is that the women do not go on and on—if anything, their thoughts are phrased in shorter units. But if the sentences of all the non-fiction authors are divided into two groups, those of twenty words or fewer ("short" sentences) and those of more than twenty words ("long" sentences), a statistical analysis indicates that the women use significantly more short sentences—58 percent, versus 48 percent of the men's sentences.

Generally speaking, the longer the sentence, the more likely it is to be structurally complex. And, in the non-fiction studied, both the men's and the women's long sentences are certainly complex. But they are complex in different ways. The structure of the long sentences of *each author* in the men's non-fiction exhibits specific, often repeated aspects of style. Norman Mailer's long sentences, for example, are highly complicated, involving lengthy seriation, many parenthetical phrases and clauses, and many self-interrupters; Frank Mankiewicz uses many introductory and inserted adverbial phrases and clauses and many appositives; Frederick Cartwright often uses right-branching sentences; Rudolf Bing employs many complicated series, all in perfectly parallel constructions. In other words, the long sentences of each male non-fiction author usually offer readily identifiable types of complexity that are characteristic of that author.

With the exception of two women non-fiction authors, the long sentences of the women do not generally display individual patterns of complexity. The exceptions are Eda LeShan and Joyce Maynard, both of whom use dashes and parentheses in their long sentences. The constructions delineated by dashes and parentheses, however, could just as well have been delineated by periods. In other words, their long sentences do not display the subordinate constructions that are the hallmark of complexity. Their long sentences thus are not so complex as those of the men. Among the other women writers, the long sentences are carefully organized syntactically but cover a range of types of complexity. It is difficult to discern any one constructional characteristic for any one of these writers. The complexity of their sentences therefore is not so individually delineated as the complexity of the men's sentences.

As for the fiction writers, the average sentence-length for men is 17 words; for women, 16 words per sentence—again not really a significant difference. But the men tend to write longer sentences than the women and *more* longer sentences than the women. Nine men produce fourteen sentences of over 80 words, whereas only five women write even one sentence of more than 80 words, none of them longer than 90 words.

The *range* of sentence-lengths in fiction is also quite different between the two groups. Using as examples the two writers of the longest sentences in each group, we find that John O'Hara's longest sentence is 116 words, his shortest is two, and his range is 114 words; Tom Wicker's longest sentence is 104 words, his shortest is two, presenting a range of 102 words. On the other hand, Ruth Macdowell's longest sentence is 90 words, her shortest is two, and her range is 88; Daphne DuMaurier's longest sentence is 86 words, her shortest is three, and her range is 83 words. The foregoing are only examples, but the relatively narrow range of sentence-lengths is a repetitive feature of the women writers of fiction.

In fiction, sentence complexity is not a particularly cogent parameter of style, because fiction is so studded with dialogue. But in sentence-length, it does not seem that the women writers vary as widely as do the men. In this respect, their writing is perhaps less daring, more conservative.

Another aspect of style is the logical development of ideas. Examination of this feature was confined to non-fiction writers and carried out by studying the occurrence of certain words or phrases that often indicate a particular kind of logical sequence. There are, of course, many ways of indicating a particular logical process without the use of specific words. Instead of the word "because," for example, indicating that a reason is being offered, a writer may simply choose to say, "Another reason is that . . ." The existence of a logical sequence without the use of specific "signaling" words cannot be gainsaid. However, a search for what may be called "signals of logic," occurring at the beginning or within the sentence, reveals a difference in the writing of the men and the women.

Logical-sequence indicators (or the particular group of words or phrases signaling a particular process of logic) may be divided into five types:[3] (1) Illustratives ("for example," "that is," "for instance"); (2) Illatives ("therefore," "(and) so," "thus," "hence"); (3) Adversatives ("however," "but," "yet," "nevertheless," "on the other hand"); (4) Causatives ("because," "for," "since"); and (5) Additives ("and," "so . . . did").

The women use 190 of these logical-sequence indicators, whereas the men use 160. On the basis of the indicators, therefore, the women cannot be said to write illogically. But there is a difference in the type of logic used by the women writers. The men and the women use approximately the same number of Adversatives, but the women employ 50 percent fewer Illustratives and Illatives and 50 percent more Causatives and Additives. The logic of the feminine style would thus seem to depend on reasons and extra information rather than on exemplifications and conclusions. In terms of the low ratio of Illatives—those words indicating conclusions—the logic of the women is less definitive than that of the men. In terms of the high ratio of Causatives, their logic is more self-justifying. Neither the men's nor the women's style is, however, "illogical." Both are logical in different ways.

The occurrence of -*ly* adverbs offers another measure of style. Women's speech has been reported to contain many more adverbs ending in -*ly* than that of men, with high use of such words as "simply," "utterly," and "awfully" as modifiers of adjectives. The unadorned adjective is presumably the province of men.

Such may indeed be the case in women's speech, but in this study, it does not carry over into their writing. There is no significant difference between the men's and the women's writing in either the total number of -*ly* adverbs used or in the number of different adverbs, and the type-token ratio for both groups is almost exactly the same in fiction and in non-fiction. But the adverb "simply" is used more often by the men than by the women; the adverb "utterly" is rarely used by either group; and the adverb "awfully" is used only by the men.

In the interest of discovering whether women writers are, as frequently claimed, "hyperemotional," adverbs of emotion (such as "amiably," "abjectly," "coldly," "angrily," etc.) were studied. That emotion is often expressed verbally or nominally is true; the expression of emotion via adverbs is only one means. Nonetheless, the two groups' use of adverbs of emotion is startlingly different in fiction and scarcely different at all in non-fiction. In fiction, the women use twice as many adverbs of emotion as do the men, a finding that probably is the basis for calling women writers "hyperemotional."

But if another type of adverb is examined, the adverb of pace (such as "gradually," "hastily," "slowly," etc.), a reverse trend is seen. The men's fiction contains twice as many of these adverbs as the women's, and again there is no difference in the non-fiction of the two groups. The men's fiction style thus seems to be "hyperactive" as compared to the women's.

If both types of adverbs are considered together, however, a more accurate evaluation of the two fiction styles is possible. In all, the women fiction writers use approximately the same number of adverbs of emotion and adverbs of pace, whereas the men fiction writers use four times as many adverbs of pace as adverbs of emotion. Thus, in fiction, where the major differences occur, there is evidence that the feminine style balances pace of action and expression of emotionality. The women writers are not hyperemotional, except in terms of the men writers. There seems to be far less basis for labeling the feminine styles as hyperemotional than for labeling the masculine style as *hypo*-emotional.

The adverb *really* deserves special mention. The women writers use the word two and a half times more often than the men writers in non-fiction, and one and a half times as often in fiction. One male novelist (Anthony

Burgess) accounts for the lessening of the difference in fiction by using that particular adverb more often than any woman writer. If his sample is disregarded, the same high proportion of *really*'s exists in the women's fiction as in their non-fiction. The relatively high occurrence as characteristic of the feminine style is probably at least unconsciously and generally recognized. It actually is very consciously recognized in the words of one male character in a woman writer's novel when he says to a woman character, " 'Really,' 'really,' 'really'! That's all you can say!" Its use probably reflects women's feelings that they will not be believed, that they are not being taken seriously or "really." These feelings would quite naturally lead women to claim sincerity and validity more frequently than do men.

To recapitulate, in those areas of style discussed here, the way the women write emerges as distinct from the way the men write. This distinction is consistently borne out in the study of other areas of style, such as the use of similes, certain adjectives and verbs, parallel structures, and various aspects of rhetoric. There is, in other words, clear evidence of a feminine style and sound justification for the theory of group style.

But the feminine style is in fact rather different from the common assumptions about it. Solely on the basis of just those aspects discussed in this paper, it can be claimed that the feminine style is conservative, structurally sound, logical in its own way, balanced in terms of emotionality and pace. There are no excesses of length or complexity or emotion. Its only excess lies perhaps in the protesting use of *really,* an understandable protest against being disbelieved.

AFTERWORD . . . .

It is with awe that I read my 1978 Braddock essay. I knew so much then, as I slashed my way through thickets of theory and statistics and descriptors. And yet I knew so little, preoccupied as I was with IBM cards and key-punching large amounts of text.

Large amounts of text continued to interest me, however. And after the 1977 publication of The Way Women Write *and my Braddock Award, I pursued my empirical approach to writing style. As reported in my 1978 essay, the differences between men's and women's style in contemporary fiction are considerable. I asked myself whether these gender differences were stable over a long period of time, say, a hundred years.*

Being of a rather neat and tidy nature, as well as predisposed to linearity, I therefore embarked on a random selection of American fiction published one hundred years before the works in my contemporary study. In this nineteenth-century project, I was enormously assisted by Nina Baym's seminal research,

Women's Fiction: A Guide to Novels by and about Women in America, 1820–1870. *My selection process, the individual sample sizes, and the various aspects of style were the same as those described in* The Way Women Write. *The overall size of the nineteenth-century study is, however, smaller than that of the contemporary study, not only because it deals solely with fiction, but also because books printed that long ago are hard to find.*

The result is Style and the "Scribbling Women," *its title an allusion to the famous Hawthorne complaint about the "damned mobs of scribbling women" who threatened to put him out of business. A five-year administrative stint as English department chair delayed the publication of this study.*

The chief finding of Style and the "Scribbling Women" *is that in the 1870s, the gender differences were nowhere near as great as those evinced in the 1970s. There are, of course, general changes in fiction style over the century, the most obvious one being sentence length, the earlier fiction containing much longer sentences than those in the contemporary study.*

One might ask why there is such similarity between the two groups of fiction writers in the 1870s and such disparity in the 1970s. The answer probably lies in the history of women's fiction, for in the mid-1800s, women writers became enormously popular. The sturdy adventure stories of male fiction writers did not command nearly so large a market as did the women's "romances." Hence, a large number of male writers of that era consciously adopted women's matters of style, tone, and language. Gender differences in fiction style faded. One could say that in this situation, the men were riding on the women's coattails.

At this time, I am no longer a Braddock competitor. Retired from academe, I am busy writing as-yet-unpublished mystery fiction—in my terse feminine style, of course.

—MARY P. HIATT
Baruch College of the
City University of New York

1980   Teachers of Composition and Needed Research in Discourse Theory

LEE ODELL

Whether by preference or by necessity, teachers of composition tend to be pragmatists. Our response to any new theory is most likely to be: What does it imply for our teaching? What specific classroom procedures does it suggest? Are these procedures practical? Will they work for the sort of students we have in our classes? Underlying these questions is at least one major assumption: our primary obligation is to have some influence on the way students compose, to make a difference in students' ability to use written language to give order and meaning to their experience.

As though this obligation were not demanding enough, I want to argue that we have at least one other responsibility. We must not only influence our students' writing, but also help refine and shape the discourse theory that will guide our work with students. In addition to being teachers, we should also function as discourse theorists and researchers. As we try to fulfill this new obligation, we will need to ask new kinds of questions. Is a given theory valid? Does it do justice to the complexities (and the simplicities) of the writing we see every day? Are the theory's assumptions borne out in writing done by our students?

It's tempting to avoid this sort of question by assuming that the work of highly skilled writers presents the most interesting test and the most dramatic illustration and discourse theory. And, of course, it would be foolish to overlook what such writers can help us discover about the composing process and the nature of effective writing. Yet if discourse theory is to make comprehensive descriptive statements about writing, theorists will have to test their assumptions against the actual performance of writers of quite diverse abilities. In our classrooms, we have unique access to this diversity. The writing of our students represents a kind of information that is almost impossible to obtain in any context other than a course that is primarily concerned with students' writing. In the remainder of this article, I shall suggest

This essay was first published in *CCC*, Volume 30, Number 1, February 1979.

ways we might use this source of information to examine and refine assumptions from current discourse theory. My suggestions will take the form of several research questions and some recommendations about how we might try to answer these questions.

One basic assumption in current discourse theory is expressed in James Kinneavy's claim that purpose in discourse is all important: "The aim of a discourse determines everything else in the process of discourse. What is talked about, the oral or written medium which is chosen, the words and grammatical patterns used—all of these are determined by the purpose of the discourse."[1] Kinneavy bases this assertion on the work of a number of theorists and on his analysis of pieces of written discourse. Yet Kinneavy's assertion is troublesome for two reasons. First, his statement about process is based primarily on an analysis of written products, rather than an analysis of the choices writers have made as their texts evolve through a succession of drafts. Second, in analyzing a written product, Kinneavy does not usually refer to the reasoning of the writer who actually produced the discourse. Granted, analyses of written products can let us make some inferences about the composing process. Furthermore, there is no simple, quick way to determine a writer's reasons for a given choice of language, syntax, etc. Yet we have, at present, no basis for assuming that analysis of products will let us find out everything we need to know about the writing process. Nor can we assume that writers' own insights will not be useful to us as we try to understand this process. Consequently, in our complex role of teacher/theorist/researcher we need to consider this sort of research question: What reasons do our students give for the choices they make in producing a piece of writing? Answers to this question should help us raise other questions, which I shall mention below.

To obtain information which would let us answer our first question, we might proceed in one of several ways. We might identify the sort of students Richard Beach calls "extensive revisers"[2] and ask them to let us see all the drafts they create for any given writing assignment. We could then identify the specific changes they make in these drafts and ask them to explain the reasoning that led them to make each change. Or we might follow one or both of the procedures Charles Cooper and I used in a recent study of professional writers' composing process.[3] First, we could ask students to re-write a given assignment so as to achieve a different purpose and appeal to a different audience. We could then identify and ask questions about changes writers had made in their original drafts. A second procedure, one that might be especially useful with student writers who have little sense of the ways a piece of writing might be revised, would be for us to make changes in a draft students have already written. We might alter sentence length or complexity, or we might modify diction, perhaps replacing neutral words with emotive terms, general words with specific. In making such changes, we would have to assure students that we were not correcting or criticizing their work, that what we were interested in was their reasons for accepting or rejecting changes we had made.

In using any of the procedures I have mentioned, we would need to tape-record students' comments so that we could review them a number of times in order to categorize the reasons students gave for their choices. This process of devising categories for their reasons will probably be tedious. But Cooper and I found that it is possible to set up categories that another reader can use to make reliable judgments about the reasons writers give for their choices.

As we listen to students' comments, we might come up with answers to questions that do not bear directly on our central concern but that have important implications for our teaching:

> To what extent do students see composing as a process of making choices? How many of them are able to generate their own alternatives from which to choose?
>
> What proportion of our students are unable to articulate a reason—any sort of reason—for choices that they have made?
>
> Are certain kinds of choices (e.g., diction) easier for them to justify than are others?

We should also be able to answer other questions that bear directly on Kinneavy's assertion about the importance of purpose in the process of composition:

> Do students justify their choices by referring to their basic purpose in writing?
>
> Do they give other justifications for their choices?
>
> Do students give reasons that cannot be accounted for by reference to current discourse theory?
>
> Do students' reasons vary according to the kind of writing task they're doing? (For example: Are there some kinds of tasks in which purpose seems a more important consideration than it does in other kinds of tasks?)
>
> Do the kinds of reasons students give vary according to the skill of the writer?

Answers to these questions may lead us to revise discourse theory so as to accommodate new kinds of reasons students give for the choices they make in writing. Further, it may be that answers to our questions will help us re-define our job as teachers. As we understand the bases students presently use in making choices, we may be able to see how we could help them make even more effective choices.

A second major assumption in current discourse theory is that different writing tasks make quite different demands on writers. The writing strategies that are essential for success with one task may be relatively unimportant for another task. On the face of it, this assumption seems self-evidently true. A letter to a close, sympathetic friend would likely contain language and syntax that would almost never appear in, say, a formal report. Yet students (freshmen, upperclassmen, and graduate students) do not always make even the sort of gross distinctions suggested by my examples. Sometimes they approach different tasks with a single set of oversimplified rules ("Mr./Ms. X taught us that we should *never* underline words for emphasis"). At other times, students use in a new context some device (a sarcastic phrase, a sentence fragment) that had previously proved appropriate for a different sort of task. In still other circumstances, students seem to be working toward contradictory purposes or establishing different speaker-audience relationships within what would appear to be a single writing task. This seeming disparity between student performance and discourse theory leads me to raise this question: Is it in fact true that different kinds of writing tasks elicit different kinds of writing performance from students? In the following discussion, I shall be concerned only with writing tasks that teachers assign. It might also be worth our while, however, to consider tasks that students assign themselves, e.g., self-initiated writings that students do outside of class.

To answer this question, we would need to assign students three different writing tasks—for example: (1) an expressive task, in which writers articulate their ideas and attitudes in a letter to a good friend; (2) a persuasive task, in which writers try not simply to express their own feelings but also to influence the feelings and actions of audiences that might appear to have little in common with the writers; (3) an explanatory task, in which writers convey information in a straightforward and reasonable manner.

In analyzing students' work on these different tasks, we might consider rather conventional matters such as diction, syntax, and organizational patterns. With diction, we might use the categories Edward Corbett mentioned in *Classical Rhetoric for the Modern Student*.[4] Our research question would become: Does one writing task elicit a greater number of abstract (or connotative or formal . . .) word choices than do the other tasks? In analyzing syntax, we could draw on the work of Charles Cooper and Barbara Rosenberg,[5] who found that certain features of syntax are most useful in making sharp distinctions between certain kinds of expository writing. We could re-phrase our basic question thus: Do different writing tasks lead students to use, on average, longer T-units (or more final free modifiers or more adjective modifiers . . .) than do other tasks? To investigate organizational patterns, we might draw upon two different procedures. We might look for students' use of transitional relationships identified by W. Ross Winterowd.[6] Or we might pursue Richard L. Larson's claim that within a given type of discourse, paragraphs are likely to perform a relatively small number of functions.[7] Thus we might ask: Do different tasks lead students to use different types of transitional relationships or to use paragraphs that fill different types of functions?

To refine our answers to the three questions I have just mentioned, we might have all the papers in our sample evaluated. We might ask several readers, working independently, to place each paper in one of three groups: most effective responses to the task; moderately effective responses to the task; least effective responses to the task. Then we could consider only the papers in the "most effective" and "least effective" groups and re-state our basic question thus: For students whose writing is rated most effective, can we say that different writing tasks elicit different writing performances? What about students whose work is rated least effective?

Implications of our answers to these questions become clear as we consider two further assumptions from current discourse theory. As a corollary to the premise that different demands made of writers elicit different performances from them, Richard Lloyd-Jones contends that (1) writing must not be judged by general criteria for "good" writing but by what Lloyd-Jones calls "primary traits," criteria that are uniquely suited to the specific task a writer is trying to perform; (2) people who are skillful with one sort of task may not be equally skillful with some other kind of task.[8]

In devising evaluation procedures for the National Assessment of Educational Progress, Lloyd-Jones has illustrated the former assumption; he has designed different scoring guides for each of several writing tasks used in the 1974 assessment. For example, to guide the scoring of one set of persuasive essays, Lloyd-Jones instructed judges to (1) determine the number of reasons students give in support of their arguments; (2) determine whether or not students elaborate on these reasons; (3) determine what kind(s) of authorities students refer to. For one set of expressive essays, Lloyd-Jones asked judges to decide whether students (1) entered into an imaginary role specified in the writing assignment; (2) elaborated upon that role by talking about the sort of details and feelings that established a distinct personality.

These scoring guides represent a significant departure from the customary practice of judging all expository writing by a single set of criteria, e.g., the categories found in an analytic scale. And this departure raises some problems for teachers and researchers. Whereas we once could use a single, widely-agreed-upon procedure for evaluating all the writing done in a given mode, we may now have to use a variety of evaluation procedures, most of which we have to create for ourselves. Since Lloyd-Jones' evaluation procedures imply a substantial change in our evaluation of students' writing, we must consider two questions. Would different evaluation procedures lead us to make different judgments about a given student's writing performance? Is any one evaluation procedure especially helpful (or unhelpful) to students?

To answer the first question, we would need to examine one piece of writing from each of forty-five students. We would have each piece of writing judged according to several procedures such as the following:

1. Analytic scale (essays are judged on the basis of such general qualities as organization, clarity, etc.)

2. Primary traits (essays are judged on the basis of criteria that seem uniquely suited to the specific writing task. For example, persuasive essays would not be judged on some general criterion such as organization but, rather, on some quality such as writers' ability to elaborate upon the reasons they give in support of their position.)

3. Analysis of specific qualities such as
   A. use of some of the transitions that Winterowd suggests are essential to "coherence";

    B. deviations from standard usage;

    C. syntactic complexity.

I mention these specific qualities with some reluctance. They probably should be included in an analytic scale. Yet each of these qualities is often treated independently as a significant feature of "good" writing. When our colleagues complain to us that we're not teaching students to write, they often mean that they're tired of seeing misspelled words and sentence fragments.

Each of the forty-five papers would have to be rated by using each of the five procedures (once using an analytic scale, once using a primary-trait scoring guide, once according to the number and kinds of transitions used . . .). After each rating, we would need to arrange the papers into three groups of equal size: superior, average, poor. Then we would be able to ask this question: As we vary the evaluation procedure, do the same papers keep appearing in the same groups? The answer would tell us whether different evaluation procedures result in different judgments about students' writing.

To determine whether any one evaluation procedure is especially helpful to students, we might consider how that procedure affects students' writing performance and how that procedure affects students' attitudes toward writing. To carry out this investigation, we would need ten or twelve classes of students, taught by five or six teachers. We would have to be sure that students were randomly assigned to these teachers and that each class would be conducted in the same way, that the only difference would be the evaluation procedure used. For an entire semester, students would be asked to write a rough draft of each essay, receive feedback on that draft, and use that feedback to revise their rough draft. In some classes, feedback would be guided by a teacher's use of an analytic scale. In others, it would be guided by a primary-trait scoring procedure. Our analysis would be based on students' first and last writing assignments of the semester. We could give judges a pair of essays from each student, a revised draft of the student's first essay of the term and a revised draft of the student's final draft of the semester. Our question for the judges would be: Which essay in each pair is the better essay? After we have judges' evaluations, we would be able to answer these questions: In each group of students (those whose instruction included evaluation by an analytic scale and those whose instruction included evaluation by primary-trait procedures) what proportion of the students showed improvement in their final essay of the term? Is this proportion substantially higher in one group than in the other?

Answers to these questions would let us determine whether one evaluation procedure was more useful than another. To find out whether one evaluation procedure had a greater effect on students' attitudes, we could use a relatively simple measure developed by John A. Daly and Michael D. Miller.[9] This measure asks students to indicate their reactions to twenty-six statements (e.g., I'm nervous about writing; People seem to enjoy what I write) about writing. We would need to ask students to respond to these statements at the beginning of the term and at the end of the term. We would then ask (1) how many students in each group showed a decrease in their apprehension about writing and (2) was the proportion of students showing a decrease in apprehension substantially greater in one group than in the other?

Once we feel reasonably confident about the sort of evaluation procedures we need to use, we could go on to ask whether students who are successful with one sort of writing task are equally successful with other kinds of writing tasks. To answer this question, we might be able to use as few as four classes of students—two from each of two teachers—but we would need at least four pieces of writing from each student. Two of these pieces of writing might ask students to perform a persuasive task; the other two might involve expressive tasks. After collecting these papers, we would need to remove students' names and ask judges to use a specific scoring procedure to group the responses to each assignment into three sets: most satisfactory, moderately satisfactory, unsatisfactory. Once all the papers had been rated, we could identify those students whose papers were most consistently rated superior for one kind of task. Then we would need to ask if those same students were consistently rated superior for the other sort of task.

If it is true that students are likely to be more successful with one sort of writing task than with others and if it is true that we must vary our evaluation procedure according to the specific writing task at hand, we may have to make substantial changes in the way we assign and evaluate writing. We will have to structure writing tasks much more carefully, being sure that we don't equate tasks that make substantially different demands on student writers. If different kinds of tasks really do make different demands/require different skills, it seems a little unfair to treat writing performance globally, either judging all expositions by the same criterion or averaging an A in expression with a C in persuasion to produce a meaningless B that reflects neither ability.

Studies proposed in this article are relatively simple. They can be carried out by a single teacher or by a few colleagues in a single composition program. Because of their limited scope, it seems unlikely that any of these studies will be definitive. Considered individually, none will enable us to generalize about all composition students in all circumstances; none will, once and for all, refute or confirm basic assumptions in discourse theory. Yet as a number of us begin to ask the same sort of questions and pursue related studies, we should be able to obtain information that will be useful in several ways. At the very least, our work should help us insure that discourse theory does not become a procrustean bed for our own students. By testing theory against the real world of student writing, we can insure that our assumptions are reasonable, that they do justice to our students' writing. In addition, we may find that this process of testing helps us refine, or at least raise useful questions about, the assumptions of a discipline that is still in its formative stages. And finally, this testing may give us more insight into our students' writing and, consequently, into our job as teachers. If our studies do not lead us to certainty, they should enable us to fulfill our multiple roles of researchers, theorists, and teachers. Our students and our discipline can only benefit.

Over the past several decades our profession has seen the most extraordinary changes. In rough chronological order, we have seen a revival of classical rhetoric and attempts to create modern rhetorics. This was followed by widespread fascination with freewriting and sentence combining, which, in turn was followed by an emphasis on collaborative writing, peer reviews, and portfolio assessment. Subsequently, we have moved some of this work online and have also begun engaging students with "writing for the community" or, more recently, "service learning."

From my perspective, all these changes are to the good. But all of them are just that—changes, developments that will be superceded by other developments, more compelling changes. So how do we respond to these or any other changes? What stance do we take toward the ongoing, sometimes chaotic, always relentless developments in our field?

My answer begins with Richard Braddock, the person whose work this collection honors. Braddock's basic operating principle was to look around and see what was actually going on, not just in the work of professional writers but in the work of composition students as well. Was either group doing what teachers claimed, hoped, or recommended? In effect, Braddock was saying, let's take our most cherished current beliefs and ask whether they hold up to careful empirical—not experimental, but empirical*—scrutiny.*

Here, for example, are three such beliefs, all of which are associated with current changes in our profession: (1) portfolio assessment allows a dialog (between writers, peers, and teachers) that can improve students' writing; (2) online peer response removes clues to respondents' status or gender and thus promotes a more egalitarian dialog; and (3) community service learning projects allow students to negotiate new roles in relation to members of the community.

All of these beliefs have to do with process, and all of them invite us to test them by asking essentially the same question: What is going on while people are engaged in any of these processes? Is it what we hope or intend? What seems to be helping or hindering students' efforts to engage in any of these processes? Questions such as these do not require the exhaustive textual analysis or the large-scale experimental studies Braddock engaged in. Rather, they require only that we as teachers pay careful attention to what our students are doing as they interact with each other or members of the community.

Why should we do this? For one thing, it's not enough to repeat pronouncements about what should be happening in our classes. Simply to survive as teachers, we need to know what is and is not going on so we can make intelligent choices about what to start doing, stop doing, or do differently. More important, to survive as members of a profession, we can't just see ourselves as purveyors of other people's insights, of meanings someone else has constructed. Those things change, sometimes as part of a profound paradigm shift, sometimes as little more than fads. Our job is to assess those meanings, those insights, in the harsh reality of our classrooms. We can do this because our discipline does not exist on the pages of journal articles or research reports. It exists in the intersection of theory and practice, in the processes of teaching and learning. Specific theories and practices of our discipline will come and go. The one thing that does not change is our obligation to draw on the lived experience of teaching and learning as we test, refine, and sometimes reject the innovations that will continue to come our way. In the continuing flux of our discipline, our responsibility as teachers and learners seems the one thing that will stay the same.

–LEE ODELL
Rensselaer Polytechnic Institute

1981   *The Study of Error*

DAVID BARTHOLOMAE

t is curious, I think, that with all the current interest in "Basic Writing," little attention has been paid to the most basic question: What is it? What is "basic writing," that is, if the term is to refer to a phenomenon, an activity, something a writer does or has done, rather than to a course of instruction? We know that across the country students take tests of one sort or another and are placed in courses that bear the title, "Basic Writing." But all we know is that there are students taking courses. We know little about their performance as writers, beyond the bald fact that they fail to do what other, conventionally successful, writers do. We don't, then, have an adequate description of the variety of writing we call "basic."

On the other hand, we have considerable knowledge of what Basic Writing courses are like around the country, the texts that are used, the approaches taken. For some time now, "specialists" have been devising and refining the technology of basic or developmental instruction. But these technicians are tinkering with pedagogies based on what? At best on models of how successful writers write. At worst, on old text-book models that disregard what writers actually do or how they could be said to learn, and break writing conveniently into constituent skills like "word power," "sentence power," and "paragraph power." Neither pedagogy is built on the results of any systematic inquiry into what basic writers do when they write or into the way writing skills develop for beginning adult writers. Such basic research has barely begun. Mina Shaughnessy argued the case this way:

> Those pedagogies that served the profession for years seem no longer appropriate to large numbers of students, and their inappropriateness lies largely in the fact that many of our students . . . are adult beginners and depend as students did not depend in the past upon the classroom and the teacher for the acquisition of the skill of writing.

This essay was first published in *CCC,* Volume 31, Number 3, October 1980.

If the profession is going to accept responsibility for teaching this kind of student, she concludes, "We are committed to research of a very ambitious sort."[1]

Where might such research begin, and how might it proceed? We must begin by studying basic writing itself—the phenomenon, not the course of instruction. If we begin here, we will recognize at once that "basic" does not mean simple or childlike. These are beginning writers, to be sure, but they are not writers who need to learn to use language. They are writers who need to learn to command a particular variety of language—the language of a written, academic discourse—and a particular variety of language use—writing itself. The writing of a basic writer can be shown to be an approximation of conventional written discourse; it is a peculiar and idiosyncratic version of a highly conventional type, but the relation between the approximate and the conventional forms is not the same as the relation between the writing, say, of a 7th grader and the writing of a college freshman.

Basic writing, I want to argue, is a variety of writing, not writing with fewer parts or more rudimentary constituents. It is not evidence of arrested cognitive development, arrested language development, or unruly or unpredictable language use. The writer of this sentence, for example, could not be said to be writing an "immature" sentence, in any sense of the term, if we grant her credit for the sentence she intended to write:

> The time of my life when I learned something, and which resulted in a change in which I look upon life things. This would be the period of my life when I graduated from Elementary school to High school.

When we have used conventional T-unit analysis, and included in our tabulations figures on words/clause, words/T-unit and clauses/T-unit that were drawn from "intended T-units" as well as actual T-units, we have found that basic writers do not, in general, write "immature" sentences. They are not, that is, 13th graders writing 7th grade sentences. In fact, they often attempt syntax whose surface is more complex than that of more successful freshman writers. They get into trouble by getting in over their heads, not only attempting to do more than they can, but imagining as their target a syntax that is *more* complex than convention requires. The failed sentences, then, could be taken as stages of learning rather than the failure to learn, but also as evidence that these writers are using writing as an occasion to learn.

It is possible to extend the concept of "intentional structures" to the analysis of complete essays in order to determine the "grammar" that governs the idiosyncratic discourse of writers imagining the language and conventions of academic discourse in unconventional ways. This method of analysis is certainly available to English teachers, since it requires a form of close reading, paying attention to the language of a text in order to determine not only what a writer says, but how he locates and articulates meaning. When a basic writer violates our expectations, however, there is a tendency to dismiss the text as non-writing, as meaningless or imperfect writing. We have not read as we have been trained to read, with a particular interest in the way an individual style confronts and violates convention. We have read, rather, as policemen, examiners, gate-keepers. The teacher who is unable to make sense out of a seemingly bizarre piece of student writing is often the same teacher who can give an elaborate explanation of the "meaning" of a story by Donald Barthelme or a poem by e. e. cummings. If we learn to treat the language of basic writing *as* language and assume, as we do when writers violate our expectations in more conventional ways, that the unconventional features in the writing are evidence of intention and that they are, therefore, meaningful, then we can chart systematic choices, individual strategies, and characteristic processes of thought. One can read Mina Shaughnessy's *Errors and Expectations* as the record of just such a close reading.[2]

There is a style, then, to the apparently bizarre and incoherent writing of a basic writer because it is, finally, evidence of an individual using language to make and transcribe meaning. This is one of the axioms of error analysis, whether it be applied to reading (as in "miscue analysis"), writing, or second language learning. An error (and I would include errors beyond those in the decoding or encoding of sentences) can only be understood as evidence of intention. They are the only evidence we have of an individual's idiosyncratic way of using the language and articulating meaning, of imposing a style on common material. A writer's activity is linguistic and rhetorical activity; it can be different but never random. The task for both teacher and researcher, then, is to discover the grammar of *that* coherence, of the "idiosyncratic dialect" that belongs to a particular writer at a particular moment in the history of his attempts to imagine and reproduce the standard idiom of academic discourse.[3]

All writing, of course, could be said to only approximate conventional discourse; our writing is never either completely predictable or completely idiosyncratic. We speak our own language as well as the language of the tribe and, in doing so, make concessions to both ourselves and our culture. The distance between text and conventional expectation may be a sign of failure and it may be a sign of genius, depending on the level of control and intent we are willing to assign to the writer, and depending on the insight we acquire from seeing convention so transformed. For a basic writer the distance between text and convention is greater than it is for the run-of-the-mill freshman writer. It may be, however, that the more talented the freshman writer becomes, the more able she is to increase again the distance between text and convention. We are drawn to conclude that basic writers lack control, although it may be more precise to say that they lack choice and option, the power to make decisions about the idiosyncrasy of their writing. Their writing is not, however, truly uncontrolled. About the actual distance from text to convention for the basic writer, we know very little. We know that it will take a long time to traverse—generally the greater the distance the greater the time and energy required to close the gap. We know almost nothing about the actual sequence of development—the natural sequence of learning—that moves a writer from basic writing to competent writing to good writing. The point, however, is that "basic writing" is something our students *do* or *produce;* it is not a kind of writing we teach to backward or un-prepared students. We should not spend our time imagining simple or "basic" writing tasks, but studying the errors that emerge when beginning writers are faced with complex tasks.

The mode of analysis that seems most promising for the research we need on the writer's sequence of learning is error analysis. Error analysis pro-vides the basic writing teacher with both a technique for analyzing errors in the production of discourse, a technique developed by linguists to study sec-ond language learning, and a theory of error, or, perhaps more properly, a perspective on error, where errors are seen as (1) necessary stages of individ-ual development and (2) data that provide insight into the idiosyncratic strategies of a particular language user at a particular point in his acquisition of a target language. Enough has been written lately about error analysis that I'll only give a brief summary of its perspective on second language or sec-ond dialect acquisition.[4] I want to go on to look closely at error analysis as a method, in order to point out its strengths and limits as a procedure for tex-tual analysis.

George Steiner has argued that all acts of interpretation are acts of trans-lation and are, therefore, subject to the constraints governing the passage from one language to another.[5] All our utterances are approximations, at-tempts to use the language of, say, Frank Kermode or the language, perhaps, of our other, smarter, wittier self. In this sense, the analogy that links devel-opmental composition instruction with second language learning can be a useful one—useful that is, if the mode of learning (whatever the "second" language) is writing rather than speaking. (This distinction, I might add, is not generally made in the literature on error analysis, where writing and speech are taken as equivalent phenomena.) Error analysis begins with the recognition that errors, or the points where the actual text varies from a hy-pothetical "standard" text, will be either random or systematic. If they are systematic in the writing of an individual writer, then they are evidence of some idiosyncratic rule system—an idiosyncratic grammar or rhetoric, an "interlanguage" or "approximative system."[6] If the errors are systematic across all basic writers, then they would be evidence of generalized stages in the acquisition of fluent writing for beginning adult writers. This distinction between individual and general systems is an important one for both teach-ing and research. It is not one that Shaughnessy makes. We don't know whether the categories of error in *Errors and Expectations* hold across a group, and, if so, with what frequency and across a group of what size.

Shaughnessy did find, however, predictable patterns in the errors in the essays the studied. She demonstrated that even the most apparently incoher-ent writing, if we are sensitive to its intentional structure, is evidence of sys-tematic, coherent, rule-governed behavior. Basic writers, she demonstrated, are not performing mechanically or randomly but making choices and form-ing strategies as they struggle to deal with the varied demands of a task, a language, and a rhetoric. The "systems" such writing exhibits provide evi-dence that basic writers *are* competent, mature language users. Their attempts at producing written language are not hit and miss, nor are they evidence of simple translation of speech into print. The approximate systems they produce are evidence that they can conceive of and manipulate written language as a structured, systematic code. They are "intermediate" systems in that they mark stages on route to mastery (or, more properly, on route to conventional fluency) of written, academic discourse.

This also, however, requires some qualification. They *may* be evidence of some transitional stage. They may also, to use Selinker's term, be evidence of "stabilized variability," where a writer is stuck or searching rather than moving on toward more complete approximation of the target language.[7] A writer will stick with some intermediate system if he is convinced that the language he uses "works," or if he is unable to see errors *as* errors and form alternate hypotheses in response.

Error analysis begins with a theory of writing, a theory of language production and language development, that allows us to see errors as evidence of choice or strategy among a range of possible choices or strategies. They provide evidence of an individual style of using the language and making it work; they are not a simple record of what a writer failed to do because of incompetence or indifference. Errors, then, are stylistic features, information about *this* writer and *this* language; they are not necessarily "noise" in the system, accidents of composing, or malfunctions in the language process. Consequently, we cannot identify errors without identifying them in context, and the context is not the text, but the activity of composing that presented the erroneous form as a possible solution to the problem of making a meaningful statement. Shaughnessy's taxonomy of error, for example, identifies errors according to their source, not their type. A single type of error could be attributed to a variety of causes. Donald Freeman's research, for example, has shown that, "subject-verb agreement . . . is a host of errors, not one." One of his students analyzed a "large sample of real world sentences and concluded that there are at least eight different kinds, most of which have very little to do with one another."[8]

Error analysis allows us to place error in the context of composing and to interpret and classify systematic errors. The key concept is the concept of an "interlanguage" or an "intermediate system," an idiosyncratic grammar and rhetoric that is a writer's approximation of the standard idiom. Errors, while they can be given more precise classification, fall into three main categories: errors that are evidence of an intermediate system; errors that could truly be said to be accidents, or slips of the pen as a writer's mind rushes ahead faster than his hand; and, finally, errors of language transfer, or, more commonly, dialect interference, where in the attempt to produce the target language, the writer intrudes forms from the "first" or "native" language rather than inventing some intermediate form. For writers, this intrusion most often comes from a spoken dialect. The error analyst is primarily concerned, however, with errors that are evidence of some intermediate system. This kind of error occurs because the writer *is* an active, competent language user who uses his knowledge that language is rule-governed, and who uses his ability to predict and form analogies, to construct hypotheses that can make an irregular or unfamiliar language more manageable. The problem comes when the rule is incorrect or, more properly, when it is idiosyncratic, belonging only to the language of this writer. There is evidence of a idiosyncratic system, for example, when a student adds inflectional endings to infinitives, as in this sentence: "There was plenty the boy had to *learned* about birds." It also seems to be evident in a sentence like this: "This assignment calls on *choosing* one of my papers and making a last draft out of it." These errors can be further subdivided into those that are in flux and mark a fully transitional stage, and those that, for one reason or another, become frozen and recur across time.

Kroll and Schafer, in a recent *CCC* article, argue that the value of error analysis for the composition teacher is the perspective it offers on the learner, since it allows us to see errors "as clues to inner processes, as windows into the mind."[9] If we investigate the pattern of error in the performance of an individual writer, we can better understand the nature of those errors and the way they "fit" in an individual writer's program for writing. As a consequence, rather than impose an inappropriate or even misleading syllabus on a learner, we can plan instruction to assist a writer's internal syllabus. If, for example, a writer puts standard inflections on irregular verbs or on verbs that are used in verbals (as in "I used to runned"), drill on verb endings will only reinforce the rule that, because the writer is overgeneralizing, is the source of the error in the first place. By charting and analyzing a writer's errors, we can begin in our instruction with what a writer *does* rather than with what he fails to do. It makes no sense, for example, to impose lessons on the sentence on a student whose problems with syntax can be understood in more precise terms. It makes no sense to teach spelling to an individual who has trouble principally with words that contain vowel clusters. Error analysis, then, is a method of diagnosis.

Error analysis can assist instruction at another level. By having students share in the process of investigating and interpreting the patterns of error in their writing, we can help them begin to see those errors as evidence of hypotheses or strategies they have formed and, as a consequence, put them in a position to change, experiment, imagine other strategies. Studying their own writing puts students in a position to see themselves as language users, rather than as victims of a language that uses them.

This, then, is the perspective and the technique of error analysis. To interpret a student paper without this frame of reference is to misread, as for example when a teacher sees an incorrect verb form and concludes that the student doesn't understand the rules for indicating tense or number. I want, now, to examine error analysis as a procedure for the study of errors in written composition. It presents two problems. The first can be traced to the fact that error analysis was developed for studying errors in spoken performance.[10] It can be transferred to writing only to the degree that writing is like speech, and there are significant points of difference. It is generally acknowledged, for example, that written discourse is not just speech written down on paper. Adult written discourse has a grammar and rhetoric that is different from speech. And clearly the activity of producing language is different for a writer than it is for a speaker.

The "second language" a basic writer must learn to master is formal, written discourse, a discourse whose lexicon, grammar, and rhetoric are learned not through speaking and listening but through reading and writing. The process of acquisition is visual not aural. Furthermore, basic writers do not necessarily produce writing by translating speech into print (the way children learning to write would); that is, they must draw on a memory for graphemes rather than phonemes. This is a different order of memory and production from that used in speech and gives rise to errors unique to writing.

Writing also, however, presents "interference" of a type never found in speech. Errors in writing may be caused by interference from the act of writing itself, from the difficulty of moving a pen across the page quickly enough to keep up with the words in the writer's mind, or from the difficulty of recalling and producing the conventions that are necessary for producing print rather than speech, conventions of spelling, orthography, punctuation, capitalization and so on. This is not, however, just a way of saying that writers make spelling errors and speakers do not. As Shaughnessy pointed out, errors of syntax can be traced to the gyrations of a writer trying to avoid a word that her sentence has led her to, but that she knows she cannot spell.

The second problem in applying error analysis to the composition classroom arises from special properties in the taxonomy of errors we chart in student writing. Listing varieties of errors is not like listing varieties of rocks or butterflies. What a reader finds depends to a large degree on her assumptions about the writer's intention. Any systematic attempt to chart a learner's errors is clouded by the difficulty of assigning intention through textual analysis. The analyst begins, then, by interpreting a text, not by describing features on a page. And interpretation is less than a precise science.

Let me turn to an example. This is part of a paper that a student, John, wrote in response to an assignment that asked him to go back to some papers he had written on significant moments in his life in order to write a paper that considered the general question of the way people change:

> This assignment call on chosing one of my incident making a last draft out of it. I found this very differcult because I like them all but you said I had to pick one so the Second incident was decide. Because this one had the most important insight to my life that I indeed learn from. This insight explain why adulthood mean that much as it dose to me because I think it alway influence me to change and my outlook on certain thing like my point-of-view I have one day and it might change the next week on the same issue. So in these frew words I going to write about the incident now. My experience took place in my high school and the reason was out side of school but I will show you the connection. The situation took place cause of the type of school I went too. Let me tell you about the situation first of all what happen was that I got suspense from school. For thing that I fell was out of my control sometime, but it taught me

alot about respondability of a growing man. The school suspense me for being late ten time. I had accummate ten dementic and had to bring my mother to school to talk to a conselor and Prinpicable of the school what when on at the meet took me out mentally period.

One could imagine a variety of responses to this. The first would be to form the wholesale conclusion that John can't write and to send him off to a workbook. Once he had learned how to write correct sentences, then he could go on to the business of actually writing. Let me call this the "old style" response to error. A second response, which I'll call the "investigative approach," would be to chart the patterns of error in this particular text. Of the approximately 40 errors in the first 200 words, the majority fall under four fairly specific categories: verb endings, noun plurals, syntax, and spelling. The value to pedagogy is obvious. One is no longer teaching a student to "write" but to deal with a limited number of very specific kinds of errors, each of which would suggest its own appropriate response. Furthermore, it is possible to refine the categories and to speculate on and organize them according to cause. The verb errors almost all involve "s" or "ed" endings, which could indicate dialect interference or a failure to learn the rules for indicating tense and number. It is possible to be even more precise. The passage contains 41 verbs; only 17 of them are used incorrectly. With the exception of four spelling errors, the errors are all errors of inflection and, furthermore, these errors come only with regular verbs. There are no errors with irregular verbs. This would suggest, then, that when John draws on memory for a verb form, he gets it right; but when John applies a rule to determine the ending, he gets it wrong.

The errors of syntax could be divided into those that might be called punctuation errors (or errors that indicate a difficulty perceiving the boundaries of the sentence), such as

> Let me tell you about the situation first of all what happen was that I got suspense from school. For thing that I fell was out of my control sometime, but it taught me alot about respondability of a growing man.

and errors of syntax that would fall under Shaughnessy's category of consolidation errors,

> This insight explain why adulthood mean that much as it dose to me because I think it alway influence me to change and my outlook on certain thing like my point-of-view I have one day and it might change the next week on the same issue.

One would also want to note the difference between consistent errors, the substitution of "situation" for "situation" or "suspense" for "suspended," and unstable ones, as, for example, when John writes "cause" in one place and "because" in another. In one case John could be said to have fixed on a rule; in the other he is searching for one. One would also want to distinguish between what might seem to be "accidental" errors, like substituting "frew" for "few" or "when" for "went," errors that might best be addressed by teaching a student to edit, and those whose causes are deeper and require time and experience, or some specific instructional strategy.

I'm not sure, however, that this analysis provides an accurate representation of John's writing. Consider what happens when John reads this paper out loud. I've been taping students reading their own papers, and I've developed a system of notation, like that used in miscue analysis,[11] that will allow me to record the points of variation between the writing that is on the page and the writing that is spoken, or, to use the terminology of miscue analysis, between the expected response (ER) and the observed response (OR). What I've found is that students will often, or in predictable instances, substitute correct forms for the incorrect forms on the page, even though they are generally unaware that such a substitution was made. This observation suggests the limits of conventional error analysis for the study of error in written composition.

I asked John to read his paper out loud, and to stop and correct or note any mistakes he found. Let me try to reproduce the transcript of that reading. I will [italicize] any substitution or correction and offer some comments in parentheses. The reader might first go back and review the original. Here is what John read:

> This assignment calls on *choosing* one of my incident making a last draft out of it. I found this very difficult because I like them all but you said I *had* to pick one so the Second incident was decide*d on.* Because (John goes back and rereads, connecting up the subordinate clause.) So the second incident was decided on because this one had the most important insight to my life that I indeed learn*ed* from. This insight explains why adulthood *meant* that much as it dose to me because I think it always influence*s* me to change and my outlook on certain thing*s* like my point-of-view I have one day and it might change the next week on the same issue. (John goes back and rereads, beginning with "like my point of view," and he is puzzled but he makes no additional changes.) So in these *few* words *I'm* going to write about the incident now. My experience took place *because* of the type of school I went to (John had written "too.") Let me tell you about the situation (John comes to a full stop.) first of all what happen*ed* was that I got *suspended* from school (no full stop) for thing*s* that I *felt* was out of my control sometime, but it taught me a lot about *responsibility* of a growing man. The school *suspended* me for being late ten time*s*. I had *accumulated* (for "accumate") ten *demerits* (for "dementic") and had to bring my mother to school to talk to a counselor and *the Principal* of the school (full stop) what *went* on at the meet*ing* took me out mentally (full stop) period (with brio).

I have chosen an extreme case to make my point, but what one sees here is the writer correcting almost every error as he reads the paper, even though he is not able to recognize that there *are* errors or that he has corrected them. The only errors John spotted (where he stopped, noted an error and corrected it) were the misspellings of "situation" and "Principal," and the substitution of "chosing" for "choosing." Even when he was asked to reread

sentences to see if he could notice any difference between what he was saying and the words on the page, he could not. He could not, for example, see
the error in "frew" or "dementic" or any of the other verb errors, and yet he
spoke the correct form of every verb (with the exception of "was" after he
had changed "thing" to "things" in "for things that I *felt* was out of my control") and he corrected every plural. His phrasing as he read produced correct syntax, except in the case of the consolidation error, which he puzzled
over but did not correct. It's important to note, however, that John did not
read that confused syntax as if no confusion were there. He sensed the difference between the phrasing called for by the meaning of the sentence and that
which existed on the page. He did not read as though meaning didn't matter
or as though the "meaning" coded on the page was complete. His problem
cannot be simply a syntax problem, since the jumble is bound up with his
struggle to articulate this particular meaning. And it is not simply a "thinking" problem—John doesn't write this way because he thinks this way—
since he perceives that the statement as it is written is other than that which
he intended.

When I asked John why the paper (which went on for two more pages)
was written all as one paragraph, he replied, "It was all one idea. I didn't
want to have to start all over again. I had a good idea and I didn't want to
give it up." John doesn't need to be "taught" the paragraph, at least not as
the paragraph is traditionally taught. His prose is orderly and proceeds
through blocks of discourse. He tells the story of his experience at the school
and concludes that through his experience he realized that he must accept responsibility for his tardiness, even though the tardiness was not his fault but
the fault of the Philadelphia subway system. He concludes that with this re-
alization he learned "the responsibility of a growing man." Furthermore John
knows that the print code carries certain conventions for ordering and presenting discourse. His translation of the notion that "a paragraph develops a
single idea" is peculiar but not illogical.

It could also be argued that John does not need to be "taught" to produce
correct verb forms, or, again, at least not as such things are conventionally
taught. Fifteen weeks of drill on verb endings might raise his test scores but
they would not change the way he writes. He *knows* how to produce correct
endings. He demonstrated that when he read, since he was reading in terms
of his grammatical competence. His problem is a problem of performance, or
fluency, not of competence. There is certainly no evidence that the verb errors are due to interference from his spoken language. And if the errors
could be traced to some intermediate system, the system exists only in John's
performance as a writer. It does not operate when he reads or, for that matter, when he speaks, if his oral reconstruction of his own text can be taken as
a record of John "speaking" the idiom of academic discourse.[12]

John's case also highlights the tremendous difficulty such a student has
with editing, where a failure to correct a paper is not evidence of laziness or
inattention or a failure to know correct forms, but evidence of the tremen-

dous difficulty such a student has objectifying language and seeing it as black and white marks on the page, where things can be wrong even though the meaning seems right.[13] One of the hardest errors for John to spot, after all my coaching, was the substitution of "frew" for "few," certainly not an error that calls into question John's competence as a writer. I can call this a "performance" error, but that term doesn't suggest the constraints on performance in writing. This is an important area for further study. Surely one constraint is the difficulty of moving the hand fast enough to translate meaning into print. The burden imposed on their patience and short-term memory by the slow, awkward handwriting of many inexperienced writers is a very real one. But I think the constraints extend beyond the difficulty of forming words quickly with pen or pencil.

One of the most interesting results of the comparison of the spoken and written versions of John's text is his inability to *see* the difference between "frew" and "few" or "dementic" and "demerit." What this suggests is that John reads and writes from the "top down" rather than the "bottom up," to use a distinction made by cognitive psychologists in their study of reading.[14] John is not operating through the lower level process of translating orthographic information into sounds and sounds into meaning when he reads. And conversely, he is not working from meaning to sound to word when he is writing. He is, rather, retrieving lexical items directly, through a "higher level" process that by-passes the "lower level" operation of phonetic translation. When I put *frew* and *few* on the blackboard, John read them both as "few." The lexical item "few" is represented for John by either orthographic array. He is not, then, reading or writing phonetically, which is a sign, from one perspective, of a high level of fluency, since the activity is automatic and not mediated by the more primitive operation of translating speech into print or print into speech. When John was writing, he did not produce "frew" or "dementic" by searching for sound/letter correspondences. He drew directly upon his memory for the look and shape of those words; he was working from the top down rather than the bottom up. He went to stored print forms and did not take the slower route of translating speech into writing.

John, then, has reached a stage of fluency in writing where he directly and consistently retrieves print forms, like "dementic," that are meaningful to him, even though they are idiosyncratic. I'm not sure what all the implications of this might be, but we surely must see John's problem in a new light, since his problem can, in a sense, be attributed to his skill. To ask John to slow down his writing and sound out words would be disastrous. Perhaps the most we can do is to teach John the slowed down form of reading he will need in order to edit.

John's paper also calls into question our ability to identify accidental errors. I suspect that when John substitutes a word like "when" for "went," this is an accidental error, a slip of the pen. Since John spoke "went" when he read, I cannot conclude that he substituted "when" for "went" because he pronounces both as "wen." This, then, is not an error of dialect interference but an accidental error, the same order of error as the omission of "the" before "Principal." Both were errors John corrected while reading (even though he didn't identify them as errors).

What is surprising is that, with all the difficulty John had identifying errors, he immediately saw that he had written "chosing" rather than "choosing." While textual analysis would have led to the conclusion that he was applying a tense rule to a participial construction, or over-generalizing from a known rule, the ease with which it was identified would lead one to conclude that it was, in fact, a mistake, and not evidence of an approximative system. What would have been diagnosed as a deep error now appears to be only an accidental error, a "mistake" (or perhaps a spelling error).

In summary, this analysis of John's reading produces a healthy respect for the tremendous complexity of transcription, for the process of recording meaning in print as opposed to the process of generating meaning. It also points out the difficulty of charting a learner's "interlanguage" or "intermediate system," since we are working not only with a writer moving between a first and a second language, but a writer whose performance is subject to the interference of transcription, of producing meaning through the print code. We need, in general, to refine our understanding of performance-based errors, and we need to refine our teaching to take into account the high percentage of error in written composition that is rooted in the difficulty of performance rather than in problems of general linguistic competence.

Let me pause for a moment to put what I've said in the context of work in error analysis. Such analysis is textual analysis. It requires the reader to make assumptions about intention on the basis of information in the text. The writer's errors provide the most important information since they provide insight into the idiosyncratic systems the writer has developed. The regular but unconventional features in the writing will reveal the rules and strategies operating for the basic writer.

The basic procedure for such analysis could be outlined this way. First the reader must identify the idiosyncratic construction; he must determine what is an error. This is often difficult, as in the case of fragments, which are conventionally used for effect. Here is an example of a sentence whose syntax could clearly be said to be idiosyncratic:

> In high school you learn alot for example Kindergarten which I took in high school.[15]

The reader, then, must reconstruct that sentence based upon the most reasonable interpretation of the intention in the original, and this must be done *before* the error can be classified, since it will be classified according to its cause.[16] Here is Shaughnessy's reconstruction of the example given above: "In high school you learn a lot. For example, I took up the study of Kindergarten in high school." For any idiosyncratic sentence, however, there are often a variety of possible reconstructions, depending on the reader's sense of the larger meaning of which this individual sentence is only a part, but also depending upon the reader's ability to predict how this writer puts sentences together, that is, on an understanding of this individual style. The text is being interpreted, not described. I've had graduate students who have reconstructed the following sentence, for example, in a variety of ways:

> Why do we have womens liberation and their fighting for Equal Rights
> ect. to be recognized not as a lady but as an Individual.

It could be read, "Why do we have women's liberation and why are they fighting for Equal Rights? In order that women may be recognized not as ladies but as individuals." And, "Why do we have women's liberation and their fight for equal rights, to be recognized not as a lady but as an individual?" There is an extensive literature on the question of interpretation and intention in prose, too extensive for the easy assumption that all a reader has to do is identify what the writer would have written if he wanted to "get it right the first time." The great genius of Shaughnessy's study, in fact, is the remarkable wisdom and sympathy of her interpretations of student texts.

Error analysis, then, involves more than just making lists of the errors in a student essay and looking for patterns to emerge. It begins with the double perspective of text and reconstructed text and seeks to explain the difference between the two on the basis of whatever can be inferred about the meaning of the text and the process of creating it. The reader/researcher brings to bear his general knowledge of how basic writers write, but also whatever is known about the linguistic and rhetorical constraints that govern an individual act of writing. In Shaughnessy's analysis of the "kindergarten" sentence, this discussion is contained in the section on "consolidation errors" in the chapter on "Syntax."[17] The key point, however, is that any such analysis must draw upon extra-textual information as well as close, stylistic analysis.

This paper has illustrated two methods for gathering information about how a text was created. A teacher can interview the student and ask him to explain his error. John wrote this sentence in another paper for my course:

> I would to write about my experience helping 1600 childrens have a
> happy christmas.

The missing word (I would *like* to write about . . .) he supplied when reading the sentence aloud. It is an accidental error and can be addressed by teaching editing. It is the same kind of error as his earlier substitution of "when" for "went." John used the phrase, "1600 childrens," throughout his paper, however. The conventional interpretation would have it that this is evidence of dialect interference. And yet, when John read the paper out loud, he consistently read "1600 children," even though he said he did not see any difference between the word he spoke and the word that was on the page. When I asked him to explain why he put an "s" on the end of "children," he replied, "Because there were 1600 of them." John had a rule for forming plurals that he used when he wrote but not when he spoke. Writing, as he rightly recognized, has its own peculiar rules and constraints. It is different from speech. The error is not due to interference from his spoken language but to his conception of the "code" of written discourse.

The other method for gathering information is having students read aloud their own writing, and having them provide an oral reconstruction of their written text. What I've presented in my analysis of John's essay is a method for recording the discrepancies between the written and spoken versions of a single text. The record of a writer reading provides a version of the "intended" text that can supplement the teacher's or researcher's own reconstruction and aid in the interpretation of errors, whether they be accidental, interlingual, or due to dialect interference. I had to read John's paper very differently once I had heard him read it.

More importantly, however, this method of analysis can provide access to an additional type of error. This is the error that can be attributed to the physical and conceptual demands of writing rather than speaking; it can be traced to the requirements of manipulating a pen and the requirements of manipulating the print code.[18]

In general, when writers read, and read in order to spot and correct errors, their responses will fall among the following categories:

1. overt corrections—errors a reader sees, acknowledges, and corrects;
2. spoken corrections—errors the writer does not acknowledge but corrects in reading;
3. no recognition—errors that are read as written;
4. overcorrection—correct forms made incorrect, or incorrect forms substituted for incorrect forms;
5. acknowledged error—errors a reader senses but cannot correct;
6. reader miscue—a conventional miscue, not linked to error in the text;
7. nonsense—In this case, the reader reads a non-sentence or a nonsense sentence as though it were correct and meaningful. No error or confusion is acknowledged. This applies to errors of syntax only.

Corrections, whether acknowledged or unacknowledged, would indicate performance-based errors. The other responses (with the exception of "reader miscues") would indicate deeper errors, errors that, when charted, would provide evidence of some idiosyncratic grammar or rhetoric.

John "miscues" by completing or correcting the text that he has written. When reading researchers have readers read out loud, they have them read someone else's writing, of course, and they are primarily concerned with the "quality" of the miscues.[19] All fluent readers will miscue; that is, they will not repeat verbatim the words on the page. Since fluent readers are reading for meaning, they are actively predicting what will come and processing large chunks of graphic information at a time. They do not read individual words, and they miscue because they speak what they expect to see rather than what is actually on the page. One indication of a reader's proficiency, then, is that the miscues don't destroy the "sense" of the passage. Poor readers will produce miscues that jumble the meaning of a passage, as in

TEXT: Her wings were folded quietly at her sides.

READER: Her wings were floated quickly at her sides.

or they will correct miscues that do not affect meaning in any significant way.[20]

The situation is different when a reader reads his own text, since this reader already knows what the passage means and attention is drawn, then, to the representation of that meaning. Reading also frees a writer from the constraints of transcription, which for many basic writers is an awkward, laborious process, putting excessive demands on both patience and short-term memory. John, like any reader, read what he expected to see, but with a low percentage of meaning-related miscues, since the meaning, for him, was set, and with a high percentage of code-related miscues, where a correct form was substituted for an incorrect form.

The value of studying students' oral reconstruction of their written texts is threefold. The first is as a diagnostic tool. I've illustrated in my analysis of John's paper how such a diagnosis might take place.

It is also a means of instruction. By having John read aloud and, at the same time, look for discrepancies between what he spoke and what was on the page, I was teaching him a form of reading. The most dramatic change in John's performance over the term was in the number of errors he could spot and correct while re-reading. This far exceeded the number of errors he was able to eliminate from his first drafts. I could teach John an editing procedure better than I could teach him to be correct at the point of transcription.

The third consequence of this form of analysis, or of conventional error analysis, has yet to be demonstrated, but the suggestions for research are clear. It seems evident that we can chart stages of growth in individual basic writers. The pressing question is whether we can chart a sequence of "natural" development for the class of writers we call basic writers. If all nonfluent adult writers proceed through a "natural" learning sequence, and if we can identify that sequence through some large, longitudinal study, then we will begin to understand what a basic writing course or text or syllabus might look like. There are studies of adult second language learners that suggest that there is a general, natural sequence of acquisition for adults learning a second language, one that is determined by the psychology of language production and language acquisition.[21] Before we can adapt these methods to a study of basic writers, however, we need to better understand the additional constraints of learning to transcribe and manipulate the "code" of written discourse. John's case illustrates where we might begin and what we must know.[22]

I wrote "The Study of Error" in 1978. I arrived in Pittsburgh in 1975 to develop a basic writing program (work represented in Facts, Artifacts, *and* Counterfacts*). I had written on curriculum and pedagogy, as these interests were what drew me to composition as a field, but I felt pressure to define a "research" project. At Pitt, I had become acquainted with Bob Glaser and Lauren Resnick, the directors of Pitt's Learning Research and Development Center. Bob appointed me as a Center Associate. He was a cognitive psychologist; he used to joke that he would turn me into an "experimentalist."*

In a sense, he did. These were the days of residual structuralism, when it seemed possible to imagine that there were systems underlying the patterns of culture. I wanted to do something systematic, something that could be replicated in thinking about basic writers and, in particular, in thinking about error. Glaser introduced me to research on math errors, research showing the patterns in errors children made doing problems in addition and subtraction. David Brumble, a colleague, introduced me to research on error in second-language learning. Tony Petrosky introduced me to miscue analysis. A group of us, including graduate students, were reading Labov and Smitherman on Black English. And, finally, we were inspired by Mina Shaughnessy's Errors and Expectations, *both her efforts to name and categorize error and her insistence that error had its own logic and style.*

We began an attempt to gather together large numbers of placement and classroom essays, all written by students identified as "basic writers," with the idea that we would see where and how we could group and cluster what we saw, using Shaughnessy's terms and categories or, where they would not serve or fit, inventing our own. As "The Study of Error" recounts, the most interesting moments for me came when I began to interview students and, finally, to tape their reading aloud of a paper, this in advance of an interview in which I would ask them to identify an error and then explain what they were doing or intending at the moment of its commission.

As I suggested above, this was part of a very productive and exciting period on our campus, when many of us were working together teaching and designing basic writing courses. The literature on basic writing contains much of that work, work by Nick Coles, Bruce Horner, Glynda Hull, Elaine Lees, Min Lu, Tony Petrosky, Mariolina Salvatori, Bill Smith, and Susan Wall.

For about a year and a half I was committed to the idea that we could determine a grammar of error, a predictable pattern true of all learners and keyed to stages of development. This was, of course, a vain hope. I turned to think about error as a social rather than as a linguistic phenomenon. I was interested in studying the academy and the logic (and the systems) behind the regular and inevitable decisions that identified certain students as "unable" to read and write. I wrote series of papers to think this through, including an essay on Errors and Expectations, *"Released Into Language"; a paper, "Wanderings: Misreadings, Miswritings, and Misunderstandings"; and "Inventing the University." All of these pieces, and most of what I have written, could be titled "The Study of Error."*

—DAVID BARTHOLOMAE
University of Pittsburgh

The Rise and Fall of the Modes of Discourse

ROBERT J. CONNORS

The classification of discourse into different types has been one of the continuing interests of rhetoricians since the classical period. Some of these classifications have been genuinely useful to teachers of discourse, but others have exemplified Butler's damning couplet, "all a rhetorician's rules/ Teach nothing but to name his tools." To explore the question of what makes a discourse classification useful or appealing to teachers, this essay will examine the rise, reign, and fall of the most influential classification scheme of the last hundred years: the "forms" or "modes" of discourse: Narration, Description, Exposition, and Argument. More students have been taught composition using the modes of discourse than any other classification system. The history of the modes is an instructive one; from the time of their popularization in American rhetoric textbooks during the late nineteenth century, through the absolute dominance they had in writing classrooms during the period 1895–1930, and into the 1950's when they were finally superseded by other systems, the modes of discourse both influenced and reflected many of the important changes our discipline has seen in the last century. Looking at the modes and their times may also help us answer the question of what sorts of discourse classifications are most useful for writing classes today.

THE EARLY YEARS: INTRODUCTION, CONFLICT, AND ACCEPTANCE

Most short histories of the modes of discourse (which for brevity's sake will hereafter be called simply "the modes") trace them back to George Campbell's "four ends of speaking" and to Alexander Bain, the Scottish logician and educator whose 1866 textbook *English Composition and Rhetoric* made the modal formula widely known. But, as Albert Kitzhaber points out, the terms we have come to call the modes were floating about in very general use during the period 1825–1870.[1] It is not easy to trace influences among rhetoric

---

This essay was first published in *CCC*, Volume 32, Number 4, December 1981.

texts of this period, since the ideas were presumed to be in currency rather than the specific property of individuals, but the first definitive use of terms similar to our modal terms was in 1827. In that year, they appeared in a small book called *A Practical System of Rhetoric*, by Samuel P. Newman, a professor at Bowdoin College in Maine.

According to the *National Union Catalog*, Newman's text was the most widely-used rhetoric written in America between 1820 and 1860, going through at least sixty "editions" or printings between its first publication and 1856—a huge number for that time. Newman owed much to Hugh Blair's *Lectures on Rhetoric and Belles Lettres* of 1783 and something to George Campbell's 1776 treatise on *The Philosophy of Rhetoric*, but *A Practical System* differed from both books in its penchant for grouping concepts, a fascination with categories which was to become one of the hallmarks of the rigidly formalized rhetoric of the late nineteenth century. Here is Newman's description of the "kinds of composition":

> Writings are distinguished from each other as didactic, persuasive, argumentative, descriptive, and narrative. . . . Didactic writing, as the name implies, is used in conveying instruction. . . . when it is designed to influence the will, the composition becomes the persuasive kind. . . . the various forms of argument, the statement of proofs, the assigning of causes . . . are addressed to the reasoning faculties of the mind. Narrative and descriptive writings relate past occurrences, and place before the mind for its contemplation, various objects and scenes.[2]

Newman uses the term "didactic" in place of the more common "expository" and, as was common in the later nineteenth century, separates persuasion of the will from argument to the logical faculties, but it seems obvious that his is the prototype of the modal formula.

Newman's terms did not, however, fall on very fertile soil. He had a few imitators between 1827 and 1866, most notably Richard Green Parker, whose 1844 text *Aids to English Composition* added "Pathetic" to Newman's list, and George Quackenbos, who listed Description, Narration, Argument, Exposition, and Speculation in his *Advanced Course of Composition and Rhetoric* of 1854. Few other texts picked up the terms, and the modes hung in suspension, waiting for a powerful voice to solidify and disseminate a formulation.

That voice was found in Bain. Here are "the various kinds of composition" from the first American edition of *English Composition and Rhetoric*.

> Those that have for their object to inform the understanding, fall under three heads—*Description, Narration,* and *Exposition.* The means of influencing the will are given under one head, *Persuasion.* The employing of language to excite pleasurable Feelings is one of the chief characteristics of *Poetry.*[3]

Minus the reference to poetry (which Bain later admitted was extraneous), this was the modal formulation that was to prove such a powerful force in the teaching of writing in American colleges.

Why did Bain's formulation win wide adherence within two decades while Newman's earlier version was not generally accepted? There are two reasons, one having to do with the manner in which Bain used the modes in his text and the other related to the changing temperament of rhetorical education in America during the late nineteenth century.

First, unlike either Newman or Quackenbos, who merely mentioned their modal terms in passing in their texts—Newman spent only two pages on his "kinds of composition"—Bain used the modes as an organizing principle in *English Composition and Rhetoric*. Modal terms inform long sections of his discussion, and one cannot read the text without carrying away a vivid impression of their importance. This is an important key to Bain's success, for the modes were to become generally accepted not merely as a classification of discourse, but as a conceptualizing strategy for teaching composition.

The second reason for the popularity of the Bainian modes was the changing atmosphere of rhetorical education between 1830 and 1900, especially in the United States. At the beginning of this period, American colleges tended to be small and were often religion-based. Curricula were generally classical, and rhetorical study tended to follow the examples set down by the great rhetoricians of the eighteenth century. The work of Hugh Blair was especially influential, and scores of editions of his *Lectures* were printed in the United States between 1790 and 1860. The analyses of belletristic literature that made Blair's work novel had a profound impact on other elements in rhetorical study during the early nineteenth century.

When we consider the popularity of Blair's belletristic approach to rhetoric, it is not strange to find that the leading discourse classification of the time—the classification the modes were to displace—was based in belles-lettres and classified discourse "according to its literary form—epistle, romance, treatise, dialog, history, etc."[4] This belletristic classification was found in most pre–Civil War rhetorics. Although some texts included journalistic forms such as Reviews and Editorials and some went into minor forms such as Allegories and Parables, the five most common belletristic forms were Letters, Treatises, Essays, Biographies, and Fiction.

Time-proven though this classification was, it lasted only thirty years after the introduction of the modes, largely because rhetorical study in America was transformed after 1860. In tandem with the shift in the structure of higher education from a preponderance of smaller private colleges to a preponderance of larger institutions with more varied and scientific curricula, the study of rhetoric mutated from a traditional (that is, classically-derived) analysis of argument, eloquence, style, and taste into a discipline much more concerned with forms. The culture was calling for a new sort of educated man, and the "Freshman English Course" as we know it today, with its emphasis on error-free writing and the ability to follow directions, was born during this period in response to the call. The shift in classification schemes from belletristic to modal is just a part—though an important part—of this larger change. The teacher of the Gilded Age perceived his students as having needs quite different from the needs of their counterparts of 1830. Treatises, Biographies, Fiction, and such were well and good, but the essentially aristocratic educational tradition they represented was on the way out. What occurred between 1870 and 1895 was a shift from a concrete, form-based model rooted in literary high culture to a more pliable abstract model that seemed to be adaptable to anything which a rising young American might wish to say.

While the belletristic classification was waning, the modes were waxing, but only after a slow beginning. The period 1875–1890 shows no clear victor, though modal texts can be seen advancing, and general acceptance of the modes took two decades after Bain's first publication of them. *English Composition and Rhetoric* itself, after a burst of popularity in 1867, subsided into relative obscurity through the 1870's and early 1880's, and Bain's early followers were not much luckier.

The turning point, the text that really marks the paradigm shift most clearly, did not come until 1885, with the publication of *The Practical Elements of Rhetoric,* by the redoubtable John Genung. As much as Bain himself (whose sales Genung helped boost throughout the late eighties), Genung popularized the modes throughout America. *The Practical Elements* was in print from 1885 through 1904, and only Bain's text, which was in print far longer, A. S. Hill's *Principles of Rhetoric,* which had the cachet of Harvard, and Barrett Wendell's *English Composition* were more popular during the period 1865–1900. Between them, Bain and Genung greatly influenced the theoretical and practical world of rhetoric instruction between 1886 and 1891, and the popularity of their books sounded the death-knell of the belletristic classification in composition courses.

Genung, of course, did not adopt Bain's notion of four modes absolutely, as had Bain's earlier and less successful imitators A. D. Hepburn and David Hill. He distinguished between Argumentation, which he called "Invention dealing with Truths" and Persuasion, which he called "Invention dealing with Practical Issues."[5] These two sorts of arguments were copied and used by derivative textbook authors after Genung until about 1910, when the four standard terms swept all before them. Genung himself adopted the four terms of the standard modes in 1893 in his *Outlines of Rhetoric,* the follow-up text to *The Practical Elements.*

THE REIGN OF THE MODES

Of the textbook authors that Kitzhaber calls "The Big Four" of the late nineteenth century—Barrett Wendell, John Genung, Adams Sherman Hill, and Fred Newton Scott (who wrote his texts in collaboration with Joseph V. Denney)—all had implicitly accepted the modes by 1894, and by 1895 all except Wendell were using them as important parts of their texts. Wendell merely mentioned the modes as an accepted convention in his *English Composition,* using instead as an organizing structure his famous trinity of Unity-Mass-Coherence (which he adopted, incidentally, from Bain's discussion of the paragraph). Though he did not use the modes in an important way, Wendell at least advanced no competitive classification, and many later texts adopted both the modes and the trinity as important elements.[6]

A. S. Hill, Boylston Professor of Rhetoric at Harvard, denied the modes throughout the eighties in his text *The Principles of Rhetoric,* which omitted Exposition from its scope. Hill saw the handwriting on the wall in the early nineties, however, when sales of his book dropped off sharply. There was no edition of *The Principles of Rhetoric* in 1894, and when the book reappeared in 1895 in a "New Edition, Revised and Enlarged," the revision recited the modal litany in perfect chorus. So fell into line many of the partially-converted.

Fred N. Scott and Joseph Denney's text, *Paragraph-Writing,* in 1891, dealt as much with paragraphs as with whole essays—using, of course, the paragraph model that Bain had originated 25 years earlier—but the four sorts of essays that Scott and Denney do mention are the familiar quartet. *Paragraph-Writing* was Scott and Denney's most popular text, and aside from its use of the modes it is important for another reason. It is the first truly popular codification of "the means of developing paragraphs" which were to become more and more important in the fifty years following Scott and Denney. Adapted from the classical topics, these "means" included Contrast, Explanation, Definition, Illustration, Detail, and Proofs. Watch these terms, for they will reappear, both as methods of paragraph development and more importantly as the "methods of exposition" that will come to supplant the modes.

This reappearance was not to happen, though, for many years. After 1895, the modes were the controlling classification, having driven the belletristic forms from the field. During the late nineties, non-modal texts almost completely disappeared; of 28 books dating between 1893 and 1906 surveyed by Kitzhaber, only four made no mention of the modes.[7] There was for a while some disagreement about whether argument and persuasion were truly separate, but by 1910 even these internecine quarrels had died out. That the modes were accepted almost absolutely was evidenced by the growth and spread of texts devoted to treating only one of them, such as George Pierce Baker's influential *The Principles of Argumentation* in 1895, Carroll L. Maxcy's *The Rhetorical Principles of Narration* in 1911, and Gertrude Buck's *Expository Writing* in 1899. As we shall see, these single-mode texts would have an important effect on the future of the modes as a system.

With single-mode and four-mode textbooks controlling the lists, the reign of modal text organization was long and ponderous, lasting from the mid-1890's through the mid-1930's. During this time there were no theoretical advances. Most textbooks were written by followers of Genung and Wendell, and a typical organizing structure of the time was a combination of Wendell's trinity of Unity-Mass-Coherence—later modernized to Unity-Coherence-Emphasis—with "the four traditional forms of discourse." (By 1920 the origin of the modes was lost in the mists of time; they had presumably been carved in stone during the Paleolithic Age.) In terms of new insights, the teaching of composition was frozen in its tracks between 1900 and

1925, and despite a few novel treatments and up-to-date appearances, I cannot find a single text that is not derivative of the authors of the nineties.

Partially this stasis was due to the changing backgrounds of textbook authors, a change which in turn was the result of new directions in the discipline of English. During this period, "philology" was coming more and more to mean the criticism and scholarly study of literature, and rhetoric was being displaced in many schools from English departments. The composition texts of the nineteenth century had generally been written by rhetorical scholars (Barrett Wendell is a notable exception), but in the early years of the new century, the majority of composition texts began to be written by literary scholars who were producing derivative texts in order to put bread on their tables. The pure fire of Bain was kept alive during this period by such literary figures as Percy Boynton, John C. French, and Raymond Pence.

From the middle of the last decade of the nineteenth century, through the Great War, and into the middle of that disillusioned decade following it, the modes controlled the teaching of composition through complete control of textbooks. Nothing threatened, nothing changed. But the world was turning, and the modes were about to be challenged.

THE MODES UNDER ATTACK

It is relatively simple to detail the hegemony of the modes up until the mid-twenties, but at that time, in composition as in the culture at large, great shifts began to occur. Not all of these shifts can be satisfactorily analyzed, but beginning in the late twenties we can note the rise of two trends that would fragment the discipline and result in the gradual diminution of the importance of the modes. The first—which was, ironically, a by-product of the vast popularity the modes had had—was the rise of single-mode textbooks, especially those dealing with exposition. The second was the appearance of a new sort of textbook which I call the "thesis text." Let us examine these trends.

To begin with, single-mode texts had been popular as far back as the nineties, as we have seen, but in the twenties and thirties the texts on argumentation and narration were far outstripped by the ultimate victor: texts concerned with exposition. Books like Maurice Garland Fulton's *Expository Writing*, which was first published in 1912 and which survived until 1953 (making it, by my calculations, the longest-lived text of the century) found new popularity in the thirties, and dozens of new expository-writing texts appeared after 1940. Fulton's text, the grandfather to most which followed it, was organized by what he called "Expository Procedures and Devices." Among them are the following: Definition, Classification and Division, Contrast, Comparison or Analogy, Examples, and Descriptive Exposition. You will notice that these overlap to a large degree with Scott and Denney's 1891 list of "Methods of Paragraph Development." Fulton's Procedures and Devices were to be the first important prototypes for the "methods of exposition" still being retailed (sometimes under different names) in many texts today.

Fulton's list was followed and augmented by many other writers throughout the twenties and thirties. There were disagreements about what the "genuine" methods of exposition were, with different texts offering different choices. By the late thirties, though, the list had largely standardized itself, and the techniques of exposition, as they appeared in a whole series of widely-used texts from the forties through the present time, consisted of selections from this final list: definition, analysis, partition, interpretation, reportage, evaluation by standards, comparison, contrast, classification, process analysis, device analysis, cause-and-effect, induction, deduction, examples, and illustration.[8]

By the 1940's exposition had become so popular that it was more widely taught than the "general" modal freshman composition course. This does not, of course, mean that the other modes had ceased to be taught, but more and more they retreated out of composition classes into specialized niches of their own. Narration and description seceded to become the nuclei of creative writing courses, and argumentation, finding itself more and more an orphan in English departments, took refuge in Speech departments and became largely an oral concern for many years. The very success of the modes—and the fact that exposition was the most "practical" of them in a business-oriented culture—was destroying their power as a general organizational strategy throughout the thirties and forties. The modes were still used in many texts, but by the end of World War II they no longer controlled composition or defined discourse except in a relatively general way.

The second trend that was to result in the passing of the modes was the rise of a new sort of composition textbook, different in its angle of approach from modal texts. Prior to 1930, nearly all composition texts were organized according to a hierarchical view of discourse in which the levels were discussed impartially—modal organization, the Bain-Wendell trinity of Unity-Coherence-Emphasis, the Bainian paragraph model, traditional three-element sentence theory, and a few other ritual topics. The order of presentation of material in texts was arbitrary, and occasionally the trinity and the modes would change positions in the hierarchy, but the most important classification discussed in the texts was always the modal, and the controlling assumptions about writing underlying these texts were drawn from the theory of modes, as well. Up until the thirties there were few departures from this line.

Then, beginning in 1930 and in larger numbers throughout the forties and fifties, we begin to see this new type of textbook. It is not a text in purely expository writing; it does not use pragmatic classification exclusively; and it certainly does not treat the levels in writing impartially. This new kind of text does, of course, contain a great deal of traditional rhetorical material, but it is marked by an important change in focus: *it announces that one powerful "master idea" about writing should control the way that students learn to write, and it cites precedence to this central thesis, subordinating all other theoretical material to it.* For this reason, I call these new textbooks thesis texts (without at all implying that they focus attention on the need for a thesis in the student's paper).

They are *the* modern composition texts, and today they control the textbook world almost completely.

It would not be hard to make a case for Barrett Wendell's *English Composition* in 1891 as the first thesis text. In that book Wendell observed that rhetoric texts in his time consisted

> . . . chiefly of directions as to how one who would write should set about composing. Many of these directions are extremely sensible, many very suggestive. But in every case these directions are appallingly numerous. It took me some years to discern that all which have so far come to my notice could be grouped under one of three simple heads. . . . The first of these principles may conveniently be named the principle of Unity; the second, the principle of Mass; the third, the principle of Coherence.[9]

There in a nutshell is the central doctrine of the thesis text: "All else is essentially subordinate to this." Wendell spent the rest of his book explicating how his three principles could be applied to sentences, paragraphs, and whole themes.

Despite the success of *English Composition* and the flock of slavish imitators it spawned, Wendell did not have a spiritual successor for over forty years; the period following his text, as we have seen, was marked by conventionality and reliance upon modal organization of texts. In 1931, though, a text appeared which was to signal an important departure: Norman Foerster and J. M. Steadman's *Writing and Thinking.* This extremely popular text was in print for over twenty years, and it exerted a profound influence on later authors. Foerster and Steadman's dual thesis was announced on their first page: "Writing and thinking are organically related," and "Writing, in other words, should be organic, not mechanic."[10] The authors then went on to subordinate the rest of their material—not much of which was genuinely original—to this thesis.

Although *Writing and Thinking* was a popular book, the new trend in texts began slowly; there are only a few books identifiable as being controlled by non-modal theses in the thirties and early forties. The theses that truly established thesis texts, that tipped the balance away from the domination of the modes in the late forties, reflected the two most popular intellectual movements in composition theory at that time: the general education movement with its "language arts/communications" approach, and the General Semantics movement. This essay is not the place for a history of these movements, fascinating as one might be. In brief, the general education/"communications" movement grew out of the Deweyite interest in "English for Life Skills" during the thirties and emphasized the whole continuum of language activities—reading, writing, speaking, and listening—rather than writing alone. The Conference on College Composition and Communication was formed in 1948 by "communications" enthusiasts. (That's where the "communication" comes from.) General Semantics, of course, was based on the work of Alfred Korzybski as popularized by S. I. Hayakawa in his influential *Words in Action* of 1940, and is most interested in language as a symbol system liable to abuse. Together, communications and General Semantics provided theses for more than half of the new composition texts that appeared between 1948 and 1952.

There were, of course, some thesis texts not based on either communications or on General Semantics. One of the best of them is still going strong: James McCrimmon's *Writing With A Purpose,* the thesis of which is, of course, the importance of the writer's controlling purpose. Most thesis texts not based on communications or General Semantics used theses based on some version of favorite old notions, writing and thinking, writing and reading, the unique demands of American writing. Later the theses in texts would grow out of concepts more complex and interesting: writing and perception, writing and cognition, writing and process. Most expository writing texts also took on characteristics of thesis texts during the fifties, and more and more thesis texts came to use the "methods of exposition."

FALL AND ABANDONMENT OF THE MODES

And where stood the Bainian modes in this avalanche—for an avalanche it became after 1950—of expositionists and thesis texts? As has been suggested, the modes did not completely disappear, but they were certainly changed, truncated, and diminished in power. The new texts that appeared did not subvert the modes because they proved them theoretically erroneous, but rather because their theses or listing of methods took over the role in organizing texts that the modes had earlier played. McCrimmon makes a telling statement in the Preface to the first edition of *Writing With A Purpose* in 1950: "The decision to make purpose the theme of the book made the conventional fourfold classification of writing unnecessary. Therefore Exposition, Narration, Description, and Argument are not considered as special types of writing."[11] Even when thesis texts mentioned the modes, they were a minor consideration. Essentially, the modes were ignored to death after 1950.

The new thesis texts used a number of original classifications of discourse, and the modes were everywhere being replaced by these novel classifications. After 1955 or so the modes are seen in new texts only when those texts have specifically traditional intent: for instance, Richard Weaver's *Composition* and Hughes and Duhamel's *Rhetoric: Principles and Usage.* Though the theses of the thesis texts would continue to change—from propositions based upon General Semantics or communications in the forties and fifties to propositions developed from transformational grammar, problem solving, and pre-writing in the sixties to theses about invention, process, cognition, and syntactic methods in the seventies—all these theses (of which some texts contain several) have one thing in common: they bypass or ignore the modes of discourse. W. Ross Winterowd spoke for authors of thesis texts when he stated in a 1965 textbook that the modal classification, "though interesting, isn't awfully helpful."[12]

In rhetoric texts today, the modes are still expiring. A few texts still mention them as minor elements, but their power in rhetorics is gone. Of the fifteen or so most widely-used freshman rhetoric texts, only one still advances the modal classes as absolute. Though the modes still retain a shadow of their old puissance as an organizing device in certain freshman anthologies of essays, their importance in modern pedagogy is constantly diminishing, and the only teachers still making real classroom use of the modes are those out of touch with current theory. Stripped of their theoretical validity and much of their practical usefulness, the modes cling to a shadowy half-life in the attic of composition legends.

L'ENVOI—THE MODES AS PLAUSIBLE FICTION

Why did the modes of discourse rise to such power, hold it for so long and so absolutely, and then decline so rapidly? At least part of the answer has to do with the relative vitality of the rhetorical tradition during the period 1870–1930, an era when hardly any progressive theoretical work was done in the field. Alexander Bain, Fred N. Scott, and perhaps Barrett Wendell are the greatest figures writing during the period, and (except for Scott, whose influence was limited) they cannot stand beside Campbell in the eighteenth century or Burke in the twentieth. The modes became popular and stayed popular because they fit into the abstract, mechanical nature of writing instruction at the time, and they diminished in importance as other, more vital, ideas about writing appeared in the 1930's and after. Like the "dramatic unities" that ruled the drama of the seventeenth and eighteenth centuries until exploded by Samuel Johnson's common sense, the modes were only powerful so long as they were not examined for evidence of their usefulness.

One of the most damning assessments of the modes' use in the nineteenth century is that of Albert Kitzhaber:

> Such convenient abstractions as . . . the forms of discourse were ideally suited to the purpose of instruction in a subject that had been cut off from all relation with other subjects in the curriculum and, in a sense, from life itself. . . . They represent an unrealistic view of the writing process, a view that assumes writing is done by formula and in a social vacuum. They turn the attention of both teacher and student toward an academic exercise instead of toward a meaningful act of communication in a social context. Like Unity-Coherence-Emphasis—or any other set of static abstractions concerning writing—they substitute mechanical for organic conceptions and therefore distort the real nature of writing.[13]

The weakness of the modes of discourse as a practical tool in the writing class was that they did not really help students to learn to write. When we look closely at the nature of modal distinctions, it is not hard to see why: the modes classify and emphasize the product of writing, having almost nothing to do with the purpose for which the writer sat down, pen in hand. Modal distinctions are divorced from the composition process. As James Kinneavy puts it,

...a stress on modes of discourse rather than aims of discourse is a stress on "what" is being talked about rather than on "why" a thing is talked about.... This is actually a substitution of means for ends. Actually, something is narrated for a reason. Narration, as such, is not a purpose. Consequently, the "modes" periods in history have never lasted very long.[14]

In our time, the modes are little more than an unofficial descriptive myth, replaced in theory by empirically-derived classifications of discourse and in practice by the "methods of exposition" and other non-modal classes. The important theoretical classification schemas of today are those of James Moffett, whose Spectrum of Discourse consists of Recording, Reporting, Generalizing, and Theorizing; of James Kinneavy, who divides discourse into Reference, Scientific, Persuasive, Literary, and Expressive types; and of James Britton, with its triad of Poetic, Expressive, and Transactional discourse. All of these classification schemes have one thing in common: they are based on the writer's purposes, the ends of his or her composing, rather than merely being classifications of written discourse.

In current textbooks, too, the modes are largely displaced by more process-oriented considerations or by heuristic theses that see classification of discourse as unimportant. The most popular discourse classification still found in textbooks is Fulton's "methods of exposition," updated and augmented, of course. Doubtless the most complete system using the methods of exposition is Frank D'Angelo's system of "discourse paradigms." We do not yet know whether the paradigms will become as rigid, abstract, and useless as did their progenitors, the modes.

"Anytime a means is exalted to an end in history of discourse education, a similar pattern can be seen," writes Kinneavy; "the emphasis is short-lived and usually sterile." The modes of discourse controlled a good part of composition teaching during one of rhetoric's least vigorous periods, offering in their seeming completeness and plausibility a schema of discourse that could be easily taught and learned. For years the fact that this schema did not help students learn to write better was not a concern, and even today the modes are accepted by some teachers despite their lack of basis in useful reality. Our discipline has been long in knuckling from its eyes the sleep of the nineteenth and early twentieth centuries, and the real lesson of the modes is that we need always to be on guard against systems that seem convenient to teachers but that ignore the way writing is actually done.

AFTERWORD . . . .

The role played by chance in constructing us—in constructing me as a teacher, researcher, writer, anyway—seems overwhelming. The story: At CCCC 1980, some graduate school friends at Ohio State University decided to propose a panel for the following year, something on "The Modes of Discourse," which I recognized vaguely as old-timey textbook stuff. One person wanted to speak on the modes and sentence combining; another was interested in Kenneth Burke and the modes. But what was I to do? "How about the history?" someone suggested. Well, Edward P. J. Corbett and James Golden had taught me rhetorical history, and Richard Altick had drilled me in literary-historical skills. "Okay, sure, I'll give it a shot," I replied. And when I reached my first job that fall, at Louisiana State University in Baton Rouge, and found a fantastic stack collection of nineteenth-century textbooks in the Middleton Library there, the task almost organized itself. Out of such small, glancing impacts are our lives shaped.

But when Jack Maxwell, the executive director of NCTE, called me in January, 1982, to tell me that I had won the Richard Braddock Award, I looked around the crowded basement office, where I was in my second year of directing the Writing Lab. "Is this a joke?" I asked, smiling but wary. After all, I was a new assistant professor who had published almost nothing before; "The Rise and Fall of the Modes of Discourse" was the first essay I had ever written after graduate school. How could it be that somehow it had been chosen over essays published that year by authors far better known than some kid running a writing lab in the deep south?

I now see the Braddock Award given to "The Modes" as an early signal of the growth of historical consciousness in the rapidly organizing field of composition studies. In 1980, only a few people had ever done serious historical work in composition. But the time was right for it in a field becoming self-aware, and I tend now to view the award given to me in 1982 more as a signal about what composition studies wanted and needed from scholarly work than as a recognition of personal merit. "The Modes" is a workmanlike enough piece, but its real importance lies in the signal its recognition gave to other scholars—Jim Berlin, John Brereton, Sharon Crowley, Nan Johnson, Bill Woods—that composition studies was ready to welcome history as an important subfield.

"Now that we're almost settled in our house," wrote Yeats, "I'll name the friends that cannot sup with us": Ed Corbett read my very rough draft; Don Stewart, to whom Ed suggested I send the draft, advised me on it out of his deep knowledge of nineteenth-century rhetoric. Dick Larson was CCC editor, and though he made many of us dance smartly in revision, his detailed criticism was all constructive. Though the plaque and the honor went to me that March, I can only repeat now the single line I recall saying then, which is another line from Yeats: "Say my glory was I had such friends."

—ROBERT J. CONNORS
University of New Hampshire

1983 Responding to Student Writing

NANCY SOMMERS

ore than any other enterprise in the teaching of writing, responding to and commenting on student writing consumes the largest proportion of our time. Most teachers estimate that it takes them at least 20 to 40 minutes to comment on an individual student paper, and those 20 to 40 minutes times 20 students per class, times 8 papers, more or less, during the course of a semester add up to an enormous amount of time. With so much time and energy directed to a single activity, it is important for us to understand the nature of the enterprise. For it seems, paradoxically enough, that although commenting on student writing is the most widely used method for responding to student writing, it is the least understood. We do not know in any definitive way what constitutes thoughtful commentary or what effect, if any, our comments have on helping our students become more effective writers.

Theoretically, at least, we know that we comment on our students' writing for the same reasons professional editors comment on the work of professional writers or for the same reasons we ask our colleagues to read and respond to our own writing. As writers we need and want thoughtful commentary to show us when we have communicated our ideas and when not, raising questions from a reader's point of view that may not have occurred to us as writers. We want to know if our writing has communicated our intended meaning and, if not, what questions or discrepancies our reader sees that we, as writers, are blind to.

In commenting on our students' writing, however, we have an additional pedagogical purpose. As teachers, we know that most students find it difficult to imagine a reader's response in advance, and to use such responses as a guide in composing. Thus, we comment on student writing to dramatize the presence of a reader, to help our students to become that questioning reader themselves, because, ultimately, we believe that becoming such a

This essay was first published in CCC, Volume 33, Number 2, May 1982.

reader will help them to evaluate what they have written and develop control over their writing.[1]

Even more specifically, however, we comment on student writing because we believe that it is necessary for us to offer assistance to student writers when they are in the process of composing a text, rather than after the text has been completed. Comments create the motive for doing something different in the next draft; thoughtful comments create the motive for revising. Without comments from their teachers or from their peers, student writers will revise in a consistently narrow and predictable way. Without comments from readers, students assume that their writing has communicated their meaning and perceive no need for revising the substance of their text.[2]

Yet as much as we as informed professionals believe in the soundness of this approach to responding to student writing, we also realize that we don't know how our theory squares with teachers' actual practice—do teachers comment and students revise as the theory predicts they should? For the past year my colleagues, Lil Brannon, Cyril Knoblauch, and I have been researching this problem, attempting to discover not only what messages teachers give their students through their comments, but also what determines which of these comments the students choose to use or to ignore when revising. Our research has been entirely focused on comments teachers write to motivate revisions. We have studied the commenting styles of thirty-five teachers at New York University and the University of Oklahoma, studying the comments these teachers wrote on first and second drafts, and interviewing a representative number of these teachers and their students. All teachers also commented on the same set of three student essays. As an additional reference point, one of the student essays was typed into the computer that had been programed with the "Writer's Workbench," a package of twenty-three programs developed by Bell Laboratories to help computers and writers work together to improve a text rapidly. Within a few minutes, the computer delivered editorial comments on the student's text, identifying all spelling and punctuation errors, isolating problems with wordy or misused phrases, and suggesting alternatives, offering a stylistic analysis of sentence types, sentence beginnings, and sentence lengths, and finally, giving our freshman essay a Kincaid readability score of 8th grade which, as the computer program informed us, "is a low score for this type of document." The sharp contrast between the teachers' comments and those of the computer highlighted how arbitrary and idiosyncratic most of our teachers' comments are. Besides, the calm, reasonable language of the computer provided quite a contrast to the hostility and mean-spiritedness of most of the teachers' comments.

The first finding from our research on styles of commenting is that *teachers' comments can take students' attention away from their own purposes in writing a particular text and focus that attention on the teachers' purpose in commenting.* The teacher appropriates the text from the student by confusing the student's purpose in writing the text with her own purpose in commenting. Students make the changes the teacher wants rather than those that the student perceives are necessary, since the teachers' concerns imposed on the text create the reasons for the subsequent changes. We have all heard our perplexed students say to us when confused by our comments: "I don't understand how you want me to change this" or "Tell me what you want me to do." In the beginning of the process there was the writer, her words, and her desire to communicate her ideas. But after the comments of the teacher are imposed on the first or second draft, the student's attention dramatically shifts from "This is what I want to say," to "This is what you the teacher are asking me to do."

This appropriation of the text by the teacher happens particularly when teachers identify errors in usage, diction, and style in a first draft and ask students to correct these errors when they revise; such comments give the student an impression of the importance of these errors that is all out of proportion to how they should view these errors at this point in the process. The comments create the concern that these "accidents of discourse" need to be attended to before the meaning of the text is attended to.

It would not be so bad if students were only commanded to correct errors, but, more often than not, students are given contradictory messages; they are commanded to edit a sentence to avoid an error or to condense a sentence to achieve greater brevity of style, and then told in the margins that the particular paragraph needs to be more specific or to be developed more. An example of this problem can be seen in the following student paragraph:

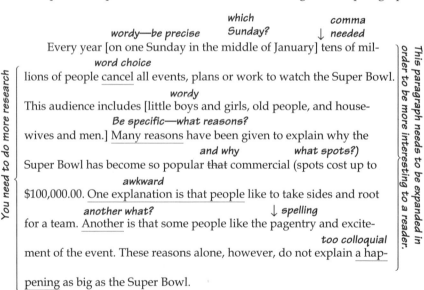

In commenting on this draft, the teacher has shown the student how to edit the sentences, but then commands the student to expand the paragraph in order to make it more interesting to a reader. The interlinear comments and the marginal comments represent two separate tasks for this student; the interlinear comments encourage the student to see the text as a fixed piece, frozen in time, that just needs some editing. The marginal comments, however, suggest that the meaning of the text is not fixed, but rather that the student still needs to develop the meaning by doing some more research. Students are commanded to edit and develop at the same time; the remarkable contradiction of developing a paragraph after editing the sentences in it represents the confusion we encountered in our teachers' commenting styles. These different signals given to students, to edit and develop, to condense and elaborate, represent also the failure of teachers' comments to direct genuine revision of the text as a whole.

Moreover, the comments are worded in such a way that it is difficult for students to know what is the most important problem in the text and what problems are of lesser importance. No scale of concerns is offered to a student, with the result that a comment about spelling or a comment about an awkward sentence is given weight equal to a comment about organization or logic. The comment that seemed to represent this problem best was one teacher's command to his student: "Check your commas and semi-colons and think more about what you are thinking about." The language of the comments makes it difficult for a student to sort out and decide what is most important and what is least important.

When the teacher appropriates the text for the student in this way, students are encouraged to see their writing as a series of parts—words, sentences, paragraphs—and not as a whole discourse. The comments encourage students to believe that their first drafts are finished drafts, not invention drafts, and that all they need to do is patch and polish their writing. That is, teachers' comments do not provide their students with an inherent reason for revising the structure and meaning of their texts, since the comments suggest to students that the meaning of their text is already there, finished, produced, and all that is necessary is a better word or phrase. The processes of revising, editing, and proofreading are collapsed and reduced to a single trivial activity, and the students' misunderstanding of the revision process as a rewording activity is reinforced by their teachers' comments.

It is possible, and it quite often happens, that students follow every comment and fix their texts appropriately as requested, but their texts are not improved substantially, or, even worse, their revised drafts are inferior to their previous drafts. Since the teachers' comments take the students' attention away from their own original purposes, students concentrate more, as I have noted, on what the teachers commanded them to do than on what they are trying to say. Sometimes students do not understand the purpose behind their teachers' comments and take these comments very literally. At other times students understand the comments, but the teacher has misread the text and the comments, unfortunately, are not applicable. For instance, we repeatedly saw comments in which teachers commanded students to reduce and condense what was written, when in fact what the text really needed at this stage was to be expanded in conception and scope.

The process of revising always involves a risk. But, too often revision becomes a balancing act for students in which they make the changes that are requested but do not take the risk of changing anything that was not commented on, even if the students sense that other changes are needed. A more effective text does not often evolve from such changes alone, yet the student does not want to take the chance of reducing a finished, albeit inadequate, paragraph to chaos—to fragments—in order to rebuild it, if such changes have not been requested by the teacher.

The second finding from our study is that *most teachers' comments are not text-specific and could be interchanged, rubber-stamped, from text to text.* The comments are not anchored in the particulars of the students' texts, but rather are a series of vague directives that are not text-specific. Students are commanded to "Think more about [their] audience, avoid colloquial language, avoid the passive, avoid prepositions at the end of sentences or conjunctions at the beginning of sentences, be clear, be specific, be precise, but above all, think more about what [they] are thinking about." The comments on the following student paragraph illustrate this problem:

> *Begin by telling your reader*
> ↓ *what you are going to write about.*
> In the sixties it was drugs, in the seventies it was rock and roll.
> *avoid—"one of the"*
> Now in the eighties, one of the most controversial subjects is nuclear
> *elaborate*
> power. The United States is in great need of its own source of power.
>
> Because of environmentalists, coal is not an acceptable source of energy.
> *be specific*
> [Solar and wind power have not yet received the technology necessary
> *avoid — "it seems"*
> to use them.] It seems that nuclear power is the only feasible means
>
> right now for obtaining self-sufficient power. However, too large a per-
>
> centage of the population are against nuclear power claiming it is un-
> *be precise*
> safe. With as many problems as the United States is having concerning
>
> energy, it seems a shame that the public is so quick to "can" a very fea-
>
> sible means of power. Nuclear energy should not be given up on, but
>
> rather, more nuclear plants should be built.

(right margin annotation: Think more about your reader.)

(left margin annotation: Thesis sentence needed)

One could easily remove all the comments from this paragraph and rubber-stamp them on another student text, and they would make as much or as little sense on the second text as they do here.

We have observed an overwhelming similarity in the generalities and abstract commands given to students. There seems to be among teachers an accepted, albeit unwritten canon for commenting on student texts. This uniform code of commands, requests, and pleadings demonstrates that the teacher holds a license for vagueness while the student is commanded to be specific. The students we interviewed admitted to having great difficulty with these vague directives. The students stated that when a teacher writes in the margins or as an end comment, "choose precise language," or "think more about your audience," revising becomes a guessing game. In effect, the teacher is saying to the student, "Somewhere in this paper is imprecise language or lack of awareness of an audience and you must find it." The problem presented by these vague commands is compounded for the students when they are not offered any strategies for carrying out these commands. Students are told that they have done something wrong and that there is something in their text that needs to be fixed before the text is acceptable. But to tell students that they have done something wrong is not to tell them what to do about it. In order to offer a useful revision strategy to a student, the teacher must anchor that strategy in the specifics of the student's text. For instance, to tell our student, the author of the above paragraph, "to be specific," or "to elaborate," does not show our student what questions the reader has about the meaning of the text, or what breaks in logic exist, that could be resolved if the writer supplied specific information; nor is the student shown how to achieve the desired specificity.

Instead of offering strategies, the teachers offer what is interpreted by students as rules for composing; the comments suggest to students that writing is just a matter of following the rules. Indeed, the teachers seem to impose a series of abstract rules about written products even when some of them are not appropriate for the specific text the student is creating.[3] For instance, the student author of our sample paragraph presented above is commanded to follow the conventional rules for writing a five-paragraph essay— to begin the introductory paragraph by telling his reader what he is going to say and to end the paragraph with a thesis sentence. Somehow these abstract rules about what five-paragraph products should look like do not seem applicable to the problems this student must confront when revising, nor are the rules specific strategies he could use when revising. There are many inchoate ideas ready to be exploited in this paragraph, but the rules do not help the student to take stock of his (or her) ideas and use the opportunity he has, during revision, to develop those ideas.

The problem here is a confusion of process and product; what one has to say about the process is different from what one has to say about the product. Teachers who use this method of commenting are formulating their comments as if these drafts were finished drafts and were not going to be revised. Their commenting vocabularies have not been adapted to revision and they comment on first drafts as if they were justifying a grade or as if the first draft were the final draft.

Our summary finding, therefore, from this research on styles of commenting is that the news from the classroom is not good. For the most part, teachers do not respond to student writing with the kind of thoughtful commentary which will help students to engage with the issues they are writing about or which will help them think about their purposes and goals in writing a specific text. In defense of our teachers, however, they told us that responding to student writing was rarely stressed in their teacher-training or in writing workshops; they had been trained in various prewriting techniques, in constructing assignments, and in evaluating papers for grades, but rarely in the process of reading a student text for meaning or in offering commentary to motivate revision. The problem is that most of us as teachers of writing have been trained to read and interpret literary texts for meaning, but, unfortunately, we have not been trained to act upon the same set of assumptions in reading student texts as we follow in reading literary texts.[4] Thus, we read student texts with biases about what the writer should have said or about what he or she should have written, and our biases determine how we will comprehend the text. We read with our preconceptions and preoccupations, expecting to find errors, and the result is that we find errors and misread our students' texts.[5] We find what we look for; instead of reading and responding to the meaning of a text, we correct our students' writing. We need to reverse this approach. Instead of finding errors or showing students how to patch up parts of their texts, we need to sabotage our students' conviction that the drafts they have written are complete and coherent. Our comments need to offer students revision tasks of a different order of complexity and sophistication from the ones that they themselves identify, by forcing students back into the chaos, back to the point where they are shaping and restructuring their meaning.[6]

For if the content of a student text is lacking in substance and meaning, if the order of the parts must be rearranged significantly in the next draft, if paragraphs must be restructured for logic and clarity, then many sentences are likely to be changed or deleted anyway. There seems to be no point in having students correct usage errors or condense sentences that are likely to disappear before the next draft is completed. In fact, to identify such problems in a text at this early first draft stage, when such problems are likely to abound, can give a student a disproportionate sense of their importance at this stage in the writing process.[7] In responding to our students' writing, we should be guided by the recognition that it is not spelling or usage problems that we as writers first worry about when drafting and revising our texts.

We need to develop an appropriate level of response for commenting on a first draft, and to differentiate that from the level suitable to a second or third draft. Our comments need to be suited to the draft we are reading. In a first or second draft, we need to respond as any reader would, registering questions, reflecting befuddlement, and noting places where we are puzzled about the meaning of the text. Comments should point to breaks in logic, disruptions in meaning, or missing information. Our goal in commenting on early drafts should be to engage students with the issues they are considering and help them clarify their purposes and reasons in writing their specific text.

For instance, the major rhetorical problem of the essay written by the student who wrote the second paragraph (the paragraph on nuclear power) quoted above was that the student had two principal arguments running through his text, each of which brought the other into question. On the one hand, he argued that we must use nuclear power, unpleasant as it is, because we have nothing else to use; though nuclear energy is a problematic source of energy, it is the best of a bad lot. On the other hand, he also argued that nuclear energy is really quite safe and therefore should be our primary resource. Comments on this student's first draft need to point out this break in logic and show the student that if we accept his first argument, then his second argument sounds fishy. But if we accept his second argument, his first argument sounds contradictory. The teacher's comments need to engage this student writer with this basic rhetorical and conceptual problem in his first draft rather than impose a series of abstract commands and rules upon his text.

Written comments need to be viewed not as an end in themselves—a way for teachers to satisfy themselves that they have done their jobs—but rather as a means for helping students to become more effective writers. As a means for helping students, they have limitations; they are, in fact, disembodied remarks—one absent writer responding to another absent writer. The key to successful commenting is to have what is said in the comments and what is done in the classroom mutually reinforce and enrich each other. Commenting on papers assists the writing course in achieving its purpose; classroom activities and the comments we write to our students need to be connected. Written comments need to be an extension of the teacher's voice—an extension of the teacher as reader. Exercises in such activities as revising a whole text or individual paragraphs together in class, noting how the sense of the whole dictates the smaller changes, looking at options, evaluating actual choices, and then discussing the effect of these changes on revised drafts—such exercises need to be designed to take students through the cycles of revising and to help them overcome their anxiety about revising: that anxiety we all feel at reducing what looks like a finished draft into fragments and chaos.

The challenge we face as teachers is to develop comments which will provide an inherent reason for students to revise; it is a sense of revision as discovery, as a repeated process of beginning again, as starting out new, that our students have not learned. We need to show our students how to seek, in the possibility of revision, the dissonances of discovery—to show them through our comments why new choices would positively change their texts, and thus to show them the potential for development implicit in their own writing.

Responding to student writing is complex and puzzling. Words enscribed from one writer to another, but words haunted by both the presence and absence of the other writer. Often I am thrilled by what I read in a student draft, a stunning advance, an exploration into an interesting argument, a struggle with a supple idea. But too often my students' drafts reveal the "brutality of good intentions," to borrow a phrase from Henry James, showing me the consequences of what I forgot to teach, or what I forgot to emphasize in the swirl of instructions and exhortations surrounding the assignment. What strikes me after all these years of teaching is the difficulty of composing a humane, thoughtful, and inspiring comment.

I had the great fortune in 1980 to teach in the New York University Writing Program with Lil Brannon and Cy Knoblauch. The three of us were fierce and passionate about the subject of teacher commentary, and we spent months researching, debating, and theorizing what goes wrong when teachers comment and students revise. My 1983 essay, "Responding to Student Writing," was greatly influenced by the excitement and energy of working with gifted colleagues and graduate students who shared this commitment. If this essay, written fifteen years ago, is still readable, durable, and useful to new writing teachers, I am pleased.

The Braddock Award meant more to me than any prize is intended to mean. After teaching for one year at NYU, I took five years off "in service of the species," while my daughters, Rachel and Alixandra, were young. In 1983 I thought of myself as a housewife from New Jersey, someone who between changing diapers and playing with her children, watched soap operas, cruised the aisles of the A&P looking for excitement. I felt as if I had been put out to pasture in rural New Jersey, isolated from the passionate exchange with colleagues and students which nurtures teaching and writing. The Braddock Award encouraged me to stay in the profession.

If I were to write "Responding to Student Writing: Part Two," I would try to write less in the voice of a self-righteous researcher, pointing her finger at her fellow teachers, and more like a fellow teacher. For it is as a teacher that I am curious about the ways in which students read and interpret my comments, why they find some comments useful, others distracting, and how these comments work together with the lessons of the classroom. I am also curious about the ways in which our colleagues across the disciplines respond to student writing.

As I reread my 1983 essay, I feel the absence of any "real" students whose voice, expertise, and years of being responded to could offer valuable perspective, and the absence of any "real" teachers, other than the stereotypical composition teacher, who seems in my essay strangely devoid of expertise. Fifteen years later I remain curious and engaged by a subject that won't let go.

—NANCY SOMMERS
Harvard University

Topical Structure and Revision:
An Exploratory Study[1]

STEPHEN P. WITTE

t is unfortunate that so many college teach-
ers of writing and composition textbooks describe revision as the process by
which a writer merely cleans up the mechanical and stylistic infelicities of an
otherwise completed text. This simplistic view presupposes something akin
to the three-stage linear model of composing set forth by Rohman and
Wlecke in the 1960's.[2] Research during the past decade, particularly that of
Emig and Sommers, challenges the assumption underlying such a view of revision by demonstrating that revision is not the end of a linear process, but is
rather itself a recursive process,[3] one which can occur at any point during
composing. Recent research also shows that different groups of writers revise
in different ways, a finding reflected in, for example, the work of Beach,[4]
Bridwell,[5] Faigley and Witte,[6] Flower,[7] and Murray,[8] as well as Sommers. Finally, recent research has developed classification systems to explain those
revisions. Such efforts appear, for example, in the work of Sommers,[9] Bridwell,[10] and Faigley and Witte.[11]

However much this body of research helps us to understand the results
or effects of revision, it does considerably less to help us understand what
causes writers to revise. The most promising research on the causes of revision, of course, is that of Flower and Hayes. Reporting on their use of
composing-aloud protocols in a case study format,[12] they conclude that when
expert writers redefine or clarify the audience and the goals of their texts,
they frequently revise.[13] This research offers the best hypotheses about the
situational or contextual causes of revision. But while Flower and Hayes suggest that the "text produced so far" becomes part of the situational context,
they do not adequately explore specific textual cues that may prompt revisions. Indeed, apart from what little can be gleaned from studies which look
to errors[14] in the text for causes of revision, we know very little about the textual cues that prompt writers to alter texts to fit specific audiences and specific communication goals.

This essay was first published in *CCC*, Volume 34, Number 3, October 1983.

In the present study, I explore some of the textual causes and effects of revision which previous research has not examined. Although the study examines t-unit, clause, and text length, it focuses on the relationships between revision and *topical structure,* at the level of both the sentence and the whole discourse. More specifically, the present essay explores the use of topical structure analysis as a way to understand some textual cues which may prompt revision and as a way to describe the effects of revision. The essay consists of four sections. The first section examines theoretically and historically the concept of topical structure and suggests its relevance to revision. The second explains the procedures used to collect and analyze the controlled revisions examined in the present study. The third section discusses the results. And the final section points out the implications of the present study for subsequent research.

TOPICAL STRUCTURE IN EXTENDED TEXTS

The concept of topic in extended discourse is not new to either rhetoricians or teachers of writing. It is implicit in any application of Aristotle's *topoi* and explicit in terms such as "topic sentence."[15] However, except for various expositions of and arguments about the nature of paragraphs,[16] modern composition researchers have generally not systematically examined how topics affect the structure of extended texts, nor have they examined the relationship of sentences to topics within extended texts.[17] Some of the most important modern research on topic in discourse appears in the work of Prague School linguists such as Vilem Mathesius,[18] Jan Firbas,[19] Petr Sgall,[20] and František Daneš.[21] Although Mathesius is generally regarded as the father of the Prague School's work on topic, his views probably derive from speculations dating to at least eighty years earlier.[22] Unlike many modern linguists who, following Bloomfield,[23] have been primarily concerned with features at or below the level of the sentence, Prague School linguists have focused on relationships between and among sentences. Consequently, one of the more important contributions of Mathesius to our understanding of discourse is his emphasis on sentences in the context of whole texts, a concern later developed somewhat differently by M. A. K. Halliday.[24]

Working largely with Slavic languages, in which word order is less rigid than in English, Mathesius used the term *theme* to identify "what the sentence is about" and the term *enunciation* to refer to "what is said about" the theme. For Mathesius, the *theme* of a sentence announces "what is known or at least obvious in a given situation and from which the speaker proceeds in his discourse," while the *enunciation* adds new or unknown information to the discourse. According to Mathesius, in Slavic languages the *theme* of a sentence usually precedes the *enunciation*. Extending his study to English, Mathesius contended that the more rigid word order of English usually means that *theme* coincides with the grammatical subject and that English therefore has a higher frequency of passive constructions than Slavic languages.

Building on Mathesius' earlier work, Firbas developed the notion of "communicative dynamism" to describe the relationship between old and new information in texts. According to Firbas, the *theme* of a sentence contributes least to the "communicative dynamism" of a text because, even though it tells what the sentence is about, it delivers the least amount of new information. For Firbas, "communicative dynamism" is defined by the amount of new information a text delivers. In place of Mathesius' *enunciation,* Firbas employed the term *rheme* to refer to that element of a sentence which contributes most to "communicative dynamism." For Firbas, the *rheme* delivers new information and usually appears toward the end of the sentence.

Drawing on such Prague School concepts as *old-new, given-new, theme-enunciation,* and *theme-rheme,* Daneš has shown that Prague School theories can be used to identify basic text patterns. In one such pattern, successive sentences express the same *theme* or *topic.*[25] In the following text, which illustrates this text pattern, I have italicized the *topic* of each sentence:[26]

> (1-a) *The theory of "Functional Sentence Perspective"* derives from the work of Mathesius during the late 1920's. (1-b) *The theory* attempts to explain the relationship of individual sentences within the context of extended texts. (1-c) *It* hypothesizes that the themes of sentences usually appear first in English sentences, expressing old or given information that provides a semantic link with the preceding sentence and hence the preceding elements of the discourse. (1-d) *The theory of "Functional Sentence Perspective"* also hypothesizes that new information introduced into the text typically appears near the end of a sentence as the rheme.

In a second text pattern, the *comment* portion of the previous sentence becomes the *topic* of the following sentence:[27]

> (2-a) *The theory of "Functional Sentence Perspective"* derives from the work of Mathesius during the 1920's. (2-b) *Mathesius* attempted to explain the relationship of individual sentences within the context of extended texts. (2-c) *This relationship* was explained with reference to two concepts, theme and rheme. (2-d) *The theme* of a sentence usually appears first and provides a semantic link to the preceding sentence by expressing old or given information derived from the rheme of the preceding sentence. (2-e) In contrast, *the rheme* usually appears near the end of the sentence and introduces information which is new to the text.

In a third pattern, the topics of successive sentences are identified with reference to their relationship to a "hypertheme," in effect a *discourse topic* which is not explicitly stated in the text itself:[28]

> (3-a) During the 1920's, *Mathesius* studied sentences in the context of extended texts. (3-b) *The concepts of "theme" and "rheme" or "given" and "new" information in sentences* grew out of Mathesius' work. (3-c) Examinations of Slavic languages, as well as English, led to *the hypothesis* that the theme of a sentence usually appears first, often as the grammatical subject, and that the rheme appears near the end of the sentence. (3-d) For some textlinguists, *the theme of a sentence* thus provides a semantic

link within the text by reiterating information recoverable from the rheme of the previous sentence.

For this third informative text, Daneš would probably maintain that the "hypertheme" is something like "Mathesius' contributions to functional sentence perspective."

Although analyzing texts from the standpoint of *topics* is not devoid of problems,[29] the approach does suggest some potentially useful concepts. One of the most important is Daneš' notion of "hypertheme" and its relationship to *sentence topics* within the context of the whole discourse. But what is the source of a text's "hypertheme," or *discourse topic*—a topic which controls or governs the meaning of the topics of individual sentences? Any satisfactory answer to this question must meet two related criteria. First, it must account for the relationship of the *discourse topic* to the text itself, the surface representation of what the writer intends to communicate to an audience. Second, because the text provides the only certain common ground between writer and reader, any answer must account for the perception of the *discourse topic* by the reader. The paragraphs which follow provide at least a partial answer to the question.

When I stated the "hypertheme" or *discourse topic* for the text consisting of sentences (3-a) through (3-d), I—as the writer of both the paragraph and the present essay—assumed that most readers agreed with me, primarily because the earlier portions of the present essay established for them what might be called a common knowledge frame,[30] a common body of knowledge together with common schemes for organizing it. This frame, in turn, permitted them to construct that "hypertheme." Had I included sentences (3-a) through (3-d) instead of (1-a) through (1-d) and (2-a) through (2-e) at the very beginning of the present essay, readers familiar with Prague School theories would likely have been able to derive that particular *discourse topic* from the interaction of their prior knowledge with the information supplied by the text. In contrast, readers not already familiar with those theories would likely have constructed a somewhat different *discourse topic*, probably something along the lines of "the relationship among sentences in extended texts." The point is that what Daneš calls "hypertheme"—and what I call the *discourse topic*—is not derived from the text alone, but from the interaction of the text with the reader's prior knowledge. Indeed, the Prague School notion of *topic* at the sentence level presupposes an audience for the text, someone in whose consciousness resides "what is known."

This point can be illustrated in another way. Consider the above text consisting of sentences (1-a) through (1-d). For that text, most readers would probably construct a *discourse topic* like the one I offered for sentences (3-a) through (3-d). But less knowledgeable readers would probably construct a different *discourse topic* from this sequence:

(4-a) From his work during the 1920's, *Mathesius* attempts to explain the relationship of individual sentences within the context of extended texts.
(4-b) *He* hypothesizes that the themes of sentences usually appear first in

English sentences, expressing old or given information that provides a semantic link with the preceding sentence and hence the preceding elements of the discourse. (4-c) *Mathesius* also hypothesizes that new information introduced into the text typically appears near the ends of sentences as the rheme.

Readers with limited knowledge might construct a *discourse topic* as specific as "Mathesius' view of the relationships between sentences in a text" or as general as "Mathesius," depending on how much or how little prior knowledge they have. On the other hand, readers with considerable prior knowledge would likely construct a *discourse topic* such as "Mathesius' contributions to a theory of functional sentence perspective." While one cannot overemphasize the importance of the reader's knowledge for identifying *discourse topics* in texts such as those represented by sentences (3-a) through (3-d) and (4-a) through (4-c), prior knowledge may be less important for identifying *discourse topics* in texts such as sentences (2-a) through (2-e) and still less important for texts such as sentences (1-a) through (1-d). The difference between the first two texts above and the last two is, I would argue, that in the first two explicit signals for identifying the *discourse topic* are embedded in a *sentence topic* in at least one of the sentences in each of the two texts. That is to say, in (1-a) through (1-d) and in (2-a) through (2-e), at least one of the *sentence topics* in each text serves to mark or signal the *discourse topic*. In contrast, the *discourse topic* of neither the third nor fourth text is stated explicitly as a *sentence topic* and must, therefore, be inferred or constructed from the interaction of the reader's prior knowledge with the information supplied by the text.

The point of all this is that *discourse topics* do not reside in the text alone, but rather reflect the interaction of text features with the reader's knowledge. This is not to say, however, that the derivation of a *discourse topic* is an altogether subjective matter: such a position would ignore the textual contributions to that derivation. In fact, one of the purposes of the present essay is to identify some of the textual cues which influence readers' constructions of *discourse topics*. Texts cannot be artificially separated from the communication process—a process which involves the text, the writer, *and* the reader.

In answer to the question I posed about a text's *discourse topic*, I have shown that it results, in part, from the interaction of the reader with the text. But I have not addressed explicitly the relationship between *discourse topics* and *sentence topics*, two concepts which must be kept separate,[31] even though the *discourse topic* may be signalled one or more times as a *sentence topic* in a particular text, as in (1-a) through (1-d) and in (2-a) through (2-e).

The relationship between the text itself and its *discourse topic* can be demonstrated by applying Liisa Lautamatti's work on the development of *discourse topics*.[32] Lautamatti's work complements a parallel line of research in this country, namely, that dealing with "staging" in discourse, a construct introduced by Joseph Grimes[33] and refined and tested empirically by Peter Clements.[34] Lautamatti, Clements, and Grimes view the contribution of *sen-*

tence topics to the development of the *discourse topic* semantically; *sentence topics* are seen as units of meaning organized hierarchically in the text. Using the term "sentence" to refer to simple and complex sentences, Lautamatti explains:

> We [readers] expect sequences making up a piece of discourse to be related, however indirectly, to the . . . *discourse topic*. This relation may be direct, especially in short texts, or indirect, based on the development of subordinate ideas, *subtopics* [i.e., *sentence topics*], which in their turn relate to the discourse topic. The development of the discourse topic within an extensive piece of discourse may be thought of in terms of a succession of hierarchically ordered subtopics, each of which contributes to the discourse topic, and is treated as a sequence of ideas, expressed in the written language as sentences. We know little about restrictions concerning the relationship between sentences and subtopics, but it seems likely that most sentences relating to the same subtopic form a sequence. The way the written sentences in discourse relate to the discourse topic is . . . called *topical development* of discourse. (p. 71)

Such a view of the relationship of *subtopics* (i.e., *sentence topics*) to the *discourse topic* surmounts the problems of using the orthographic boundaries of sentences and paragraphs as the principal semantic or meaning markers in extended discourse.[35] (Sentence boundaries can vary independently of meaning when writers choose to produce compound or compound-complex sentences, and I can find no evidence that writers segment texts into paragraphs in consistent ways.) The particular *sentence topics* which appear in a text probably result directly from a writer's implicit sense of the *discourse topic* and from the writer's decisions[36] about how to make the *discourse topic* accessible to the reader. During the production of a well-formed text, these decisions reflect the writer's concern for what Hobbes and his colleagues have termed "global coherence" and "local coherence,"[37] which are necessary conditions for a well-formed text. To meet the condition of "global coherence," writers establish relationships between their sentence topics and their discourse topic; to meet the condition of "local coherence," they establish relationships between the topics of successive sentences, often by creating text patterns such as those identified by Daneš.

If well-formed texts cohere both locally and globally, then we have to view sentences, not only as autonomous syntactic structures, but as the vehicles by which information is distributed throughout a text; such a view makes it possible to talk about semantic relationships which extend across the formal boundaries of sentences. In coherent texts—texts which allow communication to occur between writer and reader—these relationships are expressed through sequences of sentences. Sequences of sentences contribute to the *discourse topic* by developing a succession of *sentence topics*, sequences which Lautamatti calls *topical progressions*.

Lautamatti identifies only three such progressions, although there are probably more. These progressions help describe how individual sentences cohere locally and how all sentences within a text cohere globally. The first type of *topical progression* is a *parallel progression*. It corresponds to Daneš' first text pattern, represented by sentences (1-a) through (1-d) above. In a parallel progression, the *topics* of the various sentences are referentially identical, using repeated lexical items, synonyms, near-synonyms, or pronouns. The second type, called a *sequential progression,* corresponds to Daneš' second text pattern, represented above by sentences (2-a) through (2-e). In a *sequential progression,* the *comment* of a preceding sentence, usually the adjacent sentence, becomes the *topic* of the following sentence. The third type, an *extended parallel progression,* refers simply to a parallel progression which is temporarily interrupted by a sequential progression. These *topical progressions* are illustrated in the following text.[38] For ease of reference, I have italicized the *topic*[39] of each sentence:

(5-a) When a *human infant* is born into any language community in any part of the world, it has two things in common with every other infant, provided neither of them has been damaged in any way either before or during birth. (5-b) Firstly, and most obviously, *new born children* are completely helpless. (5-c) Apart from a powerful capacity to draw attention to their helplessness by using sound, there is nothing the *new born child* can do to ensure his own survival. (5-d) Without care from some other human being or beings, be it a mother, grandmother, sister, nurse, or human group, a *child* is very unlikely to survive. (5-e) *This helplessness of human infants* is in marked contrast with the capacity of many new born animals to get to their feet within minutes of birth and run with the herd within a few hours. (5-f) Although *young animals* are certainly at risk, sometimes for weeks or even months after birth, compared with human infants they very quickly develop the capacity to fend for themselves. (5-g) It would seem that *this long period of vulnerability* is the price that the human species has to pay for the very long period which fits man for survival as a species.

(5-h) It is during this very long period in which the *human infant* is totally dependent on others that it reveals the second feature which it shares with all other undamaged human infants, a capacity to learn language. (5-i) For this reason, biologists now suggest that *language* is "species specific" to the human race, which means they consider the human infant to be programmed in such a way that it can acquire language. (5-j) This suggestion implies that just as *human beings* are designed to see three-dimensionally and in colour, and just as they are designed to stand upright rather than to move on all fours, so are they designed to learn and use language as part of their normal development as well-formed human beings.

For this passage, most readers of the present essay would probably formulate a general statement of "what the passage is about" something like the following: "language development in the vulnerable human infant." This general *discourse topic* is nowhere stated explicitly in the text; however, through the interaction of their prior knowledge about language acquisition with their understanding of how extended texts work, readers can infer or construct that discourse topic. Lautamatti maintains that the progression of sentence topics in a text partly determines how we understand or comprehend it. Whether we use the phrase *progression of sentence topics* or the term "staging" to describe the textual phenomenon, what is important is the semantic hierarchy of sentence topics within the text.

As a way of indicating the relationship between the progression of sentence topics and the semantic hierarchy, Lautamatti employs the expression *topical depth*. According to Lautamatti, the *sentence topic* stated first in a text is often at the highest level in the semantic hierarchy, a hypothesis which finds some support in the work of Kieras[40] and which is fairly consistent with the "staging rules" outlined by Clements (see especially pp. 291–292 and 296–298). For Lautamatti, the concepts of *topical progression*—the *progression of sentence topics*—and *topical depth* are combined to represent the *topical structure* of a text. Following Lautamatti (p. 87), we can thus graphically depict (see Figure 1 below) the relationship between *topical progression* and *topical depth* for the above passage.

As Figure 1 indicates, the *Language and Community* passage contains five distinct sentence topics, with one of them repeated in six of the ten sentences,[41] a ratio which Lautamatti (p. 87) contends may affect the semantic complexity of the text. Because the first four sentence topics are semantically identical, sentences (5-a) through (5-d) form a *parallel progression*. Sentences (5-d) through (5-g)—because the topic of each is different—constitute a *sequential progression*, as do sentences (5-h) and (5-i). Collectively, sentences (5-a), (5-b), (5-c), (5-d), (5-h), and (5-j) make up an *extended parallel progression*.

FIGURE 1   The *Topical Structure* of the *Language and Community* Passage

Sentence No.	Topical Depth 1	2	3	4	Topic No.
5-a	human infant				1
5-b	children				1
5-c	child				1
5-d	child				1
5-e		this helplessness			2
5-f			animals		3
5-g				this period	4
5-h	human infant				1
5-i		language			5
5-j	human beings				1

The progression of sentence topics is called *extended* because the progression of the same topic through the text leaves off after (5-d), picks up with (5-h), and picks up again with (5-j). The *topical depth* of the passage is determined by the number of different sentence topics in the longest sequential progression, here sentences (5-d) through (5-g). *Thus while the passage contains five different sentence topics, it has a topical depth of four.* According to Lautamatti (p. 87), of the five sentence topics, *human infant,* or its equivalent, is the most important: it is mentioned first; it occurs most frequently; and it stands at the highest level in the semantic hierarchy of information in the text. Put somewhat differently, "human infant" or its semantic equivalent is the concept around which all other concepts in the text revolve.

The representation in Figure 1 of the *topical structure* of the passage ought to enable us to identify more specifically the *discourse topic* of the passage. I believe it does. From the prominence given the first sentence topic, we would infer that the discourse is, first, about *human infants* (who are included within the superordinate term *human beings*); second, from the other sentence topics, we can infer that the text is about *language in human infants* during a *long period of vulnerability* when they are *helpless.* The *discourse topic,* then, may be stated as follows: "language in vulnerable human infants." When what is said (by the principal verbs in the text) *about the discourse topic* is combined with the *discourse topic,* the product is the "macroproposition," "gist," or "point"[42] of the text: "Human infants are unique in that they learn language during a period of vulnerability when they are completely helpless." In short, the features of *topical structure analysis* I have outlined suggest that it is possible to construct the macroproposition for a well-formed text without the cumbersome and time-consuming business of analyzing texts into propositions, as outlined by Kintsch and van Dijk[43] and as applied to the study of revision by Faigley and Witte.

As I have explained it, *topical structure analysis* would seem to be a useful tool for studying the textual cues which may prompt revision and for studying the effects of revision on text structure, primarily because it accounts for and illuminates the interaction of reading and writing during the revision process. *Topical structure analysis* should enable researchers to chart more efficiently the actual decisions writers make as they revise texts. In the remaining sections of this essay, I report on a study designed to explore these hypotheses.

A Controlled Study of Revisions

Design and Methodology

To explore these hypotheses, I asked approximately 80 students with varying abilities as writers[44] to revise the *Language and Community* passage. Although this task may be somewhat artificial, its use in a revision study can be defended in three ways. First, as a recent survey shows, nearly three-fourths of all college graduates write collaboratively on the job.[45] When people write collaboratively, they often must revise drafts which they themselves did not write. Second, two recent national surveys—one of writing program directors and one of teachers of writing—show that collaborative learning, peer tutoring, and peer editing are among the most successful instructional activities in college writing courses.[46] All three methods of instruction presuppose the ability of students either to revise or to suggest revisions for texts other than their own. Third, such a revision task provides a useful way of exploring the relationship between reading and writing: it controls both the text features and the content to which writers must respond during revision.

The students were given 40 minutes in which to "read the passage carefully" and then to "revise it" so that it would be "easier to read and understand" but would retain "its character as a piece of informative discourse." The students were also asked to assume that they were revising for a "college-educated audience" that had a general knowledge of the subject matter of the text.

After the revised texts were collected, student names removed, and an identification number assigned to each, I gave them to four raters at different times. One rater was a lawyer; one was an insurance company executive. The two other raters were teachers of writing: one had sixteen years of experience as a teacher of writing at all levels in the university curriculum and as a technical writer; the other had taught writing in ESL classes for three years and had had experience adjusting texts so that they would be more accessible to ESL students. I employed lay raters and particular kinds of academic raters because I believed that they could provide a good estimate of the needs of the general audience I had specified for the revisions. Each rater rated the papers in random order and recorded a score from "1" (difficult to read and understand) to "4" (easy to read and understand) on separate score sheets.[47]

The ratings of all four raters for each revision were summed, yielding a total score which ranged from 4 to 16. The scores assigned by the raters were used to form two groups of revised texts, one a "low-score" group (N = 20) which had been judged relatively "difficult to read and understand" and one a "high-score group" (N = 24) which had been judged relatively "easy to read and understand." Revisions making up the low-score group had summed scores ranging from 4 to 9 (I had planned to use scores from 4 to 8, but I had to opt for the 4-to-9 range in order to meet my prior condition of having at least 20 revisions in each group). Revisions making up the high-score group had summed scores ranging from 12 to 16.

After the two groups of texts had been formed, the 44 revisions were randomly sequenced and then stored. About a month later, I analyzed the revisions in terms of several features: number of (1) words; (2) t-units; (3) clauses; (4) sentence topics; (5) parallel, sequential, and extended parallel progressions; and (6) t-units in each type of topical progression. Using these raw data, I created five computed variables for subsequent analyses: (1) words per sentence topic (words/sentence topics); (2) t-units per sentence topic (t-units/sentence topics); (3) percentage of t-units in the three types of topical progressions (e.g., t-units in parallel progressions/t-units); (4) words per clause (words/clauses); and (5) words per t-unit (words/t-units).

Two raw data variables—number of words and number of sentence topics—and the five computed variables figured importantly in the analyses of the revised texts. The two raw data variables were used as gross indices of the amount of content or information the texts delivered. Two of the computed variables—number of words per t-unit and number of words per clause—have been widely used as indices of "syntactic complexity."[48] These syntactic indices were used in the present study to provide something of a context for the topical structure analysis and to help identify additional causes and effects of revision. The three computed topical structure variables were used either to measure how much a given *sentence topic* was elaborated on or to identify differences in the ways the revised texts were structured.

Using t-tests, I then compared the two groups of texts to determine whether they differed significantly in terms of the variables I had selected for analysis. For all tests, the .05-level of confidence determined statistical significance.

Results

The results of the t-tests indicate that the two sets of revisions differ significantly in five ways.[49] First, the two sets of revisions differ significantly with respect to text length. The texts in the low-score group contain on the average 27.6% more words than those in the high-score group. The low-score revisions are on the average 93.9 (sd = 29.8) words shorter than the original *Language and Community* passage, which contains 326 words, while the high-score revisions are on the average 158.2 (sd = 46.1) words shorter. Second, the means for the number of sentence topics in the two sets of revisions also differ significantly. On the average the low-score revisions contain 49.2% more sentence topics than do the high-score revisions. The low-score revisions contain on the average 1.45 (sd = 1.54) more sentence topics than the original passage, while the high-score revisions contain on the average 1.13 (sd = 1.12) fewer sentence topics than the original.

Of the two computed syntactic variables, only the means for clause length are significantly different, with the clauses of the low-score revisions about 10% longer than those of the high-score revisions. The difference between the two groups of texts in mean t-unit length approaches statistical significance (p < .08). T-units in the low-score group average 20.06 words (sd = 3.68), while t-units in the high-score group average 18.12 words (sd = 3.61).

Comparisons of the low- and high-score revisions in terms of the computed "topical structure" variables reveal the fourth and fifth significant differences. The two sets of revisions differ significantly with respect to the mean number of t-units per sentence topic. The high-score revisions average about 27% more t-units per sentence topic than the low-score revisions. In addition, the two sets differ significantly with respect to the mean percentage of t-units in sequential progressions: 15% more of the t-units appear in sequential progressions in the low-score revisions than in the high-score revisions.

Discussion of Results

In the previous section, I reported the statistically significant and near-significant differences between the two sets of revisions. I did not, however, indicate whether such differences are meaningful. In short, the results demand interpretation. To provide a context for this interpretation, I have included a sample low-score revision and a sample high-score revision. In each revision, I have italicized the sentence topics:[50]

Example of Low-Score Revision

(6-a) In studying the *differences between human infants and other newborn animals,* we need to look at several distinguishing characteristics between and among the species, keeping in mind that neither species has been damaged in any way either before or during birth.

(6-b) Firstly, and most obviously, *newborn children* are completely helpless, as opposed to young animals at birth. (6-c) Apart from a powerful capacity to draw attention to their helplessness by using sound, there is nothing the infant can do to insure his own survival. (6-d) *This helplessness of human infants* is in contrast with the capacity of newborn animals. (6-e) *They* can get to their feet within minutes and run with the herd within hours. (6-f) Although *young animals* are at risk for some time compared with children, they are soon able to fend for themselves.

(6-g) We may look at the *ability to use language,* which is the second characteristic human infants share. (6-h) Because acquired only by humans, biologists now suggest that *language* is "species specific" to the human race. (6-i) *They* consider the *human infant* to be genetically programmed in such a way that it can acquire a language. (6-j) Biologists also consider *the long period of vulnerability and dependency on others,* during which language is learned, necessary to language development. (6-k) This suggestion implies that *children* are designed to learn and use language as part of their normal development as well-formed human beings.

Example of High-Score Revision

(7-a) All *human infants,* which are not born defective, share a common feature that distinguishes them from the other animal species. (7-b) This feature is the ability of the new born infant to communicate with sounds that eventually develop into language as we know it.

(7-c) Unlike most animal species, *human infants* are born completely helpless and must rely on another person to insure their survival. (7-d) *Children* must be fed and sheltered for many months, whereas many other animals are able to fend for themselves only hours after they are born.

(7-e) It is during this period of complete helplessness that *infants* utter sounds to communicate with others. (7-f) For example, *infants* cry when they are hungry or wet. (7-g) Later on during this period of dependency, *infants* reveal their capacity to learn language. (7-h) All normal *infants* can repeat sounds and eventually associate these sounds with objects and feelings. (7-i) For this reason, biologists now suggest that *language* is "species specific" to the human race and that all normal infants are capable of communicating through it.

Ideally, of course, these two example revisions would reflect exactly the statistical means for the different discourse features examined in the two sets of texts. While no such "average" texts exist, the two example revisions do help illustrate the differences between the two sets of revisions and between the revisions and the original text. They also help illustrate some of the text features which both the four raters and the student writers apparently associate with an informative text that is "easy to read and understand." In addition, the two examples suggest some of the features of the original text which appear to have cued particular revisions.

Syntactic "Complexity." Sentence length is one of the most obvious differences between the revisions and the original text. Both sets of revisions exhibited mean clause and t-unit lengths considerably shorter than those for the original text. The original's mean t-unit length is 30.55, and its mean clause length is 12.44. Thus the low-score revisions contain t-units about 34% shorter (10.49 words) than those of the original; the high-score texts contain t-units about 40% shorter (12.43 words). The low-score revisions contain clauses over 9% shorter (0.75 words) than those in the original; the high-score texts have an average clause length about 15% shorter (1.87 words) than that of the original.

These findings may suggest to some that, given the particular revision task, both groups of writers saw reducing "syntactic complexity" as an important goal. Perhaps these students assumed what those who have created readability formulae assumed—that shorter sentences are easier to read.[51] The shorter clauses and t-units in the high-score texts suggest that for the better writers such reduction was either more important to them or easier for them to do. Compared to those of the original text, the shorter t-units and clauses in both sets of revisions may also suggest that both groups of revisers were less capable of writing "syntactically complex" sentences than the authors of the original.

Although measures of "syntactic complexity" can be used to distinguish between the two sets of revisions and between the two sets and the original text, neither the measures nor the concept is particularly useful in pinpointing either the causes or the effects of revision. Observing that t-units and clauses in revisions are longer or shorter than those in the original text is not to explain why or how those differences occur or what they might mean for the revised texts. Such differences can, however, be accounted for in at least two ways: by examining the relationship between deleted and retained content (a matter discussed in the following section) and by examining the relationship between the placement of *sentence topics* and sentence structure and length.

Lautamatti's work (pp. 72–83) is again useful. She distinguishes among five types of sentences on the basis of the relationship between "initial sentence elements," "topical subjects" (i.e., sentence topics), and "mood subjects" (i.e., grammatical subjects of independent clauses).

Each of these sentence types is illustrated in the original *Language and Community* passage. In *Type 1* sentences—such as (5-e)—the grammatical subject, the initial sentence element, and the topical subject are identical.[52] In *Type 2* sentences—of which (5-b) and (5-d) are examples—the initial sentence element (e.g., "Firstly, and most obviously" in [5-b]) differs from the grammatical subject and the topical subject, which are themselves identical.[53] In *Type 3* sentences—of which (5-g), (5-h), and (5-j) are examples—the grammatical subject and the initial sentence element are the same, but both differ from the topical subject.[54] *Type 4* sentences—(5-a) and (5-f) in the original passage—have a topical subject which coincides with the initial sentence element and a grammatical subject which differs from both.[55] In *Type 5* sentences, such as (5-c) and (5-i), the initial sentence element, the topical subject, and the grammatical subject all differ.[56]

Although the differences between the two sets of revisions with regard to the average number of sentences of each type are not statistically significant,[57] the effect of the placement of *sentence topics* on "syntactic complexity" can be seen in a comparison of the percentages of each sentence type across the original text and the two sets of revisions. In the original passage, 10% of the sentences are *Type 1* sentences, 20% are *Type 2*, 30% are *Type 3*, 20% are *Type 4*, and 20% are *Type 5*. In the low-score revisions, approximately 31% of the sentences are *Type 1* sentences, 23% are *Type 2* sentences, 16% are *Type 3*, 11% are *Type 4*, and 19% are *Type 5*. In the high-score revisions, approximately 30% are *Type 1* sentences, 28% are *Type 2* sentences, 11% are *Type 3* sentences, 9% are *Type 4*, and 21% are *Type 5*.

These figures indicate that the percentages of *Type 5* sentences—sentences in which the initial sentence element, grammatical subject, and topical subject are all different—do not differ substantially across the low- and high-score revisions. Neither do the two sets of revisions differ substantially from the original passage in this regard. The revisions depart most dramatically from the original with respect to the percentages of *Type 1* sentences, sentences in which the grammatical subject, the topical subject, and the initial sentence element all coincide. In both sets of revisions, the percentage of *Type 1* sentences is about three times larger than it is for the original passage. In both sets of revisions, the percentage of *Type 2* sentences—in which the initial sentence element differs from the topical and the grammatical subjects, which are identical—is also larger than the corresponding percentage for the original text. For the high-score revisions the percentage of *Type 2* sentences is somewhat larger than it is for the low-score revisions. The percentages of *Type 3* and *Type 4* sentences in the revised texts are also larger than the corresponding percentages for the original text; and the low-score revisions contain higher percentages of both *Type 3* and *Type 4* sentences than do the high-score revisions.

These differences in the occurrence of the five types of sentences are important for several reasons. Among other reasons, such modifications as occur in the revisions result in shorter clauses and t-units, thus making the two sets of revisions less complex syntactically than the original text. Consider, for example, *Type 1* sentences. Because the initial sentence element, the grammatical subject, and the topical subject are identical in a *Type 1* sentence, *Type 1* sentences will generally be shorter than sentences in which all three elements are different or sentences in which two of the elements differ from the third. Both sets of revisions used about three times more *Type 1* sentences than did the original, and they used on the average fewer than half as many *Type 3* and *Type 4* sentences as the original. With the exception of *Type 5* sentences—which the writers of the revised texts may have found difficult to convert—both groups of revisions tended to reduce the relative frequency of sentence types in which the grammatical subject and the topical subject do not coincide (*Types 3, 4,* and *5*) and to increase the frequency of sentence types in which the grammatical subject and the topical subject are the same (*Types 1* and *2*). These findings suggest that one of the goals of the student writers may have been to structure or focus their sentences so as to make their grammatical and topical subjects coincide with each other. Perhaps the students believed that *Type 1* and *Type 2* sentences are easier to read and understand than the other three types. Whatever their reasons for choosing *Type 1* and *Type 2* sentences over the other three, the effects of their choices are levels of "syntactic complexity" in the revised texts that are lower than the level of "syntactic complexity" in the original passage.

Semantic Complexity.   The lower levels of "syntactic complexity" may also result from the students' efforts to reduce the amount of information in the original text. If reducing "syntactic complexity" were the primary goal of the student writers, then the length in words of the revised texts would have been greater than that of the original. "Syntactic complexity" increases as more and more independent clauses are reduced to less-than-clause status and then embedded in other independent clauses. Such embedding, as virtually all the sentence-combining books demonstrate, (1) reduces the number of independent clauses, (2) increases the average length of those clauses, and (3) reduces the number of words required to deliver the same content. In the present study, the average number of words in both sets of revisions is substantially smaller than the number of words in the original text. The writers of the low-score revisions reduced the number of words by an average of 31%; their high-score counterparts reduced it by an average of 50%. We can reduce text length *and* "syntactic complexity" *only* if we also eliminate some of the semantic content, content which is often expressed in the form of deletable syntactic units within sentences.

Both groups of writers reduced "syntactic complexity" by eliminating semantic content. For example, all of the high-score revisions and many of the low-score revisions deleted the two prepositional phrases embedded in the introductory subordinate clause of (5-a) in the original text. The students may have reasoned that "into any language community in any part of the world" was either implicit in the generic "human infant," or could be inferred from "human infant," or added a kind of qualification unnecessary for an audience of college-educated readers. Similarly, both groups of writers either eliminated completely or reduced substantially this phrase from sentence (5-f): "sometimes for weeks or even months after birth." In the low-score example, the eight-word phrase of the original becomes "for some time"; but the phrase is not retained in the high-score example. Such revisions may have been prompted by the belief that such phrases are redundant.

But while the two groups often eliminated or reduced similar semantic elements, they frequently did not treat such elements similarly. For example, the two groups of writers tended to treat the participial phrase at the end of (5-a) in very different ways. Most of the low-score revisions retained the phrase almost verbatim, as in (6-a): "keeping in mind that neither species has been damaged in any way either before or during birth." In contrast, the high-score revisions substantially reduced the length of the phrase, often transforming it into a nonrestrictive relative clause: "which are not born defective," as in (7-a). Most important, because the participial phrase in the low-score example refers to "species," it probably misrepresents the intended meaning of the original text. In the high-score revision, however, because the relative clause modifies "human infants," it remains true to the sense of the original. It would appear that the two groups of writers not only made different decisions about "necessary" and "unnecessary" information, but that they made those decisions in very different ways.

Sentence Topics and Semantic Content. But on what basis did the two groups decide which elements of the original text to delete? I suspect that they based such decisions on their constructions of a *discourse topic* or a *gist* for the original text, because those constructions seem to differ in important ways. This is suggested if we compare the *topical structure* of each sample revision. I have displayed the topical structure of the two example revisions in Figure 2 and Figure 3.

These two figures suggest that the two writers understood the original text in different ways. The high-score example contains three sentence topics—"infants" or its semantic equivalent, "feature," and "language"—which allow the construction of the same general *discourse topic* as for the original. In contrast, the low-score example contains seven sentence topics. The progression of these seven topics gives no certain clues to the *discourse topic* of the original text. On one level of analysis, the quantitative difference in the number of sentence topics carried over from the original text to the revisions appears to be a qualitative one as well: as the number of sentence topics increases, the rating decreases. Such a conclusion, however, is misleading because it suggests that a high-score revision simply reduces the number of

FIGURE 2   The *Topical Structure of the Sample Low-Score Revision* as Reflected in Its
Progression of Sentence Topics and Its Topical Depth

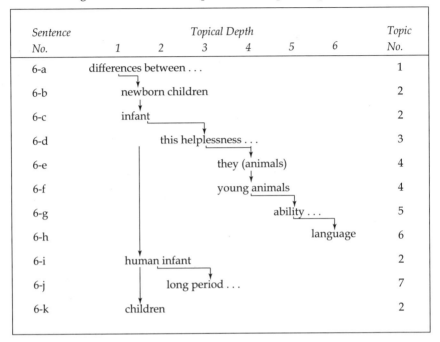

FIGURE 3   The *Topical Structure of the High-Score Sample* as Reflected in Its
Progression of Sentence Topics and Its Topical Depth

sentence topics contained in the original passage when, in fact, something quite different has occurred. As the high-score revisions illustrate, their authors were apparently able to distinguish among sentence topics in the original text according to whether particular topics were crucial to understanding the *gist* of the original; and as the low-score revisions show, their authors could not.

Given the particular sentence topics selected and the order of their appearance in the text, it is reasonable to infer from the high-score example that the writer saw the *gist* of the original as embodying the following proposition: "The ability to acquire language is unique to human infants." That proposition seems to be the *macroproposition* of the high-score revision as well. In fact, the writer of the high-score revision appears so committed to that proposition that she passed up several opportunities to introduce other sentence topics. For example, she might have made—as her low-score counterpart in fact did in sentences (6-e) and (6-f) of his revision—"animals" the topical subject of the two sentences contained in the second paragraph. Instead, the writer of the high-score revision chose to make "human infants" and "children" the topical subjects of those two sentences, thus maintaining and reinforcing the limited focus established in the first paragraph.

The two groups' differing constructions of the *gist* of the original governed their choices of sentence topics. These different sentence topics, in turn, led to different decisions about content which could be deleted from the original. This point is illustrated by the second paragraph in each of the example revisions. In its second paragraph, the low-score revision develops much more extensively the idea "young animals" than does the high-score revision, even making "young animals" the topic of sentences (6-e) and (6-f). The low-score example also retains a good deal of information about "young animals" from the original that is not retained in the high-score revision. It seems probable that if the same *gist* for the original text had been constructed by both groups of writers, then their revisions would have been much more alike than they are.

Topical Focus. Compared to the high-score example and to the original text, the low-score example lacks a clear focus. The writer of the low-score revision may have been uncertain of the *gist* of the original—and, consequently, of how to revise it—because his revision seems to shift focus at the beginning of the third paragraph. In his first paragraph, he signals a commitment to examine "*differences* between human infants and other newborn animals," a commitment honored, but not honored particularly well, in his second paragraph. However, with his third paragraph, he seems no longer to be addressing those differences: with the third paragraph, he shifts the focus to "the second characteristic human infants share." This shift makes it difficult for us to identify the gist of the low-score revision, as we were able to do for the high-score revision. The ambiguous focus in the low-score example— which, of course, threatens coherence—is fairly typical of all revisions in the low-score group.

One reason for the ambiguity or lack of focus in the low-score example is that the writer only belatedly connects "the helplessness of human infants" and language development. That connection could have been made in the second paragraph—which treats the concept of helplessness and alludes to the infant's ability to use sound to its advantage—had the writer at that point seen the connection. Instead, the connection is awkwardly made in the third paragraph, in sentence (6-j), which does not really fit conceptually between the two sentences where it appears. The writer of the low-score revision seems not to have been able to see the semantic connections among the sentence topics in the original passage; and he seems not to have had adequate criteria for distinguishing between "necessary" and "unnecessary" information in either the original text or his revision. As a result, he produced a text lacking in focus.

Although the greater number of sentence topics in the low-score revision may seem to lie at the heart of the qualitative difference between the two texts, such is not the case. The difference in the number of sentence topics is not a cause, but a symptom. In fact, the original text demonstrates that a coherent, well-formed text can embody virtually the same sentence topics as the low-score example. What is crucial is that the low-score writer apparently failed to understand the semantic relationships among the various sentence topics and between the sentence topics and a discourse topic, both in his revision and in the original text. As a result, the low-score revision is ambiguous, failing to achieve either local or global coherence through the selection and ordering of sentence topics.

All of this obviously suggests that a successful reviser must understand the topical structure and the macrostructure of the text being revised. Certainly, most people would agree, writers must understand their texts before they can revise them to better meet the needs of an audience or to realize particular discourse goals. Indeed, such understanding is a prerequisite for the writer of "reader-based prose." The low-score revisions analyzed in the present study almost always reflect their authors' inadequate understanding of the original. If students similarly misunderstand the relationship between their own texts and their purposes, they may not be able to revise them except by making, as Faigley and I observed in our sample of "inexperienced" writers, surface-level changes which do not affect the macrostructure, or gist, of their texts.

Topical Development. Differences between the two sets of revisions can also be attributed to differences in the mean number of t-units per sentence topic. The low-score revisions averaged 1.89 t-units per sentence topic, while the high-score revisions averaged 2.59, about 27% more than the low-score ones. In light of the average number of sentence topics in the two sets of revisions (6.45 in the low-score, compared with 3.88 in the high-score), these figures indicate that the high-score revisions developed or elaborated on a given sentence topic significantly more than did the low-score ones. This difference in topical development is illustrated by the two sample revisions. The high-score revision averages three t-units for every sentence topic (nine t-units divided by three sentence topics), whereas the low-score revision averages 1.57 t-units per sentence topic. In contrast, the original text averages two t-units for each of its five sentence topics. This index—the average number of t-units per sentence topic—may thus identify both the comprehensibility and the quality of texts directed toward the same audience and with the same purpose. Thus in revising the original text, the high-score writers chose to reduce the number of sentence topics and to develop more fully those retained, whereas the writers of the low-score texts chose to increase the number of sentence topics and to develop each of them less fully.

These choices with regard to the number of sentence topics and the degree to which they are developed are illustrated by the mean percentage of t-units in sequential progressions in the two sets of revisions. In the low-score revisions, 55% of the t-units are in sequential progressions, compared with 40% in the high-score revisions. With an average of 2.55 more sentence topics in the low-score revisions, more of the sentence topics would have to fall in sequential progressions, a phenomenon reflected in the mean topical depth for the low-score revisions.

Although they differ somewhat in this respect from the two sets of revisions, the two example revisions illustrate the importance of sequential progressions and topical depth. As Figure 3 indicates, the high-score example contains two sequential progressions, one formed by (7-a) and (7-b) and the second by (7-h) and (7-i). Thus about 44% of the t-units in the high-score example fall into sequential progressions. The low-score example, as Figure 2 shows, contains four sequential progressions—the first formed by (6-a) and (6-b); the second by (6-c), (6-d), and (6-e); the third by (6-f) and (6-g); and the fourth by (6-i) and (6-j). Thus about 91% of the t-units in the low-score revision appear in sequential progressions.

At first glance, it may seem that the low-score revision more closely resembles the original text in this regard than does the high-score example. However, the reverse is probably closer to the truth. As Figure 1 indicates, six (60%) of the 10 t-units or sentences in the original are in two sequential progressions—with (5-d), (5-e), (5-f), and (5-g) forming one and (5-h) and (5-i) forming the other. As Figure 3 shows, the high-score revision also contains two sequential progressions. The sequential progressions do not overlap in either the original text or the high-score revision. That is to say, the sequential progressions are not interrupted by parallel progressions below the first level of topical depth. Such interrupted sequential progressions do appear, however, in the low-score example. In the low-score example, which contains four sequential progressions, the first and second progressions share a common sentence topic, as do the second and third. In both cases, the common sentence topics are below the first level of topical depth. In the first instance of such overlapping of common sentence topics, (6-b) and (6-c) themselves form a parallel progression. The same holds true for (6-e) and (6-f), which represent the second instance. In addition, in the low-score revision, one of the overlapping sentence topics ("animals") appears only once in the original text as a sentence topic and does not appear as a sentence topic in the high-score revision at all. The other overlapping sentence topic ("newborn children"), which is at the first level of topical depth in both the original text and the high-score revision, appears at the second level of topical depth in the low-score revision. At least one such overlap occurs in each of the low-score revisions. The cause of such overlaps may be the writers' misunderstanding of the original text, but the effect is a lack of focus in the low-score revisions.

The overlapping of sequential progressions explains why the two sets of revisions display similar percentages of t-units falling into parallel and extended parallel progressions. In the original text, six of the ten t-units (60%) are in parallel or extended parallel progressions. Each parallel and extended parallel progression appears at the first level of topical depth. In the high-score example, seven of the nine t-units (77.8%) are in parallel or extended parallel progressions. As in the original text, each is at the first level of topical depth. In the low-score example, however, six of the 11 t-units (55%) appear in parallel or extended parallel progressions, and all of them occur at either the second or fourth level of topical depth. Thus while the writer of the original text and the writer of the high-score revision maintain a consistent and clear focus on the most important sentence topic by using that topic, at the uppermost level of topical depth, in parallel or extended parallel progressions, the writer of the low-score revision uses important sentence topics at lower levels of topical depth, and also develops, at even lower levels, sentence topics not crucial to the development of the discourse topic. The writer of the low-score revision does not seem to recognize which are the important sentence topics and which are not.

The importance of topical focus cannot be overemphasized, either in texts to be revised or in revisions of them. As the preceding analyses suggest, the low-score writers in the present study could neither perceive the topical structure of the original text nor create a suitable topical structure for their revisions. Why the low-score writers could not do this is open to speculation. Perhaps the subject matter of the text was beyond their ken or interest. Perhaps the topical structure of the original was too difficult for them to process. Perhaps "unnecessary" information in the original text erected a barrier between them and the text. Or perhaps, to use the terminology Faigley and I borrowed from Kintsch and van Dijk, they could not distinguish between the *microstructure* and the *macrostructure* of the original, between "content" which could be deleted without altering the *gist* of the text and "content" whose deletion would alter the *gist*. Probably because they could not accurately process the original text, the writers of the low-score revisions generally failed to produce texts which had a clear topical structure and, consequently, a clear topical focus.

The analyses reported above suggest why the low-score texts are less effective than the high-score texts. First, the low-score revisions contain a larger number of sentence topics than do the high-score texts, perhaps making the writers' task in controlling the topical structures of those revisions more difficult. Second, the low-score writers tend to use parallel, extended parallel, and sequential progressions in different ways than do their high-score counterparts. Perhaps because they do not know how to form effective sequential progressions such as the one represented by Daneš' second text pattern, the writers of the low-score revisions often bury in sequential progressions the most important sentence topics of the original text, topics which appear at higher levels of topical depth in both the original and in the high-score revisions.

Some Implications for Subsequent Research

Although making inferences about composing processes from written products is somewhat risky, the method I have outlined and applied to controlled revisions of college writers appears to be a promising one for studying the textual causes and effects of revision. It is a method which may allow researchers and teachers alike to study the decision-making processes writers use during revision. Although the present study examined controlled revisions, the method can be used to study naturally occurring revisions, whether by experienced or inexperienced writers. Indeed, the method effectively identifies problems in student texts and suggests revisions which would make those texts more accessible to their intended audiences and closer to their authors' intended meanings.

The present essay, however, is only exploratory. Whatever it suggests about the nature of readable texts must be verified through subsequent research. In the present study, I used a somewhat artificial task; and operating under that constraint, the students produced but one kind of text. Whether the findings hold for other kinds of texts collected under different circumstances and evaluated by different kinds of raters remains an open question. Yet the method I have outlined and applied seems conceptually sound, even if subsequent research suggests that texts of different kinds and purposes differ from the texts used in the present study. Perhaps most important, topical structure analysis seems a particularly good way of examining the close relationship between the reading and writing skills necessary for effective revision. In this regard, topical structure analysis—unlike the analytic methods designed to examine the effects of the revision—enables the researcher to explore the relationship between the textual causes of revision, the text features to which the writer as reader responds, and the effects those changes have on the revised text. How students decide to revise a text is largely dependent on their understanding of the text, an understanding garnered only through reading. If writers cannot read and understand their own texts, or those of others, it is difficult to see how they could ever become effective revisers. Perhaps unskilled writers tend to revise primarily at the word or sentence level because they have never learned how to read and evaluate texts in their entirety, to respond to the overall semantic structure of texts, or to evaluate semantic structure against their intentions. Because topical structure analysis can be used to compare original texts with revised texts, it should help us to understand why writers make the revisions they do.

AFTERWORD . . . .

An hour ago, a colleague and I left a meeting during which we observed two groups of engineers working jointly to develop the "set of standards," in the form of specifications and drawings, that will govern bids for contracts awarded by a city. We attended the meeting as part of one of several projects affiliated with the Center for Research on Workplace Literacy. My colleague and I believe our study of the engineers will further ground our new doctoral major in Literacy, Rhetoric, and Social Practice as well as provide multiple opportunities for graduate student research.

Such studies on the functions and uses of literacy (and other technologies of representation) in workplaces provide a context for how I now think of "Topical Structure and Revision," just as my early forays into workplace literacy prompted me to speculate about the relation of "topic" and "revision" to situated acts of writing and reading, to contexts of text production and use more generally, and to the collaborative nature of writing (including revision) among college graduates in workplaces.

The focus of one study I was beginning when I wrote the essay was L. C.—a successful mechanical engineer (at the time, his name appeared on at least nine patents) who had become a vice president for engineering development. However, L. C. had been "severed" when the engineering company for which he worked was sold to a larger one. As a child victim of polio whose physical condition had continued to deteriorate (only his repeated redesigning and remaking of his leg braces, from components of airplane wings, permitted him to walk at all), L. C. decided to "retool" himself as an independent software designer rather than extend his twenty-two-year career as an engineer. L. C.'s transition from one career to a very different one (which entailed transforming his extant knowledge and developing new performance knowledge) was part of what prompted my interest in how people deal with unfamiliar or novel topics in "texts."

Before and after I wrote "Topical Structure and Revision," L. C. taught me a great deal about topics, "texts," and human performance. One thing in particular that L. C. helped me to see was that many workplace "texts"—like L. C.'s latest annotated sketches of leg-brace modifications—treat important topics not easily represented linguistically, a problem the engineering groups this after-

noon spent much time discussing. Relatedly, L. C. and writers like the engineers observed today taught me that many topics treated in workplace "texts" of college graduates are grounded in the material circumstances of human life and directed toward the modification or amelioration of those circumstances. Third, L. C. and others—like the engineers working at City Hall—taught me that using "text" to bring about change in material circumstances of human life often affects (in many cases, positively) the nature and quality of social life. Fourth, L. C. and others taught me that "texts," topics, and acts of "text" production and use are embedded within larger contexts and knowledge domains of work activity, whether software design, engineering, law, management, or something else, and that various knowledge domains intersect in the production and use of many workplace "texts." Fifth, L. C. taught me—and the engineers today confirmed—that if we are to help our students make transitions from classrooms to work or across different work contexts and knowledge domains, then we must attend better to how "topics" and "topicalization" in "texts" relate to expertise, to the successful workplace performances that we hope our students, too, will one day achieve.

On reflection, I think "Topical Structure and Revision" either hinted at or touched upon such matters.

–STEPHEN P. WITTE
Kent State University

*Audience Addressed/Audience Invoked:
The Role of Audience in Composition
Theory and Pedagogy*

LISA EDE AND ANDREA LUNSFORD

One important controversy currently engaging scholars and teachers of writing involves the role of audience in composition theory and pedagogy. How can we best define the audience of a written discourse? What does it mean to address an audience? To what degree should teachers stress audience in their assignments and discussions? What *is* the best way to help students recognize the significance of this critical element in any rhetorical situation?

Teachers of writing may find recent efforts to answer these questions more confusing than illuminating. Should they agree with Ruth Mitchell and Mary Taylor, who so emphasize the significance of the audience that they argue for abandoning conventional composition courses and instituting a "cooperative effort by writing and subject instructors in adjunct courses. The cooperation and courses take two main forms. Either writing instructors can be attached to subject courses where writing is required, an organization which disperses the instructors throughout the departments participating; or the composition courses can teach students how to write the papers assigned in other concurrent courses, thus centralizing instruction but diversifying topics."[1] Or should teachers side with Russell Long, who asserts that those advocating greater attention to audience overemphasize the role of "observable physical or occupational characteristics" while ignoring the fact that most writers actually create their audiences. Long argues against the usefulness of such methods as developing hypothetical rhetorical situations as writing assignments, urging instead a more traditional emphasis on "the analysis of texts in the classroom with a very detailed examination given to the signals provided by the writer for his audience."[2]

To many teachers, the choice seems limited to a single option—to be for or against an emphasis on audience in composition courses. In the following essay, we wish to expand our understanding of the role audience plays in composition theory and pedagogy by demonstrating that the arguments ad-

This essay was first published in *CCC*, Volume 35, Number 2, May 1984.

vocated by each side of the current debate oversimplify the act of making meaning through written discourse. Each side, we will argue, has failed adequately to recognize 1) the fluid, dynamic character of rhetorical situations; and 2) the integrated, interdependent nature of reading and writing. After discussing the strengths and weaknesses of the two central perspectives on audience in composition—which we group under the rubrics of *audience addressed* and *audience invoked*[3]—we will propose an alternative formulation, one which we believe more accurately reflects the richness of "audience" as a concept.*

AUDIENCE ADDRESSED

Those who envision audience as addressed emphasize the concrete reality of the writer's audience; they also share the assumption that knowledge of this audience's attitudes, beliefs, and expectations is not only possible (via observation and analysis) but essential. Questions concerning the degree to which this audience is "real" or imagined, and the ways it differs from the speaker's audience, are generally either ignored or subordinated to a sense of the audience's powerfulness. In their discussion of "A Heuristic Model for Creating a Writer's Audience," for example, Fred Pfister and Joanne Petrik attempt to recognize the ontological complexity of the writer-audience relationship by noting that "students, like all writers, must fictionalize their audience."[4] Even so, by encouraging students to "construct in their imagination an audience that is as nearly a replica as is possible of *those many readers who actually exist in the world of reality*," Pfister and Petrik implicitly privilege the concept of audience as addressed.[5]

Many of those who envision audience as addressed have been influenced by the strong tradition of audience analysis in speech communication and by current research in cognitive psychology on the composing process.[6] They often see themselves as reacting against the current-traditional paradigm of composition, with its a-rhetorical, product-oriented emphasis.[7] And they also frequently encourage what is called "real-world" writing.[8]

Our purpose here is not to draw up a list of those who share this view of audience but to suggest the general outline of what most readers will recognize as a central tendency in the teaching of writing today. We would, however, like to focus on one particularly ambitious attempt to formulate a theory and pedagogy for composition based on the concept of audience as

---

*A number of terms might be used to characterize the two approaches to audience which dominate current theory and practice. Such pairs as identified/envisaged, "real"/fictional, or analyzed/created all point to the same general distinction as do our terms. We chose "addressed/invoked" because these terms most precisely represent our intended meaning. Our discussion will, we hope, clarify their significance; for the present, the following definitions must serve. The "addressed" audience refers to those actual or real-life people who read a discourse, while the "invoked" audience refers to the audience called up or imagined by the writer.

addressed: Ruth Mitchell and Mary Taylor's "The Integrating Perspective: An Audience-Response Model for Writing." We choose Mitchell and Taylor's work because of its theoretical richness and practical specificity. Despite these strengths, we wish to note several potentially significant limitations in their approach, limitations which obtain to varying degrees in much of the current work of those who envision audience as addressed.

In their article, Mitchell and Taylor analyze what they consider to be the two major existing composition models: one focusing on the writer and the other on the written product. Their evaluation of these two models seems essentially accurate. The "writer" model is limited because it defines writing as either self-expression or "fidelity to fact" (p. 255)—epistemologically naive assumptions which result in troubling pedagogical inconsistencies. And the "written product" model, which is characterized by an emphasis on "certain intrinsic features [such as a] lack of comma splices and fragments" (p. 258), is challenged by the continued inability of teachers of writing (not to mention those in other professions) to agree upon the precise intrinsic features which characterize "good" writing.

Most interesting, however, is what Mitchell and Taylor *omit* in their criticism of these models. Neither the writer model nor the written product model pays serious attention to invention, the term used to describe those "methods designed to aid in retrieving information, forming concepts, analyzing complex events, and solving certain kinds of problems."[9] Mitchell and Taylor's lapse in not noting this omission is understandable, however, for the same can be said of their own model. When these authors discuss the writing process, they stress that "our first priority for writing instruction at every level ought to be certain major tactics for structuring material because these structures are the most important in guiding the reader's comprehension and memory" (p. 271). They do not concern themselves with where "the material" comes from—its sophistication, complexity, accuracy, or rigor.

Mitchell and Taylor also fail to note another omission, one which might be best described in reference to their own model (Figure 1). This model has four components. Mitchell and Taylor use two of these, "writer" and "written product," as labels for the models they condemn. The third and fourth components, "audience" and "response," provide the title for their own "audience-response model for writing" (p. 249).

Mitchell and Taylor stress that the components in their model interact. Yet, despite their emphasis on interaction, it never seems to occur to them to note that the two other models may fail in large part because they overemphasize and isolate one of the four elements—wrenching it too greatly from its context and thus inevitably distorting the composing process. Mitchell and Taylor do not consider this possibility, we suggest, because their own model has the same weakness.

Mitchell and Taylor argue that a major limitation of the "writer" model is its emphasis on the self, the person writing, as the only potential judge of effective discourse. Ironically, however, their own emphasis on audience leads to a similar distortion. In their model, the audience has the sole power of evaluating writing, the success of which "will be judged by the audience's

FIGURE 1   Mitchell and Taylor's "General Model of Writing" (p. 250)

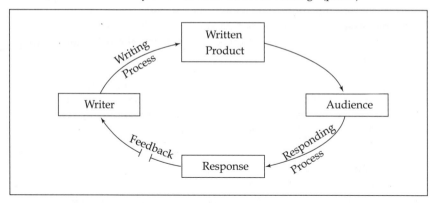

reaction: 'good' translates into 'effective,' 'bad' into 'ineffective.'" Mitchell and Taylor go on to note that "the audience not only judges writing; it also motivates it" (p. 250),[10] thus suggesting that the writer has less control than the audience over both evaluation and motivation.

Despite the fact that Mitchell and Taylor describe writing as "an interaction, a dynamic relationship" (p. 250), their model puts far more emphasis on the role of the audience than on that of the writer. One way to pinpoint the source of imbalance in Mitchell and Taylor's formulation is to note that they are right in emphasizing the creative role of readers who, they observe, "actively contribute to the meaning of what they read and will respond according to a complex set of expectations, preconceptions, and provocations" (p. 251), but wrong in failing to recognize the equally essential role writers play throughout the composing process not only as creators but also as *readers* of their own writing.

As Susan Wall observes in "In the Writer's Eye: Learning to Teach the Rereading/Revising Process," when writers read their own writing, as they do continuously while they compose, "there are really not one but two contexts for rereading: there is the writer-as-reader's sense of what the established text is actually saying, as of this reading; and there is the reader-as-writer's judgment of what the text might say or should say...."[11] What is missing from Mitchell and Taylor's model, and from much work done from the perspective of audience as addressed, is a recognition of the crucial importance of this internal dialogue, through which writers analyze inventional problems and conceptualize patterns of discourse. Also missing is an adequate awareness that, no matter how much feedback writers may receive after they have written something (or in breaks while they write), as they compose writers must rely in large part upon their own vision of the reader, which they create, as readers do their vision of writers, according to their own experiences and expectations.

Another major problem with Mitchell and Taylor's analysis is their apparent lack of concern for the ethics of language use. At one point, the authors ask the following important question: "Have we painted ourselves into a corner, so that the audience-response model must defend sociologese and its related styles?" (p. 265). Note first the ambiguity of their answer, which seems to us to say no and yes at the same time, and the way they try to deflect its impact:

> No. We defend only the right of audiences to set their own standards and we repudiate the ambitions of English departments to monopolize that standard-setting. If bureaucrats and scientists are happy with the way they write, then no one should interfere.
> But evidence is accumulating that they are not happy. (p. 265)

Here Mitchell and Taylor surely underestimate the relationship between style and substance. As those concerned with Doublespeak can attest, for example, the problem with sociologese is not simply its (to our ears) awkward, convoluted, highly nominalized style, but the way writers have in certain instances used this style to make statements otherwise unacceptable to lay persons, to "gloss over" potentially controversial facts about programs and their consequences, and thus violate the ethics of language use. Hence, although we support Mitchell and Taylor when they insist that we must better understand and respect the linguistic traditions of other disciplines and professions, we object to their assumption that style is somehow value free.

As we noted earlier, an analysis of Mitchell and Taylor's discussion clarifies weaknesses inherent in much of the theoretical and pedagogical research based on the concept of audience as addressed. One major weakness of this research lies in its narrow focus on helping students learn how to "continually modify their work with reference to their audience" (p. 251). Such a focus, which in its extreme form becomes pandering to the crowd, tends to undervalue the responsibility a writer has to a subject and to what Wayne Booth in *Modern Dogma and the Rhetoric of Assent* calls "the art of discovering good reasons."[12] The resulting imbalance has clear ethical consequences, for rhetoric has traditionally been concerned not only with the effectiveness of a discourse, but with truthfulness as well. Much of our difficulty with the language of advertising, for example, arises out of the ad writer's powerful concept of audience as addressed divorced from a corollary ethical concept. The toothpaste ad that promises improved personality, for instance, knows too well how to address the audience. But such ads ignore ethical questions completely.

Another weakness in research done by those who envision audience as addressed suggests an oversimplified view of language. As Paul Kameen observes in "Rewording the Rhetoric of Composition," "discourse is not grounded in forms or experience or audience; it engages all of these elements simultaneously."[13] Ann Berthoff has persistently criticized our obsession with one or another of the elements of discourse, insisting that meaning arises out of their synthesis. Writing is more, then, than "a means of acting upon a receiver" (Mitchell and Taylor, p. 250); it is a means of making meaning for writer *and* reader.[14] Without such a unifying, balanced understanding of language use, it is easy to overemphasize one aspect of discourse, such as audience. It is also easy to forget, as Anthony Petrosky cautions us, that "reading, responding, and composing are aspects of understanding, and theories that attempt to account for them outside of their interaction with each other run the serious risk of building reductive models of human understanding."[15]

AUDIENCE INVOKED

Those who envision audience as invoked stress that the audience of a written discourse is a construction of the writer, a "created fiction" (Long, p. 225). They do not, of course, deny the physical reality of readers, but they argue that writers simply cannot know this reality in the way that speakers can. The central task of the writer, then, is not to analyze an audience and adapt discourse to meet its needs. Rather, the writer uses the semantic and syntactic resources of language to provide cues for the reader—cues which help to define the role or roles the writer wishes the reader to adopt in responding to the text. Little scholarship in composition takes this perspective; only Russell Long's article and Walter Ong's "The Writer's Audience Is Always a Fiction" focus centrally on this issue.[16] If recent conferences are any indication, however, a growing number of teachers and scholars are becoming concerned with what they see as the possible distortions and oversimplifications of the approach typified by Mitchell and Taylor's model.[17]

Russell Long's response to current efforts to teach students analysis of audience and adaptation of text to audience is typical: "I have become increasingly disturbed not only about the superficiality of the advice itself, but about the philosophy which seems to lie beneath it" (p. 221). Rather than detailing Long's argument, we wish to turn to Walter Ong's well-known study. Published in *PMLA* in 1975, "The Writer's Audience Is Always a Fiction" has had a significant impact on composition studies, despite the fact that its major emphasis is on fictional narrative rather than expository writing. An analysis of Ong's argument suggests that teachers of writing may err if they uncritically accept Ong's statement that "what has been said about fictional narrative applies ceteris paribus to all writing" (p. 17).

Ong's thesis includes two central assertions: "What do we mean by saying the audience is a fiction? Two things at least. First, that the writer must construct in his imagination, clearly or vaguely, an audience cast in some sort of role. . . . Second, we mean that the audience must correspondingly fictionalize itself" (p. 12). Ong emphasizes the creative power of the adept writer, who can both project and alter audiences, as well as the complexity of the reader's role. Readers, Ong observes, must learn or "know how to play the game of being a member of an audience that 'really' does not exist" (p. 12).

On the most abstract and general level, Ong is accurate. For a writer, the audience is not *there* in the sense that the speaker's audience, whether a single person or a large group, is present. But Ong's representative situations—the orator addressing a mass audience versus a writer alone in a room—oversimplify the potential range and diversity of both oral and written communication situations.

Ong's model of the paradigmatic act of speech communication derives from traditional rhetoric. In distinguishing the terms *audience* and *reader,* he notes that "the orator has before him an audience which is a true audience, a collectivity. . . . Readers do not form a collectivity, acting here and now on one another and on the speaker as members of an audience do" (p. 11). As this quotation indicates, Ong also stresses the potential for interaction among members of an audience, and between an audience and a speaker.

But how many audiences are actually collectives, with ample opportunity for interaction? In *Persuasion: Understanding, Practice, and Analysis,* Herbert Simons establishes a continuum of audiences based on opportunities for interaction.[18] Simons contrasts commercial mass media publics, which "have little or no contact with each other and certainly have no reciprocal awareness of each other as members of the same audience" with "face-to-face work groups that meet and interact continuously over an extended period of time." He goes on to note that: "Between these two extremes are such groups as the following: (1) the *pedestrian audience,* persons who happen to pass a soap box orator . . . ; (2) the *passive, occasional audience,* persons who come to hear a noted lecturer in a large auditorium . . . ; (3) the *active, occasional audience,* persons who meet only on specific occasions but actively interact when they do meet" (pp. 97–98).

Simons' discussion, in effect, questions the rigidity of Ong's distinctions between a speaker's and a writer's audience. Indeed, when one surveys a broad range of situations inviting oral communication, Ong's paradigmatic situation, in which the speaker's audience constitutes a "collectivity, acting here and now on one another and on the speaker" (p. 11), seems somewhat atypical. It is certainly possible, at any rate, to think of a number of instances where speakers confront a problem very similar to that of writers: lacking intimate knowledge of their audience, which comprises not a collectivity but a disparate, and possibly even divided, group of individuals, speakers, like writers, must construct in their imaginations "an audience cast in some sort of role."[19] When President Carter announced to Americans during a speech broadcast on television, for instance, that his program against inflation was "the moral equivalent of warfare," he was doing more than merely characterizing his economic policies. He was providing an important cue to his audience concerning the role he wished them to adopt as listeners—that of a people braced for a painful but necessary and justifiable battle. Were we to examine his speech in detail, we would find other more subtle, but equally important, semantic and syntactic signals to the audience.

We do not wish here to collapse all distinctions between oral and written communication, but rather to emphasize that speaking and writing are, after all, both rhetorical acts. There are important differences between speech and writing. And the broad distinction between speech and writing that Ong makes is both commonsensical and particularly relevant to his subject, fictional narrative. As our illustration demonstrates, however, when one turns to precise, concrete situations, the relationship between speech and writing can become far more complex than even Ong represents.

Just as Ong's distinction between speech and writing is accurate on a highly general level but breaks down (or at least becomes less clear-cut) when examined closely, so too does his dictum about writers and their audiences. Every writer must indeed create a role for the reader, but the constraints on the writer and the potential sources of and possibilities for the reader's role are both more complex and diverse than Ong suggests. Ong stresses the importance of literary tradition in the creation of audience: "If the writer succeeds in writing, it is generally because he can fictionalize in his imagination an audience he has learned to know not from daily life but from earlier writers who were fictionalizing in their imagination audiences they had learned to know in still earlier writers, and so on back to the dawn of written narrative" (p. 11). And he cites a particularly (for us) germane example, a student "asked to write on the subject to which schoolteachers, jaded by summer, return compulsively every autumn: 'How I Spent My Summer Vacation'" (p. 11). In order to negotiate such an assignment successfully, the student must turn his real audience, the teacher, into someone else. He or she must, for instance, "make like Samuel Clemens and write for whomever Samuel Clemens was writing for" (p. 11).

Ong's example is, for his purposes, well-chosen. For such an assignment does indeed require the successful student to "fictionalize" his or her audience. But why is the student's decision to turn to a literary model in this instance particularly appropriate? Could one reason be that the student knows (consciously or unconsciously) that his English teacher, who is still the literal audience of his essay, appreciates literature and hence would be entertained (and here the student may intuit the assignment's actual aim as well) by such a strategy? In Ong's example the audience—the "jaded" schoolteacher—is not only willing to accept another role but, perhaps, actually yearns for it. How else to escape the tedium of reading 25, 50, 75 student papers on the same topic? As Walter Minot notes, however, not all readers are so malleable:

> In reading a work of fiction or poetry, a reader is far more willing to suspend his beliefs and values than in a rhetorical work dealing with some current social, moral, or economic issue. The effectiveness of the created audience in a rhetorical situation is likely to depend on such constraints as the actual identity of the reader, the subject of the discourse, the identity and purpose of the writer, and many other factors in the real world.[20]

An example might help make Minot's point concrete.

Imagine another composition student faced, like Ong's, with an assignment. This student, who has been given considerably more latitude in her choice of a topic, has decided to write on an issue of concern to her at the moment, the possibility that a home for mentally-retarded adults will be built in her neighborhood. She is alarmed by the strongly negative, highly emotional reaction of most of her neighbors and wishes in her essay to persuade them that such a residence might not be the disaster they anticipate.

This student faces a different task from that described by Ong. If she is to succeed, she must think seriously about her actual readers, the neighbors to whom she wishes to send her letter. She knows the obvious demographic factors—age, race, class—so well that she probably hardly needs to consider them consciously. But other issues are more complex. How much do her neighbors know about mental retardation, intellectually or experientially? What is their image of a retarded adult? What fears does this project raise in them? What civic and religious values do they most respect? Based on this analysis—and the process may be much less sequential than we describe here—she must, of course, define a role for her audience, one congruent with her persona, arguments, the facts as she knows them, etc. She must, as Minot argues, *both* analyze and invent an audience.[21] In this instance, after detailed analysis of her audience and her arguments, the student decided to begin her essay by emphasizing what she felt to be the genuinely admirable qualities of her neighbors, particularly their kindness, understanding, and concern for others. In so doing, she invited her audience to see themselves as *she* saw them: as thoughtful, intelligent people who, if they were adequately informed, would certainly not act in a harsh manner to those less fortunate than they. In accepting this role, her readers did not have to "play the game of being a member of an audience that 'really' does not exist" (Ong, "The Writer's Audience," p. 12). But they did have to recognize in themselves the strengths the student described and to accept her implicit linking of these strengths to what she hoped would be their response to the proposed "home."

When this student enters her history class to write an examination she faces a different set of constraints. Unlike the historian who does indeed have a broad range of options in establishing the reader's role, our student has much less freedom. This is because her reader's role has already been established and formalized in a series of related academic conventions. If she is a successful student, she has so effectively internalized these conventions that she can subordinate a concern for her complex and multiple audiences to focus on the material on which she is being tested and on the single audience, the teacher, who will respond to her performance on the test.[22]

We could multiply examples. In each instance the student writing—to friend, employer, neighbor, teacher, fellow readers of her daily newspaper—would need, as one of the many conscious and unconscious decisions required in composing, to envision and define a role for the reader. But *how* she defines that role—whether she relies mainly upon academic or technical writing conventions, literary models, intimate knowledge of friends or neighbors, analysis of a particular group, or some combination thereof—will vary tremendously. At times the writer may establish a role for the reader which indeed does not "coincide with his role in the rest of actual life" (Ong, p. 12). At other times, however, one of the writer's primary tasks may be that of analyzing the "real life" audience and adapting the discourse to it. One of the factors that makes writing so difficult, as we know, is that we have no recipes: each rhetorical situation is unique and thus requires the writer, catalyzed and guided by a strong sense of purpose, to reanalyze and reinvent solutions.

Despite their helpful corrective approach, then, theories which assert that the audience of a written discourse is a construction of the writer present their own dangers.[23] One of these is the tendency to overemphasize the distinction between speech and writing while undervaluing the insights of discourse theorists, such as James Moffett and James Britton, who remind us of the importance of such additional factors as distance between speaker or writer and audience and levels of abstraction in the subject. In *Teaching the Universe of Discourse*, Moffett establishes the following spectrum of discourse: recording ("the drama of what is happening"), reporting ("the narrative of what happened"), generalizing ("the exposition of what happens") and theorizing ("the argumentation of what will, may happen").[24] In an extended example, Moffett demonstrates the important points of connection between communication acts at any one level of the spectrum, whether oral or written:

> Suppose next that I tell the cafeteria experience to a friend some time later in conversation. . . . Of course, instead of recounting the cafeteria scene to my friend in person I could write it in a letter to an audience more removed in time and space. Informal writing is usually still rather spontaneous, directed at an audience known to the writer, and reflects the transient mood and circumstances in which the writing occurs. Feedback and audience influence, however, are delayed and weakened. . . . *Compare in turn now the changes that must occur all down the line when I write about this cafeteria experience in a discourse destined for publication and distribution to a mass, anonymous audience of present and perhaps unborn people.* I cannot allude to things and ideas that only my friends know about. I must use a vocabulary, style, logic, and rhetoric that anybody in that mass audience can understand and respond to. I must name and organize what happened during those moments in the cafeteria that day in such a way that this mythical average reader can relate what I say to some primary moments of experience of his own. (pp. 37–38; our emphasis)

Though Moffett does not say so, many of these same constraints would obtain if he decided to describe his experience in a speech to a mass audience — the viewers of a television show, for example, or the members of a graduating class. As Moffett's example illustrates, the distinction between speech and writing is important; it is, however, only one of several constraints influencing any particular discourse.

Another weakness of research based on the concept of audience as invoked is that it distorts the processes of writing and reading by overemphasizing the power of the writer and undervaluing that of the reader. Unlike Mitchell and Taylor, Ong recognizes the creative role the writer plays as reader of his or her own writing, the way the writer uses language to provide cues for the reader and tests the effectiveness of these cues during his or her own rereading of the text. But Ong fails to adequately recognize the constraints placed on the writer, in certain situations, by the audience. He fails, in other words, to acknowledge that readers' own experiences, expectations, and beliefs do play a central role in their reading of a text, and that the writer who does not consider the needs and interests of his audience risks losing that audience. To argue that the audience is a "created fiction" (Long, p. 225), to stress that the reader's role "seldom coincides with his role in the rest of actual life" (Ong, p. 12), is just as much an oversimplification, then, as to insist, as Mitchell and Taylor do, that "the audience not only judges writing, it also motivates it" (p. 250). The former view overemphasizes the writer's independence and power; the latter, that of the reader.

RHETORIC AND ITS SITUATION[25]

If the perspectives we have described as audience addressed and audience invoked represent incomplete conceptions of the role of audience in written discourse, do we have an alternative? How can we most accurately conceive of this essential rhetorical element? In what follows we will sketch a tentative model and present several defining or constraining statements about this apparently slippery concept, "audience." The result will, we hope, move us closer to a full understanding of the role audience plays in written discourse.

Figure 2 represents our attempt to indicate the complex series of obligations, resources, needs, and constraints embodied in the writer's concept of audience. (We emphasize that our goal here is *not* to depict the writing process as a whole—a much more complex task—but to focus on the writer's relation to audience.) As our model indicates, we do not see the two perspectives on audience described earlier as necessarily dichotomous or contradictory. Except for past and anomalous audiences, special cases which we describe paragraphs hence, all of the audience roles we specify—self, friend, colleague, critic, mass audience, and future audience—may be invoked or addressed.[26] It is the writer who, as writer and reader of his or her own text, one guided by a sense of purpose and by the particularities of a specific rhetorical situation, establishes the range of potential roles an audience may play. (Readers may, of course, accept or reject the role or roles the writer wishes them to adopt in responding to a text.)

Writers who wish to be read must often adapt their discourse to meet the needs and expectations of an addressed audience. They may rely on past experience in addressing audiences to guide their writing, or they may engage a representative of that audience in the writing process. The latter occurs, for instance, when we ask a colleague to read an article intended for scholarly publication. Writers may also be required to respond to the intervention of others—a teacher's comments on an essay, a supervisor's suggestions for improving a report, or the insistent, catalyzing questions of an editor. Such intervention may in certain cases represent a powerful stimulus to the writer, but it is the writer who interprets the suggestions—or even commands—of

FIGURE 2   The Concept of Audience

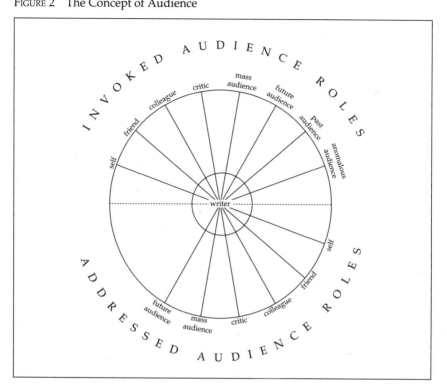

others, choosing what to accept or reject. Even the conscious decision to ac-
cede to the expectations of a particular addressed audience may not always
be carried out; unconscious psychological resistance, incomplete understanding, or inadequately developed ability may prevent the writer from following through with the decision—a reality confirmed by composition teachers
with each new set of essays.

The addressed audience, the actual or intended readers of a discourse,
exists outside of the text. Writers may analyze these readers' needs, anticipate their biases, even defer to their wishes. But it is only through the text,
through language, that writers embody or give life to their conception of the
reader. In so doing, they do not so much create a role for the reader—a
phrase which implies that the writer somehow creates a mold to which the
reader adapts—as invoke it. Rather than relying on incantations, however,
writers conjure their vision—a vision which they hope readers will actively
come to share as they read the text—by using all the resources of language
available to them to establish a broad, and ideally coherent, range of cues for
the reader. Technical writing conventions, for instance, quickly formalize any
of several writer-reader relationships, such as colleague to colleague or expert to lay reader. But even comparatively local semantic decisions may play
an equally essential role. In "The Writer's Audience Is Always a Fiction,"

Ong demonstrates how Hemingway's use of definite articles in *A Farewell to Arms* subtly cues readers that their role is to be that of a "companion in arms . . . a confidant" (p. 13).

Any of the roles of the addressed audience cited in our model may be invoked via the text. Writers may also invoke a past audience, as did, for instance, Ong's student writing to those Mark Twain would have been writing for. And writers can also invoke anomalous audiences, such as a fictional character—Hercule Poirot perhaps. Our model, then, confirms Douglas Park's observation that the meanings of audience, though multiple and complex, "tend to diverge in two general directions: one toward actual people external to a text, the audience whom the writer must accommodate; the other toward the text itself and the audience implied there: a set of suggested or evoked attitudes, interests, reactions, conditions of knowledge which may or may not fit with the qualities of actual readers or listeners."[27] The most complete understanding of audience thus involves a synthesis of the perspectives we have termed audience addressed, with its focus on the reader, and audience invoked, with its focus on the writer.

One illustration of this constantly shifting complex of meanings for "audience" lies in our own experiences writing this essay. One of us became interested in the concept of audience during an NEH Seminar, and her first audience was a small, close-knit seminar group to whom she addressed her work. The other came to contemplate a multiplicity of audiences while working on a textbook; the first audience in this case was herself, as she debated the ideas she was struggling to present to a group of invoked students. Following a lengthy series of conversations, our interests began to merge: we shared notes and discussed articles written by others on audience, and eventually one of us began a draft. Our long distance telephone bills and the miles we travelled up and down I-5 from Oregon to British Columbia attest most concretely to the power of a co-author's expectations and criticisms and also illustrate that one person can take on the role of several different audiences: friend, colleague, and critic.

As we began to write and rewrite the essay, now for a particular scholarly journal, the change in purpose and medium (no longer a seminar paper or a textbook) led us to new audiences. For us, the major "invoked audience" during this period was Richard Larson, editor of this journal, whose questions and criticisms we imagined and tried to anticipate. (Once this essay was accepted by *CCC*, Richard Larson became for us an addressed audience: he responded in writing with questions, criticisms, and suggestions, some of which we had, of course, failed to anticipate.) We also thought of the readers of *CCC* and those who attend the annual CCCC, most often picturing you as members of our own departments, a diverse group of individuals with widely varying degrees of interest in and knowledge of composition. Because of the generic constraints of academic writing, which limit the range of roles we may define for our readers, the audience represented by the readers of *CCC* seemed most vivid to us in two situations: 1) when we were concerned about the degree to which we needed to explain concepts or terms;

and 2) when we considered central organizational decisions, such as the most effective way to introduce a discussion. Another, and for us extremely potent, audience was the authors—Mitchell and Taylor, Long, Ong, Park, and others—with whom we have seen ourselves in silent dialogue. As we read and reread their analyses and developed our responses to them, we felt a responsibility to try to understand their formulations as fully as possible, to play fair with their ideas, to make our own efforts continue to meet their high standards.

Our experience provides just one example, and even it is far from complete. (Once we finished a rough draft, one particular colleague became a potent but demanding addressed audience, listening to revision upon revision and challenging us with harder and harder questions. And after this essay is published, we may revise our understanding of audiences we thought we knew or recognize the existence of an entirely new audience. The latter would happen, for instance, if teachers of speech communication for some reason found our discussion useful.) But even this single case demonstrates that the term *audience* refers not just to the intended, actual, or eventual readers of a discourse, but to *all* those whose image, ideas, or actions influence a writer during the process of composition. One way to conceive of "audience," then, is as an overdetermined or unusually rich concept, one which may perhaps be best specified through the analysis of precise, concrete situations.

We hope that this partial example of our own experience will illustrate how the elements represented in Figure 2 will shift and merge, depending on the particular rhetorical situation, the writer's aim, and the genre chosen. Such an understanding is critical: because of the complex reality to which the term *audience* refers and because of its fluid, shifting role in the composing process, any discussion of audience which isolates it from the rest of the rhetorical situation or which radically overemphasizes or underemphasizes its function in relation to other rhetorical constraints is likely to oversimplify. Note the unilateral direction of Mitchell and Taylor's model (p. 5), which is unable to represent the diverse and complex role(s) audience(s) can play in the actual writing process—in the creation of meaning. In contrast, consider the model [Figure 3] used by Edward P. J. Corbett in his *Little Rhetoric and Handbook*.[28] This representation, which allows for interaction among all the elements of rhetoric, may at first appear less elegant and predictive than Mitchell and Taylor's. But it is finally more useful since it accurately represents the diverse range of potential interrelationships in any written discourse.

We hope that our model also suggests the integrated, interdependent nature of reading and writing. Two assertions emerge from this relationship. One involves the writer as reader of his or her own work. As Donald Murray notes in "Teaching the Other Self: The Writer's First Reader," this role is critical, for "the reading writer—the map-maker and map-reader—reads the word, the line, the sentence, the paragraph, the page, the entire text. This constant back-and-forth reading monitors the multiple complex relationships between all the elements in writing."[29] To ignore or devalue such a central

FIGURE 3   Corbett's Model of "The Rhetorical Interrelationships" (p. 5)

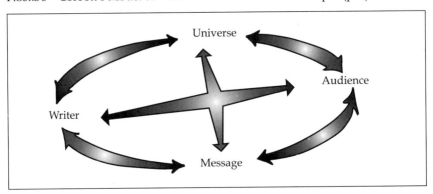

function is to risk distorting the writing process as a whole. But unless the writer is composing a diary or journal entry, intended only for the writer's own eyes, the writing process is not complete unless another person, someone other than the writer, reads the text also. The second assertion thus emphasizes the creative, dynamic duality of the process of reading and writing, whereby writers create readers and readers create writers. In the meeting of these two lies meaning, lies communication.

A fully elaborated view of audience, then, must balance the creativity of the writer with the different, but equally important, creativity of the reader. It must account for a wide and shifting range of roles for both addressed and invoked audiences. And, finally, it must relate the matrix created by the intricate relationship of writer and audience to all elements in the rhetorical situation. Such an enriched conception of audience can help us better understand the complex act we call composing.

AFTERWORD . . . .

During the conversations we engaged in as we wrote this brief afterword, we found ourselves circling around the notion of the epideictic, particularly as it relates to professional awards. Until quite recently, the CCCC Richard Braddock Award was one of a limited number of honors a person professing rhetoric and composition could receive. As winners of this award, we benefitted in a number of ways—from the personal pleasure of the epideictic moment itself to the professional capital that accrued as a result. Yet even at the time, and certainly since, we have had mixed feelings about this (or perhaps any) award: Who wins such honors, and for what reasons? Who does not win and why not? These questions underscore an obvious point: the epideictic moment celebrates—but also inevitably excludes.

We make these comments to emphasize the professional, political, ethical, and rhetorical situatedness of the Braddock Award and to highlight the ways in which the award serves to authorize the work of those recognized. This authorized work may of course reify the status quo, but it may also open a space for different and possibly more productive scholarly moves. In accepting the Braddock Award, we hoped out loud that "Audience Addressed/Audience Invoked" (AA/AI), the first coauthored essay to win the award, would help lead to growing acceptance of collaboration in our academic homes. We also hoped it would help generate more complex thinking about audience.

Subsequent years have seen such work—by Gesa Kirsch and Duane Roen, Peter Elbow, Jack Selzer, James Porter, Robert Roth, Douglas Park, Bennett Rafoth, Mary Jo Reiff, Rosa Eberly, and others. We have learned much from these efforts. But when we decided in the mid-1990s to talk and think again about the question of audience, we did not directly engage this conversation, choosing instead to revisit AA/AI. As we indicate in "Representing Audience: 'Successful' Discourse and Disciplinary Critique," the essay that resulted from that revisiting, we did so because we wished to "embrace multiple understandings of [AA/AI], and to acknowledge the extent to which any discursive moment contains diverse, heterodox, and even contradictory realities" (169).

Particularly relevant here is our recognition that AA/AI itself enacts exclusionary gestures by failing to explore the ways "audiences cannot only enable but also silence writers and readers" (170) and by unconsciously but persistently turning away from tension and contradiction in its consideration of both writing and schooling. In making these and other observations, we hoped to emphasize that "'success' is—in every case—more charged with tensions, competing motives, and trade offs than we would have imagined, tensions that . . . can and should inform our teacherly and writerly practices" (177).

To which we would now add: and professional practices (like the Braddock Award) as well. For certainly such awards, such markings of "success," are charged with precisely the kinds of tensions and competing motives we note. One useful way to begin unpacking these tensions might be to think about the audiences which such awards not only address and invoke but exclude, ignore, or transform.

—LISA EDE
Oregon State University

—ANDREA LUNSFORD
The Ohio State University

The Shifting Relationships between Speech and Writing

PETER ELBOW

Paradoxes . . . beset the relationships between the original spoken word and all its technological transformations. . . . [I]ntelligence is relentlessly reflexive, so that even the external tools that it uses to implement its workings become "internalized," that is, part of its own reflexive process. (Ong, *Orality*, 81)[1]

We have seen interesting work in recent years on the nature of speech and writing and the mentalities associated with each. The insights from these investigations are extremely valuable, but a dangerous assumption is sometimes inferred from them: that speech and writing are distinctly characterizable media, each of which has its own inherent features and each of which tends to foster a particular cognitive process, or "mentality."[2] I am interested in the cognitive processes associated with speech and writing, but instead of saying that each medium has a particular tendency, I will argue that each medium can draw on and foster *various* mentalities. This essay is a call for writers and teachers of writing to recognize the enormous choice we have and to learn to take more control over the cognitive effects associated with writing. This essay is in three parts—each showing a different relationship between speech and writing.

I. The Traditional View: Indelible Writing, Ephemeral Speech

Obviously writing is more indelible or permanent than speech. Speech is nothing but wind, waves of temporarily squashed air, waves that begin at once to disperse, that is, to lose their sound. Writing, on the other hand, stays there—"down in black and white." Once we get it on paper it takes on a life of its own, separate from the writer. It "commits us to paper." It can be brought back to haunt us: read in a different context from the one we had in

This essay was first published in *CCC*, Volume 36, Number 3, October 1985.

mind—read by any audience, whether or not we know them or want them to see our words.

Where the *intention* to speak usually results automatically in the *act* of speech, writing almost always involves delay and effort. Writing forces us not only to form the letters, spell the words, and follow stricter rules of correctness (than speech); we must also get into the text itself all those cues that readers might need who are not present to us as we write, who don't know the context for our words, and who don't know us or how we speak. In addition to this "contextualizing," we must capture onto the page some substitute for all those vocal and visual cues for listeners that we give without effort or attention in speaking. We can take nothing for granted in writing; the text has to say it all.

In the effort to do all these things as we write, how can we help but pause and reflect on whether what we are engaged in putting down is really right—or even if it is, whether it is what we really wanted to say? If we are going to take the trouble to write something down, then, we might as well get it right. *Getting it right,* then, feels like an inherent demand in the medium itself of writing.

Research (see Tannen, "Oral and Literate Strategies") shows that speech tends to carry more "phatic" messages than writing—messages about the relationship between the speaker and the listener or between the speaker and his material (e.g., "I know you're my friend"), even when the ostensible function of the spoken words is purely substantive or informational. Thus writing tends to carry a much higher proportion of "content" messages to absent readers—more permanent messages which are judged for validity and adequacy, not just accepted as social interchange.

This feeling that we must get things right in writing because written words are more indelible than speech is confirmed when we look to the *history* of speech and writing. The development of writing as a technology seems to have led to the development of careful and logical thinking—to a greater concern with "trying to get it *really* right" (see Ong, *Orality,* and his other works; Goody, *Domestication;* Havelock, *Plato*). Ong claims that the development of writing gave us a new "noetic economy," that is, a wholly new relationship to words and knowledge—new habits of shaping, storing, retrieving, and communicating what we know.[3]

We see a parallel argument about the teaching of writing. That is, leading theorists tell us that the poor thinking we see in many of our students stems from their not yet having made that great developmental leap from oral language strategies to written or literate language strategies (Lunsford, "Cognitive Development"; Shaughnessy, *Errors*). Obviously, students can think better when they can examine their thoughts more self-consciously as a string of assertions arranged in space. The technology of indelible writing permits students in a sense to step out of the flux of time: to detach themselves from oral discourse, from the context in which words are uttered and first thought about, and from the tendency in speech to rely on concrete and experiential modes of discourse. As Havelock emphasizes, writing helps to separate the knower from the known.

This contrast between the two media is reinforced when we turn to the story of how we learn to speak and to write as individuals. We learn speech as infants—from parents who love us and naturally reward us for speaking at all. Our first audience works overtime to hear the faintest intention in our every utterance, no matter how hidden or garbled that meaning may be. Children aren't so much criticized for getting something wrong as praised for having anything at all to say—indeed they are often praised even for emitting speech as pure play with no message intended.

What a contrast between that introduction to speech and the introduction to writing which most children get in school. Students can never feel writing as an activity they engage in as freely, frequently, or spontaneously as they do in speech. Indeed, because writing is almost always a requirement set by the teacher, the act of writing takes on a "required" quality, sometimes even the aspect of punishment. I can still hear the ominous cadence in my ears: "Take out your pens." Indeed, in the classic case of school punishment the crime is speech and the punishment is writing ("I will not talk in class. I will not talk in class."). Do some teachers still insist, as some of mine did, that ink must be used? The effect was to heighten our sense of writing as indelible, as the act of making irrevocable choices—as though there were something wrong about changing our minds.

I don't want to imply gradgrindish conditions which may no longer be widespread. But the school setting in which most of us learn to write and have most of our writing experiences till we leave school is just one more reason why we experience writing as more indelible than speech—and why we experience writing as inherently a medium for *getting it right.*[4]

But we need to turn this accustomed picture upside down.

II. Speech as Indelible, Writing as Ephemeral

As Roland Barthes says, "it is ephemeral speech which is indelible, not monumental writing. . . . Speech is irreversible: a [spoken] word cannot be retracted . . ." ("Death of the Author"). Precisely because speech is nothing but temporary crowdings in air molecules, we can never revise it. If we speak in the hearing of others—and we seldom speak otherwise—our words are heard by listeners who can remember them even (or especially) if we say something we wish they would forget. Once we've said (as a joke), "I've never liked that shirt you gave me," or (in a fight), "Well damn it, that *is* a woman's job," or even (in a seminar, without thinking about what our colleagues might think of us), "I've never been able to understand that poem"— or once Jesse Jackson refers to Jews in public as "hymies"—once any of these words are spoken, none can be undone.

Speech is inherently more indelible than writing also because it is a more vivid medium. When we speak, listeners don't just see our words, they see us—how we hold and move ourselves. Even if we only hear someone over the phone or on the radio—perhaps even someone we've never met—still we experience the texture of her talk: the rhythms, emphases, hesitations, and other tonalities of speech which give us a dramatized sense of her character or personality. And if we *don't* reveal ourselves more through our speech than our writing, that too is taken as a revelation: someone will say, as of Gary Hart, "he seems a bit cool and aloof."

But perhaps you will reply that *casual speech* is more ephemeral than writing. Yet there are plenty of occasions when we are trying as hard as we can to "get it right" in speech—because our speech is "a speech," or an "oral report," or discourse to strangers; or for some reason we feel we are being carefully judged for our speech, as in a job interview. Perhaps casual speech is more common in our culture—or in literate or print cultures—than in others. In oral cultures such as the Homeric Greek, the Anglo-Saxon, and the Native American, there was scorn for anyone who spoke hasty unplanned words. Perhaps we fall into the assumption that speech is ephemeral because we live in a blabbing culture.

In short, our sense of speech as ephemeral and writing as indelible stems not so much from the nature of speech and writing as media but from how and where they are most often used. (And researched. See Schafer, "Spoken and Written," for a corrective view.) Our paradigm for speech is casual conversation among trusted friends; our paradigm for writing is more formal discourse to a little-known audience or an audience that is likely to judge us on our utterance.

So far from speech being ephemeral, then, the problem with speech is that it isn't ephemeral enough. What we need is a mode of discourse that really *is* ephemeral—we need the luxury of being able to utter everything on our minds and not have anyone hear it until *after* we decide what we really mean or how we want to say it. Interestingly enough, the most indelible medium of all is also the most ephemeral: writing.

However indelible the ink, writing can be completely evanescent and without consequences. We can write in solitude—indeed we seldom write otherwise—we can write whatever we want, we can write as badly as we want, and we can write one thing and then change our mind. No one need know what we've written or how we've written it. In short, writing turns out to be the ideal medium for *getting it wrong*. (This evanescence of writing is enormously enhanced by the new electronic media where words are just electrical or magnetic impulses on a screen or a disk.)

Perhaps there's nothing new in the idea of writing as ephemeral. Perhaps the phrase from Barthes has tempted me into that Gallic weakness for trying to phrase the obvious as a scandal. In the days of parchment people wrote to last, but now we are flooded with ephemeral temporary documents.[5]

But though we float on a rising tide of ephemeral writing, our writing habits and instincts are dominated by the old assumption that writing is indelible. That is, most people, even when they are writing a draft that no one will read, nevertheless write by habit *as though readers were going to see it.* Do I exaggerate? Plenty of people experiment or make a mess as they write. Yet what do most people do when they are writing along and they suddenly wonder whether they really believe what they are about to write, or whether it holds up on examination, or even whether it is well phrased. Most people stop writing and don't resume writing till they have figured out what they want to say. This *feels* like a reasonable and normal way to behave, but notice the assumption it reveals: that the function of writing is to record what we have *already* decided—not to figure out *whether* we believe it. If we were speaking, we would be much more likely to speak the train of thought as it comes to mind even though we're not sure of our final opinion—as a *way* of making up our minds. It is almost as though we fear, as we write, that someone might at any moment swoop down and read what we have just written and see that it is rubbish.

Thus writing for most people is dominated by the experience of not writing: of elaborate planning beforehand to decide what to write and frequent pausing in midcourse to search for the right word or the right path. This nonwriting behavior is not surprising since *planning* is probably stressed more than anything else in advice to writers. (This advice is stressed not only in traditional textbooks but in recent ones such as Linda Flower's.) But because of my own difficulties in writing, I have come to notice the enormous cognitive and linguistic leverage that comes from learning to avoid the mentality dominated by the indelibility of writing and learning instead to exploit the ephemeral or "under" side of writing. It feels very different to put down words not as commitment but as trial, or as Barthes and some of the deconstructionists say, as play, *jouissance,* or the free play of language and consciousness. Thinking is enriched. Writing in this mode can produce an *immersion in discourse itself* that doesn't occur when we sit and think—an immersion in language that can entice us into ideas and perceptions we could not get by planning.

Exploiting the ephemeral quality of writing is often a matter of exploiting chaos and incoherence. Often I find I cannot work out what I am trying to say unless I am extremely disorganized, fragmented, and associative, and let myself go down contrary paths to see where they lead. (Note that what one is *trying to say* is more than what one *has in mind*—see Perl on "felt sense" in "Understanding Composing.") I can't be that incoherent when I start off trying to write it right. I can't even be that incoherent in speech. My listeners are too impatient for sense, for my main point. (Now I know why I often close my eyes when talking about something difficult: it is an instinctive attempt to blot out the audience and their implicit demand that I be clear and come to the point.) So when trying to write it right, and even in speaking, I must usually settle for the short run of *some* coherence—making *some* sense —and abandon the thread (only it's not really a thread because it's so broken) of the long-run, incipient, more complex meaning which has been tickling the back of my mind. But when I write in the ephemeral and fully exploratory mode for myself alone, I can usually find that meaning by inviting myself to wander around it and finally stumble into it. Thus whereas the commonsense view is that planning is more appropriate to writing than to speaking, the opposite is also true: we badly need arenas for *nonplanning* in our discourse, and speech is too constricting. For nonplanning we need private writing.

We think of the mind's natural capacity for chaos and disorganization as the *problem* in writing—and before we finish any piece of indelible public writing, of course, that incoherence must be overcome. But what a relief it is to realize that this capacity for ephemeral incoherence is valuable and can be harnessed for insight and growth. The most precious thing in this kind of writing is to find one contradicting oneself. It guarantees that there will be some movement and growth in one's thinking; the writing will not just be a record of past thoughts or prejudices. (Good teachers, in commenting on student papers, have learned to see contradictions in the text as positive opportunities for mental action and growth, not just as problems.)

But even when we have the safety of knowing that our words are private and ephemeral and that we will revise them into coherence, we often feel there is something dangerous about letting ourselves write down what is wrong or doubtful or ungainly, or even just something we are not sure we believe. To do so seems to violate a taboo that derives from a magical sense that writing is indelible even if no one else ever sees the words. We stop and correct our words or crumple up the sheet because it feels as though if we leave the wrong words there, they will somehow pollute us. Words on paper will "take"—debilitate the mind. Yet we cannot exploit the ephemerality of language unless we are willing to take the risk.

But why not use the *mind* for all this ephemeral work? Would God have given us a mind if he'd wanted us to waste all this paper writing down what's wrong or badly put? But that internal thinking process lacks a dimension which writing provides. When we just think inside our heads, the cycle of language is incomplete; we are prey to obsession. The thoughts, sentences, images, or feelings that play in our heads continue to play round and round. But when we write down those thoughts or feelings, the sterile circle is often broken: they have a place on paper now; they evolve into another thought or even fade away. Writing is a way to get what is inside one's head outside, on paper, so there's room for more.[6] (Of course speaking too can have this same function—"getting things out"—but sometimes the presence of a listener is a hindrance.)

I come here to what I most want to emphasize: the *mentalities* related to speech and writing. Ong and the others emphasize how the use of writing enhances logical, abstract, and detached thinking. True enough. But there is a very different kind of good thinking which we can enhance by exploiting the underside of writing as ephemeral. And like the effect Ong speaks of, this kind of thinking is not just an occasional way of considering things but a pervasive mode of cognitive functioning. I'm talking about the mentality that gradually emerges when we learn how to put down what's in mind and invite that putting down to be *not* a committing ourselves to it but the opposite, a letting go of the burden of holding it in mind—a letting go of the burden of having it shape our mind. Having let it go, our mind can take on a different shape and go on to pick up a different thought.

In this way writing can function as a prosthesis for the mind—a surrogate mind instead of just a mouthpiece for the mind. For the mind is a structure of meaning and so too is a piece of writing. The mind, as a structure of meaning, can grow and develop through stages and so too can a piece of writing. Thus writing provides us with two organisms for thinking instead of just one, two containers instead of just one; the thoughts can go back and forth, richen and grow. We think of writing as deriving meaning from the mind that produces it, but when all goes well the *mind* derives meaning from the text it produces. (Organization, or meaning, or negative entropy, can flow in both directions.)

I don't mean to sound too mysterious here. I am just talking about the common phenomenon of people's ideas developing and changing as a result of their thinking. It often happens as people live and talk and write over months and years. But in truth, people tend to stay stuck in their points of view. They are prevented from growing until they get out of or move past the structure of meaning that *is* their mind. Ong might say that indelible, careful writing enhances such growth. Yes, that's true when all goes well. But the crucial mental event in growth is often the *abandonment* of a position we hold. Ephemeral writing is usually better than careful writing at helping us abandon what we start out thinking. (See Elbow, *Teachers,* Appendix essay.)

Thus the potentiality in writing that I want to highlight here does not just involve generative techniques for getting first drafts written quicker, but rather a genuine change in mentality or consciousness. The original development of writing long ago permitted a new mentality that fostered thinking that was more careful, detached, and logical. But along with it and the indelibility that makes writing valuable came also a mentality that tends to lock us into our views once we have carefully worked them out in writing. In contrast, the cultivation of writing as ephemeral fosters the *opposite* mentality whereby we use discourse (and writing in particular) not so much to express what we think but rather to develop and transform it.

Before going on to Section III, I should emphasize that the opposite claims in the first two sections—that writing is both *more* and also *less* indelible than speech—do not really undercut each other. My celebration of writing as ephemeral in no way diminishes the fact that writing is also the best medium for being careful, for getting things right, for "quality." I am unrepentant about insisting that we can have it both ways—if we learn how.

We need writing to help domesticate our minds (the title of Goody's book about the development of literacy is *The Domestication of the Savage Mind*), but we also need writing as a way to unleash some cognitive savagery—which is often lacking in a "literate" world too often lulled into thinking that picking up a pencil means planning and trying to get things right. And speech, being a social medium, seldom leads us to the conceptual wilderness we sometimes need.

For not only is there no theoretical contradiction between the two functions of writing, it turns out that they enhance or reinforce each other. People can be *more* careful and get their final drafts *righter* when they spend some of their time unhooking themselves from the demands of audience and inviting themselves to get it wrong. And contrarily, people can be more fruitful in the mentality of nonsteering when they know they will turn around and shift consciousness—impose care and control and try for indelibility—before their text goes to the real audience.

III. WRITING AS SIMILAR TO SPEECH

Having indicated two ways in which speech and writing are *different* or *opposite* from each other, finally I want to argue how they are or can be essentially similar. I will proceed by focusing on a series of features characteristic of speech, and argue in each case why we should seek to foster them in writing.

To exploit the speech-like qualities of writing as we teach is a way of teaching to strength: capitalizing on the oral language skills students already possess and helping students apply those skills immediately and effortlessly to writing—a way of helping with the crucial process Ong calls the "internalization of the technology of writing."

(1) In informal speech situations we can utter our words spontaneously—comfortably, naturally, unselfconsciously—with full attention on our meaning and no attention on how we actually *form* the signs or symbols that convey our meaning. We can come close to achieving this situation in writing through the use of "spontaneous writing" or "freewriting": writing in which we put down whatever words come to mind—without regard to the conventions of forming words and without regard to the quality of the writing. We don't give the writing to an audience—or if we do, the audience merely "listens" to it for the meaning and doesn't respond (see Elbow, *Power*, 13–19). The work of Graves and Calkins shows how much we have tended to overestimate the amount of special knowledge or control of the medium people need for fluent and comfortable writing.

Speech is usually social and communal, writing solitary. But we can make writing communal too by having people write together and to each other in ways that are worth spelling out in more detail below.[7]

(2) Speech usually responds to a particular occasion and fits a particular context. It's not usually meant to last or be recorded—it's for a particular audience which is right there when the discourse is uttered and hears it right away. We can make all this happen in writing if we have students write in class or in small groups—particularly if they write about some issue or situation in which they are involved—and have them immediately share with each other what they write. The audience is right there and known; the writing is part of the context and the interaction of a particular group on a particular day. In speech, when something isn't clear, the audience asks for clarification right away. We can invite this naturally to happen in response to writing.

(3) In speech, the response—immediate, of course—is usually a *reply* to *what* has been said, not an *evaluative comment* on *how* it was said. And the reply is almost invariably an invitation to the speaker to reply to the reply. We can make this happen too in our teaching (though students often need

coaching to get out of the assumption that the only way to respond to a text is to criticize it).

For of course the point of speech is often not to be a final or definitive statement but rather to keep the discourse going and produce more discourse in response—to sustain an ongoing dialogue or discussion. We can easily give writing this quality too by making our course a forum for constant writing-in-response-to-each-other's-writing, that is, by stressing the ways in which writing naturally functions as an invitation to future writing or a reply to previous writing—which is how most writing in the world actually occurs. Paradoxically, it turns out that if we invite much of the writing in a course to be more temporary and speech-like (that is, if we relax some of the pretense of chirographic, i.e., formal, definitiveness), students often manage to achieve *higher* levels of text-like definitiveness or indelibility on the fewer pieces where we stress revision and transcendence of local context.

For obviously I am not arguing that we should exploit similarities to speech in *all* the writing we ask of students. Many of our assignments should stress indelibility—stress the need for tight, coherent, final drafts which are statements that could survive outside the context of local author and local audience. We can decide on how much writing to treat in one mode or the other depending on the students we are teaching. For example, if the course is for weak students who are scared or uncomfortable in their writing, I would go quite far in exploiting speech similarities.

Thus the teaching practices I have just described *could* be called condescending strategies: ways to manage the writing context so as to *relax* temporarily some of the inherent difficulties in writing as a medium.[8] But I wish to go on now to stress how writing of the very highest quality—writing as good as any of us could possibly hope to achieve—not only can but should have many of the essential qualities somewhat misguidedly labelled "inherent in speech."

(4) The best writing has *voice:* the life and rhythms of speech. Unless we actively train our students to *speak onto paper,* they will write the kind of dead, limp, nominalized prose we hate—or *say* we hate. We see the difference most clearly in extreme cases: experienced teachers learn that when they get a student who writes prose that is so tied in knots that it is impenetrable they need only ask the student to *say* what she was getting at and the student will almost invariably speak the thought in syntax which is perfectly clear and lively, even if sometimes inelegantly colloquial. If the student had known enough to "speak the thought onto paper" and then simply cleaned up the syntax, the writing would have been much better than her best "essay writing."

(5) Excellent writing conveys some kind of involvement with the audience (though sometimes a quiet non-obtrusive involvement). This audience involvement is most characteristic of oral discourse. The best writing has just this quality of being somehow a piece of two-way communication, not one-way—of seeming to be an invitation to the audience to respond, or even seeming to be a reply to what the audience had earlier thought or said. This

ability to connect with the audience and take its needs into account is *not* lacking in most students—contrary to much recent received opinion. Students use this social skill quite spontaneously and well in much of their speech to a present audience, but they naturally enough neglect to use it in much of their writing since the audience is less clear to them. We can easily help students transfer to writing their skill in connecting with an audience by having them write more often in a local context to a limited and physically present audience (as when they talk).

I am speaking here to what I see as a growing misconception about the inability of adolescents to "decenter": a dangerous tendency to make snap judgments about the level of a student's cognitive development on the basis of only a text or two—texts which are anything but accurate embodiments of how the student's mind really operates. Teachers and researchers sometimes describe the weakness of certain student writing as stemming from an inability to move past oral language strategies and a dependence on local audience and context.[9] But in reality the weakness of those pieces of writing should often be given the *opposite* diagnosis: the student has drifted off into writing to *no one in particular*. Often the student need only be encouraged to use *more* of the strategies of oral discourse and the discourse snaps back into good focus, and along with it usually comes much more clarity and even better thinking.

(6) Commentators like to distinguish speech from writing by saying that speech is reticent: it invites listeners to fill in meanings from their involvement in the context and their knowledge of the speaker. Good writing, on the other hand (so this story goes), must make all the meanings explicit, must "lexicalize" or "decontextualize" all the meanings, and not require readers to fill in. But here too, this talk about the inherent nature of speech and writing is misguided. It is precisely a quality that distinguishes certain kinds of good writing that it makes readers *contribute to* or *participate in* the meanings, not just sit back and receive meanings that are entirely spelled out.

Deborah Tannen, a speech researcher, illuminates this confusion ("Oral and Literate," 89):

> If one thinks at first that written and spoken language are very different, one may think as well that written literature—short stories, poems, and novels—are the most different from casual conversation of all. Quite the contrary, imaginative literature has more in common with spontaneous conversation than with the typical written genre, expository prose.
>
> If expository prose is minimally contextualized—that is, the writer demands the least from the reader in terms of filling in background information and crucial premises—imaginative literature is maximally contextualized. The best work of art is the one that suggests the most to the reader with the fewest words. . . . The goal of creative writers is to encourage their readers to fill in as much as possible. The more the readers supply, the more they will believe and care about the message in the work.

Although we can *maximize* the unstated only in imaginative literature, nevertheless, I believe it is unhelpful to go along with Tannen's oversimple contrast between imaginative and expository writing. Surely it is the mark of really good essays or expository writing, too, that they bring the reader *in* and get him or her to fill in and participate in the meanings, and thereby make those written meanings seem more real and believable. (I think of the expository writing of writers like Wayne Booth, Stephen Gould, or Lewis Thomas.) And even to the degree that imaginative literature is different from expository prose, we must not run away from it as a model for what gives goodness to good expository prose.

If we accept uncritically the assumption that "cognitive development" or "psychological growth" consists of movement from concrete "oral" modes to abstract "literate" modes, we are left with the implication that most of the imaginative literature we study is at a lower developmental and cognitive level than most of the expository writing turned in by students. I'm frightened at the tendency to label students cognitively retarded who tend to exploit those oral or concrete strategies that characterize so much good literature, namely narration, description, invested detail, and expression of feeling. I'm not trying to deny the burden of Piaget, Bruner, etc., etc., namely, that it is an important and necessary struggle to learn abstract reasoning, nor to deny that teaching it is *part* of our job as teachers of writing. Again I claim both positions. But there is danger in *over*emphasizing writing as abstract and non-speech-like. (Even Bruner makes a similar warning in his recent work "Language, Mind.")

(7) Commentators on orality and literacy tend to stress how speech works in time and writing in space. Ong is eloquent on the evanescence of speech because it exists only as sound and thus is lost in the unstoppable flow of time. In speech, past and future words *do not exist* (as they would do if they were part of a text): the only thing that exists is that fleeting present syllable that pauses on the tongue in its journey to disappearance. Speech and oral cultures are associated with narration—which takes time as its medium. Writing and literate cultures are associated with logic—which exists outside of time.

This is an important distinction and people like Ong are right to exploit its remarkably wide ramifications, but there is a danger here, too. In truth, writing is also essentially time-bound. Readers are immersed in time as they read just as listeners are when they hear. We cannot take in a text all at once as we can a picture or a diagram. We see only a few written words at a time. It is true that if we pause in our reading, we can *in a sense* step outside the flow of time and look back to earlier sections of the text, or look forward to later sections; I don't mean to underestimate the enormous contrast here with speech where such "back-" or "forward-scanning" is impossible. Nevertheless the essential process of reading a text is more like listening than looking: the essential phenomenology involves being trapped in time and thus unable to take in more than a few words at a time.

This point is not just theoretical. The problem with much poor or need- lessly difficult writing is the way it pretends to exist as it were in space rather than in time. Such writing is hard to read because it demands that we have ac- cess all at once to the many elements that the writer struggled to get into the text. The writer forces us repeatedly to stop and work at finding explanations or definitions or connections which he *gave,* it is true, or *will* give in a few pages, but which he does not bring to our minds now when we need them. (It often feels to the writer as though he's *already* given us the material we need when we are reading page two—even though we don't get it till page six—because he's *already* written page six when he rewrites page two.) Poor writers often assume that because they are making a document rather than a talk, they are *giving us a thing in space* rather than *leading us on a journey through time,* and that therefore they can pretend that we can "look at the whole thing."[10]

One of the marks of good writers, on the other hand, is their recognition that readers, like listeners, are indeed trapped in the flow of time and can take in only a few words at a time. Good writers take this as an opportunity, not just a problem. The drama of movement through time can be embodied in thinking and exposition as naturally as in stories. And the ability to en- gage the reader's time sense is not a matter of developing some wholly new skill or strategy, it is a matter of developing for writing that time-bound fac- ulty we've all used in all speaking.

(8) By reflecting on how writing, though apparently existing in space, is essentially speech-like in that it works on readers in the dimension of time, we can throw important light on the peculiar *difficulties of organizing or struc- turing a piece of writing.*

In thinking about organization in writing we are tempted to use models from the spatial realm. Indeed our very conception of organization or struc- ture tends to be spatial. Our *sense,* then, of what it means to be well organized or well structured tends to involve those features which give coherence to space—features such as neatness, symmetry, and non-redundancy. Giving good organization to something in time, however, is a different business be- cause it means giving organization or structure to something of which we can grasp only one tiny fraction at any moment.

A thought experiment. Imagine a large painting or photograph that looks well organized. Imagine next an ant crawling along its surface. How would we have to modify that picture to make it "well organized" for the ant? Since he cannot see the picture all at once, we would have to embed some tiny, simplified reductions or capsule "overviews" of the whole picture at periodic points in his path—especially where he starts and finishes. Oth- erwise he could never make sense of the barrage of close-up details he gets as he crawls along; he would have no overall "big picture" or gestalt into which to integrate these details. But if we should make such modifications we would make the picture much "messier" from a visual point of view.

The plight of our ant points to the interesting work in composition the- ory and cognitive science about "chunking" and short- and long-term memory and the magic number seven. (In effect, the ant needs the visual information "chunked" for him.) Because language is time-bound, its meanings cannot actually enter our minds through our eyes—its meanings must detour through memory. If eyes were enough, "chunking" would be much easier, for as gestalt psychology has shown, vision as a cognitive process involves the making of gestalts, i.e., automatic chunking. (See G. A. Miller's classic essay, "The Magical Number Seven.")

Thus the test of good organization in writing—as in speech—is not whether the text *looks* neat when diagrammed in an outline or some other visual scheme, but whether it produces an *experience* of structure and coherence for the audience in time. But how is this effect achieved? The issue is complex, but I would suggest that certain common features of speech help discourse function as coherent in time—and thus are helpful for creating the sense of good structure in a text. We are more likely in speaking than in writing to give the quick forward- and backward-looking structural aids that readers need when they are trapped in the flow of time. When we are speaking we are less likely to put our heads down and forget about the structural needs of our audience because our audience is right there before us.

Discourse is sometimes given coherence by the use of cyclical or spiral patterns characteristic of speech—or a kind of wave-like repetition in which new material is introduced only after some allusion (however brief) to the past material needed for understanding the new material. This is the archetypal back-and-forth movement of waves on a beach which Auerbach (*Mimesis*) relates to the rhythm of Old Testament poetry—or the homely "mowing long grass" pattern of movement where repeatedly you push the mower forward four feet and back two feet, so each piece of ground is covered twice: there is always a quick summary before going forward.[11]

Oddly enough, *lists* (that feature of oral and epic poetry) are remarkably effective ways to give structure to discourse in time. As researchers into document design have noticed, written texts are often much more coherent to readers when a connected chain of statements is reshaped into a main statement and a *list* of supporting or following items. Lists have an interesting cognitive characteristic: as we take in each item we tacitly rehearse our sense of what that item is an instance *of*. Thus, a list is a way of increasing unity and also giving readers a reiterated sense of the main point without having to repeat it explicitly for them.

Discourse is sometimes given coherence in time by the use of recurring phrases, metaphors, images, or resonant examples (not merely decorative or illustrative but structural) which "chunk" or function as micro-summaries. Such recurring miniature units are characteristic of oral discourse (and music). A phrase can continue to ring in the reader's ear or an image continue to appear in the mind's eye while we are trapped in the underbrush of prose, and thus give structure or coherence to an experience in time.

The big picture problem is really a problem of how to get readers to hold in mind a *pattern* or *relationship* among elements while having to focus attention on only one of those elements. Imagine an essay with three major points or sections (as with the present essay). If we think of it "structurally" or "from above"—that is, spatially—we see three emphases or focuses of attention, as so many paintings and photographs are organized triangularly. But what holds the picture together is the fact that in the realm of vision we can focus on one of the three main areas yet simultaneously retain our view of the other two and our sense of how they relate to the one we are looking at. With an essay, on the other hand, we can read *only* one small part at a time, and so it is hard to experience the *relationship* or *interaction* of the three parts.

Thus the problem of structure in a temporal medium is really the problem of how to *bind time*. Whereas symmetry and pattern bind space (and also bind smaller units of time—in the form of rhythm), they don't manage very well to hold larger units of time together. What binds larger units of time? Usually it is the experience of anticipation or tension which then builds to some resolution or satisfaction. In well-structured discourse, music, and films (temporal media) we almost invariably see a pattern of alternating dissonance-and-consonance or itching-and-scratching. Narrative is probably the most common and natural way to set up a structure of anticipation and resolution in discourse.

But how do we bind time with patterns of anticipation and resolution in *essays or expository writing?*[12] Here the tension or itch that binds the words is almost always the experience of some *problem* or *uncertainty*, that is somehow conveyed to the reader. Unless there is a felt question—a tension, a palpable itch—the time remains unbound. The most common reason why weak essays don't hang together is that the writing is all statement, all consonance, all answer: the reader is not made to experience any cognitive dissonance to serve as a "net" or "set" to catch all these statements or answers. Without an itch or a sense of felt problem, nothing holds the reader's experience together—however well the text itself might summarize the parts. (This is a common problem in the essays of students since they so often suppose that essays are only for telling, not for wondering.) I wish workers on coherence and cohesion would focus more on the ways in which writers convey a sense of felt problem or itch. Surely that does more to hold texts together than repeated words or phrases.

If it seems as though I'm trying to fiddle with our sense of structure in texts, I must plead guilty. For I think that we often call texts well structured when they are merely "neat" or symmetrical, but really don't *hold* together: we "look through" our temporal experience of the text to a projected outline of the meanings. Particularly as academics, we are trained to read this way. Other readers—"popular" or informal readers—often do not notice that atemporal neatness and so feel such texts as incoherent. Yet on the other hand such readers are sometimes *satisfied* with the structure of texts that are less "neat"—we would call them sprawling—because the writer has been able to string those sprawling elements together experientially in time.

Have I gone too far? Obviously this is a tangled matter. For we yearn for neatness, economy, and spatial structure in our texts: poor writing is often poor because of the lack of these features. The problems of structure in writing are subtly difficult. Because of the confusion introduced into our very notion of structure by the pervasive metaphor of space, I suspect that we are still waiting for the help we need in showing us simple and valid models of good structure in time. If we want to explain the structure of well-ordered expository writing, we probably would do well to look to studies of the structure of music and film and poetry. (See, for example, Meyer and Zuckerkandl on music.)

Yet we mustn't plead ignorance too fast. As speakers, everyone has had extensive experience organizing discourse in time to make it coherent to listeners. (I admit that coherent speech is rare—but not as rare as coherent writing. And it is true that we speak in dialogue more often than in monologue—but we have had more experience with monologue than with writing.) Thus, continual experience with speaking of all sorts—even experience in not being understood and then clarifying our meaning—has built up for all speakers extensive intuitive skill at organizing discourse in time.

Thus we do well to exploit these intuitive, time-oriented speech skills when we try to organize our writing (particularly expository or conceptual writing where organizational problems are most difficult). When we tell ourselves to "be careful about organization" or to "give good structure" to our text, we tend to think in terms of building blocks laid out in space, and thus we often fail to give our readers an experience of coherence and clarity (however neatly we pattern our blocks). If, on the other hand, we think of our structural problem as that of trying to speak a long monologue so it is coherent to listeners in time, we are more likely to invoke crucial temporal organizational skills at two levels:

(a) In the large, overall structure of our text, we are more likely to "tell the story" as it were of our thinking. This doesn't usually mean turning it into actual narrative (although that needn't be ruled out as the most natural and effective structure for thinking), but rather saying, "Where does this thinking *start*? Where is it *going*? And where is it trying to *get to*?" Our attempt to speak a monologue will get us to find the larger *movement* of thought and help us intuitively to appeal to the faculty of hearing and memory, not visual schematics.

(b) In the smaller structures of our text, we are even more likely to appeal directly to hearing if we think of ourselves as speaking a monologue, and this will help us naturally chunk shorter sequences of information or thinking (from one to several paragraphs) into "heard" units which will cohere and thus be more easily understood and remembered.

So here again my point is that in order to make writing good we should try to make it like speech. When we structure speech we naturally exploit our time sense, our hearing, and our memory; and we naturally build in patterns of tension and resolution, not just arrangement of parts.

(9) A final reason why writing needs to be like speech. Perhaps it is fanciful to talk of speech having a magic that writing lacks—call it presence, voice, or *pneuma*—but the truth is that we tend to experience meaning some-

how more *in* spoken words than written ones. (Socrates and Husserl make this point: see Searle, "The Word Turned Upside Down.")

This vividness of speech is illustrated in academic conferences where people speak written papers out loud. Because we are listening to *writing* presented orally, we may notice in a curiously striking way how it seldom seems as semantically "inhabited" or "presenced" as speech.

Of course most of us can convey *more* meaning by reading a written essay out loud than by trying to give a speech from notes—more precisely, clearly, and quickly too. Yet the moment-to-moment language of a recited essay (even if more precise) is almost invariably less "full of meaning" than the language of our actual live speech (even if that speech has some stumbling and lack of precision). In short, writing seems to permit us to get *more* meaning into words (get more said more quickly), but speech helps get our meanings integrated more *into* our words.

But why should it be that we seem to experience the meaning more in spoken words than written words? Is it just because spoken words are *performed* for us and so we get all those extra cues from seeing the speaker, hearing how she speaks—all those rhythms and tonalities? That is important, but there's something else that goes deeper: in listening to speech we are hearing mental activity going on—live; in reading a text we are only encountering the record of completed mental events. It's not that the audience has to *receive* the words while the mental activity is going on, but that the language has to be *created* while the mental activity is going on: the language must embody or grow out of live mental events. The important simultaneity is not between meaning-making and hearing, but between meaning-making and the production or emergence of language. The crucial question for determining whether discourse achieves "presence" is whether the words produced are *an expression of something going on* or *a record of something having gone on.*

To speak is (usually) to give spontaneous verbal substance to mental events occurring right at that moment in the mind. Even when we are stuck or tongue-tied we seldom remain silent for long: Billy Budd is the exception. Usually we say something about our inability to figure out what to say. To write, however, is usually to *rehearse* mental events inside our heads before putting them down. (Someone's speech usually sounds peculiar if he rehearses his words in his head before speaking them.)

My hypothesis then is that when people produce language *as* they are engaged in the mental event it expresses, they produce language with particular features—features which make an audience feel the meanings very much *in* those words. Here then is an important research agenda for discourse analysis: what are the language features that correlate with what people experience as the semantic liveness of speech? (See Halpern, "Differences," for a start at this job.)

Such research would have very practical benefits for writing theory, since of course writing *can* be as alive as speech. What characterizes much excellent writing is precisely this special quality of lively or heightened semantic presence. It's as though the writer's mental activity is somehow there in the words on the page—as though the silent words are somehow alive with her meaning.

When a writer is particularly fluent, she has the gift of doing less internal rehearsal. The acts of figuring out what she wants to say, finding the words, and putting them down somehow coalesce into one act—into that integrative meaning-making/language-finding act which is characteristic of speech. But even beginners (or writing teachers) can achieve this liveliness and presence when they engage in freewriting or spontaneous writing. It is this semantic presence which often makes freewriting seem peculiarly lively to read. One of the best directions for coaching freewriting is to tell oneself or one's students to "talk onto the paper."

Of course we cannot usually produce a carefully-pondered and well-ordered piece of writing by talking onto paper. In any piece of writing that has been a struggle to produce, there is often a certain smell of stale sweat. And freewriting or spontaneous speech may be careless or shallow (the meaning is *in* the words but the *amount* of meaning is very small). But if we learn to talk onto paper and exploit the speech-like quality possible in writing, we can have the experience of writing words with presence, and thereby learn what such writing *feels* like—in the fingers, in the mouth, and in the ear. This experience increases our chances of getting desirable speech qualities into the writing we revise and think through more carefully.

IV. Conclusion

I have argued three contrary claims: writing is essentially unlike speech because it is more indelible; writing is essentially unlike speech because it is more ephemeral; and writing is essentially *like* speech. My goal is to stop people from talking so much about the inherent nature of these media and start them talking more about the different ways we can *use* them. In particular I seek to celebrate the flexibility of writing as a medium, and to show that we need to develop more control over ourselves as we write so that we can *manage* our writing process more judiciously and flexibly. Let me end with three images for the writer (one to match each claim)—and with each image a mentality.

First, I see the writer clenched over her text, writing very slowly—indeed pondering more than writing—trying to achieve something permanent and definitive: questioning everything, first in her mind before she writes the phrase, then after she sees it on paper. She is intensely self-critical, she tries to see every potential flaw—even the flaws that some unknown future reader might find who is reading in an entirely different context from that of her present audience. She is using the "new" technology of indelible writing that Ong and others speak of and thereby enhancing her capacity for careful abstract thinking by learning to separate the knower from the known. She is learning the mentality of detachment.

Second, I see the writer in a fine frenzy: scribbling fast, caught up in her words, in the grip of language and creation. She is writing late at night—not because of a deadline but because the words have taken over: she wants to go to bed but too much is going on for her to stop. She has learned to relinquish some control. She has also learned to let herself write things she would never show to anyone—at first anyway. By exploiting the ephemeral underside of writing, she learns to promote the mentality of wildness with words—the mentality of discourse as play. And perhaps most important, she has learned to promote the mentality of involvement in her words rather than of detachment or separation. But because that involvement is so totally *of the moment,* she knows she may well write a refutation tomorrow night of what she is writing tonight. She writes to explore and develop her ideas, not just express them.

Third, I see the writer at her desk conjuring up her audience before her in her mind's eye as she writes. She is looking *at* them, speaking *to* them— more aware of the sound of her spoken words in her ear than the sight of her written words on paper. She is the writer as raconteur, the writer with the gift of gab. She is not "composing" a text or "constructing" a document in space—she is "uttering" discourse in time; she is not "giving things" to her readers, she is leading readers on a mental journey. She is a bit of a dramatist, using discourse as a way to *do* things to people. She is involved with her discourse through being involved with her audience. Often her audience is a genuine community and her writing grows out of her sense of membership in it.

Is one of these modes of writing better? I don't believe so. Yet in the end I think there *is* a single best way to write: to move back and forth among them. And I believe there is a particular mentality which the technology of writing is peculiarly suited to enhance (as speech is not), namely *the play of mentalities.* We can learn to *be* all three writers imaged above. Writing can show us how to move back and forth between cognitive processes and mentalities which at first may seem contradictory, but which if exploited will heighten and reinforce each other.

AFTERWORD . . . .

What a relief and pleasure it is to get the Braddock Award when you are scared that maybe you are all wrong. It didn't prove I was right, but it sure made me feel better.

The first thing that hit me when I read back over my essay and some of the notes is my memory of working with Richard Larson. He was a powerful and effective editor who played a big role in helping make composition a more scholarly and professional field. Not that I always enjoyed it. I might have guessed what was in store when his reply to my initial submission said, "I'd like to have the essence of your paper." And here's another classic Larson line: "Your point, though not easy and obvious, isn't complicated."

But looking forward rather than back, I'd love to see these Braddock essays serve as seeds for further research and study. Two issues of phenomenology continue to gnaw at me from my essay.

1. What is structure *in writing? Not as we think of it in diagrams, but as readers really experience structure. Even though texts are layed out on paper in space, they are actually* experienced *in the dimension of time. Our concept of structure and most of our words for it are built on visual/spatial metaphors—and tend to imply visual/spatial experience rather than aural/temporal experience. The test of good structure in a piece of writing is not whether the text* looks *neatly structured when outlined or shown in some visual scheme, but whether it produces an* experience of coherence in time—*a sense of felt connectedness among parts. The problem then is how to bind time—how to get a reader to* feel together *events that take place ten or fifty minutes apart. A lot of competent writing by skilled writers that doesn't really work well for readers may suffer from the writer's trying to apply spatial models of neatness and structure to temporal phenomena.*

I am not satisfied with the light thrown on all this by traditional studies of coherence and cohesion. I'd urge graduate students and mature scholars to look at successful speeches and successful music (phenomena in time)—and at good theorists of speeches and music. I have a hunch that a key is the experience of anticipation, tension, dissonance or itch—and especially how that can bind stretches of time when it is answered with experiences of resolution, relief, and harmony.

2. What is felt meaning *in words? It is often said that spoken words tend to thrust their meanings into our minds more vigorously and actively than written words do. But this formulation distracts from an important question for writing: some* written words *convey more felt meaning than others. We need to know more about this. I'd love to see more phenomenological investigation.*

—Peter Elbow
University of Massachusetts, Amherst

Detection, Diagnosis, and the
Strategies of Revision

LINDA FLOWER, JOHN R. HAYES,
LINDA CAREY, KAREN SCHRIVER,
AND JAMES STRATMAN

evision is a perplexing subject. Everyone, including the students who don't do it, seems to acknowledge its virtue. Yet the research on revision points up a decided split between teachers' claims and students' performance. Teachers assert that the practice of multiple drafts is the key to good writing; it is the professional's method of choice. Furthermore, they define the goal of revision as substantive change: revision can lead to re-seeing, restructuring, even reconceptualizing the entire discourse. Revision, the establishment asserts, is a powerful, generative process.

Many students, however, seem to operate with a different definition. A number of studies, including one by the NAEP (National Assessment of Educational Progress), suggest that by and large students simply don't revise (NAEP, *Write/Rewrite*). If they do, their texts may get worse (Perl, "Composing"; Beach, "Self-Evaluation"). For many writers, revising is not a generative practice, but appears to be a set of rule-governed actions for proofreading and correcting. This working definition of revision is strongly at odds with the teachers' generative theory. Why?

If teachers and professionals are right about the nature and power of revision, why are students slow to take advantage of such a good thing? One answer may be that revision requires ability, not just motivation. Or it may be that we haven't succeeded in making our generative version seem practical or operational enough to use. For example, just how does one go about the business of "reseeing" anything? In writing this paper, we feel that one step in understanding and teaching this art may be to translate our enlarged notion of revision into a more explicit description of the thinking processes this act requires. Doing so is not without hazard. It means translating a complex process with many variables into a necessarily limited set of heuristics—hoping we have discovered those powerful heuristics which have a far-reaching effect. However, as teachers we constantly gamble on doing just this—on capturing the key variables, on teaching the intellectual skills that make a difference in

This essay was first published in *CCC,* Volume 37, Number 1, February 1986.

performance. As researchers we are attempting the same thing. This paper is an effort to describe some of the key intellectual actions which underlie the process of revising and which most affect its practice.

Descriptions of Revision Practice in Expert and Novice

Research suggests that experienced and novice writers differ in their implicit theories of the revision process, in how they behave during revision, and in the changes they are likely to make in the text. To begin with, they bring different assumptions and language to the task. Sommers' students faced revision like the grim reaper, prepared to tramp through a text cutting and "slashing out." The goal, as they describe it, is to fix errors rather than rethink; the primary tool is deletion. In contrast, many experienced writers conceptualize the task as discovering content, structure, and voice (Sommers, "Revision"; Murray, "Revision"). Likewise, Beach's extensive revisers expected their revisions to make major alterations to the substance of a draft, and they brought a working vocabulary to the task that made such holistic revamping possible. Unlike the nonrevisers who "mimicked formulaic textbook language" (e.g., "sounds choppy") in evaluating drafts, the extensive revisers were able to generalize about their plans and problems. Even though the extensive revisers were not necessarily the best writers, Beach observed that their more abstract representation of a text in terms of key points or patterns of development often provided a "reference point for work on the next draft" (Beach, "Self-Evaluation," pp. 161–162).

Secondly, experienced and novice writers make different use of their reading of drafts. The good writers in Bridwell's study (who were defined by their highly-rated papers) made nearly 30% of their revisions *after rereading* the first day's work during the period between drafts. Poor writers made little use of this time, making 96% of their changes *as they were writing* one draft or the other. "The possibility exists that these students hardly re-read their papers before they began again with a new version . . . or merely re-copied with a few minor changes" (Bridwell, "Revising," p. 216). Likewise, the students (of average ability) in a study by Atwell reread their text twice as often as the basic writers. Yet, when these students were prevented from reading, it affected them less (Atwell, "Text"). We suspect that the key variable here is not reading itself. Rather, the better writers are using reading of drafts to construct a sense of the text's current gist and/or to form a rhetorical plan which will guide revision. Under normal conditions the building and retrieval of this plan is prompted by rereading. If the text is removed, as it is in blind writing experiments (cf. Blau, "Invisible"), then the plan must be held in memory. The key process here may not be reading but building that working image of the text.

Finally, experts and novices make different kinds of changes with strikingly different frequencies. Typically, novices focus on convention and rule-governed features (Nold, "Revising"; Sommers, "Revising"). More importantly, as Faigley and Witte show, these changes have little effect on the text's meaning. By analyzing the propositional structure of the text, Faigley and Witte were able to distinguish revisions which alter meaning from those which change only the surface structure. Their student writers kept meaning changes to a cautious 12%, whereas advanced students and adults more than doubled that figure at 24% and 34% respectively (Faigley and Witte, "Revision").

These and other studies build a consistent picture of differences between experts and novices. However, these correlational results don't let us build a prescriptive pattern for how one should revise. For one thing, we don't know if the features we see in expert behavior are really the cause of the expert's success. Would students who mimicked this behavior by revising more and changing meaning produce expert revisions? Does the outward behavior capture the essential process? We think not, for this reason.

Revision is by nature a strategic, adaptive process, not a predictable procedure. One revises only when the text needs to be better. What the expert actually does will be highly sensitive to what Faigley and Witte have called "situational variables," such as, how good the text is to begin with, how much the writer knows about this topic or genre, and how high his standards for success are. These variables govern the goals, the procedures, and the kinds of text changes an expert would make (e.g., even an expert doesn't make meaning-level changes if he doesn't *need* to). As Halpern and Liggett ("Computers") astutely point out, our current image of revision as an extended, discovery-based process reflects the habits of the novelists, journalists, essayists, and academicians usually studied. We often assume that substantial revision is an obligatory part of invention. However, studies of writers on the job reveal quite different strategies adapted to the technology of word processing or the demands of first-time-final drafts (Gould, "Letters"; Van Dyke, "Executives"). Dictating, for example, encourages writers to do advance rather than on-line planning and to remember plans and current text rather than review or "reread" the tape as they compose (Halpern and Liggett, "Computers").

A complex decision process underlies the visible behavior of revising. That is why a description of statistically typical group behavior is not a prescription for how to do it. For example, even though our research shows that expert writers happily ignore many surface problems of spelling, grammar, and style, it seems unlikely that advising students to do the same would produce equally expert revisions. Or consider the common-sense assumption that more revision would mean better papers (Beach, "Self-Assessing"), which was disproved in Bridwell's study ("Revising"), in which the most extensively revised papers were at the top and bottom of the quality scale. In a study of younger writers, the revisions of eighth-graders actually lowered the quality of the text (Bracewell, Bereiter, and Scardamalia, "Control"). The *amount* of revision is simply not the key variable. And revision as an obligatory *stage* required by teachers doesn't necessarily produce improvement, especially if the writer has put effort into the planning and writing. Revision, then, is a strategic action, adapted to the necessities of the task.

A Theoretical Perspective on Revision

In modeling the intelligent revision process of real writers, it seems to us that the key variables will not be how many or what kind of changes writers make, but how well they adapt the text they have to the goals they want to achieve. From our theoretical perspective, the two key variables underlying expert performance are likely to be *knowledge* and *intention*. Each needs the other.

1. **Knowledge.** When a writer chooses to go beyond simply redrafting (i.e., creating a new rather than improved text), revision can make a surprisingly heavy demand on a writer's knowledge. To begin with, the skilled reviser must be able to recognize conceptually complex features of a text, such as its argument, and detect weak ones, as well as recognize more explicit errors such as a comma splice. Skilled revision also involves the ability to use tests and procedures. Supposedly simple activities such as proofreading can often be hard to do even when one knows the rules and tries hard (Shaughnessy, "Errors"). Finally, the writer must possess strategies for dealing with the problems detected. Responding to problems in texts draws on both declarative knowledge about texts and their features and procedural or how-to knowledge such as strategies for making revisions. Perceptivity, for instance, can depend on both one's schemas and one's mental procedures for reading and testing a text. Although some of this knowledge, such as our grammar, is quite unconscious and automatic, revision often involves making the tacit explicit. It demands active usable knowledge.

2. **Intention.** Intention determines whether a reviser actually "uses" the knowledge she may be said to "possess." Intention enters the process in two places: in the form of an initial problem representation—the reviser's image of the task itself (cf. Sommers, "Revision")—and in the form of the goals and criteria she brings to bear during evaluation. Many of these guiding intentions are tacit: an argumentative essay is likely to activate automatically such criteria as "be logical," whereas another genre, such as a love note, might not. One's intentions, goals, or criteria are often built into the representation of the task. That is to say, they are built into the experienced writer's representation. Some intentions, however, are the result of more conscious decisions. In practice, the experienced writer may have automated some of this decision process, while the inexperienced writer may be only dimly aware that other decisions are possible. However, both writers are, willy nilly, making choices with consequences. Intentions affect performance in a number of ways: by directing the writer to set goals which define a level of satisfaction and level of effort (Halpern and Liggett, "Computers"), by directing a trade-off of speed for quality (Gould, "Letters"), and by leading the writer to choose some strategies over others, such as to recast the discussion or merely patch up the text. We suspect that in some instances, "poor" revisers are simply students whose intentions and goals differ—whether through ignorance or choice—from the intentions and expectations of the instructor. Knowing when to use knowledge can be as difficult as acquiring it.

If a given performance in revision depends on a dynamic interplay of knowledge and intentions, how can we model the process of an effective reviser? A gross behavioral description (e.g., time on task, amount of reread-ing) would have to be qualified into oblivion. An analysis of final products alone would be misleading. For example, we would not say that a good re-viser would always make more revisions, change the macrostructure, or dis-cover new meanings, even though we value these relatively difficult actions when the situation demands them. In turning descriptive research into pre-scriptions, we must avoid creating new rigid rules of the kind Rose ("Rules") saw operating in invention. We must deal with the fact that revision in ex-perts is based on a highly conditional decision process.

One approach to this problem is to step back and describe or model the basic thinking process which underlies revision itself and then to look within that process for those places where experts and novices make different deci-sions or handle the process itself differently. We might think of these as "gates" or hurdles in the process—places that make special demands on the writer and make a visible difference in performance.

Perhaps a word about how process models of this sort work as theories would be in order. The cognitive process model we will present here is an at-tempt to identify the central, underlying processes a writer naturally goes through and to propose a working hypothesis about how these processes are organized. In the working hypothesis we will present, revision is a process that not only draws on the writer's knowledge, but actively generates new knowledge. Its two major processes, **evaluation** and **strategy selection,** work in an active interplay with three kinds of knowledge: the goals a writer has (and may modify as a result of evaluation); the **problem representation** the writer creates during revision; and the **strategies** he or she can bring to bear.

It is easy to misread a cognitive model, such as the one in Figure 2, as if it were a more familiar kind of document—a recipe for revision or a pre-scribed set of steps. A model does contain temporal information about the or-ganization of processes in terms of what must precede or will affect other processes. But note that the model shows the flow of *information,* not stages in observable behavior. For instance, the act of evaluating may force a change in the writer's goals (or flow of new information back to the writer), while the focus of the writer's attention remains on the task of rewriting.

The cognitive process model presented here differs from a textbook or "how-to" model in yet another way. It is a guide to research in expert/novice differences rather than a model of an expert. It gives us the superstructure of the process; however, it doesn't try to assert how a given subprocess should be handled. Like the obligatory program in a piano competition or a fiddler's contest, the model only asserts that everyone is playing the same song (e.g., doing evaluation). It isn't intended to describe just how the experts (or novices) will do it. On the other hand, like any theory, it exerts a strong influ-ence on what questions seem worth asking, such as, do the problem repre-sentations experts build look different from those of novices? A model leads us to consider certain basic processes and ask how people use them and what difficulties they are most likely to have.

Finally, a cognitive process model of the sort presented here is both a theory and a distillation of data. It represents in our case the range of processes observed in detailed data on fourteen writers, whose behavior, we should add, invalidated a number of other "reasonable" models we constructed along the way (Hayes, Flower, Schriver, Stratman, and Carey, "Revision"). Because such a model is data-based rather than speculative, it reflects the behavior of individual writers rather than of the world as a whole. However, this means that it can offer us a concrete working hypothesis which can be tested against new evidence.

The theory of revision that stands behind this model is presented in detail elsewhere. Here we wish to *use* the model to look at three major "gates" or hurdles that the revision process presents to beginning writers: detecting problems in text, diagnosing those problems, and selecting a strategy. Our plan for the paper then is to begin with a quick walk through the model, looking at the major cognitive processes a writer must manage, and then to focus on these three sources of expert/novice differences. Within each section we try to combine previous research with our own work in order to build an integrated picture of what we do know about the revision process and to point out what we don't. An overview of the paper's organization may be helpful.

    I. A Working Model of Revision

   II. Detecting Problems in Texts

  III. Diagnosing Problems

  IV. Selecting a Strategy

   V. Models and Individual Differences

I. A Working Model of Revision

The REVIEW Process: Evaluation and Revision

Our walk through the process of revision will begin with a writer in the midst of composing. Whether this act of revision lasts for five seconds or twenty-five minutes, it begins with the writer's evaluative review of either written text, mental text, or a writing plan. In terms of our earlier model of cognitive processes in writing (Flower and Hayes, "Theory"), the writer has entered the REVIEW process. As Figure 1 shows, the writer's focus of attention has changed; she has chosen at this instant neither to PLAN nor to TRANSLATE (produce text) but to initiate the REVIEW process with the act of Evaluation. We use the word "choose" to suggest a change in the dominant focus in the writer's attention; however, we observed earlier that Evaluation (like idea Generation) can act as a priority interrupt that can burst into any other process without notice. The process modeled in Figure 1 is a hierarchical process; that is, sub-systems or processes are nested within more inclusive processes. The REVIEW process is defined or carried out by its twin processes

FIGURE 1   A Model of Cognitive Processes in Composing

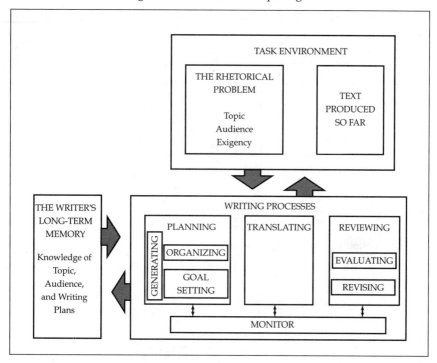

of Evaluating and Revising. With this paper we hope to go more deeply into how these two sub-processes are in fact conducted.

Experienced writers appear to do a good deal of evaluation—constantly monitoring their progress, evaluating not only the text but their own current writing strategy, and even themselves as writers (Elbow, "Teachers"; Murray, "Revision"). Although excessive monitoring and the judgments of an overbearing internal critic can stifle the process (Rose, "Rules"), much evaluation is positive, appearing in protocols as brief interjections of "O.K.," "good," "all right now," often located at the end of composing episodes (Flower and Hayes, "Pause"). A positive evaluation usually leads the writer back into the task—a return to PLANNING or TRANSLATING. The event we wish to explore in detail is the other possibility—the negative evaluation of a current text or plan.

The theory of revision on which this paper is based is embodied in the shorthand of a cognitive process model in Figure 2. Seen in overview its main elements are these:

Task Definition.   Our hypothetical instance of revision began in a sense much earlier when the writer set up an image of the revision task itself, deciding, for instance, to work at the level of the whole text or merely to proofread.

FIGURE 2   Cognitive Processes in Revision

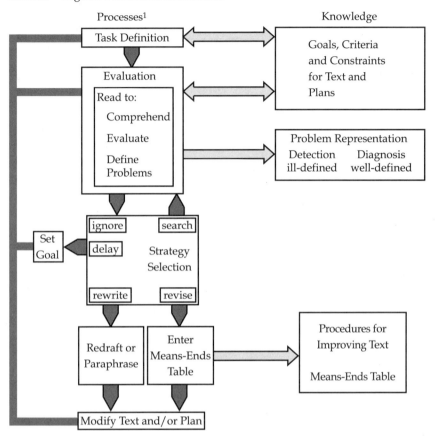

1. Cognitive process models such as this one are conventionalized ways to describe two important features of a process: 1) the way information flows during the process and 2) the structure of the process, in the sense of the options people appear to have (or the actions they in fact take) given a previous action.

Reading the structure of this model involves noting three things:

1. The Processes (represented on the left) result in the creation of, or call for the use of, Knowledge (represented on the right). See the light arrows.

2. Information of a different sort flows between Processes (as indicated by the dark arrows). In practical terms, a flow of information from one Process to another entails a change in the writer's attention, as control of the writer's cognition passes from one subprocess of revision to another. (Note how the dark shading represents this flow of control; the light shading indicates the flow of Knowledge.)

3. The flow of information between Knowledge and Processes and between different Processes in this system is highly reciprocal. The cognitive process of revision as a whole which is hypothesized here has a great deal of *potential* for feedback among the subprocesses.

For example, we could follow the sequence of a reviser in the process of Evaluation. We observe that within that process she has given herself the goal of Defining a Problem. (The fact that she has chosen to set this more demanding goal for her Evaluation process, rather than simply reading to detect problems, may lead us to infer that she is an experienced writer. As our study observed, novices typically set lower aims for their Evaluation process.)

The output of this subprocess of Evaluation is a Problem Representation (see the box on the right) which can range from an ill-defined representation, or simple detection, with little information about the problem to a well-defined representation or diagnosis. The output of our reviser's Evaluation turns out to be a Diagnosis of a problem with the tone of the text. In effect, her act of evaluation has created a fairly well-defined representation of a problem. The next question is what to do about it. When her attention moves to the process of Strategy Selection, she decides, as it happens, that the better part of wisdom

Evaluation. In a simpler model of Evaluation this process would be limited to fault-finding or the detection of dissonance. The model presented in Figure 2, however, attempts to account for the far more generative and complex process we in fact observed. To begin with, Evaluation is a constructive process, based on the process of reading for comprehension. In reading for Comprehension (i.e., trying to build a mental representation of the text), the reader imposes certain constraints on that process. That is, a person who is reading for comprehension has certain goals a text must meet (e.g., truthfulness, logical consistency, etc.), and will automatically detect if a text fails to meet these goals. So some evaluation can occur simply as a side effect of reading.

When that same reader reads to Evaluate (e.g., to see if the text has any problems; to give it a grade; or to decide if it is finished), he or she chooses, in effect, to raise the ante and to entertain a larger, more inclusive set of constraints. The reader as evaluator imposes additional goals or criteria on the text (e.g., this technical description which I understand must also appear clear and interesting to an audience of freshmen). In a sense then, the process of evaluation simply turns up the power on the reading process: it enlarges the set of constraints that the mental representation one is building must meet and turns reading into testing.

This escalation is even clearer when that same reader accepts the even more demanding goal of Defining the Problem he or she detects. When a teacher, for example, goes beyond evaluation to diagnosis, or when a writer does the same with her own text, they are placing an even greater burden on the Evaluation process, asking it to entertain even more inclusive goals, such as, "discover why this description seems unclear."

Our model of Evaluation, then, describes a generative process built on the principle of a *progressive enlargement of the goals and constraints one entertains.* This has a number of implications which we will only mention here. One is that Evaluation itself can lead to the discovery of new possibilities, not

---

would be to Delay work on this tone problem. So she Sets a Goal (in this case to read for tone later) and this change in goal becomes part of her Task Representation and a part of the Goals and Criteria she has for the text (see the boxes at the top of the model). Notice how information has flowed from one process to another. The shaded channels/arrows on the left of the model represent these active lines of communication between processes and the way control of the writer's mental activity can shift from one process to another. In fact, pondering her Strategy Selection an instant later, she decides that this is not enough; the tone problem she has diagnosed is so significant that she wants to change her whole rhetorical stance and create a different relation with her reader—and in doing so she alters the content of her Goals and Criteria in a significant way.

The processes of Evaluation, Diagnosis, and Strategy Selection have led our reviser to rethink her goals for the text and to make some far-reaching changes in the revision task which she gave herself. Such a decision may well lead her into either a fresh attempt—a Rewrite—or it may lead her to Revise by turning to her repertory of revision strategies. This knowledge of what to do (one's "means") given the problem one sees (one's "ends") is defined in the model as a Means-Ends table. Finally, one of the most important links, which is implicit in the lowest box of this diagram, is the link which may lead our reviser out of revision, back into either planning or text production (see Figure 1). Revision is only a part of the larger action.

In a process as complex and interactive as revision, there are many actions and relations one cannot hope to capture in a graphic model; nevertheless, models are a way of turning our observations of this dynamic process into more explicit and testable hypotheses.

just errors. Secondly, it can operate as a relatively automatic process in response to the reviewer's standard goals and criteria for texts or for a given type of discourse. Third, this basic cognitive process operates not only on written text, but on mental text and even plans. Finally, because Evaluation is sensitive to permutations in the reviewer's goals, knowledge, and current process, it lets us see the source of some striking differences in expert and novice performance.

Consider, in our hypothetical instance of revision, some of the possible paths an expert or novice might be likely to take through Evaluation. One of the obvious central components in reading to Evaluate or to Define Problems is the process of testing the text against one's intentions. However, such testing could be either an automatic output of reading or a conscious choice. And what entity is the reviser going to test—her written text, her mental text, or her plans? Finally, we must remember that "intention" is only a term of convenience to indicate the amazing array of goals, constraints, criteria, and expectations writers bring to evaluation. These may range from standard expectations for discourse and text in general, to vague intentions for this text (e.g., "sound sensible"), to specific rhetorical plans.

The dynamic interplay between what a writer knows, intends, and does becomes more open to observation if we view evaluation as a generative, constructive act. The output of this process—the writer's problem representation—can tell us still more about the goals and criteria the writer is actively entertaining.

Problem Representation.   The problems which writers represent to themselves range along a continuum, going from quite ill-defined problems (e.g., "this just doesn't sound quite right") to extremely well-defined ones (e.g., "I forgot the second 'l' in 'speling'"). Although ill-defined representations, at the lower left end of the continuum, are common and often necessary, they are little more than mere Detections. They recognize that a problem exists, but contain very little information about the problem. Representations in the right half of the spectrum take on the character of a Diagnosis: as the problem becomes more well-defined, the representation carries both more information about the problem and more implied strategies for solving it.

Strategy Selection.   On the basis of his or her representation of the problem, the writer must determine an action, which includes the possibility of searching for more information (i.e., *re*representing the problem in a more elaborated way), delaying action, or ignoring it altogether. The major strategic choice, however, appears to be between the two processes of Rewrite and Revise. We are using these two terms in a particular sense to capture an important difference we observed. Writers who choose the Rewrite process simply extract the gist from their extant text (written or mental) and use that to generate *new text*. In essence they try to say it again, say it differently with *little or no input from an analysis of the problem*. This is a fast, efficient process that can work at both global levels (Redrafting the whole text) or local ones (Paraphrasing the current sentence). In the Revise process, on the other hand, the act of writing is guided by the Diagnosis and any revision strategies the writer may have attached to that diagnosis. We can think of this set of strategies and goals as the writer's Means-Ends table. This repertory of Ends (recognized problems) and Means (possible actions for dealing with those problems) spans the entire range of actions we normally associate with revising, from rule-governed procedures for "fixing" a text to wholesale plans for "reseeing" it.

This theory of revision has a number of distinctive features. First, it describes revision as the interaction of knowledge (on the right hand side of the model) and a set of underlying processes (noted on the left). Distinguishing these elements helps us track the path of strategic choice through revision and will help us discover which parts of this process experts and novices handle differently.

Secondly, it treats Evaluation as a constructive, generative process and tries to account for some important sources of variability within it. Just as the evaluative process reflects changes in the scope of the reviser's goals, the output of Evaluation—the Problem Representation—also varies in the amount of information this evaluative process generates.

Finally, this model of revision describes a process with many gates or hurdles: there are many places where knowledge and intention interact (e.g., the goals you entertain in evaluation affect which problems you detect). There are also many places in this process where the results of a prior act determine the course of the next (e.g., you are only likely to fix the problems you represent). The model helps us predict points in this interactive process that might make special demands on a writer or be a source of trouble for the novice. In the discussion which follows we will focus on three major gates: *detecting* that a problem exists; *building a diagnostic representation* of that problem, and *selecting a strategy.*

II. Detecting Problems in Texts

Some of the problems people detect during Evaluation are the spontaneous result of reading for comprehension. However, as teachers we are particularly interested in what happens when the writer/reader takes on the additional goals of reading to evaluate and define. When this happens additional standards, demands, and/or expectations for the text (i.e., the goals, constraints, and criteria noted in Figure 2) come into play. In a sense the reader's standards for what is judged as "comprehensible" simply go up from, say, "must have a discernible topic" to "must have a tightly-knit, logical exposition of a topic." The attempt to build such a mental representation from the current text (e.g., a well-knit, logical one) constitutes a *test* of that text. We believe it is this *constructive* process which underlies what others have described as comparison or detecting dissonance.

Let us ask then, what allows this constructive test to succeed or fail? Evaluation or testing is often understood as a process of comparison, pattern matching, or category recognition. As such it underlies many complex cognitive acts, including concept recognition (Bruner, Goodnow, and Austin, *Thinking*). Yet how can we say that a writer detects a dissonance or a failed comparison between text and intention when the second side of the equation, an "ideal" or "correct" or intended text, doesn't exist—when there is no template to "match" the current text against? As we hope to show, evaluation depends on two constructive processes which often affect the reviser's ability to detect problems: representing both the text and one's intentions to one's self.

Representing the Text.   Revisers must read the text as an input to revision, but it is important to think of reading as a metaphor for **represent to oneself.** The reader in this sense is constructing his or her own internal, mental representation of the text. Revisers read not only the surface written text but also unwritten text in their heads. Or they may read/represent the underlying text base or gist, as when skimming an entire section for its drift or focus. (Cf. Witte's discussion of revising a "pre-text," in "Revising.") This form of reading is especially evident when people read to revise someone else's text. In addition, our model asserts, people not only operate on the text or text base, they also "read" and revise their own plans. The same cognitive processes we see people using to evaluate and modify text are also used to revise their plans and goals. A text is simply one instantiation of the writer's meaning; a plan represents that meaning in another, less elaborated, less constrained form (Flower and Hayes, "Images"). Revision operates on meaning in all its forms. The experienced writers in this study were particularly adept at working with the larger, more abstract units of plans and gists. It may even be that substantive revision or "reseeing" cannot go on unless a writer has created a manageable representation (e.g., a gist or a plan) to work with.

These experts also revealed another creative aspect of the Evaluation process. They used it to observe what they had wrought and in the process to discover fresh, even surprising aspects of the text and to set up new, potential plans and goals (e.g., "now, that's a good point; I could use it as an example"). Evaluation as discovery can change the intentions by which the text is subsequently tested.

"Reading text" as we use the term, then, refers to the act of representing to oneself this rich mix of written texts, and unwritten gists, plans, goals, and possibilities (Flower and Hayes, "Images"; "Cognitive Theory").

Representing One's Intentions.   In order to evaluate a current "text," a reviser must also represent her intentions. A negative evaluation is a sense of dissonance between these two internal representations of text and intention. As Gabriel Della-Piana puts it, "revision is not 'making a poem better,' it is making the poem more consonant or congruent with one's image of what the piece of writing is intended to accomplish" ("Poetry," p. 106).

Intentions take many forms. In a cognitive sense, intentions are one's goals and plans for the current text as well as the criteria and models for texts in general that one brings to the task. They are not defined by what one may "know" or have been taught but by the knowledge that is actively brought to the task, that is, by the criteria you "think" to apply. Even then, people's intentions are often so abstract and ill-defined that evaluation can be a very imprecise matter of judgment. In fact, writers' failures to detect (what others consider) blatant problems are sometimes dramatic. For example, Bond, Hayes, and Flower ("Law") asked a group of Washington lawyers to revise a piece of tortured federal regulation prose for the benefit of lay readers. According to one lawyer, the sentences were long enough to choke a horse. But some of the lawyers simply couldn't find anything to revise. Although they had agreed to be subjects, were giving verbal protocols of their revision efforts, and were diplomatically given a second try at the task, they simply *failed to see* problems a normal reader would have with that impenetrable legal text. They failed to detect a dissonance.

The point is that, in evaluation, writers are comparing the text *as they read it* to that set of intentions and criteria *which they represent to themselves.* And unfortunately this representation of intention is not a nicely-formed, idealized version of a text—a sort of Platonic template for easy comparison. Instead, it is likely to consist of 1) a unique network of goals and intentions built up during planning which is guiding the act of writing, and 2) a vast set of standard and genre-specific tests and criteria for good writing already stored in the writer's long term memory. (Cf. Nold's ["Intentions"] classification of writing subtasks, which is ordered from Intentional features, such as the writer's purpose and topic, to Conventional features such as usage and spelling.) This representation of goals and criteria may also be quite abstract (e.g., make this "interesting"; the ideas should "flow"). And at any given time some intentions may be much more active than others. This changing salience creates that surprising day-after experience of seeing one's text with fresh eyes. Furthermore, the recognition of one type of problem may block awareness of another by preempting attention or highlighting certain criteria or goals at the expense of others. To sum up, detecting problems in a text— even achieving that initial sense of dissonance—calls on two non-trivial constructive processes: representing a "text" through reading (or memory), and representing one's intentions. And both are affected by the writer's willingness to entertain dissonance itself (Young, "Rhetoric").

Research on revision suggests that the process of detection often goes awry for two major reasons: the writer who is attempting to compare intention and text has either a poor representation of the text before him, or an inadequate representation of the intentions (goals and criteria) he should be using. Revision depends heavily on both skill in reading the text and on the adequacy of one's planning and one's repertory of standards. A number of recent studies have begun to fill in our picture of Evaluation by describing some of the intellectual operations it requires and some of the ways it can go wrong.

An Inaccurate Representation of the Text

Some writers have difficulty with revision because they are content to work with a vague or approximate representation of the text. David Bartholomae found that when basic writers read their own texts aloud, they unconsciously "corrected" a high percentage of the errors in verb endings, noun plurals, syntax, and spelling appearing in the text ("Error"). Yet when asked to locate the errors in the text, they were unable to detect the difference between their "correct" intentions (e.g., "I was suspended from school") and the actual text (e.g., "I was suspense from school"). Perhaps, as Bartholomae suggests, these students are still learning the conventions of the print code which translates oral discourse into writing. Patricia Laurence diagnoses this problem as a form of "perceptual recklessness": the meaning of the sentence dominates attention, squeezing out awareness of surface structure ("Error").

This problem is not confined to basic writers. Professional proofreaders accommodate the difficulty of actually seeing the text as it is by techniques such as working in pairs (with one person to read the original, spell words, verbalize commas, etc.) or by reading from the bottom line up in order to defeat the clever attempts of inference to fill in the words that should be there. These detection techniques, however, depend on having that perfect "original" for a template, and they can't deal with the more important problems of logic, organization, and meaning.

Some of the most intransigent detection problems occur when the text neglects to specify something, such as a referent, that is already obvious to the writer. In reviewing, the writer can blithely "read" her intended meaning into the text. Writers try to outmaneuver their memory by leaving time between composition and revision for intentions to fade. However, as Bracewell, Bereiter, and Scardamalia ("Control") have shown, a mere time lag has no effect on the revisions of younger writers (grades 4–12). They argue that the real issue is not time but the presence or absence of the cognitive process of comparison itself. Time makes the process easier, but only if you are already doing it.

One of the unanswered questions for writing research is, how do writers in fact distinguish their intended meaning from a text's meaning? This question is raised experimentally in Bartlett's ("Learning") study of how children learn to handle anaphora or reference devices and to detect ambiguity. In order to create cohesion and suggest that two noun phrases share the same referent, English uses three main devices: definite articles, lexical repetitions, and pronouns. However, as Bartlett's example below illustrates, this process of signaling anaphoric reference often goes awry in children's texts:

> One day a man left his house. Another man was standing outside. The man took out a letter and gave it to him.

The intended referent would no doubt be crystal clear to the writer who is visualizing the whole event, but the reviser must detect the difference between her intention and the information actually available in the text. Intentions have a way of muscling into the reading. As Bartlett showed, it is much easier to spot rule-governed errors than it is to spot ambiguity (in which one must distinguish between an intended meaning and an explicit meaning available in the text). Bartlett's fifth-grade students did equally well at detecting missing subjects or predicates and detecting faulty referents when they occurred in *other* students' texts (detecting about 50% of the planted errors). However, when asked to edit their *own* texts (which also contained a sizable sample of these same errors), their ability to detect the ambiguous references dropped to only 10% (5 of 52), while performance on the rule-governed missing subjects or predicates stayed the same (17 out of 30). Bartlett's study as well as Bartholomae's suggests that seeing the text and not one's intentions is no mean feat. It may involve not only knowing written conventions but also imagining an *inferred meaning* created by the interaction of a reader and the text.

If these studies suggest that managing one's attention and accurately decoding text are important, Witte ("Topical Structure") shows how students' sense of the top-level propositions (or gist) of a text can have an even broader effect on the topical structure of their revisions. When students were asked to revise a well-structured but complex paragraph from a textbook to make it clearer, both good and poor revisers appeared to bring similar goals to the task: everyone tried to create shorter sentences, reduce syntactic complexity, and make the sentence topic coincide with the grammatical subject and initial position where possible. However, only the high-scoring revisers reconstructed the paragraph around the gist of the original paragraph (i.e., around its central proposition about its major topic), organizing their sentences to support its meaning. The low-scoring revisers appear neither to have perceived the original gist nor to have constructed a coherent topical focus of their own.

This is a provocative study; it argues that there is a direct connection between the focus and meaning one constructs from reading a text and the topical structure and coherence one constructs in revision. Since many writers work collaboratively (i.e., on each other's texts) or from pre-existing texts, the accuracy of such reading could have a large effect on their ability to evaluate and to revise. More broadly, it suggests one way the text one has already written could affect the subsequent course of composing. The question is, when writers explore their knowledge and try to discover meaning by writing, do they always emerge at the end of composing a paragraph, for example, with a clear conceptualization of their gist (i.e., of a top-level assertion about their topic)? Or do they have to go back at times as *readers of their own text* to construct a discourse topic, much as the subjects in the Witte study did? We think revisers do depend on reading. Various studies suggest that many times writers *do not* have a clear representation of the gist in their own minds, especially if their knowledge is complex or if it has a list-like or narrative structure in memory (Bereiter and Scardamalia, "Conversation"; Flower, "Writer-Based Prose"; Langer, "Topic Knowledge"). Creating such gists from one's drafts is a demanding intellectual maneuver (Elbow, "Teachers"). This suggests that writers, like their audience, are at times required to "read" and construct a more condensed representation of their own text—of the gist of a paragraph or the focus of the text as a whole—in order to revise effectively.

Our emphasis here on "representation" helps explain why students have some of the problems they do. To wit: the process of Reading to Evaluate requires the reviser to construct a representation of his own text or text plan as a basis for comparing intention and text. As one reads, even more information and more constraints are added to working memory. As the richness of the information grows, so does the problem of managing it. From various studies, we can piece together some of the ways revisers, trying to limit these added constraints, can fail to "see" problems in texts. To begin with, some people, like Calkins' fourth-grade Random Drafters ("Children's Rewriting"), simply don't read their texts at all or do so only in a cursory fashion (Bridwell, "Revising"), using the text as merely a stimulus to generate new material—a different rather than better text (Bracewell, Bereiter, and Scardamalia, "Myths"). Handwritten drafts are often so illegible that the writer trying to "figure out the rough draft" (Bean, "Word-Processing") sees only local problems and emerges with a fragmented picture of the meaning. Here is where the real benefit of word processors to composing may lie—the writer can work with readable, updated texts. Yet even with good copy, the reader may have trouble or not take the trouble to construct an image of the gist, discourse topic, or focus that does justice to what he actually said (Witte, "Topical Structure"). A writer who does not perceive a focus, a rhetorical plan, or a schema for the larger units may simply use reading to handle local transitions, looking back only a sentence or two at a time, testing the current sentence against the semantic and syntactic patterns of its close neighbors rather than against the larger rhetorical plan (Atwell, "Text"; Perl, "Composing"). Recent studies with word processors show how "seeing" the text is more of a strategic than a physical problem. Text editors seem to help the good writer get better, i.e., to do more of what he already did. But they don't change the tendency of both good and poor student writers to make local changes and to avoid making additions at the level of the paragraph or idea cluster (Collier, "Word Processor"). Learning to "see" extended pieces of discourse as chunks held together by a unifying purpose and a gist is a matter of construction as much as perception. As a strategy for dealing with the extra information and constraints rereading supplies, seeing gists is clearly a desirable advance over the alternative strategies of ignoring the text or representing it in discrete, bite-sized pieces. But it is also hard to learn and rarely directly taught.

To sum up, the reviser's ability to detect problems depends on her ability to provide an accurate representation of the text itself, separate from her own internal representation of meaning. And it may depend on her ability to "read" a draft text and construct a sense of its discourse topic, its gist, or its underlying plan or purpose, which can then be tested against the writer's broad rhetorical intentions. As this reminds us, the Evaluation process also depends on the reviser's representation of intentions, which we shall consider now.

A Limited Representation of Intentions

A second reason writers fail even to detect problems (i.e., problems *we* perceive) can be traced to their own inadequate representation of the intentions of the text (defined as including goals, constraints, and criteria). Such a writer might perceive the text quite clearly, as Bond's ("Law") lawyers no doubt did. But he might bring to the task such a limited set of criteria for good writing and such an impoverished set of goals for the text (e.g., "I [the writer] should be able to understand it") that his detector would only pick up a narrow range of mismatches. Like a radio with a narrow bandwidth, or like Sommers' ("Revision") student writers primed to locate and slash out "unnecessary" words, a reviser will detect only events that violate his own actively represented internal standards. Beach and Eaton ("Factors") found that college students do have difficulty trying to articulate their own goals and intentions. When asked to state the content, function, and intended effect on the reader for each paragraph in an essay, students often gave content summaries in response to all three questions. Their notion of intention seemed limited to a restatement of the gist.

Intention is in part a mirror of one's knowledge. The store of rich, easily accessed criteria available to a solid grammarian, an accomplished stylist, or an experienced journalist allows them to detect whole categories of difficulty unknown to the novice. Faigley and Witte's comparison of the revisions made by inexperienced and expert writers is a dramatic case in point ("Revision"). Unlike previous research on revision, this study distinguished between surface and meaning changes: that is, between those surface changes which preserve meaning or affect only the microstructure of the text, and those changes which alter the macrostructure in a way that would change a summary of the text. The inexperienced student writers behaved in the manner we have come to expect, sticking to surface and formal, microstructure changes (e.g., there were only 1.3 macrostructure changes per 1000 words [.13%]). In contrast, when the adults (experienced journalists) were given the drafts of three of these inexperienced students' papers to revise, 65% of their changes were macrostructure or meaning-level changes. Yet this striking difference is not so surprising if we look at the criteria these writers brought to the task—criteria and goals the novices probably never thought of. One of the originals, a rather pedestrian piece of student prose, began:

> Our state capital is a beautiful structure that is very unique. When entering the city of Austin, it is a site that stands out amongst the skyrises that surround it. This building is known for its architecture, the craftsmanship inside the building and the history that it holds.

The revision by the expert seems to share little more than a common topic. It begins:

> The Capitol of Texas remains the most impressive building in Austin, even though bank skyscrapers and university towers have challenged its one time dominance of the skyline. The Capitol will never

again be as prominent as the Nation's Capitol in Washington, where surrounding buildings have been kept in scale, but the richness of the structure itself has not been diminished. It remains a statement of the grandiose vision of the makers of modern Texas.

The basis of this journalist's revision was not a recrafting faithful to the original plan, but rather wholesale importation of more sophisticated, "expert" intentions. His detection is based on his own wider knowledge and different standards. As the rewriter said:

> The story lacked information. It needed an angle. State capitols are normally uninteresting, so I used the Texas angle. Texans do things differently.

In this example, the writer's intentions are fully conscious and explicit, but what does it mean, in the heat of revision, to actively "represent" one's intentions, especially when certain goals or criteria are considered only if they are violated? One answer is that much of the knowledge of an experienced writer is stored in the form of automatic condition/action rules. That is, the writer has developed a body of standard criteria for acceptable text—expectations for grammatical form, logical flow, or a plain style—as well as special sets of criteria appropriate to the task or genre. A violation of any of these expectations becomes the "condition" for the condition/action rule to fire, and it triggers an immediate awareness or detection. This sort of knowledge depends very little on conscious attention. Because it is stored as condition/action rules, whenever a condition is met (e.g., when a noun and verb disagree), its appropriate action (i.e., call out a fault) is triggered.

Yet even these "automatic" processes seem to be subject to the focusing effects of intention. Proofreaders traditionally try to manage their attention by working in two passes: one to "proof" for errors and the other to "read" for logic and content. Why does this practice seem necessary? Halpin ("Editing") found that certain kinds of errors—spelling, subject-verb agreement, pronoun case, and dangling modifiers—could be accurately detected with a single search process. That is, it took no more time to search a text with multiple potential error types than it did to scan for the most time-consuming error type, which was spelling. For errors of this sort, revisers can apparently rely on condition/action rules and on efficient parallel mental processing. There is no need for separate passes. However, reading for rhetorical problems calls for a more active process that we are just beginning to understand.

Knowledge stored as condition/action pairs is extremely convenient: it helps us stop automatically at red lights, hit the carriage return without thinking, and detect many problems in texts with little demand on our attention. Having sophisticated goals and well-learned criteria of this sort is obviously important. However, the assumptions and conscious intentions we bring to a text may carry even more weight; failures to detect may also be failures to use or activate the knowledge one has. The goals and criteria one *actively* represents to oneself gain an important place in focal attention where they exert an even stronger influence on what one sees and the absences one detects. For example, because Faigley and Witte's expert represented his goals as journalistic success, the lack of information he noted in the text was a salient omission. If, as we might imagine, the novice writer had modeled his intentions on the high school "hot-air" essay, such solid information would scarcely be thought necessary—its omission would go undetected. We should note that people set their own threshold for acknowledging a detection (e.g., faint warning bells don't count), just as they can later choose to ignore even the clangers they do hear.

The point here is that what a writer "knows" may have less effect on performance than what part of the information he actively "represents" as relevant. When writers plan, or when editors size up the goals of the text to be edited, or when teachers remember problems from the student's last paper, this effort serves a priming function for detection: it brings certain areas of knowledge to attention and makes others more accessible and likely to be recalled. This priming effect depends on the difference between active and quiescent knowledge. It operates even when the writer is only partly aware of the goals and criteria (e.g., the intentions) she has represented to herself.

We can see the dramatic effect intention has on student revision in a study by Hays ("Audience") in which a group of advanced peer tutors and basic writers wrote an essay to high school students on using marijuana. Using a combination of protocol analysis and interviewing, she found that roughly half the advanced and half the basic writers (total of 5) approached this task with "both a strong sense of a general audience and a strong degree of purpose vis-à-vis that audience" (Hays, p. 10). The other students focused on the teacher, had slight awareness of audience, or simply intended to express their own point of view regardless of the audience. When the papers were evaluated on a primary trait scale, the group with a strong sense of purpose and audience swept the boards: the advanced high-purpose students wrote the four top ranked papers and the high-purpose basic writers in the group even scored above some of their more advanced peer tutors. The surprising result of this study for our purposes is that the high-purpose group not only wrote better papers, but made far more substantive revisions. Although the size of this sample is small, Hays' basic writers violated our assumptions about what basic writers look for when they revise. The basic writers with a high sense of purpose and audience made 80% of their revisions for substantive reasons; the low-purpose group averaged 33% such revisions. (Even though they were assigning different tasks, compare Faigley and Witte's 1981 study in which only 12% of the revisions made by inexperienced writers involved meaning changes.) Although these high-purpose writers had a number of low-level errors to detect (and did so), it appears that they chose to suspend concern about style and correctness in order to focus on larger problems such as anticipating the reader's needs and objections. Their strong sense of intention and elaborated representation of the audience appeared to have a dramatic effect on the kinds of problems they detected and revised.

To sum up, Evaluation that leads to a problem detection is in part an automatic process. Reading itself can flag some problems; and the more condition-action pairs one has learned, the larger one's repertory of relatively automatic procedures. However, Evaluation is also a constructive, goal-driven process guided by the intentions (e.g., goals and criteria) one brings to the task. The way in which a reviser represents her intentions not only activates awareness of certain features of texts, but focuses and in turn limits attention.

Is Detection Enough?

Detection is a necessary and potentially difficult process. Without that initial sense of dissonance between intention and text, nothing else happens. However, detecting a problem doesn't mean that the writer can solve it—he may not even know what the problem is. In trying to isolate some of the component skills a reviser must manage, Scardamalia and Bereiter ("Development") have hypothesized that children possess many of the production skills necessary for rewriting, but simply fail to use them because of the excessive demands that writing places on attention. They were able to test this hypothesis experimentally through "procedural facilitation"—a research method that "facilitates" by reducing the demands made by one particularly difficult process which blocks the exercise of other skills. Those blocked skills then have a chance to operate, if the child possesses them (Bereiter and Scardamalia, "Conversation"). In the case of revision, they hypothesized that the difficult process which blocked other skills was simply the effort that had to be exerted to monitor and direct one's attention—to *remember* to revise. In order to remove this "hobble" on performance, they supplied some of the executive control that children lack, in the form of a game-like routine the child applied to every sentence he or she wrote. This routine is based on a theoretical model of the revision process they call the CDO routine—a three-step process of Compare, Diagnose, and Operate. The child is asked to apply this routine to each sentence as he or she writes: 1) first, evaluate the current sentence; 2) if something is wrong, try to diagnose the trouble; and then 3) attempt to fix it. The child is given further help with the first and third steps (Compare and Operate) by having a set of cards which suggest typical evaluations ("this is good," "people may not believe this") and typical revision tactics ("I'd better give an example," "I think I'll leave it this way," "I'd better change the wording").

The results of this study help us tease apart the subskills that support adult revision. To begin with, the children not only appreciated and used the rather cumbersome CDO procedure, they all thought it helped them do something they normally didn't do (evaluate their texts), and 74% said it made the process of writing easier. Furthermore, their choice of general evaluative statements from the set of cards resembled that of an adult. But when asked to explain their choice (to diagnose the problem they had detected), many children were unable to go beyond the original evaluative phrase. Their comments often focused on specific details or tried to justify why the faulty sentence was written that way in the first place. Furthermore, their writing itself did not improve, and in fact the revisions of the eighth-graders were actually changes for the worse. Scardamalia and Bereiter suggest that children may often carry out this initial comparison (a part of the process we are calling Evaluate) and then go no further. Diagnosing, selecting tactics, and handling sentence production are more demanding subskills which the children are still learning.

The picture of revision emerging from the research surveyed here suggests that the revision process presents a series of hurdles for the writer: it includes a series of semi-independent subprocesses any one of which may be the source of difficulty. For example, in analyzing a group of students' detailed self-evaluations done over an entire term, Rubin ("Self-Evaluation") found that even the "A" students missed 75% of the problems their instructor identified, and they were correct in the problems they did identify only slightly more than half the time. In a task which encouraged self-assessment before revision, Beach and Eaton ("Self-Assessing") found that at best college freshmen attempted to change only 52% of the problems they had themselves noted. (And the average number of attempted revisions appeared to be closer to 24%.)

These studies are starting to identify derailing points in the revision process; Bartlett ("Learning") shows one reason why it stops. We can see clear evidence of the difference between detecting a problem and fixing it in the performance of sixth- and seventh-graders who were given two kinds of pronoun referent problems. In one case, students had only to repeat a proper name to clarify the text (as in "John and Joe lived on Elm Street. He . . ."). In the other, students had to generate new information (as in "A boy lived on Elm Street. Another boy lived next door. The boy . . ."). Students detected the two problems with almost equal frequency (62% and 52% respectively) and were able to fix 95% of the instances of the first type they detected. However, when they had to generate new information to disambiguate the sentence (as in "A boy *named Charles* lived on Elm Street . . ."), the ability to fix problems fell to 58%. Taken together, these studies suggest that while detection can be a difficult process itself, it is only the first step in revision. The entire process asks writers to coordinate yet other skills, each of which, like detection, must be learned.

In our research on revision we tried to extend this inquiry in two ways. First we wanted to see how adults carry out these component processes in the context of a natural task. Accordingly, we asked questions such as these: what problems do writers detect? do writers normally diagnose? if so, what form does diagnosis take? Secondly, we wanted to know how adults with different skills—students, English professors, and professional writers—handled each of these processes. Our model (Figure 2) reflects the basic processes these groups of writers had in common; our results, however, suggest that they conduct these processes in quite different ways. This research project, supported by a grant from the National Science Foundation, is reported in Hayes, Flower, Schriver, Stratman, and Carey ("Cognitive

Processes in Revision"). The present paper does not attempt to summarize that study, since it was devoted to the close tracking of cognitive processes in revision, to discovering individual and group differences, and to exploring a theory of Evaluation based on current theories of reading and knowledge construction. In this paper we wish to put the model to more direct use. Can it, first of all, help us *predict where* the revision process breaks down? That is, can it help us see where beginning writers may slip from the current of revision's powerful and generative process into more limited and passive encounters with plans and text? Secondly, can it help us go beyond describing students' under-revised products to *diagnosing what* those writers are actually doing?

Fourteen subjects (7 students, 4 teachers, 3 professionals) were given a letter, written from one college coach to another, discussing why women are unnecessarily reluctant to participate in college sports. The subjects were asked to revise this letter (written to the Carnegie-Mellon University coach) into a handout for freshman women at the University. We designed the task to be a naturalistic one demanding both high- and low-level revision: that is, although the information in the letter was appropriate, the task implicitly called for changes in voice, genre, format, rhetorical stance, perceived audience, and style. In addition, we planted a set of stylistic and rule-governed errors in the text, including errors in spelling, punctuation, sentence style, and diction. The questions then were, how would writers choose to represent this task to themselves, what problems would they detect, what problems would they diagnose, and how would they fix the problems they found? Each of these questions is being investigated in more detail in subsequent studies; only the revision of planted errors is discussed here.

In order to provide converging, independent measures of performance and to distinguish the knowledge these writers might *have* from the knowledge they *used* in the heat of revision, we collected 1) concurrent protocols of their revising, 2) extensive cued recalls on all changes (i.e., retrospective responses to the question, "what did you do here?" which were elicited immediately after the task and cued by the subject's own text), and 3) a week or more after the task, the results of a test of each reviser's ability to detect and diagnose our set of 26 "planted" problems when they were presented one by one out of context. (This was called the Single Sentence task.)

The results of this study for detection were surprising. During revision the experts actively detected only 58% of the planted problems (based on clear evidence in the text or protocol). However, there is evidence that the experts sometimes chose to halt the Detection process on a given sentence or paragraph. They appeared to possess either a **precedence** rule that said, "If you find an important or global problem, let it take precedence; stop the search for minor errors," or a **density** rule that said, "If you see a growing number of difficulties, stop looking for individual problems and just rewrite."

Yet even in the Single Sentence task, which presented sentences with potential problems one sentence at a time, the experts detected only an average of 66% of the "plants." Why wasn't it 100%? One answer supports our hypothesis about the influence Intention has even on Detection: in the Single Sentence task, the experts often ignored problems of style, such as wordiness, that they had vigorously attacked in the context of a real revision. They seemed to narrow their criteria to clear, certifiable errors. Nevertheless, the fact remains: the experts were not absolutely reliable detectors of even standard problems. However, they were still considerably better than the novices, who detected only 58% during revision and 42% on the Single Sentence task.

These raw figures don't tell the whole story. When the experts revised, they succeeded in fixing or eliminating 91% of the planted problems. Even when they had not actively noted some individual problems, their revisions often replaced whole multi-error units with acceptable text. However, the novices, who often retained these errors in their revised text, removed only 64% of the planted problems. We assume that everyone noticed some problems they didn't verbalize or mark; however, this additional difference in the number of problems retained in the text suggests that the novices' low detection scores are indeed a meaningful indicator of their real Detection skills. Not only did they miss many problems, but the protocols show the novices reading out loud and actively approving of some of the most blatantly tortured prose. When they rewrote, they retained errors and added new ones.

These results suggest that detecting even common, rather obvious errors may not be as easy as teachers often suppose. More importantly, a student's failure to revise may be a failure even to detect problems. The revision process may end at its beginning as the writer enters the constructive process of Evaluation lightly equipped with a limited set of intentions or an inadequate representation of either plan or text.

III. DIAGNOSING PROBLEMS

The preceding section looked at what it takes even to get on the board in revision—to detect that a problem exists. Let us now look at the Problem Representations which are constructed in the process of Evaluation (see Figure 2). Having detected a problem, the writer's work has just begun. The output of Evaluation is merely a shout (or a whisper) that says "a problem exists." One of the central questions of our study was, how do adults actually represent these problems to themselves? And what effect does that representation have on what they do next?

A negative evaluation may give the reviser little information beyond the fact that a piece of text doesn't measure up to expectations. A useful Problem Representation must supply enough information to allow the reviser to act. The representations writers create appear to exist along a continuum (see Figure 3). At the low or left end of the scale are representations such as "this just doesn't sound right" or "awful." We have called these representations "simple Detects." They are the sparest sort of representation and appear to offer the reviser meager information about the nature or source of the problem. Even

FIGURE 3 The Strategic Choices Allowed by DETECTION and DIAGNOSIS

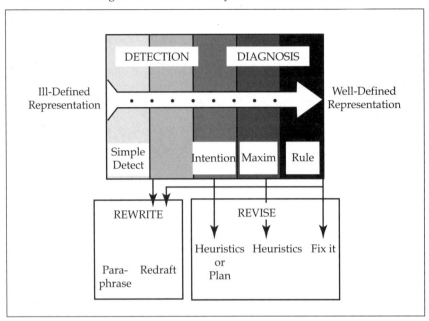

comments such as "this word, I just don't like it" take the reviser a little further to the right on the scale by adding information about the locus of the problem.

We can also look at problem definitions as implicit instructions for what to do. Representations which are low in information about the nature or locus of the problem create what are called "ill-defined problems"—neither the procedures nor the criteria for action are apparent in the definition. Many complex problems, such as "I have to make this argument work," necessarily begin as ill-defined problems. By contrast, the representations on the far right end of the continuum create extremely "well-defined" problems, such as spell "receive" with an "i" before "e" except after "c." These high-information, procedurally explicit, "fix-it" representations are usually available only for rule-governed problems of spelling, grammar, and usage.

Along this continuum from "simple Detects" to "fully explicit" representations lie important differences in how people represent problems in texts. For instance, the older children in the Scardamalia and Bereiter study ("Development") were surprisingly good (e.g., agreed with adults) at choosing an appropriate problem definition from among a set of general and abstract descriptions on cards. But when asked to specify the problem further or locate it in the text, they could not explain their choice or define the problem more explicitly, nor could they select a means of dealing with it. In terms of our model, they could not move their sense of the problem to the well-defined end of the continuum and create a more information-laden, action-oriented representation. In a study of good and poor student editors, Hull ("Editing") also noticed that the experts not only knew more rules and conventions but were better at problem-solving and experimenting with the text until they discovered the error and its correction.

Although it is important to see that problem representations exist on a continuum defined by the amount of information they contain, the representations that fit on the upper end of this continuum form an interesting and distinctive group. As Figure 3 indicates, we have reserved the term Diagnosis, which is often applied to any problem representation, for this special group of more sophisticated, high-information definitions of the problem (Flower, Carey, Hayes, "Diagnosis"). A Diagnosis, such as "wordy" or "this is going to bore freshmen," differs from a Detection in important ways: first, it places the problem in a conceptual category—"a whatchamacallit I've seen before"—even if the writer does not have a name for the category. Secondly, because it makes contact with a known category, a Diagnosis calls up additional information about the problem. Finally, it points the way to solution procedures. Diagnosis constitutes a particularly powerful form of problem representation. As an act of concept recognition it draws on prior knowledge to identify and define problems in a way that points to revision.

Unlike the all-purpose definitions of Detection (e.g., "this sounds bad, it won't work, and I don't like it"), Diagnosis brings new information to the task. We make this distinction between detection and a *bona fide* diagnosis in other areas. For instance, if a friend looked at us and said, "you're looking peaked today; you'd better get some rest," we would be pleased they cared and even detected our terminal condition. If, however, our doctor said that after we had dragged our sorry case to his office, we would no doubt be annoyed, since from him we expect a well-defined, informed diagnosis that provides specific information about the problem and a suggestion for what to do (e.g., "You have infectious mononucleosis with a white blood count of 12,000. I want you to plan on no alcohol and sleeping 10 hours a night for the next two weeks"). A diagnosis, in this setting, is a problem representation you would be willing to pay for.

Given the important differences between a Detection such as "I have to say this better," and a Diagnosis, such as "those things aren't parallel" or "this idea doesn't logically follow from that," which is better? Is the extra information of a Diagnosis worth the price of the extra learning or processing it may take to create it?

One way to answer this question is to study expert problem representations. And the obvious expert model would appear to be an English instructor. The English teacher's stock-in-trade is high-level diagnosis, whether the problem is simply grammatical (e.g., a run-on sentence), technical and stylistic (e.g., the confusing syntax created by a double dependent clause), or rhetorical (e.g., a disconcerting switch of voice or an example that won't persuade). On top of this, teachers have names and categories for everything—even code words such as "awk" that fit conveniently in the margin. This image of the expert as fluent diagnostician might seem the obvious choice if there weren't a competing model. This competing model suggests that although diagnosis may be a necessary skill for teachers, who comment on papers for a living, it isn't nearly as significant to people who actually *rewrite* the papers. Perhaps (this model of rewriting might say) we teachers have imagined revision in our own image and ignored the final stage of the student's revision process which teachers don't go through—rewriting.

From the perspective of a rewriter, diagnosis looks less essential. A minimal problem representation may be perfectly adequate since the goal is simply the extended growth of one's ideas through the continuation of writing itself. Diagnosis necessarily directs attention to one's previous draft or train of thought. But the freewriter/rewriter may choose simply to write, and when she detects that something is wanting, simply abandon the first effort and jump into the breech again. We should note that this sketch may not characterize the freewriter as Elbow describes her ("Teachers"), since that writer may resort to a good deal of analytical diagnosis when it comes to summing up, finding a gist, and dealing with stuck points, as Elbow's own diary entries suggest. Our own results suggest that expert writers use both Detection and Diagnosis, for different reasons, at different times. Having the capacity to Diagnose when she needs to seems to be the defining feature of the expert, since the most important distinction between Detection and Diagnosis is that they can lead to different actions.

IV. SELECTING A STRATEGY

As the model in Figure 2 suggests, writers have a number of options at this point. These range from cycling back through the problem representation process searching for more information, to delaying action till later, to deciding to ignore the problem altogether (Hayes, Schriver, and Flower, "Decisions"). This set of options is constrained, however, in an important way. The only way to enter the REVISE process is to go through Diagnose first. This is because REVISE is, by definition, a process that depends on the new information generated in a diagnosis, whereas REWRITE, like original text production, does not.

In this part of our paper we will consider two of the major paths of action we see writers choosing: the Detect/Rewrite strategy and the Diagnose/Revise strategy (see Figure 3). In choosing the Diagnose/Revise route, the writer has access to a variety of strategies tied to the problem he defines (that is, he consults his own internal means-ends table which offers strategies ranging from simple fix-it routines to global planning). A mere Detection, on the other hand, offers fewer choices and commits the writer to the Rewrite strategy. Although our choice of terms here, REWRITE VS. REVISE, is partially arbitrary, we want to use the distinction to point to an important difference in the writer's process. Let us consider the Detect/Rewrite strategy first.

The Detect/Rewrite Strategy

Rewriting is a delightfully simple and efficient procedure. Upon detecting that a phrase, sentence, or section of text-plan fails to fit her intentions, the writer then spends no more time or attention on the faulty text. She recalls or reads it only to get its gist—what it was trying to do or say. That is, the rewriter may extract only propositions from the original text, keeping little or even none of its original wording. She then consults her goals and has a fresh try at producing text. The Rewrite process simply replicates the writer's original attempt to produce text, shaping intention once again into a different syntactic and semantic representation. Rewriting takes both a global and local form, which can be described respectively as Redrafting and Paraphrasing (see Figure 2). In the more global Redrafting process, extant text is discarded wholesale. The writer carries forward two things: her current intention and the gist of what was said in the first draft. A writer who chooses the Detect and Rewrite/Redraft sequence makes a speedy exit from the REVIEW process and returns to the basic processes of PLANNING and TRANSLATING. Her effort is neither encumbered with nor is it guided by a diagnosis of earlier problems or by a plan based on that diagnosis. If the act of writing has itself modified the writer's original goals or criteria, Redrafting allows a fresh start. But it can also lead to a series of merely different—not better—texts. This choice of action appears to describe the students Calkins called Random Drafters ("Children's") and Schwartz called Restarters ("Journeys").

A more local form of Rewriting which we saw in many of our student writers is more aptly defined as Paraphrase. The writer, typically working with individual sentences or even clauses, attempts to capture the same propositional information (or a loose approximation of it) in a different semantic or syntactic form. The writer is likely to go through a series of generate-and-test loops, subjecting each new candidate to an Evaluation that leads to a fresh Detection and a return to Rewrite.

In the Rewrite process in general, the writer returns to square one—a set of propositions or a gist—and runs those same propositions through her mental sentence generator again (cf. Mann and Moore, "Text"). This process of "generate and test" goes on constantly during composing, of course, as writers use successive approximations to capture or even discover their meaning. This "don't look back; just keep writing it" technique for revision seems particularly valuable when one is using writing for discovery (Elbow, "Teachers"; Murray, "Revision") or when the text is too garbled to be worth diagnosis, or when one needs to be free of the text's influence, or (in the case of another person's text) when the Rewriter would rather just do it his way. The power of this strategy does, however, depend on the power of one's sentence generator, that is, on one's fluency in creating sentences in the first place. When experts revise the work of novices, they may not only represent the goals of the text differently, but may have much more flexible, sophisticated, and fluent linguistic skills at their disposal as well. Rewriting also has the merit of being efficient when there is little to be gained by figuring out *why* the first version *didn't* work. It is often much faster simply to say it again. For example, teachers reading student papers often encounter sentences with strange modifications or awkward syntax which they could easily rewrite but whose shortcomings they find exceedingly difficult to explain.

Despite its simplicity, there are problems with the rewrite strategy. If the writer is not particularly fluent or if the sentence is complex, his attempt to juggle multiple versions of the text can soon overload short term memory. At times Rewriters appear to juggle internal representations of meaning, of the new text *and* of the text to be avoided. This original text can be a powerful *misleading stimulus* for a writer in Paraphrase (Bereiter and Scardamalia, "Conversation"). In experiments with revision of sentences, children produce better revisions when they can work from a matrix of information or a list of propositions rather than from full sentences (Bracewell, "Control").

By depending on a simple generate-and-test procedure (especially if one's fluency is limited), the writer can find herself caught in the frustrating round of playing the same sentence with variations over and over in her head. The protocol below (Figure 4) illustrates how this process can work and some of the difficulties of a novice writer who depends solely on the Detect/Rewrite strategy. In this case, the writer has detected a problem, but, as we later confirm, she doesn't know exactly where or what it is, so she begins rewriting, trying to generate a new sentence that will eliminate the problem. Notice first how this strategy of writing "by ear" in the sense in which some musicians play by ear depends on repeated passes at the offending sentence. It uses the running start procedure Sondra Perl noticed in basic writers: one repeats the beginning of the sentence, then forges ahead until it falls apart ("Composing"). In this case, our writer continues until she detects a new instance of (what some would recognize as) faulty parallelism.

Notice that her solution to the problem is largely local—a bit-by-bit accrual of prepositional phrases and clauses added to the base clause. Her chief criterion appears to be this: does this new element violate the syntax of what I have already said. There is no global plan for revision. As you can see in the schematic version of the sentence at the bottom of Figure 4, her final solution is in fact a piecemeal rendition of the original that does avoid syntactic "errors" but fails to reflect the underlying parallelism of the ideas. One irony of this supposedly simpler piecemeal approach is that a proposed change can be tested only by returning to and replaying the entire confusing sentence. The writer then ends up having to hold an entire syntactically-complicated unit in short term memory. The protocol in Figure 4 reflects both the simplicity and potential difficulty of a Detect/Rewrite strategy. This sentence appeared in the context of a paragraph on the benefits of college sports.

In contrast to this student's frustrating and time-consuming efforts, one of our experienced writers simply read the sentence and revised it in one pass through, commenting as he wrote, "I love infinitives, obviously." What was he doing that made it so easy? The protocol shows us that a part of his performance can be attributed to the same Rewrite strategy our novice tried to use: extracting the gist and recasting the sentence. In this case, the expert asked himself, with a slight edge in his voice, "What *do* sports help freshmen to do?" His revision uses the propositions from the original to answer the question: "Sports help freshmen, in particular, to meet new people; they help all students to learn to work together, to cooperate, to be responsible and to handle competition whether one wins or loses." However, guiding this revision, and the key to his effortless correction of the original syntax, was an act of diagnosis. That is, he recognized and defined a specific problem which

FIGURE 4 Protocol of a Novice Using the Rewrite Strategy

ORIGINAL TEXT

Students also learn to interact with people, cooperation, punctuality, responsibility, how to win and lose correctly, and how to treat your opponents.

REWRITE COMMENTS

(Changes which the subject proposes orally as she talks have been underlined for easier comparison; the text she actually writes is in bold, including some revisions later rejected.)

1. **Students also learn to interact with people** [. . .]
2. — interact with people—cooperation, punctuality, responsibility, how to win and lose correctly, and how to treat your opponents.
3. Students also learn to interact with people through cooperation, punctuality.
4. Students also learn to interact with people through cooperation, punctuality, and responsibility, how to win or lose correctly, and how to treat their opponents.
5. Students also learn to interact with people.
6. Students learn responsibility.
7. Students also learn to interact with people by cooperating—by cooperating, being punctual.
8. Students also learn to interact with people.
9. Students also learn to interact with people. They must be punctual, they must cooperate—be punctual, learn to win or lose correctly.
10. Students also learn to interact with people by coop—cooperation.
11. Students also learn to interact with people.
12. This is one heck of a sentence you know.
13. Students also learn to interact with people. **They learn to cooperate, be punctual**.
14. **They are given much responsibility, and** learn to cooperate, be punctual, and learn to win or lose correctly . . . and how to treat their opponents.
15. Final reread: Students also learn to interact with people. They are given much responsibility and must cooperate, be punctual, **learn to win or lose correctly and how to treat their opponents properly.**

Final version:
Students also learn to interact with people.
They are given much responsibility and must cooperate,
                       be punctual,
                       learn to win and lose correctly
                       and treat their opponents
                         properly.

called for specific kinds of rewriting. When asked on the cued recall to comment on any changes he made, this writer made it clear that he not only knew exactly what the problem was, but had a vocabulary for thinking about it: "First of all it's not a parallel structure. It starts with an infinitive . . . and then we go to cooperation, punctuality, responsibility, and then back to the infinitive." He also noted the switch in voice. Furthermore, he knew exactly which strategy he would use to fix the sentence: "I like the idea of a list of things that sports help one to do. My first tendency whenever I'm setting up a list is to use infinitives." He later noted that this means/ends plan was so habitual he often had to go back and cut infinitives out. In addition to parallelism, he noted two other problems and/or goals: keeping all the terms at the same level of abstraction and eliminating some of the conceptual redundancy in the list.

When we compare the performance of our expert and novice on this single sentence, we can see the added power diagnosis can give a reviser. The expert's diagnostic process defines the problem to be solved, calls in a vocabulary for analyzing it, and supplies strategies for solving it. It activates a body of goals, criteria, and options which support revision, and it draws on the writer's metaknowledge of his own writing to monitor the process itself. The novice on the other hand is bound to her text, rewriting by ear, rather than revising by design. Her performance on the protocol and cued recall indicates that she simply didn't have a clue to what the problem was. When later asked specifically to diagnose the problem, on the Single Sentence task, she clearly *detected* the locus of (at least part) of the difficulty: "I don't know how to explain it, but the 'ity's' don't fit in with the 'learning to interact.'" However, when she tried to categorize or define the problem, she began grasping for straws:

> I mean you have a present tense verb and then you have an explanation of — a word explaining what they learn. Now how do I explain that? . . . It also doesn't seem to me, maybe because of the way cooperation, punctuality, responsibility, fit in with interact. It doesn't seem like a full sentence even though it is. It does have its subject and its verb. . . .

Although this writer could accurately detect at least a part of the non-parallel terms (the "ity's"), she remained unable to diagnose the problem she detected. Her comments suggest that she resorted to what few tools of analysis she had: checking for tense, full sentences, and subject and verb agreement. In this case, the writer had no choice but to use the Rewrite strategy, whether it was efficient for her or not.

To sum up, the Detect/Rewrite strategy has some special strengths. First, it has the virtue of simplicity: the writer merely plunges again into the stream of language production. No special knowledge or analytical effort is required. All of the writer's energy is devoted to what really matters — finding a different and better way to represent meaning or intention. Secondly, Rewriting has the full power of the writer's language production system behind it. Each act of Rewriting (at least in Redrafting) is in principle a fresh pass at making meaning—a pass that, unlike a diagnosis, is unconstrained by the pattern and focus of one's first attempt.

On the other hand, if the revision task is complex, Rewriting can be a difficult process to carry off. If, for example, a number of elements in a sentence or paragraph must interact, or the passage is long, Rewriting puts a heavy load on short term memory. Trying to hold the subject in memory until its verb comes along is a simple case of this phenomenon, which often undoes the basic writer (Shaughnessy, 1977; Daiute, 1981) and which plagues us all. This does not mean that Rewriting is the wrong strategy: it may be necessary as well as difficult. After all, writing is difficult. However, let us suppose that the problem is susceptible to diagnosis, whether it is a simple case of faulty parallelism or a complex case of unsupported claims. If the writer is not fluent at generating alternatives, rewriting can be a poor strategy. It fails to recognize that a definable problem—and a strategy made for the job—may exist. The Detect/Rewrite strategy allows one to make a straightforward, but relatively blind, leap into ill-defined problems.

The Diagnose/Revise Strategy

Diagnosis is the act of recognizing and categorizing the problem one detects in the text. We have reserved the term for those problem representations that, unlike Detections, are high in information and high on the continuum from ill- to well-defined problems. Choosing to diagnose appears to be primarily the expert's option; however, the quality of information in expert diagnoses may be even more significant than their frequency (Flower, Carey, and Hayes, "Diagnosis"). Diagnosis draws on one of the skills that separates experts from novices in many domains—skill in pattern recognition. For example, people traditionally assumed that the special strength of chess masters was their ability to think ahead and plan an entire series of moves in advance. However, DeGroot discovered that master and weaker players alike look only two to three moves ahead, both considering between 30 and 50 alternative actions. The masters planned no further ahead than normal players—they simply made better plans; they planned the *right* moves. One key difference, it turned out, was that chess masters are able to recognize somewhere between 10,000 and 100,000 chess board patterns. This vast store of familiar patterns and their outcomes allowed the expert to look at the current situation on the chess board and "see" it as sets of moves and their results that he had tried before. We should note that this is not simply a general perceptual skill. Masters are no better than novices at remembering random (non-chess) arrangements. Rather, in the 10,000–20,000 hours of study a chess master has typically logged, he has built up a repertory of meaningful patterns or categories which are rich in information. In the process of pattern matching, the expert categorizes the new situation as a version of an older one, and, in doing so, taps information stored in memory on what to do about it (see Hayes, "Thinking," for a discussion of this research).

The process of diagnosis in writing depends on the same ability to categorize, that is, to see a problem in the text as a meaningful, familiar pattern. When the writer can say, "Oh, it's one of those again" (e.g., this sounds "wordy" or "it's got to have a more positive tone"), that knowledge carries important implications:

1. Categorizing or recognizing helps the writer separate the problem from the noise by focusing attention on the features that matter. In diagnosis, unlike detection, the writer devotes attention to the problematic text itself. This attempt to define the qualities that triggered detection can turn a wide-open, ill-defined problem (e.g., "I don't like the way this sounds") into a more sharply focused problem the writer can work on. It is the principle of modern medicine: why take a general purpose dose of castor oil for "whatever ails you" when what you really need is eight hours of sleep and half as much coffee. If your argument doesn't "flow" because of a missing inference, you don't want to rewrite the entire discussion to fix it.

2. Diagnosis can operate at many levels of awareness. Although it is clearly a problem-solving procedure, we do not want to suggest that it is always a self-conscious procedure or a highly technical response. In experienced writers some Diagnoses may be quite automatic, demanding little time, attention, or comment. More importantly, writers do not need a **name** for a pattern, category, or concept in order to use it. Many problems may not have or need a conventional name. Consider the following diagnosis: "This paragraph seems to concentrate on all the mistakes athletes make when what I really want people to appreciate is the inherent difficulty of the game." Here diagnosis takes the form of a prediction about the reader's response and a description of how the faulty text organization is working. Nevertheless, the statement is an effective diagnosis because it locates and defines a meaningful problem type (i.e., a misleading focus) that the writer can solve.

Diagnosis can also operate on unnamed linguistic patterns and relationships. For instance, it is possible for you to pinpoint and recognize (as a modification or connection problem) the tangled modification created by a double dependent clause, even if you don't know the technical terms, as the syntax of this sentence demonstrates. (If you had trouble with the preceding sentence, you may have tried to determine why the syntax seemed derailed. Breaking the sentence down into its intuitively meaningful units produces a non-technical but informative diagnosis: the logically-related phrases are physically separated in the sentence.) Let us put this important point another way. The power of diagnosis is not based on knowing the technical vocabulary of a college handbook—one can be innocent of grammar and recognize an agreement problem, and one can have never heard of "squinting modifiers" or "undistributed middles" and still recognize the pattern, diagnose its logic, and know what to do. On the other hand, one premise of education is that having a language helps you see and think about what you see (Freedman, "Review"). The question is, how much of what do we need to teach writers? If, for example, extensive instruction in formal grammar has a quickly diminishing return, would instruction in more basic structural units, as de Beaugrande ("Step") has proposed, provide a more practical conceptual framework? Pattern recognition and *bona fide* diagnosis can go on without the benefit of technical vocabulary or even names. On the other hand, the growth of conscious and articulate knowledge often goes hand in hand with conceptual sophistication and the power to use and control what one knows.

3. A third effect of categorizing is that it brings relevant past experience and specialized knowledge to bear on the problem. For an experienced writer, the notion of "stuffy"-sounding prose brings with it clues to where the problem might lie. It tells him to look for formal diction, Latinate constructions, and long embedded sentences. It then supplies a raft of optional strategies for solving the problem, such as, try to transform some Latinate nouns into verbs, or walk around the room and try to say what you mean out loud.

4. Even global, ill-defined problems at the "whole-text" level are susceptible to the categorizing power of diagnosis. One way writers represent such problems is by simulating a reader's response. These small scenarios help define the problem, even though the category they supply is often more implicit than stated, as in the comment "I think I'd just read that first sentence and say 'why bother?'" Diagnoses that deal with questions of intention and audience are by nature complex and relatively ill-defined, as we have suggested in Figure 3. An intentional diagnosis, such as "this has to be more upbeat and positive to work as a handout," is more specific about text features and explicit about the problem type than an imagined reader's response, but both diagnoses tend to deal with relatively broad, complex problems. This means that the action suggested by such a diagnosis is likely to be a heuristic procedure, not a rule; it can even call for a return to planning itself. Berkenkotter's ("Decisions") study of Donald Murray's process as a professional writer documents a series of just such "intentional" diagnoses which led to sessions of high-level planning. Diagnoses such as these often call for sophisticated strategies in response to complex problems.

Rule-governed diagnoses, at the other end of the diagnosis continuum, are more narrow, but they do lead to explicit fix-it rules for action. Diagnoses which depend on maxims, such as "wordy," appear to be somewhere in the middle between these two extremes and to lead to a variety of heuristics. In fact, the set of actions writers attach to these supposedly standard maxims is an important source of difference in the revisions that expert and novice writers produce (Flower, Carey, and Hayes, "Diagnosis"). It is important to remember that stylistic diagnoses, on which handbooks and their maxims typically focus, represent only a portion of the rhetorical knowledge writers can use. For instance, the social contract between writer and reader may be a far more useful basis for diagnosis and revision than our traditional text-based criteria of readability (Beach, "Self-Assessing"). As Beach describes it, the reader is imagined to process information according to Grice's four Maxims, that is, to expect informativeness, truth, relevance, and clarity. The reviser evaluates the text on the basis of inferences about this Gricean reader (e.g., will the reader consider this new information?) and by simulating the reader's response to current text.

Revision, as Beach describes it, draws on a highly conscious mix of analysis, inference, and the comparison of rhetorical options. Our own research suggests that in order to carry out global or whole-text revisions, experts depend heavily on Diagnosis to help them recognize and plan around problems. The following excerpt from an expert's protocol shows how the various processes of Rewriting, Diagnosing, Goal Modification, and Evaluation can work together in a rapid interplay of conscious and automatic processes. [See Figure 5.]

FIGURE 5   Interplay between Detection, Diagnosis, and Goal Setting (Proposed Text Underlined)

	Line	
	1	I hope you will consider—this is the beginning of the final paragraph—consider—a—joining
Evaluate	2	Oh, I like that
State Criteria	3	Joining one of the—I hate the word participate
Rewrite: Paraphrase	4	Hope you will consider being a part of women's athletics at CMU. I hope you will consider being a part of women's athletics at CMU.
A Current Goal	5	Here's where I get that fun bit in here
	6	You will
Diagnose: Reader Response	7	No you won't either, not necessarily . . .
Diagnose: Category	8	I'm coming on strong
A Current Goal	9	For space [on the piece of paper] really. I believe
Change in Goal	10	(Experimenter gives him some paper) Oh, can I?
Change in Goal	11	I believe you will enjoy it
Diagnose: Uncertain Rule	12	Let's see, is athletics a singular or a plural word?
	13	I hope you will consider being a part of women's athletics, I think you will enjoy . . .
Define Problem Further	14	Athletics "is" my favorite activity
	15	Athletics "are" my favorite activity
	16	is
	17	I hope you—I believe you will enjoy

The passage begins with the writer trying to create the "final pitch" — an earlier goal based on his diagnosis of what the handout needs but lacks. He interrupts himself with a positive evaluation and then (Line 3) a reference to one of his standard criteria, probably activated by the word "joining" he has just considered. Line 4 suggests that the writer detected something still inappropriate about the wording, since he here generates a paraphrase of the candidate in Line 1. At Line 5, the writer reports a goal that has now entered his attention ("getting the fun bit in"), which is probably a part of his plan for the "final pitch." Line 6 is cut short by a Diagnosis that simulates a reader's response: The writer had said "you will" and the imagined reader has replied, "no I won't." The writer then re-represents the problem, defining it more categorically as an instance of "coming on too strong."

Line 9 shows how trivial and unexamined goals, such as fitting your words to the paper available, can affect sentence generation. When the experimenter offers the writer a piece of paper and explicit permission to move off the page, the writer returns to the text with a revised set of intentions. With the comment, "Oh, can I?" in Line 9, we can infer that the writer's active, current intentions now include a new process goal (write anywhere) and a new content goal based on his diagnosis of a simulated reader's response, in lines 7 and 8: a goal that might be something like "qualify my assertion, change my persona, or soften my tone." The protocol naturally doesn't reveal the full detail of the decision-making that leads from the diagnosis "Coming on strong" to the addition of "I believe," but it shows how the writer tried to move his problem representation from the response of an imagined reader along the continuum toward a more well-defined problem, and it shows how diagnosis led in one instance to a change in goals, and in the other to further specification of goals. The final lines show how the detection of even rule-governed errors can send an expert into a self-conscious attempt at pattern matching and a focused diagnosis of a problem.

V. MODELS AND INDIVIDUAL DIFFERENCES

Although all parts of the revision process must work in concert, a process model tries to partition that whole into meaningful conceptual entities—to recognize those places where individual subprocesses make distinct contributions to the whole and create their own special problems for the writer. The value of such a model will lie not only in its truthfulness to the data it represents, but in its power to do three things: first, to offer a framework for integrating research on revision into a steadily growing picture of the process as a whole; secondly, to put hypotheses into a testable form and create an agenda for theory-conscious research; and finally, to address some of the important issues teachers and researchers have raised about the nature of revision.

This model describes the underlying general processes of Reviewing— and their range of variation—as we saw them in our subjects. It offers us testable hypotheses about the distinctive contributions of these key subprocesses, about the role of reading and the influence of the reviser's goals and criteria on Evaluation, about the options offered by the Detect-Diagnose continuum, and about other parts of the process. Finally, we believe that this description helps us locate parts of the process, such as diagnosis and the representation of intention and text, that cause writers difficulty.

However, this study, like all exploratory research and theory building, is just a beginning. A cognitive process model by itself cannot tell us how different writers, with different levels of skills or experience, would carve out strategic paths through these processes. As people begin to explore these developmental, expert/novice, and background differences, we see research questions in four areas which merit real attention since they will help us discover some of the distinctive features of the expert's revision process that we might be able to teach.

1. What part of this process creates the greatest difficulty for inexperienced writers? Or, to put it positively, what would give the greatest boost to performance: help in detection, diagnosis, or actual revision strategies?

2. Various studies suggest that even some inexperienced writers may do a good deal of diagnosis and possess a reasonable repertory of maxims. Is there, however, a significant difference in the quality of information contained in those diagnoses or in the knowledge embedded in a given maxim? What does a writer really know when she says "wordy" or "I'm coming on too strong?"

3. Is there a "best strategic path" through the review process? Is the Diagnose/Revise strategy more desirable to use and to teach than a Detect/Rewrite strategy? Diagnose and Revise clearly reflects the teacher's process and allows for the teacher/editor's intervention. Is it also a powerful and efficient strategy for writers?

4. Finally, can an understanding of the reviser's underlying cognitive processes give more direction to teaching? In their review of the literature on teacher commentary, Knoblauch and Brannon suggest that students have trouble translating teacher's comments into new strategies: "the depressing trouble is, we have scarcely a shred of empirical evidence to show that students typically even comprehend our responses to their writing, let alone use them purposefully to modify their practice" ("Teacher," p. 1). For instance, Newkirk ("Barriers") has suggested that teachers' comments are typically plans for revision (e.g., "try to be more specific"). Students may learn to follow such plans where indicated yet never learn to detect or diagnose the underlying problem themselves. Are we offering local remedies for text, when what students really need is the strategic knowledge that will let them generate such plans on their own?

We believe that seeing revision as a distributed process of detection, diagnosis, and strategic action lets us make distinctions of just this sort. One goal of further research will be to answer the four questions we have posed: to discover the knowledge revisers do use and how they manage the options this complex process offers them.

Researchers talk about "letting the data speak to you." This notion can be problematic if we forget that what we hear from data depends, in part, on our prior assumptions and frames of reference. Collaborative research can help us grapple with this problem by forcing us to confront competing interpretations and, thus, to recognize and negotiate our personal biases in listening to the data.

For two years of weekly meetings we analyzed the transcripts, texts, and cued recalls that led to "Detection, Diagnosis, and the Strategies of Revision" and to a later more elaborated account ("Cognitive Process in Revision"). What stands out from those sessions is the intractable voices of our participants. A typical scenario: One member of the team, who has spent the week deep in the texts and transcripts of Participants A & B, comes in with a fascinating answer to one of the questions we have been wrestling with (such as, how are detection and diagnosis related; are they really distinctive "steps" as other accounts suggest? Or how do a reviser's goals or attitudes affect what she sees or how she interprets it?) So as this Team Member regales us with her shiny new explanatory theory based on Participants A & B, another team member starts to fidget. He has been "listening" all weekend to patterns in the performance of Participants C & D and what they are doing simply won't support the lovely, rational, coherent story suggested by the actions of Participants A & B. It could have even made an elegant paper . . . until the data started to "talk back." And it is back to the drawing board. Indeed, going back to the drawing board is a process that has continued. One of our team members, John R. Hayes, has recently proposed a rather different model to account for these data in his essay "A New Framework for Understanding Cognition and Affect in Writing."

Those meetings called us, with a persistent regularity (which one may appreciate more warmly in retrospect than at the time), to the fragility of hypotheses based on the comforting logic of a theory or the compelling evidence of a great "example." John Dewey describes the latter as a quest for certainty, drawn to a hope that the conditional and unpredictable nature of reality can be avoided by operating in a world of theory ruled by the logic of our language. In contrast, research projects like these, with a team of colleagues happily ready to "have at it," seem to thrive in what Dewey calls an "experimental way of knowing." That is, a situated inquiry where one's examples and interpretations are systematically and unavoidably accountable to other voices from the same data. Looking back, it is easy to see ways to expand that metaphor and recognize other "voices" in this data supplied by the social and cultural contexts we invoked and the writers constructed. And to recognize some important voices this kind of data makes very difficult to hear. But the big challenge, it seems, lies in the willingness to listen.

—LINDA FLOWER

—JOHN R. HAYES

Carnegie Mellon University

Underlife and Writing Instruction

ROBERT BROOKE

This article uses the sociological concept of underlife to explain several aspects of writing instruction. In sociological theory, "underlife" refers to those behaviors which undercut the roles expected of participants in a situation—the ways an employee, for example, shows she is not just an employee, but has a more complex personality outside that role.

In contemporary writing instruction, both students and teachers undercut the traditional roles of the American educational system in order to substitute more complex identities in their place. On the one hand, students disobey, write letters instead of taking notes, and whisper with their peers to show they are more than just students and can think independently of classroom expectations. On the other, writing teachers develop workshop methods, use small groups, and focus on students' own "voices" in order to help students see themselves as writers first and students second. Both sets of behaviors are underlife behaviors, for they seek to provide identities that go beyond the roles offered by the normal teacher-as-lecturer, student-as-passive-learner educational system.

These forms of underlife, moreover, are connected to the nature of writing itself. Writing, in the rich sense of interactive knowledge creation advocated by theorists like Ann Berthoff in *The Making of Meaning* and Janet Emig in *Web of Meaning,* necessarily involves standing outside the roles and beliefs offered by a social situation—it involves questioning them, searching for new connections, building ideas that may be in conflict with accepted ways of thinking and acting. Writing involves being able to challenge one's assigned roles long enough that one can think originally; it involves living in conflict with accepted (expected) thought and action.

This article will explore student and teacher behavior in writing instruction as the underlife of the current educational system, and will suggest that the identities which may be developing for students in writing classrooms

This essay was first published in *CCC,* Volume 38, Number 2, May 1987.

are more powerful for real academic success than the traditional identity of the successful student. It may be that the process of allowing a particular kind of identity to develop is what contemporary writing instruction is all about.

THE CONCEPT OF UNDERLIFE

My understanding of "underlife" stems from Erving Goffman's books *Asylums* and *Stigma,* although the concept has long been accepted in sociology. As presented in these books, the concept of underlife rests on three assumptions about social interaction. First, a person's identity is assumed to be a function of social interaction. Second, social interaction is assumed to be a system of information games. Third, social organizations are assumed to provide roles for individuals which imply certain kinds of identities. With these assumptions in mind, "underlife" can be understood as the activities (or information games) individuals engage in to show that their identities are different from or more complex than the identities assigned them by organizational roles. In this section, I will describe these assumptions and the concept of underlife that emerges from them.

Identity as Social Interaction.   In *Stigma,* Goffman explains that we understand another person's identity as a product of (1) how they immediately appear to us through dress, bearing, accent, physical features, and the like; (2) what we know about their history; and (3) the stances they take towards the groups we assume they belong to. We may initially assume, for example, that the young man in the front row of a new class is a typical "fraternity boy" because of (1) his haircut, his polo shirt, and his brand name tennis shoes. As we get to know (2) his history, we may find out that he comes from a wealthy family, that his parents hope he will become a doctor, and that he struggles with this because he has a hard time keeping up his grades. We will also begin to get a sense of him as a unique individual when we find out (3) he is troubled by his relationship to his family, more interested in English than in medicine, and feels in conflict because he would like to drop medicine, reject the family, and go into graduate school, but also wants to marry his sorority sweetheart, keep the family fortune, and lead a "successful" life. We (and he) use all three forms of information in assigning to him a particular identity.

Information Games.   The identity we assign such a young man is greatly determined, however, by the kinds of information he chooses to give us. If he dressed differently, we would see him differently. Perhaps if we knew more of his history we would see him in a different light. Perhaps we may think that his choice to tell us of his interest in English is a calculated choice, intended to get us to grade easier. The identity assigned an individual by other people is largely the product of the "information games" people play when interacting with each other. By what each person chooses to reveal about himself in each context, we develop a sense of that person's identity. Central to Goffman's conception of the human person, then, is a sense of the "information games" nature of interaction—people are assumed to attempt to develop the best defensible portrait for themselves in social interactions.

Organizational Roles. The kind of portrait a person can develop for herself, however, is a function of the organizations (businesses, families, clubs, hospitals, etc.) she operates in. As Goffman explains, social organizations are places where individuals are placed into certain roles. Appropriate activity in these roles carries with it implications about identity. In a school classroom, for example, prompt and accurate completion of tasks set by the teacher carries with it a "good student" identity, and a student who always complies pleasantly will be understood as smart, well-mannered, possibly a teacher's pet.

Underlife. Exactly because organizations offer definitions of identity, they also offer individuals the opportunity to respond to the definitions in creative ways. Because definitions of self exist in organizations, individuals can give information about how they see themselves by rejecting the definition offered. Institutional underlife is exactly such a case: actors in an institution develop behaviors which assert an identity different from the one assigned them.

In *Asylums,* Goffman studies the underlife of a major American mental hospital, and comes to the conclusion that underlife activities take two primary forms. First, there are *disruptive* forms of underlife, like those engaged in by union organizers, "where the realistic intentions of the participants are to abandon the organization or radically alter its structure." Second, there are *contained* forms of underlife, which attempt to fit into "existing institutional structures without introducing pressure for radical change" (199). Most forms of underlife are of the second kind—they work around the institution to assert the actor's difference from the assigned role, rather than working for the elimination of the institution. In the mental hospital, Goffman finds many examples of such contained underlife patterns, including identity jokes and challenges (where staff and inmates would kid each other about having attributes of the other class), attempts to "get around" established procedures (such as dumping dinner in the garbage and having a friend who works in the kitchen smuggle out a plateful of boiled eggs), and explicit attempts to express rejection of inmate status (like withdrawing from interaction with other patients, parodying psychological theory, claiming it was all a mistake, and engaging in violent behavior). The point of each of these behaviors, claims Goffman, is to show that one has a self different from the patient-self assigned by the hospital.

The prevalence of such behaviors throughout the hospital and other institutions leads Goffman to conclude that underlife behaviors are a normal part of institutional life. All members of the institution—staff, patients, technicians, janitors, doctors—engaged in such behaviors. Consequently, Goffman claims, institutional underlife must be understood as an activity closely related to individual identity. "I want to argue," he writes, "that this recalcitrance is not an incidental mechanism of defense but rather an essential constituent of the self" (319). For Goffman, looking at those activities through which individuals resist or reject the identity assigned them by institutions is a way of looking at how individuals form their sense of identity. No one but the complete fanatic completely associates herself with only one role—instead, the self is formed in the distance one takes from the roles one is assigned. In such an analysis, activities which aren't "on task" become as important as activities which are, for besides the task itself there is also always the formation of identity.

Underlife in a Writing Class

Underlife activities, as Goffman describes them, are the range of activities people develop to distance themselves from the surrounding institution. By so doing they assert something about their identity. Underlife allows individuals to take stances towards the roles they are expected to play, and to show others the stances they take. When the kinds of student behaviors normally seen as misbehavior are examined in writing classrooms, what appears is exactly this sort of constructive, individual stance-taking. It is exactly in these underlife behaviors that students are developing their individual stances towards classroom experience.

I would like to discuss several examples of underlife in the writing classroom from this perspective. The examples all come from a semester-long participant-observation study of a freshmen writing class in spring 1986. As a participant-observer, I was able to hear and record many behaviors I am unable to attend to while teaching my own courses. These behaviors include the private conversations students have with one another, the notes they write to themselves and then scratch out, the things they're writing when the teacher thinks they're taking notes, and other such activities. What surprised me was the extent and content of these activities—even in the most docile class hour, such activities are constantly going on, and (significantly) they are usually connected to the class activities in some way. The students are developing their own stances towards class activity, not whispering about unrelated subjects like parties and dates as I had always assumed.

In the classroom I observed, the students' underlife activities divided fairly cleanly into four major types, which I will discuss in order of frequency.

First, students tend to find creative uses for classroom activities and materials which are purposefully different from those the teacher intended. Usually, these creative uses show that classroom ideas could be used outside of class in ways more interesting to the students. During a class period devoted to using Young, Becker, and Pike's tagmemic matrix in *Rhetoric: Discovery and Change*, for example, two male students found ways of thinking about the subject that asserted their own interests. The teacher had brought in a bag of potatoes to serve as an example, and was having the class use the tagmemic matrix to explore "how many ways they could think about something as simple as a potato." While the class was discussing how a potato might change over time and in what contexts this change would be interesting, these students began a private discussion of how to ferment the potato to get vodka. When asked by the teacher what they were talking about, one of the two (looking nervous) explained that the process of fermentation was obviously a "change over time" and that this process was interesting "in the context of alcohol production." In this example, the students had openly ceased to participate in class, and seemed (from their giggles) to be "telling jokes" behind the teacher's back. But the content of their "jokes" was actually a way of applying the class concepts to their own late-adolescent interests in alcohol. Their retreat from class participation was a retreat which took a class concept with it, and which applied that concept in a highly creative and accurate way.

In the classroom I studied, this kind of creative use of classroom ideas was the most frequent form of underlife behavior. Most of the private conversations I heard applied a class concept to the students' world. In fact, particularly striking images or ideas frequently sparked several private conversations throughout the room. When the class discussed Annie Dillard's "Lenses," for example, a student pointed out Dillard's comparison of feeling disoriented to the shock of coming out of a really good movie and realizing you'd forgotten where you parked the car. Immediately, several private conversations started up throughout the room—the ones I could hear focused on how that feeling had happened to them too, in situations they could share with their peers.

To a teacher thinking only of how well her point is getting across, what seems to be going on in these cases is disruptive: students aren't paying attention, but are talking to one another about things that don't have to do with class. But to a teacher thinking about how students are using classroom information, these diversions should seem positive. In them, no matter how jokingly, students are actively connecting ideas in the classroom to their own lives outside the classroom, and are discovering ways in which classroom knowledge seems useful even when (or especially when) it isn't used for classroom purposes.

The second most frequent kind of underlife was student comments on the roles people were taking in the classroom, or the roles the classroom was asking them to take. Students, for example, frequently focused on the "games-playing" nature of student participation in college courses. Consider, for example, the following interaction which occurred during a small group discussion of a chapter from Margaret Laurence's *A Bird in the House:*

> MICK: "You know, everyone in the story tries to make themselves seem better than they are, you know, but Vanessa finds out every one of them is worse than they seem. It's like *all* of them are lying."
>
> MEL: "Good point. She[the teacher]'ll like that."

CHUCK: "Yeah. Home run. Three strikes."

MEL (laughing): "Big bucks."

CHUCK: "Yeah, big bucks, no whammies."

General laughter, and the conversation immediately turned to discussion of a TV game show called "Press Your Luck!" On this show, contestants played a form of roulette to get "big bucks," but lost everything if they landed on a "whammie." The whammies, incidently, were animated cartoon characters which would ramble across the screen and devour the hapless contestant's earnings. The group's discussion (which went on for several minutes, the assigned task having been forgotten) focused on how "lucky" players had to be to win anything on "Press Your Luck!" and how in general the game was a rip-off — as a contestant, nine times out of ten you got to get humiliated for nothing.

What struck me most about this interaction was not that students were avoiding the official task, nor that they were avoiding my presence enough to feel comfortable avoiding the task, but that the interaction highlighted (and sprung from) a deep-rooted sense of their experience with classrooms. Their comments, and the quick shift from doing a classroom exercise to discussing a game show, pointed out that they thought of the classroom as a "games-playing" environment, where "points" accumulated "big bucks," where one might get "whammied," where you always had to "press your luck." They thought of themselves as contestants in a game of luck, nerves, and skill, in which those who scored the most points survived, and those who didn't went home humiliated. They were aware, in short, that the classroom environment demanded certain actions of them which were as formal and arbitrary as the actions demanded in games-playing. The purpose of their interaction was to show each other that they all recognized this, that they as individuals were different from the roles they were being asked to play, and that they were all aware of each other as fellow games-players.

As a consequence of this mutual recognition of each other as games-players, students frequently engaged in conversations about how to "get by" effectively in the classroom. Especially in the few minutes before class when the teacher was not yet in the room, students would openly discuss strategies they'd used to succeed in the classroom. One woman told another, for example, that she'd written in her journal (which the teacher would see) an entry describing how hard the last paper was to write and how long it took her because that was the sort of thing the teacher wanted — even though she'd actually written the paper in an hour and a half after midnight the night before. Similarly, students would often share the comments they received on papers, and discuss what in the papers might have sparked the teacher to make these comments. These conversations occurred especially when one student had done well on a paper, and another hadn't, as if the students were together trying to pinpoint what was expected of them for success in this classroom. In all these activities, it was clear that students were not immediately evaluating each other on their success and honesty in embracing the classroom roles, but were instead mutually helping each other to succeed in "getting by" in the classroom without losing themselves in its expectations.

Such "role-recognition" activities on the part of students seem very similar to the "identity jokes" Goffman found in the hospital he studied. The purpose for commenting on the roles that exist in the classroom is the same purpose for kidding a staff member for acting like an inmate—such comments show that the speaker is aware of and different from the roles assigned in the situation, that there is more to the speaker than that. The quantity of such comments in the classroom I studied suggests that students are highly aware of the roles the classroom asks them to play, and highly defensive of their differences from these roles.

A third major category of underlife activities involves evaluations of what is going on in the classroom. In these comments, students explicitly took a stance towards some aspect of the classroom, and evaluated it as good or bad. Often, these evaluations focused on their own performance:

> CHUCK: Did you bring your paper?
>
> BEN: That damn thing—
>
> CHUCK: Pretty "damn," huh?
>
> BEN: It's so "damn" I keep forgetting it.

or on the course materials:

> JANE (holding up book): Did you think this was all right?
>
> HOLLY: Dumb.
>
> JANE: Dumb?
>
> HOLLY: I hated it. Let me read your journal.
>
> JANE: No, it's stupid.—No, don't take it.—Give it back. (whispers) Teacher! Teacher! (Teacher comes into the classroom, and both students straighten in their seats.)

or on the day's activity:

> NELLIE (to those around her during potato description day): I can't believe this! (She closes her book and starts writing a letter to a friend).

These activities, also relatively common, allow the individual students to claim explicitly whether or not they accept the activity going on around them. Interestingly, most of these in-class comments expressed negative evaluations, even though formal student evaluations of the course showed most students thought this was the best writing course they'd ever taken. The purpose of these evaluative comments, it seems, is the same purpose as the other underlife activities—to assert one's fundamental distance from the classroom roles. Negative evaluations show that one can think independently; positive evaluations would show compliance with the course expectations. The purpose of such an evaluative comment has nothing to do with what the student really thinks of the class when comparing it to other classes. Instead, it has to do with asserting the student's ability to think in ways other than those expected in the classroom.

The last major category of underlife activity involved those private activities whereby an individual divides her attention between the class activity and something else. The most common example of divided attention was reading the student newspaper while the teacher was beginning class, but more interesting examples occurred. In this class, students were required to turn in a one-page journal entry every day—in a typical class period, four or five students could be observed writing their journals. Sometimes they would write these in such a way that the teacher would think they were taking notes. Sometimes they would write them as they were participating in small group discussions. In each case, however, they would be dividing their attention between the journal page and the activity that the teacher had set up. Both activities, of course, were connected to class demands; what was rebellious about writing the journal in class was that it took full and undivided attention away from the prescribed activity in the classroom.

The point of all these underlife activities is clearly to distance oneself from the demands of the classroom while hopefully remaining successful within it. All would be considered examples of "contained" underlife by Erving Goffman. The point is not to disrupt the functioning of the classroom, but to provide the other participants in the classroom with a sense that one has other things to do, other interests, that one is a much richer personality than can be shown in this context. All these activities, in short, allow the student to take a stance towards her participation in the classroom, and show that, while she can succeed in this situation, her self is not swallowed up by it. The interesting parts of herself, she seems to say, are being held in reserve.

Underlife and the Writing Teacher

If student underlife within the writing classroom is "contained" underlife, then the writing teacher's position can only be considered "disruptive." Students merely try to gain a little psychic distance from the roles they must inhabit in the classroom, but writing teachers clearly see themselves as engaged in the process of changing classroom roles. In fact, many writing teachers explain their position as one of "struggle" against the prevailing educational institution because the goals of writing are finally different from the goals of traditional education. Adrienne Rich, for example, claims in "Teaching Language in Open Admissions" that her goal of helping underprivileged writers find ways of writing powerfully in their own contexts comes into conflict with large social institutions which would prefer these individuals remained inarticulate. Mike Rose's article, "The Language of Exclusion," describes the writing teacher's plight, aware of the importance of writing for learning and thinking on the one hand, but forced by institutional administrators to test, remediate, and exclude students because of their poor writing "skills" on the other, and claims teachers must strive for the first while combating the second. In "Reality, Consensus, and Reform," Greg Myers shows how wanting to teach writing as a freeing process has historically been in conflict with (and undercut by) the ideological purposes of the educational institution, and argues that writing teachers need to recognize that "our interests are not the same as those of the institutions that employ us, and that the improvement of our work will involve social changes" (170). Similarly, Pamela Annas' "Style as Politics" shows how, for writers who are disadvantaged within the current social structure, writing is always a complex political act of finding language to express other possibilities than those offered by the current sociopolitical climate, and that this finding of language is in conflict with the standards of accepted writing. In each case, these writing teachers feel themselves to be after something different from what the traditional education system produces—instead of traditional "good students," they want students who will come to see themselves as unique, productive writers with influence on their environment.

They would like their students to see themselves as writers rather than as students, and their pedagogical changes are attempts to facilitate this shift in roles. Writing teachers change the classroom to help students extend their identities.

Writing teachers, however, are more likely to speak of "voice" than of "identity," for the first is a rhetorical concept and the second a sociological concept. But the two are very closely related, since both have to do with the stance an individual takes towards experience. In writing theory, a writer's "voice" is most often described as the unique stance she takes towards experience, and the unique way she relates herself to her context. In sociological theory, as we have seen, "identity" develops out of the individual's stance towards experience and out of the way she relates herself to the roles assigned her in the context. The ideas are closely connected: when a writing teacher worries about her student's "voice," she is also worrying about her student's "identity."

In writing classrooms, "voice" is often felt to be the paradox that prompts pedagogical change—as teachers, we want students to write in their own voices, but how can they when we *assign* them to? And how can their voices really be their own when they are evaluated by us? Knoblauch and Brannon explain in their *Rhetorical Traditions and the Teaching of Writing:*

> How can teachers hope to encourage engaged writing, particularly given the fact that classroom composing is, to a degree, inevitably artificial since the impulse to write comes from outside the writers? . . . Any school writing alters the normal circumstances in which a writer takes initiative to communicate to some reader, and in which the reader is interested in the substance of that particular text but not especially interested in the writer's overall ability or continuing maturation. (108)

If our goal as writing teachers is to enable students to see themselves as and to act as writers, then our role as teachers making assignments and evaluating their performance can only get in the way. In the classroom, students write to comply with our demands—they don't write because they see themselves as writers. The need for writers to develop their own voices is the central place where writing pedagogy comes into conflict with itself. If students really are to develop their own voices, they will need to ignore the requirements set for them by outsiders and write instead as they want—they would need, in short, to engage in a kind of underlife in relation to the classroom.

What's at stake, it seems, is a part of their "identity"—we would like them to think of themselves as *writers* rather than as *students*. We would hope they see purposes for writing beyond the single purpose of getting us to give them good grades. We would like them to take initiative to communicate with readers, to use writing to help better their world, to use writing to help them understand their world. Instead, we worry that they may see themselves only as games-players, as individuals forced to play the student role and who consequently distance themselves from that role as anyone working in an organization does. As writing teachers, we want them to *own* their writing, rather than attributing it only to the classroom—rather than claiming it's only a game we play in class.

If we wish them to see themselves as writers, we must help both them and ourselves to see our interaction in writing classrooms as cut from a different mold than "regular" classrooms. The roles must be different.

In fact, it is exactly such problems with classroom roles that lurk behind current calls to change writing pedagogy. The range of such suggested changes is staggering. Janet Emig's "Non-Magical Thinking" and Peter Elbow's *Writing Without Teachers* both argue that the teacher should become "a writer among writers," and that the first requirement of the writing teacher is that she must write herself, often and in many modes. Knoblauch and Brannon's *Rhetorical Traditions* suggests changing the structure of the classroom to a "writing workshop" where students and teacher can really talk to one another "as members of the same community of learners" (111). Donald Murray's *A Writer Teaches Writing* argues for one-on-one conferences between writer and teacher, in which the teacher takes a secondary place to the writer's own talk about her work and acts mainly as a fellow writer-editor and not as a teacher. Alongside these suggestions for classroom reform are powerful indictments of the traditional writing classroom for being teacher-centered rather than student-centered, focused on the product rather than process, being oppressive rather than liberating.

The whole call for pedagogical shift is most powerfully a call for a shift in the identity roles offered in the classroom. In other words, although we haven't clearly articulated it, the organizing assumption of composition instruction, in theory and practice, is that the primary function of the composition classroom is to foster a particular identity or stance towards the world. Writing teachers want to produce writers, not students, and consequently we seek to change our pedagogy to allow the possibility of the writer's identity.

CONCLUSION: WRITING, AUTONOMY, AND ACTION

The reasons writing teachers seek to alter normal classroom practice and the reasons students express their distance as individuals from classroom roles thus seem intimately connected: both have to do with a concern for the student's identity. Neither writing teacher nor student is content to rely on the expected roles of teacher and student. Both want there to be more to the self, and both show this desire—the student by distancing herself from classroom expectations, the teacher by structuring the course so that normal classroom expectations are only partly in effect.

What is at stake, in other words, is who the individuals in the classroom will be. Student underlife primarily attempts to assert that the individuals who play the role of students are not only students, that there is more to them than that. It is thus a *contained* form of underlife, a form which (as Goffman would say) attempts to exist within the existing structure without introducing too much friction. But writing teachers would have students go further—they would have students see themselves as writers, as people who use the processes writing offers to explore, question, and change elements of their social lives. Writing instruction is thus a *disruptive* form of underlife, a form which tries to undermine the nature of the institution and posit a different one in its place.

When we look at writing instruction from the perspective of underlife, it appears that the purpose of our courses is to allow students to substitute one kind of underlife for another. Instead of the naive, contained form they normally employ, we're asking them to take on a disruptive form—a whole stance towards their social world that questions it, explores it, writes about it. We ask them to stand apart from the roles they normally play, and instead to try exploring what they normally think and what they'd normally do through writing. We would like them to become distanced from their experience, and consider it. As their underlife behavior shows, they are of course already distanced, already posing as "different from" the roles they play every day. They *are* different from these roles. But they aren't conscious of how they are different, and how they work to maintain their difference. And that, it seems, is what writing instruction tries to do—get them to become conscious of their differences from their normal roles, get them to accept that they are different, get them to explore and write out of these differences. Writing, finally, asks individuals to accept their own underlife, to accept the fact that they are never completely subsumed by their roles, and instead can stand apart from them and contemplate. Writing instruction seeks to help the learner see herself as an original thinker, instead of as a "student" whose purpose is to please teachers by absorbing and repeating information.

It is in this desire to shift roles, from student to writer, from teacher-pleaser to original thinker, that writing instruction comes into greatest conflict with the existing educational system, and also has the most to offer to it. For the shift begun in writing classrooms is a shift that would improve education in other classrooms as well. If the student in a chemistry class grew to think of herself as someone who thinks in certain ways to solve certain problems rather than as someone who must "learn" equations to pass tests, then the student would begin to see herself as a chemist, and to act accordingly. In other words, if all our classrooms were to focus on fostering the identities of students as thinkers in our disciplines rather than merely on transmitting the knowledge of our fields, then students might easily see the purpose for these particular "information games." But for students to see themselves as chemists, or social scientists, or writers, they must first see themselves as more than just students in our classrooms, as real thinkers with power and ability in this area. To help students make this change, of course, would require just as far-reaching pedagogical changes in other areas as writing teachers have begun to make in theirs. It would need much that is now only offered in writing classes—small class size, student-directed projects, peer interaction, chances for revising work and ideas as the course progresses. In all these changes, writing teachers could lead the way. For the student's identity of writer as original thinker, as able to step outside expectations and think creatively on one's own, may be the identity that would make the other identities possible, in the same way that the identity of "good student" (complete with study skills and time management behaviors) is now what makes traditional academic learning possible. Such a shift in education would be a far-reaching and beneficial shift, focusing on the identity and abilities of the student as an original thinker, rather than on the student's ability to comply with classroom authority.

Writing, in short, is "about" autonomy and action—to really learn to write means becoming a certain kind of person, a person who accepts, explores, and uses her differences from assigned roles to produce new knowledge, new action, and new roles. The concept of underlife shows us this process, a process at work in every classroom and at the core of our discipline. It suggests we think carefully about the identities we have, the identities we model, and the identities we ask students to take on, for the process of building identity is the business we are in.

AFTERWORD . . . .

Rereading "Underlife and Writing Instruction" in 1998, I notice the focus on identity and conflict. "Writing involves being able to challenge one's assigned roles long enough that one can think originally; it involves living in conflict," I wrote then. Now, in 1998, these ideas resonate with many of the movements energizing composition: cultural studies viewing identity as a product of cultural literacies; critical pedagogies asking students to critique their cultural places; postcolonial and feminist compositionists describing the self as torn between opposing discourses. All these movements developed independently, yet I note the resonance now and can't help thinking this article would have been richer had I access to such material then.

But beyond that, the difference in myself as a reader/writer of this article involves exactly the kind of identity shift I was struggling to articulate. In 1987, I was a beginning assistant professor, fresh from graduate school, fascinated by the "disruptive" side of underlife. Goffman's concept helped me articulate something I was feeling: skepticism about the coercive forces of power that pushed all of us (students, teachers, administrators) into institutional roles. I wanted to find and name my own individual stance amongst these forces. But now, in 1998, my identity has shifted as my relations to power and institutions have changed. Now, I'm a full professor working with the National Writing Project and several state agencies to develop programs which might help revitalize Nebraska rural communities. I still see the coercive force of power (it's hard not to in a world as inequitable as ours), but I focus more on the productive possibilities of institutions and communities, the roles they create. I watch an oral history project develop in Aurora, Nebraska, through which high school students create web pages to record the wisdom of elderly community members, or I watch elementary teachers in Albion, Nebraska, pair students and community members to adopt local buildings, find their archives, interview any surviving past owners. Such school projects are, of course, necessarily coercive in their reading, writing, and research requirements. But at the same time they produce new roles and relationships. Teenagers and the elderly get to know each other, value each other's stories. Kids and businesses become jointly interested in their town's past, perhaps seeing themselves as part of ongoing rural change in relation to American history. These emerging programs create identity options for rural people that weren't fully there before. They enrich the range of roles we all might choose.

"The process of building identity is the business we are in," I wrote in 1987. Much of the work of compositionists in the 1990s, by minds far better than my own, has been to develop deep connections and conflicts between identity and discourse and community. Now that we, as a field, understand this, perhaps the task of the next ten years will be to imagine programs which increase the self's possible roles, widening the ways literacy is used in the celebration and establishment of viable, sustainable communities.

–ROBERT BROOKE
University of Nebraska–Lincoln

Rhetorical Reading Strategies
       and the Construction of Meaning

CHRISTINA HAAS
AND LINDA FLOWER

*T*here is a growing consensus in our field
that reading should be thought of as a constructive rather than as a receptive
process: that "meaning" does not exist in a text but in readers and the representations they build. This constructive view of reading is being vigorously
put forth, in different ways, by both literary theory and cognitive research. It
is complemented by work in rhetoric which argues that reading is also a discourse act. That is, when readers construct meaning, they do so in the context
of a discourse situation, which includes the writer of the original text, other
readers, the rhetorical context for reading, and the history of the discourse. If
reading really is this constructive, rhetorical process, it may both demand
that we rethink how we teach college students to read texts and suggest useful parallels between the act of reading and the more intensively studied
process of writing. However, our knowledge of how readers actually carry
out this interpretive process with college-level expository texts is rather limited. And a process we can't describe may be hard to teach.

We would like to help extend this constructive, rhetorical view of reading, which we share with others in the field, by raising two questions. The
first is, how does this constructive process play itself out in the actual, thinking process of reading? And the second is, are all readers really aware of or in
control of the discourse act which current theories describe? In the study we
describe below, we looked at teachers trying to understand a complex
college-level text and observed a process that was constructive in a quite literal sense of the term. Using a think-aloud procedure, we watched as readers
used not only the text but their own knowledge of the world, of the topic,
and of discourse conventions, to infer, set and discard hypotheses, predict,
and question in order to construct meaning for texts. One of the ways readers
tried to make meaning of the text was a strategy we called "rhetorical reading," an active attempt at constructing a rhetorical context for the text as a
way of making sense of it. However, this valuable move was a special strat-

This essay was first published in *CCC*, Volume 39, Number 2, May 1988.

egy used only by more experienced readers. We observed a sharp distinction between the rhetorical process these experienced readers demonstrated and the processes of freshman readers. It may be that these student readers, who relied primarily on text-based strategies to construct their meanings, do not have the same full sense of reading as the rhetorical or social discourse act we envision.

Some of the recent work on reading and cognition gives us a good starting point for our discussion since it helps describe what makes the reading process so complex and helps explain how people can construct vastly different interpretations of the same text. Although a thinking aloud protocol can show us a great deal, we must keep in mind that it reveals only part of what goes on as a reader is building a representation of a text. And lest the "constructive" metaphor makes this process sound tidy, rational, and fully conscious, we should emphasize that it may in fact be rapid, unexamined, and even inexpressible. The private mental representation that a reader constructs has many facets: it is likely to include a representation of propositional or content information, a representation of the structure—either conventional or unique—of that information, and a representation of how the parts of the text function. In addition, the reader's representation may include beliefs about the subject matter, about the author and his or her credibility, and about the reader's own intentions in reading. In short, readers construct meaning by building multi-faceted, interwoven representations of knowledge. The current text, prior texts, and the reading context can exert varying degrees of influence on this process, but it is the reader who must integrate information into meaning.

We can begin to piece together the way this constructive, cognitive process operates based on recent research on reading and comprehension, and on reading and writing. Various syntheses of this work have been provided by Bransford; Baker and Brown; Flower ("Interpretive Acts"); and Spivey. To begin with, it is helpful to imagine the representations readers build as complex networks, like dense roadmaps, made up of many nodes of information, each related to others in multiple ways. The nodes created during a few minutes of reading would probably include certain content propositions from the text. The network might also contain nodes for the author's name, for a key point in the text, for a personal experience evoked by the text, for a striking word or phrase, and for an inference the reader made about the value of the text, or its social or personal significance. The links between a group of nodes might reflect causality, or subordination, or simple association, or a strong emotional connection.

The process of constructing this representation is carried out by both highly automated processes of recognition and inference *and* by the more active problem-solving processes on which our work focuses. For instance, trying to construct a well-articulated statement of the "point" of a text may require active searching, inferencing, and transforming of one's own knowledge. The reason such transformations are constantly required can be explained by the "multiple-representation thesis" proposed by Flower and

Hayes ("Images" 120). It suggests that readers' and writers' mental representations are not limited to verbally well-formed ideas and plans, but may include information coded as visual images, or as emotions, or as linguistic propositions that exist just above the level of specific words. These representations may also reflect more abstract schema, such as the schema most people have for narrative or for establishing credibility in a conversation. Turning information coded in any of these forms into a fully verbal articulation of the "point," replete with well-specified connections between ideas and presented according to the standard conventions of a given discourse, is constructive; it can involve not only translating one kind of representation into another, but reorganizing knowledge and creating new knowledge, new conceptual nodes and connections. In essence, it makes sense to take the metaphor of "construction" seriously.

It should be clear that this image of "meaning" as a rich network of disparate kinds of information is in sharp contrast to the narrow, highly selective and fully verbal statement of a text's gist or "meaning" that students may be asked to construct for an exam or a book review. Statements of that sort do, of course, serve useful functions, but we should not confuse them with the multi-dimensional, mental structures of meaning created by the cognitive and affective process of reading.

If reading, then, is a process of responding to cues in the text and in the reader's context to build a complex, multi-faceted representation of meaning, it should be no surprise that different readers might construct radically different representations of the same text and might use very different strategies to do so. This makes the goals of teacher and researcher look very much alike: both the teacher and the researcher are interested in the means by which readers (especially students) construct multi-faceted representations, or "meaning." The study we are about to describe looks at a practical and theoretical question that this constructive view of reading raises: namely, what strategies, other than those based on knowing the topic, do readers bring to the process of understanding difficult texts—and how does this translate into pedagogy?

Seeing reading as a constructive act encourages us as teachers to move from merely *teaching texts* to *teaching readers*. The teacher as co-reader can both model a sophisticated reading process and help students draw out the rich possibilities of texts and readers, rather than trying to insure that all students interpret texts in a single, "correct" way—and in the same way. Yet this goal—drawing out the rich possibilities of texts and of readers—is easier to describe than to reach.

What Is "Good Reading"?

The notion of multiple, constructed representations also helps us understand a recurring frustration for college teachers: the problem of "good" readers who appear to miss the point or who seem unable or unwilling to read critically. Many of our students are "good" readers in the traditional sense: they have large vocabularies, read quickly, are able to do well at comprehension tasks involving recall of content. They can identify topic sentences, introductions and conclusions, generalizations and supporting details. Yet these same students often frustrate us, as they paraphrase rather than analyze, summarize rather than criticize texts. Why are these students doing less than we hope for?

To interpret any sophisticated text seems to require not only careful reading and prior knowledge, but the ability to read the text on several levels, to build multi-faceted representations. A text is understood not only as content and information, but also as the result of someone's intentions, as part of a larger discourse world, and as having real effects on real readers. In an earlier study, we say that experienced readers made active use of the strategy of rhetorical reading not only to predict and interpret texts but to solve problems in comprehension (Flower, "Construction of Purpose"). Vipond and Hunt have observed a related strategy of "point-driven" (vs. "story-driven") reading which people bring to literary texts.

If we view reading as the act of constructing multi-faceted yet integrated representations, we might hypothesize that the problem students have with critical reading of difficult texts is less the representations they *are* constructing than those they *fail to construct*. Their representations of text are closely tied to content: they read for information. Our students may believe that if they understand all the words and can paraphrase the propositional content of a text, then they have successfully "read" it.

While a content representation is often satisfactory—it certainly meets the needs of many pre-college read-to-take-a-test assignments—it falls short with tasks or texts which require analysis and criticism. What many of our students *can* do is to construct representations of content, of structure, and of conventional features. What they often *fail* to *do* is to move beyond content and convention and construct representations of texts as purposeful actions, arising from contexts, and with intended effects. "Critical reading" involves more than careful reading for content, more than identification of conventional features of discourse, such as introductions or examples, and more than simple evaluation based on agreeing or disagreeing. Sophisticated, difficult texts often require the reader to build an equally sophisticated, complex representation of meaning. But how does this goal translate into the process of reading?

As intriguing as this notion of the active construction of meaning is, we really have no direct access to the meanings/representations that readers build. We cannot enter the reader's head and watch as the construction of meaning proceeds. Nor can we get anything but an indirect measure of the nature, content, and structure of that representation. What we can do, however, is to watch the way that readers go about building representations: we can observe their use of *reading strategies* and so infer something about the representations they build.

In order to learn something about the construction of meaning by readers, we observed and analyzed the strategies of ten readers. Four were experienced college readers, graduate students (aged 26 to 31 years), three in engineering and one in rhetoric; six were student readers, college freshmen aged 18 and 19, three classified "average" and three classified "above average" by their freshman composition teachers.

We were interested in how readers go about "constructing" meaning and the constructive strategies they use to do so. However, we suspected that many academic topics would give an unfair advantage to the more experienced readers, who would be able to read automatically by invoking their knowledge of academic topics and discourse conventions. This automaticity would, however, make their constructive reading harder for us to see. We wanted a text that would require equally active problem solving by both groups. So, in order to control for such knowledge, we designed a task in which meaning was under question for all readers, and in which prior topic knowledge would function as only one of many possible tools used to build an interpretation. Therefore, the text began *in medias res,* without orienting information about author, source, topic, or purpose. We felt that in this way we could elicit the full range of constructive strategies these readers could call upon when the situation demanded it.

The text, part of the preface to Sylvia Farnham-Diggory's *Cognitive Processes in Education,* was like many texts students read, easy to decode but difficult to interpret, with a high density of information and a number of semi-technical expressions which had to be defined from context. The readers read and thought aloud as they read. In addition, they answered the question "how do you interpret the text now?" at frequent intervals. The question was asked of readers eight times, thus creating nine reading "episodes." The slash marks indicate where the question appeared, and also mark episode boundaries, which we discuss later. To see the effect of this manipulation on eliciting interpretive strategies, you might wish to read the experimental text before going further. (Sentence numbers have been added.)

But somehow the social muddle persists.[s1] Some wonderful children come from appalling homes; some terrible children come from splendid homes.[s2] Practice may have a limited relationship to perfection—at least it cannot substitute for talent.[s3] Women are not happy when they are required to pretend that a physical function is equivalent to a mental one.[s4] Many children teach themselves to read years before they are supposed to be "ready."[s5] / Many men would not dream of basing their self-esteem on "cave man" prowess.[s6] And despite their verbal glibness, teenagers seem to be in a worse mess than ever.[s7] /

What has gone wrong?[s8] Are the psychological principles invalid?[s9] Are they too simple for a complex world?[s10] /

Like the modern world, modern scientific psychology is extremely technical and complex.[s11] The application of any particular set of psychological principles to any particular real problem requires a double specialist: a specialist in the scientific area, and a specialist in the real area.[s12] /

Not many such double specialists exist.[s13] The relationship of a child's current behavior to his early home life, for example, is not a simple problem—Sunday Supplement psychology notwithstanding.[s14] / Many variables must be understood and integrated: special ("critical") periods of brain sensitivity, nutrition, genetic factors, the development of attention and perception, language, time factors (for example, the amount of time that elapses between a baby's action and a mother's smile), and so on.[s15] Mastery of these principles is a full-time professional occupation.[s16] / The professional application of these principles— in, say a day-care center—is also a full-time occupation, and one that is foreign to many laboratory psychologists.[s17] Indeed, a laboratory psychologist may not even recognize his pet principles when they are realized in a day care setting.[s18] /

What is needed is a coming together of real-world and laboratory specialists that will require both better communication and more complete experience.[s19] / The laboratory specialists must spend some time in a real setting; the real-world specialists must spend some time in a theoretical laboratory.[s20] Each specialist needs to practice thinking like his counterpart.[s21] Each needs to practice translating theory into reality, and reality into theory.[s22]

The technique of in-process probing tries to combine the immediacy of concurrent reporting with the depth of information obtained through frequent questioning. It can of course give us only an indirect and partial indication of the actual representation. What it does reveal are gist-making strategies used at a sequence of points during reading, and it offers a cumulative picture of a text-under-construction.

Aside from our manipulation of the presentation, the text was a typical college reading task. Part of the author's introduction to an educational psychology textbook, it presented an array of facts about the social reality of learning, problems of education, and the aims of research. *Our* reading of the text, obviously also a constructed one, but one constructed with the benefit of a full knowledge of the source and context, included two main facts and two central claims. In a later analysis, we used these facts and claims to describe some of the transactions of readers and text.

FACT: Social problems exist and psychological principles exist, but there's a mismatch between them.

FACT: There are two kinds of educational specialists—real-world and laboratory.

CLAIM (EXPLICIT IN TEXT): The two kinds of specialists should interact.

CLAIM (IMPLICIT): Interaction of the two specialists is necessary to solve social problems.

The differences in "readings" subjects constructed of the text were striking and were evidenced immediately. For instance, the following descriptions of three readers' readings of the text suggest the range of readers' concerns and begin to offer hints about the nature of their constructed representations of the text. These descriptions were what we called "early transactions" with the text—an analysis based on readers' comments during reading of the first two paragraphs, or ten sentences, of the text.

Seth, a 27-year-old graduate student in Engineering, by his own account a voracious reader of literature in his own field, of travel books, history, and contemporary novels, is initially confused with the concepts "physical function and mental one" (sentence 4). He then explains his confusion by noting the nature of the materials: "well, that's got some relationship with something that came before this business."

Kara, a freshman who does average college work, also thinks the text is confusing; specifically, she says "I don't know what 'glibness' means" (sentence 7). But whereas Seth sets up an hypothesis about both the content of the text and its source—"I think it's part of an article on the fact that the way you turn out is not a function of your environment"—and reads on to confirm his hypothesis, Kara's reading proceeds as a series of content paraphrases—"It's talking about children coming from different homes . . . and women not being happy." She continues to interpret the text a chunk at a time, paraphrasing linearly with little attempt to integrate or connect the parts. She reacts positively to the text—"I love the expression 'what has gone wrong'" (sentence 8)—and, despite her initial confusion with "glibness," she seems satisfied with her simple reading: "I just feel like you're talking about people—what's wrong with them and the world."

Not all the freshman student readers' transactions with the text were as superficial and oversimplified as Kara's—nor were they all as contented with their readings of the text. Bob—an above-average freshman with a premed major—paraphrases content linearly like Kara, but he also sets up a hypothetical structure for the text: "It seems that different points are being brought out and each one has a kind of a contradiction in it, and it seems like an introduction. . . ." Unlike Kara, however, he becomes frustrated, unable to reconcile his own beliefs with what he's reading: "Well, I don't think they're too simple for a complex world. I don't think these are very simple things that are being said here. I think the situations—women, children, and men— I think they're pretty complex . . . so I don't understand why it said 'too simple for a complex world'" (sentence 10).

Our more experienced reader, Seth, also sets up an hypothesis about the text's structure: "Maybe he's [the author] contrasting the verbal glibness with caveman instinct." But Seth goes further: "I think the author is trying to say that it's some balance between your natural instinct and your surroundings but he's not sure what that balance is." These hypotheses try to account for not only the propositional content of the text, but also the function of parts ("contrasting"), the author's intent, and even the author's own uncertainty.

Seth continues to read the text, noting his own inexperience with the area of psychology—"I'm thinking about Freud and I really don't know much about psychology"—and trying to tie what he has just read to the previous paragraph: "I guess the psychological principles have something to do with the way children turn out. But I don't know if they are the physical, environmental things or if they're a function of your surroundings and education."

In these "early transactions" with the text, we see a range of readings and vast differences in the information contained in the readers' representations: Kara is uncertain of the meaning of a word and somewhat confused generally; she paraphrases content and is satisfied with the text and her reading of it. If we have a hint about the representations of text that Kara is building it is that they are focused primarily on content and her own affective responses and that they are somewhat more limited than those of the other readers. Bob's comments suggest that he may be building representations of structure as well as content, and that he is trying to bring his own beliefs and his reading of the text into line.

Seth is concerned with the content, with possible functions—both for parts of the text and for the text as a whole—with the author's intentions, with the experimental situation and with missing text; he also attends to his own knowledge (or lack of it) and to his prior reading experiences. What this suggests is that Seth is creating a multi-dimensional representation of the text that includes representations of its content, representations of the structure and function of the text, representations of author's intention and his own experience and knowledge as a reader of the text.

The "texts" or representations of meaning that the readers created as they were wrestling with the text and thinking aloud were dramatically different in both **quantity**—the amount of information they contained—and **quality**—the kinds of information they contained and the amount of the original text they accounted for. However, with no direct access to the internal representations that readers were building, we looked instead at the overt strategies they seemed to be using.

STRATEGIES FOR CONSTRUCTING MEANING

The initial transactions with text suggested some differences among readers. Our next move was to more systematically analyze these differences. Each protocol contained two kinds of verbalizations: actual reading of the text aloud and comments in which the readers were thinking aloud. About half of these comments were in response to the question, "How do you interpret the text now?" and the rest were unprompted responses. Each comment was sorted into one of three categories, based on what the readers seemed to be "attending to." This simple, three-part coding scheme distinguished between Content, Function/Feature, and Rhetorical reading strategies. These strategies are readily identifiable with some practice; our inter-rater reliability, determined by simple pair-wise comparisons, averaged 82%. Later, after about 20 minutes' instruction in the context of a college reading classroom, students could identify the strategies in the reading of others with close to 70% reliability.

Comments coded as *content strategies* are concerned with content or topic information, "what the text is about." The reader may be questioning, interpreting, or summing content, paraphrasing what the text "is about" or "is saying." The reader's goal in using content strategies seems to be getting information from the text. Some examples of comments coded as content strategies:

> "So we're talking about psychological principles here."

> "I think it's about changing social conditions, like families in which both parents work, and changing roles of women."

> "I don't know what glibness is, so it's still confusing."

As Table 1 shows, both students and more experienced readers spent a large proportion of their effort using content strategies. On the average, 77% of the reading protocol was devoted to content strategies for students, 67% for the older readers. Building a representation of content seems to be very important for all of the readers we studied.

Function/feature strategies were used to refer to conventional, generic functions of texts, or conventional features of discourse. These strategies seemed closely tied to the text: readers frequently named text parts, pointing to specific words, sentences, or larger sections of text—"This is the main point," "This must be an example," "I think this is the introduction." While content strategies seemed to be used to explain what the text was "saying," function/feature strategies were often used to name what the text was "doing": "Here he's contrasting," "This part seems to be explaining. . . ." In short, the use of these strategies suggests that readers are constructing spatial, functional, or relational structures for the text. Some examples of comments coded as function/feature strategies:

> "I guess these are just examples."

> "Is this the introduction?"

> "This seems to be the final point."

Predictably, these strategies accounted for less of the protocol than did the content strategies: 22% for students, 20% for more experienced readers (see Table 1). And the groups of readers looked similar in their use of this strategy. This, too, may be expected: identifying features such as introduc-

TABLE 1   Mean Proportion of Strategies Used

	Students	Experienced Readers
Content Strategies	77% (58.1)	67% (58.0)
Feature Strategies	22% (15.8)	20% (18.0)
Rhetorical Strategies	1%* (.3)	13%* (9.3)

*Difference significant at .05 level. Numbers in parentheses indicate the mean number of protocol statements in each category.

tions, examples, and conclusions is standard fare in many junior high and high school curricula. In addition, these students are of at least average ability within a competitive private university. We might ask if more basic readers—without the skills or reading experiences of these students—might demonstrate less use of the function/feature strategies. Further, these readers were all reading from paper; people reading from computer screens—a number which is rapidly increasing—may have difficulty creating and recalling spatial and relational structures in texts they read and write on-line (Haas and Hayes 34–35).

Rhetorical strategies take a step beyond the text itself. They are concerned with constructing a rhetorical situation for the text, trying to account for author's purpose, context, and effect on the audience. In rhetorical reading strategies readers use cues in the text, and their own knowledge of discourse situations, to recreate or infer the rhetorical situation of the text they are reading. There is some indication that these strategies were used to help readers uncover the actual "event" of the text, a unique event with a particular author and actual effects. One reader likened the author of the text to a contemporary rhetorician: "This sounds a little like Richard Young to me." Readers seem to be constructing a rhetorical situation for the text and relating *this* text to a larger world of discourse. These examples demonstrate some of the range of rhetorical strategies: comments concerned with author's purpose, context or source, intended audience, and actual effect. Some examples of rhetorical reading strategies:

> "So the author is trying to make the argument that you need scientific specialists in psychology."
>
> "I wonder if it [the article] is from *Ms.*"
>
> "I don't think this would work for the man-in-the-street."
>
> "I wonder, though, if this is a magazine article, and I wonder if they expected it to be so confusing."

While the groups of readers employed content and function/feature strategies similarly, there is a dramatic difference in their use of the rhetorical strategy category. Less than 1% (in fact, one statement by one reader) of the students' protocols contained rhetorical strategies, while 13% of the experienced readers' effort went into rhetorical strategies. This is particularly striking when we consider the richness and wealth of information contained in these kinds of comments. For instance, setting this article into the context of *Ms.* magazine brings with it a wealth of unstated information about the kind of article that appears in that source, the kind of writers that contribute to it, and the kind of people who read it.

Rhetorical reading appears to be an "extra" strategy which some readers used and others did not. Mann-Whitney analyses show no significant differences in the use of content or function/feature strategies, and an interesting—$p < .05$—difference between the two groups in use of rhetorical strategies. The small numbers in parentheses indicate the mean number of protocol statements in each category for each group of readers; the significance tests, however, were performed on the proportions of strategies used by each reader.

An example of two readers responding to a particularly difficult section of text reveals the differences in the use of strategies even more clearly than do the numbers.

> STUDENT READER: Well, basically, what I said previously is that there seems to be a problem between the real-world and the laboratory, or ideal situation versus real situation, whatever way you want to put it—that seems to be it.

> EXPERIENCED READER: OK, again, real world is a person familiar with the social influences on a person's personality—things they read or hear on the radio. . . . And laboratory specialists is more trained in clinical psychology. And now I think this article is trying to propose a new field of study for producing people who have a better understanding of human behavior. This person is crying out for a new type of scientist or something. (Ph.D. Student in Engineering)

While the student reader is mainly creating a gist and paraphrasing content, the experienced reader does this and more—he then tries to infer the author's purpose and even creates a sort of strident persona for the writer. If readers can only build representations for which they have constructive tools or strategies, then it is clear that this student reader—and in fact all of the student readers we studied—are not building rhetorical representations of this text. In fact, these student readers seem to be focused almost exclusively on content. The student reader above is a case in point: her goal seems to be to extract information from the text, and once that is done—via a simple paraphrase—she is satisfied with her reading of the text. We called this type of content reading "knowledge-getting," to underscore the similarity to the knowledge-telling strategy identified by Bereiter and Scardamalia (72) in immature writers. In both knowledge-getting and knowledge-telling, the focus is on content; larger rhetorical purposes seem to play no role.

It is useful to see rhetorical reading not as a separate and different strategy but as a progressive enlargement of the constructed meaning of a text. These student readers seldom "progressed" to that enlarged view. Reading for content is usually dominant and crucial—other kinds of strategies build upon content representations. Functions and features strategies are generic and conventional—easily identified in texts and often explicitly taught. Rhetorical strategies include not only a representation of discourse as discourse but as *unique* discourse with a real author, a specific purpose, and actual effects. This possible relationship between strategies may point to a building of skills, a progression which makes intuitive sense and is supported by what we know about how reading is typically taught and by teachers' reports of typical student reading problems.

The difference in the use that experienced and student readers make of these strategies does not in itself make a convincing case for their value. Rhetorical reading strategies certainly *look* more sophisticated and elaborate, but an important question remains: What does rhetorical reading *do* for readers? We might predict that constructing the additional rhetorical representation—requiring more depth of processing—would be an asset in particularly problematic reading tasks: texts in a subject area about which the reader knows little, or texts complex in structure. It might also be important in those reading tasks in which recognizing author's intention is crucial: propaganda, satire, even the interpretation of assignments in school.

However, let us consider a rival hypothesis for a moment: maybe rhetorical strategies are simply "frosting on the cake." Maybe good readers use these strategies because reading for information is easier for them, and they have extra cognitive resources to devote to what might be largely peripheral concerns of the rhetorical situation.

We suspect that this was not the case, that rhetorical reading is not merely "frosting on the cake" for several reasons: first, in the absence of a rhetorical situation for the text, *all* experienced readers constructed one. Second, the more experienced readers seemed to be using all the strategies in tandem; i.e., they used the rhetorical strategies to help construct content, and vice versa. They did not "figure out" the content, and then do rhetorical reading as an "embellishment." Rhetorical reading strategies were interwoven with other strategies as the readers constructed their reading of the texts.

And third, in the "tug of war" between text and reader which characterizes constructive reading (Tierney and Pearson 34), we found that the rhetorical readers seemed to recognize and assimilate more facts and claims into their reading of the text. Recall that there were two facts and two claims which we felt constituted a successful reading of this text. We used readers' recognition of these facts and claims to gauge and to describe the kind of representation they had constructed.

FACT: Social problems exist and psychological principles exist, but there's a mismatch between them.

FACT: There are two kinds of educational specialists—real-world and laboratory.

CLAIM (EXPLICIT IN TEXT): The two kinds of specialists should interact.

CLAIM (IMPLICIT): Interaction of the two specialists is necessary to solve social problems.

In recognizing facts in the text, both groups of readers did well. But there were very interesting differences in the patterns of recognition of claims in the text. Readers who used the rhetorical strategies, first, recognized more claims, and second, identified claims sooner than other readers. As we described earlier, our presentation of the text to the readers created nine reading episodes; each asked for the readers' interpretation of "the text so far" at the end of the episode. This allowed us some measure of constructed meaning by plotting the points at which readers recognized each fact or claim. We said that readers recognized a claim when they mentioned it as a possibility. This "recognition" was often tentative; readers made comments such as "So maybe this section is saying the two kinds of scientists should communicate," or "I guess this could solve the stuff at the beginning about social muddle."

The "episode line" in Figure 1 shows the points at which two readers (a student and a more experienced reader) recognized Claim 1, plotted in relation to the point at which the text would reasonably permit such recognition. Figure 2 shows this information for the same readers recognizing Claim 2. Claim 2 is never explicitly stated, it only becomes easy to infer in the final episode. Of all the implicit meanings the text *could* convey, we saw this second claim as central to the coherence of the argument.

As Figure 3 illustrates, all student readers got Claim 1, but only at episode 9, where it was explicitly stated—for the second time—in the text. (Claim 1 is first stated in episode 8.) More experienced readers, on the other hand, had all inferred Claim 1 much earlier—by episode 7. In addition, student readers did not recognize the unstated second claim at all, although all experienced readers inferred it, some as early as episode 8.

At episode 4 (the first point at which it would be possible to infer Claim 1), 25% of the experienced readers had inferred and mentioned this idea. At

FIGURE 1   When did a reader recognize Claim 1? "The two kinds of specialists should interact."

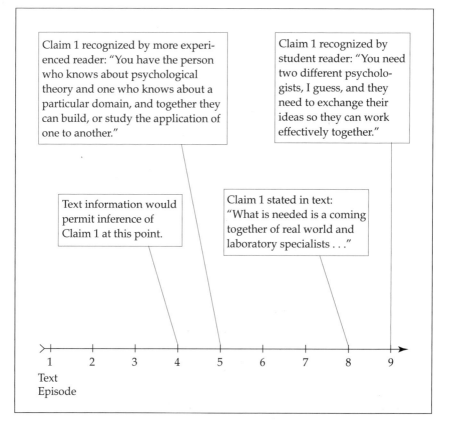

FIGURE 2 When did a reader recognize Claim 2? "Interaction of two kinds of specialists is necessary to solve social problems."

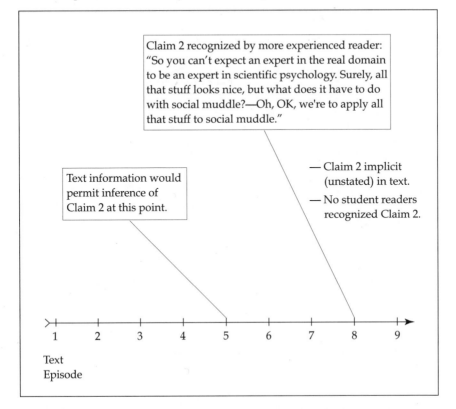

Claim 2 recognized by more experienced reader: "So you can't expect an expert in the real domain to be an expert in scientific psychology. Surely, all that stuff looks nice, but what does it have to do with social muddle?—Oh, OK, we're to apply all that stuff to social muddle."

— Claim 2 implicit (unstated) in text.

— No student readers recognized Claim 2.

Text information would permit inference of Claim 2 at this point.

1   2   3   4   5   6   7   8   9

Text
Episode

episode 5, 50% of these readers recognized it, at episode 6, 75% saw it, and by episode 7 all of the experienced readers had inferred Claim 1. In contrast, none of the student readers recognized this claim until episode 8, when it was cued in the text. At that point, 33% of the students noted it. At episode 9, when Claim 1 was restated, the rest of the students recognized it.

Claim 2 was never explicitly stated in the text, but half the experienced readers had inferred this claim at episode 8 and all had inferred it at episode 9. None of the student readers offered any hints that they had recognized this implicit claim. It seems that the rhetorical readers were better able to recognize an important claim that was *never explicitly spelled out in the text*. In sophisticated texts, many important high-level claims—like Claim 2—remain implicit, but are crucial nonetheless.

This study, because it is observational rather than experimental, does not allow us to conclude that the rhetorical reading we observed in the more experienced readers—and only in the more experienced readers—was the only or even the dominant cause for their ability to recognize claims. However, it makes sense that readers who are trying to make inferences about au-

FIGURE 3   Readers' Recognition of Claim 1

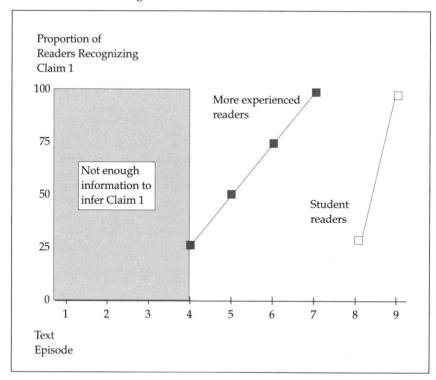

thor, context, purpose, and effect, who are trying to create a representation of the text as the result of a purposeful action, would be more likely to recognize the claims—both implicit and explicit—within a text.

THE ROLE OF RHETORICAL READING

This study suggests that the strategy of rhetorical reading may be an important element in the larger process of critical reading. The constructive process we observed in readers actively trying to understand the author's intent, the context, and how other readers might respond appears to be a good basis for recognizing claims, especially unstated ones the reader must infer. Speaking more generally, this act of building a rich representation of text—larger than the words on the page and including both propositional content and the larger discourse context within which a text functions—is the kind of constructive reading we desire our students to do.

However, is rhetorical reading a strategy students could easily adopt if cued to do so? Being able to see one's own text and the texts of others as *discourse acts*—rather than bodies of facts and information—is desirable, useful, and important for reading and writing of all kinds. This is the kind of meaning building we would like students to do, and rhetorical reading is one strategy that may help them do it. In saying this, however, we recognize that this knowledge will do us little good if we can't use it to help students. People must be *able* to construct elaborate representations of meaning, and they must have the strategies to do so. How this is to come about is not clear.

Our first attempt at "suggestive" teaching—introducing the students to the concept of rhetorical reading and encouraging them to use it—found that while students could identify the rhetorical reading strategy in the reading of others, they were less successful at using it. Can we expect merely to hand students tools for building rich representations of text and set them to work? Or will rhetorical reading require active teaching—teaching by direct instruction, by modelling, and by encouraging students to become contributing and committed members of rhetorical communities?

Although the answers to these questions are not yet clear, we offer here our own reading of these results: first, some readers are actively concerned with the situations from which texts arise. These readers seemed to expend some effort in representing the rhetorical situation of a text they are reading. However, reading is a complex cognitive activity. It involves constructing representations on several levels, and student readers, even good students, seem to be bogged down in content: they focus on knowledge-getting while reading.

We believe that teaching students to read rhetorically is genuinely difficult. It is difficult in the way that teaching students to *write* rhetorically is difficult. In fact, this work with student and experienced *readers* provides a potential parallel to research results with student and expert *writers*. While expert writers, like those Flower, Hayes, Shriver, Carey, and Haas have studied, work within a rhetorical framework—imagining audience response, acknowledging context and setting their own purposeful goals—student writers often concentrate on content and information—they "knowledge tell," in Bereiter and Scardamalia's terms. Similarly, these student readers seem to concentrate on knowledge, content, what the text is about—not taking into account that the text is the product of a writer's intentions and is designed to produce an effect on a specific audience.

While experienced readers may understand that both reading and writing are context-rich, situational, constructive acts, many students may see reading and writing as merely an information exchange: knowledge-telling when they write, and "knowledge-getting" when they read. Helping students move beyond this simple, information-exchange view to a more complex rhetorical model—in both their reading and their writing—is one of the very real tasks which faces us as teachers. And research with real readers and writers continues to offer insights into the equally complex ways all of us construct meaning.

It is interesting—if a bit humbling—to reflect back on earlier work, and we have appreciated the opportunity to do so. In some ways, it is tempting for us to "read" our essay as a culmination *of the events and influences around us at the time. Indeed, we were profoundly influenced by work in cognitive psychology (we were both collaborating with Dick Hayes at the time, and Chris was taking classes in the Psychology Department at Carnegie Mellon), by reading research and theory (where constructivist accounts of meaning making were opening new avenues for research), and of course by scholars of rhetoric (including especially the rhetoricians in our own department, Rich Enos, Dave Kaufer, and Richard Young). So, in one sense, this work is a culmination of the events surrounding it.*

Read another way, however, it is equally tempting to see our essay as the commencement *of the work that has kept each of us busy for the decade since. That is, we could view this work as leading to Chris's longitudinal study of rhetorical development in college, her interest in the reciprocity between text, tool, and agent, and her ongoing research on situated literacy with colleagues in Kent State University's Center for Research on Workplace Literacy. Or we could see this paper as an early step in Linda's work toward an expanded social/cognitive account of writing, or as the beginning of her recent theory building work, following writers into the process of constructing negotiated meaning.*

But constructing this text—or any text—as culmination or as commencement *necessarily entails a fallacy in historical thinking, what theorist of technology Wiebe Bijker calls a "Whiggish view of history," or a view in which past events necessarily culminate in a new—and better—present. In short, one of the dangers inherent in this kind of reflective exercise is a tendency to overlay a developmental narrative, a narrative only available in hindsight, onto one's own work or onto the work of the discipline as a whole. We have tried to avoid the temptation to see the "event" of our Braddock essay as part of a narrative of linear development and thereby avoid the teleology that that kind of narrative implies.*

To counter a "Whiggish" view, we offer two rival metaphors: rather than seeing our own scholarship, or the collective work of our discipline as represented in the Braddock essays, as a developmental narrative, in which events and acts build on one another, we propose seeing it as "stream," to use the metaphor of historians Neustadt and May. In their view, one avoids the fallacy of "Whiggish" history by recognizing that "time is a stream." Although the stream may be different (wider, faster, more powerful, more peaceful) at particular points, it never ceases to remain "the stream." A second metaphor which appeals to us—in thinking about our own work as well as the last twenty-five years in composition studies—is the Burkean parlor conversation: rather than seeing our essay as "prior to" Cushman's or "post–" Ede and Lunsford, we would like to think of our piece as in dialog or conversation with those pieces—and with many more besides, both in this volume and beyond.

–CHRISTINA HAAS
Kent State University

–LINDA FLOWER
Carnegie Mellon University

The Idea of Community in the Study of Writing

JOSEPH HARRIS

f you stand, today, in Between Towns Road, you can see either way; west to the spires and towers of the cathedral and colleges; east to the yards and sheds of the motor works. You see different worlds, but there is no frontier between them; there is only the movement and traffic of a single city.

—RAYMOND WILLIAMS
Second Generation (9)

In *The Country and the City,* Raymond Williams writes of how, after a boyhood in a Welsh village, he came to the city, to Cambridge, only then to hear "from townsmen, academics, an influential version of what country life, country literature, really meant: a prepared and persuasive cultural history" (6). This odd double movement, this irony, in which one only begins to understand the place one has come from through the act of leaving it, proved to be one of the shaping forces of Williams's career—so that, some 35 years after having first gone down to Cambridge, he was still to ask himself: "Where do I stand . . . in another country or in this valuing city?" (6)

A similar irony, I think, describes my own relations to the university. I was raised in a working-class home in Philadelphia, but it was only when I went away to college that I heard the term *working class* used or began to think of myself as part of it. Of course by then I no longer was quite part of it, or at least no longer wholly or simply part of it, but I had also been at college long enough to realize that my relations to it were similarly ambiguous— that here too was a community whose values and interests I could in part share but to some degree would always feel separate from.

This sense of difference, of overlap, of tense plurality, of being at once part of several communities and yet never wholly a member of one, has accompanied nearly all the work and study I have done at the university. So when, in the past few years, a number of teachers and theorists of writing

This essay was first published in *CCC,* Volume 40, Number 1, February 1989.

began to talk about the idea of *community* as somehow central to our work, I was drawn to what was said. Since my aim here is to argue for a more critical look at a term that, as Williams has pointed out, "seems never to be used unfavourably" (*Keywords* 66), I want to begin by stating my admiration for the theorists—in particular, David Bartholomae and Patricia Bizzell—whose work I will discuss. They have helped us, I think, to ask some needed questions about writing and how we might go about teaching it.[1]

Perhaps the most important work of these theorists has centered on the demystifying of the concept of *intention*. That is, rather than viewing the intentions of a writer as private and ineffable, wholly individual, they have helped us to see that it is only through being part of some ongoing discourse that we can, as individual writers, have things like points to make and purposes to achieve. As Bartholomae argues: "It is the discourse with its projects and agendas that determines what writers can and will do" (139). We write not as isolated individuals but as members of communities whose beliefs, concerns, and practices both instigate and constrain, at least in part, the sorts of things we can say. Our aims and intentions in writing are thus not merely personal, idiosyncratic, but reflective of the communities to which we belong.

But while this concern with the power of social forces in writing is much needed in a field that has long focused narrowly on the composing processes of individual writers, some problems in how we have imagined those forces are now becoming clear. First, recent theories have tended to invoke the idea of community in ways at once sweeping and vague: positing discursive utopias that direct and determine the writings of their members, yet failing to state the operating rules or boundaries of these communities. One result of this has been a view of "normal discourse" in the university that is oddly lacking in conflict or change. Recent social views of writing have also often presented university discourse as almost wholly foreign to many of our students, raising questions not only about their chances of ever learning to use such an alien tongue, but of why they should want to do so in the first place. And, finally, such views have tended to polarize our talk about writing: One seems asked to defend either the power of the discourse community or the imagination of the individual writer.

WILLIAMS AND THE PROBLEM OF COMMUNITY

In trying to work towards a more useful sense of *community*, I will take both my method and theme from Raymond Williams in his *Keywords: A Vocabulary of Culture and Society*. Williams's approach in this vocabulary reverses that of the dictionary-writer. For rather than trying to define and fix the meanings of the words he discusses, to clear up the many ambiguities involved with them, Williams instead attempts to sketch "a history and complexity of meanings" (15), to show how and why the meanings of certain words—*art, criticism, culture, history, literature,* and the like—are still being contested. Certainly *community*, at once so vague and suggestive, is such a word too, and I will begin, then, with what Williams has to say about it:

> *Community* can be the warmly persuasive word to describe an existing set of relationships, or the warmly persuasive word to describe an alternative set of relationships. What is most important, perhaps, is that unlike all other terms of social organization (*state, nation, society,* etc.) it seems never to be used unfavourably, and never to be given any positive opposing or distinguishing term. (66)

There seem to me two warnings here. The first is that, since it has no "positive opposing" term, *community* can soon become an empty and sentimental word. And it is easy enough to point to such uses in the study of writing, particularly in the many recent calls to transform the classroom into "a community of interested readers," to recast academic disciplines as "communities of knowledgeable peers," or to translate standards of correctness into "the expectations of the academic community." In such cases, *community* tends to mean little more than a nicer, friendlier, fuzzier version of what came before.

But I think Williams is also hinting at the extraordinary rhetorical power one can gain through speaking of community. It is a concept both seductive and powerful, one that offers us a view of shared purpose and effort and that also makes a claim on us that is hard to resist. For like the pronoun *we, community* can be used in such a way that it invokes what it seems merely to describe. The writer says to his reader: "We are part of a certain community; they are not" — and, if the reader accepts, the statement is true. And, usually, the gambit of community, once offered, is almost impossible to decline — since what is invoked is a community of those in power, of those who know the accepted ways of writing and interpreting texts. Look, for instance, at how David Bartholomae begins his remarkable essay on "Inventing the University":

> Every time a student sits down to write for us, he has to invent the university for the occasion — invent the university, that is, or a branch of it, like history or anthropology or economics or English. The student has to learn *to speak our language, to speak as we do,* to try on the peculiar ways of knowing, selecting, evaluating, reporting, concluding, and arguing that define *the discourse of our community.* (134, my emphases)

Note here how the view of discourse at the university shifts subtly from the dynamic to the fixed — from something that a writer must continually reinvent to something that has already been invented, a language that "we" have access to but that many of our students do not. The university becomes "our community," its various and competing discourses become "our language," and the possibility of a kind of discursive free-for-all is quickly rephrased in more familiar terms of us and them, insiders and outsiders.

This tension runs throughout Bartholomae's essay. On one hand, the university is pictured as the site of many discourses, and successful writers are seen as those who are able to work both within and against them, who can find a place for themselves on the margins or borders of a number of discourses. On the other, the university is also seen as a cluster of separate communities, disciplines, in which writers must locate themselves through taking on "the commonplaces, set phrases, rituals and gestures, habits of mind, tricks of persuasion, obligatory conclusions and necessary connections that determine 'what might be said'" (146). Learning to write, then, gets defined both as the forming of an aggressive and critical stance towards a number of discourses, and as a more simple entry into the discourse of a single community.

Community thus becomes for Bartholomae a kind of stabilizing term, used to give a sense of shared purpose and effort to our dealings with the various discourses that make up the university. The question, though, of just who this "we" is that speaks "our language" is never resolved.[2] And so while Bartholomae often refers to the "various branches" of the university, he ends up claiming to speak only of "university discourse in its most generalized form" (147). Similarly, most of the "communities" to which other current theorists refer exist at a vague remove from actual experience: The University, The Profession, The Discipline, The Academic Discourse Community. They are all quite literally utopias—nowheres, meta-communities—tied to no particular time or place, and thus oddly free of many of the tensions, discontinuities, and conflicts in the sorts of talk and writing that go on every day in the classrooms and departments of an actual university. For all the scrutiny it has drawn, the idea of community thus still remains little more than a notion—hypothetical and suggestive, powerful yet ill-defined.[3]

Part of this vagueness stems from the ways that the notion of "discourse community" has come into the study of writing—drawing on one hand from the literary-philosophical idea of "interpretive community," and on the other from the sociolinguistic concept of "speech community," but without fully taking into account the differences between the two. "Interpretive community," as used by Stanley Fish and others, is a term in a theoretical debate; it refers not so much to specific physical groupings of people as to a kind of loose dispersed network of individuals who share certain habits of mind. "Speech community," however, is usually meant to describe an actual group of speakers living in a particular place and time.[4] Thus while "interpretive community" can usually be taken to describe something like a world-view, discipline, or profession, "speech community" is generally used to refer more specifically to groupings like neighborhoods, settlements, or classrooms.

What "discourse community" means is far less clear. In the work of some theorists, the sense of community as an active lived experience seems to drop out almost altogether, to be replaced by a shadowy network of citations and references. Linda Brodkey, for instance, argues that:

> To the extent that the academic community is a community, it is a literate community, manifested not so much at conferences as in bibliographies and libraries, a community whose members know one another better as writers than speakers. (12)

And James Porter takes this notion a step further, identifying "discourse community" with the *intertextuality* of Foucault—an argument that parallels in interesting ways E. D. Hirsch's claim, in *Cultural Literacy*, that a literate community can be defined through the clusters of allusions and references that its members share. In such views, *community* becomes little more than a metaphor, a shorthand label for a hermetic weave of texts and citations.

Most theorists who use the term, however, seem to want to keep something of the tangible and specific reference of "speech community"—to suggest, that is, that there really are "academic discourse communities" out there somewhere, real groupings of writers and readers, that we can help "initiate" our students into. But since these communities are not of speakers, but of writers and readers who are dispersed in time and space, and who rarely, if ever, meet one another in person, they invariably take on something of the ghostly and pervasive quality of "interpretive communities" as well.

There have been some recent attempts to solve this problem. John Swales, for instance, has defined "discourse community" so that the common space shared by its members is replaced by a discursive "forum," and their one-to-one interaction is reduced to a system "providing information and feedback." A forum is not a community, though, so Swales also stipulates that there must be some common "goal" towards which the group is working (2–3). A similar stress on a shared or collaborative project runs through most other attempts to define "discourse community."[5] Thus while *community* loses its rooting in a particular place, it gains a new sense of direction and movement. Abstracted as they are from almost all other kinds of social and material relations, only an affinity of beliefs and purposes, consensus, is left to hold such communities together. The sort of group invoked is a free and voluntary gathering of individuals with shared goals and interests—of persons who have not so much been forced together as have chosen to associate with one another. So while the members of an "academic discourse community" may not meet each other very often, they are presumed to think much like one another (and thus also much *unlike* many of the people they deal with every day: students, neighbors, coworkers in other disciplines, and so on). In the place of physical nearness we are given like-mindedness. We fall back, that is, on precisely the sort of "warmly persuasive" and sentimental view of community that Williams warns against.

Insiders and Outsiders

One result of this has been, in recent work on the teaching of writing, the pitting of a "common" discourse against a more specialized or "privileged" one. For instance, Bartholomae argues that:

> The movement towards a more specialized discourse begins...both
> when a student can define a position of privilege, a position that sets
> him against a "common" discourse, and when he or she can work self-

consciously, critically, against not only the "common" code but his or her own. (156)

The troubles of many student writers, Bartholomae suggests, begin with their inability to imagine such a position of privilege, to define their views against some "common" way of talking about their subject. Instead, they simply repeat in their writing "what everybody knows" or what their professor has told them in her lectures. The result, of course, is that they are penalized for "having nothing really to say."

The task of the student is thus imagined as one of crossing the border from one community of discourse to another, of taking on a new sort of language. Again, the power of this metaphor seems to me undeniable. First, it offers us a way of talking about why many of our students fail to think and write as we would like them to *without* having to suggest that they are somehow slow or inept because they do not. Instead, one can argue that the problem is less one of intelligence than socialization, that such students are simply unused to the peculiar demands of academic discourse. Second, such a view reminds us (as Patricia Bizzell has often argued) that one's role as a teacher is not merely to inform but to persuade, that we ask our students to acquire not only certain skills and data, but to try on new forms of thinking and talking about the world as well. The problem is, once having posited two separate communities with strikingly different ways of making sense of the world, it then becomes difficult to explain how or why one moves from one group to the other. If to enter the academic community a student must "learn to speak our language," become accustomed and reconciled to our ways of doing things with words, then how exactly is she to do this?

Bizzell seems to picture the task as one of assimilation, of conversion almost. One sets aside one's former ways to become a member of the new community. As she writes:

> Mastery of academic discourse must begin with socialization to the community's ways, in the same way that one enters any cultural group. One must first "go native." ("Foundationalism" 53)

And one result of this socialization, Bizzell argues, may "mean being completely alienated from some other, socially disenfranchised discourses" (43). The convert must be born again.

Bartholomae uses the language of paradox to describe what must be accomplished:

> To speak with authority [our students] have to speak not only in another's voice but through another's code; and they not only have to do this, they have to speak in the voice and through the codes of those of us with power and wisdom; and they not only have to do this, they have to do it before they know what they are doing, before they have a project to participate in, and before, at least in the terms of our disciplines, they have anything to say. (156)

And so here, too, the learning of a new discourse seems to rest, at least in part, on a kind of mystical leap of mind. Somehow the student must "invent the university," appropriate a way of speaking and writing belonging to others.

WRITING AS REPOSITIONING

The emphasis of Bartholomae's pedagogy, though, seems to differ in slight but important ways from his theory. In *Facts, Artifacts, and Counterfacts*, a text for a course in basic writing, Bartholomae and Anthony Petrosky describe a class that begins by having students write on what they already think and feel about a certain subject (e.g., adolescence or work), and then tries to get them to redefine that thinking through a seminar-like process of reading and dialogue. The course thus appears to build on the overlap between the students' "common" discourses and the "academic" ones of their teachers, as they are asked to work "within and against" both their own languages and those of the texts they are reading (8). The move, then, is not simply from one discourse to another but towards a "hesitant and tenuous relationship" to both (41).

Such a pedagogy helps remind us that the borders of most discourses are hazily marked and often travelled, and that the communities they define are thus often indistinct and overlapping. As Williams again has suggested, one does not step cleanly and wholly from one community to another, but is caught instead in an always changing mix of dominant, residual, and emerging discourses (*Marxism* 121–27, see also Nicholas Coles on "Raymond Williams: Writing Across Borders"). Rather than framing our work in terms of helping students move from one community of discourse into another, then, it might prove more useful (and accurate) to view our task as adding to or complicating their uses of language.

I am not proposing such addition as a neutral or value-free pedagogy. Rather, I would expect and hope for a kind of useful dissonance as students are confronted with ways of talking about the world with which they are not yet wholly familiar. What I am arguing against, though, is the notion that our students should necessarily be working towards the mastery of some particular, well-defined sort of discourse. It seems to me that they might better be encouraged towards a kind of polyphony—an awareness of and pleasure in the various competing discourses that make up their own.

To illustrate what such an awareness might involve, let me turn briefly to some student writings. The first comes from a paper on *Hunger of Memory*, in which Richard Rodriguez describes how, as a Spanish-speaking child growing up in California, he was confronted in school by the need to master the "public language" of his English-speaking teachers and classmates. In her response, Sylvia, a young black woman from Philadelphia, explains that her situation is perhaps more complex, since she is aware of having at least two "private languages": a Southern-inflected speech which she uses with her parents and older relatives, and the "street talk" which she shares with her friends and neighbors. Sylvia concludes her essay as follows:

> My third and last language is one that Rodriguez referred to as "public language." Like Rodriguez, I too am having trouble accepting and using "public language." Specifically, I am referring to Standard English which is defined in some English texts as:
>
> > "The speaking and writing of cultivated people ... the variety of spoken and written language which enjoys cultural prestige, and which is the medium of education, journalism, and literature. Competence in its use is necessary for advancement in many occupations."
>
> Presently, I should say that "public language" is *becoming* my language as I am not yet comfortable in speaking it and even less comfortable in writing it. According to my mother anyone who speaks in "proper English" is "putting on airs."
>
> In conclusion, I understand the relevance and importance of learning to use "public language," but, like Rodriguez, I am also afraid of losing my "private identity"—that part of me that my parents, my relatives, and my friends know and understand. However, on the other hand, within me, there is an intense desire to grow and become a part of the "public world"—a world that exists outside of the secure and private world of my parents, relatives, and friends. If I want to belong, I must learn the "public language" too.

The second passage is written by Ron, a white factory worker in central Pennsylvania, and a part-time student. It closes an end-of-the-term reflection on his work in the writing course he was taking.

> As I look back over my writings for this course I see a growing acceptance of the freedom to write as I please, which is allowing me to almost enjoy writing (I can't believe it). So I tried this approach in another class I am taking. In that class we need to write summations of articles each week. The first paper that I handed in, where I used more feeling in my writing, came back with a ($\checkmark$–) and the comment, "Stick to the material." My view is, if they open the pen I will run as far as I can, but I won't break out because I have this bad habit, it's called eating.

What I admire in both passages is the writer's unwillingness to reduce his or her options to a simple either/or choice. Sylvia freely admits her desire to learn the language of the public world. Her "I understand ... but" suggests, however, that she is not willing to loosen completely her ties to family and neighborhood in order to do so. And Ron is willing to run with the more free style of writing he has discovered, "if they open the pen." Both seem aware, that is, of being implicated in not one but a number of discourses, a number of communities, whose beliefs and practices conflict as well as align. And it is the tension between those discourses—none repudiated or chosen wholly—that gives their texts such interest.

There has been much debate in recent years over whether we need, above all, to respect our students' "right to their own language," or to teach them the ways and forms of "academic discourse." Both sides of this argument, in the end, rest their cases on the same suspect generalization: that we and our students belong to different and fairly distinct communities of discourse, that we have "our" "academic" discourse and they have "their own" "common" (?!) ones. The choice is one between opposing fictions. The "languages" that our students bring to us cannot but have been shaped, at least in part, by their experiences in school, and thus must, in some ways, already be "academic." Similarly, our teaching will and should always be affected by a host of beliefs and values that we hold regardless of our roles as academics. What we see in the classroom, then, are not two coherent and competing discourses but many overlapping and conflicting ones. Our students are no more wholly "outside" the discourse of the university than we are wholly "within" it. We are all at once both insiders and outsiders. The fear (or hope) of either camp that our students will be "converted" from "their" language to "ours" is both overstated and misleading. The task facing our students, as Min-zhan Lu has argued, is not to leave one community in order to enter another, but to *reposition* themselves in relation to several continuous and conflicting discourses. Similarly, our goals as teachers need not be to initiate our students into the values and practices of some new community, but to offer them the chance to reflect critically on those discourses—of home, school, work, the media, and the like—to which they already belong.

COMMUNITY WITHOUT CONSENSUS

"Alongside each utterance . . . off-stage voices can be heard," writes Barthes (21). We do not write simply as individuals, but we do not write simply as members of a community either. The point is, to borrow a turn of argument from Stanley Fish, that one does not *first* decide to act as a member of one community rather than some other, and *then* attempt to conform to its (rather than some other's) set of beliefs and practices. Rather, one is always *simultaneously* a part of several discourses, several communities, is always already committed to a number of conflicting beliefs and practices.[6] As Mary Louise Pratt has pointed out: "People and groups are constituted not by single unified belief systems, but by competing self-contradictory ones" (228). One does not necessarily stop being a feminist, for instance, in order to write literary criticism (although one discourse may try to repress or usurp the other). And, as the example of Williams shows, one does not necessarily give up the loyalties of a working-class youth in order to become a university student (although some strain will no doubt be felt).

In *The Country and the City*, Williams notes an "escalator effect" in which each new generation of English writers points to a lost age of harmony and organic community that thrived just before their own, only of course to have the era in which they were living similarly romanticized by the writers who come after them (9–12). Rather than doing much the same, romanticizing academic discourse as occurring in a kind of single cohesive community, I would urge, instead, that we think of it as taking place in something more like a city. That is, instead of presenting academic discourse as coherent and well-defined, we might be better off viewing it as polyglot, as a sort of space in which competing beliefs and practices intersect with and confront one another. One does not need consensus to have community. Matters of accident, necessity, and convenience hold groups together as well. Social theories of reading and writing have helped to deconstruct the myth of the autonomous essential self. There seems little reason now to grant a similar sort of organic unity to the idea of community.

The metaphor of the city would also allow us to view a certain amount of change and struggle within a community not as threats to its coherence but as normal activity. The members of many classrooms and academic departments, not to mention disciplines, often seem to share few enough beliefs or practices with one another. Yet these communities exert a very real influence on the discourses of their members. We need to find a way to talk about their workings without first assuming a consensus that may not be there. As Bizzell has recently come to argue:

> Healthy discourse communities, like healthy human beings, are also masses of contradictions. . . . We should accustom ourselves to dealing with contradictions, instead of seeking a theory that appears to abrogate them. ("What" 18–19)

I would urge an even more specific and material view of community: one that, like a city, allows for both consensus and conflict, and that holds room for ourselves, our disciplinary colleagues, our university coworkers, *and* our students. In short, I think we need to look more closely at the discourses of communities that are more than communities of discourse alone. While I don't mean to discount the effects of belonging to a discipline, I think that we dangerously abstract and idealize the workings of "academic discourse" by taking the kinds of rarified talk and writing that go on at conferences and in journals as the norm, and viewing many of the other sorts of talk and writing that occur at the university as deviations from or approximations of that standard. It may prove more useful to center our study, instead, on the everyday struggles and mishaps of the talk in our classrooms and departments, with their mixings of sometimes conflicting and sometimes conjoining beliefs and purposes.

Indeed, I would suggest that we reserve our uses of *community* to describe the workings of such specific and local groups. We have other words — *discourse, language, voice, ideology, hegemony* — to chart the perhaps less immediate (though still powerful) effects of broader social forces on our talk and writing. None of them is, surely, without its own echoes of meaning, both suggestive and troublesome. But none, I believe, carries with it the sense of like-mindedness and warmth that make community at once such an appealing *and* limiting concept. As teachers and theorists of writing, we need a vocabulary that will allow us to talk about certain forces as social rather than communal, as involving power but not always consent. Such talk could give us a fuller picture of the lived experience of teaching, learning, and writing in a university today.

AFTERWORD . . . .

In the years after I published "The Idea of Community," I was often asked if I was doing any more work on the subject—a sensible question but one which I never felt I had much of an answer to since I thought that I had already pretty much said what I had to say in that essay, and what I thought I'd said was that community didn't strike me as a useful term to use in theorizing writing and its teaching. In part this points to a limit of critique as a form of writing— which is that defining the problems with certain positions doesn't always lead to a sense of what to do instead, to new perspectives and practices. But I also just felt stuck. I wasn't much drawn to a kind of theorizing that seemed to grow more abstruse and strident as it became less responsive to the actual difficulties of writing, but I also didn't know exactly what I had to offer in its place. I had a sense of what I wanted: a critical approach to teaching centered in the values of American pragmatism and liberalism. But I wasn't sure how to articulate this without seeming to fall into simple nostalgia.

I'm still not sure. But there are two moves in the community essay that I might still draw on in working towards more open and democratic forms of teaching. The problem, though, is that they are two very different, and perhaps even contradictory, moves. The first is to rethink *the metaphors we use in imagining the aims of our teaching. In my essay, I quoted Raymond Williams observing that community has no "positive opposing or distinguishing term"—that we are instead given a stark choice between community (good) and noncommunity (bad). But I now think that Williams was wrong, that the term* public *describes a form of social organization that rests not on likemindedness but on a more limited willingness to argue out differences, to coexist in what Richard Sennett has called a "community of strangers." This is the sort of view I was fumbling for when, near the end of my essay, I suggested replacing community with* city *as a metaphor for writing spaces. And I continue to think that imagining ourselves as teaching toward a public sphere, a discursive commons which none of us owns, leads to more interesting writing than viewing ourselves as bringing students into a kind of gated community of academic discourse whose keys we already hold.*

But the other move, which I hinted at in my essay but failed to develop, is to resist *such metaphors of space in order to look closely at the material sites in which writing and teaching go on. We need to study the micropolitics of actual classrooms: how new perspectives come into play or get shut down; how student writings repeat, contest, parody, or transform the ideas and phrasings of their books and teachers. And we need to attend to the curricular and economic structures that we work in — to the roles composition plays in our departments and universities, and to who gets paid how much for doing what. Such a focus on the local and material, I believe, will tell us much about the dynamics of language and power.*

–JOSEPH HARRIS
University of Pittsburgh

1991　　　*"This Wooden Shack Place": The Logic of an Unconventional Reading*

GLYNDA HULL AND MIKE ROSE

*T*his is a paper about student interpretations of literature that strike the teacher as unusual, a little off, not on the mark. When we teachers enter classrooms with particular poems or stories in hand, we also enter with expectations about the kind of student responses that would be most fruitful, and these expectations have been shaped, for the most part, in literature departments in American universities. We value some readings more than others—even, in our experience, those teachers who advocate a reader's free play. One inevitable result of this situation is that there will be moments of mismatch between what a teacher expects and what students do. What interests us about this mismatch is the possibility that our particular orientations and readings might blind us to the logic of a student's interpretation and the ways that interpretation might be sensibly influenced by the student's history.

The two of us have been involved for several years in a study of remedial writing instruction in American higher education, attempting to integrate social-cultural and cognitive approaches to better understand the institutional and classroom practices that contribute to students being designated remedial (Hull and Rose). One of the interesting things that has emerged as we've been conducting this research is the place of reading in the remedial writing classroom, particularly at a time when composition professionals are calling for the integration of reading and writing while affirming, as well, the place of literature in remedial instruction (Bartholomae and Petrosky; Salvatori, "Reading and Writing"). As this integration of reading, and particularly the reading of literature, into the remedial writing classroom continues, composition teachers will increasingly be called on to explore questions of interpretation, expectation, and background knowledge—particularly given the rich mix of class and culture found in most remedial programs. We would like to consider these issues by examining a discussion of a poem that was part of a writing assignment. Specifically, we will analyze a brief stretch of

This essay was first published in CCC, Volume 41, Number 3, October 1990.

discourse, one in which a student's personal history and cultural background shape a somewhat unconventional reading of a section of a poem. We will note the way the mismatch plays itself out in conversation, the logic of the student's reading and the coherent things it reveals about his history, and the pedagogical implications of conducting a conversation that encourages that logic to unfold.

The stretch of discourse we're going to analyze comes from a conference that immediately followed a classroom discussion of a poem by the contemporary Japanese-American writer Garrett Kaoru Hongo. The class is designated as the most remedial composition class at the University of California; it is part of a special program on the Los Angeles campus (the Freshman Preparatory Program) for students determined by test scores to be significantly at-risk. (The SAT verbal scores of this particular section, for example, ranged from 220 to 400.) Mike Rose taught the class at the time he was collecting data on remedial writing instruction at the university level, and though his class was not the focus of his research, he did keep a teaching log, photocopy all work produced by the class, and collect sociohistorical and process-tracing data on several students and tape-record selected conferences and tutorial sessions with them. For reasons that will shortly be apparent, a student named Robert was one of those Rose followed: he will be the focus of this paper. Let us begin this analysis with the poem Robert and the others in the class read; the discussion took place during the third week of the fall quarter:

And Your Soul Shall Dance
  for Wakako Yamauchi

Walking to school beside fields
of tomatoes and summer squash,
alone and humming a Japanese love song,
you've concealed a copy of *Photoplay*
between your algebra and English texts.
Your knee socks, saddle shoes, plaid dress,
and blouse, long-sleeved and white
with ruffles down the front,
come from a Sears catalogue
and neatly complement your new Toni curls.
All of this sets you apart from the landscape:
flat valley grooved with irrigation ditches,
a tractor grinding through alkaline earth,
the short stands of windbreak eucalyptus
shuttering the desert wind
from a small cluster of wooden shacks
where your mother hangs the wash.
You want to go somewhere.
Somewhere far away from all the dust
and sorting machines and acres of lettuce.
Someplace where you might be kissed

by someone with smooth, artistic hands.
When you turn into the schoolyard,
the flagpole gleams like a knife blade in the sun,
and classmates scatter like chickens,
shooed by the storm brooding on your horizon.

Garrett Kaoru Hongo

The class did pretty well with "And Your Soul Shall Dance." They followed the narrative line, pictured the girl, and understood the tension between her desires (and her dress) and the setting she's in. The ending, with its compressed set of similes and metaphors, understandably gave them some trouble—many at first took it literally, pictured it cinematically. But, collaboratively, the class came to the understanding that the storm meant something powerful and disquieting was brewing, and that the girl—the way she looks, her yearning for a different life—was somehow central to the meaning of the storm. The class was not able, however, to fit all the pieces together into one or more unified readings. And during the discussion—as members of the class focused on particular lines—some students offered observations or answers to questions or responses to classmates that seemed to be a little off the mark, unusual, as though the students weren't reading the lines carefully. Rose wondered if these "misreadings" were keeping the students from a fuller understanding of the way the storm could be integrated into the preceding events of the poem. One of these students was Robert.

A brief introduction. Robert is engaging, polite, style-conscious, intellectually curious. His father is from Trinidad, his mother from Jamaica, though he was born in Los Angeles and bears no easily discernible signs of island culture. His parents are divorced, and while he spends time with both, he currently lives with his mother in a well-kept, apartment-dense area on the western edge of central Los Angeles. Robert's family, and many of their neighbors, fall in the lower-middle-class SES bracket. He was bused to middle and high school in the more affluent San Fernando Valley. His high-school GPA was 3.35; his quantitative SAT was 410, and his verbal score was 270. In class he is outgoing and well-spoken—if with a tinge of shyness—and though his demeanor suggests he is a bit unsure of himself, he volunteers answers and responds thoughtfully to his classmates.

During the last half hour of the class on the Hongo poem, the students began rough drafts of an interpretive essay, and in his paper Robert noted that his "interpretation of this poem is that this girl seems to want to be different from society." (And later, he would tell his teacher that Hongo's poem "talked about change.") Robert clearly had a sense of the poem, was formulating an interpretation, but he, like the others, couldn't unify the poem's elements, and Rose assumed Robert's inability was caused by his misreading of sections of the poem. Here is Rose's entry in his teacher's log:

> Robert was ok on the 1st third of the poem, but seemed to miss the point
> of the central section. Talk with the tutor—does he need help with close
> reading?

Rose decided to get a better look, so he moved his regularly-scheduled conference with Robert up a week and tape-recorded it. In the three-minute excerpt from that conference that follows, Robert is discussing the storm at the poem's conclusion—the foreboding he senses—but is having some trouble figuring out exactly what the source of this impending disruption is. Rose asks Robert if—given the contrast between the farming community and the girl's dreams and appearance—he could imagine a possible disruption in her not-too-distant future. We pick up the conversation at this point. To help clarify his own expectations, Rose replayed the stretch of tape as soon as Robert left, trying to recall what he intended in asking each of his questions.

1a   Rose: What do you think . . . what, you know, on the one hand what might the reaction of her parents be, if she comes in one day and says, "I, I don't like it here, I want to leave here, I want to be different from this, I want to go to the city and . . ." [*Expectation:* Robert will say the parents will be resistant, angry—something rooted in the conservative values associated with poor, traditional families.]

1b   Robert: Um, that would basically depend on the wealth of her family. You'd wanna know if her parents are poor . . . (mumbling) . . . they might not have enough money, whereas they can't go out and improve, you know . . . [Responds with a *qualification* that complicates the question by suggesting we need to know more. This further knowledge concerns the family's economic status, something Rose had assumed was evident.]

2a   Rose: OK. OK. [*Acknowledges with hesitation*] From what we see about the background here and the times and the look, what can . . . can we surmise, can we imagine, do you think her parents are wealthy or poor? [*Focuses* on the poem, asking for a conjecture. *Expectation:* Robert's attention will be drawn to the shacks, the hand laundering, the indications of farm labor.]

2b   Robert: I wouldn't say that they're wealthy but, again, I wouldn't say that they are poor either. [Responds with a *qualification*]

3a   Rose: OK. [*Acknowledges with hesitation*] And why not? [Requests *elaboration. Expectation:* Robert will provide something from the poem, some line that explains the ambiguity in his answer.]

3b   Robert: Because typical farm life is, you know, that's the way that you see yourself, you know, wear jeans, just some old jeans, you know, some old saddle shoes, boots or something, some old kinda shirt, you know, with some weird design on the shoulder pad . . . [Responds by creating a *scenario*]

3c   Rose: Uh huh . . . [*Unsure about direction,* but *acknowledges*]

3d   Robert: . . . for the guys. And then girls, probably wear some kind of plain cloth skirt, you know, with some weird designs on it and a weird shirt. I couldn't really . . . you really wouldn't know if they're . . . whether they were rich or not. Cause mainly everyone would dress the same way . . . [Continues *scenario* leading to an observation]

4a   Rose: Yeah. [Sees the purpose of the scenario] That's right, so you wouldn't be able to tell what the background is, right? [*Confirms* Robert's observation and *reflects back*] Let's see if there's anything in the poem that helps us out. (pause) "All of this sets you apart..." this is about line twelve in the poem, "All of this sets you apart from the land-scape: / flat valley grooved with irrigation ditches, / a tractor grinding through alkaline earth, / the short stands of windbreak eucalyptus / shuttering the desert wind / from a small cluster of wooden shacks / where your mother hangs the wash." [*Focuses* on poem] Now if she lives with her mother in a wooden shack, a shack ... [*Begins line of reasoning*]

4b   Robert: OK. OK. Oh! [*interrupts*] Right here—is it saying that she lives with her mother, or that she just goes to this wooden shack place to *hang* her clothes? [*Challenges* teacher's line of reasoning]

4c   Rose: Oh, I see. So you think that it's possible then that her mother ... [*Reflects back*]

4d   Robert: [*picks up thought*] washes her clothes probably at home some-where and then walks down to this place where the wind ... the wind ... so the eucalyptus trees block this wind, you know, from ... [*Elaborates*]

4e   Rose: [*picks up thought*] so that the clothes can dry.

4f   Robert: Right. [*Confirms*]

5a   Rose: Well, that's certainly possible. That's certainly possible. [*Confirms*] Um, the only thing I would say if I wanted to argue with you on that would be that that's possible, but it's also the only time that this writer lets us know anything about where she might live, etc. .... [*Begins to ex-plain his interpretation*—an interpretation, we'd argue, that is fairly con-ventional: that the family is poor, and that poverty is signaled by the shacks, the place, most likely, where the family lives]

Certainly not all of Robert's exchanges—in classroom or conference—are so packed with qualification and interruption and are so much at cross purposes with teacher expectation. Still, this stretch of discourse is represen-tative of the characteristics that make Robert's talk about texts interesting to us. Let us begin by taking a closer look at the reasoning Robert exhibits as he discusses "And Your Soul Shall Dance." To conduct this analysis, we'll be in-tersecting socioeconomic, cognitive, and textual information, bringing these disparate sources of information together to help us understand Robert's in-terpretation of sections of "And Your Soul Shall Dance," explicating not the poem, but a particular reading of it in a particular social-textual setting.

Here are a few brief comments on method:

Our data comes from the stretch of discourse we just examined, from other sections of the same conference, from a stimulated-recall session (on an essay Robert was writing for class) conducted one week prior to the confer-ence,[1] and from a follow-up interview conducted four months after the con-ference to collect further sociohistorical information.

To confirm our sense of what a "conventional" reading of this section of the poem would be, we asked six people to interpret the lines in question.

Though our readers represented a mix of ages and cultural backgrounds, all had been socialized in American literature departments: two senior English majors—one of whom is Japanese-American—two graduate students—one of whom is African-American—and two English professors—one of whom is Mexican-American. Regardless of age or cultural background, all quickly offered the same interpretation we will be suggesting is conventional.[2]

ANALYSIS

1a–1b

1a   Rose: What do you think . . . what, you know, on the one hand what might the reaction of her parents be, if she comes in one day and says, "I, I don't like it here, I want to leave here, I want to be different from this, I want to go to the city and . . ."

1b   Robert: Um, that would basically depend on the wealth of her family. You'd wanna know if her parents are poor . . . (mumbling) . . . they might not have enough money, whereas they can't go out and improve, you know . . .

Robert claims that the reaction of the girl's parents to "I want to leave here . . . [and] go to the city . . ." would "depend on the wealth of her family." This qualification is legitimate, though the reasoning behind it is not quickly discernible. In the follow-up interview Robert elaborates: "[If she goes to the city] she's gonna need support . . . and if they're on a low budget they won't have that much money to be giving to her all the time to support her." The social context of Robert's reasoning becomes clearer here. He comes from a large family (11 siblings and half-siblings), some members of which have moved (and continue to move) across cultures and, to a degree, across class lines. It is the parents' obligation to help children as they make such moves, and Robert is aware of the strains on finances such movement brings—he is in the middle of such tension himself.

2a–4f

This segment includes Robert's qualified response to "do you think her parents are wealthy or poor?", his farm fashion scenario, and his perception of the "small cluster of wooden shacks." As we've seen, we need to understand Robert's perception of the shacks in order to understand his uncertainty about the parents' economic status, so we'll reverse the order of events on the transcript and deal first with the shacks.

4a   Rose: Yeah. That's right, so you wouldn't be able to tell what the background is, right? Let's see if there's anything in the poem that helps us out. (pause) "All of this sets you apart . . ." this is about line twelve in the poem, "All of this sets you apart from the landscape: /flat valley grooved with irrigation ditches, / a tractor grinding through alkaline earth, / the short stands of windbreak eucalyptus / shuttering the desert wind / from a small cluster of wooden shacks / where your mother hangs the wash." Now if she lives with her mother in a wooden shack, a shack . . .

4b   Robert: OK. OK. Oh! Right here—is it saying that she lives with her mother, or that she just goes to this wooden shack place to *hang* her clothes?

Those of us educated in a traditional literature curriculum, and especially those of us trained in an English graduate program, are schooled to comprehend the significance of the shacks. We understand, even if we can't readily articulate them, the principles of compression and imagistic resonance that underlie Hongo's presentation of a single image to convey information about economic and historical background. Robert, however, isn't socialized to such conventions, or is only partly socialized, and so he relies on a model of interpretation Rose had seen him rely on in class and in the stimulated-recall session: an almost legalistic model, a careful, qualifying reasoning that defers quick judgment, that demands multiple sources of verification. The kind of reasoning we see here, then, is not inadequate. In fact, it's pretty sophisticated—though it is perhaps inappropriately invoked in a poetic world, as Rose begins to suggest to Robert in 5a. We'll come back to this momentarily, but first we want to address one more issue related to Robert's uncertainty about the income level of the girl's parents.

We would like to raise the possibility that Robert's background makes it unlikely that he is going to respond to "a small cluster of wooden shacks" in quite the same way—with quite the same emotional reaction—as would a conventional (and most likely middle-class) reader for whom the shacks might function as a quickly discernible, emblematic literary device. Some of Robert's relatives in Trinidad still live in houses like those described in the poem, and his early housing in Los Angeles—further into central Los Angeles than where he now lives—was quite modest. We would suggest that Robert's "social distance" from the economic reality of poor landscapes isn't as marked as that of the conventional/middle-class reader, and this might make certain images less foreign to him, and, therefore, less emotionally striking. This is certainly *not* to say that Robert is naive about his current position in American society, but simply to say that the wooden shacks might not spark the same dramatic response in him as in a conventional/middle-class reader. The same holds true for another of Hongo's indicators of economic status—the hanging of the wash—for Robert's mother still "likes to wash her clothes by hand." Paradoxically, familiarity might work against certain kinds of dramatic response to aspects of working-class life.

In line with the above assertion, we would like to consider one last indicator of the girl's economic status—the mention of the Sears catalogue. The Sears catalogue, we believe, cuts two ways in the poem: it suggests lower-income-level shopping ("thrifty," as one of our readers put it) and, as well, the importing of another culture's garments. But the catalogue also carries with it an ironic twist: it's not likely that conventional readers would con-

sider a Sears catalogue to be a source of fashion, so there's a touch of irony—
perhaps pity mixed with humor—in this girl fulfilling her romantic dreams
via Sears and Roebuck. We suggest that Robert's position in the society
makes it difficult for him to see things this way, to comply with this conventional reading. He knows merchandise from Sears is "economical" and "af-
fordable," and, to him, there's nothing ironic, pitiable, or humorous about
that. When asked if he sees anything sad or ironic about the girl buying there
he responds, "Oh, no, no," pointing out that "some of the items they sell in
Sears, they sell in other stores." He then goes on to uncover an interesting
problem in the poem. He uses the Sears catalogue to support his assertion
that the family isn't all that poor (and thus doesn't necessarily live in those
shacks): "She couldn't be really poor because she has clothes from the Sears
catalogue." Robert knows what real poverty is, and he knows that if you
have enough money to buy at Sears, you're doing OK. He goes on to speculate—again with his careful, qualifying logic—that if she is as poor as the
shacks suggest, then maybe the Sears clothes could be second-hand and sent
to her by relatives, in the way his family sends clothes and shoes to his relatives in Trinidad. Hongo's use of the Sears catalogue is, in some ways, undercut by other elements in his poem.

> 3b   Robert: Because typical farm life is, you know, that's the way that you
> see yourself, you know, wear jeans, just some old jeans, you know, some
> old saddle shoes, boots or something, some old kinda shirt, you know,
> with some weird design on the shoulder pad . . .
>
> 3c   Rose: Uh huh . . .
>
> 3d   Robert: . . . for the guys. And then girls, probably wear some kind of
> plain cloth skirt, you know, with some weird designs on it and a weird
> shirt. I couldn't really . . . you really wouldn't know if they're . . .
> whether they were rich or not. Cause mainly everyone would dress the
> same way . . .

Now we can turn to the farm fashion scenario. Given that the "small
cluster of wooden shacks" doesn't seem to function for Robert as it might for
the conventional reader, he is left more to his own devices when asked: "do
you think her parents are wealthy or poor?" What begins as a seeming non
sequitur—and a concrete one at that—does reveal its purpose as Robert
plays it out. Though Robert has a frame of reference to understand the eco-
nomics of the scene in "And Your Soul Shall Dance" and the longing of its
main character, he is, after all, a city boy, born and raised in central Los Angeles. What he does, then, when asked a question about how one determines
the economic background of people moving across a farm landscape is to access what knowledge he does have about farm life—things he's read or
heard, images he's gleaned from movies and television shows (e.g., *The Little
House on the Prairie*)—and create a scenario, focusing on one indicator of socioeconomic status: fashion. (And fashion is a sensible criterion to use here,
given the poem's emblematic use of clothing.) Classroom-observational and
stimulated-recall data suggest that Robert makes particularly good use of

visual imagery in his thinking—e.g., he draws pictures and charts to help him comprehend difficult readings; he rehearses sentences by visualizing them before he writes them out—and here we see him reasoning through the use of scenario, concluding that in certain kinds of communities, distinctions by readily discernible indicators like dress might not be all that easy to make.

4d   Robert: washes her clothes probably at home somewhere and then walks down to this place where the wind . . . the wind . . . so the eucalyptus trees block this wind, you know, from . . .

4e   Rose: so that the clothes can dry.

4f   Robert: Right.

This section also involves the wooden shacks, though the concern here is Robert's assertion that the mother doesn't have to live in the shacks to hang the wash there. Robert's reasoning, again, seems inappropriately legalistic. Yes, the mother could walk down to this place to hang her clothes; the poem doesn't specify "that [the girl] lives with her mother, or that [the mother] just goes to this wooden shack place to *hang* her clothes." But to Rose during the conference this seemed like a jurisprudential rather than a poetic reading. In the follow-up interview, however, Robert elaborated in a way that made Rose realize that Robert might have had a better imagistic case than his teacher first thought—for Rose missed the full visual particulars of the scene, did not see the importance of the "tractors grinding through alkaline earth." Robert elaborates on "this place where . . . the eucalyptus trees block this wind." He describes this "little shack area where the clothes can dry without being bothered by the wind and dust . . . with all this . . . the tractor grinding through the earth. That brings up dust." Robert had pictured the surrounding landscape—machines stirring up grit and dust—and saw the necessity of trees to break the dust-laden wind so that wash could dry clean in the sun. The conventional reader could point out that such a windbreak would be necessary as well to protect residents, but given Robert's other interpretations, it makes sense, is coherent, to see the shacks—sheds of some kind perhaps or abandoned housing—as part of this eucalyptus-protected place where women hang the wash. What's important to note here is that Robert was able to visualize the scene—animate it, actually—in a way that Rose was not, for Rose was focusing on the dramatic significance of the shacks. Robert's reading may be unconventional and inappropriately jurisprudential, but it is coherent, and it allows us—in these lines—to animate the full landscape in a way that enhances our reading of the poem.

CONCLUSION

We hope we have demonstrated the logic and coherence of one student's unconventional reading. What we haven't addressed—and it could certainly now be raised—is the pedagogical wisdom of encouraging in a writing classroom the playing out of such unconventional readings. Reviewing the brief stretch of Rose's and Robert's discourse, we see how often teacher talk is qualified, challenged, and interrupted (though not harshly), and how rarely teacher expectations are fulfilled. If the teacher's goals are to run an efficient classroom, cover a set body of material, and convey certain conventional reading and writing strategies to students who are on the margin of the academic community, then all these conversational disjunctions are troubling.

What we would like to suggest, though, is that the laudable goal of facilitating underprepared students' entry into the academic community is actually compromised by a conversational pattern that channels students like Robert into a more "efficient" discourse. The desire for efficiency and coverage can cut short numerous possibilities for students to explore issues, articulate concerns, formulate and revise problems—all necessary for good writing to emerge—and can lead to conversational patterns that socialize students into a mode of interaction that will limit rather than enhance their participation in intellectual work.[3] We would further suggest that streamlined conversational patterns (like the Initiation-Comment-Response pattern described by Mehan) are often reinforced by a set of deficit-oriented assumptions about the linguistic and cognitive abilities of remedial students, assumptions that are much in need of examination (Hull et al.; Rose, *Lives*).

We would pose instead a pedagogical model that places knowledge-making at its center. The conversational techniques attending such a model are not necessarily that demanding—Robert benefits from simple expressions of encouragement, focusing, and reflecting back—but the difference in assumptions is profound: that the real stuff of belonging to an academic community is dynamic involvement in generating and questioning knowledge, that students desperately need immersion and encouragement to involve themselves in such activity, and that underprepared students are capable— given the right conditions—of engaging in such activity. We would also underscore the fact that Robert's reading (a) does bring to light the problem with the Sears catalogue and (b) animates the landscape as his teacher's reading did not do. Finally, we would suggest that engaging in a kind of "social-textual" reading of Robert's reading moves us toward deeper understanding of the social base of literary interpretation (cf. Salvatori, "Pedagogy").

In calling for a richer, more transactive model of classroom discourse, we want to acknowledge that such a model removes some of the control of teacher-centered instruction and can create moments of hesitance and uncertainty (as was the case with Rose through the first half of the transcript). But hesitancy and uncertainty—as we all know from our own intellectual struggles—are central to knowledge-making. Furthermore, we are not asking teachers to abandon structure, goals, and accountability. A good deal of engineering still goes on in the transactive classroom: the teacher focusing discussion, helping students better articulate their ideas, involving others, pointing out connections, keeping an eye on the clock. Even in conference, Rose's interaction with Robert is clearly goal-driven, thus Rose's reliance on focusing and reflecting back. Rose operates with a conventional reading in mind and begins moving toward it in 5a—and does so out loud to reveal to

Robert the line of such reasoning. Robert's interpretation, though, will cause his teacher to modify his reading, and the teacher's presentation of his interpretation will help Robert acquire an additional approach to the poem. (In fact, the very tension between academic convention and student experience could then become the focus of discussion.) This, we think, is the way talk and thought should go when a student seems to falter, when readings seem a little off the mark.[4]

AFTERWORD . . . .

About ten years ago we began to study the ways those students—variously labeled "remedial," "underprepared," "at risk," "nontraditional"—had historically been taught and depicted. Our empirical data included fieldnotes on and videotapes of instruction; transcriptions of tutorial sessions; school literacy materials; survey information on students' work, communities, and daily lives; everyday literacy materials from sports magazines to romances, coupons to workplace forms to devotional tracts; detailed tracing of cognitive and linguistic processes that unfolded as students read and wrote; and interview, survey, and archival information on the institutions and programs the students were attending.

We hoped that such historical, cultural, and psychological studies would lead to a new conceptualization of problematic literacy performance, one that would help educators better understand the complex mix of social and psychological forces at play in the production of a flawed piece of writing, and the cognitive and linguistic ability that often gets lost in the assessment of the piece of writing.

Looking back on our two CCC articles, and looking forward from them, we are struck by several generative tensions.

1. There are increasing attempts—via action research, teacher-research, and feminist methods—to create research projects that involve students more directly, often with the goal of providing assistance. The challenge, it seems to us, is how to develop both systematic, principled methodologies and appropriate intervention. With the means available to us at the time, we hope we worked out of that productive tension.

2. The past decade has seen a significant shift in composition studies toward social and political analysis, providing much-needed awareness of the broad contexts that inform writing and writing instruction. The concern we have is how

*to continue to develop ways to use social analysis with close examination of lan-
guage used in the complex settings that people inhabit. Such a development
could move us beyond the current "theory" vs. "empiricism" divide and into
generative paradox: What might a critical empiricism look like? Is a data-driven
post-post-structuralist theory possible?*

*3. Over the past decade, some writing programs, concerned about the limi-
tations of remedial instruction, have experimented successfully with courses
that incorporate underprepared students into the standard curriculum. Any effective instructional response to the varied and complex needs of students—
whether in a comprehensive curriculum or special program—is, we think, worthy of study, with an eye toward replication. There is no one right way. But this
issue of programmatic response brings us to the third, and most materially con-
sequential tension: How to respond when we have accumulated knowledge of the
problems with conventional instruction, when a significant number of students
need assistance, when programs are being cut, when powerful conservative
forces—using a language of standards and equality—are threatening to abolish
all remedial and preparatory programs, and in places like New York already
have. Response in such environments must, of course, be multilayered and
strategic, and, we hope, might include to good effect the kinds of understandings
that emerge from research of the sort represented here.*

–Glynda Hull
University of California, Berkeley

–Mike Rose
University of California, Los Angeles

1992

Remediation as Social Construct: Perspectives from an Analysis of Classroom Discourse

GLYNDA HULL, MIKE ROSE,
KAY LOSEY FRASER,
AND MARISA CASTELLANO

n this paper, we examine remediation as a social construct, as the product of perceptions and beliefs about literacy and learning, and we illustrate some ways in which inaccurate and limiting notions of learners as being somehow cognitively defective and in need of "remedy" can be created and played out in the classroom. We will look closely at one student in one lesson and detail the interactional processes that contribute to her being defined as remedial—this specific case, however, is also representative of common kinds of classroom practices and widespread cultural assumptions, ones we've seen at work in our other studies (Hull and Rose, "Rethinking"). In order to better understand these cultural assumptions and the ways they can affect classroom practices, we will attempt to combine an empirical, fine-grained analysis of classroom discourse with broader historical and cultural analyses. We want to place a teacher's instructional and evaluative language in the contexts that we believe influence it, that contribute to the practice of defining students as remedial.

We write this paper believing that, however great the distance our profession has come in understanding the students and the writing we call "remedial," we have not yet come far enough in critically examining our assumptions about our students' abilities—assumptions which both shape the organization of remedial programs and orient daily life in remedial classrooms. Engaging in such an examination is not so easy, perhaps because as teachers of remedial writing, we have good intentions: we look forward to our students' growth and development as writers; we want to teach our students to be literate in ways sanctioned by the academy and the community beyond. And, knowing our intentions, we can forget to examine our assumptions about remediation—assumptions that are deeply held and so ingrained as to be tacit, that can, without much conscious choice on our part, drive the way we structure a course and circumscribe the learning that students will do in it. Our hope, then, is that this paper will be an occasion to re-

This essay was first published in *CCC*, Volume 42, Number 3, October 1991.

flect on the ways we, as teachers, can inadvertently participate in the social construction of attitudes and beliefs about remediation which may limit the learning that takes place in our classrooms, and to consider some ways in which we can begin to examine these basic assumptions, building from a different ground our notions about our students' abilities and the nature of literacy learning.

ANALYZING CLASSROOM DISCOURSE

The centerpiece of our discussion—a fifty-minute classroom lesson on writing conducted in a remedial classroom at an urban college[1]—was one of several that we videotaped across a semester. As regular observers in the class, we also collected field notes and records of reading and writing assignments and homework and essays. We conducted interviews with students and teachers as well, sometimes asking them to comment on the videotapes we had recently made of classroom lessons. Outside of class, we served as tutors and thereby were able to audiotape our conferences with students and to elicit additional writing and reading performances.

In our studies, we have worked only with teachers rated highly by their departments and students. The teacher in this study was June, a recent and respected graduate of a long-standing composition program and a candidate for an advanced degree in literature. Our work with June confirmed her commitment to teaching. She spent a great deal of time responding to papers at home and meeting with students in conferences, and she was interested in discussing composition research and finding ways to apply it in her classroom. In fact, she volunteered to participate in our study because she saw it as an occasion to be reflective about her own teaching and to improve instruction for students in remedial classes.

The composition program in which June had studied was also a part of the college and included reading on and discussion of new composition theory and practice. The size of the class she taught was reasonable (approximately 15 students), though June taught three sections requiring two different preparations while completing graduate school. A remedial writing course and a complementary reading course were required for entering students depending on their scores on entrance tests. In the writing course, students kept a journal, made summaries of short reading passages, and wrote essays on assignments common to the program. Most of these assignments asked students to read short passages as background material and to use them as the basis for writing an essay on a specified topic related to the reading. One of these assignments gave rise to the classroom talk that we will analyze.

In this lesson, which took place the fourth week of the semester, June held a discussion to prepare students to write an essay on music videos and their appropriateness for viewers. The essay assignment consisted of a set of brief readings: a magazine article describing recently released and acclaimed rock videos; an editorial from a local newspaper on censorship; a review of the music video, *Thriller;* a list of recent music videos with brief descriptions. The assignment then asked students to take part in current debates about the regulation of music videos, developing a position on the issue perhaps by arguing that videos ought to be banned from television, or that there should be no censorship, or that some kind of rating system should be developed. The assignment emphasized that students should justify their arguments and make clear their reasoning.

In the class, June introduced the topic of music videos and, in preparation for the writing assignment, led a class discussion on accessibility and censorship issues. The discussion was, then, a kind of "pre-writing" activity, an attempt, June told us, to help students access their own knowledge and experiences and to draw upon them when writing an academic essay. "Many of these students don't have a lot to bring with them in terms of academic experience," she explained, "but they do have some life experiences to bring with them." What we want to do in our analysis of this lesson is to look closely at the conversation June had with her class, characterizing it in terms of its interactional patterns and the kinds of classroom discourse such patterns allow, and to consider the relationship between one student's pattern of talk and the teacher's perception of her cognitive abilities.

Let us explain why we have chosen to examine talk as a way to study this writing class. In *The Social Construction of Literacy,* Jenny Cook-Gumperz reminds us that literacy learning consists of more than the acquisition of cognitive skills; it also involves the "social process of demonstrating knowledgeability" (3). In other words, competence in classrooms means interactional competence as well as competence with written language: knowing when and how and with whom to speak and act in order to create and display knowledge. In the same way, then, that there are cultural "rules" for how to have conversations in particular contexts—the kinds of replies that are appropriate, the points at which it is acceptable to interrupt, the ways one might indicate attentiveness and interest—so there are rules for the talk that goes on in classrooms, rules students will need to know, at least tacitly.[2] From a significant amount of research on Western schooling, it is clear that a great deal of classroom talk is led by the teacher, and that a particular kind of participant structure—or way of arranging verbal interaction (Philips)—dominates classroom conversations. This structure consists of a tripartite series of turns in which a teacher *initiates,* a student *replies,* and the teacher *evaluates* the student's response—the IRE sequence (Cazden; Mehan, *Learning;* Sinclair and Coulthard).[3] In the initiation, or opening turn, the teacher can inform, direct, or ask students for information. The student's reply to this initiation can be non-verbal, such as raising a hand or carrying out an action, or it can be a verbal response. In the evaluation turn, the teacher comments on the student's reply.

Here is an example of an IRE sequence in which June asks about music videos that students have seen lately. We first provide a plain transcript of this brief stretch of talk between teacher and students, and then we follow it with a second transcript (Figure 1) in which we attempt to capture some of the elements of speech that are lost when talk is written down—pauses, stress, and tempo, for instance—elements which suggest a speaker's communicative intentions. Such features, known as contextualization cues (Gumperz, "Contextualization," *Discourse*), signal how an utterance is to be understood, including how it relates to what precedes or follows. According to this system, speakers' turns are segmented into idea or information units[4] on the basis of both semantics and intonation (rising or falling contours). Other features are also represented: lexical prosody, such as vowel elongation or fluctuation, and overlapping speech, where more than one person talks at a time. We think this method enhances the understanding of classroom interaction, and we will incorporate it into our discussion accordingly.[5]

Transcript #1

Initiation	*Reply*	*Evaluation*
1. TEACHER: How 'bout *I Want Your Sex,* Matt? What would [you rate] that?		
	2. MATT: R.	
		3. TEACHER: R. All right. The title of it might indicate right off the bat that it should be an R rated video. Okay.
4. TEACHER: How 'bout some of the rest of you?		
	5. MARIA: I, I, just seen *Like a Prayer.*	
		6. TEACHER: Okay, *Like a Prayer,* all right, good.
7. TEACHER: What, do you know what the rating would be on that one?		

Here is the same segment of classroom talk, this time with contextualization cues marked. The most prominent symbols in this segment are slash marks (/ and //), which signal a drop in voice tone and the end of a speaker's turn; double equal signs (= =), which indicate overlap (that more than one person is speaking at once—e.g., lines g, h, and i in Figure 1) or latching (that they are speaking in rapid succession—e.g., lines a and b in Figure 1); asterisks (*), which label words that speakers are stressing; and indications of volume, pitch, and tempo in brackets—e.g., [p] means quieter speech, [f] means louder speech, [hi] means high-pitched speech.

FIGURE 1   Transcript with Contextualization Cues Marked

a Teacher: how about i want your sex matt what would you rate that?
b Matt: == r/
c Teacher: r// alright//
d   the *title of it might-
e Maria: == [laughs] ==
f Teacher: == indicate right
            off the bat that it should be . . an r rated video, okay/
g   how 'bout some of the rest == of you?
h Unidentified Speaker: == (all last == summer)
i Maria: == {[f] uh
            uh} . . i i just seen like a pray {[laugh]er}/
j Teacher: == okay like *a prayer alright, {[hi] *good}/
k   what-, do you know what the rating would be {[p] on that
            one}?

Selected Contextualization Cues
Symbol   Significance
//   turn-final falling intonation
/   slight falling intonation suggesting more to come
. .   pauses of less than .5 seconds
<2>   pauses timed precisely (= 2 second pause)
==   overlapping or latching speech
~   fluctuating intonation
*   accent, normal prominence
CAPS   accent, extra prominence
( )   unintelligible speech
(xxx)   unclear word, each "x" = one syllable
[ ]   non-lexical phenomena which interrupts the lexical stretch
{[ ]}   non-lexical phenomena which overlays the lexical
               stretch, such as:
            [p]   quieter speech
            [f]   louder speech
            [hi]   high pitch
            [lo]   low pitch
            [ac]   accelerated speech

In this exchange, we see a series of initiations in the form of teacher questions, student replies, and teacher evaluations of those replies—these evaluations often signalled by the word "okay." Throughout the semester, we noticed that "okay" was June's most frequent evaluation token—whether or
not a student's response was acceptable—but early on we learned to differentiate her positive "okays" from negative ones by means of intonation
patterns. Here the first "okay" was pronounced with a slight falling intonation—a signal that the student's response had been appropriate. (Contrast
this positive or at least neutral intonation pattern with the negative one for

"okay" found below in line e of Figure 2.) Also apparent from Figure 1, but not from Transcript 1, is that there is a fair amount of simultaneous talk going on. Note that Maria overlaps her teacher's talk with a laugh in line e and then again in line i, but more loudly the second time, as she attempts to gain the floor. Paying attention to these kinds of contextualization cues helped us more confidently understand and interpret the dynamics of talk and interaction that characterized this particular lesson.

The majority of the conversational turns which occurred in this lesson— some 52 percent—followed the IRE pattern. There were portions of the class time, however, which did not strictly fit this pattern—such as teacher lectures, student initiations, and teacher responses to student initiations. One particularly salient participant structure we call the "mini-lecture." Teacher evaluations often led into these pieces of extended discourse, which served either to elaborate on information already provided or discussed, or to introduce new material. A noticeable feature of mini-lectures was that during them June did not acknowledge interruptions or entertain questions. Students who attempted to interrupt were not given the floor. Of the six attempts to interrupt her lectures during this particular class, June gave only one of these any attention, and that one just enough to work the topic into the mini-lecture.

The predominance of IRE sequences and mini-lectures suggests a discourse that is very much teacher-led. And, in fact, of all the exchanges that occurred during this lesson, 83 percent were directed by June. Two of the twelve students in the class, Andrea and Maria, made the majority of student initiations and responses—19 percent and 16 percent respectively—and also the majority of student responses to teacher initiations—24 percent and 20.5 percent. For the most part, the rest of the class sat quietly—at times they whispered or laughed to each other—but they answered few of June's questions, and they asked fewer questions still. In other words, they adhered to the participant structures that normally characterized interaction in this classroom.

Except, that is, for Maria. We now want to look closely at the talk of one student whose discourse patterns stood out, who did not always abide by the tacit rules that governed talk in this classroom. In fact, she often and obviously pressed at the boundaries of what was permissible conversationally. Of Spanish and Italian descent, Maria was born in El Salvador and moved to the United States with her parents when she was almost two years old. Although all her schooling had taken place in the United States, her first language was Spanish, and through a bilingual program in elementary school she had learned to read and write Spanish before she learned English. Maria told us that her parents don't speak English very well today, although they have been in the United States since 1971, and Spanish continues to be the language of their home, except between Maria and her thirteen-year-old sister.

What Maria told us about her experiences in school prior to college suggests that there she had been a successful student, particularly in English and foreign language classes. She claimed to enjoy writing and said that she had written a romance novel in high school. Her worst subject in high school, she reported, was math, in which she improved from a C to a B (suggesting that she was at least a B student in her other subjects). Maria told us that she had traveled with her high-school speech team and had won a $1000 scholarship to college. As a college freshman, she still enjoyed writing, especially short stories, and she also kept a journal regularly, writing in it about once a week.

Maria sat in the front row of her remedial writing class. She attended every class and turned in all of her homework on time. She also chose to get tutoring when it was offered. In many respects, then—her scholastic history, her engagement in the course, her goals for the future—she seemed very much the dutiful student, dedicated to schooling and willing to work hard. But as we will illustrate with examples of talk from this lesson, her rules for classroom discourse did not map well onto the norm for this class, particularly her strategies for gaining the floor. And this mismatch, this small but noticeable discontinuity, was to work to her disadvantage.

The difficulty was with turn-taking. In ordinary conversation, the potential exists for the speaker to change after every speaker's turn. That is, once a person has concluded her turn, unless she designates the next speaker, then anyone can take a turn (Sacks, Schegloff, and Jefferson). There are differences, of course, in conversational style: "high involvement" speakers tend to take more turns, talk more, and overlap their speech more than other speakers (Tannen). Generally, though, in an ordinary conversation, a speaker has the opportunity to talk after the current speaker finishes. But this state of affairs does not, as we illustrated above, exist in certain kinds of classroom conversations. When a teacher initiates, he takes the floor, his students reply, and then the teacher takes the floor back as he evaluates the reply. This IRE structure, this set of interactions, constitutes an integral unit. The appropriate time for students to gain access to the floor is after an IRE sequence. It's not appropriate in an IRE classroom for students to speak after any speaker's turn except the teacher's initiation, and certainly not during a turn. But this is what Maria does.

Maria not only speaks before an IRE sequence has been completed, interjecting between an initiation and a directed response, she also, on occasion, interrupts during a mini-lecture—an extended piece of teacher discourse which is supposedly non-interruptable—with an "Ohhh!" or "Huh Hmmm!" loud enough to be picked up by the audio recorder. Here is an example of such an interruption. Following a lively discussion of a potential rating system for music videos, June begins an explanation of the writing assignment:

Transcript #2

1. TEACHER: Yeah, all right. Very frightening, traumatic, (kind of) blood and gore. [Laughter from the class.] Okay, yeah. All right, yeah. And they, yeah, there's a problem with the accessibility of music videos on television right now, and that's really what we're going to be dealing with in this essay, is

the issue of music videos that is being considered right now, and you're going to have a chance to . . .

2. MARIA: Oh.

3. TEACHER: . . . try to convince your audience of your position. Okay?

When we analyzed this excerpt—in the manner of Figure 1—it was clear that June/the teacher intends this explanation of a new writing assignment to be non-interruptable: she completes the sentence she had begun as if Maria had not spoken. While Maria's "Oh" is not a lengthy interruption, it is a loud one, and we can also note that she is the only student to interrupt mini-lectures during this lesson.

In addition to interrupting the IRE sequence and mini-lectures inappropriately, Maria sometimes pursued topics for a longer time than June seemed to prefer, continuing to initiate statements about a topic after June was ready to move on. In fact, in the example above, when Maria interrupts the beginning of the mini-lecture with her "Oh," she seems to do so because she is still pursuing a topic that she had initiated moments earlier. Here is the larger context for that interruption, several turns both preceding and following it:

Transcript #3

1. TEACHER: Any other music videos that you feel should have been rated in some way or another? [6 second pause]

2. MARIA: How about those scary ones like, um, *Thriller?*

3. TEACHER: Okay. All right. How could-, well, how could you rate those?

4. MARIA: Uh, R. But they're, the, the, they're very, very—I don't like them 'cause they're very scary.

5. TEACHER: Okay.

6. ANDREA: That's why we should create another rating between R and X, 'cause it would-

7. MARIA: No, because it's not only about, um, sex, about that, but it's those, those, those, those traumatic-

8. TEACHER: Okay.

9. MARIA: You hear about blood and-[Laugh]

10. TEACHER: Yeah, all right. Very frightening, traumatic, (kind of) blood and gore.
    [Laughter from the class.]
    Okay, yeah. All right, yeah.
    And they, yeah, there's a problem with the accessibility of music videos on television right now, and that's really what we're going to be dealing with in this essay, is the issue of music videos that is being considered right now, and you're going to have a chance to . . .

11. MARIA: Oh.

12. TEACHER: . . . try to convince your audience of your position. Okay?

13. MARIA: When I saw the first part of *Thriller* and that, that part when the first part about that corpse?

14. TEACHER: Mmhmm.

15. MARIA: And, and, he jumped up with blood and that was, I, I haven't seen a scene like that in a video before. (It was) scary. Very scary!

[Laughter]

16. TEACHER: Yeah, I can tell just from the publicity which videos I'm gonna avoid just because of those kinds of scenes. So, okay. Wh-, tell me a little about whether you think music videos that you have seen should be allowed on TV. What kinds of things . . um . . should determine whether they can be on TV?

17. ANDREA: Language.

18. TEACHER: Okay, language . . .

The contextualization cues at the opening of the transcript suggest that something may be amiss conversationally right from the start. Note the overlap between June's and Maria's speech in lines b, c, and d, and the fluctuating intonation of June's "okay" and "all right" in line e, the intonation indicating that, in this teacher's repertoire, these are not affirmative responses.

FIGURE 2   Section of Transcript with Contextualization Cues Marked

> a Teacher: {[f] any other music videos that you felt should . . be rated, that should have been rated in some way or another?}
> <6>
> b Maria: = = how about = = those scary ones-
> c Teacher: = = (xxx) = =
> d Maria: = = like um, thriller?
> e Teacher: ok~ay, all r~ight/ {[hi] how could, well how could you rate those?}

We can see from the extended portion of classroom talk in Transcript 3 that Maria interrupts the mini-lecture apparently to continue talking about a topic that she had brought up just moments earlier—the frightening violence in the video *Thriller*—but that June had discouraged. In fact, Maria pursues this topic quite persistently: she ignores June's question in turn 3 about how such movies are rated to comment further on their frightfulness in turn 4; she heads off Andrea's comment about a new rating proposal in turn 6 to argue for the salience of trauma over sex in turn 7; and she interrupts June's mini-lecture (which starts in line 10) to describe a particularly scary incident from *Thriller* in turn 13. We can see June responding to Maria's initiations with brief or disapproving responses (see turn 3/line e; see also turn 16) and finally taking hold of the discourse once again.

We think June's response in this instance is understandable: Maria appears to be reintroducing a topic that had been completed; June had shifted from discussion of specific videos to the essay question of whether or not music videos should be regulated. It is interesting to note, though, that the

question June asks to bring the discourse round again to the essay topic—
what kinds of things should determine whether a video could be aired on
television?—was answered implicitly by Maria in her discussion of the violence in *Thriller*, but her contribution wasn't explicitly acknowledged.

In fact, June didn't appear to value what seemed to us appropriate responses from Maria, even when those responses did fit the pattern of classroom talk. Toward the end of Transcript 3 (turn 16), June asked what might
determine how a movie video would be rated. In response to her question,
students suggested "language," "sex," and "violence," and there were brief
discussions of each in turn. June then asked the question again, for the fourth
time, and when there was no response for several seconds, she explained that
nudity might be another factor and explained how it's not to be confused
with sexual scenes. Then, again, she asks the "what else" question; there's a
long pause, and Maria replies:

Transcript #4

1. TEACHER: Okay, can you think of anything else that might, they might consider when they're trying to decide how to rate a music video? (pause)

2. MARIA: Um, is it like . . ( ) . . something to do with somebody that criticizes
somebody else, like political issues, something like that?

3. TEACHER: Um, I don't know, um, that-

4. MARIA: Seems like, um, yeah-

5. TEACHER: That's not a widely recognized one but it might be one that is sort of
subtle that's-

6. MARIA: Yeah. Like talking about like if you ( ) somebody, like race or something like that, ( ) video ( ) something like that.

7. TEACHER: Um, I don't know. Um, who would that kind of a video appeal to?

8. MARIA: Um, I don't know, um.

9. TEACHER: Would that appeal to children?

10. MATT: What music video is this?

11. TEACHER: If, a music video about some kind of a political issue.

12. MARIA: Yeah.

13. MATT: Oh, you mean like *Graceland* or something by U2?

14. TEACHER: Yeah, something like that. Now is that the kind of video that would
really appeal to children?

15. ANDREA: No.

16. TEACHER: Or who would that appeal to?

In the following analysis of turns 1–7, notice that after line a, there is a long
pause—one that perhaps gives Maria and the rest of the class enough time to
provide thoughtful responses. It's also noteworthy that in line b we see some
indications—from her pauses, soft voice, and tentative questions—that
Maria is struggling to articulate a partly formed idea. Notice, though, that in

line f Maria takes on steam as she thinks of race as a possible example and speeds up her talk.

FIGURE 3   Section of Transcript with Contextualization Cues Marked

a Teacher:	. . . okay, {[hi] can you think of anything else that might}-, they might consider when they're trying to decide how to rate a music video? <5>
b Maria:	Uhhm, is it like <4> {[p] ( ) uh <3> something to do with . . somebody that criticizes somebody else}, like . . political issues? something like that?
c Teacher:	uh [sigh] <2.5> i don't know/ um = = that-
d Maria:	= = seems like um, yeah-
e Teacher:	= = {[f] that's not a widely recog}nized one but . . it might be one that is sort of subtle that's-
f Maria:	y~eah like {[ac] [p] talking about like if you ( ) somebody, like race or something like that ( ) video ( ) something like that}
g Teacher:	{[p] mm hmm/} uhhm, {[hi] i don't know}/
h	um, WHO would that kind of video appeal to?

In this exchange, it seems to us that Maria brings up a new way to think about what influences ratings: a video with political overtones certainly could arouse concern or anger. Maria's comment, then, could have been an occasion for a discussion of censorship. For such a discussion to happen, however, June would need to provide some assistance, some verbal scaffolding, for Maria is struggling to express a partly formed idea about the importance of political contexts for music videos. But June does not assist this potential contribution; in fact, she disallows Maria's answer by undercutting it. (Notice June's use of "I don't know" in the evaluation slot in contrast to her usual, more ostensibly neutral, "Okay.") June shifts the discussion away from political censorship and toward the issue of age by asking an unexpected question: "Who would that kind of a video appeal to?" (In line h this shift is signaled by June's intonation, a specific use of a contextualization cue that we observed at other places in the lesson.) This question departs from the pattern she had earlier established—the repeated question of "what else" might determine how a video gets rated—and it has a silencing effect on Maria. The conversation gets short-circuited, and Maria's moment for contributing a piece of knowledge is lost, and so is an opportunity for the class to consider an important issue.

Soon after the lesson, June viewed the videotape we had made of it, and she commented on Maria's classroom talk:

Maria is becoming to me the Queen of the Non Sequiturs. You know, she really is just not quite. . . . That's, that's why I'm sort of amazed at times at, at her writing level, which is not really too bad. . . . Because her thinking level seems to be so scattered that I would expect that her writing would be a lot more disorganized and disjointed.

June was amazed at the level of Maria's writing, which was "not really too bad," given the scattered cognition she surmised from Maria's oral performance in class. In fact, June actually awarded Maria's written logic and organization with steadily improving grades and positive comments on her essays: "I like the way you made distinctions between facts and opinions." "You are very thorough and your thinking about the advice is very clear and logical." But, in spite of such evidence, June seemed to be greatly influenced in her assessment of Maria's abilities by her talk in the classroom, using "talking" as a barometer for "thinking," labeling Maria the "Queen of the Non Sequiturs." At the end of the semester, when summing up her evaluations of students, June confided that Maria "was a sweet girl, but she drove me crazy." She accounted for the improvement Maria had made in her writing by surmising that she had probably gotten help from her parents. (This was unlikely, however, since Maria's parents spoke little English.) June then made a final comment about her thinking: "Maria has thinking continuity problems." She predicted Maria wouldn't pass the next writing class the first time through "because it requires coherent thinking."

We think we can outline the process by which June constructed her view of Maria. When we looked over our field notes and our videotapes, there was abundant evidence that Maria did violate some of this classroom's rules for talk. Over the course of the semester, Maria made twenty-eight statements that were recorded in our fieldnotes. Ten of these were responses that fit the IRE question/answer structure; the remaining eighteen were initiations in the form of questions, and of these questions, six were procedural—how long does our essay have to be? must we type or can we write by hand? what page did you say that exercises are on?—a type of question that may be bothersome, particularly if its timing is a little off and it occurs after the conversation has turned to other matters. And, in fact, June did notice Maria's questioning patterns, and commented at the end of the semester that Maria asked a lot of questions in class but didn't answer many that June had posed to her.

Maria did, then, seem to initiate more than she responded—asking questions, taking the floor, diverting the course of classroom talk—and hers was not exactly the expected posture for a student in an IRE classroom. There were times when her interjections did suggest that she was not paying attention or was involved in something else related to the class, like reading over the assignment sheet while June was talking. This, we would argue, led to June's construction of Maria as the "Queen of the Non Sequiturs," the student who could be trusted to make a comment that was inappropriate or off-target. Given the way Maria's conversational habits stood out, it seems likely that June's view of Maria as an inappropriate talker would eventually become salient enough to affect her perception of Maria even when she interjects in a way that is appropriate. Join this perception of a particular student with this teacher's strong predilection for an IRE participant structure, and you won't be surprised that Maria's chances to be heard would be undercut. The cycle continues as Maria's interactional patterns in class become not just an annoying conversational style, but the barometer by which to measure her cognitive abilities. Her bothersome conversational habits become evidence of a thinking problem—evidence that is so salient that it goes unqualified even in the face of counter-evidence that Maria, in fact, wrote rather well.

But though we can explain at least some of the steps in the construction of Maria as a scattered thinker, we are left with a troubling question: how is it that annoying conversational style can become a measure of intellectual ability? What we have seen here is a relatively minor disjunction between teacher expectation and student behavior, an irritating mismatch of styles that, perhaps, chafes at a teacher's sense of authority. But given that irritations with students can lead to a range of outcomes, what made June's judgment of cognitive deficiency possible? To answer this question, we believe we need to consider the broader educational and cultural context in which this teacher lives—the received language and frames of mind she works within. Put another way, we need to consider the ways our schools have historically judged mental ability from performance that is somehow problematic and the sanctioned paths of inference from behavior to cognition that emerge from such judgments. We will begin by describing what we think of as this larger context for remedial writing instruction with a brief history of "low achievers" in American education.

The Cultural Context of School Failure

There is a long, troubling history in American education of perceiving and treating low-achieving children as if they were lesser in character and fundamental ability. Larry Cuban and David Tyack, citing work by Stanley Zehm, trace this history by examining the labels that have been attached to students who are low-achievers, for "contained in a name, either explicitly or implicitly, is both an explanation and a prescription" (4). In the first half of the nineteenth century the poor performer was a "dunce," "shirker," "loafer," "reprobate," or "wrong-doer" who was "stupid," "vicious," "depraved," "wayward," or "incorrigible." Some of these labels imply that students lacked intelligence, but the majority suggest a flawed character. Such assessments, note Cuban and Tyack, reveal "a set of religious and moral convictions that placed responsibility for behavior and achievement in the sovereign individual" (4). During the last half of the nineteenth century, the labels shifted somewhat toward intelligence rather than character, though with a developmental or organic cast: students were "born late," "sleepy-minded," "overgrown," "immature," "slow," or "dull." "The condemnatory, religious language used earlier was diminishing," note Cuban and Tyack, "but the notion that academic failure came from defects of character or disposition continued" (4). As we moved into the twentieth century, notions of developmental and intellectual normalcy—evident in the abnormalcy of labels like "born late" and "sleepy-minded"—continued to evolve and were applied, in a negative way, to poor performers. And with the advent of the IQ movement, the assessment of intelligence, as Stephen Jay Gould has observed, was pseudoscientifically reified into a unitary measure of cognitive—and human—worth. Class and race prejudice, xenophobia, and the social engineering of Social Darwinists and Eugenicists absorbed the new technology of mental measurement, and the deficiency of those who performed poorly in school could, it was said, be precisely and scientifically assessed.

Though the ways of thinking about thinking generated by the IQ movement are still very much with us, we have changed perspectives somewhat since the heyday of the Eugenicists. The social reform movements of the 50s and 60s shifted the discussion of school failure from the character and ability of the individual toward the society that produces "alienated" and "socially maladjusted" youth and, as well, toward the economic conditions that have a negative impact on a lower-class child's readiness for school. Yet such social theories often reflected the influence of the theories that preceded them. Cuban and Tyack point out that along with the sociologically oriented analyses of the 50s—with their discussions of "social maladjustment" and "dropping out"—came designations of students as "immature learners," "unwilling learners," and "dullards." And many of the economic analyses of the 60s discussed minority and working-class culture in terms of deficit and pathology. A number of linguistic, psychological, and social psychological studies—focused, to a great extent, on African Americans—were designed and interpreted in such a way as to demonstrate impoverishment of language, maladaptive mother-child interaction, inadequate environmental stimuli for the development of cognition, and so on. (See Mitchell for a good overview.) Education tried to move beyond the moralistic, characterologic, deficit orientation of a previous era only to enshrine such orientations in a seemingly reform-minded social science research—and to continue to fault children for educational failure.

Through the 70s and 80s, two other perspectives on school failure have emerged: the effect cultural differences can have on communication and learning in the classroom (see, e.g., Au; Heath; Philips), and the effect class- and race-based resistance to socialization into the mainstream can have on school performance (see, e.g., Chase; Everhart; Giroux; Ogbu and Matute-Bianchi; Willis). We see these perspectives as powerful advances and—like many researchers of our generation—have been deeply influenced by them. But what concerns us is the ease with which older deficit-oriented explanations for failure can exist side by side with these newer theories, and, for that fact, can narrow the way such theories are represented and applied, turning differences into deficits, reducing the rich variability of human thought, language, and motive (Rose, "Language"; "Narrowing").

We think here of another teacher at another school in our study—a very good teacher, respected by colleagues and warmly regarded by students—a teacher who, upon receiving an assignment to teach his institution's most "remedial" course, dutifully sought out the program's expert in applied linguistics and schooling. The expert told the teacher, among other things, about research on differences in socialization for schooling. Our teacher later told a colleague that he was "in despair," fearful that he "may not be able to help these kids." Given their early socialization patterns "they barely have a chance. They're doomed by the time they enter school." There may be a harsh truth in the teacher's despair—poor kids do fail in disproportionate numbers—but note how variability disappears as rich differences in background and style become reduced to a success-failure binary and the "problem"—as has been the tendency in our history—shifts from the complex intersection of cognition and culture and continues to be interpreted as a deficiency located within families and students. In this perspective, school performance, as Ronald Edmonds once put it, "derives from family background instead of school response to family background" (23).

It is difficult to demonstrate causal relationships across the level of individual functioning and the levels of social, cultural, and historical contexts, what Erickson calls "system levels" or "levels of organization" (166–67). It is difficult to demonstrate, in our case, that pervasive, shared assumptions about ability and remediation influenced a teacher's interaction with and assessment of a student. One way to gain some reasonable evidence of influence, however, is to look closely at the language the teacher uses, and we have done that. Another way is to find institutional mechanisms that might serve to instantiate influential cultural assumptions. One such mechanism seemed to be the college's training program in which this teacher participated. In such programs, readings on topics like the composing process, the social context of schooling, and error analysis are sometimes combined, we have observed, with skills-and-drills materials and deficit-oriented theories and assessments. From what we could tell from the teacher's discussion of the program with us, this mix seemed to obtain. In addressing it, we can treat more fully a point we made earlier: the lasting power of deficit notions in our society and the way they can blend with and subvert more forward-looking notions about language and cognition. This blend is evident in two excerpts from June's commentary on the videotapes of the previous lesson and a present one.

In the first, June and the interviewer have been talking about the difficulty her students have with academic writing, particularly papers requiring categorization and comparison:

TEACHER: They don't have those skills. Many of them don't. And many don't have an attention to detail that's necessary for some kinds of things; for instance, for classification, uh, exercises there's a need to look at, at specifics and at detail at times in order to be thorough, you know, to deal with that. They just don't have the practice in doing that. Uh, I think what I'm trying to do is, um, make sure that I tie as much as I possibly can into their own experience. Um, because many of these students don't have a lot to bring with them in terms of academic experience, but they do have some life experience to bring with them so. . . .

INTERVIEWER: Okay.

TEACHER: So, for instance, what I did in class about, um, having them write about what they think the educational system should do. Uh, ideally I would have liked them to do that before they ever read the article on, uh, Wednesday, just to get them thinking about what they're, what they already know about it, what, you know, what experience has already shown them about the things or what they've heard somewhere. . . . A lot of these kids have problems with connections between things. They, they don't see the connection between what goes on in their lives and what happens in the classroom, what happens, uh, at home. . . .

June notes, accurately we think, that many of her students haven't had sufficient practice in writing academic papers in which they must classify phenomena and attend closely to detail. She then observes that while her students may not have had a certain kind of privileged education, they certainly do have life experience and a history of schooling—both of which can be tapped and reflected upon, activating background knowledge that can help them with college assignments. But then look at the interesting thing that happens—a move that we witnessed in a number of our studies—the leap is made from an accurate description of particular difficulties (students have trouble writing certain kinds of papers) to a judgment about a general cognitive capacity: "A lot of these kids have problems with connections between things." Note, as well, the acknowledgment of a problem with the educational system—the segmentation of home and school knowledge—but the locating of it within the individual's cognition ("They don't see the connection") rather than within the system.

Now to the second excerpt:

INTERVIEWER: Maria said something real interesting today. I asked them . . . to tell me what they think good writing or good reading is, and . . . she just immediately said "Good writing is creative writing."

TEACHER: She's written a novel—incredible!

INTERVIEWER: Yes, she told me that (both laugh).

TEACHER: She's written about it in her journal and I, I, you know I thought that was neat. . . .

INTERVIEWER: You know I asked her . . . if she tried to apply creativity in her writing, and she said, "Oh, yes!"

TEACHER: Well, she doesn't. . . . (laughs) She doesn't understand the difference between creative writing and expository prose.

INTERVIEWER: I'm not sure.

TEACHER: Yet.

INTERVIEWER: I'm not sure.

TEACHER: Well, that's not really something they get until, um, English 20A anyway. We don't really start talking about those distinctions until then. . . .

June wants to "tie as much as [she] possibly can into [her students'] own experience"; she also thinks it's a good thing that Maria wrote about her novel in her journal. But almost in the same breath she devalues Maria's extra-institutional literary activity and negates the possibility that she could learn things about literacy from it. The closing remark about English 20A is telling, we think, for with it June suggests that it is only through a lockstepped, carefully segmented curriculum that students like Maria can eventually develop the ability to understand the characteristics of different literacies and make distinctions between them. Perhaps because this teacher views fundamental cognitive abilities as deficient—thinking continuity problems, problems seeing connections—she suggests that it is only through the remedial therapy of a series of self-contained, carefully sequenced treatments that literacy knowledge can be developed. In a different guise, this is a skills-and-drills philosophy in which instructional scaffolding is replaced by curricular prostheses.

The point we want to make is that June is not alone in her judgments. For almost two centuries the dominant way to think about underachieving students has been to focus on defects in intellect or character or differences in culture or situation that lead to failure, and to locate the causes within the mind and language of the individual.[6] We are primed by this history, by our backgrounds and our educations, to speak of students as deficient,[7] even as we attempt to devise curricula we call forward-looking,[8] and this is true despite the great awakening that has occurred since the publication of Shaughnessy's *Errors and Expectations* in 1977. To be sure, we have found ways to understand our students' writing and promote its development, even when that writing differs markedly from the academic standard; we have come to see our courses as entry points to the academy, safe ground where students who have not had sufficient experience with academic reading and writing can make up for lost time, and do so without censure. Often, however, these new understandings come mixed with deeply held, unarticulated assumptions about remediation and remedial students, deficit assumptions that have been part of educational thought for a long time. Our unexamined cultural biases about difference, our national habits of mind for sorting and labeling individuals who perform poorly, our legacy of racism and class bias—these are the frames of mind which make it possible, even unremarkable, to assume that talk that is occasionally non-synchronous with the talk in a classroom indicates some fundamental problem in thought, to assume "thinking continuity problems" from a difference in conversational style. In examining June's ways of assessing cognition, then, we hope to set the foundation for ongoing self-examination, for we are all enmeshed in culture, and, even as we resist them, we are shaped by its forces.

EXAMINING ASSUMPTIONS

How can we as teachers and researchers examine our assumptions about remediation and remedial writing and remedial students? How can we be alert to deficit explanations for the difficulties that students experience in our classrooms? We have four suggestions: remembering teacher development, attending to classroom discourse, making macro-micro connections, and re-thinking the language of cultural difference.

Remembering Teacher Development

When basic writing was just emerging as a course worth a teacher's serious attention and commitment, Mina Shaughnessy pointed out that most work was focusing on what was wrong with students rather than with teacher development. The effect of this tendency was the erroneous notion "that students, not teachers, are the people in education who must do the changing" ("Diving In" 234). Shaughnessy reminded us that students aren't the only people in a classroom who develop and grow, and she proposed a kind of impressionistic developmental scale for teachers of basic writing, each stage of which she named with a common metaphor: "Guarding the Tower," "Converting the Natives," "Sounding the Depths," and "Diving In." The significant thing to us about these metaphors is that they focus on teachers' attitudes about students' abilities. Teachers who guard the tower are so stunned by fractured writing that they believe the students who produced it have no place in the academy, for they will never be able to live up to the ideal of academic prose. Once this shock abates, and teachers begin to believe that students are educable, they proceed with conversion by offering them a steady flow of "truth" without thinking too much about the skills and habits students bring with them, often unconsciously, to their interactions with texts. The third stage involves the recognition that the writing behavior these students display has a logic that merits careful observation. At this point, then, a teacher is moving away from deficit notions and towards an appreciation of students' abilities. The last stage takes place when a teacher is willing to "remediate himself, to become a student of new disciplines and of his students themselves in order to perceive both their difficulties and their incipient excellence" (239). It is not at all easy, cautioned Shaughnessy, for a college teacher to assume that the students in a class, already labeled "remedial," possess this incipient excellence.

We want to argue that the situation Shaughnessy described is still with us. Granted, we have made much progress in learning about the writing process, in conducting interdisciplinary research, in imagining liberatory pedagogies, even in establishing composition programs which include some kind of training for teachers.[9] But what we have been much less successful in doing is promoting teacher development of the sort Shaughnessy described. We have assumed, as a best-case scenario, that if new teachers are introduced to writing theory and research as a part of their graduate training, and if they have the chance to prepare and develop curricular materials for their classes (conditions that are all too rare), then they will necessarily acquire whatever it is they need to know about remedial students. Maybe we have also assumed that teachers automatically move from "guarding the tower" to "diving in" just as a function of experience. Our studies make us question these assumptions. Because deficit notions of abilities are so deeply ingrained in most of us, it seems very unlikely that most teachers, pressed as they are by constraints of time and curricula, will discover serendipitously more productive ways to view students' abilities.

And how we view students' abilities, we have tried to illustrate in this paper, can have profound effects. A great deal of research has shown that students whose teachers expect them to do well, tend to do well, while students whose teachers expect them to do poorly, do poorly. These findings hold firm, even in cases of mistaken placement or misinformation. That is, "bright" students who are mistakenly expected to perform poorly in the classroom will often do poorly, while students labeled "average" will often excel if their teacher believes that this is what they are supposed to do (Brophy). We have illustrated that Maria's discourse style did not fit well with the IRE participant structure of her remedial writing class. It also occurred to us that Maria's conversational patterns more closely resembled the talk that is allowed in classrooms geared to the honors student. Perhaps Maria, who placed in non-remedial classes in high school and was on the speech team, was accustomed to speaking up with her own opinion, which she expected to be acknowledged by her teachers and to be of some import to the lesson. She displays an eagerness to be involved, to interact with her teacher.[10] By the end of the semester, the mismatch between Maria's discourse style and that of the classroom seemed to be taking a toll. Maria told us in her last tutoring session that she now "had some problems with . . . English," that her writing had gotten "longer" but not necessarily better, and that she was "not a very good speaker." Perhaps it is also noteworthy that she expressed interest at the end of the semester in teaching students who were poor performers in the classroom. In any case, her negative self-assessments are very different from the successful Maria we saw at the beginning of the semester — the student who loved writing and who'd been a member of the speech team — and suggest that she had perhaps begun to internalize her teacher's opinions of her abilities.

Research on expectancy theory thus supports Shaughnessy's claims about teacher development: the beliefs we construct of our students' abilities can influence their lives in our classrooms and beyond in profound ways. We want to suggest that it would be unwise just to rely on process pedagogy and experience in the classroom to foster the development of non-deficit attitudes among teachers and teacher-trainees. We need to spend some time thinking about teacher development — not just what knowledge to impart about writing, but how to develop the ability to question received assumptions about abilities and performance, how to examine the thinking behind the curricula we develop and the assessments we make.[11]

We might, for a start, look closely at writing instruction to identify moments when teachers transcend deficit attitudes, when teaching serves to invite rather than to deny. Roger Simon has written about "the contradictory character of the work of teaching" (246), illustrating that "what teachers choose to signify at any particular moment in time may present meanings which are ideologically inconsistent with meanings present at other times" (248). He locates the origin of these contradictions not in the individual but in the larger social and institutional context, and he sees contradictory moments as potentially liberatory, for they make possible the inclusion of oppositional knowledge in educational practice. In a related way, we might think of teaching as an ongoing flow of moments of invitation and moments of denial. The better, the more effective the teaching, the richer and more frequent the moments of invitation, encouragement, and assistance (though no extended period of teaching will be free of constraint, limit, even rejection). What has interested us in this paper is the way in which culturally sanctioned, deficit-oriented assumptions about learning and cognition can tip the scale. But what we need to do as well is identify, understand, and learn to foster those moments in which teachers encourage rather than restrict their students' potential.

Attending to Classroom Discourse

One of the things we have learned in doing this paper is the value of looking closely at the talk that transpires in classrooms. We have been interested particularly in conversational patterns—rules for turn-taking and the special participant structure that characterizes so much of talk in school, the IRE sequence. But this work on turn-taking, interesting and revealing though it can be, was a means to another end. In the classroom, it is through talk that learning gets done, that knowledge gets made. Using conversational turns as a unit of analysis gave us a window on knowledge-making.

In the analysis reported in this paper, we focused on a moment when Maria didn't get to make knowledge, when her chance to contribute a special piece of information, one that would have deepened the discourse at hand, was denied. We have argued that the reason her contribution was denied had to do with her teacher's construction of her as a particular kind of remedial student, a scattered thinker, and that such a construction likely had its origin in long-standing, widespread beliefs about low-achieving students, beliefs that such students are deficient and that the locus of any academic difficulty they have lies within them. In this instance, then, we saw faulty notions about cognition being played out and reinforced within a certain participant structure, the IRE sequence.

This finding raised for us the possibility that the IRE sequence could be the vehicle for a discourse of remediation, a discourse where most questions have "known" answers, where the teacher maintains tight control over conversation, where students are not allowed to participate in free-ranging talk. In the literature on classroom talk, many objections have been raised about the IRE participant structure in terms of the role that more free-ranging talk can play in knowledge construction (see, e.g., Applebee; Barnes; Cazden; Dillon; Edwards and Furlong; Moffett; Tharp and Gallimore). We too see a place for free-ranging, student-led discussion (Hull and Rose, "'This Wooden'").[12] But we would also suggest that the IRE participant structure does not itself circumvent knowledge-making and engagement; the kinds of questions that teachers ask and the kinds of evaluations that they give to students' responses will more often affect what knowledge gets made and who makes it. Questions that are genuine questions, that don't have pre-specified answers, and evaluations that validate students' contributions are going to create a different kind of classroom discourse and a different level of engagement.[13]

Let us look at some bits of conversation from our classroom lesson which do just that.

> TEACHER: Well, tell me a little bit about what would go into determining how the music videos that you have seen might be rated. What kinds of things, um, would be used to determine how, what, how a movie gets rated?
>
> STUDENT: Language.
>
> TEACHER: Okay, language (writes it on the board). Like what, tell me, give examples. I mean . . . You don't have to swear but. . . .

In this IRE sequence, June asks a follow-up question, incorporating the student's answer into her next question in order to elicit an elaboration on the student's answer. She considers the student's answer important enough to spend time on it, to work it into the exchange, to allow it to modify the subsequent discussion. And in so doing, she bestows value on it.

> TEACHER: Or who would that appeal to?
>
> MATT: I don't think that—
>
> SUSAN: ( ) over 18.
>
> MATT: Children of what age level?
>
> TEACHER: Okay, that's a good question: children of what age?

Here June accepts a student's initiation and sanctions it as the topic of the next series of questions. This move shows, again, a willingness to accept students' ideas and to value them.

> TEACHER: What, what are some of the music videos you've seen recently?
>
> ANDREA: *Thriller.*
>
> TEACHER: *Thriller.*
>
> MATT: *Graceland.*
>
> TEACHER: Okay, *Thriller* . . . and *Graceland.* I'll, I'll come back to that one, but *Thriller,* what's the rating on *Thriller?*

Here June acknowledges that a student's comment, although it cannot immediately be responded to, is nevertheless important and will eventually be discussed.

And those moments when June was able to shift out of the IRE pattern— mixing conversation styles, encouraging other modes of participation—gave rise to yet other opportunities for fruitful talk. For example, when one student proposes that music videos could be rated by a quantitative tally of objectionable language, June responds:

> TEACHER: Okay. Now that's something I had not heard before, but that kind of makes sense.

Here, then, is an admission from June that a student knows something that she doesn't—an admission that might lessen the power differential in the classroom and make authentic discourse more possible. Another such moment occurred when a student points out that the same kind of violence that would result in a restrictive rating for a music video regularly occurs as part of on-the-scene reporting in newscasts—an assertion, by the way, that challenged the position June had adopted. The student then goes on to give an example of a murder shown recently on a local television news program:

> MATT: I saw the shooting.
>
> ANDREA: Yeah, I've seen the shooting.
>
> JASON: Yeah, ( ) They shot 'im like from, from where I'm at to where you're at. . . .

Following the above excerpt, the conversation takes off and continues for another two pages in our transcript. June does evaluate a few times during this conversation, but she sees that it is clearly a topic of concern for the students—a number of different students initiate during this discussion—and she lets it go longer than any other student conversation in the lesson. She also becomes an "equal" participant at times, no longer evaluating but asking questions for which she doesn't have a particular answer in mind. These are not remarkable exchanges, but they were rare in the lessons we analyzed, and they do illustrate a capacity to engage in kinds of classroom conversation other than those we saw with Maria.

We want to recommend that attention be paid to the talk that goes on in our writing classrooms—analyses of the participant structures, whether they be IRE sequences or other patterns of interaction—with an eye for determining the kind of talk those structures allow. We have seen that discourse structures direct talk in particular ways and that certain moves within those structures can instantiate assumptions about cognition and undercut creative thinking and engagement. If we look closely at the talk we allow, we may also get a new sense of our own assumptions about our students' capabilities.

Making Macro-Micro Connections

What has frequently happened in the study of reading and writing is that researchers have conducted either fine-grained analyses of texts or of the cognitive processes involved in text comprehension and production *or* have produced studies of wider focus of the social and political contexts of reading, writing, and schooling. Such a separation isn't peculiar to literacy research, but characterizes as well divisions among disciplines. As anthropologist

Frederick Erickson has pointed out, "Individual cognitive functioning has been largely the purview of cognitive psychologists who have often attempted to study thinking apart from the naturally occurring social and cultural circumstances of its use," while "the anthropology of education often has studied *anything but* deliberately taught cognitive learning" (173). Erickson goes on to suggest that "some rapprochement is needed, from the direction of the (more cognitively sophisticated) psychology of learning to the (more contextually sophisticated) anthropology of learning" (173).

Such calls to systematically integrate social and cognitive perspectives are increasing (Freedman, Dyson, Flower, and Chafe; Michaels; Rose, "Complexity"). Sociologist Aaron Cirourel argues that "the study of discourse and the larger context of social interaction requires explicit references to a broader organizational setting and aspects of cultural beliefs often ignored by students of discourse and conversational analysis" (qtd. in Corsaro 22). At the same time, educational anthropologist Henry Trueba reminds us, "the strength of ethnographic research [on school achievement] and its contribution to theory building . . . will depend on the strength of each of the microanalytical links of the inferential chains that form our macrotheoretical statements" (283). To adequately study language in society, then, one has to take into account "interrelationships among linguistic, cognitive, and sociocultural elements" (Cirourel quoted in Corsaro 23).

Moving between micro-level, close examination of oral or written discourse and macro-level investigations of society and culture—seeking connections between language, cognition, and context—is, we feel, particularly important in the case of students designated remedial and for our efforts to examine our assumptions about these students' abilities (Hull and Rose, "Rethinking"). Without the microperspective, one runs the risk of losing sight of the particulars of behavior; without the macroperspective, one runs the risk of missing the social and cultural logic of that behavior. In the case of Maria, micro-level analyses enabled us to examine closely the conversational processes by which a student was defined as a scattered thinker and the ways her opportunities to participate in and contribute to knowledge production were narrowed. Macro-level analyses can encourage a consideration of Maria's discourse processes in contexts other than the individual cognitive one provided by her teacher and, as well, encourage reflection on the very language June uses in making her assessment. So, let us now play out some macro-level considerations of Maria's conversational style.

Reproduction-resistance theorists and cultural-difference theorists, both mentioned earlier, would raise questions about the broader political and cultural contexts of Maria's behavior. The former group would wonder if Maria's conversational style was an attempt to resist an educational system that does not serve her well, while the latter group would wonder if Maria's conversational style reflected communication patterns shaped by her cultural inheritance and/or her family background. The focus of the "problem" of Maria's conversational style wouldn't automatically be on the isolated processes of her own cognition, but on the possible role played by other political or cultural influences. A somewhat related perspective would focus on

Maria's history in classrooms—wondering what prior socializing experiences in school might have influenced her interactional style. A further perspective would tighten the contextual focus to the immediate psychosocial context of Maria's current instruction. Was there something about the way Maria expressed her need to be involved in the class and her teacher's conscious or unconscious reaction to it that affected Maria's conversational style?

In posing these perspectives, we do not want to suggest that each has equal explanatory power for Maria's case. For example, our data don't seem to support reproduction-resistance theory. Maria was an eager participant in the classroom community, taking part dutifully in virtually every aspect of her course. Her interruptions of classroom talk did not appear to us to be interruptions for the sake of disruption; rather she seemed to want to take part in class, to make a contribution, or to keep track of assignment information she may have missed. (The value of this perspective in Maria's case may be more general, however, in that it can lead one to examine the political context of schooling and the inequities of class in American educational history.) The applicability of the cultural-differences perspective is a more complicated issue. There may well be home/school differences at work in Maria's conversational style; unfortunately we were not able to visit Maria's home or collect information from other sources that could shed light on this hypothesis directly. One could argue, though, against the applicability of the cultural-differences hypothesis here in any strong way. While Maria may have operated with different cultural assumptions about communication when she first began elementary school in the United States, it seems unlikely that she would not have become aware of the dominant discourse of schooling, the IRE participant structure, by the time she entered college. Still, there is real value, it seems to us, in speculating on the possible conversational dynamics within Maria's family that might influence what she does in the classroom, especially under the pressure to articulate an idea. We have very limited data on the third perspective offered above—Maria's history of interaction with teachers—though this seems a good possibility to pursue, especially given her participation on a speech team, where somewhat more interactive conversational patterns could have existed. We think the fourth perspective—the psychosocial context of Maria and her teacher—is also promising, especially when we consider the less excitable Maria observed in our tutorial sessions.

Our best, and cautious, guess about the context of Maria's conversational style in this classroom, then, would be that three possible influences are at work: (a) Maria's previous experience in classrooms or other school contexts that were less teacher-centered, (b) characteristics of her non-classroom conversational style, possibly shaped by family dynamics, and (c) Maria's eagerness—perhaps tinged with anxiety—to do well and be part of things and the growing number of disapproving cues she picks up from her teacher, which could lead to further uncertainty and anxiety, and with that, further communicative missteps.

Attempting to link micro-level with macro-level analysis—shuttling in a systematic way between close linguistic and cognitive study and studies of broader contexts—can, we think, provide a richer understanding of the history and logic of particular behaviors. It might provide, as well, checks and balances on the assessments we make about ability, and perhaps it can lead us to raise to conscious examination our assumptions about the nature and cause of performance that strikes us as inadequate or unusual. But even as we use this micro-macro metaphor, we are unhappy with it, for we recognize that it still separates cognitive behaviors and social contexts into different domains. In fact, one reason for much recent interest in Vygotsky and the extension of his work called "activity theory" (Wertsch; Minick) is that his sociocultural theory of mind provides an alternative to the division of cognition from context, mind from culture, knowing from acting. We see a need to work toward holistic conceptions of the study of schooling and students' performance which take as a given that linguistic and cognitive behaviors occur within, and can best be understood within, their particular institutional, cultural, and historical milieus.

Rethinking the Language of Cultural Difference

Our last suggestion for examining our assumptions about remediation and remedial students is to work toward a conceptualization of discourse that undercuts easy thinking about difference. This call is difficult, for it requires an engagement of the very language currently available to us to discuss school failure in a progressive way.

Research on cultural and class differences in communication and learning styles has revealed the coherence, purposiveness, and richness of behavior that has puzzled mainstream educators and resulted in harmful explanations and assessments of poor performance. Such research has moved us significantly toward a more democratic vision of learning and schooling and, in some cases, has helped us successfully tailor instruction to fit students' needs (e.g., Au; Heath). But our time spent in remedial programs—reviewing curricula, talking to teachers and administrators, catching our own disturbing reactions to the literacy performances we saw—has made us uncomfortable with much of the research that focuses on differences, whether such difference grows out of the recognition that communication styles at school aren't like those at home or that people come to intellectual tasks in different ways. The problem is that all American educational research—ours and everyone else's—emerges from a culture in the grips of deficit thinking, and any analysis that delineates differences will run the risk of being converted to a deficit theory (Rose, "Narrowing"). We believe that a focus on differences, while potentially democratic and certainly instructive, can lead us to forget two things: (1) in fundamental ways, we all possess the means to use language to make meaning; we all participate in fundamental linguistic and cognitive processes by virtue of our common humanity and (2) human beings, given the right social conditions, are astoundingly adaptive, and to determine what works against this adaptability, we need to look at the social and instructional conditions in the classroom rather than assume the problem is to be found in the cultural characteristics students bring with them. Two research-based observations are pertinent here. The first is from Asa Hilliard, and the second comes from Luis Moll and Stephen Diaz:

> I do believe that greater sensitivity to [learning] style issues will make meaningful contributions to pedagogy in the future. Yet I remain unconvinced that the explanation for the low performance of culturally different "minority" group students will be found by pursuing questions of behavioral style. Since students are adaptable, the stylistic difference explanation does not answer the question of why "minority" groups perform at a low level. . . . [C]hildren . . . are failing primarily because of systematic inequalities in the delivery of whatever pedagogical approach the teachers claim to master—not because students cannot learn from teachers whose styles do not match their own. (Hilliard 68)

> Although student characteristics certainly matter, when the same children are shown to succeed under modified instructional arrangements it becomes clear that the problems . . . working-class children face in school must be viewed primarily as a consequence of institutional arrangements that constrain children *and* teachers by not capitalizing fully on their talents, resources, and skills. (Moll and Diaz 302)

It is useful here to recall Ray McDermott's discussion of the way our society "keep[s] arranging for school failure to be so visible." "We might do better," he continues,

> to ask how it is a part of the situation of every minority group that it has had to be explained, or about the degradation every minority group has had to suffer from our explanations. . . . By making believe that failure is something that kids do, as different from how it is something that is done to them, and then by explaining their failure in terms of other things they do, we likely contribute to the maintenance of school failure. (McDermott 362–63)

McDermott takes us all to task for our manufacture of failure, our entrapment in a way of thinking and of organizing society that virtually assures failure. We struggle within a discourse that yearns for difference, and difference, in our culture, slides readily toward judgment of better-or-worse, dominance, otherness.

Yet the moment we express our concerns about a focus on difference, we must stop short. Without such a focus one can easily forget that "intellectual development is socially and culturally based, and that what happens in the home, school, and local community . . . is crucial to understanding the learning processes and academic achievement of all children, including minority children" (Trueba 279). Such a perspective can lead to a greater appreciation of the richness of background, language, and gesture that comprise America. In fact, a focus on cognitive and linguistic *similarity* can shift readily to a leveling vision that not only reduces the variability that should be a cause for celebration, but, in its way, can also blind us to the political and economic consequences of difference. As Linda Brodkey puts it, a focus on similarity can distract us "from noticing the consequences of difference, namely, inequity" (599). Given a history of diminishment, of a devaluation and ridicule of difference, it is not surprising that some members of historically subjugated groups want to move beyond an embrace of cognitive and linguistic similarity to an elevation of difference. Within French feminism and African-American cultural studies, for example, some writers are arguing for the existence of distinctive female and Afrocentric epistemologies. Their move is to turn otherness on its head, to celebrate ways of knowing that have been reduced and marginalized.

Given the culturally received ways we have to think about school failure in America, it seems that we have to keep these two perspectives in dynamic tension, see them as elements in a complex dialectic, a dialectic that can lead us to be alert to the ease with which we can make limiting, harmful judgments about linguistic and cognitive ability, the ease with which rich differences can be ignored or converted to deficits, but the ease, as well, with which differences can be represented in essentialistic and deterministic ways that reduce human variability and adaptability. For that fact, we need to be vigilant that the very dialectic we want to honor does not degenerate into the kind of bi-polar, better-worse scheme that has been so characteristic of our thinking about language use. To focus on the possible cultural or class differences of a student like Maria can both reveal the logic of her behavior and— given the ways we carry with us to react to difference—blind us to the shared cognitive and linguistic processes she displays. But to focus on the shared nature of Maria's cognitive and linguistic processes can blind us to the specifics of her background, and, further, can lead us to downplay variability and the way difference has been historically embedded in inequity. To talk about difference in America, given our legacy of racism and class prejudice, requires us to talk, as well, about the many reductive, harmful ways difference has historically been represented. What we need to develop are conceptual frameworks that *simultaneously* assert shared cognitive and linguistic competence while celebrating in a non-hierarchical way the play of human difference.[14]

A F T E R W O R D   . . . .

In revisiting "Remediation as Social Construct" and reviewing the list of Braddock Award–winning essays, we were struck by the extent to which so many are products of their time. The essays of the 1980s reflect that decade's cognitive science focus, when research that considered problem solving strategies and the "logic" of seemingly illogical writing behaviors was highly valued. By the 1990s, the focus had shifted to the social and interactive aspects of writing, due

*in part to context-dependent activity. "Remediation as Social Construct"
sounds another dominant theme of the early 90s: integrating micro and macro
levels of analysis in order to gain a fuller picture of current practices in writing
instruction. Using techniques adapted from anthropology and sociolinguistics,
we engaged in both macrolevel ethnographic classroom observation and micro-
level analysis of the participant structures in the classroom in order to create a
more complete understanding of how writing instruction may fail the developmental student. This approach struck a chord with others in composition studies, and we believe the essay was honored because it presented to the field an explicit method of analyzing spoken discourse that helped us understand success
and failure in the classroom. The conclusions reached through this dual method
of analysis revealed a participant structure in the classroom that stifled individual differences and became a way for the instructor to judge cognitive ability.*

*One of our goals in "Remediation" was to remind the field that when in-
struction fails, we should consider not only the role of the student in that failure
but also the instructor as an active participant in the interaction that led to failure. We needed to be reminded of that fifteen years after reading it in Mina
Shaughnessy's* Errors and Expectations, *and even now we still need to be reminded. We hope that the legacy of the article is that it causes writing instructors to reflect on how they structure their classrooms and on the opportunities
for participation that they afford. In addition, we hope they also examine their
attitudes about their developmental students and how those attitudes can be revealed in subtle ways by their interactions in the classroom.*

*At the end of "Remediation" we did not reach one sole conclusion. We did
not want to claim that any one explanation could do justice to the complexity
that lies behind every teacher-student interaction. Instead, our goal was to lay
out what some of those complexities were, and to point to specific directions in
which composition studies could go in order to capture, describe, and understand that complexity.*

—Marisa Castellano
University of California, Berkeley

—Kay M. Losey
State University of New York at Stony Brook

Between the Drafts

NANCY SOMMERS

cannot think of my childhood without hearing voices, deep, heavily-accented, instructive German voices.

I hear the voice of my father reading to me from *Struvelpater*, the German children's tale about a messy boy who refuses to cut his hair or his fingernails. Struvelpater's hair grows so long that birds nest in it, and his fingernails grow so long that his hands become useless. He fares better, though, than the other characters in the book who don't listen to their parents. Augustus, for instance, refuses to eat his soup for four days, becomes as thin as a thread, and on the fifth day he is dead. Fidgety Philip tilts his dinner chair like a rocking horse until his chair falls backwards; the hot food falls on top of him, and suffocates him under the weight of the table cloth. The worst story by far for me is that of Conrad, an incorrigible thumb-sucker, who couldn't stop sucking his thumb and whose mother warned him that a great, long, red-legged scissor-man would—and, yes, did—snip both his thumbs off.

As a child, I hated these horrid stories with their clear moral lessons, exhorting me to listen to my parents: do the right thing, they said; obey authority, or else catastrophic things—dissipation, suffocation, loss of thumbs—will follow. It never occurred to me as a child to wonder why my parents, who had escaped Nazi Germany in 1939, were so deferential to authority, so beholden to sanctioned sources of power. I guess it never occurred to them to reflect or to make any connections between generations of German children reading *Struvelpater*, being instructed from early childhood to honor and defer to the parental authority of the state, and the Nazis' easy rise to power.

When I hear my mother's voice, it is usually reading to me from some kind of guide book showing me how different *They*, the Americans, were from us, the German Jews of Terre Haute. My parents never left home without their passports; we had roots somewhere else. When we traveled westward every summer from our home in Indiana, our bible was the AAA

This essay was first published in *CCC*, Volume 43, Number 1, February 1992.

tour guide, giving us the officially sanctioned version of America. We attempted to "see" America from the windows of our 1958 two-tone green Oldsmobile. We were literally the tourists from Terre Haute, those whom Walker Percy describes in "The Loss of the Creature," people who could never experience the Grand Canyon because it had already been formulated for us by picture postcards, tourist folders, guide books, and the words *Grand Canyon.*

Percy suggests that tourists never see the progressive movement of depths, patterns, colors, and shadows of the Grand Canyon, but rather measure their satisfaction by the degree to which the canyon conforms to the expectations in their minds. My mother's AAA guide book directed us, told us what to see, how to see it, and how long it should take us to see it. We never stopped anywhere serendipitously, never lingered, never attempted to know a place.

As I look now at the black-and-white photographs of our trips, seeing myself in pony-tail and pedal pushers, I am struck by how many of the photos were taken against the car or, at least, with the car close enough to be included in the photograph. I am not sure we really saw the Grand Canyon or the Painted Desert or the Petrified Forest except from the security of a parking lot. We were travelling on a self-imposed visa that kept us close to our parked car; we lacked the freedom of our own authority and stuck close to each other and to the book itself.

My parents' belief that there was a right and a wrong way to do everything extended to the way they decided to teach us German. Wanting us to learn the correct way, not trusting their own native voices, they bought language-learning records with an officially sanctioned voice of an expert language teacher; never mind that they spoke fluent German.

It is 1959; I am 8 years old. We sit in the olive-drab living room with the drapes closed so the neighbors won't see in. What the neighbors would have seen strikes me now as a scene out of a *Saturday Night Live* skit about the Coneheads. The children and their parental-unit sitting in stiff, good-for-your-posture chairs that my brother and I call the electric chairs. Those chairs are at odd angles to each other so we all face the fireplace; we don't look at each other. I guess my parents never considered pulling the chairs around, facing each other, so we could just talk in German. My father's investment was in the best 1959 technology he could find; he was proud of the time and money he had spent, so that we could be instructed in the right way. I can still see him there in that room removing the record from its purple package, placing it on the hi-fi:

> Guten Tag.
> Wie geht es Dir?
> Wie geht es Werner/Helmut/Dieter?
> Werner ist heute krank.
> Oh, das tut mir Leid.
> Gute Besserung.

We are disconnected voices worrying over the health of Werner, Dieter, and Helmut, foreign characters, names, who have no place in our own family. We go on and on for an eternity with that dialogue until my brother passes gas, or commits some other unspeakable offense, something that sets my father's German sensibility on edge, and he finally says, "We will continue another time." He releases us back into another life, where we speak English, forgetting for yet another week about the health of Werner, Helmut, or Dieter.

I thought I had the issue of authority all settled in my mind when I was in college. My favorite T-shirt, the one I took the greatest pleasure in wearing, was one with the bold words *Question Authority* inscribed across my chest. It seemed that easy. As we said then, either you were part of the problem or you were part of the solution; either you deferred to authority or you resisted it by questioning. Twenty years later, it doesn't seem that simple. I am beginning to get a better sense of my legacy, beginning to see just how complicated and how far-reaching is this business of authority. It extends into my life and touches my students' lives, reminding me again and again of the delicate relationship between language and authority.

In 1989, 30 years after my German lessons at home, I'm having dinner with my daughters in an Italian restaurant. The waiter is flirting with 8-year-old Rachel, telling her she has the most beautiful name, that she is *una ragazza bellissima*. Intoxicated with this affectionate attention, she turns to me passionately and says, "Oh, Momma, Momma, can't we learn Italian?" I, too, for the moment am caught up in the brio of my daughter's passion. I say, "Yes, yes, we must learn Italian." We rush to our favorite bookstore where we find Italian language-learning tapes packaged in 30-, 60-, and 90-day lessons, and in our modesty buy the promise of fluent Italian in 30 lessons. Driving home together, we put the tape in our car tape player, and begin lesson number 1:

> Buon giorno.
> Come stai?
> Come stai Monica?

As we wind our way home, our Italian lessons quickly move beyond preliminaries. We stop worrying over the health of Monica, and suddenly we are in the midst of a dialogue about Signor Fellini who lives at 21 Broadway Street. We cannot follow the dialogue. Rachel, in great despair, betrayed by the promise of being a beautiful girl with a beautiful name speaking Italian in 30 lessons, begins to scream at me: "This isn't the way to learn a language. This isn't language at all. These are just words and sentences; this isn't about us; we don't live at 21 Broadway Street."

And I am back home in Indiana, hearing the disembodied voices of my family, teaching a language out of the context of life.

In 1987, I gave a talk at CCCC entitled "New Directions for Researching Revision." At the time, I liked the talk very much because it gave me an opportunity to illustrate how revision, once a subject as interesting to our profession as an autopsy, had received new body and soul, almost celebrity status, in our time. Yet as interesting as revision had become, it seemed to me that our pedagogies and research methods were resting on some shaky, unquestioned assumptions.

I had begun to see how students often sabotage their own best interests when they revise, searching for errors and assuming, like the eighteenth-century theory of words parodied in *Gulliver's Travels,* that words are a load of things to be carried around and exchanged. It seemed to me that despite all those multiple drafts, all the peer workshops that we were encouraging, we had left unexamined the most important fact of all: revision does not always guarantee improvement; successive drafts do not always lead to a clearer vision. You can't just change the words around and get the ideas right.

Here I am four years later, looking back on that abandoned talk, thinking of myself as a student writer, and seeing that successive drafts have not led me to a clearer vision. I have been under the influence of a voice other than my own.

I live by the lyrical dream of change, of being made anew, always believing that a new vision is possible. I have been gripped, probably obsessed, with the subject of revision since graduate school. I have spent hundreds of hours studying manuscripts, looking for clues in the drafts of professional and student writers, looking for the figure in the carpet. The pleasures of this kind of literary detective work, this literary voyeurism, are the peeps behind the scenes, the glimpses of the process revealed in all its nakedness, of what Edgar Allan Poe called "the elaborate and vacillating crudities of thought, the true purposes seized only at the last moment, the cautious selections and rejections, the painful erasures."

My decision to study revision was not an innocent choice. It is deeply satisfying to believe that we are not locked into our original statements, that we might start and stop, erase, use the delete key in life, and be saved from the roughness of our early drafts. Words can be retracted; souls can be reincarnated. Such beliefs have informed my study of revision, and yet, in my own writing, I have always treated revising as an academic subject, not a personal one. Every time I have written about revision, I have set out to argue a thesis, present my research, accumulate my footnotes. By treating revision as an academic subject, by suggesting that I could learn something only by studying the drafts of other experienced writers, I kept myself clean and distant from any kind of scrutiny. No Struvelpater was I; no birds could nest in my hair; I kept my thumbs intact. I have been the bloodless academic creating taxonomies, creating a hierarchy of student writers and experienced writers, and never asking myself how I was being displaced from my own work. I never asked, "What does my absence *signify?*"

In that unrevised talk from CCCC, I had let Wayne Booth replace my father. Here are my words:

> Revision presents a unique opportunity to study what writers know. By studying writers' revisions we can learn how writers locate themselves

316 ON WRITING RESEARCH

within a discourse tradition by developing a persona—a fictionalized self. Creating a persona involves placing the self in a textual community, seeing oneself within a discourse, and positing a self that shares or antagonizes the beliefs that a community of readers shares. As Wayne Booth has written, "Every speaker makes a self with every word uttered. Even the most sincere statement implies a self that is at best a radical selection from many possible roles. No one comes on in exactly the same way with parents, teachers, classmates, lovers, and IRS inspectors."

What strikes me now, in this paragraph from my own talk, is that fictionalized self I invented, that anemic researcher, who set herself apart from her most passionate convictions. In that paragraph, I am a distant, imponderable, impersonal voice—inaccessible, humorless, and disguised like the packaged voice of Signor Fellini giving lessons as if absolutely nothing depends on my work. I speak in an inherited academic voice; it isn't mine.

I simply wasn't there for my own talk. Just as my father hid behind his language-learning records and my mother behind her guide books, I disguised myself behind the authority of "the researcher," attempting to bring in the weighty authority of Wayne Booth to justify my own statements, never gazing inward, never trusting my own authority as a writer.

Looking back on that talk, I know how deeply I was under the influence of a way of seeing: Foucault's "Discourse on Language," Barthes' *S/Z*, Scholes' *Textual Power,* and Bartholomae's "Inventing the University" had become my tourist guides. I was so much under their influence that I remember standing in a parking lot of a supermarket, holding two heavy bags of groceries, talking with a colleague who was telling me about his teaching. Without any reference, except to locate my own authority somewhere else, I felt compelled to suggest to him that he read Foucault. My daughter Alexandra, waiting impatiently for me, eating chocolate while pounding on the hood of the car with her new black patent-leather party shoes, spoke with her own authority. She reminded me that I, too, had bumped on cars, eaten Hershey Bars, worn party shoes without straps, never read Foucault, and knew, nevertheless, what to say on most occasions.

One of my colleagues put a telling cartoon on the wall of our Xerox room. It reads "Breakfast Theory: A morning methodology." The cartoon describes two new cereals: Foucault Flakes and Post-Modern Toasties. The slogan for Foucault Flakes reads: "It's French so it must be good for you. A breakfast commodity so complex that you need a theoretical apparatus to digest it. You don't want to eat it; you'll just want to read it. Breakfast as text." And Post-Modern Toasties: "More than just a cereal, it's a commentary on the nature of cereal-ness, cerealism, and the theory of cerealtivity. Free decoding ring inside."

I had swallowed the whole flake, undigested, as my morning methodology, but, alas, I never found the decoding ring. I was lost in the box. Or, to use the metaphor of revision, I was stuck in a way of seeing: reproducing the thoughts of others, using them as my guides, letting the post-structuralist vocabulary give authority to my text.

Successive drafts of my own talk did not lead to a clearer vision because it simply was not my vision. I, like so many of my students, was reproducing acceptable truths, imitating the gestures and rituals of the academy, not having confidence enough in my own ideas, nor trusting the native language I had learned. I had surrendered my own authority to someone else, to those other authorial voices.

Three years later, I am still wondering: Where does revision come from? Or, as I think about it now, what happens between the drafts? Something has to happen or else we are stuck doing mop and broom work, the janitorial work of polishing, cleaning, and fixing what is and always has been. What happens between drafts seems to be one of the great secrets of our profession.

Between drafts, I take lots of showers, hot showers, talking to myself as I watch the water play against the gestures of my hands. In the shower, I get lost in the steam. There I stand without my badges of authority. I begin an imagined conversation with my colleague, the one whom I told in the parking lot of the grocery store, "Oh, but you must read Foucault." I revise our conversation. This time I listen.

I understand why he showed so much disdain when I began to pay homage to Foucault. He had his own sources aplenty that nourished him. Yet he hadn't felt the need to speak through his sources or interject their names into our conversation. His teaching stories and experiences are his own; they give him the authority to speak.

As I get lost in the steam, I listen to his stories, and I begin to tell him mine. I tell him about my father not trusting his native voice to teach me German, about my mother not trusting her own eyes and reading to us from guide books, about my own claustrophobia in not being able to revise a talk about revision, about being drowned out by a chorus of authorial voices. And I surprise myself. I say, Yes, these stories of mine provide powerful evidence; they belong to me; I can use them to say what I must about revision.

I begin at last to have a conversation with all the voices I embody, and I wonder why so many issues are posed as either/or propositions. Either I stop sucking my thumb *or* the great long-legged scissor-man will cut it off. Either I cook two chickens *or* my guests will go away hungry. Either I accept authority *or* I question it. Either I have babies and be in service of the species *or* I write books and be in service of the academy. Either I be personal *or* I be academic.

These either/or ways of seeing exclude life and real revision by pushing us to safe positions, to what is known. They are safe positions that exclude each other and don't allow for any ambiguity, uncertainty. Only when I suspend myself between either *and* or can I move away from conventional boundaries and begin to see shapes and shadows and contours—ambiguity, uncertainty, and discontinuity, moments when the seams of life just don't want to hold; days when I wake up to find, once again, that I don't have enough bread for the children's sandwiches or that there are no shoelaces for their gym shoes. My life is full of uncertainty; negotiating that uncertainty day to day gives me authority.

Maybe this is a woman's journey, maybe not. Maybe it is just my own, but the journey between home and work, between being personal and being authoritative, between the drafts of my life, is a journey of learning how to be both personal and authoritative, both scholarly *and* reflective. It is a journey that leads me to embrace the experiences of my life, and gives me the insight to transform these experiences into evidence. I begin to see discontinuous moments as sources of strength and knowledge. When my writing and my life actually come together, the safe positions of either/or will no longer pacify me, no longer contain me and hem me in.

In that unrevised talk, I had actually misused my sources. What they were saying to me, if I had listened, was pretty simple: don't follow us, don't reproduce what we have produced, don't live life from secondary sources like us, don't disappear. I hear Bob Scholes' and David Bartholomae's voices telling me to answer them, to speak back to them, to use them and make them anew. In a word, they say: revise me. The language lesson starts to make sense, finally: by confronting these authorial voices, I find the power to understand and gain access to my own ideas. Against all the voices I embody—the voices heard, read, whispered to me from off-stage—I must bring a voice of my own. I must enter the dialogue on my own authority, knowing that other voices have enabled mine, but no longer can I subordinate mine to theirs.

The voices I embody encourage me to show up as a writer and to bring the courage of my own authority into my classroom. I have also learned about the dangers of submission from observing the struggles of my own students. When they write about their lives, they write with confidence. As soon as they begin to turn their attention toward outside sources, they too lose confidence, defer to the voice of the academy, and write in the voice of Everystudent to an audience they think of as Everyteacher. They disguise themselves in the weighty, imponderable voice of acquired authority: "In today's society," for instance, or "Since the beginning of civilization mankind has. . . ." Or, as one student wrote about authority itself, "In attempting to investigate the origins of authority of the group, we must first decide exactly what we mean by authority."

In my workshops with teachers, the issue of authority, or deciding exactly what we mean by authority, always seems to be at the center of many heated conversations. Some colleagues are convinced that our writing programs should be about teaching academic writing. They see such programs as the welcome wagon of the academy, the Holiday Inn where students lodge as they take holy orders. Some colleagues fear that if we don't control what students learn, don't teach them to write as scholars write, we aren't doing our job and some great red-legged scissor-man will cut off our thumbs. Again it is one of those either/or propositions: either we teach students to write academic essays or we teach them to write personal essays—and then who knows what might happen? The world might become uncontrollable: Students might start writing about their grandmother's death in an essay for a sociology course. Or even worse, something more uncontrollable, they might just write essays and publish them in professional journals claiming the authority to tell stories about their families and their colleagues. The uncontrollable world of ambiguity and uncertainty opens up, my colleagues imagine, as soon as the academic embraces the personal.

But, of course, our students are not empty vessels waiting to be filled with authorial intent. Given the opportunity to speak their own authority as writers, given a turn in the conversation, students can claim their stories as primary source material and transform their experiences into evidence. They might, if given enough encouragement, be empowered not to serve the academy and accommodate it, not to write in the persona of Everystudent, but rather to write essays that will change the academy. When we create opportunities for something to happen between the drafts, when we create writing exercises that allow students to work with sources of their own that can complicate and enrich their primary sources, they will find new ways to write scholarly essays that are exploratory, thoughtful, and reflective.

I want my students to know what writers know—to know something no researchers could ever find out no matter how many times they pin my students to the table, no matter how many protocols they tape. I want my students to know how to bring their life and their writing together.

Sometimes when I cook a chicken and my children scuffle over the one wishbone, I wish I had listened to my grandmother and cooked two. Usually, the child who gets the short end of the wishbone dissolves into tears of frustration and failure. Interjecting my own authority as the earth mother from central casting, I try to make their life better by asking: On whose authority is it that the short end can't get her wish? Why can't both of you, the long and the short ends, get your wishes?

My children, on cue, as if they too were brought in from central casting, roll their eyes as children are supposed to do when their mothers attempt to impose a way of seeing. They won't let me control the situation by interpreting it for them. My interpretation serves my needs, temporarily, for sibling compromise and resolution. They don't buy my story because they know something about the sheer thrill of the pull that they are not going to let *me* deny *them*. They will have to revise my self-serving story about compromise, just as they will have to revise the other stories I tell them. Between the drafts, as they get outside my authority, they too will have to question, and begin to see for themselves their own complicated legacy, their own trail of authority.

It *is* in the thrill of the pull between someone else's authority and our own, between submission and independence that we must discover how to define ourselves. In the uncertainty of that struggle, we have a chance of finding the voice of our own authority. Finding it, we can speak convincingly . . . at long last.

My essay "Between the Drafts" came out of my frustration in not being able to revise a talk I had delivered on revision. No matter how many words I carried around and exchanged, no matter how many drafts I scribbled, revising did not lead to a clearer vision. So where does revision come from, I wondered. And what is supposed to happen between the drafts? At that time I was teaching a course on the essay, intrigued by the gathering exploratory spirit of the essays I was reading. I gave my students the assignment of writing an exploratory essay, and I decided to write my own. After years of writing thesis-driven academic prose, I found the exploratory essay with its twists and turns, its complications and unfolding, the hardest piece I had ever written.

Hard, but great fun. Images, stories, conversations, decades of experience, began to unfold and present themselves to me for the picking, waiting to see what I could make of them. They seemed to have a magnetic force, and I couldn't stop them. For the first time I was writing from abundance, a fortunate place to be. This was a new kind of writing for me, and I found it liberating, engaging, and surprisingly fun.

Between the drafts I had to figure out what was at stake for me, both intellectually and personally, in the language and ideas I claimed. Why did I care about revision, a subject that had gripped, probably obsessed me since graduate school? Where was I in the hierarchy I had created of student writers and experienced writers? I wanted to figure out how to treat revision not as an academic subject but as a personal subject. At the same time, I wanted to figure out how to bring my writing and my life together so I could write in a way that bridged the personal with the academic. Not easy tasks for one exploratory essay. The Braddock Award encouraged me to continue experimenting with my writing, learning to balance passion with critical distance, commitment with interpretation, never leaving myself behind when I write academic essays.

—NANCY SOMMERS
Harvard University

1994   *On Authority in the Study of Writing*

PETER MORTENSEN
AND GESA E. KIRSCH

f the author is dead, as Roland Barthes con-
tends, then what about authority? It, too, has passed from our midst, if we
are to believe Hannah Arendt. In the end, it seems that both author and authority suffered the same fate. Succumbing to modernity unraveled, theories
of authorship and authority supposedly ceased to explain the production
and reception of written discourse. Language itself—and not the human
agents and agency of its performance—thus emerged as the central concern
of English studies. This turn of events continues to pose a perplexing question for those of us who study and teach writing. How are we to account for
the theoretical erasure of the authority that constitutes the writers—the authors—we face every day in our composition classrooms?

One answer to this question, an answer that motivates this essay, suggests that authority may not be dead after all, and even if it is, it hardly matters. Contemporary myths of authority are so prevalent that authority remains for many a simple matter of common sense. Indeed, in the literature of
composition studies, mention of authority is so frequent as to demand an assessment of its status, of how it functions for those who talk and write about
acts of composing. So alive or dead, functional or not, the concept of authority is very much with us. Or perhaps we should speak of *concepts* of authority, concepts that we might array from the most contingent to the most determined.

Composition studies now struggles with two fairly distinct views of "authority," yet the term is trusted as stable and uniform by a range of authors
who otherwise appear to hold differing assumptions about the nature of
language and the world. While both views assume that authority attends
the negotiation of power within the context of communities, they diverge
in assumptions about how communities function and, consequently, how
authority is to be defined and engaged (see Harris). In one view, community evolves from consensus and authority compels assimilation. That is,

This essay was first published in *CCC*, Volume 44, Number 4, December 1993.

individuals gain discursive authority by submitting to the explicit and tacit conventions of discourse which obtain in the community (see Bartholomae). An alternative view is more suspicious of authority: assimilation is seen as uncritical accommodation of authority. Thus, a properly critical stance toward authority warrants resistance to the hegemony of conventional ways of knowing (see Chase; Trimbur).[1]

Both the assimilation and resistance models of authority have certain limitations. Among these limits is a tendency to objectify authority, to cast it as something fixed and *autonomous* that writers or writing can possess. We propose, instead, a *dialogic* model of authority, one which infuses authority with ethics. Such a dialogic model of authority addresses an issue generally ignored in models of autonomous authority: the asymmetrical power relations that situate participants in institutional cultures such as the academy. In constructing this model we consider feminist critiques of authority as one way to move beyond a notion of authority based on autonomy, individual rights, and abstract rules, and we move toward a model based on dialogue, connectedness, and contextual rules. Specifically, we examine how authority might be recast if informed by an "ethic of care," as some feminist scholars have proposed. An ethic of care, we argue, presents one possibility for rethinking notions of objectified, stable, autonomous authority. And while imbuing authority with care is hardly unproblematic (especially when care is conflated with nurturing), we believe that doing so yields a plan for subverting authority conceived as singular and monologic.

SITUATING AUTHORITY

Meditating on Arendt's obituary for authority, we come to wonder why such a supposedly hollow phenomenon continues to preoccupy so many in composition studies. "[A]uthority has vanished from the modern world," Arendt claims, and "if we raise the question what authority is, we can no longer fall back upon authentic and undisputable experiences common to all" (81). But authority need not derive from common experience or coherent tradition. Rather, as Henry Giroux contends, it is "a historical construction shaped by diverse, competing traditions which contain their own values and views of the world" (*Schooling* 74). As a result, authority has "no universal meaning simply waiting to be discovered" (74). Authority, then, can carry positive connotations, as it often does in politically conservative discourse, or it can be implicated in all that is unjust, as might be stressed from a politically radical perspective. In the middle sits a liberal critique of authority, inquiry that illuminates the dialectical nature of authority, yet fails to comprehend "how power is asymmetrically distributed within and between different communities" (78).

Models of autonomous authority presuppose that discourse communities function largely as egalitarian forums. But while equality might be an ideal characteristic of community, we know of no community in which it consistently prevails. This is because relations in communities are in part defined by differences in knowledge, experience, and status—differences in power that endlessly shift within and across social contexts. A dialogic model of authority addresses such asymmetrical power relations by linking them to an ethical concern for the well-being of community members. In describing this concern as an "ethic of care," Patrocinio Schweickart urges us to confront power differentials (especially those inscribed in language) and to refrain from developing utopian theories that ignore difference. Schweickart's formulation of ethics, which we discuss in greater detail later, resonates with Giroux's remark that ethics, conceived within a radical framework,

> becomes more than the discourse of moral relativism or a static transmission of reified history. Ethics becomes, instead, a continued engagement in which the social practices of everyday life are interrogated in relation to the principles of individual autonomy and democratic public life—not as a matter of received truth but as a constant engagement. ("Liberal" 134)

Ethics here illuminates the tension between authority as enabling individual autonomy and authority as engendering democratic, dialogic public life.

In the past decade or so, composition scholars have argued about authority mainly from the liberal and radical positions Giroux stakes out. Illustrative of the liberal position, David Bartholomae has suggested that students entering the university must learn how to adopt voices of institutional authority if they are to produce successful academic prose. And Patricia Bizzell has argued that discourse communities assert a great deal of authority over newcomers (basic writers, for example) by demanding that they change not only their ways of talking and writing, but also their ways of thinking, reasoning, and seeing the world ("What Happens"). Susan Wall and Nicholas Coles have criticized the early work of scholars such as Bartholomae and Bizzell for emphasizing accommodation over resistance, for claiming, as Bartholomae does in "Inventing the University," that students must learn to speak "our language." Quoting Bartholomae, Wall and Coles explain that

> What troubles us about this formulation of the problem [students must learn to speak academic language] is the way in which it can be, and in fact is now being, appropriated by those educators who want to argue for an unambiguously accommodationist Basic Writing pedagogy, a return to a new set of "basics," the conventions of academic discourse "written out, 'demystified,' and taught in our classrooms." (230–31)

In contrast, composition scholars writing from a radical perspective have insisted that we account for authority in discourse by examining attempts to subvert it. Geoffrey Chase, for example, describes writing students' failure to adopt the authoritative voice of the institution as something which "grows out of a larger sense of the individual's relationship to liberation" (15). In other words, resistance to authority signals a "movement against the dominant ideology" in sympathy with a "movement toward emancipation" (15). Resisting institutional authority to achieve emancipation would seem, then, to imply formation of a personal authority by which students might "affirm their own voices, learn how to exercise the skills of critical interrogation, and, finally, exercise the courage to act in the interests of improving the quality of human life" (21–22). In a similar vein, John Trimbur advocates teaching writing students to replace "the 'real world' authority of consensus with a rhetoric of dissensus [that] can lead students to demystify the normal workings of discourse communities" (615). Both Chase and Trimbur emphasize that critical, effective writing pedagogy must interrogate the very epistemological assumptions it inscribes.

But, as Chase and Trimbur acknowledge, such interrogation is itself problematic. From a poststructuralist perspective, it can be argued that we can never succeed in "objectively" questioning the epistemological assumptions of the cultures we inhabit or, for that matter, the pedagogies we practice. Such questioning fails, finally, because it feigns critical distance from subjects in which it is thoroughly interested. And relying on abstract arguments to achieve this critical distance amounts to nothing more than abject "theory hope" (Fish 342).

Of course, this is not to say that poststructuralist theories eschew critical inquiry. On the contrary, they permit interested reflection on authority, allowing this reflection to grow in diversity and sophistication within the context of argument. We should not, then, abandon poststructuralist theories simply because they do not answer all of the questions composition scholars have asked about authority. What is of value here is the insistent questioning that can—better than reified answers—yield insight into the diffuse and polymorphous condition of authority.

QUESTIONING AUTHORITY

To begin this exploration, we examine authority figured as autonomous, as unified and coherent. We then point to the tension between acts of assimilation and resistance, tension that disrupts the unity and coherence of autonomous authority. Finally, we argue for a dialogic model of authority, one that foregrounds rather than suppresses contending notions of the concept.

The *Oxford English Dictionary* posits authority within a fairly narrow compass. Since the fifteenth century, authority has designated both the "power to enforce obedience" and the "power to influence action, opinion, belief." The theoretical distinction between power to enforce and power to influence is key here, a distinction that maps onto two functional categories: the authority of office and the authority of expertise.[2] In either case, authority channels power. It acts as a conduit to translate power into effect, at times to traduce power as enlightened, rational behavior. This conduit often materializes in discourse, and thereby discourse legitimates the enforcement of obedience and the containment of action.

Obedience and containment are crucial to keeping order in the discursive universe of institutions. In hierarchical institutions (e.g., the academy), authority is the legitimate force that attenuates raw power: authority conditions the power to persuade, the power to coerce, the power to initiate or mandate action. True, power in academic communities may be possessed, conferred, and exercised by individuals at many levels—but ideally only as authorized by convention. Authority thus bears the burden of domesticating power, where power is always much "more complicated, dense and pervasive" than the explicit authority of law or institutions (Foucault, "The Eye of Power" 158). From this perspective, then, authority functions to conceal the wide dispersion of power in society, leaving the potentially false impression that authority, and the power behind it, can be located in a particular position or person (see Herzberg 71).

The idea of authority invoked most commonly today resembles what Max Weber terms "legal authority," an impersonal, rational authority inherent in specific social positions and secured by the possession of expertise, defined as technical knowledge (328). Knowing how to do and say things a certain way entitles one to authority and its exercise. Weber labels this sort of authority impersonal because it inheres in positions, not people. Thus, in place of a personal standard, the autonomous self appeals to authority validated by logic and dictated by law.

Weber, however, does not deny the existence of personal authority. He locates it in "traditional" and "charismatic" forms, both of which are personal insofar as in each "obedience is owed to the *person*," whether ancient monarch or modern dictator (328). While traditional forms of personal authority ebbed with the post-Enlightenment ascendance of rational ideology, Weber observes that charismatic forms of personal authority emerged to exploit any failure of the rational social order. However, he envisions no place for personal authority in the modern constitutional state because it poses a threat to the autonomous authority of law which, Weber believes, aggregates individuals into functional democratic communities. While Weber notices that authority can never be quite autonomous and is, for better or worse, always tied to personal authority, feminist scholars have further noted that autonomous authority is conceived within a particular kind of personal authority that is distinctly male-marked. It is so marked because men have traditionally held most positions of authority, and acts of asserting authority are often marked as masculine, regardless of the actor's gender. The link between authority and masculinity, some feminist scholars conclude, has led to a privileging of individual rights over community relations, and to an absence of care in those relations (see Jones, "The Trouble with Authority"; Rosenblum).

How this might happen becomes clearer upon examining Mikhail Bakhtin's theorizing of community as the ground upon which various forms of discourse and authority meet. For Bakhtin, communities always contain forces contending oppositely for stasis and change (270–72). On the one hand, community members maintain a predictable state of affairs through acts of accommodation. That is, for the sake of mutual benefit, people accept the conventions which constitute authorized ways of doing things in the community—like interpreting discourse. Certainly, conventions specify what counts as what in a given situation, but they may serve other functions as well: to regulate behavior, to establish and uphold tradition. Bakhtin labels this conservative force "centripetal," designating that force which pulls things inward toward a systemic center of gravity. On the other hand, community members can agitate for change by resisting conventional action. Such resistance—or "centrifugal" force, in Bakhtin's vocabulary—is part of the "game" of community life, and can be valued just as accommodating participation is valued.

But resistance requires authority, and the source of that authority in Bakhtin's universe comes from what he calls "internally persuasive discourse" (342). Internally persuasive discourse is the constellation of voices we appropriate as we learn how to differentiate ourselves as individuals in a particular social setting. These voices speak through us, and allow us to "be" who we need to be in a given circumstance. (Manipulating these internal voices to good effect relates, in Aristotelian terms, to *ethos*.) But it is also possible—and much easier—to speak with authority by repeating what Bakhtin calls "authoritative" utterances: discourse the community generates over time to preserve its structure, to maintain the status quo (342–43). In other words, repetition of a community's standard arguments supports its discursive traditions; utterances spoken from an individual's fund of internally persuasive discourse can question conventions, and thereby challenge traditions.

In *Feminist Dialogics,* Dale Bauer examines what happens to Bakhtin's notions of discourse and authority when community is conceived as a gendered space. Bauer argues that Bakhtinian communities figured with attention to gender appear to be "ambivalent territory" for women because in them women are generally compelled to speak from marginal positions (xiv). Accordingly, communities become sites of repression and subversion—of silence—for women. And if male voices dominate in the everyday discourse of community, they are likely to determine most of the conventions that regulate choices communities make in valuing the authority of utterances.

In fact, authority and gender are so closely linked that we often have trouble recognizing authoritative gestures that arise particularly from women's experience. On this point Kathleen Jones has argued that "the roots of the dichotomy experienced by women between being in authority and being subject to it stem from the separation of public life and political authority from private life and the passions" ("On Authority" 152–53). She also suggests that if "the dichotomy between compassion and authority contributes to the association of the authoritative with a male voice, then the implication is that the segregation of women and the feminine from authority is internally connected to the concept of authority itself" (152). Nancy Rosenblum makes a similar observation, arguing "[t]hat authority is almost always male, to say nothing of patriarchal, [and] overwhelms differences between authority of office and knowledge" for women (117). She concludes that because women have been taught to be submissive to *all* forms of authority, the distinctions they make among various types of authority more often than not blur together. Feminist scholars, then, trace the separation of authority from the feminine to the same gender dichotomies that assign women to the realm of the private and the affective, and keep men separate from it.

It is precisely by examining the gendered nature of authority that we can break open definitions of autonomous authority and use a feminist perspective to develop a more dialogic model of authority. But before discussing the consequences of this feminist critique, we will briefly examine how deeply rooted are notions of autonomous authority in theories of rhetoric, even those theories informed by social-constructionist perspectives.

AUTHORITY IN RHETORICAL THEORY

The notion of autonomous authority appears implicit in rhetorics past and present. Medieval rhetorics located authority in the word received: the word set down in classical antiquity, the word inscribed by God. But early modern thinkers—Bacon and Descartes among them—rejected discourse authorized historically or divinely. Eighteenth- and nineteenth-century rhetorics prescribed methods that would stimulate the sovereign mind to produce properly logical and, consequently, authoritative discourse (see Crowley; Berlin). These methods, many have argued, characterize the "current-traditional" rhetorics which today still strongly influence the teaching and practice of college composition (see Miller, 106–07; Hamilton-Wieler).

Even the most effective challenges to current-traditional rhetoric—the various process-oriented theories of composing—still tend to align authority with technique. Granted, process technique generally accounts for the subjectivities of readers and writers, not just the objectivity of texts. Nevertheless, "expressive," "cognitive," and "social" process theories all exhibit some investment in autonomous authority, although the site of that authority shifts across categories (Faigley, "Competing" 527–28). A brief overview of process perspectives establishes their positions on autonomous authority, as well as the varying terms—self, mind, text—in which autonomy is expressed, and points to the need for rethinking process perspectives with a dialogic model of authority in mind. Although we cannot attend to the subtle differences among process theories and risk oversimplifying, we review process perspectives for two reasons: to demonstrate how they incorporate a sense of authority as autonomous, and to discuss, at the same time, how process perspectives set the stage for reconceptualizing authority in dialogic terms.[3]

Generally, expressive theories of composing have evolved in part out of attacks on the autonomous authority which current-traditional rhetorics sited solely in discourse. In various ways, these theories wrest authority from the word and claim it for writers. Peter Elbow's *Writing with Power* provides a representative example. He argues that "everyone, however inexperienced or unskilled, has real voice available; everyone can write with power" (304). Here "voice" corresponds with self, "power" with authority. Writers can claim authority if their writing has voice, and if that voice allows readers access to the writer's "mind" and "experience" (317). The effect of Elbow's expressive approach is to create an autonomous self: a private subjectivity defined, for better or worse, by how arresting a voice it can "breathe" into accounts of lived experience.

Cognitive theories of writing, like more general theories of cognition, assume that the mental processes that shape and transform representations of knowledge can be inferred from human behavior (Mandler 11). The individual mind and the autonomous text thus become twin seats of authority, for they both "contain" the source of authority — knowledge. Building on such assumptions, developmental-cognitive studies of writing investigate college students' attitudes toward the authority of knowledge as they compose. Some cognitive theories attempt to account for the influence of social context (see Berkenkotter; Flower, Stein, Ackerman, Kantz, McCormick and Peck 14–26; Schriver). But even so, in the developmental-cognitive view, authority emphasizes the introspective acts of autonomous minds.

Social theories of writing stress the influence of context on composing, influence thought to be ignored in most studies of individual cognition. In the social view, authority is never inherent in texts or minds, but rather is negotiated and constructed in discourse by individuals who observe conventions for the representation of knowledge. Conventions test the authority of knowledge; conventions provide the standard for assessing whether a person or text possessing knowledge is authoritative. In locating authority in convention, social theories of composing reject a model of authority grounded in absolute, transcendent truth. What counts as authoritative knowledge, then, has no putative "foundation" in a bedrock of truth. "Anti-foundationalist" theories of composing attempt to break down the autonomy of authority and feature it as something available to those who, through practice, learn to discern and produce fluent forms of communal discourse.

But even in the social view, authority remains strictly a function of a body, albeit a metaphorical body, a community. It is still a function constructed and construed in terms of foundational epistemology, wherein knowledge, authority, and "success are seen to flow from the community automatically to those who before their apprenticeship lacked any relevant cognitive or social abilities" (Cooper 216). While these arguments stress the social nature of writing, they still figure individual consciousness as bending to conform to conventions in order to claim authority.

Thus we might expect an expressly anti-foundationalist perspective on composing to figure forms of authority that are not autonomous. In practice, though, it is not figured at all. Because autonomous authority is held to be so central to foundationalist systems of thought, it has no legitimate place in the anti-foundationalist world view. Bizzell argues that exponents of the anti-foundationalist perspective remain steadfast in

> the conviction that the question about foundational knowledge and unimpeachable authority is the single most important question, even if it has to be answered in the negative. Hence, because they must answer no to the all-important question, they feel they have no authority to offer

any strong alternatives. . . . All they feel they can do is to speak up for their own and everyone else's autonomy. ("Beyond" 667)

Bizzell suggests that one way around this problem is to invoke rhetoric, a rhetoric that addresses both civic and personal ethics. She believes that doing so would enable speakers, especially traditionally marginalized speakers, to "define a rhetorical situation that leaves room for change because none of the parties in the conversation is wholly determined either by material circumstances, such as biological gender, or discursive constructions, such as the current cultural interpretations placed on gender" (673). With gender as a lens, we can re-envision autonomous authority that goes beyond assimilation and resistance. We thus turn to feminist critiques of authority that consider the interplay of authority and gender.

FEMINIST CRITIQUES OF AUTHORITY

One critique of autonomous authority favored by feminist scholars situates authority on a trajectory from personal to impersonal, from visible to invisible, from the pretense of care to no care at all. Resonant with this logic, the genealogy of modern authority can be arranged along a continuum anchored at its extremes by paternalism and autonomy. Paternalism represents "an authority of false love," while autonomy is "an authority without love" (Sennett 50, 84). Paternalistic authority may promise "nurturance," but it finally fails to enact the pledge "that one's care will make another person grow stronger" (82). And autonomous authority—the prevailing legal-rational authority Weber theorized—denies care altogether because it denies its own influence. Of course, this denial is shot through with irony. Autonomy derives from an "imbalance" of influence: it comes from asserting authority which holds in abeyance the influence of others, *and* from concealing this very gesture (103). In this double move, autonomous authority attempts to exempt itself from scrutiny and critique. Indeed, it is nostalgia for the caring component of traditional order that signals the modern moment of authority. What completes the invention of modernity is a collective forgetting that authority ever had an aspect of care (84–121).

In the *OED*'s discursive history of authority, we find a tertiary sense in which a traditional authority might treat "kindly" its subject. As individuals, traditional and charismatic authorities were obliged by divine or natural law to show concern for the well-being of their subjects. But that sense, dated to the mid-eighteenth century, again could be mere nostalgia for the care lost as the dominant meaning of authority shifted to suit the rise of industrial capitalism. No such obligation to care binds the authority appointed by vernacular law, by the legal-rational rule of governmental and institutional bureaucracies.

Some feminist scholars gesture to the limitations of autonomous authority—to a striking absence of care for community relations and ethics—and suggest that we must recuperate authority by inflecting it with care. Care, as we understand it, connotes an asymmetrical relationship between "one car-ing" and "one cared for." In such a relationship, the "one caring" experiences deep engagement with the other; he or she "assumes a dual perspective and can see things from both his [or her] own pole and that of the cared-for" (Noddings qtd. in Schweickart 88). This definition exposes the assumption of asymmetry in human relations as the essential connection between authority and care. And because authority is male-identified and care female-identi-fied, we see potential for a critical reassessment of *both* terms by exploring their nexus. We recognize that defining the concept of care is no less prob-lematic than defining authority. Care can easily lapse into paternalism—care imposed through authoritarian acts—and so presuppose the superiority of individual subjectivity and agency.

Furthermore, as Sarah Hoagland notes, an ethics of care can reinforce stereotypical female roles and continue to oppress women—or men—who act in "caring" roles. Hoagland suggests that an ethics of care can only be successful if it includes a critique of "dominance and subordination" and consequently encourages change of existing hegemonic relations in society (252):

> If an ethics of caring is going to be morally successful in replacing an ethics located in principles and duty, particularly within the context of oppression, then . . . it must consider analyses of oppression, it must ac-knowledge a self that is both related and separate, and it must have a vi-sion of, if not a program for, change. (261)

Caring can be imagined not as nurturing, then, but as more literally "tak-ing care of" an obligation to another. In the case of writing instruction, this means that teachers assume an institutional role of caring—caring, per-haps, that students understand both the ethical and logical demands of dis-course in academic communities. So conceived, there is no requirement that writing teachers *like* the students they care for. The teacherly obligation cen-ters instead on taking care that the diffusion of authority in the writing class-room promotes learning for all of the competing constituencies represented there.

We entertain this discussion of care and authority not because we see it as a simple or even necessary approach to interrogating authority, but be-cause it provides a heuristic for thinking through alternative ways of re-conceptualizing authority. Yet unlike authority, care can never be fully autonomous, autonomous care being essentially narcissism. Rather, care in-heres in relations between people and, therefore, assumes community as its first domain.

The suggestion to couple authority and care has potentially radical im-plications: instead of authority that delineates individual, autonomous sub-jects, we might envision authority that "augments" social relationships. To-ward this end, Jones proposes giving "community . . . ontological priority" in definitions of authority so that

> authority as a system of rules for securing private rights, structuring in-
> dividual obligations, or protecting autonomy through reciprocal duties
> gives way to authority as a way of cohering and sustaining connected-
> ness. . . . In this female perspective, the quest for authority becomes the
> search for contexts of care that do not deteriorate into mechanisms of
> blind loyalty. ("On Authority" 160–61)

Authority so figured enables the formation of communities by weaving together those experiential differences that falsely make autonomy seem a
"natural" aspect of some "universal" human condition. Rather than understanding authority as stemming from a totalizing impulse, then, it becomes a
phenomenon knowable only in context, as it continually constitutes (and is
constituted by) particular communities. Along similar lines, Schweickart has
pointed to the limitations of autonomous authority inherent in contemporary
theories of reading and writing. She notes that "current theories of reading,
no less than theories of discourse, are imbued with the sensibility of an ethic
of rights" (86), an ethic that presupposes symmetrical relations between participants engaged in discourse. "What is lacking, clearly," Schweickart observes, "is any concession to the fact that the ability to argue, and even the capacity for articulate speech, is not uniformly distributed in the population
and that this model of ideal discourse effectively rules out those who, for
whatever reason, lack the capacity or inclination for competitive argumentation" (91). Drawing on the work of Nel Noddings, Schweickart urges us to
integrate an ethic of care into theories of reading and writing, thereby accounting for asymmetry in the textually mediated relations of readers and
writers. She consequently proposes a conception of reading and writing that
manifests authority as commitment to community, as caring for the well-
being of others.

Still, feminist scholars do not deny that under local circumstances authority can be quite hierarchical, a powerful force in assigning and denying
value. This, however, is an inevitable part of community life, according to
scholars such as Jones. It is best, then, to reform authority primarily by recon-
sidering its aims in evaluation and decision-making ("The Trouble" 108–09).
That is, we should, in dialogue with others, shape what authority *does* rather
than simply attempting to alter what it *is*.

A feminist critique of authority has important consequences for composition classrooms and theories of writing. For example, incorporating a dialogic model of authority into our pedagogical practices means that we must
teach students how and when authority can be negotiated. We must help
them understand—and utilize—the many forms authority can take. Of
course, at the same time, we need to consider how much authority college
composition students bring with them to the classroom.[4] Given students' authority, is everything in the composition classroom negotiable, open to challenge? May students reject an ethic of care if they so choose? We do not believe so. As should be evident, we are not arguing for a relativistic brand of
authority; we do not hold that one notion of authority is as good as the next.

Rather, by giving "ontological priority to community," in Jones's terms, we are arguing for more dialogic uses of authority, for a reinvigoration of Giroux's idea of "democratic, public life." We must, therefore, avoid displacing autonomous authority with just another monologic model of text-mediated human relations. Consequently, dialogic authority can finally only be defined and negotiated according to the circumstances in which it occurs, changing along with the social actors engaged in the drama of community life. A "messy pluralism" (Rosenblum 119)—the likes of which academics generally disdain—is sure to accompany any effort to refigure authority. But a local, provisional, messy pluralism may be what is necessary to provide composition studies with multiple senses of authority that are inclusive and heterogeneous.

Rosenblum reminds us that people can choose many different positions in relation to authority:

> individuals require different situations for expressivity and creativity. We know that some people work most productively within a hierarchy and others under conditions of cooperation or even isolation; less apparent is the fact that the same individuals may need all of these. It bears mentioning that it is not always weakness, infirmity, or moral cravenness to choose to be subject to authority, even in situations where autonomy is expected of us or considered ideal. (125)

In other words, we must not stop at encouraging students to seize authority, as liberal/radical educators typically advocate. We must also help students choose how to be subject to authority without being coerced. Bizzell, for example, has recently argued that the difference between using coercion and authority lies in an act of persuasion. She suggests that a teacher can persuade students that their "best interests ultimately will be served" if on appropriate occasions they subject themselves to the teacher's authority ("Classroom" 851). Once students grant such authority to a teacher, the student-teacher relationship changes; the teacher can exercise authority with students without having to renegotiate authority every step of the way. Such dialogic authority allows teachers to engage students in discourse that can be difficult and even painful, yet crucial to their learning—such as asking students to examine their own race and gender biases (851–52). Bizzell cites the pedagogical practice of bell hooks *(Talking Back: Thinking Feminist, Thinking Black)* as an example of how dialogic authority can be used to engage students in difficult but critical learning experiences (see also Bizzell, "Power, Authority, and Critical Pedagogy").

Exercising authority over students, then, does not necessarily implicate us in acts of coercion. Amplifying this point, Lisa Delpit argues that writing teachers who assert authority might better serve some students' educational needs than those "progressive" teachers who turn much or all of their authority over to students. Specifically, Delpit is critical of teachers who refrain from authoritative gestures so that students feel free to develop a fluent voice. She says that this approach ignores the fact that many African American students already possess fluent voices, and that what they need are "technical skills" taught *within the context of* critical and creative thinking," skills that will help them adapt their voices to the demands of academic audiences (55). Here Delpit is not arguing for an authoritarian paradigm in the composition classroom. Rather, her point is that authority is constructed and construed differently for various members of communities, specifically school communities. Thus to meet the educational needs of *all* of our students, we must understand and address the various (perhaps conflicting) notions of authority students bring with them to our classrooms.

To help us enact a feminist critique of authority in the composition classroom, we need to investigate the discursive practices writers use to invoke authority and the ways readers judge and respond to that authority. As we suggested in our review of rhetorical theory, academic writing practices are thoroughly grounded in autonomous authority. Such practices conflate good technique—fluency in conventional forms—with authority. Conventional forms, or rather the processes by which writers achieve them, tend to disguise human subjectivity and thereby anchor authority in the truth-telling power of method. In turn, without traces of authoritative technique, truths proffered by unconventional texts are suspect; unorthodox forms of academic discourse win less acclaim from readers.

Not only is academic discourse grounded in autonomous authority, but so is the language of its teaching (e.g., war metaphors like "attacking the opponent" typically used to describe argumentative strategies). Jane Tompkins goes so far as to compare the nature of academic arguments to the violence depicted in the Hollywood "Western":

> Violence takes place in the conference rooms at scholarly meetings and in the pages of professional journals; and although it's not the same thing to savage a person's book as it is to kill them with a machine gun, I suspect that the nature of the feelings that motivate both acts is qualitatively the same. This bloodless kind of violence that takes place in our profession is not committed by other people; it's practiced at some time or other by virtually everyone. *Have gun, will travel* is just as fitting a theme for academic achievers as it was for Paladin. (589)

Traditional discussions of argument usually do not consider the "losers" of arguments, nor is there often assessment of the intellectually limiting effects on forums in which argument is the dominant or sole mode of discourse. In this regard, Olivia Frey speaks of the "literary Darwinism" that forces some women to write in "inauthentic" voices for the sake of professional survival, while other women are silenced altogether by the adversarial tone of traditional academic argumentation (507–08).

The preceding critiques of academic discourse ultimately raise the question of how and whether academic discourse can be reconfigured so that it might go beyond simply inverting the hierarchy of authorized discourse types. We need to ask, then, whether academic arguments can be written and taught in alternative ways, ways that sidestep the epistemological traps laid by autonomous authority.

Catherine Lamb, among others, has taken up this task with engaging success. She draws on psychological and sociological notions of mediation and negotiation to define argument as cooperative, not competitive. Lamb explains that "[w]e need . . . to consider a feminist response to conflict, at the very least to recast the terms of the dichotomy so that 'argumentation' is opposed not to 'autobiography' but, perhaps, to 'mediation'" (13). Lamb's proposal is appealing because it calls for redefining normal discourse as a wide field in which sources of authority are visible and open to contest, in which meaning is negotiable, never predetermined.

Implicit in Lamb's argument is this imperative: we must broaden our understanding of authority if it is to complement, not undermine, mediation and negotiation in argument. Avoiding autonomous authority in academic argumentation would require, among other things, that writers *take care* to declare their interests in sources of authority relevant to their arguments. Such a move would permit readers to understand writerly authority as necessarily conflicted, subject to change given the variety of audiences within the discursive world of the academy. Declarations of this sort would not, we think, legislate a comprehensive expressionist rhetoric, despite its desirable insistence on open-ended, exploratory inquiry. Rather, skepticism about autonomous authority should do the opposite, should encourage broadening the range of rhetorics that lend texture to knowledge and life.

Of course, studying authority and identifying its manipulative aspects might simply permit us to imagine (and act out of) ever more insidious forms of authority. But studying authority might also prompt serious inquiry that would open authoritative practices to negotiation. By mapping the manifold ways in which authority defines people and relations of power—the discursive landscapes we and our students traverse—we can resurrect authority and make it more democratic, better suited to voices of both consensus *and* conflict.[5]

AFTERWORD . . . .

"On Authority in the Study of Writing" grew from inquiries we began individually while graduate students at the University of California, San Diego. It was the late 1980s when we began this work, and composition studies struggled with keywords—discourse, power, community—*all of which signified the field's strong interest in the social construction of knowledge.* Authority, *too, was a keyword. To some, it represented a tradition that exerted positive influence on writers and writing. To others,* authority *was synonymous with coercion, antithetical to pedagogies aimed at empowerment through literacy. We entered the conversation arguing that authority is neither inherently good nor bad, but*

rather an inevitable presence in institutional life: a presence to be named and known in critical fashion. This project of naming and knowing continues to pre-occupy our work, as it does that of many colleagues. For example, we believe that the field's present interest in ethics represents an attempt to understand how power and authority flow through currents of literacy, currents that carry some toward intellectual and material prosperity and others away from it.

In recent years, we have been particularly interested in how authority shapes the formal study of literacy. Editing Ethics and Representation in Qualitative Studies of Literacy *underscored for us the extent to which what we see when we study literacy is influenced by what we are authorized to see, and, crucially, what research participants feel authorized to disclose or withhold. But contributors to* Ethics and Representation *drove home another point worth consideration: purely ethical thinking tends to fix our attention on singu-lar figures—"researchers" and "subjects." It is only when we think politically as well as ethically that we animate these figures, that we comprehend both "re-searchers" and "subjects" as dynamic subjectivities whose authority is cultur-ally and historically situated.*

Situated—but not wholly determined. The distinction here is important, and one that feminist theories of language and pedagogy have helped us to make. Indeed, authority has remained a useful concept in our work precisely because feminist theorizing has led us to imagine a world in which individuals possess the agency to use institutional power toward liberatory ends. So whether ana-lyzing gender, race, age, or other social phenomena, studying authority in dis-course lets us map cultural conditions as they are and illuminate pathways to-ward changing them for the better.

Most memorable about composing "On Authority" are the circumstances of our collaboration. We were fortunate to be working in departments that deemed scholarly collaboration acceptable. And we were fortunate, too, to have access to computing resources, however rudimentary, that significantly narrowed the dis-tance between Detroit and Lexington. Yet we are all too aware that our circum-stances were (and are) privileged, this in a profession where intellectual and ma-terial support for collaboration is quite unevenly developed. The irony of "On Authority," then, is that it speaks from a position of well-grounded institutional authority and so can only begin to say all that must be said on the subject.

—Peter Mortensen
University of Kentucky

—Gesa E. Kirsch
National Council of Teachers of English

sex, lies, and manuscript: Refiguring Aspasia in the History of Rhetoric

CHERYL GLENN

A fellow rhetorician recently gave me a nineteenth-century print entitled "Alcibiades and Aspasia." In beautiful detail, French artist J. L. Gerome (best-known for transfusing his journeys to the East with an exotic and erotic charm) presents Aspasia reclining seductively on Alcibiades, her hand cupping his breast, her head suspiciously near his stomach and wide-spread legs, while Alcibiades looks away from her and reaches out to grasp Socrates' hand. Thus Aspasia comes down to us as an odalisque, while Alcibiades, the object of her attention, comes to us wreathed in laurel.[1]

For the past 2500 years in Western culture, the ideal woman has been disciplined by cultural codes that require a closed mouth (silence), a closed body (chastity), and an enclosed life (domestic confinement).[2] Little wonder, then, that women have been closed out of the rhetorical tradition, a tradition of vocal, virile, public—and therefore privileged—men. Women's enclosed bodies provide lacunae in the patriarchal territory of rhetorical practices and displays, a gendered landscape, with no female rhetoricians clearly in sight. But just as recent feminist scholarship has begun to recover and recuperate women's contributions in the broad history of culture-making—in philosophy, literature, language, writing, societal structure, Christianity, history, education, reading, psychology, and gender—so too have feminist historians of rhetoric begun to re-map rhetorical history.[3] In her "Opportunities for Feminist Research in the History of Rhetoric," Patricia Bizzell accounts for various disruptions that could realign and regender the rhetorical terrain and anticipates the consequences of refiguring the role of women on that terrain.[4] And in "Coming to Terms with Recent Attempts to Write Women into the History of Rhetoric," Barbara Biesecker works to "forge a new storying of our tradition that circumvents the veiled cultural supremacy operative in mainstream histories of Rhetoric" (147). Such challenges not only restore women to rhetorical history and rhetorical history to women, but the restoration itself

---

This essay was first published in *CCC*, Volume 45, Number 2, May 1994.

revitalizes theory by shaking the conceptual foundations of rhetorical study.[5] More than theory is, of course, at stake here. For in challenging the dominant stories of the West, feminist scholars are challenging the contemporary academic and cultural scene as well.

ASPASIA OF MILETUS

As part of the feminist challenge to the history of rhetoric, I want to reconstruct and refigure a woman whose texts, life, and manuscripts have been annexed by men: Aspasia of Miletus. In fifth-century BC, Miletus was a Far-Eastern Greek subject-ally, a cultivated city (in what is now Turkey) renowned for its literacy and philosophies of moral thought and nature.[6] A non-Athenian, citizen-class Greek, Aspasia arrived in Athens brilliantly educated by means that have never been fully explained.[7] Whether she was educated within a literate Milesian family or within a school for *hetaerae* (upper-class courtesans), she was exceptionally fortunate, for "there is no evidence at all that in the classical period girls attended schools, and it is entirely consistent with what we know about the seclusion of women in Athens that Athenian girls did not do so (some other cities may have been less benighted in this respect)" (Harris 96).[8] Married at an early age, Athenian women neither attended schools nor participated in the *polis*.[9] Yet the system of the *polis*, which implied both civic consciousness and "the extraordinary preeminence of speech over all other instruments of power" (Vernant, *Origins* 49), tripped the mechanism that powered the active diffusion and acquisition of literacy among Greek males (proper citizens). And we must assume that at least a

Alcibiades and Aspasia (J. L. Gerome)

few Athenian or Athenian-colony women of the citizen class, even those defined by good families and cultural constraints, became literate—and became conscious of civic rights and responsibilities (Cole 222–23; Harris 103, 107).[10] Aspasia of Miletus was one of those women.

As a free woman brought up in the transitional society of Asia Minor, Aspasia was freed from the rigidity of traditional marriage and from the identity that arose from that fixed role. And upon emigrating from Miletus, Aspasia emerged in Athens linked with the great statesman Pericles (fl. 442 BC), the aristocratic democrat who placed Athenian democratic power "in the hands not of a minority but of the whole people," with everyone equal before the law (Thucydides 2.37.1). Thus this non-Athenian, or "stranger-woman," was subject to Athenian law but did not have citizen rights. Nor was she accountable to the severe strictures of aristocratic Athenian women, whose activity, movement, education, marriage, and rights as citizens and property-holders were extremely circumscribed by male relatives. Aspasia could ignore—even rupture—the traditional enclosure of the female body. She could subvert Pericles' advice for ideal womanhood: "Your greatest glory is not to be inferior to what God has made you" (Thucydides 5.46.2). She could—and she did.

We know about Aspasia much the same way we know about Socrates: from secondary sources, for neither of their work exists in primary sources. Although the historical tradition has readily accepted secondary accounts of Socrates' influence, teaching, and beliefs, the same cannot be said about any female counterpart, especially a woman described so briefly and in so few accounts. But the fact that Aspasia is even mentioned by her male contemporaries is remarkable, for rare is the mention of any intellectual woman. Surviving fragments and references in the work of male authors provide tantalizing indications that the intellectual efforts of Aspasia were, at least occasionally, committed to writing—and to architecture. Aspasia is memorialized in a fresco over the portal of the University of Athens, in the company of Phidias, Pericles (on whom she leans), Sophocles, Antisthenes, Anaxagoras, Alcibiades, and Socrates.

When other women were systematically relegated to the domestic sphere, Aspasia seems to have been the only woman in classical Greece to have distinguished herself in the public domain. Her reputation as both a rhetorician and philosopher was memorialized by Plato (437–328 BC), Xenophon (fl. 450 BC), Cicero (100–43 BC), Athenaeus (fl. AD 200), and Plutarch (AD 46–c. 120)—as was, of course, her enduring romantic attachment to Pericles. For those authors, Aspasia clearly represented the intelligentsia of Periclean Athens. Therefore, I want to consider seriously this historical woman who merited such documentation, for the story of her intellectual contributions to rhetoric may suggest the existence of an unrecognized subculture within that community, and the artistic and literary uses of Aspasia of Miletus may configure an emblem of Woman in rhetorical history.

The best-known source of information about Aspasia is Plutarch's *Lives of the Noble Grecians and Romans* (AD 100), an account written several hundred years after her existence. Nevertheless, all earlier mentions of Aspasia confirm this

> inquiry about the woman, what art or charming facility she had that enabled her to captivate, as she did, the greatest statesmen, and to give the philosophers occasions to speak so much about her, and that, too, not to her disparagement. That she was a Milesian by birth, the daughter of Axiochus, is a thing acknowledged. And they say it was in emulation of Thargelia, a courtesan of the old Ionian times, that she made her addresses to men of great power. Thargelia was a great beauty, extremely charming, and at the same time sagacious; she had numerous suitors among the Greeks. . . . Aspasia, some say, was courted and caressed by Pericles upon account of her knowledge and skill in politics. Socrates himself would sometimes go to visit her, and some of his acquaintances with him; and those who frequented her company would carry their wives with them to listen to her. Her occupation was anything but creditable, her house being a home for young courtesans. . . . [I]n Plato's *Menexenus*, though we do not take the introduction as quite serious, still thus much seems to be historical, that she had the repute of being resorted to by many of the Athenians for instruction in the art of speaking. Pericles's inclination for her seems, however, to have rather proceeded from the passion of love. He had a wife that was near of kin to him, who had been married first to Hipponicus, by whom she had Callias, surnamed the Rich; and also she brought Pericles, while she lived with him, two sons, Xanthippus and Paralus. Afterwards, when they did not well agree, nor like to live together, he parted with her, with her own consent, to another man, and himself took Aspasia, and loved her with wonderful affection; every day, both as he went out and as he came in from the market-place, he saluted and kissed her. (200–01)

By every historical account, Aspasia ventured out into the common land, distinguishing herself by her rhetorical accomplishments, her sexual attachment to Pericles, and her public participation in political affairs. Her alleged connection with the courtesan life is only important so far as it explains her intellectual prowess and social attainments—and the surprise of an Athenian citizenry unaccustomed to (or perhaps jealous or suspicious of) a public woman.[11] As Marie Delcourt wrote in her study of Pericles:

> No one would have thought the less of Pericles for making love to young boys . . . but they *were* shocked by his treating [Aspasia] like a human being—by the fact that he *lived* with her instead of relegating her to the *gynaikeion* [women's quarters], and included his friends' wives when he issued invitations to dinner. It was all too amazing to be proper; and Aspasia was so brilliant she could not possibly be respectable. (77)

Aspasia opened an academy for young women of good families (or a school for *hetaerae,* according to some sources) that soon became a popular salon for the most influential men of the day: Socrates, Plato, Anaxagoras, Sophocles, Phidias, and Pericles.[12] Aspasia's appearance was unprecedented at a time when the construction of gender ensured that women would be praised only for such attributes as their inherent modesty, for their inborn reluctance to join males (even kinsmen) for society or dining, and for their absolute incapacity to participate as educated beings within the *polis;* at a time when a woman's only political contribution was serving as a nameless channel for the transmission of citizenship from her father to her son (Keuls 90); and at a time when Pericles pronounced that "the greatest glory of a woman is to be least talked about by men, whether they are praising . . . or criticizing" (Thucydides 5.46.2).[13] It is difficult to overemphasize how extraordinary the foreign-born Aspasia—a public woman, philosopher, political influence, and rhetorician—would have been in fifth-century BC Athenian society.

Fifth-Century BC Athens

In the burgeoning democracy of Periclean Athens, men were consciously forming human character in accordance with the new cultural ideals of military strength and justice *(diké)* tempered by the traditional concepts of *areté* (excellence of virtue, usually associated with the well-born and wealthy citizen-class).[14] Only aristocratic male citizens, equal in their *homonoia* (being of one mind), argued for civic and political *areté,* the essential principle of government by the elite—a democratic oligarchy. Yet the Platonic Socrates called for *areté* according to social role, be it male or female, free or slave (*Republic* 353b), and later Aristotle would write that both the rulers and the ruled, males and females alike, "most possess virtue" and that "all must partake of [moral virtues] . . . in such measure as is proper to each in relation to his own function" (*Politics* 1260a5; 1260a7). Thus was manifested the complex tension between the elitist *areté* and a more democratic *homonoia.*

In *The Origins of Greek Thought,* Jean-Pierre Vernant tells us that "Greek political life aimed to become the subject of public debate, in the broad daylight of the agora, between citizens who were defined as equals and for whom the state was the common undertaking" (11). Such public oratory fed the spirit of panhellenism, a doctrine sorely needed to unify the Greek city-states, just as it satiated the male appetite for public display. Vernant describes the *polis* as a system implying "the extraordinary preeminence of speech over all other instruments of power, [speech becoming] the political tool par excellence, the key to authority in the state, the means of commanding and dominating others" (49). In what would be an inestimable contribution to a democratic oratory possessed by aristocratic characteristics, former logographer (speech writer) Isocrates practiced rhetoric as a literary form, one imbued with civic, patriotic, and moral purpose. Confident in the power of words, he practiced and taught a morally influenced and rhetorically based system of general culture that propounded individual responsibility as well as political and social action. No longer were men deferring to their sovereign or the gods, who could reinforce *nomos* (beliefs, customs, laws, as enforced by universal opinion) with *physis* (nature, reality). "With this denial of the absolute status of law and moral things, the stage [was] set for a controversy between the two . . . [and for drawing] different practical conclusions from it" (Gutherie III: 60). Individuals would be responsible for their own actions and collectively responsible for the actions of the democratic state, the *polis.*

The Athenian *polis* was founded upon the exclusion of women, just as, in other respects, it was founded upon the exclusion of foreigners and slaves (Vidal-Naquet 145). Although females born of Athenian-citizen parents were citizen-class and subjects within the *polis,* they were not actual citizens in any sense. Nor could foreign-born women or men hope for citizenship, regardless of their political influence, civic contributions, or intellectual ties with those in power. Therefore, noncitizens such as Protagoras, Gorgias, Prodicus, Thrasymachus, Anaxagoras, and Aspasia functioned within the *polis,* yet outside its restraints.

If we think of gender as a cultural role, a social rank, "a social category imposed on a sexed body" (Scott 32), or as "a primary way of signifying relations of power" (Laqueur 12), then we can more easily trace Aspasia's movement across gendered boundaries of appropriate roles for women and men in fifth-century BC Athens. She seems to have profited by her excursion into the male domain of politics and intellect, even at the expense of her respectability, reputation, and authority. Named among the rather short "list of Athenian citizen [class] women" known to us from literature (Schaps 323), the assertively intelligent Aspasia has been interpreted as self-indulgent, licentious, immoral. Historical records have successfully effaced the voice of the ideal Greek woman, rendering silent her enclosed body. And those same historical records have defaced any subversion of that ideal woman, rendering her unconfined body invalid.

Thus, even though her contributions to rhetoric are firmly situated and fully realized within the rhetorical tradition, those contributions have been directed through a powerful gendered lens to both refract toward and reflect Socrates and Pericles. Ironically, then, Aspasia's accomplishments and influence have been enumerated by men, and most often attributed to men—or installed in the apocryphal, the safest place for wise (and therefore fictitious) women. And as for Aspasia's popular salon, it's often accredited to Pericles instead of to his female companion.

ASPASIA, PERICLES, AND THE FUNERAL ORATION

Pericles, perhaps the most socially responsible, powerful, and influential of Athenians, was indeed surrounded with the greatest thinkers of his age—with Sophists, philosophers, architects, scientists, and rhetoricians. In his *Mass and Elite in Democratic Athens,* Josiah Ober refers to Pericles' intellectual circle as the "'educated' of late fifth-century Athens" and "a brain trust," describes the Sophists as "experts in political manipulation who were flocking to Athens from other Greek poleis," and places the "educated courtesan Aspasia . . . among Pericles' closest associates," calling her "the power behind the throne" (89–90).[15] For forty years, the Athenians applauded Pericles' eloquence, often invoking his wise and excellent companions, including rhetorician Aspasia and philosopher Anaxagoras. In the *Phaedrus,* the Platonic Socrates calls Pericles "the most perfect orator in existence" and attributes Pericles' eloquence to the successful combination of his natural talents with the high-mindedness he learned from Anaxagoras, who "filled him with high thoughts and taught him the nature of mind . . . and from these speculations [Pericles] drew and applied to the art of speaking what is of use to it" (269e4 ff.). Cicero later concurred that Pericles' teacher was indeed Anaxagoras, "a man distinguished for his knowledge of the highest sciences; and consequently Pericles was eminent in learning, wisdom and eloquence, and for forty years was supreme at Athens both in politics and at the same time in the conduct of war" (*De Oratore* III.xxxiv. 138–39).

Yet several centuries later, Philostratus (fl. AD 250) wrote in his *Epistle* 73 that "Aspasia of Miletus is said to have sharpened the tongue of Pericles in imitation of Gorgias," with "the digressions and transitions of Gorgias' speeches [becoming] the fashion" (qtd. in Sprague 41–42). Philostratus echoes Plato, the earliest writer to mention Aspasia. In the *Menexenus,* the Platonic Socrates reveals Aspasia to be the author of Pericles' Funeral Oration *(Epitaphios),* an assertion I explore below. Aspasia becomes implicated even more in Pericles' education if we consider the "familiar knowledge at Athens that Aspasia had sat at the feet of Anaxagoras in natural philosophy" (Courtney 491). And several hundred years later, when Quintilian (AD 100) examined Pericles' written works, he concluded that some other pen had composed them: "I have been unable to discover anything in the least worthy of [Pericles'] great reputation for eloquence, and am consequently the less surprised that there should be some who hold that he never committed anything to writing, and that the writings circulating under his name are the works of others" (*Institutio Oratoria* 3.1.12). The rhetorician most closely associated with Pericles would no doubt have served as his logographer, as logography (the written composition of speech) was commonly the province of rhetoricians. Hence, Aspasia surely must have influenced Pericles in the composition of those speeches that both established him as a persuasive speaker and informed him as the most respected citizen-orator of the age.

Although Plutarch credits Aspasia with contributing greatly to intellectual life, specifically to philosophy, politics, and rhetoric, many scholars have since discredited her. In the aforementioned "Life of Pericles," Plutarch draws on a now-incomplete work of Aeschines (450 BC) to describe Aspasia, but neither his nor Aspasia's case has been strengthened by the fragments of Aeschines that survived. Those fragments present a controversial statement on gender equality: "the goodness of a woman is the same as that of a man," an assertion Aeschines illustrates with the political abilities of Aspasia (qtd. in Taylor 278).[16] Both Xenophon and Cicero (and later, medieval abbess Heloise, perhaps best-known for her attachment to Abelard), however, tap that same complete text, giving credence to the text—as well as to the existence of a historical Aspasia.[17]

According to several ancient authors, all of whom knitted together secondary sources to shape a reliable Socrates, Socrates deeply respected Aspasia's thinking and admired her rhetorical prowess, disregarding, it seems, her status as a woman and a *hetaera*. In Xenophon's *Memorabilia,* for instance, Socrates explains to Critobulus the "art of catching friends" and of using an intermediary:

> I can quote Aspasia. . . . She once told me that good matchmakers are successful only when the good reports they carry to and fro are true; false reports she would not recommend for the victims of deceptions hate one another and the matchmaker too. I am convinced that this is sound, so I think it is not open to me to say anything in your praise that I cannot say truthfully. (II. 36)

In Xenophon's *Oeconomicus,* Socrates ascribes to Aspasia the marital advice he gives to Critobulus: "There's nothing like investigation. I will introduce Aspasia to you, and she will explain the whole matter [of good wives] to you with more knowledge than I possess" (III. 15). Plutarch writes that "Socrates sometimes came to see her [Aspasia] with her disciples, and his intimate friends brought their wives to her to hear her discourse . . . as a teacher of rhetoric" (200); Athenaeus calls Aspasia "clever . . . Socrates' teacher in rhetoric" (V.29) and goes on to account for the extent of Aspasia's influence over Socrates:

> [I]n the verses which are extant under her name and which are quoted by Herodicus . . . [she says]: "Socrates, I have not failed to notice that thy heart is smitten with desire for [Alcibiades]. . . . But hearken, if thou wouldst prosper in thy suit. Disregard not my message, and it will be much better for thee. For so soon as I heard, my body was suffused with the glow of joy, and tears not unwelcome fell from my eyelids. Restrain thyself, filling thy soul with the conquering Muse; and with her aid thou shalt win him; pour her into the ears of his desire. For she is the true beginning of love in both; through her thou shalt master him, by offering to his ears gifts for the unveiling of his soul."
> So, then, the noble Socrates goes a-hunting, employing the woman of Miletus as his preceptor in love, instead of being hunted himself, as Plato has said, [Socrates] being caught [as he was] in Alcibiades' net. (V.219)

Furthermore, in the *Menexenus,* the Platonic Socrates agrees that were the Council Chamber to elect him to make the recitation over the dead (the *Epitaphios*) he "should be able to make the speech . . . for she [Aspasia] who is my instructor is by no means weak in the art of rhetoric; on the contrary, she has turned out many fine orators, and amongst them one who surpassed all other Greeks, Pericles" (235–36). But it was Pericles—not Aspasia—who delivered that speech.

The *Menexenus* contains Plato's version of Socrates' version of Aspasia's version of Pericles' Funeral Oration, further recognition of Aspasia's reputation as rhetorician, philosopher, and as influential colleague in the So-phistic movement, a movement devoted to the analysis and creation of rhetoric—and of truth. Moreover, the Funeral Oration itself held political, philosophical, and rhetorical significance: by its delivery alone, the Funeral Oration played out "rhetoric's important role in shaping community" (Mackin 251). In *The Invention of Athens: The Funeral Oration in the Classical City*, Nicole Loraux clarifies the funeral oration as an "*institution*—an institu-tion of speech in which the symbolic constantly encroached upon the func-tional, since in each oration the codified praise of the dead spilled over into generalized praise of Athens" (2). Besides conflating praise of the Athenians with praise of Athens, this institutionalized and specialized epideictic was useful for developing "consubstantiality *[homonoia]*" and creating a "similar rhetorical experience" for everyone present, be they citizens, foreigners, or women related to the dead.[18] The shared experience of this rhetorical ritual linked everyone present even as it connected them "with other audiences in the past" (Mackin 251). As "one of the authorized mouthpieces of classical Athens," the funeral oration translated into "Greek patriotism," for it was "Athenian eloquence" "adapted to the needs of a given historical situation" (Loraux 5). As such, the issues of translation and adaptation easily connect the *Epitaphios* with Sophistic philosophy.

In *Rereading the Sophists*, Susan Jaratt reminds us that "for the Sophists, human perception and discourse were the only measure of truths, all of which are contingent" (64); therefore, they focused on "the ability to create accounts of communal possibilities through persuasive speech" (98). And Loraux tells us that in every epitaphios, "a certain idea that the city wishes to have of itself emerges, beyond the needs of the present" (14). Thus the be-liefs and practices of Sophists overlapped beautifully with one basic require-ment of an epitaphios: "the personality of the orator has to yield to the impersonality of the genre . . . as an institution and as a literary form" (11). Aspasia's Sophistic training, political capacity, and powerful influence on Pericles' persuasive oratory easily translated into Socrates' pronouncement to Menexenus that she composed the famous funeral oration delivered by Pericles:

> I was listening only yesterday to Aspasia going through a funeral speech for [the Athenians] . . . [S]he rehearsed to me the speech in the form it should take, extemporizing in part, while other parts of it she had previously prepared, . . . at the time when she was composing the funeral oration which Pericles delivered. (236b)

That Aspasia may well have composed Pericles' speech makes sense, since after all, being honored by the opportunity to deliver the *Epitaphios*, he would have prepared well, seeking and following the advice of his col-leagues, including Aspasia, on points of style and substance. That she wrote it becomes more convincing when we consider Loraux's assurance that "the political orator must have the ascendant over the logographer" (11) and that the Sophist would preserve the "essential features of the civic representations" (107). For reasons of Aspasia's proximity to Pericles and her intellectual training, Quintilian was right, then, to doubt the originality of Pericles' work.

Before demonstrating her expertise at composing moving, patriotic epideictic oratory, Aspasia reminds Socrates of the efficacy of rhetoric. In the *Menexenus*, the Platonic Aspasia explains that "it is by means of speech finely spoken that deeds nobly done gain for their doers from the hearers the meed of memory and renown" (236e)—an accurate description of contingent truth. Jarratt explains the sophistic rhetorical technique and its social-constructionist underpinning with her definition of *nomos* as a "self-conscious arrangement of discourse to create politically and socially significant knowledge . . . thus it is always a social construct with ethical dimensions" (60).

Hence, the author of the *Epitaphios*—whether viewed as Aspasia or Pericles—makes clear the power of oratory to influence the public's belief that its history was other than it was. Loraux explains that "a Sophist and a rhetor [would have] used the official oration in order to write a fictitious logos; within the corpus, then, the 'false' follows hard upon the 'true'" (9). Accordingly, the most aggressive exploits of Attic imperialism are represented as "[bringing] freedom [to] all the dwellers of this continent" (*Menexenus* 240e), as "fighting in defence of the liberties of the Boeotians" (242b), as "fighting for the freedom of Leontini" (242a), as "setting free . . . friends" (243c), and as "saving their walls from ruin" (244c). In offering this version of Pericles' Funeral Oration, an exaggerated encomium abounding with historical misstatements and anachronisms, Plato makes explicit his own feelings about the use of rhetoric—just as Thucydides uses his own version of the *Epitaphios* to make explicit his belief in the necessary subjection of individual citizenship to the polis: "A man who takes no interest in politics is a man . . . who has no business here at all" (II.40).

Thinly disguised in the *Menexenus* is Plato's cynicism. In his opinion, the development of oratory had negative consequences for Athens, the most glaring defect of current oratory being its indifference to truth. A rhetorician such as Aspasia was, indeed, interested more in believability than in truth, more interested in constructing than delivering truth, more interested in *nomos* than *physis*—interests leading to Thucydides' claims that such "prose chroniclers . . . are less interested in telling the truth than in catching the attention of their public" (I.21). In the opening dialogue of the *Menexenus*, the Platonic Socrates disparages the orators in much the same way he does in the *Symposium*, saying that "in speeches long beforehand . . . they praise in such splendid fashion, that . . . they bewitch our souls. . . . [E]very time I listen fascinated [by their praise of me] I am exalted and imagine myself to have become all at once taller and nobler and more handsome . . . owing to the persuasive eloquence of the speaker" (235b). Thus Plato recoils from the touch of rhetoric.

ASPASIA'S INFLUENCE

Aspasia was an active member of the most famous intellectual circle in Athens, her influence reaching such well-known thinkers as Socrates and such exemplary orators as Pericles. Most importantly, her influence extended to Plato, coloring his concept of rhetoric as well. Like Aspasia, Plato taught that belief and truth are not necessarily the same, a sentiment he makes evident in his *Gorgias* when Gorgias admits that rhetoric produces "[mere] belief without knowledge" (454). Plato also agrees with Aspasia that rhetoric, which is the daughter of truth-disclosing philosophy, does not always carry on the family tradition; rhetoric can be used to obscure the truth, to control and deceive believers into belief. In the *Gorgias,* his Socrates says, "[R]hetoric seems not to be an artistic pursuit at all, but that of a shrewd, courageous spirit which is naturally clever at dealing with men; and I call the chief part of it flattery" (463). And in the *Phaedrus,* Plato writes that "in the courts, they say, nobody cares for truth about these matters [things which are just or good], but for that which is convincing; and that is probability" (272e).

Like Aspasia, Plato approved of a rhetoric of persuasion; he too sees the political potential of public rhetoric. But his rhetoric is foremost a search for the truth; only truth—not fictive effect over accuracy—should constitute persuasive rhetoric. His perfect orator of the *Phaedrus* "must know the truth about all the particular things of which he speaks and writes . . . [and] must understand the nature of the soul" (277c), for the ideal rhetorician speaks "in a manner pleasing to the gods" (273e). What Plato could have learned, then, from Aspasia was the potentially harmful uses of rhetoric as a branch of philosophy—as well as the as-yet uncalibrated potential of rhetoric to create belief.

In addition to influencing Socrates and Plato, Aspasia also influenced Xenophon and his wife, specifically in the art of inductive argument. In *De Inventione,* Cicero uses her lesson in induction as the centerpiece for his argumentation chapter. Like others before him, Cicero too acknowledges Aspasia's influence on Socrates as well as the existence of the Aeschines text:

> [I]n a dialogue by Aeschines Socraticus[,] Socrates reveals that Aspasia reasoned thus with Xenophon's wife and with Xenophon himself: "Please tell me, madam, if your neighbour had a better gold ornament than you have, would you prefer that one or your own?" "That one," she replied. "Now, if she had dresses and other feminine finery more expensive than you have, would you prefer yours or hers?" "Hers, of course," she replied. "Well, now, if she had a better husband than you have, would you prefer your husband or hers?" At this the woman blushed. But Aspasia then began to speak to Xenophon. "I wish you would tell me, Xenophon," she said, "if your neighbour had a better horse than yours, would you prefer your horse or his?" "His," was the answer. "And if he had a better farm than you have, which farm would you prefer to have?" "The better farm, naturally," he said. "Now if he had a better wife than you have, would you prefer yours or his?" And at this Xenophon, too, himself was silent. Then Aspasia: "Since both of you

have failed to tell me the only thing I wished to hear, I myself will tell you what you both are thinking. That is you, madam, wish to have the best husband, and you, Xenophon, desire above all things to have the finest wife. Therefore, unless you can contrive that there be no better man or finer woman on earth you will certainly always be in dire want of what you consider best, namely, that you be the husband of the very best of wives, and that she be wedded to the very best of men." To this instance, because assent has been given to undisputed statements, the result is that the point which would appear doubtful if asked by itself is through analogy conceded as certain, and this is due to the method employed in putting the question. Socrates used this conversation method a good deal, because he wished to present no arguments himself, but preferred to get a result from the material which the interlocutor had given him—a result which the interlocutor was bound to approve as following necessarily from what he had already granted. (I.xxxi.51–53)

Few women participated in the intellectual life of ancient Greece. Aspasia was a striking exception.

Although Aspasia was a powerful force in Periclean Athens and seems to have affected the thinking of Plato and Socrates, few Greek thinkers accepted women as mental equals. Aristotle makes no provision for the intellectual woman, except for his nod to Sappho: "Everyone honours the wise. . . . [T]he Mytilenaeans [honour] Sappho, though she was a woman" (*Rhetoric* 1389b.12). Otherwise, Aristotle denied any philosophical or rhetorical contributions of women. He quotes Sophocles when he writes, "'Silence gives grace to woman'—though that is not the case likewise with a man" (*Politics* I.v.9). Reasoning from Aristotle's basic premise, Aspasia could not have become a teacher, much less a rhetorician. By the principle of *entelechy* (the vital force urging one toward fulfilling one's actual essence), she would have naturally followed her predetermined life course, her progress distinctly marked off and limited to a degree of perfection less than that for a man. The power politics of gender, the social category imposed on each sexed body, both gives rise to and then maintains the social creation of ideas about appropriate roles for women and men. Denied the *telos* of perfect maleness, Athenian women were denied a passport into the male intellectual battleground of politics, philosophy, rhetoric. But Aspasia had approached the border— and trespassed into masculine territory.

For the most part, Aristotle's accounts of woman, buttressed by the defective scientific understanding of reproduction and biological processes, belie woman's participation in the making of culture, leaving her daughters without access to any knowledge of a female tradition or intellectual underpinning. For Aristotle, men and women differed only in outward form—but the inequality is permanent. Unlike Plato, he could not see beyond the contemporary and seemingly permanent inferior status of Greek women. In the *Politics*, Aristotle writes "between the sexes, the male is by nature superior and the female inferior, the male ruler and the female subject" (I.ii.121); in the *Poetics*, he pronounces goodness as possible "even in a woman . . . though

[she] is perhaps an inferior . . . but it is not appropriate in a female Character to be manly, or clever" (15.1454a.20–24); and in the *Rhetoric,* he writes that "one quality or action is nobler than another if it is that of a naturally finer being: thus a man's will be nobler than a woman's" (I.9.15).

And those naturally finer beings (men) were awarded a public voice, which enabled them to participate as speakers, thinkers, and writers in the *polis,* in the "good" of public life. A public voice was the right and privilege of those who were declared to possess reason and goodness to its fullest extent—men only. In the *polis*—the public sphere of action, the realm of highest justice, the world of men—women and slaves should be invisible and aphonic. "Naturally" then, women and slaves—inferior beings in every way —were condemned to silence as their appointed sphere and condition. And most women spoke no memorable alternative—that is, except for Aspasia. But even Aspasia's voice is muted, for she speaks only through men.

ASPASIA'S CHALLENGE TO THE HISTORY OF RHETORIC

Aspasia colonized the patriarchal territory, but her colony was quickly appropriated by males. Although she herself escaped enclosure, although she publicly articulated her intelligence and her heterosexual love, she did not escape those who defined her. Her influence has been enclosed within the gendered rhetorical terrain—and neutralized. "And the trouble is," Myra Jehlen writes, "that the map of an enclosed space describes only the territory inside the enclosure. Without knowing the surrounding geography, how are we to evaluate this woman's estate . . ." (80). Few of us have ever heard of Aspasia of Miletus, teacher of rhetoric. But if we locate her colony within "its larger context" and "examine the borders along which [she] defined herself" (81)—the writings of the men she influenced, Plato, Socrates, and Pericles— we can better map out how Aspasia was perceived by those men and, perhaps, how she might have perceived her estate within the surrounding geography.

But even now, Aspasia's intellectual estate seems to be "off-limits," except in that her story serves as a morality tale for women who insist on entering the rhetorical arena: such a woman will be used, misappropriated, and eventually forgotten. Or worse, perhaps, they will be disfigured in artistic renderings such as Gerome's, inscribed with masculine fantasy and curiosity. Gerome's idyllic rendition of Aspasia and Alcibiades is both inaccurate and unfair: Our Mother of Rhetoric, life-long companion of Pericles and influential colleague of famous men, is the harem girl to the arrogant, dissolute, untrustworthy, love-object of Socrates, Alcibiades. Thus the example of Gerome's print brings to the fore the whole notion of women's place in rhetoric. Where on that landscape we call rhetorical history should we begin to look for women? How many women remain hidden in the shadows of monumental rhetoricians? How many others remain misidentified as holes and bulges on out-of-the-way territories? And how much of rhetorical history is itself, as Carole Blair describes, "rhetorical iterations, saturated with the impure representations, intrinsic interestedness, and general obstreper-ousness of any discourse" (417)?

By acknowledging that rhetorical history is not neutral territory, the re-figuring of Aspasia's role in the history of rhetoric has ramifications on past study as well as implications for future study. The most powerful ramifica-tion is an awareness of women's place on the rhetorical terrain. Until most re-cently, we had not even thought of looking for a woman in rhetoric. It had al-ready been assumed, *a priori*, that no woman participated in the rhetorical tradition. We had been willing to believe the tautology that no women have been involved in rhetorical history because not a single rhetorical treatise by a woman appears in lists of primary works (we resolutely ignore Lucia Olbrechts-Tyteca) and because not a single woman appears in the indices of the most comprehensive histories of Western rhetoric. But upon examination, the fault line of gender reveals that women have indeed participated in and contributed to the rhetorical tradition, and that fault line reverberates down the corridors of past scholarship to the foundations of the Greek intellectual tradition.

Our first obligation, then, as rhetorical scholars is to look backwards at all the unquestioned scholarship that has come before; then, we must begin to re-map our notion of rhetorical history. By simply choosing which men and women to show and how to represent them, we subtly shape the percep-tions of our profession, enabling the profession to recognize and remember—or to forget—the obvious and not-so-obvious women on our intellectual landscape. But looking backwards will not be enough; we must attend to the current professional scene as well. For example, the early and influential work of Ann Berthoff, Janet Emig, Janice Lauer, and Mina Shaughnessy could easily fade out of our professional consciousness if we don't keep these foremothers of composition studies in our professional narratives, if we don't know or remember the scholarship on which we're building our own work. Perhaps the most important consequence of refiguring rhetorical history, however, is the effect on our students, for we also shape the perceptions of them. By writing a more inclusive history of rhetoric, we can more easily en-able and encourage both our female and male students to participate in a lit-erature, in a history, in a profession, or in communities of discourse from which they may feel excluded and detached.

Fortunately, rhetorical scholars—females and males alike—around the country are involved in various feminist historiographic projects.[19] And their archeological findings are serving to challenge the history of rhetoric to rec-ognize the full range of its texts, its lies, its manuscripts, its practices, and its theories. In fact, it's the "theoretical understanding of rhetorics of the past [that] underwrites our capacity for further theorizing" (Blair 404). And Aspa-sia's contribution to rhetoric is just one of many stories that disrupt, refigure, and then enrich what has long been held as patriarchal territory. Until re-cently, we didn't seem to realize that the rhetorical map had flattened out the truth, leaving scarcely a ridge on the surface that could suggest all the women, and the otherwise disenfranchised, that are buried beneath the surface. The significance of Aspasia's challenge lies in recharting the plains, valleys, and borders of rhetoric, and accounting for all the pockets of as-yet-unaccounted-for activity. Having passed through the familiar and patriarchal territory of exclusionary rhetoric, we are moving into a frontier—the rhetorics of the future that await our exploration, our settlements, and our mapping.

AFTERWORD . . . .

As I prepared to write this commentary, I thought of how I came to the title of my essay: it's from sex, lies, and videotape, *a movie that, among other things, features women telling their private, until-then untold stories. Women and their untold stories provided the basis for my essay and for my larger research agenda at the time.*

By winning the Braddock Award, "sex, lies, and manuscript" also won, I imagine, a measure of respectability and publicity, especially for the then-controversial idea that women played roles in rhetorical history and theory. In fact, when I reread the piece now, I wonder at all the research I (felt I) had to do to rationalize bringing one female rhetor into our view. My initial conference paper (1992 CCCC) on the subject had met with some resistance. For example, one agitated audience member whispered loudly to the woman beside him, asking her to "tell Cheryl not to say that." "Say what?" I wondered. And when I got to the part in my paper about studying rhetoric in graduate school but never considering even one female figure, my former professor, Ed Corbett, rose up from the audience and apologized to us all for "being a sexist." After the laughter subsided, I assured him that he was teaching what he knew at the time. Back in 1985, our class wasn't giving much thought to why we weren't studying women in rhetorical history.

The research and methodology of the 1994 "sex, lies, and manuscript" had been vetted and sanctioned by specialists in our field, so I continued to rely upon it to write Rhetoric Retold: Regendering the Tradition from Antiquity Through the Renaissance. *Now, just a few years after that initial essay, I can appreciate the many other rich and successful ways to do feminist historiography, the various measures and kinds of archival and library research that reveal many more compelling stories. JoAnn Campbell, Mary Garratt, Catherine Hobbs, Susan Kates, Shirley Wilson Logan, Kris Ratcliffe, Molly Meijer Wertheimer, and Hui Wu are just a few of the scholars who are bringing into focus the untold stories and rhetorical lives of women from the seventeenth through twentieth centuries.*

If my essay did anything, maybe it called attention to the continued exploration of a practical, historical, and theoretical rhetorical terrain that engenders and spans the sexes, disciplines, cultures, ethnicities, and racial constructions. After all, the recent resurgence of rhetorical studies hasn't so much been a discovery of new rhetorics; it has been a recognition of already/always rhetorical activities, of our new-found ability and willingness to listen to unheard and untold stories: feminist, womanist, activist, religious, medical, African American, Native American, Hispanic, and Asian rhetorics, for example. Our attention to additional, previously neglected rhetorics is invigorating our field in new ways. And this is what I'm enjoying the most these days—the pluralization of "rhetoric" to "rhetorics." That little "s" alone signifies our progress—and our possibilities.

–CHERYL GLENN
Pennsylvania State University

Importing Composition: Teaching and Researching Academic Writing Beyond North America

MARY N. MUCHIRI,
NSHINDI G. MULAMBA, GREG MYERS,
AND DEOSCOROUS B. NDOLOI

*T*his seems to be a period in which composition as a field takes stock of its history and position among research fields and in the university. One distinctive feature of its development that has not been much discussed is the fact that for all its huge growth and institutionalization in conferences, journals, and departments, composition remains largely restricted to the United States and Canada. Copies of *CCC*, like boxes of Baker's unsweetened chocolate, find their way abroad only by accident, or when ordered by some obsessive expatriate. The large and elegantly produced freshman composition textbooks that seem so ubiquitous in university bookstores sell their tens of thousands of copies entirely in the North American market.

In some ways this is appropriate. Composition research remains local, in a way other areas of academic research do not, because it has been tied to teaching in specific programs, and innovations in testing or syllabi or tutoring fit specific institutional needs; it is local because it is concerned with practice. But as composition research has developed it has come to see itself as the study of writing in general, and academic writing in particular. In those terms it might be of interest beyond universities in the United States and Canada. But when it is exported, it changes meaning and serves different needs in the new context, just as the work of Foucault, or Bakhtin, or Ngugi changes meaning when it is imported into the US.[1]

We are university lecturers teaching in four different university systems who share a research interest in academic writing; the chances of careers and funding brought us together in Lancaster for the last three years. Mary is studying how students at Kenyatta University, in Kenya, interpret examination prompts, and how they draw on the local culture of the institution to do this. Ndoloi is studying the ways first-year students at the University of Dar es Salaam, in Tanzania, represent themselves in their writing. Mulamba is analyzing texts of the final dissertations of students doing degrees in English

This essay was first published in *CCC*, Volume 46, Number 2, May 1995.

at the University of Lubumbashi, in Zaire. Greg is studying writing by academic researchers in UK universities.[2]

The purpose of this paper is to open a discussion of what happens to the published literature on composition in these new contexts. In the Teaching of Writing Group at Lancaster, we often have this discussion with teachers of communication skills or English for Academic Purposes (EAP) from many countries, all trying to adapt composition research to their settings. We believe such a discussion can be useful to composition researchers, in reminding them what they take for granted that is local to their institutions and nation. Composition research makes assumptions about students, teachers, language, and universities. Some of the assumptions from US research are refreshing in these new contexts; some have to be questioned, and some seem bizarre.

COMPOSITION AND ENGLISH FOR ACADEMIC PURPOSES

While there is no composition industry outside the US and Canada, that is not to say that there is no interest or research in academic writing. But most studies are done to support programs for students whose first language is not English—the idea of teaching English to English speakers (L1, or first language, students) is seen as rather odd. Academic writing is studied in applied linguistics or English language teaching departments under such headings as English for Academic Purposes (EAP) or English for Specific Purposes (ESP). As the name suggests, institutions around English for Academic Purposes have a more limited view of their mission than English Departments in the US. Rather than offer a theory of communication or language use or academic knowledge in general, EAP tries to analyze the immediate needs of students, to define a register of English on this basis, and to suggest the most efficient ways of teaching it, so that students can get on with their studies.[3]

English language teachers around the world may start reading composition research, when they can get it, because the titles sound relevant, but they often stop reading because what is said seems to apply only to the US and Canada—not even to acknowledge that there might be other systems. Of course part of the problem is that composition research is devoted largely to teaching those for whom English is a first language (L1), while English Language Teaching (ELT) is aimed at those for whom English is a second (or third or fourth) language, but who must use it in their studies. But the differences also have to do with the educational systems. In their own universities, the ELT teachers say:

> Courses do not focus just on writing, to the exclusion of reading, speaking, and listening;
>
> Students do not write personal essays, with no disciplinary content;
>
> Assessment is by examination with only a small coursework component;

Students who cannot write competently fail the entrance exam, so the teachers don't see them;

Their institutions lack the resources—and the postgraduate students—for extensive essay-marking.

So they may dismiss the whole composition literature on "L1 writing," and go back to *TESOL Quarterly, ELT Journal, Applied Linguistics,* and *English for Specific Purposes Journal,* all of which report enough research on academic writing to keep them busy reading, without trying to track down hard-to-get composition articles.

Yet there is work done in composition research that we can't get elsewhere.[4] This is partly just because in the US and Canada there are so many postgraduate degree programs, meetings, books, and funded projects; most of all, there are so many students, and teachers to teach them, and even some relatively secure positions for researchers, something the ELT world does not provide. Also, the composition literature has produced some inspiring accounts of teaching and learning in difficult situations. Writers like Mina Shaughnessy, Patricia Bizzell, David Bartholomae, and Mike Rose have offered powerful accounts of what it is like to come as a new student to a university. They have helped us imagine how strange the conventions of academic writing might seem to those unfamiliar with them, and have challenged the naturalness of disciplinary expectations. There are writers who do this in the English Language Teaching and Communication Skills literatures.[5] But composition researchers have given particular importance to this imaginative leap, perhaps because the field is still defined in part by freshman composition.

We would like to add to this literature by comparing entry processes in our universities. The problem we share is how students can enter universities without intellectual brutality, loss of identity, and waste of talents—how all students, and not just those with special preparation, can have a chance to succeed. But in different countries, both the universities and the worlds outside them can be different. So the process of entry, and the part in it played by writing, may also differ crucially. We will outline differences in the geographical place of the university, in the view of students as individuals, the view of teachers as researchers, the view of English as a language, and the stability of the university as an institution.

THE JOURNEY

One common metaphor for the changes a student undergoes on entering university is that of the journey from home: across town from East LA to UCLA, or down to Pittsburgh from the coal-mining towns of western Pennsylvania, or taking the IND subway uptown to City College, Willie Morris leaving Mississippi for Austin, Jude Frawley entering Christminster, or Julie Walters walking onto campus for the first time in *Educating Rita*. Even at an urban community college just a mile from home, some separation seems to be part of the ritual of beginning.

It is helpful to remind ourselves that one of the things a university does is alter one's sense of geography. This journey is part of what defines the relation between the university and the rest of society. In the US, especially at elite universities, it may be a journey to a protected enclave; students remember nostalgically their days in Ann Arbor, or Berkeley, or Cambridge, or even across Los Angeles in Westwood. While secondary schools are usually tied to one community, universities get students from all over town, or the whole state, or the whole country. Thus they have an important social function, not only setting up new social links, but breaking the ties to home.

Of course students at Kenyatta, Dar es Salaam, and Lubumbashi have also left family and friends and journeyed to get there, often spending days on the matatu, daladala, bus, or train.[6] But the journey is in one sense further for them, because it is not out to a protected enclave, but in to the heart of the nation. Benedict Anderson has noted how universities under colonial domination (his case was Indonesia) contributed in unintended ways to the sense of a national identity, because they brought to one place students from throughout the country (as it was defined by imperial maps) to an administrative centre (again, as defined by the empire). At Nairobi or Dar es Salaam or Lubumbashi, a student met others from all over the country and learned to take them as part of his or her community, while those from just beyond the national boundaries went to some other center. Even today, there are only four state universities in Kenya, three in Tanzania (counting the medical school), and three in Zaire, so in going away to one of them one is becoming a part of the national life in a new way.[7] It is not surprising that in these countries (unlike in the US) universities are centers of political resistance, and may be closed whenever a government feels vulnerable.

Another way in which the journey is different is that university attendance remains in most countries in the world the privilege of a tiny minority. It is easy to forget in the US just what a difference this makes to students. Students in these countries may come to university bearing not just the hopes of their family, but the hopes of an entire village, for whom they will become an important link to the worlds of government and business.[8] The pressure to succeed, or at least to survive, is enormous. Teachers in these universities recognize the experience of their students in Mike Rose's powerful descriptions, in *Lives on the Boundary,* and recognize the stresses on those who are the first in their families to attend university. But they may be less likely to recognize the complete break with the past that Rose describes in his own college career and in that of some of his students. For these African students, the journey to university is also a journey back to those who sent them.

What does this journey have to do with students' writing? One might think that this exciting transformation of students' lives would make their prose burst out with discoveries. And yet, in all forms of students' writing, Mary, Ndoloi, and Mulamba find again and again a dull correctness and caution. Where is the richness of experience we see in their journey? We will

come back to some of the pedagogical factors that might contribute to the
bland impersonality of their writing, but part of it may have to do with the
distance of the journey. Where the university system is centralized and
highly selective, students may have too much at stake to do anything but try
to get by.

There may be a more immediate fear as well; part of the caution about
personal expression may result from students' or lecturers' fears of punishment if they voice political criticisms. This does not mean there is lack of political discussion; Kenya has just had and Tanzania is to have multi-party
elections, and political talk is everywhere, wherever students meet (in contrast to many US universities). But it is too risky to let these issues get into
academic work. In Zaire, now torn by civil war, Mulamba says that topics
seen as political are strictly avoided, because group loyalties are so important
(or were, before the exile of non-Shaba teachers and the collapse of the university); they would revive political and ethnic rivalries between teachers
and students. For their part, lecturers fear that students spy for the political
leaders—that is, they side with someone who seems to promise them a future. To those outside the university, this silence may seem like selling out;
Ndoloi recalls the proverb: "The fed dog doesn't bark."

In America and Canada, the universities are scattered, and most people
have a chance to attend them. But composition teachers, too, regularly express annoyance with the dullness and correctness of the run-of-the-mill essays they receive. The annoyance arises when the dullness seems to arise
from a rejection of academic challenges. Are we saying that such dullness is
(horrible thought) a cultural universal? No, we suspect that a very similar
dullness may have quite different social causes. The fear of failure in North
American universities may not be so great (of course we cannot say). Certainly the fear of political persecution should be less. Essays may be dull because the university means too little to the student, or because it means too
much. Can we tell the difference between the dullness of boredom, the dullness of linguistic limitation, and the dullness of fear?

STUDENTS, DIFFERENCE, AND SOLIDARITY

In the African universities Mary, Ndoloi, and Mulamba studied, students are
first of all members of groups: of a small band of students with whom they
survive the university, of the body of students as a whole, and of a community beyond the university, of family, village, and tribe. These loyalties are
embodied in daily practices of academic life. Mary wanted to know how students at Kenyatta came to know just what was expected on an exam, since
the exam questions themselves did not provide explicit guidance. They were
getting much of their information, she found, from what they call "survival
groups." Students band together, sharing notes, sharing knowledge of lecturers, so that the strong help support the weak. One student she interviewed
distinguishes these survival groups from more general discussion groups.

> In the survival group you just get together, write some points some-
> where and give one person, then in the exam room you'll have to sit to-
> gether and the paper will be circulating. Or in another case, you don't
> have to write anywhere, you just discuss the major points . . . just a mat-
> ter of surviving the exam.

Everyone in such a survival group then spends less time on study, and they
are free to work on social or political activities. Mulamba notes that in his
university in Zaire, teachers' responsibility for dissertations in English is limited to the mechanics: bibliography, footnotes, endnotes. Students have to
learn everything else about format and writing on their own. They monitor
each others' work, working in groups as postgraduate students do in the US
and UK.

These survival groups may remind us of the kinds of collaborative activities many composition teachers encourage. But unlike the collaborative writing of Kenneth Bruffee, which seeks to draw students into scholarly dialogue, the collaborations we studied seem to arise from the assumption that
the university is an adversarial system, students vs. teacher. Another practice
Mary found was the use of "Mwakenya." This refers to a way of folding the
paper vertically so that one can recopy one's notes for practice, and memo-
rize them easily on, for instance, the long bus-trip home. Similar methods
seem to be developed in other systems, wherever rote memorization is necessary. But it was also suggested that this way of preparing notes made them
convenient for smuggling into an exam. It is part of the elaborate cat-and-
mouse game of any examination-based system. But what especially struck
Mary was the name the students gave this system—*Mwakenya*. Mwakenya is
the name of a pro-democracy movement, once associated with Ngugi wa
Thiongo, before his arrest and exile to the US. Similar practices in other parts
of Africa, she found, have similar names. In Tanzania, Ndoloi points out, it is
"Nondo," which is "crowbar" in Kiswahili. It can also be called "Kombora,"
Kiswahili for missile. In Nigeria the name is "Ecowas," after the Economic
Community of West African States. The name makes it clear that, whatever
the teachers may think of it, the practice is seen by students as group resistance, not just individual cheating. Even in the UK, which is in some ways
more like the US, and where neither study groups nor cheating seem to be so
organized, Greg finds a powerful sense of a group of all students vs. all
teachers, that he did not have in the US.

The sense of group loyalty can also apply to a wider community, of village or people beyond the university. This long-held loyalty can make it hard
to take on the kind of academic voice that stresses argument, difference, distinction, personality. Recent historians of composition have tended to trace
the concern with voice in an expressivist view of the writing process, but the
rhetoric carries through all the schools of composition. In contrast, other cultures may value a voice that identifies one with a group and doesn't make
one stand out. Ndoloi found in his analysis of Tanzanian students' writing a
tendency to take on various collective personae, associated with traditional

speech events. For instance, one first-year project in Commerce and Management requires the student to take a position on a plan to locate a coffee curing plant in a remote, economically depressed region. Rather than marshal economic arguments, some students may take on the voice of the Wise Man, the older brother or village leader who is qualified to make judgments for the group:

> In this case what I can advise the people of this region is that economically there is no possibility of constructing a coffee curing plant in Singida region.

Or another example:

> As for advice, I would like to ask interested parties to get themselves acquainted with the Tanzanian government policies . . .

Ndoloi points out to his Communication Skills students that these pronouncements or appeals to authority are inconsistent with the kinds of authority favored in academic writing. Called upon to make a judgment, his students take up the rhetoric they knew best before they came to university. This rhetoric depends, not on the marshalling of impersonal arguments or a persona of objectivity, but on a confident assertion of one's right to make such a judgment. And that right is a function of one's place in a family or community or party organization. There are probably similar kinds of authority in American communities, but if there are, they do not seem to be acknowledged by most textbooks and research.

Mulamba, in Zaire, found indications of loyalties to tribe and village even in the highly conventionalized genre of English Language and Literature dissertations. What first interested him in this genre was the strangeness of some of the introductory material. Students would first write many pages maintaining a fairly rigid academic genre (Mulamba's dissertation shows just how rigid they are). But when at the end they came to write dedications and acknowledgements, they would often switch to their home languages (rather than the English of the dissertation or the French of the rest of the university). Clearly there was some powerful desire to link the work back to some group.

Another way Zairean students express a collective persona is by insisting on using "we" rather than "I." Here is a typical example from a student of literature working towards a second degree:

> We may finally assume that our dissertation has not treated prejudices and interracial union exhaustively.

Who is *we* here? The *we* seems to be the conventional academic usage that includes the reader. Mulamba gives it a different reading, tracing it to the French use of a magisterial *nous* (see Muhlhausler and Harré). But it could also suggest a different sort of community from that assumed in academic discourse. When teachers try to get them to change to English conventions, students justify "we" on the grounds that the dissertation has been a collective achievement both intellectually (help from supervisor, lecturers, class-mates) and financially (contribution from almost the whole tribe). As with the acknowledgements, they insist on expressing their indebtedness to all concerned in a more permanent form (after all, as Mulamba puts it, *verba volant, scripta manent*). Mary points out how this desire to acknowledge the community contrasts to her Ph.D. viva (oral defense) in the UK, where she could not acknowledge her supervisor's input. For the purposes of the viva, she had to treat the dissertation as entirely an individual product, while she felt it was really a collaborative product.

How do these senses of group identity relate to composition teaching? Part of the liveliness of articles in composition journals results from their dealing with and quoting individual students. The goal of a one-to-one teacher-student relationship underlies much of the comment on teaching writing, even when it is recognized that, with heavy teaching and large classes, that goal is far off. Mike Rose and Maxine Hairston, like other teach-ers of writing, often make their points by characterizing individual students:

> At twenty-eight, Lucia was beginning her second quarter at UCLA. There weren't many people here like her. She was older, had a family, had transferred in from a community college. (Rose 181)

> Imagine, for example, the breadth of experience and range of difference students would be exposed to in a class made up of students I have had in recent years. One student would be from Malawi. The ivory bracelet he wears was put on his arm at birth and cannot be removed; he writes about his tribal legends. Another student is a young Vietnamese man who came to America when he was eight; he writes about the fear he felt his first day in an American school because there were no walls to keep out bullets. Another is a young Greek woman whose parents brought her to America to escape poverty; she writes about her first conscious brush with sexism in the Greek orthodox church . . . (Hairston 190–91)

Both Rose and Hairston get emotional effect by breaking with the usual ten-dency to generalize in writing about education. They treat students as indi-viduals, even while placing them in familiar social categories (such as ethnic groups). This sort of social background is common. But somehow the rela-tions between students, in a group, or their relations to teachers, as a group, remain mysterious. They appear as a group only when they become a prob-lem, such as when the class attacks an individual student or resists some goal of the teacher. Collaborative writing is something to be promoted, against the grain of student experience, by careful organization. How much do we know about actual collaborative practices? Plagiarism is often, though not always, seen as a problem with individual students and their knowledge of conven-tions. But how much do we know about organized plagiarism, such as through fraternity files, and how it works? In the composition literature, stu-dents may come from communities, but at university they succeed or fail on their own. The strain of individualism in writing instruction has often been pointed out by composition researchers, both those who critique it and those who seek to promote it (compare, for instance, the critique in Lester Faigley's *Fragments of Rationality* with the comments in Hairston's "Diversity").

We do not mean to over-simplify the group loyalties of students by attributing to them some special social consciousness or warm tradition known only to those outside Europe and North America, and we do not mean to deny the multiplicity of cultures in the US, which has been a key topic of recent *CCC* articles. And we are not saying that it is always a good thing to identify oneself with a group. Current events in Kenya and Zaire show that loyalties to village and tribe and group and nation can clearly be dangerous, as well as liberating. Our point is that there are ways of belonging to a group, in one's student life and in one's writing, that differ from the life of the isolated, aspiring, and expressive individual assumed in some composition literature. It differs also from the rather abstract community proposed in some writing on social construction (that's why Mary, Ndoloi, and Mulamba sometimes find Greg's research on academic writing rather odd). This belonging is a matter of daily practices (such as copying), traditional echoes (such as acknowledging the home village in its language), and powerful, sometimes even unwilling, ethnic and linguistic loyalties.

TEACHERS: GETTING ON THE MAP

Why is it that Mary, Ndoloi, and Mulamba had to leave their families and friends and work, and leave large cosmopolitan cities, to come to Lancaster, a small university in a small town in a country where it always rains, in order to study the writing done back at their own universities? Clearly there is something rather odd about the academic map, so that hundreds of small institutions in North America and Europe are on it, and others elsewhere are off it. Of course, there has been research done by faculty at Kenyatta, Dar es Salaam, and Lubumbashi, in languages and in other fields. But there is a widespread assumption that validation of knowledge comes from distant and powerful research centers. And that changes the whole approach to academic writing.

It is important to stress that lack of money and time by faculty members is as important in marginalizing research as geography. Ndoloi points out the significance of the fact that university lecturers at Dar drive pick-ups. It seems they do at the other universities in Africa as well. This is because they must also have something going on the side, delivering vegetables from one's village to the city, or keeping hens, or having a little cafe. In Kenya these moonlighting jobs are called "Jua kali," after the open air workshops around Nairobi. These other jobs are of course unofficial, but the university salary is so small and so unreliable that they are usually necessary. It is difficult to do research, even if the materials are available, if one has to juggle several jobs at once. Many composition teachers trying to do some research while working on temporary contracts, perhaps at different institutions across town, already know this. The difference is that in Africa, all university teachers must struggle this way. It is only by going abroad on a fellowship—

as Mary, Ndoloi, and Mulamba did—that one can get the money and time to do the research. Thus knowledge remains identified with other centers. Students at Kenyatta, Dar, and Lubumbashi find they have come to the center of things, in their country, but they have come to the margins of the world of research. Ideas in composition research about the function of academic writing assume that the university is at least notionally a place of research as well as teaching, where new knowledge is produced. What happens to this assumption if a university denies that research is done there?

This issue came up when Mulamba and Greg were discussing whether what the students were doing at Lubumbashi could be called "knowledge-making."[9] If knowledge is ultimately validated elsewhere—in North American and European journals, conferences, experts, and textbooks—then the function of the lecturer is just to pass it on, more or less efficiently. This means the lecturers have a frustratingly limited job; it also means the students become skeptical about just how much some of their lecturers know, and how up to date their knowledge could be. The students in Mary's interviews said it isn't worth reading beyond the one book the lecturer happens to know, because to know more on an exam could be dangerous. It is important to stay within circumscribed areas. In this context, a teacher who tried to open up study, to include a range of reading and the students' own findings and conclusions, would be seen as raising and blurring the requirements, changing the rules in the middle of the game.

In his detailed study of dissertations, Mulamba traces the appearance and disappearance of the review of the literature as a section. This section would not have been found in any of the French texts that students might have used as models of academic writing. It does not seem to have made sense to them, as they collected what they could find in the library at Lubumbashi. But Mulamba has a few papers with reviews of the literature, all from before 1983, when the department had Peace Corps volunteers or Fulbright scholars visiting. They brought the literature review with them, and it duly went in. When the foreign lecturers left (the university no longer provided accommodation for them), the review of the literature left with them.

Mulamba pursued this issue further in interviews with the lecturers. They recalled having done some essay-writing themselves, but said that now students no longer read (a familiar complaint all around the world). Students could point out, in their defense, that the books are old, and the library is almost permanently locked. Since 1991 (when the government of General Mobutu began its long and continuing collapse), the library at the American Cultural Centre, which did have some recent publications, has been ransacked. So students write up their dissertations based on other, earlier dissertations still available in the department (preferring to use those written by the lecturers themselves when they were students). It is not surprising that under these conditions the literature review disappears.

While students do not expect their teachers to be models of research, this does not mean they don't respect them. But they have difficulty finding what form this respect should take. Ndoloi has found signs that the university can be treated as an extension of family and community. For instance, a typical acknowledgement of assistance concludes:

> First and foremost I am indebted to my supervisor Mrs. R—— of the Foreign Languages for her motherly supervision, which really uplifted me. . . . May God the almighty bless her abundantly.

The language here is sufficiently odd for Ndoloi to mark it for discussion. But the attitude, he believes, is typical. And it differs from acknowledgements in North America, where teachers can certainly be nurturing and parental, but where students are unlikely to have the language or assumptions that enable them to celebrate this role. The student at Dar finds a way to define the teacher-student relation by treating it as being like that between a mother and child, close and nurturing, and invokes a shared religious belief. The teacher may be parent, as here, or may be impersonal judge, a representative of the state, but it is hard for the teacher to be a mentor, a research model, a link to a larger conversation.

Of course all North American universities, even the most prestigious, also have many faculty who mainly teach, rather than publish. And at some North American universities, only a very few can ever publish or get a research grant. Still it is possible to maintain the notion that every community college and isolated campus is an outpost of the academic world. Look at the notes on the authors in this journal. If this is a typical issue of *CCC* there will not only be authors from the predictable places, research universities with graduate programs, there will also be authors from small and relatively isolated colleges and large teaching institutions. Why do the more than a thousand US colleges and universities remain in touch, while a university in the huge and cosmopolitan city of Nairobi does not? Again there are matters of history (no colonial legacy), and geography (the distances are less great), and institutions (like annual conferences), and, underlying all this, money. The links are also embodied in the everyday mechanics of academic life. It is not too much to say that the photocopier, personal computers, and regular mail make North American academic life possible. (Both Mary and Ndoloi point out that even the high-quality paper for photocopiers can be scarce and expensive.)

What does this contrast tell us about academic writing? The academic networks that we take for granted in any composition textbook are politically, geographically, and historically contingent. Academic networks define concepts like novelty, evidence, and discipline that are the basis of much of composition teaching. The ideal is to invite the students into an ongoing conversation. Charles Bazerman has dramatized the sense of a network in *The Informed Writer*, trying to get students to see they are entering an ongoing conversation, even in a first year essay. David Bartholomae argues that the main characteristic distinguishing less advanced from more advanced writers in a placement test is not the presence or absence of sentence-level errors, but the way the more advanced writers establish their authority as *writers;* they claim their authority, not by simply claiming they are skiers or that they have done something creative [as in earlier examples], but by placing themselves both within and against a discourse, or within and against competing discourses, and working self-consciously to claim an interpretive project of their own, one that grants them their privilege to speak. (158)

We wonder to what degree this modelling of an academic conversation depends on the sense that the student is entering a world of research and debate. The "research essay" that takes up so much of many composition handbooks seems to assume the student links into a network of new knowledge, through the library and the teacher. Composition teachers may forget just how fragile these links are.

ENGLISH AS *A* LANGUAGE OR AS *THE* LANGUAGE

Recall the tongue-tied, conventional students who wrote the weaker passages in Bartholomae's "Inventing the University." Now imagine that these placement essays had to be written in Latin. (Only a century ago they might have been.) That gives some notion of the problem for African students, even in a country like Kenya where English is the medium of instruction throughout the schools and is widely spoken. English will always be one language among many, a student's third, fourth, or fifth language (after Gikuyu and Kiswahili, or Kichaga and Kiswahili, or Ciluba and Kikongo and French), one marked for special purposes, such as school or church or business. One problem is that it is, of course, hard to learn so many languages well, and most students give up well before they reach university. But the most determined or fluent students do learn (remember these are highly selective universities), and their English is pretty good by any standard. The more interesting issue for us is that choosing English as a language in a multilingual setting always conveys a social and political meaning.[10]

The use of English has a different meaning in Kenya, Tanzania, and Zaire.[11] In Zaire, French is the main European language of the university and of public life, and English is left with a tiny niche. English is not the language of the former colonial power; the desire to learn English may mean, for instance, that one hopes for a career in business, perhaps as a translator or bilingual secretary. It is a marketable, practical skill, like computer programming. In Kenya and Tanzania, English can never be considered apart from the colonial past. In Kenya, English is widely used in education, government, and business, though Kiswahili is also an official language. In Tanzania, Kiswahili is widely used as a national language, which means that special fluency in writing English can still be a distinctive personal skill.

The students at Kenyatta, Dar es Salaam, or Lubumbashi have already learned English to a certain level, or they wouldn't have gotten through the rather strenuous exams. But many of them still have problems with their written work at the university. Administrators, teachers in other departments, and the students themselves may attribute the difficulty to lack of knowledge of the English language. Their assumption is that the students just need to continue English lessons to the next level, not having been taught properly earlier. Students may become defensive—after all, it is their examinable knowledge of English that got them here, and to challenge it is a direct threat to their self-esteem and future careers. Ironically, the effect of the focus on language difficulties is to conceal the other difficulties students have in entering a university, and in seeing themselves as part of the process of making knowledge. If a student uses an odd verb tense in the introduction to a paper, the teacher could assume he or she just didn't know English verbs, and call for more drill. Thus there would be no thinking about why the verb tenses shift as they do in introductions. Composition research can help the teachers argue that the main problem is not some specific competency in a language, but the social uses of language as communication within academic institutions.

What relevance do these multilingual settings have for the US (a multilingual country that keeps insisting it is monolingual), and the institutionalized bilingualism of Canada? English teachers in other countries, including Britain, are puzzled that institutions in the US and Canada would expend such huge efforts and resources to teach English to university-level students, most of whom speak it as a native language. The justification offered by the profession is that composition teachers are not teaching English as a language alongside French or German or Kiswahili, but are rather teaching a kind of language *use*. So while some faculty members and legislators may think that composition classes should teach prescriptive grammar, the classes are more likely to teach processes of invention, or arrangement, or stylistic choice. The composition industry is based on an equivocation between these two senses of "English"—as a language (a lexicon and grammar that can be contained in a handbook), or as the language of academic discourse (which is both a narrower and a broader topic).

This may seem to overstate the contrast with the US. After all, composition teachers have long stressed the social context of language, from Labov's "The Logic of Nonstandard English" to multiculturalism today. Teachers actually have to argue, against the opposition of "English Only," that the US is and should be culturally and linguistically diverse. But discussions of bilingualism or bidialectalism usually assume these islands of difference exist within a sea of monolingual English culture. For monolinguals in the US, ideas like "speech community" or "code-switching" or "register" have to be painstakingly established as abstractions and illustrated with data. In Africa, as in all multilingual countries, people do sociolinguistics on every streetcorner. Someone in Nairobi market who switches from English to Kiswahili to Gikuyu in the course of buying a *kiondo* (a bag) is changing footing, and knows just what is going on. (People do the same thing with registers in English, but it takes them a whole seminar to show that that is what they're doing.) In Africa, the diversity of cultures, sometimes explosive, is a given, not an ideal to be defended, and academic life must work with it, one way or another.

One effect of a largely monolingual society is to contribute to the apparent authority and generality of academic knowledge. Patricia Bizzell comments on the omnivorousness of academic discourse:

> It seems, then, that bi-culturalism is likely to be very difficult when the academic world view is one of the world views involved, because the academic seeks to subsume other world views to which the students may retain allegiance. (Bizzell, *Academic Discourse* 171)

Much of the work of teaching composition critically is making students aware of the tricks of language, the way academic language is different from everyday language and may take on unjustified authority. Researchers like Shaughnessy, Bartholomae, and Bizzell have written eloquently to show how strange the language of the university can seem from outside. Others, like Peter Elbow, have lamented the fact that academic language is cut off from everyday language. But it remains true that a US teacher must convince each new group of students that there are different uses of English that need to be learned even by fluent speakers of English.[12]

English for Academic Purposes works in multilingual settings by narrowing the range of English until it is considered teachable. Its researchers and teachers have something to learn from the broader range of English use considered in composition research and literacy studies. But composition teachers and researchers also have something to learn from settings in which English is a minority language. One effect of a multilingual society is to frame academic knowledge as a distinct and limited institution: there is English for Academic Purposes as there is English for diamond dealing, for diplomacy, or for working in hotels. For students at Kenyatta, Dar es Salaam, or Lubumbashi, academic knowledge is already in a box marked, "treat this with awe, but with skepticism." Again, imagine if the academic journals you read were all in Latin. It could give them prestige, but could also serve as a kind of warning: everything here is not just in language (the code of thought) but is in *a* language (a particular code, among others).

THE UNIVERSITY, THE DEGREE, AND TIME

A freshman composition program is built around cycles so regular that people hardly notice them: essay deadlines, course syllabi, degree years. These cycles carry two assumptions: (1) that individual students develop in coherent stages, and (2) that the university goes on permanently without major change. The assumption of coherent development does not seem to be made in all systems. The three African universities, like most European universities, focus on a single moment, rather than on the long story; they conceive of the student career as an examination, preceded by a period of preparation. The examination is one more step in the rigid ladder of selection that led the student to secondary school and university attendance. As in most European universities, there is not much conception of how the student develops over his or her time there.

The whole idea of a first year as a preparation for entry into the university has until recently been alien to both African systems and the European systems on which they were based. Looking at a first-year course in a US university, the European or African lecturers would ask just what US students *did* learn in secondary school. The ideal of higher education in the US is that it is open to all, like the public schools; only on that assumption does Mike Rose's powerful indictment of waste have its force. In most universities elsewhere, those who are ready will go on, those who are not ready will fail, and there will be no Mike Rose to call it an injustice. A high failure rate may be taken as an indication of institutional failure (as in recent reports in Kenya) or as a sign that standards are being maintained (as in Zaire). In either case vast failure is taken for granted.

Mary and Ndoloi are involved in Communication Skills courses aimed at reducing this failure rate, but these are relatively new operations.[13] The idealism of Shaughnessy, Bartholomae, Bizzell, and Rose is part of what makes the enterprise of composition interesting[14] to them, and it is interesting to those teaching study skills in other elite systems where the intake of students is expanding (such as the UK, or now, South Africa). All composition research assumes that students must be prepared explicitly for the tasks before them. Ideally, they must be given a series of chances to practice any skill on which they might be assessed, and given support, through writing labs and basic writing courses, if they have difficulties. It is as if composition courses came with an entirely different conception of human nature and of education. Certainly they come with a different conception of time. Instead of the once and for all judgment of exams, the career of a US student is to be broken down into smaller and smaller units; it is bumpy road rather than a cliff-face.

The developmental view of a student's career, planning for the future and offering support where necessary, is linked to a second key assumption, of the overwhelming stability of the university. The reality in Africa, as in most countries outside North America and Europe, is that universities are very fragile. Mary, Ndoloi, and Mulamba had three-year grants to study writing at their respective universities, and in the course of that time all three universities were closed for some period. In Kenya the universities were closed between January and August 1992, during the political struggles that finally led to the first multi-party elections. Now, as Mary plans her return, Kenyatta university is closed again, in a lecturers' strike over resources for teaching. In Tanzania all universities were closed in May 1990 for a whole year, and again in February 1992, as students rebelled over "cost sharing," the demand that for the first time they pay fees to attend.[15] Lubumbashi University has been closed during the civil war raging throughout Zaire as other parties challenged the ruling party, and as part of a staff strike over pay. More recently, the English Department in particular suffered as hundreds of thousands of members of other ethnic groups, particularly the Baluba people from Eastern Kasai, were driven out of Lubumbashi and the rest of Shaba (Katanga) Province.[16]

The effect of this constant threat to the continuity of studies does not seem to be, as one might expect, wholesale abandonment of the educational system. When the universities reopen, as they usually do, students return, deposit their dissertation, and sit their exams. Staff put on extra sessions, as they did at Kenyatta, to handle the now double load of students, or students have to wait a year to enter, as they do at Dar. Of course, some kinds of damage to the students are permanent. As Lubumbashi University closed again last year, Mulamba thought first of the students who had completed years of work, and might now be denied the chance to get a degree, since the department was so depleted. Everything is at risk, and not just from the usual individual threats—the disk is erased, money runs out, glandular fever strikes—but from historic changes. It affects the students knocking on the door of the university if they know that there might be no door out the other side. For instance, Mulamba has observed how students have tended to choose shorter, more practical, if less prestigious courses, that they will have a better chance of finishing in the coming years of unrest. For those who remain, English becomes more and more a short-term acquirement, and each written exercise becomes a hurdle rather than an opportunity for development. In the US, first-year composition students could believe they were learning for their third year (we do not know if they do). In Zaire now, that third year looks very far off indeed.

The apparent stability of US universities may help explain the difference in political focus in North American composition studies and in language studies in some other countries. There has been a debate in composition studies about whether composition courses should or should not take social change and cultural diversity as a topic.[17] To Greg's surprise, at first, this debate has not particularly interested Mary, Ndoloi, and Mulamba, partly because they take the involvement of the university in politics as a perhaps painful fact of its life, not as a link either to be strenuously asserted or equally strenuously denied.[18] Mary points out that a course stressing cultural diversity (Development Studies) is a part of the foundation year at Kenyatta, but it is seen as supporting the status quo. Ndoloi quotes national documents that define the political role of university education. Mulamba traces thought on *négritude* and the codification of four national languages in Zaire. In each case, what counts as radical for them seems to be different from what counts as radical in the North American debates. The educational ideal for them is not the pursuit of diversity and an active role for universities, but the pursuit of consensus and some new and as yet undefined sort of continuity.

THE LOCAL AND THE GLOBAL

As we four have discussed this paper, we have kept coming back to the word "importing" in our title. In earlier drafts we used the word "exporting," but that seemed to suggest that this flow of ideas is part of neocolonialism, the way that, for instance, the export of an examination system, or European ideas of research, has been considered part of colonialism. This is a familiar and important line of criticism of the transfer of educational ideas. Patricia Irvine and Nan Elsasser compare the importation of composition standards to the West Indies to the misguided application of inappropriate agricultural technologies.

> By importing a curriculum and applying it as if West Indian students had practised the forms of writing integral to a North American education, we contribute to confusion and lack of learning. To improve writing qualitatively at the college, we must . . . incorporate the social, economic, and political realities in bold, innovative curricula. (Irvine and Elsasser 318)

Gloria Paulik Sampson defends Chinese language teaching methods, involving memorization, focus on reading, and teacher-centered classrooms, against the "technocratic imperialism" of methods imported from North America. Mary has insisted, in similar terms, on the importance of taking local cultures into account in planning educational change (Muchiri).

There certainly are elements of neocolonialism in the educational systems of Kenya, Tanzania, and Zaire—for instance, the examination systems that are taken for granted. Even the Overseas Development Administration aid and British Council fellowships that took Mary, Ndoloi, and Mulamba to Britain are part of a larger strategy of development and trade links. For better *and* worse, their universities remain tied to the former imperial powers. Following this line of critique, North American institutions, including universities, step in with a new colonialism, as unidirectional and potentially inappropriate as the old. But the relation of methods from North American composition to these universities is more complex than this. Unlike the flow of British language teaching and testing methods, sponsored by the British Council, the flow of ideas from US universities is accidental, unsponsored, and erratic. It has the same dangers of inappropriate application in a new context, but not the same political associations. Nor can it really be compared to McDonalds or CNN or the World Bank, all powerful multinationals. What we need is not a colonial metaphor, as conventionally applied, but some way to go from the global circulation of writing research to the local contexts of writing.

North American and European academics may be struck each day by how institutions of knowledge become more and more global in their reach. This change is particularly striking in composition research, as it achieves academic respectability, but it is true to different degrees in all fields. Journals, conferences, publishers, and research projects are international, linked by e-mail, photocopies, faxes, and airlines. But this apparent globalization is deceptive. Everyday academic work is still overwhelmingly determined by its national setting. The funding, the geography, the politics, the national ideology determine daily concerns like hours, class size, assessment, careers. And access to that global network of contacts is by no means equally apportioned.

Let us say that Mary, at Kenyatta University, wanted to try to institute the kind of responses to students' essays urged in the composition literature.

What would she need? First of all, she would need a lot of money; there is no chance of such comments when each tutor has hundreds of students. She would need a course based on coursework instead of exams, and for that she would need a different relation of students to teachers, and a different university year. But she might need different students, as well, since those selected by a ruthless examination system may not be those most likely to benefit from comments intended to develop their own voices. She would need students confident enough in their English to bear comments on it that had nothing to do with its correctness. She would need somehow to be able to cut free from institutional hierarchies and ethnic divisions and regional origins and suspicions of bias, all of which she found in her research, and institute a kind of free trade zone in which these comments could be taken as one to one, teacher to student. She would need to know the student was coming back next week, next term, next year. She would need to know the university would still be there. She would need an ideology of opportunity and fairness to fall back on, to persuade people that this sort of education was characteristically Kenyan. And when she became discouraged, as she would, she would need to be able to turn to other writing researchers and teachers at the next CCCC, who would say she was doing the right thing. If Ndoloi wanted to introduce process pedagogy, or Mulamba to change the way students used references, or if Greg wanted to start freshman composition and placement exams in the UK, they might find in a similar way that they had to reconstruct a whole institution and culture.

One response by North American composition teachers to this experiment in transporting composition might be a sigh of relief, that their universities have composition classes of large but manageable size (not 500, as at Kenyatta), that they have access to research and libraries, that sequences of courses consider the preparation of students, that universities can remain open, that lecturers are not summarily arrested. That is true enough, but rather complacent. A more useful response to the uneven spread of composition research would be to see how much of the work is tied to the particular context of the US. When composition researchers make larger claims about academic knowledge and language, it needs to acknowledge these ties. The very diversity rightly celebrated in the composition literature may lead a teacher to forget that it is diversity joined in a peculiarly American way, within American institutions, in an American space. The teacher in New York or Los Angeles may look out over a classroom and think, "The whole world is here." It isn't.

If one grants the local origins of composition research, there are two kinds of messages that one might draw from this exercise in following composition research in other systems. One is that composition researchers and ELT teachers are reminded just how radical composition ideas can be, perhaps not in their own local settings, but transplanted into a setting with different assumptions. The assumptions about malleable writer identities in composition meet the rigidities of the European and colonial examination systems. The recognition of links *and* differences between academic and non-academic languages contrasts with the tendency of some EAP needs analyses to isolate and reify language. The insistence on the teacher as a link into a larger conversation challenges stereotypical roles of teachers confronting suspicious students in a hierarchical system. Composition researchers take a surprisingly long view of development, of students and of the university, that can be refreshing and sometimes astonishing in the scramble of teaching and learning in African universities. All that is for the good, at least in these new contexts.

Lest the composition researchers get too complacent, one should look for places where composition is difficult to transplant, and ask if these difficulties don't sometimes arise closer to home. We have mentioned the dull errorlessness of the prose, and wondered how it relates to similarly depressing prose in North American students, perhaps seeing a variety of causes, not all of them matters of laziness or lack of imagination. We have mentioned apparently absurd arguments from authority in essays, vague reliance on consensus, uncritical use of written sources, treatment of teachers as parents, invocation of religious belief, all of which can be dismissed as simply conformist, but all of which may be valued differently from other perspectives. North American teachers develop ways of dismissing some kinds of resistance to their reforming message as not worthy, while other kinds of resistance are to be promoted as progressive. Mary, Ndoloi, and Mulamba reconsider some of these distinctions.

As we said at the outset, we mean this essay only to open a discussion, one involving North Americans but also, we hope, writing teachers elsewhere. We can perhaps sum up our intervention with three questions for composition teachers and researchers. Imagine you could pack something of the world of composition, just enough to fit in a small box that would fit under an airline seat. It is not for foreign aid, or for trade, both of which can be exploitive; let us think of it as barter. What would you pack in this box; what is essential in the composition enterprise? That's the fun part. Now here comes the hard part: Where would you send it? And even harder: What would you expect to get in return?

A F T E R W O R D . . . .

We are pleased to see that papers making similar points were in press at the same time as ours. We stressed the importance of group practices in many university settings, such as the Mwakenya; Alistair Pennycook has taken up similar issues. We noted the practical and material difficulties of research in countries outside the circle of North American and European scholarship, such as those posed by the long-term civil unrest; Suresh Canarajah gives a poignant account of publication from Sri Lanka. We asked readers to imagine the teaching of writing in a context in which English was one choice, invested with specific meanings in Kenya, Tanzania, or Zaire. Tony Silva, Ilona Leki, and Joan Carson raise similar issues in relation to the teaching of English as a Second Language in the U.S.

Mary Muchiri notes that the situation we described in 1996, in terms of "the view of teachers as researchers," seems to be moving from bad to worse, due to many factors, especially the collapse of many African economies. Teachers, especially in private universities, have little time for research. Students are normally better in negotiating their terms, through group pressure, than teachers. Consequently, they are provided with facilities such as computer labs before the lecturers have even a limited access to them. Research funding is available to bring in outside speakers, but not for local researchers. African Nations and institutions only pay lip service to the importance of research. Though Kenya has plans to become a developed country by 2020, it has no funds set aside for research in 1998! Mary has managed to pursue some of her work on writing and study practices, in relation to the Christian goals of her university, but apparently our comments on the sense of isolation of scholars in Africa are even more true today.

Nshindi Mulamba notes that his approach to academic writing has changed considerably because of his Ph.D. on undergraduate dissertations and the Braddock Award; he has come to consider himself an "agent of change" in his university in central Zaire, a context where he feels no one else seems to care about the basics of composition. Few students there are socialized into academic writing, and few supervisors of dissertations are willing to embark on new training. They cling to their intuitions about academic writing, and their indirect means of training, because their jobs are secure, there are no incentives, they would lose face if they changed, and anyway the library is poor. He has a paper on the student viva (the oral examination of a thesis) in Les Annales de L'Université de Mbujimayi.

Greg and Mary have exchanged e-mails to prepare this comment, and Mulamba managed to send his comments by post. We were unable to contact Deoscorous B. Ndoloi, who has returned to the University of Dar es Salaam; we do know that one of his projects is a study of supervisors' written comments on Ph.D. dissertations.

—MARY N. MUCHIRI
Daystar University, Nairobi

—GREG MYERS
Lancaster University, U.K.

The Rhetorician as an Agent
of Social Change

ELLEN CUSHMAN

n his "Afterthoughts on Rhetoric and Pub-
lic Discourse," S. Michael Halloran finds that "the efforts of citizens to shape
the fate of their community . . . would surely have been of interest to American neoclassical rhetoricians of the late eighteenth and early nineteenth centuries" (2). Unfortunately, he sees an "apparent lack of interest in such 'Public Discourse' among new rhetoricians of late twentieth-century English
departments" (2). One way to increase our participation in public discourse
is to bridge the university and community through activism. Given the role
rhetoricians have historically played in the politics of their communities, I believe modern rhetoric and composition scholars can be agents of social
change outside the university.

Some critical theorists believe that the primary means of affecting social
change is to translate activism into liberatory classroom pedagogies. This
paper seeks to address other ways in which we can affect social change,
something more along the lines of civic participation. As Edward Schiappa
suggests, "pedagogy that enacts cultural critique is important but it is not
enough. . . . We should not allow ourselves the easy out of believing that
being 'political' in the classroom is a substitute for our direct civic participation" (22). I agree. I hope here to suggest ways we can empower people in
our communities, establish networks of reciprocity with them, and create solidarity with them. Using a self-reflexive rhetoric, I'll describe the limitations
of my own role as a participant observer in a predominately Black (their
term) neighborhood in a city in upstate New York. I hope to reveal a tentative model of civic participation in our neighborhoods which I believe illuminates some paradoxes in postmodern approaches to composition.*

---

*This paper is a multivoiced, self-reflexive look at our roles as rhetoricians. As
such, I hope to turn our work as scholars inside out, upside down, back in upon itself.
I've included many voices in this paper because this was the only way I seemed able

This essay was first published in *CCC,* Volume 47, Number 1, February 1996.

APPROACHING THE COMMUNITY

One of the most pressing reasons why composition scholars may not work in the community has to do with deeply rooted sociological distances between the two. Many universities sit in isolated relation to the communities in which they're located—isolated socially and sometimes physically as well. Rensselaer, for example, where I'm a fourth year aPhiD candidate[#], is isolated socially and physically from the community.

The Hudson borders Troy on the East, rolling hills on the West. Most of downtown developed along the river valley, while RPI expanded up one of these hills. People in the city generally call those associated with RPI "higher ups." Rensselaer students often call people in Troy "Troylets," "trash," or "low lifes." RPI was originally built closer to the city, beginning at the West edge of the valley, but for reasons too complicated to go into here, RPI expanded up the hill. The relationship between Rensselaer and Troy is best symbolized by the Approach, what used to be a monument of granite stairs, pillars, and decorative lights, but is now barely recognizable as a walkway.[1] (See Figure 1.)

The city gave the Approach to Rensselaer in 1907 as a sign of the mutually rewarding relationship between the two. Once an access way to the university on the hill, literally and figuratively, the stairway was pictured on many of the notebooks of students in the Troy City school district. Walk into

---

to capture the range of reactions I've had to the theories and practices of critical pedagogues and cultural studies theorists—from initial enthusiasm to disillusionment to frustration and anger. And so I've organized this paper as a hall of mirrors. The central image is the argument that rhetoricians can be agents of social change outside the university and a brief explanation of how this plays out in research. To create this image, I use a narrative voice to tell a story of possibility. The footnotes with various markers are the next set of mirrors and reveal more background for my argument. In these footnotes, I use a self-critical voice hoping that we will pause for a brief moment to examine our discourse. The numbered endnotes include the theorists I find most useful in reflecting my argument. Here I use an academic voice in a conscious effort to work within the system. Finally, we have the appendices. In these I don't want to cite specific authors because the onus to consider the ramifications of using critical discourse remains on all of our shoulders. Yours and mine. With these asides, I want to point to trends in the discourse I've heard at conferences and read in the work of many composition scholars. I've appended these, first, because they reflect the main argument by revealing my initial frustration and, many times, anger, which prompt this paper; and, second, because they're written from this anger, I risk being dismissed as inflammatory, a risk I hope to reduce by making them an aside; third, these asides have significant personal value to me. They're the best translation of my street-tough, face-breaking, fight-picking voice that I can manage for an academic audience. Given this activist research, my white trash history, and being only one pay check away from returning to the streets, I'm never very far from that voice, that way of being, no matter how many books, computers, students, and teachers I sit in front of.

[#]An aphid is a type of louse. So an aPHiD brings the "lo" together with "use." The plural of louse is lice. When I graduate, I'll have a License to create knowledge from the people I study. Do da. Do da.

FIGURE 1   View of "The Hill" and the Approach in the early 1900s.

RPI Archives.

any diner in the city and folks can remember the Approach pictured on their notebooks when they were growing up. Even in the late 1950s, students and city officials worked together to maintain this connection as part of a "civic betterment project." (See Figure 2.)

Unfortunately, the Approach fell into disrepair during the early 1970s as a result of disagreements between the city and university about who should have responsibility for maintenance. Now angry graffiti, missing stairs, and overgrowth symbolize the tattered relationship between the city and RPI. (See Figure 3.) Young fraternity boys are rumored to use the Approach for initiation during rush week, and certain ski club members have skied down the Approach as a testament to their ability and courage. While Troy natives look at the Approach in fury and disgust, the city and RPI continue to negotiate over its upkeep and hopeful repair.

I spend time describing this symbol of the relationship between the university and the city because I don't think this relationship is an isolated example of the sociological distance between the university and the community. It's precisely this distance that seems to be a primary factor in prohibiting scholars from Approaching people outside the university. Every day, we reproduce this distance so long as a select few gain entrance to universities, so long as we differentiate between experts and novices, and so long as we value certain types of knowledge we can capitalize on through specialization.[2] This history of professionalization might be one reason academics have so easily turned away from the democratic project that education serves to ensure—civic participation by well-rounded individuals.[3]

FIGURE 2   Rensselaer students clean up the Approach in 1959.

RPI Archives.

Malea Powell, an Eastern Miami and Shawnee Indian, suggests that the theorizing of academics necessitates a distance from the daily living of people outside academe, particularly those people we study. Although she's found "a location for healing in theory," she also knows these theories are used to "civilize unruly topics," with a similar assumption of manifest destiny that colonists use(d) to civilize unruly Native Americans. "Central to telling the 'American' story is the settlers' vision of the frontier, a frontier that is 'wilderness,' empty of all 'civilized' life." In order to colonize, the

FIGURE 3   The Approach in 1995.

Photo by Chris Boese.

settlers denied the very existence of Turtle Island's original people. Powell sees that

> this denial, this un-seeing . . . characterizes our "American" tale. For the colonizers it was a necessary un-seeing; material Indian "bodies" were simply not seen . . . the mutilations, rapes, and murders that made up 'the discovery' and 'manifest destiny' were also simply not seen. Un-seeing Indians gave (and still gives) Euroamericans a critical distance from materiality and responsibility, a displacement that is culturally valued and marked as "objectivity."

Scholars reproduce this colonizing ideology when we maintain a distance from people. In search of an area of interest, we look to stake our claim over a topic, or in Powell's words, "define a piece of 'unoccupied' scholarly territory . . . which will become our own scholarly homestead." If the scholarly territory happens to be occupied by other scholarly endeavors, our job demands that we show how these original scholars fail to use their territory well, thereby giving us manifest justification for removing their theories from the territory through expansion, co-option, or complete dismissal. In some fundamental ways, we shirk our civil responsibility and always already enact violence under the guise of objective distance, and the thin veil of 'creating' knowledge.

Powell (and I) "don't mean to disable scholarly work here." But I believe that in doing our scholarly work, we should take social responsibility for the people from and with whom we come to understand a topic. I'm echoing Freire who shows that when we theorize about the oppressed, we must do "authentic thinking, thinking that is concerned about *reality*, does not take place in ivory tower isolation, but only in communication" (64). Once we leave the classroom, we're again in ivory tower isolation, unless we actively seek our students in other contexts—particularly the community context.

Activism begins with a commitment to breaking down the sociological barriers between universities and communities. And if we see ourselves as both civic participants and as preparing students for greater civic participation, then activism becomes a means to well defined end for Approaching the community. Recent work by Bruce Herzberg reveals one model for how rhetoricians can enter into the community. His thoughtful article on "Community Service and Critical Teaching" shows how he manages to link his writing courses with community agencies.

> The effort to reach into the composition class with a curriculum aimed at democracy and social justice is an attempt to make schools function . . . as radically democratic institutions, with the goal not only of making individual students more successful, but also of making better citizens, citizens in the strongest sense of those who take responsibility for communal welfare. (317)

I'm not asking for composition teachers to march into the homes, churches, community centers, and schools of their community. I'm not asking for us to become social workers either. I am asking for a deeper consideration of the civic purpose of our *positions* in the academy, or what we do with our knowledge, for whom, and by what means. I am asking for a shift in our critical focus away from our own navels, Madonna, and cereal boxes to the ways in which we can begin to locate ourselves within the democratic process of everyday teaching and learning in our neighborhoods. For the remainder of this paper, let me offer some brief considerations of what such activism might ideally entail, as well as some practical limitations of trying to live up to this ideal. For these considerations, I draw upon my own activist research in a primarily African-American inner city.

SHORT CHANGED

Most current accounts of activism in cultural studies don't do justice to social change taking place in day-to-day interactions. I think activism can lead to social change, but not when it's solely measured on the scale of collective action, or sweeping social upheavals. (See the appendix on "Slippery Discourse.") Rather, we need to take into our accounts of social change the ways in which people use language and literacy to challenge and alter the circumstances of daily life. In these particulars of daily living, people can throw off the burdens placed upon them by someone else's onerous behavior. In other words, social change can take place in daily interactions when the regular flow of events is objectified, reflected upon, and altered. Daily interactions follow regular patterns of behavior, what sociologist Anthony Giddens terms "routinization." These interactions result from every individual re-enacting the social structures that underpin behaviors. Giddens' notion of the "duality of structure" captures the ways in which individuals' behaviors manifest overarching social structures. When the routine flow of events is impeded or upset, we have an example of deroutinization—of what can be the first steps to social change on microlevels of interaction. I've found that people disrupt the status quo of their lives with language and literacy and that the researcher, when invited to do so, can contribute resources to this end.

For instance, Raejone, a 24-year-old mother of two, applied to a local university. As she composed her application essay, I offered some tutoring and access to Rensselaer computers. This was the first time she had applied to college. In another example, Lucy Cadens moved to a safer, suburban apartment complex. With my (and others') letters of recommendation, she obtained decent housing that accepts her Section 8. To facilitate the process of transferring her social services from one county to another, she asked me to complete a letter of certification which stated how many children she has in her new apartment. This is the first time Lucy has lived outside of the inner city. These precedents mark the very places where people deroutinize the status quo of wider society, together, during activist research.[4] Over the course of two and a half years of research, these people and I have worked together during numerous literacy events to create possibilities, the promising, if minute, differences in opportunity: together we've written resumes, job applications, college applications, and dialogic journals; when asked to do so, I've written recommendations to landlords, courts, potential employers, admissions counselors, and DSS representatives; one teen and I co-directed a literacy program that allowed six children to read and write about issues important to them and that united resources from Rensselaer, Russell Sage College, the public library, and two philanthropic organizations. Since together we unite resources and grease the mechanisms of wider society institutions, all of these literacy acts carve possibilities from the routine ways these institutions, agencies, courts, and universities have historically worked in constraining ways.

I need to emphasize the difference between missionary activism, which introduces certain literacies to promote an ideology, and scholarly activism, which facilitates the literate activities that *already* take place in the community. For example, the Cadens' household had become too crowded with extended family. Lucy's daughter, Raejone, and her two children decided to seek housing from the philanthropic organization that rented to Raejone's mother. This agency had many units available and a short waiting list, but as the months passed, Raejone realized that her name never moved up the list. Her sisters also applied for housing but encountered similar foot dragging. Raejone found housing through a private landlord and then wrote a letter to this housing agency. In it she protested the inadequate treatment she received. Raejone and the directors of this housing program met to discuss the letter, and since then, Raejone's sisters have been offered housing by this agency. Raejone's letter caused the people who were simply reproducing their typical behavior to pause and consider the impact of their actions. In effect, the people in this housing program have altered the ways in which they treat Raejone and her family. Raejone, without any of my assistance, potently enacts her agency in order to challenge the routine foot dragging she faced.

Often this type of social change would be overlooked or underestimated with the emancipatory theories we currently use. Those who choose to say resistance only counts when it takes the form of overt and collective political action might describe us as using nothing more than coping devices with this literacy. Choosing to see this interaction in isolation, they may be correct; however, Scott reminds us that thousands of such "'petty' acts of resistance have dramatic economical and political effects" (*Domination* 192). These daily verbal and literate interactions mark the very places where composition teachers can begin to look for the impact of our critical pedagogy and activism, both in the classroom and when we approach the community.[5]

RED ROBIN HOODS

If we view social change at a micro level of interaction, we can begin to see where activism fits into the particulars of daily living. Activism means accepting a civic duty to empower people with our positions, a type of leftist stealing from the rich to give to the poor. To empower, as I use it, means: (a) to enable someone to achieve a goal by providing resources for them;

(b) to facilitate actions—particularly those associated with language and literacy; (c) to lend our power or status to forward people's achievement. Often we are in a position to provide the luxuries of literacy for people. Since we're surrounded with the tools for literacy all day long, we often take for granted the luxury of the time and space needed for our literacy events. We schedule our work days around papers we read and write; our research is often carried out in libraries—clean, well lit, with cubicles and desks to use as we silently mine books for information;* and we return to our homes or offices to trace out an idea with pen and paper or at the keyboard. Our time is devoted to reading and writing with spaces and institutional resources often provided for us. But when we approach the community, often we will be forced "to recall the material conditions of writing," to remember that "we do confront such complex material questions as how to provide equality of access to computers for word processing" (Gere 87).

The reading and writing used for individual development in many communities is a valued, scarce, and difficult endeavor. We may say to ourselves that reading and writing is more important than some daily worries, such as cleaning, taking care of children and grandparents, and cooking, but often one of the primary ways people build a good name for themselves outside of work is to be solid parents, providers, doers. Mike Rose reminds us in *Lives on the Boundary* as he describes Lucia, a returning student and single mother, and notes "how many pieces had to fall in place each day for her to be a student. . . . Only if those pieces dropped in smooth alignment could her full attention shift to" the challenges of literacy for her own development (185). In *All Our Kin*, Carol Stack also describes similar domestic demands which must take priority over time for oneself in order for people to maintain their social networks of reciprocity. In other words, before people can devote their time to reading and writing to improve themselves, their social and family duties must be in place. Many women in the neighborhood in which I am immersed say they "wish there were more than 24 hours in a day," or they qualify their literate goals with, "if I had time, I could study that driver's manual." Yet, for a researcher, seeing the need for time is only half of the equation; the other half is doing something about those needs.

Empowering people in part enables them to achieve a goal by providing resources for them. Since it's difficult for many of these women to clear time alone while they're at home, we often schedule one or two hours to be together during the week when they know they won't be missed. We've spent time in places where we have many literate resources at our disposal including bookstores, libraries, my apartment (not far from this neighborhood), as well as the Rensselaer computer labs and Writing Center. During these times we've cleared together, we've studied driver's manuals, discussed books, gone through the college application process, as well as worked on papers,

---

*We mine data in our scholarly homeplots looking for a gem of an idea others will value.

resumes and letters they wanted to write. Because we have worked together, these people who want time away from the neighborhood have achieved their literate goals.

Empowerment also happens when we facilitate people's oral and literate language use as well as lend our status for their achievement. The people in this neighborhood recognize the prestige of the language resources and social status I bring from Rensselaer and ask for assistance in a number of their language use activities.[+] One woman had just received an eviction notice and asked me to "help [her] get a new place." She asked if we could practice mock conversations she might have with landlords over the phone. She thought this practice would "help [her] sound respectable, you know, white." As we practiced in her dining room, she wrote what we said on the back of a Chinese take-out menu for future reference. Once she set appointments to see an apartment, she contacted me so we could view the apartments together because "having you with me will make me seem respectable, you being from RPI and all." She differentiates between the social languages we speak and she wants to practice these languages with me.[6] She also identifies one way she can use my position for her own ends. She eventually got an apartment and thanked me for what she saw as my contribution. (See the appendix on "False Consciousness.") I've found that the luxury of literacy can easily be transferred from the university to our neighborhoods when we expand the scope of our scholarly activities to include activism. While empowerment may seem one-sided, as though the scholar has a long arm of emancipating power, the people in communities can empower us through reciprocity.

MUCH OBLIGED

The terms governing the give-and-take (reciprocity) of involvement in the community need to be openly and consciously negotiated by everyone participating in activist research. As Bourdieu terms it, reciprocity describes a gift-giving and receiving behavior which can produce a mode of domination if the gift is not returned. "A gift that is not returned can become a debt, a lasting obligation" (126). Depending on the terms of the exchange, this obligation can either be in the form of a monetary debt, which imposes "overtly economic obligations by the usurer," or, in the form of an ethical debt, which produces "moral obligations and emotional attachments created and maintained by the generous gift, in short, overt violence or symbolic violence" (126). Reciprocity in exchange networks quickly produces power relations where the likelihood of oppression depends upon the terms of the giving and receiving.

[+]In addition to language resources, I make available many of my material resources: clothes, small amounts of money, food, and rides to the doctor, stores, and DSS offices.

While Bourdieu depicts reciprocity networks by studying the bonds maintained in relations between kin-people and tribal chiefs, this notion of reciprocity applies to the ways in which we enter into the community. With an idea of how exchanges create and maintain oppressive structures, activists can pay conscious attention to the power structures produced and maintained during their interactions with others outside of the university. Reciprocity includes an open and conscious negotiation of the power structures reproduced during the give-and-take interactions of the people involved on both sides of the relationship. A theory of reciprocity, then, frames this activist agenda with a self-critical, conscious navigation of this intervention.

Herzberg's work exemplifies reciprocity well when interpreted in terms of the give-and-take relationship between the researcher and community. Through a "service-learning program," students at Bentley became adult literacy tutors at a shelter in Boston and wrote about their experiences in Herzberg's composition classroom. At the outset, the rules were established for what types of information could be exchanged between the tutor and learners. The students "were not allowed (by the wise rules of the shelter and good sense) to quiz their learners on their personal lives and histories" (315). Before these tutorial sessions began, the boundaries for exchange of information were set. Students tutored, wrote, and received college credit; Herzberg gave his time and energy, which eventually earned him a spot in this journal; and although this article does not make clear what the people in the shelter received and gave from this involvement, he indicates "the tutoring, as best [as they] could determine, appeared to be productive for the learners at the shelter" (316). From his work, we begin to see how bridging the university and community establishes give-and-take relationships that must be openly and carefully navigated.

It may seem that the activist research I described in the previous section is one-sided, that I may sound like a self-aggrandizing liberator of oppressed masses. But this just isn't the case, since these people empower me in many ways. Referring back to my original definition of empowerment, they've enabled me to achieve a primary goal in my life: getting my PhD. They've let me photocopy their letters, personal journals, essays, and applications. They've granted me interviews and allowed me to listen to their interactions with social workers, admissions counselors, and DSS representatives. They've told me stories and given me the history of this area through their eyes. They've fed me, included me in their family gatherings for birthdays and holidays, and have invited me to their parties and cook outs. They've read my papers and made suggestions; they listened to my theories and challenged them when I was off mark. (See the appendix on "In Ivory Towers, We Overlook.") As I write my dissertation, they add, clarify and question. In some very important ways, we collaborate in this research. In fact, the two women whose writing I refer to most frequently in this article signed a release form so that you may read about them today. To quote from the *CCC* "consent-to-reprint" forms, Raejone and Lucy understood that they "will receive no compensation" for their work and that they "assign publishing rights for the contribution to NCTE, including all copyrights." They have given me the right to represent them to you and have facilitated my work in doing so. They've also lent me their status. They've legitimized my presence in their neighborhood, in masque, and in some institutions simply by associating with me. Through reciprocity, they've enabled me to come closer to achieving my goal every day; they've facilitated my actions; and they've lent me their status.

THE ACCESS IN PRAXIS

Often we don't have to look far to find access routes to people outside of the university. Any kind of identification we may have with people in our communities, to some extent, acts as a point of commonality where our perspectives overlap, despite our different positions. These points of convergence, I think, come closest to Freire's notion of solidarity. Solidarity manifests itself when there are common threads of identity between the student and teacher. To achieve empowerment through critical consciousness, the teacher "must be a partner of the students in his relations with them" (62). A partnership connotes people working together toward common goals. Freire finds "one must seek to live with others in solidarity . . . [and] solidarity requires true communication" (63). I believe that access to people with whom we identify is the initial building block for the solidarity and communication needed in activism.

Many access routes into the community have been established by philanthropic organizations, churches, community centers, and businesses. Before an access route is chosen, though, significant research needs to be done to see how the community developed, what types of contributions are needed, and whether or not there's precedent for the work proposed. After I spoke with representatives in many philanthropic and social service agencies, I volunteered in a bridge program between Rensselaer and a community center. Once there, I proposed a summer literacy program, but when this was over, I soon realized that I needed to reposition myself in the community. When I stopped volunteering, the women in this community found it easier to identify with me as a person and not as an organizational member.

Although I'm white, the women in this neighborhood and I identify with each other in many ways: we're no strangers to welfare offices, cockroaches, and empty refrigerators. We've held our chins out and heads up when we haven't had enough food stamps at the check out line. We've made poor (and good) choices in men and have purple and pink scars to prove it. We know enough to take out our earrings before we fight. We know abuses and disorders and the anonymous places people turn to for them. Since many of these people came from the Carolinas, and since my great-great-grand parents were in the Trail of Tears, we know why, on a crisp January day, a cardinal in a pine tree gives us hope.

Once we locate an access route into the community, we can begin the long process of self disclosure and listening from which we can begin to identify with each other. For Freire, communication is the main way to achieve this identification: "Through dialogue, the teacher-of-the-students and the students-of-the-teacher cease to exist and a new term emerges: teacher-student with students-teachers. The teacher is no longer the-one-who-teaches, but one who himself is taught in dialogue with the students, who in turn while being taught also teach" (67). Through communication, the exchange of questioning and asserting, we come to identify with each other and challenge the bases for our differences.

While this type of dialogue can take place in the classroom, the very power structure of the university makes it difficult to establish and maintain dialogue and solidarity. There's only so much we can get to know about our students within the sociological confines of the academic composition classroom. (See the appendix on "Freired Not.") Yet when we approach the community, we maneuver around the sociological obstacles that hinder us in the classroom from communicating with our students in ways that show our identification with them. Said another way, activism starts with some kind of identification with people outside of the university, an identification that often can flourish in a context where both the scholar and people together assess and redraw lines of power structures between them.

No Mother Teresas Here

With the initial components of activism roughed out this way, I need to provide some important caveats. Let me show a few of the limitations of this kind of praxis with reference to shortcomings and mishaps in my own ethnographic fieldwork. My first concern in folding open activism this way is that these principles will be read as altruistic, when in my experience activism establishes an interdependency. Activism can't be altruistic because we have to be in a position to participate in our communities. The very same position as scholar which distances us from the community also invests us with resources we can make available to others. And we need these luxuries in order to be stable enough to give our time, knowledge, and resources. This means we must work very hard in the academy with the support of our community in order to garner the status and resources that we then return to the community.

I don't mean to simplify the process of gaining luxury here because I recognize that becoming an agent of social change in our neighborhoods requires time and energy. As a funded graduate student, I'm particularly fortunate to have the time and money to do this activist research. My teaching assistantship requires an average of twenty hours of work per week, and since I'm through with course work, I'm only on campus when I'm teaching, writing on the computers, or researching in the library. While I know my professors have 3/2 and 3/3 course loads, I've heard of other professors who have 5/5 course loads and hundreds of students every semester.[7] Yet, at the risk of sounding pollyannic, we've already seen precedents for the type of scholarly civic participation I suggest. Perhaps through the reciprocity of activism, we might fold together our scholarly and civic duties.

Since the relationship established in activism centers upon reciprocity, an interdependency emerges. One of the ways in which we've maintained a mutually empowering relationship is through open and careful navigation of the reciprocity we've established. While this reciprocity may sound easy to maintain, many times requests have to be turned down. I've asked to record certain people and have been refused; I've also asked for examples of certain types of writing people didn't feel comfortable giving me, so I went without. Likewise, one person asked me to co-sign on a car loan (which I couldn't); and another person asked me to sign over any royalties I receive from a possible book to the families on the block (which I'm still considering). Everyone in this research realizes what we stand to gain from the work, and reciprocity helps prevent the work from becoming altruistic.

If we ignore the give-and-take established in activist research and instead choose to paint ourselves in the bright colors of benevolent liberators, we risk becoming what Macedo so delicately terms "literacy and poverty pimps" (xv). When we adopt a fashionable theory of emancipatory pedagogy and activism without considering the structural constraints imposed by reciprocity, we capitalize on others' daily living without giving any of these benefits in return. But here's the paradox—we need to make activism part of our research and teaching, so that we can make a living in the university. How else will we be able to give in equal amount to what we take?

ACCESSIVE FORCE

The degree to which we gain entrance into the daily lives of people outside the university in some measure depends upon who we are. The boundaries of our access must be negotiated with the people. Often, leftist posing assumes a here-I-am-to-save-the-day air, takes for granted immediate and complete entrance into a community, presumes an undeniably forceful presence. In my own work, I've overstepped the boundaries of my access working under similar assumptions. Six months into this research on a summer afternoon, I joined a large group of teens and adults playing cards, sipping beer, and talking on a front stoop. I was dealt into a game of 21 and listened to gossip and news. Lucy Cadens had a boyfriend (Anthony) who was seated in one of the folding chairs at the end of the stoop. Lucy had been gone for a few minutes, and he and I chatted until it was my turn to deal.

Later that day, Lucy called me away from the stoop and asked, "You want to tell me about Anthony?" I thought she was referring to a complaint a parent made to the center staff about him, and told her I wasn't at liberty to talk about it. She looked confused and asked me if I was talking to him that day. I told her of what I thought was an innocent conversation about gambling in Atlantic City. "They told me he was fishing with you," she said with her hands on her hips. I was shocked; what I thought was a simple conversation was actually him flirting with me. I told Lucy that I would keep a much safer distance from him and asked if she thought I should make that a unilateral decision about interacting with men in the neighborhood. She said I should be careful about who I talked to and about what, but that I could be polite to them. Since then, I've negotiated this boundary much more carefully and have gathered the majority of my notes from the children and women of the neighborhood. In this way, the access I presumed I had was fundamentally limited along gender lines. The lines of access must be charted, recharted, and respected in activist research. I had overstepped a boundary, albeit unintentionally, and realized my liberal presumption of unlimited access was pompous and shortsighted.

THE BEST LAID APPROACHES

Civic participation requires careful understandings of how our position will work, or not, within the given organizations of people. As mentioned earlier, I originally gained access to this neighborhood as a literacy volunteer and researcher through a bridge program between Rensselaer and the neighborhood center located in the heart of this community. As a volunteer, the social workers expected that I follow the same rules of conduct that they were institutionally bound to follow. However, I soon realized that the roles of researcher and volunteer contradict each other in important ways.

As a volunteer, a team player, I was expected to tell the social workers any details I might be privy to which concerned the private lives of the people in this neighborhood. I often visited the homes and sat on the stoops with people when the social workers were bound to stay in the center—their liability insurance did not cover them if something happened to them outside the center. As a researcher, though, I needed to walk between both worlds, the home and community center, but I was bound to the ethics of participant observation which dictate I cannot reveal information about my informants. Unfortunately, the center staff felt threatened by my peculiar position and worried that I would jeopardize their standing within the community with the information I had about the workings of their institution. As a result, they asked me to discontinue my volunteer work with them.

When we first consider bridging with communities, especially if we hope to do research at the same time, we must chart the internal workings of the institutions in order to see the ways we might, or might not, fit in. I initially believed I could simply volunteer and do research—"surely people will welcome the time and resources I offer." Here I was guilty of leftist posing disguised as philanthropy. Because I assumed this, I didn't negotiate my role within this organization well at all.

Even with these limitations, we can begin to participate in our communities despite (to spite) the sociological distances we must cross. Cultural studies models of empowerment and critical pedagogues are derelict in their civic duties by not including an expanded version of activism. Through activism, we've taken the first, tentative steps toward social change outside of the social confines of the university classroom. Finally, we not only fill a civic responsibility with activism, but also inform our teaching and theories with the perspectives of people outside the university. We begin to see just how deficient our estimations of our students are when we immerse ourselves and contribute to their everyday literacy and hidden belief systems.

The roads into the communities aren't paved with yellow bricks and sometimes may seem unapproachable, but access can generally be gained with observation and informal interviews to see who is already in the neighborhood and how they got there. Along the way relationships need to be navigated openly and consciously with close attention paid to boundaries and limitations in our access and intervention. Of course, I'm ignoring one potential means of access into the community—our students. But then, this assumes that we have solid enough relations with them to be able to follow them beyond the moat surrounding the ivory tower.

• • •

APPENDICES

Slippery Discourse

Many researchers believe that they can promote *social change* and *empower* students through critical literacy and emancipatory pedagogy. Yet we often hear the terms *social change* and *empowerment* used as though the nature of their outcomes is clearly established and reflected upon. This slippery discourse leads us to believe that we're all after the same ends: "enfranchising outsiders," having "social impact," creating a more "just society," offering a "liberating ideology," honing students' "awareness and critical consciousness," challenging "the oppressive system," "encouraging resistance," and of course, "interrogating dominate hegemony."[†] Just how these end products of critical pedagogy lead to social change and empowerment isn't clear to me from these discussions. In fact, some scholars make no distinctions between social *change* and *empowerment,* as though to empower is to liberate, and to liberate is to produce social change.[8] Underpinning this slippery discourse is an equally slick assumption—*social change* and *empowerment* lead to some kind of collective action or resistance involving the masses of people we teach.[9] When we view the impact of critical pedagogy from these grand levels, though, we miss the particular ways in which our teaching and research might contribute to students' abilities to take up their civic responsibilities once they leave our classrooms. We need a theory of social change and empowerment that captures the complex ways power is negotiated at micro levels of interaction between people, which would allow us to better characterize the impact of our work. With such a theory, we're less likely to paint ourselves as great "liberators of oppressed masses."

[†]These trends in discourse I culled from many of the collected essays in *Composition and Resistance*. Since these discourses often make one think of saviors, the footnote marker seems particularly apt.

False Consciousness

Many critical theorists portray themselves as brokers of emancipatory power, a stance that garners them status at the expense of students. One way to make a position for themselves in the academy is to diagnose their students as having "false consciousness." Once labeled as having "false consciousness," students can be easily dismissed and diminished by critical theory.[10] Yet, the many scholars who do immerse themselves into the daily living of people find, predictably, hidden ideologies—belief systems that contain numerous, clever ways to identify and criticize onerous behavior.[11] In some fundamental sense, the discursive posturing we so frequently hear would not be able to legitimize itself, if it didn't diminish others in its wake. The label of false consciousness, then, reveals more about the speaker's limited access to students and communities, than it reveals about the level of people's critical abilities. If cultural studies theorists were to visit the homes and streets of the people attending their classes, they would likely hear critiques of the dominating sociological forces.[12] Therein we see the fundamental problem in building our models of cultural studies: we're sociologically distanced from the cultures we study.

In Ivory Towers, We Overlook

When we fail to consider the perspectives of people outside of the academy, we overlook valuable contributions to our theory building. Without a praxis that moves between community and university, we risk not only underestimating our students' pre-existing critical consciousness, but we also risk reproducing the hegemonic barriers separating the university from the community. That is, we become guilty of applying our theories from the sociological "top-down," instead of informing our theories from the "bottom-up." In fact, it appears many value the idea more than the people, a value that bolsters the sociological distance of the university from the community. I've even read arguments *supporting* the social isolation of theorists in the academy from people in communities. In other words, we exclude many of the people we're trying to empower for the sake of positing (what we sure as hell hope will be) liberating ideas. The flaw in this logic seems so obvious: How can we study ideologies, hegemonies, power structures, and the effects of discursive practices when we overlook community discursive dispositions—the place where these language practices are first inculcated, generated and consequently reproduced in the social habitus?[13] Thus, many postmodern theorists remain tucked within their libraries and don't engage the very people they hope to help. They will send their theories down to the people and engage each other in postmodern conversations (over pomo tea perhaps) in their postmodern universities.

Freired Not

When we begin to turn cultural studies in on itself in a self-reflexive manner, we see its limiting assumptions and paradoxical stances as it's applied to composition studies. And this is indeed a shame, because the political and sociological theories it employs are very useful in expanding our roles as rhetoricians to include more perspectives from the margins. In the opening of *Pedagogy of the Oppressed,* Freire evaluates the oppressors in society: "To affirm that men are persons and persons should be free, and yet, to do nothing tangible to make this affirmation a reality, is a farce" (35). What he means by tangible is left up to interpretation; I suggest he means activism.[14] If we let *tangible* be synonymous with activism, then to what extent is promoting critical consciousness in our classrooms "activist"? My sense is that we're not doing enough because we're acting within the role of the teacher that has been perpetuated by the institution, and thus keeps us from breaking down the barriers between the university and community. In fact, many critical pedagogues have betrayed their activist agenda in their classrooms by characterizing their students as "dull," "numb," "dumbly silent," "unreflective," "yearning" and/or "resentful."[∞] They place themselves in the oppressive position by relegating students to the category of the "unfortunates." Pedagogues are only two letters shy of becoming demagogues. About these characterizations, Freire might say: "No pedagogy that is truly liberating can remain distant from the oppressed by treating them as unfortunates" (39). What these researchers fail to remember is that the students they teach are in a prime position for critical reflection precisely because they are disenfranchised: "Who are better prepared," Freire asks, "than the oppressed to understand the terrible significance of an oppressive society?" (29).

AFTERWORD . . . .

Risks. When writers take them, they need to be well aware of possible ramifications. In some fundamental sense, I wrote "Rhetorician as an Agent of Social Change" by holding at bay those nagging voices that kept warning me about the risks I was taking: "Do you want to self-disclose in this multi-voiced way? Shouldn't you try to write out the street talk? Am I playing too much with ideas people hold dear?" I suspect that other winners of the Braddock have tried to hush these nagging voices, the voices that ask you to separate what you want to say from what you should say.

Without risks—and the imagination and passion that infuse them— knowledge advances slowly indeed. The articles that garner this award venture into areas seemingly familiar, taken-for-granted even, and then complicate, revise, deepen, or broaden in some way what we think we know. Writing this piece

---

[∞]As found in the popular collection of essays, *Contending with Words.*

as a graduate student, I never would have flattered myself into believing it would be published, let alone receive a Braddock. I say this not out of false modesty, but rather from a keen sense that this piece shows some recklessness, the kind of venturing that scares people, rattles their cages a bit. It took shape from a deep seated need to do something with my scholarship, to go beyond the university classroom, to remember where I've come from. This article helped me articulate my role in the academy in ways that do justice to my sense of self and community. Rah. But it also, so I've been told, may have cost me a few jobs. Boo.

My hope remains that some readers enjoyed the edge of the piece. I hope too that it's helped scholars reconceptualize, maybe even relocate, their work in a broader public realm.

—ELLEN CUSHMAN
University of California, Berkeley

Moments of Argument: Agonistic Inquiry and Confrontational Cooperation

DENNIS A. LYNCH, DIANA GEORGE, AND MARILYN M. COOPER

riting teachers have been teaching argument for decades. As a profession, we have taken generations of students through the laws of logic, the etiquette of dispute, and the lessons of preparedness only to receive in return the same stale and flat arguments on the big issues: abortion rights, gun control, affirmative action, and others just as large and just as canned. In their writings, our students fall easily into one of two camps: for or against. They cling to their original positions as if those were sacred to home, country, and spiritual identity. Too frequently absent from these debates is any real knowledge of the issue at hand as anything more than a pointless argument among people who do not care very much about the outcome—except that it is always better, in the classroom as in many other arenas, to be on the winning rather than the losing side.

We don't blame our students. Schooled, as so many of us are lately, on the heated but shallow public debates raging on such television programs as *Firing Line* and *Crossfire,* or the broadside attacks of Rush Limbaugh, or even the sleepy This-Side-Then-That-Side interviews of *MacNeil Lehrer Newshour,* our students merely follow their models. Students have learned to argue vigorously and even angrily, but not think about alternatives, or listen to each other, or determine how their position may affect others, or see complexities, or reconsider the position they began with, or even to make new connections across a range of possible disagreements. Louis Menand points out that "[o]ne of the techniques we've perfected for screaming at one another—as the linguist Deborah Tannen has recently been complaining—is to divide every discussion, 'Crossfire'-style, into two, and only two, diametrically opposed positions, and to have the representatives of each side blast away at each other single-mindedly until interrupted by a commercial" (76). Hardly a style that will generate new, productive lines of action.

Iris Marion Young locates one source of this pattern of public discourse in what she calls interest-group pluralism. All debates over public policy in

This essay was first published in *CCC,* Volume 48, Number 1, February 1997.

our society, she argues, are reduced to debates over the distribution of wealth, income, and material goods, and interest groups are formed to ensure that particular interests get their fair share. "Public policy dispute is only a competition among claims, and 'winning' depends on getting others on your side" (72). This distributive paradigm forces even arguments for ending nonmaterially based oppression and dominance to look like arguments to attain the selfish desires of a particular interest group. Thus, for example, arguments for affirmative action programs appear not as attempts to change unconscious stereotypes that underlie biased hiring practices but as attempts to get more jobs for minorities. Young concludes, "This process that collapses normative claims to justice into selfish claims of desire lacks the element of public deliberation that is a hallmark of the political. A politicized public resolves disagreement and makes decisions by listening to one another's claims and reasons, offering questions and objections, and putting forth new formulations and proposals, until a decision can be reached" (72–73).

What we want to work out in this essay is a way of understanding and teaching argument that prepares students to participate in serious deliberations on issues that face all of us every day. It sometimes seems, in recent arguments over argument, that we must choose between two contrasting styles of argument, competitive or collaborative, but such a decision is unnecessarily abstract and ignores the historical development of thought about argument and its role in social democratic processes. Throughout most of this century, as Andrea Lunsford and Lisa Ede argue (39), we have steadily moved away from argumentation as competition and contest. Since I. A. Richards defined rhetoric as the study of misunderstanding (thereby bringing rhetoric closer to hermeneutics), the prevailing sentiment has been in favor of a more cooperative conception of rhetoric. The ultimate aim of rhetoric should be communication, not persuasion, we are told. And later, the idea that rhetoric is epistemic and the correlate notions of rhetoric as inquiry and of writing to learn have continued the same general effort to expand rhetoric's horizons while diminishing or eliminating altogether the nasty clash of individual intentions that marks much traditional rhetorical practice and its theory.

More recently, though, some rhetoricians have begun to suspect that the whole point of argumentation is being lost in our talk about cooperation and collaboration, that we are losing the value of challenging, opposing, and resisting "the interplay of social, cultural and historical forces" that structure our lives (Bizzell, *Discourse* 284). Susan Jarratt, for example, calls for composition instructors to rethink their objections to agonistic rhetoric and conflict-based pedagogy. She acknowledges that, at this historical juncture, those who advocate a "nurturing, nonconflictual composition classroom" may feel uneasy with her suggestion ("Feminism" 120). Indeed, as bell hooks points out (*Talking Back* 53), students may not leave the class feeling all that comfortable, either. Nevertheless, Jarratt and others (among them Bizzell, Bauer, Berlin, and Fitts and France) continue to argue that teachers should take a stronger, less nurturing, and more confrontational role in the classroom—especially if the aim is to prepare students to take action in a bureaucratized world that resists change.

Peter Elbow has argued that we neutralize potential hostility by emphasizing the believing game over the doubting game. While this position encourages students to listen to each other and to think about alternatives, Jarratt points out that it also leaves unexamined the social origins of difference and untouched the existing structures of privilege and authority ("Feminism" 116–17). Students—as well-schooled in the ideology of pluralism as in the habits of popular debate—are eager to grant the right of everyone to their own opinion. A theoretical openness to other perspectives is, though, easily reversed in practice, especially when the situatedness of perspectives within established power structures is ignored, as when whites insist that blacks, or men insist that women, be more open to and accepting of their perspectives.

What we are seeking is a way of reconceiving argument that includes both confrontational and cooperative perspectives, a multifaceted process that includes moments of conflict and agonistic positioning as well as moments of understanding and communication. We want to see argument as agonistic inquiry or as confrontational cooperation, a process in which people struggle over interpretations together, deliberate on the nature of the issues that face them, and articulate and rearticulate their positions in history, culture, and circumstance. And thus we join with Jarratt in hoping for writing courses where "instructors help their students to see how differences emerging from their texts and discussions have more to do with those contexts than they do with an essential and unarguable individuality" ("Feminism" 121). Such a conception can remove argument from the (televised) boxing ring and return it not to the private domestic sphere but to the many ambiguous public spaces—meeting rooms, hallways, cafeterias, and, yes, classrooms—where it has a chance to become more productive. The question that confronts us now is, what exactly might such a conception of argument look like? What kind of activity are we trying to suggest by the admittedly difficult (if not oxymoronic) expressions "agonistic inquiry" and "confrontational cooperation"?

A New Articulation

Before we describe two different courses in which we attempted to put into practice our understanding of how argument might best be approached in first-year composition, we would like to briefly articulate the theoretical perspective that emerged as we tried to find a new paradigm for the teaching of argument.

Our concern from the start was that, without knowledge of the history behind an issue of those affected or potentially affected by it, or of the complex material causes and potential real effects of the decisions being made, classrooms could easily drive students back into a narrower kind of arguing.

Jarratt, in "Feminism and Composition," shows her awareness of such a potential problem when she argues for a distinction between "eristic wrangling" and "disputation." Wrangling takes place, according to Jarratt, between people who position themselves from the start as enemies, whereas disputation acknowledges that conflict also plays a role among friends who argue with one another out of good will. Disputation, which draws on the "ability to move into different positions," should then open up the space needed for more considered judgments and disagreements.

However, the point of Jarratt's distinction often seems on the edge of slipping away, for instance, when she quotes bell hooks urging us to establish in the classroom ". . . an atmosphere where [students] may be afraid or see themselves at risk" ("Feminism" 120). If we emphasize the fear and the risk, we can see the aggressive and agonistic qualities of traditional debate returning to the classroom, together with its narrowness and simplicity. The weight placed by Jarratt on conflict, on the necessary emergence of real differences, and especially on the need for students who have been disempowered to become more "self-assertive" in the classroom may push students toward strategies of simplification as a matter of survival. But if instead we emphasize, as Jarratt later does, a classroom "in which students argue about the ethical implications of discourse on a wide range of subjects and, *in so doing, come to identify their personal interests with others,* understand those interests as implicated in a large communal setting, and advance them in a public voice" ("Feminism" 121, emphasis added), then we hear an echo of John Gage and what we have called a cooperative rhetoric of inquiry.

In an essay that in some interesting ways anticipates Jarratt's position, "An Adequate Epistemology for Composition," Gage suggests that we might clarify our disagreements over the best way to teach argument by attending to the epistemological bases of the modes of argumentation we are considering. Toward this end, he offers his own distinction among three views of argument. The first two views disconnect rhetoric from knowledge—either skeptically or positivistically—and turn it into an artifice or a vehicle. An argument, under both of these views, becomes a mere formal exercise. In the first case, unencumbered by any sense of truth or right, one concentrates on learning and employing those forms that will help one to win or survive. In the second case, one has recourse to rhetorical forms because ideas—truths—still need to be embodied and communicated: argument thus becomes a mere vehicle for leading an audience to a truth known independently of the rhetorical process. The third view, in contrast to the other two, connects rhetoric to dialectic and to the social production of knowledge, and, as we might expect, Gage associates this view with Aristotle:

> From this perspective, rhetoric aims at knowledge, or makes it available. Rather than producing persuasion without reference to truth, rhetoric aims at producing mutual understandings and therefore becomes the basis for inquiry into sharable truths. "The function of rhetoric," Aristotle asserted, "is to deal with things about which we deliberate, but for which we have no rules." ("Adequate Epistemology" 153–55)

Gage thus seeks to contain the eristic impulses within argumentation by linking argument to the production of knowledge—though disagreeing, people cooperate to make connections in the construction of "sharable truths." This is not knowledge in the modernist sense—objective and timeless truth—but a knowledge that is true only insofar as it emerges from the social, cooperative process of argumentation.

People argue, according to Gage, in order to negotiate conflicts and differences. We do not argue in order to express our inner selves or as a fun exercise, though we can approach argument in this way if we so choose. The primary function of argument, therefore, the one Young argues is necessary for public deliberation and that Gage would have us consider as teachers of writing, is to get something done in the world, including the academic world. And given the kinds of issues we tend to discuss in the academic world, according to Gage, we cannot and should not expect to rely on truths or independent formal guarantees that would render the negotiation process mechanical and easy. All we can do is come together (in some fashion), articulate our differences, listen, try hard to understand, acknowledge how thoroughgoing the differences may be, and—and here is Gage's main contribution, as he sees it—not just formulate reasons that defend our initial position, but reformulate those very positions through a process of argument ("Adequate Epistemology" 162). In other words, the real conflicts are already there at the outset of a disagreement, in the way we define the issues and set up our purposes, and thus when teachers ask students to establish their position *before* they interact with those with whom they disagree, teachers inadvertently push students to reproduce their disagreements rather than moving towards negotiated and temporary resolutions of disagreements.

Gage's approach to argument perhaps sounds closer than it probably is to the work of Jarratt, Bizzell, and others who have been critical of a humanist tradition (with its connections to Aristotle) and who look instead to postmodern theories or look behind Aristotle to the sophists. Yet even so, a lingering concern might remain for many who would read (or reread) Gage's work in the present context of composition studies: careful as he is to emphasize the thoroughly social and dialectical nature of his approach to argument, his account still lacks a fully social and political dimension. This is perhaps most visible in his characterization of conflict. When Gage sets his students up to argue with one another, the aim that he assumes will govern their efforts *is* to negotiate conflict—but the conflicts he imagines are what he calls "conflicts of knowledge." What is at stake in any argumentative situation for Gage is the current state of one's knowledge or beliefs, and even though he is careful to stress that people, not ideas, are in conflict—the "real people" that he reaches for in his account of argument often seem at the last minute to gently dissolve into mere place holders for the ideas they are committed to. The effect is especially apparent when one recalls that the conflicts our students experience are reflected in the structure of our social, political, and economic conditions—and thus are not contained in the minds of individual students. Put otherwise, the social production of knowledge that Gage so engagingly argues for remains a mostly abstract and intellectual affair because the extent to which his students enter into their arguments already positioned unequally itself remains unquestioned.

But if we hesitate to embrace the limited sense of "social" in Gage's social rhetoric of inquiry, neither are we fully satisfied with Jarratt's pedagogy of "productive conflict." In this regard, we intend our provisional and somewhat playful notion of "agonistic inquiry" to delineate an activity that is a social process of negotiating, not "conflicts of knowledge," so much as conflicts of positioning and power—conflicts in which students can discern that something is at stake, someone is affected, and someone has been silenced for reasons that can be determined.

Indeed, the differences among Gage's, Jarratt's, and our positions can perhaps better be seen in the manner in which we each describe the kind of risks we anticipate our students will face in our classrooms. In Gage's contribution to *What Makes Writing Good*, for instance, he asks his students to "risk committing yourself, if only for the time being, to an idea," and he sees such a commitment as a risk because it "means that there will be people who will not agree with you" (100). To argue is to commit yourself, not to others, but to an idea, and to be committed to an idea ensures that you will run into conflicts and disagreements with others. The risk for students, in other words, is that by connecting with an idea they will isolate themselves, which of course is what has motivated Gage's argument from the start: by risking disagreement, we stand to recoup our loss on another level, that of the social production of knowledge.

The strong focus on knowledge that Gage adopts thus threatens to hold students within a temporary state of isolation while they carefully work and rework their thesis-statements. True enough, the consideration a student gives to her opponent's position overcomes some of the effects of that isolation—but only certain intellectual effects. The fact that argumentative activity has been cut off from that which differentiates us—especially from our histories, our cultures, our various positions of power within institutions and social practices—all serves to decrease the chance that our students will feel or find new connections with those affected by an issue, especially with those whose "interests" are not readily observable within the issue as it has been divided up and handed to us historically. The possibility that traditional argumentation, even reconfigured as a rhetoric of inquiry, might still isolate students more than it connects them is finally what led Lester Faigley, in part, to explore the potential of networked classrooms—in spite of or perhaps because of their admitted messiness: "while electronic discourse explodes the belief in a stable, unified self, it offers a means of exploring how identity is multiply constructed and how agency resides in the power of connecting with others and building alliances" (199). We believe that argumentation can and should be approached in a manner that will allow this form of agency to emerge in the classroom, rather than be constrained by a particular epistemological model.

The risk Jarratt's students face is similar to the one Gage anticipates, though it is tinged with a much stronger sense of loss or threat. She also asks her students to accept the risk of encountering disagreement, to risk a public display of difference, but she anticipates much more in such a risk—much more struggle, tension, confusion, anger, embarrassment, condescension, reprisal, intractability. When Jarratt calls for a renewed commitment to "serious and rigorous critical exchange" between students, and also between teachers and students, we sense that her aim is not just to get her students to reconsider a few beliefs or opinions. Her aim is to position students in a manner that will challenge who they are—positions they might enjoy or suffer. The risk of not being connected with others, of learning that others disagree with you, thus becomes intensified for Jarratt's students, increasing the likelihood that disagreement will turn into direct challenge.

Because we are sympathetic to Jarratt's concerns—especially regarding the "unequal positioning" some people enjoy over others when arguing within institutional settings—we appreciate the urge to intensify the risks her students might experience in her classroom and the desire to make differences and disagreements more real and more risky. From our perspective, though, the risk is not merely that your social position and identity may be challenged, or not merely that someone may disagree with your intellectual position, or not even that you may lose the argument; the risk is also that you may become different than you were before the argument began. Serious argumentation requires a willingness to see things differently and to be changed in and through the dialogic process. As Gage points out, argumentation enables us to reformulate our positions through our interactions with those with whom we are in conflict; as Jarratt emphasizes, those positions are not just intellectual ones but positions of power and identity that come out of real histories.

This kind of change is not easy. In *Teaching to Transgress,* bell hooks acknowledges the pain in this process and the consequent need for teachers to show compassion:

> There can be, and usually is, some degree of pain involved in giving up old ways of thinking and knowing and learning new approaches. I respect that pain. And I include recognition of it now when I teach, that is to say, I teach about shifting paradigms and talk about the discomfort it can cause. (43)

Eloise Buker points out that the change we go through in order to understand another person or perspective is "often accomplished only through struggle," and the threat of struggle always carries with it the reflex action of retrenchment, a retreat back into isolation and defended difference. We believe that students will risk such changes only when argumentation is perceived as a social activity through which they, first and foremost, *connect* with others.

We have seen that aspects of the kind of argumentation to which we have been pointing can be found within both Gage's and Jarratt's fully articulated positions: Gage moves us toward an understanding of rhetoric as something that requires us to connect and interact with those with whom we disagree; and Jarratt insists that when we do so we must squarely confront the differences among us. Yet the pressure each puts on argumentation—as the production of knowledge (finding a sharable thesis) or as the last hope in a world of unspeakable injustices—tends to obscure these insights and thus to reduce, rather than to enhance, the chance that students will experience how argument can facilitate our "ability to move into different positions," generate new relations with others, and thus change both the inner and outer landscapes of our initial disagreements and conflicts.

Our quest to develop a new approach to teaching argumentation began, however, not with these theoretical considerations but rather developed as we together designed courses that tried to instantiate a revised sense of argument as inquiry. The two courses we describe below differ from each other in outline and content, but each course takes as its primary goal to engage students in a kind of writing that moves beyond the "opposing viewpoints," disputatious, display type of argumentation. Both courses avoid, as much as possible, rushing students to defend sides or to decide on a position. Instead, we sought to give students more time to learn and think about the issues they were engaging, with the idea in mind that in the process they will recognize that the positions we take—especially the first, easy positions that we have "accepted"—usually have been socially, culturally, and historically determined and, not coincidentally, usually have unforeseen consequences for others, others whose positions are often not even represented by the manner in which the issues are handed down to us ("pro and con").

At the same time, we wanted students to have the chance to discover that complex issues have the potential to involve us in unexpected alliances through which we can open ourselves to new possibilities and responsibilities. What we are about to offer, we acknowledge, is not so much a specific method of teaching argument that can be followed, step by step, as an approach, or a loose affiliation of approaches. Our discussion is instead meant as a part of an ongoing project we share with others to rethink the role of argument in the writing curriculum, especially as we attempt to answer the demand that our writing courses help prepare students to deal with the real conflicts that face all of us in society today.

What's Wrong with the Washington Redskins?

What the government did to the Cherokee Indians was cruel and unusual punishment. No one should be forced off their land and then forced to travel hundreds of miles. On top of this one-third of their population died along the way. Even though this type of thing would never happen in modern day, we can look back now and critique the action of the government. I feel sorry for the Indians, but if the government had not done this, America would not be what it is today. If Indians still owned most of the United States, America would be a third-world country.

The first-year MTU student whose work is excerpted above is not exceptional in his assessment that bad things just happen on the road to progress.

This is the sort of comment that is normal in many courses, at least in Michigan's Upper Peninsula, that deal with issues of American Indian rights or the history of westward expansion. This student was not taking such a course, however. He was in a second-term composition course and was asked to write a short response to a passage from *The Education of Little Tree*. That he chose to stake out a position is less interesting to us, in our discussion of argument, than is the sense we have that he feels that there is no real issue at hand. History is history. Bad things happen to good people. Let's get on with our lives. The course we will describe in the next few pages was designed partially in response to that easy way in which first-year students often seem to dismiss the many issues that surround them daily, in the news, in classes, in work situations, even in the most mundane kinds of arenas—like what to name a football team.

In this writing course, which focused on the issue of using Indian mascot names and logos for sports teams, we began working essentially from argument out: we asked students to read and to summarize two extremely opposed positions presented in two articles: "Indians Have Worse Problems," by syndicated columnist Andy Rooney, and "Crimes Against Humanity," by Cherokee activist and critic Ward Churchill. Many students found Rooney's arguments (even such claims as "American Indians were never subjected to the same kind of racial bias that blacks were," or, "While American Indians have a grand past, the impact of their culture on the world has been slight") as reasonable, even persuasive. By contrast, many were offended by Ward Churchill's charge that "the use of native names, images and symbols as sports team mascots and the like is, by definition, a virulently racist practice" (43). But by far, the most consistent response of the class, an honors section, was that the question of Indian mascot names was a non-issue. Several students, for example, wrote that demonstrations over mascot names were publicity stunts from a radical group of Indians who did not represent the majority. Moreover, the class made the charge that this issue was just another example of PC at work. Why should anyone care what a team calls itself?

It seemed to us that this was a good start for the approach to argument we had in mind. The question, "Why should anyone care?" was precisely the kind of question we wanted students to ask—and answer. Yet, at this moment in the course we also had to contend with the fact that our students were oscillating in their relation to the issue, oscillating between disengaging from the issue—calling it PC and a non-issue—and throwing themselves into a heated defense of using Indian mascot names. Clearly Ward Churchill's charges had threatened something very close to them, perhaps their loyalties to school, team, tradition, even national identity. Since team and school mascot names function to unite students' and fans' identities, in effect building both public and private loyalties, the issue of changing the name of a team can easily become tied to those and other loyalties. Such an issue threatens to polarize students as they take sides and doggedly defend their "camp"—which is precisely the behavior we had hoped to avoid. That attachment to "what is" over a willingness to debate "what might be the implications of" accounts, at least in part, for the sort of positioning we see in the passage above. To that student, America is fine as it is. This is his country. If anything else had happened, we would have some other, some less developed country—a country not his. Loyalty is a complicated bit of the puzzle of human reasoning.

What is more, an issue like the mascot one seems, for many students, to hit at political loyalties. As we noted above, by the second day of this assignment, students were already dismissing its relevance as simply another "PC debate." This turn was perhaps inevitable, for, as Gerald Graff points out, "In literature and the humanities, cultural nationalism has been the main organizing principle since the romantic period, when the doctrine became established that the quality of a nation's language and literature was the touchstone of its greatness as a nation" (151). This kind of loyalty plays itself out easily enough every time we bring cultural studies, cultural critique, or a multicultural agenda to the writing class. Such an agenda threatens nationalism. As Graff reminds us, "The rule seems to be that any politics is suspect except that kind that helped us get where we are, which by definition does not count as politics" (156). Thus, our students' easy initial acceptance of Rooney's column and their discomfort with Churchill's article. They found Rooney abrasive but acceptable and Churchill merely abrasive. (We might add here that both are openly abrasive.)

This is, of course, a paradoxical predicament for a class given over to the study of argumentation. The presumed goal is to critically examine not just one's beliefs but the decisions that are being made in our communities. The more those decisions touch students' loyalties, though, the more likely students are to retrench, not listen to others, resort to quips, and as a result lose sight of the complexity of the issue under consideration. We chose this moment of oscillation, then, to ask the students to write out (in their notebooks) their own position in this debate. Then we asked them to put that position statement away and to start a different kind of work.

At the end of the term, when they did share with their instructor that initial notebook entry, students' own inability to see any issue worth discussing here was clear. The most common reaction was anger: Indians, one student wrote, just "have to have something to cry about." They should, "GROW UP, STOP CRYING, AND GET ON WITH LIFE!" Others echoed that attitude. One admitted that when she thought of Indians, she got a picture of fat, lazy drunkards who live off the government. The class, as a whole, certainly gave the impression that they felt those arguing over mascot names were "making a big deal out of nothing." They didn't understand why anyone could get upset over such a topic. And, they felt that American Indians were simply holding onto a past they no longer had a right to. One student, for example, wrote that he lives in Keweenaw Bay, where one band of Ojibway is located, and he resents the fact that the Indians there can haul "thousands of pounds of lake trout from Keweenaw Bay with motorized boats, instead of canoes, and commercially made nets, instead of hand woven ones." A few stated very simply that Indian people ought to assimilate and get it over with.

Many agreed with the student who said, during class discussion, that the Indians have lost the big battle, and they have to understand what it means to lose. The instructor, by contrast, was not convinced that her students knew the many consequences of "losing." The class seemed comfortable with the status quo, unwilling to poke around into an argument they wished had never been brought up in the first place.

These vigorously negative stereotypes might surprise a few readers who see more romanticized images as the current media stereotype, especially from such recent popular programs and films as *Northern Exposure, Dr. Quinn: Medicine Woman, Pocahontas, Dances with Wolves,* and *The Last of the Mohicans,* to name a few. Jeffery Hanson and Linda Rouse explain this kind of contradictory stereotyping of American Indians as common. They discovered that, although the students they studied reported that most of the information they have about American Indians came from the media, the stereotype they eventually formed depended on where they were living. If they lived in areas where American Indians were not a visible minority and were not competing for resources, the stereotype tended to be overwhelmingly positive and romanticized. If they lived in a region (such as South Dakota, Wisconsin, or Minnesota) where Indian people did constitute a visible minority and might compete for resources, the stereotypes were severely negative. Our students' responses to this issue are typical of the kinds of responses Rouse and Hanson discovered among students living in this part of the country.

For this section of the term, then, the class sometimes angrily argued that we had entered into a silly, even meaningless debate. They claimed no interest in and, several of them, no knowledge of the ways each side might argue their position. And, yet, when asked to list arguments from both sides of the discussion, students found it much easier to outline the position represented by Rooney than that represented by Churchill. For the instructor, that meant that either Rooney's position was the position most available in the popular press, or that students' own loyalties or stereotypes were interfering with their ability to understand other positions.

The next step in this assignment, then, was to begin investigating the many issues, questions, and concerns that surround the arguments set forth in Rooney's and Churchill's articles. In an attempt to get students beyond polarized debate, we asked them not to look for more arguments for or against using Indian mascot names. Instead, we wanted them to ask different questions—questions that would direct their attention more broadly to the people involved in the discussion, what matters to those people, and how the debate got to the Rooney-Churchill level. Then we asked them to start looking for some possible answers to these questions: Why would anyone argue over something as seemingly harmless as a name? Why does anyone think it is an issue at all? Obviously, it wasn't just an issue with Indian people, or Andy Rooney, the Cleveland Indian fans, and others would not be so resolute in their determination to keep what they considered theirs. The argument came from somewhere, and it was about something more than naming teams. Where did it come from? What was it about? Our first strategy, then, was to ask students to question the concepts they were using (the significance of naming), to situate the issue historically (how did the problem develop?), and to find analogous problems from the past in order to resist coming to closure too quickly.

For the next six weeks, the students did research that might have seemed far afield of the initial argument. Goaded by Rooney's assertion that American Indians had contributed little to contemporary culture, they learned and wrote about separate Indian cultures. In response to Churchill's question of why it seems so much easier these days to use Indian names in ways we would not use other group names, they did research on reservation schools and acculturation—along the way learning what Richard Henry Pratt meant when he declared it a necessity that "[t]he Indian must die as an Indian in order to live as a man." During this part of the course, several students did work on stereotyping and its effects. As a result, one student compared the arguments over Indian mascot names and symbols to arguments in the sixties and seventies when a number of African American stereotyped product names and logos were changed. Another student ran across articles detailing the controversy over Crazy Horse Malt Liquor and was prompted by that controversy to learn more about Crazy Horse. He had heard the name all his life and knew nothing of the man. The student who shouted in all caps to Indian people to GROW UP! found there was much more to get over than he had anticipated. After watching *In the White Man's Image*, this student wrote,

> After watching the tape on the Indian school, I was shocked when I heard an Indian voice say that after the school, they wanted to be good and live in wood houses and settle down. They taught the Indians that their old ways were bad. I think this is horrible. It helps to destroy the heritage of the Indians.

In his paper, he acknowledged the truth that most team supporters quite honestly do not intend to demean Indian people with mascot names, but he pointed out that the intention is not necessarily the effect. He quoted Indian activist and songwriter John Trudell who told the class, "There are a million ways to put a people down and using their names and rituals is just one way." What this student did, then, was to try to understand why some people might defend the status quo while others see it as "a virulently racist practice" (Churchill).

At the end of the term, students wrote about the experience of using argument as a tool of intellectual inquiry. In portfolio cover letters, most said they had not really changed their initial position on the argument (though now most simply said that if a name offends the group named, it ought to be dropped), and they still thought the argument was a trivial one. What had changed, however, was why they thought it trivial. In the process of questioning the issue—what matters? why does naming seem both so serious and so trivial?—they felt they had discovered other, more significant (historically and culturally informed) issues within this one. They weren't ready to give either Andy Rooney or Ward Churchill the nod in terms of who they thought had "won" this debate, but they did see something much more profound embedded within the terms of the debate. One student wrote that, far from learning to keep his opinion to himself (as he had been taught to do in high school), this work had taught him that he had to more carefully understand his position and its consequences. He wrote, "[t]he research I did for essay 3 made me want to run and tell the world how I felt about the mascot issue. So I did. I was rewarded when upon reading my paper in front of the class, everyone seemed interested in it." This was the student who had done his work on Crazy Horse.

We should add that these students did not feel compelled to take the Indians' side in this debate, either. Despite fears expressed by some that introducing political dispute into the classroom is a way of forcing students to accept the instructor's politics, our experience has been that such acceptance is neither easy nor likely. For example, in this course, one student who began the class angrily declaring that Indians had to accept the fact that they were the ones who lost, wrote,

> I feel I have succeeded in showing that one of the reasons that this topic is an issue is that the American mainstream and the Indians are two separate cultures. The two most important things that I have learned from this course [are] that it is all right to think for yourself and form educated opinions . . . [and] that you have to look at every issue from many different perspectives.

He remained steadfast in his belief that the only way for this issue to be resolved would be for Indian people to accept assimilation as a goal (a position that certainly did not reflect the instructor's politics), but he no longer thought of assimilation as an easy or natural consequence of having lost the big battle. He had, in other words, uncoupled his conclusion that Indians must accept assimilation from the myth of the big battle and reconnected it to his emerging thoughts about culture and cultural conflicts. What he makes of that achievement may well take years to fully realize.

It is true that what these students ended up writing might look less like argument, as we have come to know it, and more (depending on the student's choice of topic) like analysis. And, yet, the course does not avoid argument, either. The kind of assignment we have been describing acknowledges the flat debate then leaves it alone. At the same time, the assignment leads students to an understanding that a more complex argument might be made possible through ongoing inquiry. Too many classroom strategies, too many textbooks, insist that students learn to take hold of and argue a position long before they understand the dimensions of a given issue. We would much rather our students learn to resist doggedly defending their position too soon in the discussion. That is not to suggest that students do not hold positions very early in this process. Certainly, they do, and they most likely want to defend and keep intact those positions. We won't deny that. For the students in this class, however, their initial position statements were never used during whole-class discussion. Those early statements remained theirs to do with as they pleased. Primarily, students seemed to use them as a starting point for their research or as a way to identify questions within the broader topic of the course. As their instructors, we were more interested (and we believe the class was, too) in what students learned about the issues surrounding this debate than which side they initially took in it. Moreover, we were interested in helping students realize the complications imbedded in discussions on even seemingly uncomplicated issues like what to name a football team.

A River Runs Through It

> Eventually, all things merge into one, and a river runs through it. The river was cut by the world's great flood and runs over rocks from the basement of time. On some of the rocks are timeless raindrops. Under the rocks are the words, and some of the words are theirs. I am haunted by waters.
> —Norman MacLean, *A River Runs Through It* (113)

Generally speaking, water is not a topic people in the upper midwest spend a lot of time thinking about, much less arguing about. Except in bad winters when water mains freeze, we don't worry much about where our water is coming from and whether we will have enough. So, when we announced to a first-year writing class that the topic we would be focusing on for the quarter was water resources, they were distinctly nonplused. But a few weeks into the course, many of them wrote comments like the following:

> Before entering HU 101, water resources rated just as high as the Royal Family on my list of importance. Now, after reading a few articles on the subject, I think about it quite often. What amazes me most about water resource management is its complexity.

Like the rivers of North America, the issue of water resources flows through a complex array of political positions and priorities in our society. From the James Bay hydroelectric project in Quebec to the California aqueduct, from the draining of the Everglades to proposals for a pipeline to pump Alaskan water to Texas, the questions of who owns the water in North America and how it should be used are the concern of agribusiness, golfers, small farmers, white-water rafters, mining companies, American Indians, fishermen, electrical companies, environmentalists, and urban residents, among others, and the conflicting demands of these interests result in strange and shifting alliances among groups who are often opposed on other issues. In arguing in this arena, students find it hard to locate preconstructed positions they can accept and argue for. Instead, they must sort through and negotiate competing concerns in order to construct a position they feel is justified and they want to defend.

Of course, any issue, including water resources, can be cast in the point-counterpoint argument mode: America's Rivers—Should we dam them for power or let them run free? When differences of opinion are polarized and sensationalized in this way, the emphasis in argument shifts from the issue to the skills and personalities of the combatants and the formal structures of argumentation. And while these are always a part of argument, and contribute a lot to the enjoyment some people find in argument, focusing on stark controversies at the expense of the complexities of an issue is also a way of evading or covering up the painful and complex problems that face us and that we must resolve if we want to have a society that's worth living in. We wanted to show students that arguments do matter, that the positions they take matter to them in their daily lives, and that argument serves a useful function in society, the function of helping us all make better decisions, together. We called the kind of writing they would be doing deliberative discourse, not to take the focus off the differences that lead to disputation but to emphasize that such differences are legitimate and deeply felt and must be talked about in a serious way.

We were again, in this course, concerned to not push students prematurely into taking a position on issues they knew little about and thus cared little about. Certainly, the aim of argument is to influence specific decisions in a specific context, to recommend a particular course of action, and certainly it is the pressure imposed by the need for specific decisions—should we enact NAFTA? should we raise the sales tax or the income tax to finance public schools?—that sometimes leads us to simplify what we know are complicated issues and to wrangle over them heatedly. But this is only one moment in the activity of arguing, and in many ways the end of argument. To see this moment as the whole of argumentative writing is to risk seeing all decisions as final, all positions as absolute or even natural, to see argument, paradoxically, as somehow antithetical to change.

It takes time to learn about an issue, to learn what you really think about it and how it affects your life and the lives of others. On the first day, we talked about all the ways water was important to us: in raising crops and in otherwise providing us with food; in mining resources; in manufacturing products; in disposing of waste; in transporting people and products; in providing electrical power; in providing habitats for other species, recreational opportunities, and spiritual relaxation; and in simply sustaining our lives. We then handed out the assignments for the course. We asked them to write four related papers in which they were to construct a position they believed in on a specific issue of their choice involving water resources. The assignments were designed to give students a chance to reflect on their ideas and arguments as they wrote and read and discussed and rewrote; in essence, the first three papers were simply drafts, albeit "good" drafts, steps in the process of developing a carefully considered argument for a carefully constructed position in the fourth and final paper.

The first assignment asked them simply to explore the general issue of water resources and their reactions to it, to find what aspects of this issue interested them. Some of the questions we asked them to think about in this paper were: What aspects of this issue relate to your interests and plans and how do they relate? What experiences have you had that shape how you feel about this issue? What aspects of the issue do you find interesting at this point and why? What surprised you in what we have read and discussed? What else would you like to find out about this issue? The purpose here was for them to find some way to connect to the issue, whether intellectually, experientially, or emotionally.

Many of our midwestern students who personally experienced the decline of farming in this region were struck by one of Marc Reisner's conclusions in *Cadillac Desert:* "In a West that once and for all made sense, you might import a lot more meat and dairy products from states where they are raised on rain, rather than dream of importing those states' rain" (517). One student who grew up on a farm in Michigan explained that his stepfather had committed suicide when the price of milk declined and he couldn't repay his bank loans. His experience clearly affected how he responded to much of the material we looked at in the course: he was especially sympathetic to the plight of the long-term small rancher in Nevada who lost his water to the newly irrigated large farms down the valley, to the situation of the olive farmer in California who was put out of business by Prudential Insurance's cornering the market with their five-thousand acre farm near Bakersfield, and to the Hispanic farmers in *The Milagro Beanfield War* in their fight against the developers.

Other students found less heart-rending personal connections to the issues involving water. A student who lived on a lake investigated the state laws that allowed the owner of the water rights of the lake to manipulate the water level to maximize the hydroelectric power his dam could produce. A student with a passion for golf looked into water conserving designs for the abundant golf courses in western deserts. Some students were simply moved by a question of fairness: several wrote about the treatment of the Cree Indians by the developers of the James Bay hydroelectric project. And others were interested in the technological problems involved, like the students who wrote about new methods of irrigation and power generation. The students' level of commitment to the issue—and then to the position they constructed—thus varied in strength and nature, but all understood that deliberative discourse required some kind of commitment on their part.

The second assignment asked students to begin to stake out a position they found persuasive on a specific issue, although we cautioned them to discuss *all* the positions that they found persuasive and to explain how these positions might conflict with one another and how these conflicts might be resolved. We also emphasized, both in the instructions and in comments on their drafts, that this paper was only the beginning of the process of constructing a position, that they would next need to look at the position they had stated and think about such things as whether it really represented what they believed in, what sort of actions would follow from this position, whether they really found these actions to be possible and desirable, and what questions their position raised that they would need to investigate further.

When one student, a very skilled writer, handed in the first draft of this second paper, he told the instructor he had the outline of his final paper, and all he would have to do in the rest of the course was to add in a little more information from the library. He had formulated a logical problem-solution argument: since irrigated farming in the west made no economic sense, the government should buy out western agricultural concerns and subsidize the development of more agriculture in the midwest and east. When we suggested that there were a couple of serious problems with his solution, namely that the federal government most assuredly did not have the money in these times of national debt to finance such a plan, and that people who had lived and farmed in the west for generations might not appreciate having their livelihoods eliminated in this way, he said that he was ignoring these aspects of the situation for the purposes of his argument. We said that a solution that wouldn't work isn't a solution at all, that there was more to taking a position than constructing a clear thesis and a logically argued paper.

He seemed somewhat taken aback; clearly, this strategy of quickly taking stock of the issue and offering a novel and definitive solution had worked well for him in past writing courses. We pressed our questions because we wanted to push him (and the other students) beyond the form of argument that ignores real conflicts by turning them into abstract problems to be solved or managed. In his second draft of the second paper and in the third paper, he analyzed the complexities of the situation more thoroughly. He discovered that financial incentives for more efficient use of water by farmers could and were being paid for by urban water users in the west rather than the federal government. He discovered that zoning, the establishment of agricultural districts, and cluster residential development were possible solutions to the increasing pressure of development that drives up the property values of agricultural land beyond the levels where farming is economically feasible in the midwest.

The third assignment asked students to reconsider their initial positions from the point of view of someone who would not agree with them. We told students that the reason to look at opposing positions when constructing an argument was not so much to anticipate and counter objections as it was to learn more about the issue and thus to make your own position more reasonable and practical, to take into account not only your own interests and desires and experiences but also those of others.

We had a chance to make this point clearer one day in another class that was similarly structured but focused on a different topic. A female student stated unequivocally that it was essential that one parent in a family not work so that someone would be home when the kids got back from school; a male student countered that both his parents worked and that he had not suffered at all from coming home to an empty house. The two debated this issue rather heatedly for about five minutes with the rest of the class throwing in encouraging comments or reactions. She argued that she would have felt insecure and unloved in his position; he countered that he developed a strong sense of independence and still felt close to his parents because of the time they did find to spend together. When he finally said it was clear he couldn't win this argument because she always had something to say in response, we instead asked the class to look at what had happened differently, not as simply an argument to be won or lost but as an opportunity to learn about different perspectives—to learn that your experiences and needs are not necessarily the same as those of others and that there are benefits and drawbacks to the differing decisions made by parents.

In composing this third assignment we reminded ourselves that the risk in argument is not that you may lose but rather that you may change. We asked them to think about the concerns of someone who held a position that they did not find to be persuasive and explain why someone might hold this position. Then we asked them to discuss what they might learn from this position: What beliefs and feelings did they find they could sympathize with, even if they did not agree with them? What experiences did they learn about that might help them see new aspects of the issue? How did some of the concerns expressed relate to some of their concerns? We asked these questions knowing full well that our students were in the midst of working and reworking their relations to the world around them and that our questions might contribute to that work by asking them to connect with others' concerns and needs. We also knew full well the rhetorical force of the questions we asked; thoughtfully pursued, these questions could and did prompt changes in our students.

The student who was so concerned with the plight of small farmers began his writing by adamantly opposing corporate farming, but he really did not know why he opposed corporate farming—except that it put small traditional farmers out of business and he thought that this was unfair. In the course of his work on his papers, he came across a statement by René Dubos in an essay by Edward Abbey ("farming as a way of life is a self-sustaining, symbiotic relationship between man and earth") that gave him a way of talking about the difference in attitude toward the land and toward their work he felt between traditional small farmers and corporate agribusinesses. But at the same time, he developed an understanding of the place of corporate farming in the economic system of the country. In a statement he wrote at the end of the course, he explained:

> My position on the topic of water at first was corporate farms are no good and we shut them down completely. As we read articles and wrote papers I slowly learned how complex our economic system is. I didn't realize all the jobs that would be lost and how it would affect California's economic system. Also I finally realized the fact that corporate farms just didn't appear out of nowhere. They developed over time. . . . The corporate farms that should be kept after and be taxed super high are conglomerates like Prudential, [which] would possibly force them to sell their land to people who care and respect the land and soil. These are the corporate farms that don't care for the land and if the land

becomes worthless they just buy land somewhere else and they say "oh well we lost a couple of acres of land we can just write it off as a loss." I guess I'm still against corporate farms but mostly only them being owned by conglomerates.

The student who lived on a lake came to sympathize with the owner of the water rights' desire to make a living through the sale of hydroelectric power, and he connected this situation to that of a western water dispute between a rancher and alfalfa farmers. Instead of recommending government regulation, as he had started out doing, he argued instead that people need to learn to work together so that all can make a living and be satisfied that their water is being used efficiently.

The last assignment asked students to pull together all that they had learned from writing and rewriting the first three papers, from their readings, and from our work in class. By then they had all learned a lot—and so had we—not only about the specific issue they had been researching and analyzing, but also about different attitudes toward water issues in general and different concerns that needed to be taken into account. They had lots of their own writing to read over and reflect on, to revise and reuse. They had, in short, a good place from which to begin constructing a thoughtful and informed argument. Constructing a position, we told them, means sorting through for yourself the various questions and problems and values involved in an issue and coming to a decision you can stand up for.

What this sequence of assignments allowed students to do, then, was to take some time with a single issue, to really think about it, to investigate what was involved, to respond to it in more than one way, to make assertions about it and then reconsider those assertions, to risk changing how they thought about the things that mattered to them and what they might do in the future. And students did, for the most part, change their thinking about the issues they dealt with, although, as with the students in the course discussing mascot names, they did not simply shift sides or take on the instructor's position. Despite a great deal of skepticism expressed by the instructor, the golf aficionado still argued that the desert was a good place to situate golf courses, as long as they were correctly designed. The student who first proposed that western agriculture be abandoned still argued in his final paper that we must reverse the trend toward dependence on western agriculture, but the solution he offered was much more complex—and much more realistic. In a statement about his paper, he observed, "I initially thought that farming in the desert was completely ludicrous and had no place in crop production. I've since learned that, if done correctly, irrigating farming can be a part of American farming for a long time." In his paper, he argued that "irrigating farmers in the American southwest are going to have to adapt to their regions pending water shortages," and that "planned rural developments" in the midwest "are needed to ensure that these lands remain available for farming." Almost all of the students in this class arrived at extremely complex positions, often so complex that they had to struggle hard to express them in any coherent way. But also, more importantly, students developed positions that mattered to them and that dealt with real world problems in a realistic way.

Pushing students to develop positions that take into account the complexities of real world issues not only moves argumentative writing into a more serious realm, away from display or eristic debate, it also gives them a sense of how their academic work can connect with and help them understand their everyday lives. One of the number of students who wrote about the impact of the James Bay hydroelectric project on the lifestyle of the Cree Indians attended a local round table discussion about sustainable development as part of her preparation for writing her final paper. What she learned there was more than just support for her position: "When I went to the Round Table Meeting on Monday night my thoughts about this paper strengthened even more. My feelings were really true, they weren't made up by reading about the subject in magazine articles."

Asking students to research issues and to learn from people they disagree with does not prevent them from taking strong positions, though it does result in positions that are more reasonable and thoughtful. Their work is a form of collaborative inquiry, but it is still argument, too, in that it negotiates serious differences and recommends a course of action. We also found that bringing conflicts into the classroom does not necessarily mean turning the classroom into a site of conflict. When students are aware that the differences of opinion between them exist in a broader arena—that these differences are not just their own opinions but arise from historical, social, and cultural conditions—they do not feel they need to argue so fiercely and single-mindedly, and they can take the time to listen to other voices and re-think their positions.

By Way of a Conclusion

Perhaps the most frustrating, though not surprising, thing we learned from our two courses was that the very things we set out to resist—two-sided issues, the rush to assert a thesis, and the concentration on forms—returned again and again, if we were not careful. Just as so many argument readers tell students that pro-and-con arguments are too facile and yet go on to organize their chapters in terms of pro-and-con (or speak in ways that assume students "want to take a side"), we found ourselves worrying whether our students' "positions" were clear enough, or whether they had a controversial enough "thesis." Even our examples betray the obvious, namely, that once you ask students to write through their interest in an issue, the assumption becomes that they will have a position that stands against, is differentiated from, someone else's position. And it is easier to grasp one's position, think it through, and present it to others if it is conceived in terms of an opposition.

We thus saw (and tried to understand) the forces that drove us and our students to simplify and to formalize the argumentative situation, and this is why, in the first course, we were not concerned that the papers we received did not all look argumentative. We understood that the initial disagreement (between Rooney and Churchill) would contextualize, for them and for their readers, their effort to answer questions that seemed only tangentially related to the disagreement. Their research did not preclude argument; it was infused with the initial sense of argument, and, what is most important, their answers served to modify the initial simplicity of the disagreement.

In the second class on water resources, similar doubts arose. Although we asked students to articulate their "positions," the decision to see their positions as solutions to problems, together with the scrutiny given the solutions offered (and together with the relatively "untopical" nature of the issue), encouraged students to reconfigure the conflicts, to bring in other perspectives, other complications, which then served to decenter the original disagreement in a fresh (and more complex) direction. Thus, in one case the issue shifted from "irrigated farming in the western states: yes or no?" to "how can we tilt the balance of farming back to the midwestern states (which have a natural supply of water) in a manner that increases the efficiency of western farming and discourages the selling off of good farm land to developers in the midwest?"

In our approach to argument, we share concerns with both cooperative and neosophistic rhetorics. Although we too want to teach the conflicts, at the same time we do not want to turn the classroom into the place where conflicts between students or between students and teachers erupt—not because we are reticent to allow emotion or turmoil into our classrooms, and not because we think all classrooms should be nurturing, but because we suspect, for now at any rate, that the desire to see results in the form of "critical action," when pressed too single-mindedly, may backfire and reduce a much needed understanding of the complexity of those conflicts. Wanting to have something to say and (desperately) needing to have something to say in self-defense can be productive under certain circumstances. But when arguments are entered into hastily, the complexity of the issues is often lost, and with it (we might add) the basis for introducing important, higher level concepts such as ideology, multiple subjectivity, and contingent foundations.

Neither do we wish to ignore or banish the different experiences and commitments that students bring with them into the classroom, for the expression and investigation of these differences is crucial to understanding the complexities of the problems we want to do something about. Conflicts have histories and are imbedded in more or less permanent power structures; decisions affect different people differently and have consequences that go beyond immediate situations; differences are rarely (if ever) brought permanently into consensus. What is important, to our minds, in teaching students to deal with conflict is that they experience the process of constructing a complex, historically knowledgeable position in light of what matters to, and what will result for, those affected by the positions taken.

If we believe that the writing classroom is a place to engage in serious intellectual inquiry and debate about the questions that trouble our everyday lives, we need to think again about our approach to argument. We need to see argumentation as a crucial social responsibility—an activity that requires us to position ourselves within complicated and interconnected issues. We need to see it as a complex and often extended human activity, or, rather, as an array of human activities, including institutionalized formal debate, legal trials, shouting matches that threaten to end in fist fights, conversational games of one-upsmanship, disagreements among friends, and extended deliberations within a community over what course of action to pursue. We need to see it not just as a matter of winning or losing but as a way to connect with others which may lead to change, not only in the world but also in ourselves. But, most of all, we need to see it as a means of coming to decisions, a way of getting things done in the world, that includes moments of agonistic dispute, moments of inquiry, moments of confrontation, and moments of cooperation.

AFTERWORD . . . .

We had thought we might stage a mock argument as our response but, given that we couldn't agree on what to argue, that plan was the first to be dismissed. In fact, we all did agree that this article is still very new to us. We first delivered three very separate talks in a panel chaired by John Trimbur at CCCC in Nashville in 1994. It took another three years before those papers became one article. That panel ended up somehow snagging one of those Outstanding Classroom Practice awards the organization was giving at the time. We must have thought we had something here.

In fact, whatever it was that identified that panel as worthy of one of those ephemeral awards is also what prompts this response. Emulating others' classroom practice is tricky: you always need to determine what exactly in the practice is appropriate and applicable to your own teaching situation. In the article we did try to warn readers about this: "What we are about to offer, we acknowledge, is not so much a specific method of teaching argument that can be followed, step by step, as an approach or a loose affiliation of approaches," and we did implicitly invite composition teachers to join us in rethinking "the role of argument in the writing curriculum." But classroom models are seductive, and we have had responses that suggest to us that some teachers simply try to use the courses we describe as syllabi templates, with varying degrees of success.

So let us say this again: these courses were specifically designed for our students in our program in our university, a very specific situation with its own social and cultural contexts and, thus, its own peculiar pedagogical challenges and possibilities. Our students combine the characteristics of relatively homogenous backgrounds, a willingness to investigate the world, a suspicion of new points of view, and a tendency to pull back rather than engage others; our program is inspired by critical pedagogy; our university is a small technological university in a remote corner of the north woods.

What instead we had hoped to provide teachers in this article was a way of thinking about how to approach argument in their own very particular classrooms. In particular, we hoped that teachers would see argument as developing over time, as a series of moments, rather than just as the presentation of the finished argument, and that thus it is essential to allow students the time and spaces to work through their thoughts and do some research on a topic or concern they share with others to discover how the positions they adopt might affect others. And we hoped also to suggest that argument is not just confrontational and not just cooperative, but sometimes one and sometimes the other and very often also inspires inquiry and leads to change in those arguing.

–DENNIS A. LYNCH

–DIANA GEORGE

–MARILYN M. COOPER

Michigan Technological University

1998

Dispositions toward Language:
Teacher Constructs of Knowledge
and the Ann Arbor Black English Case

ARNETHA BALL AND TED LARDNER

So here's our hypothesis: what students learn about writing depends more than anything else on the context in which they write. . . . And if the linguists are right that the social context is the driving force behind literacy acquisition, then *the social context of your English/language-arts classroom is the most powerful and important variable you can experiment with.* More important than what textbook or speller or dictionary to use; more important than what kinds of assignments to give; more important than how to set up cumulative writing folders; more important than the criteria by which you assign kids to peer response groups; more important than "teaching Graves" versus teaching Calkins or Hillocks. More important than anything.
—STEVEN ZEMELMAN AND HARVEY DANIELS (50–51)

Because composition has been organized as a field in terms of the classroom, the production, transmission, and assimilation of teacher knowledge continues to be a significant theoretical and practical concern. As John Schilb has recently pointed out, though many writing instructors attempt to separate pedagogy from theory, the "field identifies itself with pedagogy" (*Between* 30). In developing its discussion of pedagogical theory (as distinct from rhetorical theory), scholarship in composition studies has generated what we call constructs of teacher knowledge. In this essay we address competing constructs of teacher knowledge, analyzing them from a perspective which takes racially-informed language attitudes and their effects on teaching and learning in culturally diverse classrooms as its central concern. In developing this analysis, our point of departure is the 1979 Ann Arbor "Black English" court case. This case focused on the language barriers created by teachers'

This essay was first published in *CCC*, Volume 48, Number 4, December 1997.

413

unconscious negative attitudes toward students' uses of African American English and the negative effect these attitudes had on student learning.

In our reading, the Ann Arbor case is significant for composition studies for two reasons. First, it stands as a legal intervention into the educational process, disrupting business as usual by holding the school system responsible for the educational underachievement of Black students. It associated low educational achievement not with shortcomings within learners, but with inadequate, ineffective curricular and pedagogical routines. Second, in the Ann Arbor case the Court held the school district and teachers responsible for rethinking pedagogy and curriculum in light of extant information about African American English. In so doing, it raised then and continues now to pose the question of how educators accomplish the necessary but complicated task of assimilating new knowledge about race and language in order to translate that knowledge into classroom practice. We believe that barriers similar to those identified in Ann Arbor still affect teaching and learning in many secondary-level and college writing classrooms. Similarly, the complex issues surrounding teacher education and changing teachers' attitudes and behaviors in the classroom remain to be explored in the scholarly dialogue of our field.

We begin here with a summary of the Ann Arbor case, highlighting its focus on teacher attitudes and the consequent issue of teacher knowledge and practice. Next, we argue that three distinct constructs of teacher knowledge are evident in writing studies today, each of which is differentially linked to the issue of race reflected in language attitudes raised in the Ann Arbor case. We conclude with some implications for composition as a field, arguing in particular that pedagogical theory in composition needs to more adequately address questions of language diversity and race in order to affect the climate in the writing classroom.

BACKGROUND: THE COURT DECISION

In 1979, a Federal District Court handed down a decision in favor of 11 African American children, residents of a scatter-site low-income housing project and students at Martin Luther King, Jr., Elementary School, holding the Ann Arbor School District Board responsible for failing to adequately prepare the King School teachers to teach children whose home language was African American English. The case drew national and international attention to the role of language variation in the education of Black children. Stating that a major goal of a school system is to teach reading, writing, speaking, and understanding standard English (Memorandum 1391), Judge Charles Joiner wrote that "when teachers fail to take into account the home language" (1380) of their students, "some children will turn off and not learn" (1381). Challenging a pedagogical ethos grounded in the presumption of universalities, Judge Joiner observed that the teachers involved in the case all testified that they treated the plaintiff students just as they treated other students. However, in so doing they may have created a barrier to learning

(1379). In the Ann Arbor case, the Court ruled that the teachers' unconscious but evident attitudes toward the African American English used by the plaintiff children constituted a language barrier that impeded the students' educational progress (1381).

Like the recent Oakland School Board resolution on Ebonics, the Ann Arbor case stirred controversy. As in Oakland, the controversy was in part a result of inaccurate reporting in the media, some of which represented the Court as requiring teachers to teach African American English (see Smitherman, "What"). However, outside of the public furor and of much more substantive import, in ordering the defendant school board to invest time and money in a staff development program for King School teachers, the Court in the Ann Arbor case disrupted the institutional *status quo* by holding the school district accountable for the inadequate educational progress of the Black children involved. From this perspective, the Ann Arbor case can be viewed as a turning point in the history of educational justice for African American children, and the Court's Memorandum Opinion and Order signals this recognition:

> The problem posed by this case is one which the evidence indicates has been compounded by efforts on the part of society to fully integrate blacks into the mainstream of society by relying solely on simplistic devices such as scatter housing and busing of students. Full integration and equal opportunity require much more and one of the matters requiring more attention is the teaching of the young blacks to read standard English. (1381)

As much as the Court's decision can be viewed as an answer to "a cry for judicial help in opening the doors to the establishment" (1381), it must also be recognized that the overriding theme of the Court's ruling was to uphold existing linguistic, educational, and social arrangements. Many educators have viewed the Ann Arbor decision as a step forward on the same road leading from the *Brown v. Topeka* decision in 1954. Keith Gilyard, for example, calls the Ann Arbor decision a precedent-setting case which ought to have an officially established place within the educational environment (10). But while it is important to note such celebrating of the Ann Arbor case, it is also important to note that the elements of the decision which directly address language barriers and African American English have yet to be cited as a precedent in other cases aimed at school policy. Furthermore, the Court's final Memorandum Opinion and Order explicitly and unequivocally positions African American English in a subordinate relationship to the mainstream:

> Black English is not a language used by the mainstream of society— black or white. It is not an acceptable method of communication in the educational world, in the commercial community, in the community of the arts and science, or among professionals. (1378)

The Michigan Legal Services attorneys who mounted the case for the plaintiff children in Ann Arbor drew on the testimony of experts in sociolinguistics and education in order to establish two key propositions: that African American English is a rule-governed language system, and that the teachers' failure to recognize this linguistic fact led to negative attitudes toward the children who spoke it, that, in effect, their attitudes constituted a language barrier impeding students' educational progress. Establishing the first proposition, the expert testimony addressed the second by asserting that communicative interference can derive from either structural mismatches among dialects or from nonstructural phenomena. Nonstructural interference phenomena refers to differing attitudes and conflicting values about speech systems and the individuals who use them. Experts testified that negative linguistic attitudes shaped the institutional policies and practices that hindered the education of African American English speaking children. Then as now, research on language attitudes consistently indicates that teachers believe African American English speaking children are "nonverbal" and possess limited vocabularies. Speakers of African American English are often perceived to be slow learners or uneducable; their speech is often considered to be unsystematic and in need of constant correction and improvement.

In the Ann Arbor case, the Court identified teachers' language attitudes as a significant impediment to children's learning. Because the children failed to develop reading skills, they were thereby impeded from full participation in the educational program at King School. The Court enumerated multiple potential causes (absences from class, classroom misbehavior, learning disabilities, and emotional impairment and lack of reading role models [1391]) for their difficulties, but focused on one:

> Research indicates that the black dialect or vernacular used at home by black students in general makes it more difficult for such children to read because teachers' unconscious but evident attitudes toward the home language causes a psychological barrier to learning by the student. (1381)

The Court called for the Ann Arbor School District Board to develop a program to (1) help the teachers understand the problem, (2) provide them with knowledge about the children's use of African American English, and (3) suggest ways and means of using that knowledge in teaching the students to read (1381). In a court-ordered, 20-hour inservice program for the King School teachers, experts in reading and sociolinguistics furnished teachers with information on these topics. In spite of the wealth of information delivered to teachers, however, the school district's report of the results of this inservice program concludes that though teacher respondents "felt positively about all substantive issues, they were somewhat less positive about their understanding of the pedagogical issues" (Howard 17).

The nonstructural barriers resulting from negative attitudes were the focus of the Ann Arbor case, and they remain to challenge successful practice and our students' educational progress today. Survey results reported by Balester suggest that this was as true in 1992 as it was in 1979, the year of the Ann Arbor trial, or in the late 60s when scholarship in applied linguistics first took direct aim at many teachers' traditional, prescriptivist orientations. In 1994, Bowie and Bond found that teachers still continue to exhibit negative attitudes toward African American English, often stating that African American English has a faulty grammar system and that children who speak African American English are less capable than children who speak standard English.

CONSTRUCTS OF TEACHER KNOWLEDGE

It is clear that the outcome of the Ann Arbor case left many questions unanswered, including the most pressing question of how teachers are to respond to the linguistic and cultural diversity of their students. At the heart of the Ann Arbor decision was the recognition of the need for teachers to become sensitive to students' uses of African American English, to move into a way of being in the classroom which is responsive to and informed by recognition of racial and linguistic difference. However, the unresolved pedagogical issues reflected in the King School teachers' responses to their inservice program remain at the center of our reading of the Ann Arbor case in relation to composition studies: How do teachers learn and transform new knowledge into classroom practice? We argue that three competing constructs of teacher knowledge offer divergent ways of responding to this question. The three constructs we wish to describe are the *teacher as technician, teacher knowledge as lore,* and *teacher efficacy.* We distinguish these constructs from one another in terms of their approaches to the underlying issue of racially-informed language attitudes: How do they situate teachers in relation to confronting race as an element in classroom climate? How do they bring to the surface for teachers the awareness of unconscious negative language attitudes? How do they dispose teachers to be able to reflect on and move forward into alternative classroom practices?

Teacher as Technician

The teacher as technician is clearly the operative construct evident in the Ann Arbor case. This construct was a necessary feature of the "objectivist rhetoric" which made up the expert testimony in the trial, which was the dominant rhetoric in the Court's Memorandum Opinion and Order, and which continues to be the undergirding rhetoric of current scholarship on African American English in sociolinguistics, education, and literacy studies. Cy Knoblauch has identified "objectivist rhetoric" as empirical discourse which portrays knowledge as derived from unbiased observation and rigorous argumentative procedure. Because of this, the objectivist paradigm has served as a corrective to superstitions, emotional excesses, and prejudices (130). The Ann Arbor case demonstrates just this corrective potential.

One feature of objectivist rhetoric is its organization of knowledge in linear, cause-and-effect terms. A second feature, evident in the discourse of the case, is the trope of application. The Court acknowledged the necessary contributions of the King School teachers' "skill and empathy" (1391) to classroom success. But the chief significance of the trial lies in the way in which it focused on the need for teachers to apply in practice the findings of modern sociolinguistic scholarship. The process and outcome of the case reflects a technical construct of teacher knowledge in that it subordinates teachers' own reflective resources ("skill and empathy") to disciplinary (sociolinguistic) expertise. The case inscribes teachers as needy recipients of already-formed information which would, it was presumed, ameliorate their attitudes and which would (somehow) be translated into new, more effective teaching strategies.

The Final Evaluation of the results of the Ann Arbor inservice program stated that a great deal of information was available regarding such topics as the history and structure of African American English and the effect of teacher attitudes on student learning. But there was evidently little if any attention given at the time to the process of applying this knowledge in practice. Its application was apparently presumed to be automatic. Thomas Pietras, the Language Arts Coordinator for the Ann Arbor School District at the time of the King School trial, wrote that disseminating information to teachers about African American English "assumes that teacher knowledge will result in success in language arts" for speakers of African American English (qtd. in Howard et al. 59), but the results of the questionnaire that teachers filled out subsequent to the inservice speak to the disconnection between knowledge and application. The Final Evaluation distinguishes "substantive" issues from "pedagogical" issues, and the content of the inservice program itself virtually ignored questions of pedagogy, assuming perhaps that providing teachers with knowledge would lead by itself to improved student performance. How that improved student performance was (or is) to be achieved was never addressed; the teacher as technician construct doesn't ask that question, because it tends to bypass altogether the responsive decision-making that teachers must engage in.

The objectivist rhetoric exemplified in the Ann Arbor case in the testimony of experts served to move the Court to intervene in an ingrained, discriminatory institutional practice at King School. When William Labov, one of the leading expert witnesses to testify in Ann Arbor, wrote about the case saying that "negative attitudes can be changed by providing people with scientific evidence" (32), he expressed perfectly the objectivist view in which science serves as a corrective to prejudice. It also reflects a view of teachers as technicians and of pedagogy as the transparent process of translating "substantive" information in the classroom. Unfortunately, as the King School teachers' own evaluation of their training session indicates, introducing sociolinguistic information seems not to have led them to recognize avenues toward more effective classroom practice. Describing the limitations of objectivist rhetoric and the construct of teacher as technician we argue it entails, Knoblauch suggests that educators may speak of "advances" in "our knowledge of the processes of human learning, including the development of literacy" (130), and may thereby evince "a willingness to ground instruction in what we can observe about those processes" (130). However, Knoblauch goes on, "teachers and researchers accept the least advantageous assumptions of a positivist outlook . . . when they encourage [for example] the new knowledge of linguistics . . . to dictate instructional and learning agendas" (131). The practical (non-)consequences of this acceptance of a "positivist outlook" are evident in the King School teachers' responses. As much as they may have wished for it to be so, they seemed to recognize no clear way in which linguistic or sociolinguistic knowledge could "dictate" teaching and learning processes.

Teacher Knowledge as Lore

Such an impasse is perhaps what composition theorists who talk about teacher knowledge as lore might have predicted. Lore is a postmodern, "postdisciplinary" construct that rejects objectivist, linear, cause-and-effect discourse in favor of complex, multifaceted, and improvisational ways of understanding pedagogical interactions to explain how teachers know what to do.

We identify postdisciplinary views of teacher knowledge as lore with work which has emerged in composition in the last ten years—subsequent, that is, to the Ann Arbor case. Variously formulated by scholars ranging from Steven North to Louise Wetherbee Phelps and Patricia Harkin, this work has complicated the idea of disciplinary knowledge governing a teacher's practice in the classroom. In Harkin's formulation, lore is identified with teachers' informed intuitions about what works in the classroom. At the center of her discussion is the example of Mina Shaughnessy's *Errors and Expectations.* Harkin identifies Shaughnessy's book as exemplary of lore, and goes on to illustrate the disciplinary critique of lore by reference to critiques of Shaughnessy's work. Harkin writes that critics of teacher knowledge as lore see a danger in teachers who "are willfully ignorant of disciplinary knowledge," and who

> think they should be free . . . to ignore [for example] modern linguistic scholarship, free to invent their own programs as they go along . . . free to ignore evidence or theory, free to rely on their own insight, free, that is, to ignore facts. (130)

Harkin's reply is to turn aside the ethical implications (teachers ignore facts) and to deconstruct the idea of "facts" in itself: "Facts are only facts in the discipline which constitutes them," she asserts (130). Going on, she argues that because the complex scene of teaching cannot be reduced to the linear causality which disciplinary knowledge demands, teachers cannot be expected to obey disciplinary imperatives. Lore, with its improvisational logic, is the more appropriate interpretive framework with which to think about teaching, to think about how we know what to do in the classroom. The construct of teacher knowledge as lore thus turns us in the right direction as it asks directly about the process of discovery, application, and transformation of teacher knowledge in the classroom. Privileging teachers' direct experiences and reflective practice, lore draws our attention to the moment-to-moment process of observing, interpreting, and decision making that is characteristic of engaged teaching.

However, what the construct of teacher knowledge as lore works to resist—the apparent necessity for teachers to attune their practice to, for example, modern linguistic scholarship—lies at the heart of the Ann Arbor case and the intervention it represented into a discriminatory *status quo*. One unintended effect, then, of the construct of lore, of relying on teachers' informed intuitions, is to displace a direct confrontation with race as it may be manifested in students' strategic uses of African American English. In its effort to disrupt the disciplinary encroachment of, for example, sociolinguistics (we find Harkin's selection of "linguistics" as evidence quite telling), "postdisciplinary" theory substitutes for one problematic construct, the teacher as technician, an equally problematic construct of teacher knowledge as lore produced through "a process of informed intuition" when "practitioners do what works" (Harkin 134). In Ann Arbor, it took two years of legal action to force the school district to acknowledge that whatever its teachers' intuitions were, what was supposed to be working didn't work for a significant number of African American children. The case highlighted facts about language variation, race, language attitudes, and school performance which teachers ultimately were not free to ignore. Another effect of the postmodern construct of lore might thus be to undermine the strategic uses to which the objectivist discourses of the social sciences have been put. Since *Brown v. Topeka,* these discourses have been a chief weapon in the fight for educational justice for African American students. The familiar antifoundationalist critique that denies truth as a transcendent category could thus also deny access to the court of last appeal against racism in the quest for civil rights and educational equity. It is interesting to imagine but difficult to see how a postdisciplinary perspective might have carried the day in the Ann Arbor case.

The Ann Arbor case thus reveals possibilities and limitations of lore. We remain skeptical of the unintended effects of the antifoundationalism upon which lore is premised since this seems to rule out "appeals to truth, objectivity, ethics, and identity that social critics have traditionally made" (Schilb, "Cultural" 174). In terms of the issues of race and literacy highlighted by the Ann Arbor case and at play in composition classrooms today, postdisciplinarity and lore remain susceptible to such criticisms. Whereas scholars in other fields draw on postmodern theory to make race a prominent element in their analyses of cultural transactions (Cornel West, Patricia Williams), in many of composition's important discussions of postmodern theory, race is hardly mentioned. This is a striking oversight. What we are most concerned with, however, is to find ways to raise teachers' awareness of their own processes of pedagogical discovery and change, to help teachers recognize what their own habits of reflection make accessible to them, and what these habits of mind may leave out. The construct of lore moves us a long way toward the goal of seeing teachers' own reflective practice as the nexus of pedagogical theory. Our concern is that this construct does not put enough pressure on the question of "what works," thereby pushing teachers to confront the limitations of their practice—especially when for the majority of students everything seems to be running along smoothly, as was the case in Ann Arbor, where most of the students at King School were doing very well. In reference to issues of race which are raised in writing classes when students speak or draw on African American English in their writing, we see a need for teachers to avail themselves of facts which may seem external or peripheral to their experience of the classroom, but which may carry significance for some students. When lore does not confront practitioners with their own language biases, it works against change.

Teacher Efficacy

The third construct of teacher knowledge we wish to consider is teacher efficacy. It differs in one significant way from each of the first two constructs insofar as it draws attention to affect as an essential—perhaps the essential— component in teaching practice. In a field closely allied with composition, teacher educators such as Henry Giroux, Kenneth Zeichner, and Daniel Liston have offered a construct of teacher knowledge generated through reflective practice where teachers examine classroom routines in light of encompassing social and institutional pressures. We argue that the construct of teacher efficacy pushes beyond this enlarged view of reflective practice. By making affect a central issue in theorizing pedagogy, teacher efficacy moves closest to the largely unspoken dimensions of pedagogical experience when, let's say, white teachers in university writing courses attempt to mediate the discourse practices of African American English speaking students. Opening up these deeply felt but difficult to name dimensions of interaction, teacher efficacy speaks to the cumulative effect of teachers' knowledge and experience on their feelings about their students and their own ability to teach them.

This was what the Ann Arbor case was really about: the psychological barriers to learning that cause some students to dis-identify with school. Teacher efficacy as a construct of teacher knowledge places affect at the center and in so doing opens up and addresses questions of motivation and stance which are prior to and underlie curricular designs or pedagogical technique. When we speak of affect here, we refer to the emotional tone of classroom interactions. With reference to the Ann Arbor case, insofar as language variation is a factor in educational achievement, language as the medium of instruction is what counts. What is most relevant about Ann Arbor was how it drew attention to language as the medium of instruction and the interference generated by teachers' unconscious negative responses to their students' own language.

Defining affect in terms of "teachers' expectations, their empathy, and their own sense of self-efficacy" (370), Susan McLeod reminds us of the research which demonstrates the variable influence (positive or negative) of teacher affect on students' motivations for learning. Teacher efficacy refers to a teacher's beliefs about the power she or he has to produce a positive effect on students. McLeod points out that a teacher's emotional state or disposition forms one source of this sense of self-efficacy. Another source, and the most influential, is "the cultural beliefs that go to make up the macrosystem of American education," beliefs which inform teachers' common sense assumptions including "conceptions of the learner and the teacher and the role of education" (379). McLeod and others have shown that many variables contribute to teacher efficacy, including prior experience in multicultural settings, available resources, and teachers' visions of themselves as agents of social change. Teachers with high personal teaching efficacy believe that all students can be motivated and that it is their responsibility to explore with students the tasks that will hold their attention in the learning process. Valerie Pang and Velma Sablan propose that teacher efficacy is an especially important construct in the context of multicultural classrooms, and that teachers and teacher educators need to seriously examine what they believe about their ability to teach children from various cultural and linguistic backgrounds, particularly African American students. Pang and Sablan note that "when the overwhelming majority of the teaching force in this country is not from under-represented groups, the need to look at teacher misconceptions of African American culture, customs, history, and values is essential" (16).

Until the lawsuit, institutional custom invited the Ann Arbor School District to explain away African American student failure by attributing it to shortcomings in students rather than to shortcomings in the educational system or to the teachers' own lack of "skills or knowledge to help low achievers" (McLeod 380). Subsequent to the inservice program ordered by the Court, the King School teachers reflected low efficacy, that is, little confidence in their ability to adapt pedagogy to the various strengths and needs of speakers of African American English. Applied to the teaching of literacy that goes on in college writing courses, the question becomes, how do teachers become aware of unconscious negative attitudes (or even the dimly felt sense of unease resulting from lack of experience) they may bring with them to the learning environment? And, what steps can teachers take to communicate their sense of efficacy and high expectations to culturally diverse students?

Among the three constructs of teacher knowledge considered here, only that of teacher efficacy, grounded as it is in the consideration of affect in the classroom, makes these questions of felt sense, of emotional response, available for reflection. The Ann Arbor case focused on the language barrier which resulted from teachers' negative attitudes toward African American English. Racism—unconscious and institutional—was the clear subtext in the trial. Arthur Spears describes the problematic relationships among race, language variety, and school achievement. Citing dialect differences in other countries, Spears notes:

> Greater language differences are overcome elsewhere. Why can't they be overcome in American schools? The answer that comes through in a

number of studies of the issue is that the real problems are attitudinal and social. All these problems can be related to the general problem of institutional racism . . . low teacher expectations and disrespect for the home language and culture of inner-city pupils. (53–54)

Though rarely acknowledged as such, racism in the sense reflected here still remains an issue in the current teaching of writing, surfacing in the classroom in a variety of often subtle, unconscious manifestations (see Delpit). Neither of the first two constructs of teacher knowledge described offer adequate approaches to this problem; neither offers a vocabulary within which to directly address teachers' affective responses—low expectations, disrespect—which are the chief means through which institutional racism is manifested. Neither the teacher as technician construct nor lore offers direct access to unconscious negative racial stereotypes as a central issue in pedagogical theory. Our conclusion is that while unconscious attitudes are indeed, as Labov points out, partly a problem of (lack of) knowledge *per se,* they are more urgently a matter of feeling, the affective domain of racialized classroom experience which neither the technician model nor lore explicitly engages.

IMPLICATIONS FOR PRACTICE

The question remains, however: If our goal is to move urban youth in cities like Cleveland or Detroit into academic discourse communities, what stands in the way of that happening? In working toward building a sense of efficacy we need to give particular attention to staff development and writing programs in which teachers re-envision their capacity to function as catalysts of positive growth and development in students. In part, this improved sense of efficacy stems from an improved teacher knowledge base concerning the linguistic practices of diverse students. This can be accomplished by reviewing the literature diligently developed over the past four decades to provide a more complex, more complete linguistic profile of African American linguistic behavior. Characteristic features, discourse patterns, and rhetorical modes in African American English had been identified in the literature prior to the Ann Arbor case (Abrahams; Labov; Smitherman, *Talkin*). Research published since the conclusion of the case in 1979 has shed more light on distinctive discourse patterns and rhetorical modes. Much of this work has generated new knowledge of organizational patterns in the oral and written expository language of African American English speakers (Ball, "Expository"), the subtle ways that academically successful students strategically use African American English in their writing (Ball, "Cultural"), and on the assessment of writing produced by African American English speakers (Richardson). Research investigating the teaching practices of exemplary African American teachers working in community-based organizations has shown that these teachers build on the language practices of their African American students. They work explicitly to make students metacognitively aware of their oral and written uses of African American English and of alternative ways of expressing their ideas in academic and in technical, workplace English (Ball, Broussard, and Dinkins; Morgan; Ball, "Community").

Becoming informed about cultural discourse patterns and rhetorical modes is a significant resource that successful teachers can build on. Most interesting, however, is the impact of an awareness of cultural differences in discourse patterns on classroom interactions. The presence of varied patterns of discourse in classrooms can impact instruction in positive as well as in negative ways (Foster, "Effective"). Speech behavior is central to a full understanding of how a community expresses its realities, and research on teacher efficacy suggests that effective teachers develop strong human bonds with their students, have high expectations, focus on the total child, and are able to use communication styles familiar to their students. Exemplary African American teachers in community-based organizations are able to draw, to varying degrees, on primarily the rhetorical modes and discourse-level strategies of African American English in shaping interactive discourse as the medium of instruction with their students (Ball, Broussard, Dinkins; Foster "Educating"). Their practice in this regard stands as a model for other teachers to reflect on as they consider expanding their own pedagogical repertoires. We are not advocating that all teachers need to learn and teach Black English. We are arguing that the practices of exemplary African American teachers show us ways of focusing on participation patterns in interactive discourse as the medium of instruction in order to raise the awareness of teachers of the possible links between their own styles of communication and their students' responsiveness in classroom exchanges. Having high expectations and good intentions is not enough; these intentions and expectations need to be evident to students in observable or, we might say, audible behaviors in the classroom.

But as important as this knowledge base may be, it will not in and of itself activate teachers to change their practice. The cognitive internalization of information is not enough to increase teacher efficacy. The Ann Arbor case suggests that the key to effective uses of language diversity in the classroom relates fundamentally to teachers' dispositions toward literacy—that is, depends upon teachers' affective stance toward themselves, their work environment, and especially their culturally diverse students. More current research seems to confirm this. Addressing disposition as the most important variable, we have begun to push beyond internalization of knowledge about African American English in the teacher-education programs we are involved in. In doing so, we have found ourselves observing the ways preservice teachers encounter and contextualize the pedagogical ramifications of language diversity. Our observations suggest that preservice teachers who attempt to address the complex issues relating to this topic may do so by examining personal experiences of crossing borders from one speech community to another. Given these observations, we have begun to consider occasions for knowledge-making that appear in "extra-professional" sites where teachers become aware of their own culturally influenced dispositions toward literacy. We have begun to explore ways of talking that help teachers connect to parts of their experience that conventional academic, theoretical frameworks seem to silence.

IMPLICATIONS FOR PEDAGOGICAL THEORY

In 1991 Ann Dyson and Sarah Freedman challenged writing and composition professionals to take significant and positive steps toward building a more powerful theoretical framework for writing research and instruction by expanding our framework to

> include more analytic attention to how the complex of sociocultural experiences enter into literacy learning experiences that have roots in social class, ethnicity, language background, family, neighborhood, and gender. Without serious attention to the unfolding of this wider cultural frame in literacy learning, our vision of the whole remains partially obscured. (4)

This call addresses the ways we construct theory in our field, how we represent the relationships among literacy processes, pedagogy, interactions within the classroom, and cultural expectations which embed our institutions. The first two constructs—teacher as technician and teacher knowledge as lore—share a *curricular* view of the theory-practice relationship. Both of these views are consistent with extant models of pedagogical theory offered in composition studies (Brannon; Fulkerson). Each of the first two constructs we consider here analyzes the decisions teachers make in terms of the propositions of theory: a view of the writing process, the development of writing ability, the goal of writing and teaching, the ways knowledge is constructed. Each locates teacher authority within professional discourse, and assigns teachers a stable, centered, and professional subjectivity which is monologic, perhaps ungendered, and more to our point, unmarked by race. Both constructs are therefore, for teachers and the profession alike, discourses of control.

The third construct, teacher efficacy, reconfigures the representation of pedagogical theory. In particular, instead of seeing writing pedagogy as determined by a general theory of writing (in whatever versions this general theory might appear), the alternative we propose would place the teacher, the student, and the site of literacy instruction at the center, each exerting its influence on the others, each influencing an orientation toward the activity of the course, each in relationships with the others which are at best dialogical and, as some scholars have pointed out, often contradictory and conflictual (Lu). The construct of teacher efficacy does not subordinate pedagogy to a teacher's "substantive" knowledge, nor does it place teacher knowledge in dialogue with its situation, as the postdisciplinary view would have it. The construct of efficacy locates pedagogical theory in relation to three intersecting points of view: the institutional context of the writing course, the teacher's sense of herself as an actor within that institutional site, and the dialogizing, ambivalent, often resistant perspectives of students. The virtue of this model of pedagogical theory in composition is that by drawing attention to the "complex sociocultural experiences of literacy learning" Dyson and Freedman refer to, it sharpens the kinds of questions practitioners may ask about what works in and what works on the activity sponsored by the writing classroom.

CHANGING DISPOSITIONS

Disposition has two meanings which offer complementary views of the challenges surrounding literacy education in multicultural classrooms. The first meaning is "one's customary manner or emotional response; temperament." In its response to Oakland's Ebonics resolution, the American public's customary manner of emotional response toward African American English became front-page public news. The second meaning of disposition is "the power to control, direct, or dispose." These two meanings of disposition frame the interrelated issues surrounding the Ebonics controversy and the Ann Arbor "Black English" case, and the significance each holds for the field of composition. On the one hand, the Ann Arbor case came to focus on the language barrier which results from teachers' unconscious, negative attitudes toward African American English. On the other, ill-disposed toward their students' use of African American English, the Ann Arbor teachers expected less and their students not surprisingly lived down to these lowered expectations, evidence of the power of self-fulfilling prophecy.

More than 20 years ago, in response to the Ann Arbor case, the Black Caucus of NCTE and CCCC disseminated a carefully prepared "Commentary" regarding African American English. Recently reprinted in response to the Ebonics initiative, the purpose of the "Commentary" was to express the viewpoints of Black linguists and language arts educators on the topic. Briefly summarized, the "Commentary" asserts that the Black language system in and of itself is not a barrier to learning. The barrier is negative attitudes toward that language system, compounded by lack of information about the language system and inefficient techniques for teaching language skills, all of which is manifested in an unwillingness to adapt teaching styles to students' needs. Such barriers, in fact, reflect teachers', and the public's, dispositions toward literacy. In light of the public outcry over Ebonics, we ask: Have those dispositions changed today? The "Commentary" of the Black Caucus went on to say that the language of Black students is actually a strength on which teachers might draw in order to develop effective approaches to teaching. They concluded the statement with a call for thorough, unbiased research on the topic. However, based on the tone of the criticisms and emotional responses to the Ebonics issue, it became evident that society in general does not take such a detailed or objective view on the matter of the representations of diverse languages in the classroom.

After looking closely at the Ann Arbor case, it seems clear that for writing teachers today, many of the same barriers exist in the classroom that stood between the teachers at King School and their students. Because of cultural differences in patterns of language use, and because of differences in styles of interaction used to demonstrate knowledge, many students from diverse social and linguistic backgrounds are entering urban classrooms where teachers still have a difficult time recognizing and fully utilizing the wealth of language resources students use effectively outside school. These are resources that often go unrecognized and unrewarded within classroom settings. In spite of the considerable professional rhetoric over the past 20 years or so, recent research indicates that African Americans and other students of color are still faring very poorly in our nation's urban schools (Quality Education for Minorities Project). In light of the history of failure and miscommunication that marks the educational experiences of many African American English speakers, educators must continue to insist on seeking ways that the barriers created by diversity in language as the medium of instruction can become, instead, bridges between home language practices and academic registers teachers want students to learn. Making a significant place for affect within pedagogical theories is an important step toward this goal.

AFTERWORD . . . .

This award stands as a high-water mark in both of our careers. We have found the synergies of this collaborative experience to have been exhilarating, and the recognition that the Braddock Award carries gratifying. However, as we look at the list of Braddock Award essays, we note that our article is the only one that focuses on issues of African American vernacular English (AAVE) in composition classrooms. We know that our profession purports to stand as a vanguard on issues of justice, freedom, equity, and access—yet we find that we are still at odds when it comes to discussions of varieties of English as they appear in our students' written and oral discourse. We would like to believe that the work for which we have won this award might affect the teaching of composition and the lives of real students within composition classrooms. We are skeptical that it will. We believe, in fact, that few of the people we encounter on a day-to-day basis will even recognize what the Braddock Award is. Administrators at our institutions will be happy to acknowledge the winning of another award, but we believe that few other scholars or practitioners in our departments ever read College Composition and Communication.

Imagine a writing program at a modestly sized midwestern urban university. In a typical semester, sixty-nine sections of various first-year writing courses will be taught by a mix of full-time faculty and part-timers. Among the teachers who will staff these sections, perhaps two subscribe to CCC. No one, no one here has read our article. No one knows what the Braddock Award is. Furthermore, here the prevailing attitude toward first-year writing is the usual: Faculty and administrators love the credit hours it generates but hold their noses when they must teach it.

Let us put the matter where it matters most. In those sixty-nine sections of first-year writing courses, there will be five or six African American students whose stances and primary discourses put them at difficult angles with the white teachers (every section, usually) who are tasked with initiating them into the academic discourse community. Here's what happens: the failure of many of those African American students to thrive gets explained away. If the topic arises at all, it is said that most students do alright, so why should teachers change—for to reach these students changes in teachers' lives and teaching practices (and in writing programs as well) would have to be significant. In "Dispositions" we attempted to glance down the road of possible changes that writing teachers, and writing programs, would need to make if they were to make genuine attempts to respond to the needs and experiences of all of the students who enter our classrooms. We think that the Braddock Award stands as a validation of our glance down that road.

When we were asked to write this afterword, we were afforded another opportunity to glance down that road. As we paused to take that glance, we were reminded of the words of James Sledd, who once said to one of us, "Look. Look around you. What difference have departments of English made anywhere? We live because we can say every now and then 'I helped this individual student.' All right. Since that's the limit of our power, then we ought to do it. But how very tiny that is."

And as we think on these words, it makes us wonder.

—Arnetha Ball
University of Michigan

—Ted Lardner
Cleveland State University

NOTES AND
WORKS CITED*

Reading—and Rereading—The Braddock Essays

NOTES

1. See, for instance: "Teaching Writing," "Methods, Methodologies, and the Politics of Knowledge: Reflections and Speculations," "Reading the Writing Process," "Writing Centers and the Politics of Location: A Response to Terrance Riley and Stephen M. North," and (with Andrea Lunsford) "Representing Audience: 'Successful' Discourse and Disciplinary Critique."

2. Though Braddock's essay was published in *Research in the Teaching of English,* in subsequent years only essays published in *College Composition and Communication,* the journal published by CCCC, have been eligible for recognition.

3. The Outstanding Book Award and the Exemplar Award were established in 1991; the James A. Berlin Memorial Outstanding Dissertation Award, in 1992; and the Nell Ann Pickett Service Award in 1993.

4. Additional factors undoubtedly did (and do) play a role in decisions about publication in *CCC.* During most of Edward P. J. Corbett's tenure as editor of *CCC,* for instance, he encouraged those submitting articles to stay within a limit of 2500 words or eight to ten pages. The guidelines for the submission of manuscripts in the October, 1979, *CCC* (volume 30, number 3) increased the word limit from 2500 to 3500 words, or ten to fifteen pages, a practice which subsequent *CCC* editor Richard L. Larson continued. (Both Corbett and Larson stated that they would accept longer articles, though such articles needed to recommend themselves in some special way.) Under Joseph Harris's editorship, the guidelines for submission do not specify word limits.

5. In her 1991 *Textual Carnivals: The Politics of Composition,* Susan Miller makes the following calculation about the number of students and teachers engaged in the work of composition at that time: "The teaching of writing, at least according to publishers of textbooks for writing courses, engages about four million freshman-level students each year. If we consider how many additional students take upper-level writing and graduate courses in rhetoric and composition theory, adding another million to this figure is probably not an exaggeration. If we divide this expanded number by twenty-four, the mean class size reported in the Association of Departments of English '1983–84 Sample' [Huber 45], we can estimate that at least 165,000 teaching assignments are made each year in classes relevant to postsecondary writing, not counting classes offered in government or professional settings. Estimating an average load in writing courses among two- to four-year institutions would be foolish, but it is probably safe to guess that at least 25,000 individuals are engaged in college-level composition teaching each academic year" (4–5).

6. Nancy Bird narrates roughly the same story in her dissertation, adding that "hopes that . . . [the 1947 joint meeting of the Speech Association of America and the NCTE] would mark the beginning of a new organized effort to deal with the problems of communication and composition were not realized" due to "considerable differences of opinion among those attending" (33). In a 1993 interview with John Gerber, presented in Sharon Crowley's *Composi-*

*The notes and works cited for the original Braddock essays are reproduced here as they originally appeared when the essays were published. Because of changing documentation styles, formats will vary. Notes and works cited for the afterwords reflect current MLA documentation preferences.

tion in the University, Gerber contradicts Bird and Lloyd-Jones, for he dates the birth of the CCCC to a 1947 meeting of the NCTE, not 1948. A review of issues of *College English* undertaken by Robert Connors supports Bird's and Lloyd-Jones's chronology. In an email communication to me, Connors writes: " . . . it seems pretty clear that Bird's chronology is accurate. There was a meeting in Feb. 1947 about college comp, but . . . the Nov. 1947 NCTE meeting did not seem to follow it up in any meaningful way . . . and I see no indication that anything like the CCCC was planned at it. In 1948, the 'Thanksgiving Meeting' . . . did have a very active set of College Section meetings, one of which Wykoff and Gerber were at that was concerned with comp issues. And in the Feb. 1949 issue, which reported on the November NCTE of 1948, the meeting report was near a small box announcing a meeting on the composition curriculum (no name) at the Stevens Hotel on April 1–2 that had been called on the basis of a College Section meeting at Thanksgiving. . . . So the "Conference on College Freshman Courses in Composition and Communication" . . . [was] proposed, planned, and executed in four months!"

7. This curricular and administrative emphasis was so strong that, according to Nancy Bird, during early discussions of possible titles for the CCCC serious consideration was given to the name "American Association of Directors of Freshman English: A Department of the NCTE" (37). Other confirmation for this strong curricular emphasis can be found in early reports of CCCC chairs to the NCTE. Holdings in the NCTE archives indicate that the first CCCC annual report, included as part of the large NCTE annual report, appeared in 1952 and was written by Harold B. Allen, current CCCC chair. Allen began his report with this statement: "In 1952 the Conference on College Composition and Communication measurably strengthened its position as the only national group exclusively concerned with the freshman course" (9). Similarly, Karl W. Dykema begins his 1953 report to the NCTE by observing, "The CCCC was organized to deal with the college freshman course" (A-9). Finally, here is the introduction to T. A. Barnhart's 1954 CCCC report to the NCTE: "At the 1954 Spring meeting of the Conference on College Composition and Communication, former chairman Harold B. Allen spoke significantly on the new climate in which college English teachers now find themselves, saying: 'For the first time freshman English instructors and administrators are working together on a national scale to attack our common problems. In four short years the CCCC has provided extraordinary stimulus to constructive thinking and positive action about these problems'" (A-7).

8. In its early years, the CCCC's strongest base was in the midwest. The organization's first conference to be held elsewhere took place in 1956, when the conference met in New York City. The first west coast CCCC occurred in 1959 in San Francisco.

9. NCTE granted permanent status to the CCCC in 1955.

10. During the early years of the CCCC, for instance, there was tension between those who favored communication skills courses and those who emphasized composition over communication—tension that spilled over into efforts to consider changing the name of the CCCC. (Among those considered were: Conference on College Composition, Council on College Writing, and Council on College Rhetoric). An undated "Report on the Name-Change Questionnaire" drafted by Paul Roberts and housed in NCTE archives gives some sense of the nature of this conflict. Here are two representative comments included in the report:

"To drop the word 'communication' is, in my opinion, to move a step closer to the ivory tower. The current spurt of interest in composition is excellent, but it is unthinkable for colleges to neglect the communication process. Why must the professors make an issue of this? Among the suggestions listed, I have no second choice."

"My feelings on the matter are not strong. Three C's seem better than four. 'Council' seems better than 'Conference' (especially when the 'Conference' holds a conference). But if the word 'Communication' is necessary to alleviate the fears of the benighted supporters of the communication idea, I would vote for the CCCC as it now stands, 'Conference' and all. Let us not slight anyone."

11. The identification of freshman English as a "problem" to be "attack[ed]" is a recurrent theme of CCCC and *CCC* documents from the 1950s. (The 1951 volume of *CCC* included C. Harold Gray's "The Problem of Freshman English in the Professional School," Karl W. Dykema's "The Problem of Freshman English in the Liberal Arts College," and Adolphus J. Bryan's "The Problem of Freshman English in the University.")

12. The question of composition's disciplinary status from the 1970s to the present is complex. If one considers only the situation of tenure-line faculty who profess the teaching of writing, then clearly composition studies has attained a considerable foothold in the academy. In

Fragments of Rationality: Postmodernity and the Subject of Composition, Lester Faigley comments on changes in the field that took place in the 1970s and 1980s, observing, "In spite of the continuous skirmishing between literature and composition factions in English departments at public universities during the 1970s and 1980s, the institutional conditions at many schools favored the development of writing programs. If there were often snarling colleagues in traditional literary fields, there were also smiling deans and vice-presidents. Professional schools were eager to improve the writing abilities of their graduates, and as students became more career-oriented, they began to recognize that writing would be important to their future. Even the stance of many English Departments moderated when they realized that elevating the status of composition would not turn them into service departments and that large writing programs could underwrite many of their traditional activities" (67). Improvements in the status and working conditions of tenure-line faculty did not, however, extend to the many part- and full-time instructors and teaching assistants who teach the majority of writing classes in the United States.

13. During the 1970s and 1980s a number of new scholarly journals joined *College Composition and Communication, College English,* and *Research in the Teaching of English* as possible forums for researchers in composition studies. These journals, and their founding dates, include: *Freshman English News* (1971; *FEN* is now titled *Composition Studies/Freshman English News*); *Reader* (as a newsletter, 1971; as a journal, 1976); *The Journal of Basic Writing* (1975); *The Writing Lab Newsletter* (1975); *WPA: Writing Program Administration* (1977); *The Writing Center Journal* (1980); *Pre/Text* (1980); *The Journal of Advanced Composition* (1980); *The Writing Instructor* (1981); *The Journal of Teaching Writing* (1981); *Rhetoric Review* (1982); *Rhetorica* (1983); *Written Communication* (1984); and *Teaching English in the Two-Year College* (1984).

14. A "Secretary's Report" by George S. Wykoff published in the February 1951 issue of *CCC* provides evidence of this interest in the material situation of teachers of writing. The report discusses, among other things, "projects to be undertaken by the CCCC" as determined at the previous spring conference. These include:

   (a) the professional status of the composition or communication teacher
   (b) the teaching load of the composition or communication teacher
   (c) the problem of diagnostic and achievement tests (objective and essay types, etc.)
   (d) teacher training for composition or communication (graduate seminars, on-the-job training, etc.)
   (e) articulation with high schools (14)

15. Richard Lloyd-Jones took the publication *Research on Written Composition: New Directions for Teaching,* by George Hillocks, Jr—a work that presents itself as in the lineage of Braddock, Lloyd-Jones, and Schoer's earlier effort—as an opportunity to clarify his role in that project. In an introduction to Hillocks's work, Lloyd-Jones comments, "Despite the implications of my own work in testing, I do not think of myself as an empiricist; my role with Braddock and Schoer was that of the rhetorical theorist. . . . In 1962 I was not sure I shared Braddock's hope that we are emerging from an age of alchemy, and I still think of lore and other forms of experiential knowledge as essential to our crafts . . ." (xiv).

16. In "Mediating Pedagogy and Theory: CCC and the Richard Braddock Memorial Award," Thomas E. Recchio characterizes this tension as involving a "centripetal force" growing out of "the pressures of academic disciplinarity . . . that would splinter composition studies from the classroom while the daily experience of composition scholars in the classroom exerts a centrifugal force focused on questions of pedagogy" (3–4).

17. These trends are, of course, not uniform. Though a number of Braddock essays in the early and mid-1980s are grounded in cognitivist methodologies, others are not. Robert J. Connors's essay is primarily historical in its methodology, for instance, while Peter Elbow's might best be characterized as phenomenological.

18. The growing body of teacher research is an obvious exception to this statement—but the fact that this research is identified as a particular kind of research within composition studies indicates the extent to which it is still a resistant or marginalized form of inquiry.

19. The point I make in this paragraph evokes that made by Stephen M. North in *The Making of Knowledge in Composition: Portrait of an Emerging Field.* In this study North argues that ". . . the field has been driven by the need to replace practice as its primary mode of inquiry and lore as its dominant form of knowledge. That drive resulted in what I called a methodological land rush: a scramble to stake out territory, to claim power over what constitutes knowledge in Composition; and to claim, as well, whatever rewards that power might carry with it" (317). While my analysis here in some ways supports North's observation, I hope to

have portrayed a multivocal (as opposed to North's univocal) narrative, one which acknowledges the multiplicity of desires that many in composition have held.

WORKS CITED

Allen, Harold B. "Conference on College Composition and Communication." 1952 NCTE Annual Report. Box 26. National Council of Teachers of English Administrative Archives. Urbana, IL.

Anon. "MLAise in March." *Rhetoric Review* 9 (Fall 1990): 185–86.

Anzaldúa, Gloria. *Borderlands/La Frontera: The New Mestiza.* San Francisco: Aunt Lute Books, 1987.

Bakhtin, Mikhail. *The Dialogic Imagination: Four Essays by Mikhail Bakhtin.* Trans. Caryl Emerson and Michael Holquist. Ed. Michael Holquist. Austin: U of Texas P, 1981.

Barnhart, T.A. "Annual Report of the Conference on College Composition and Communication." 1954 NCTE Annual Report. Box 26. National Council of Teachers of English Administrative Archives. Urbana, IL.

Bartholomae, David. "Writing with Teachers: A Conversation with Peter Elbow." *College Composition and Communication* (Feb. 1995): 62–71, 84–87.

Berkenkotter, Carol. "Paradigm Debates, Turf Wars, and the Conduct of Sociocognitive Inquiry in Composition." *College Composition and Communication* 42 (May 1991): 151–169.

Berlin, James A. "Contemporary Composition: The Major Pedagogical Theories." *College English* 44 (Dec. 1982): 765–77.

———. "Rhetoric and Ideology in the Writing Class." *College English* 50 (Sept. 1988): 477–94.

Bird, Nancy K. "The Conference on College Composition and Communication: A Historical Study of Its Continuing Education and Professionalization Activities, 1949–75." Diss. Virginia Polytechnic Institute and State U, 1977.

Bizzell, Patricia. *Academic Discourse and Critical Consciousness.* Pittsburgh: U of Pittsburgh P, 1992.

———. "Cognition, Convention, and Certainty: What We Need to Know about Writing." *Pre/Text* 3 (Fall 1982): 213–43.

Braddock, Richard, Richard Lloyd-Jones, and Lowell Schoer. *Research in Written Composition.* Champaign: NCTE, 1963.

Bridwell-Bowles, Lillian. "Discourse and Diversity: Experimental Writing within the Academy. *College Composition and Communication* 43 (Oct. 1992): 349–68.

Brodkey, Linda. "Modernism and the Scene(s) of Writing." *College English* 49 (Apr. 1987): 396–418.

Brown, Stuart C., Paul R. Meyer, and Theresa Enos. "Doctoral Programs in Rhetoric and Composition: A Catalog of the Profession." *Rhetoric Review* 12 (Spring 1994): 240–51.

Bryan, Adolphus J. "The Problem of Freshman English in the University." *College Composition and Communication* 2 (May 1951): 6–8.

Burke, Kenneth. *Language as Symbolic Action: Essays on Life, Literature, and Method.* Berkeley: U of California P, 1966.

CCCC Committee on Professional Standards for Quality Education. "CCCC Initiatives on the Wyoming Conference Resolution: A Draft Report." *College Composition and Communication* 40 (Feb. 1989): 61–72.

Chaplin, Miriam T. "Issues, Perspectives, and Possibilities." *College Composition and Communication* 39 (Feb. 1988): 52–62.

Chapman, David W., and Gary Tate. "A Survey of Doctoral Programs in Rhetoric and Composition." *Rhetoric Review* 5 (Spring 1987): 124–85.

Charney, Davida. "Empiricism Is Not a Four-Letter Word." *College Composition and Communication* 47(Dec. 1996): 567–93.

"Conference on College Courses in Communication." Conference Program. 1947 Conference on College Courses in Communication. National Council of Teachers of English File. Record Series 15/7/760. University of Illinois Archives. Urbana, IL.

"Conference on College Freshman Courses in Composition and Communication." Conference Program. 1949 Conference on College Freshman Courses in Composition and Communication. National Council of Teachers of English File. Record Series 15/7/760. University of Illinois Archives. Urbana, IL.

Connors, Robert J. *Composition-Rhetoric: Backgrounds, Theory, and Pedagogy.* Pittsburgh: U of Pittsburgh P, 1997.

———. "Query Re Founding of CCCC." Email to Lisa Ede. 3 Sept. 1988.

Cooper, Marilyn. "The Ecology of Writing." *College English* 48 (Apr. 1986): 364–75.

Crowley, Sharon. *Composition in the University: Historical and Polemical Essays.* Pittsburgh: U of Pittsburgh P, 1998.

Dykema, Karl W. "Conference on College Composition and Communication." 1953 NCTE Annual Report. Box 26. National Council of Teachers of English Administrative Archives. Urbana, IL.

———. "The Problem of Freshman English in the Liberal Arts College." *College Composition and Communication* 2 (May 1951): 3–5.

Ede, Lisa. "Methods, Methodologies, and the Politics of Knowledge: Reflections and Speculations." *Methods and Methodology in Composition Studies.* Ed. Gesa Kirsch and Patricia Sullivan. Carbondale: Southern Illinois UP, 1992. 314–29.

———. "Reading the Writing Process." *Taking Stock: Reassessing the Writing Process Movement.* Ed. Thomas Newkirk and Lad Tobin. Portsmouth: Boynton/Cook, 1994. 31–44.

———. "Teaching Writing." *Composition Studies: Anatomy of a Discipline.* Ed. Erika Lindemann and Gary Tate. New York: Oxford UP, 1991. 118–34.

———. "Writing Centers and the Politics of Location: A Response to Terrance Riley and Stephen M. North." *Writing Center Journal* 16 (Spring 1996): 111–30.

Elbow, Peter. "Being a Writer vs. Being an Academic: A Conflict in Goals." *College Composition and Communication* 46 (Feb. 1995): 72–83, 87–92.

———. *Writing with Power: Techniques for Mastering the Writing Process.* New York: Oxford UP, 1981.

———. *Writing without Teachers.* New York: Oxford UP, 1973.

Faigley, Lester. "Competing Theories of Process. A Critique and a Proposal." *College English* 48 (Oct. 1986): 527–42.

———. *Fragments of Rationality: Postmodernity and the Subject of Composition.* Pittsburgh: U of Pittsburgh P, 1992.

Flower, Linda. *The Construction of Negotiated Meaning: A Social Cognitive Theory of Writing.* Carbondale: Southern Illinois UP, 1994.

Flynn, Elizabeth. "Feminism and Scientism." *College Composition and Communication* 46 (Oct. 1995): 353–68.

"For Administrative Head of Work in Composition and Communication." Undated Survey. National Council of Teachers of English File. Record Series 15/7/760. University of Illinois Archives. Urbana, IL.

Foucault, Michel. *Discipline and Punish: The Birth of the Prison.* Trans. Alan Sheridan. New York: Vintage, 1979.

Frey, Olivia. "Beyond Literary Darwinism: Women's Voices and Critical Discourse." *College English* 52 (Sept. 1990): 507–26.

Fulkerson, Richard. "Composition Theory in the Eighties: Axiological Consensus and Paradigmatic Diversity." *College Composition and Communication* 41 (Dec. 1990): 409–29.

Gere, Anne Ruggles. "The Extracurriculum of Composition." *College Composition and Communication* 45 (Feb. 1994): 75–92.

———. "The Long Revolution in Composition." *Composition in the Twenty-First Century: Crisis and Change.* Ed. Lynn Z. Bloom, Donald A. Daiker, and Edward M. White. Carbondale: Southern Illinois UP, 1996. 119–32.

Gerber, John C. "The Conference on College Composition and Communication." *College Composition and Communication* 1 (Mar. 1950): 12.

Gilyard, Keith. "Conference on College Composition and Communication Call for Program Proposals." Urbana: NCTE, 1998.

Gray, C. Harold. "The Problem of Freshman English in the Professional School." *College Composition and Communication* 2 (Feb. 1951): 3–6.

"Guidelines for the Workload of the College English Teacher." *College English* 49 (Sept. 1987): n. pag.

Hairston, Maxine. "Diversity, Ideology, and Teaching Writing." *College Composition and Communication* 43 (May 1992): 179–95.

———. "The Winds of Change: Thomas Kuhn and the Revolution in the Teaching of Writing." *College Composition and Communication* 33 (Feb. 1982): 76–88.

Haraway, Donna J. *Simians, Cyborgs, and Women: The Reinvention of Nature.* New York: Routledge, 1991.

Hill, James A. "Concurrent Session Program Proposal Form." Urbana: NCTE, 1981.

Hillocks, George, Jr. *Research on Written Composition: New Directions for Teaching.* Urbana: NCTE, 1986.

hooks, bell. *Talking Back: Thinking Feminist/Thinking Black.* Boston: South End, 1989.

Huber, Bettina J., and Art Young. "The 1983–84 Survey of English Sample." *ADE Bulletin* 84 (1986): 40–61.

Hunting, Robert S. "A Training Course for Teachers of Freshman Composition." *College Composition and Communication* 2 (Oct. 1951): 3–6.

Kinneavy, James L. *A Theory of Discourse: The Aims of Discourse*. New York: Norton, 1971.

Lauer, Janice. "Heuristics and Composition." *College Composition and Communication* 21 (Dec. 1970): 396–404. Rpt. in *Contemporary Rhetoric: A Conceptual Background with Readings*. Ed. W. Ross Winterowd. New York: Harcourt, 1979. 79–90.

Lindemann, Erika. *A Rhetoric for Writing Teachers*. 3rd ed. New York: Oxford UP, 1995.

Lloyd-Jones, Richard. "Who We Were, Who We Should Become." *College Composition and Communication* 43 (Dec. 1992): 486–96.

Lunsford, Andrea A., and Lisa Ede. "Representing Audience: 'Successful' Discourse and Disciplinary Critique." *College Composition and Communication* 47 (May 1996): 167–79.

Macrorie, Ken. *Telling Writing*. 3rd ed. Rochelle Park: Hayden, 1970.

Marshall, James. "'Of What Does Skill in Writing Really Consist?': The Political Life of the Writing Process Movement." *Taking Stock: The Writing Process Movement in the '90s*. Ed. Lad Tobin and Thomas Newkirk. Portsmouth: Boynton/Cook, 1994. 45–55.

Miller, Susan. *Textual Carnivals: The Politics of Composition*. Carbondale: Southern Illinois UP, 1991.

Murray, Donald. *Learning by Teaching*. Upper Montclair: Boynton/Cook, 1982.

Neel, Jasper. *Plato, Derrida, and Writing*. Carbondale: Southern Illinois UP, 1988.

North, Stephen M. *The Making of Knowledge in Composition: Portrait of an Emerging Field*. Upper Montclair: Boynton/Cook, 1987.

Peck, Wayne Campbell, Linda Flower, and Lorraine Higgins. "Community Literacy." *College Composition and Communication* 46 (May 1995): 199–222.

Purnell, Rosentene Bennet. "Concurrent Session Program Proposal Form." Urbana: NCTE, 1982.

Ray, Ruth E. *The Practice of Theory: Teacher Research in Composition*. Urbana: NCTE, 1993.

Recchio, Thomas E. "Mediating Pedagogy and Theory: CCC and the Richard Braddock Memorial Award." Unpublished essay, 1998.

RLV. "Adversaries and Mentors." *Rhetoric Review* 9 (Fall 1990): 184–85.

Roberts, Charles W. "Workshop Reports of the 1950 Conference on College Composition and Communication." *College Composition and Communication* 2 (May 1950): 3.

Roberts, Paul. "Report on the Name-Change Questionnaire." Committee Report (1959). National Council of Teachers of English File. Record Series 15/7/760. University of Illinois Archives. Urbana, IL.

Rorty, Richard. *Philosophy and the Mirror of Nature*. Princeton: Princeton UP, 1979.

Royster, Jacqueline Jones. "When the First Voice You Hear Is Not Your Own." *College Composition and Communication* 47 (Feb. 1996): 29–40.

Sheils, Merrill. "Why Johnny Can't Write." *Newsweek* 8 Dec. 1975: 56–65.

Sirc, Geoffrey. "Never Mind the Tagmemics, Where's the Sex Pistols?" *College Composition and Communication* 48 (Feb. 1997): 9–29.

SM. "Tales from the Field." *Rhetoric Review* 9 (Fall 1990): 186–87.

"Statement of Principles and Standards for the Postsecondary Teaching of Writing." Conference on College Composition and Communication. Urbana: NCTE, 1989.

Stewart, Donald C. "Concurrent Session Program Proposal Form." Urbana: NCTE, 1982.

"Students' Right to Their Own Language." *College Composition and Communication* 25 (Special Issue, 1974).

"The 1950 Spring Meeting." *College Composition and Communication* 1 (Mar. 1950): 16.

Troyka, Lynn Quitman. "New Plan for CCCC Program Proposals." *College English* 40 (1979): 936.

———. "Program Proposal Form." Urbana, NCTE, 1979.

Wykoff, George S. "Secretary's Report.: *College Composition and Communication* 2 (Feb. 1951): 13–15.

The Frequency and Placement of Topic Sentences in Expository Prose
Richard Braddock

NOTES

1. The copies were supplied through the generosity of the Department of English, University of Iowa.

2. Here and hereafter, reference to specific articles in the corpus will be made simply by using the author's last name—or, in the cases of the two articles by individuals of the same last name, by using the first initial and last name (see Table 1). The paragraph referred to here is in Lear, p. 89.

WORKS CITED

Ashida, M.E. Something for everyone: a standard corpus of contemporary American expository essays. *Research in the Teaching of English,* 1968, 2, 14–23.
Bain, A. *English Composition and Rhetoric,* enl. ed. London: Longmans, Green, 1890.
Basic skills system: writing test, Form A. New York: McGraw Hill, 1970.
Gorrell, R.M., and Laird, C. *Modern English handbook,* 4th ed. Englewood Cliffs, New Jersey: Prentice Hall, 1967.
Hunt, K.W. *Grammatical structures written at three grade levels.* Research Report No. 3. Urbana, Illinois: NCTE, 1965.
Irmscher, W.F. *The Holt guide to English.* New York: Holt, Rinehart, and Winston, 1972.
Rodgers, P. Jr. A discourse-centered rhetoric of the paragraph. *College Composition and Communication,* 1966, 17, 2–11.
Braddock, Richard, Richard Lloyd-Jones, and Lowell Schoer. *Research in Written Composition.* Champaign, IL: NCTE, 1963.

What I Learned at School
Jim W. Corder

WORKS CITED IN AFTERWORD

Corder, Jim W. "Argument as Emergence, Rhetoric as Love." *Professing the New Rhetorics.* Ed. Theresa Enos and Stuart Brown. Englewood Cliffs: Prentice-Hall. 412–28.
———. *Chronicle of a Small Town.* College Station: Texas A & M P, 1989.
———. *Contemporary Writing: Process and Practice.* Glenview: Scott, Foresman. 1979.
———. *Handbook of Current English.* 6th ed. Glenview: Scott, Foresman, 1981.
———. *Hunting Lieutenant Chadbourne.* Athens: U of Georgia P, 1993.
———. *Lost in West Texas.* College Station: Texas A & M P, 1988.
———. *Making It in Las Vegas.* Unpublished manuscript. Collection of Roberta Corder.
———. *Rhetoric, Remnants, and Regrets.* Unpublished manuscript. Collection of Roberta Corder.
———. *Scrapbook.* Unpublished manuscript. Collection of Roberta Corder.
———. *To the Carolinas.* Unpublished manuscript. Collection of Roberta Corder.
———. *Uses of Rhetoric.* New York: Lippincott, 1971.
———. *Yonder.* Athens: U of Georgia P, 1992.

The Search for Intelligible Structure in the Teaching of Composition
Frank J. D'Angelo

NOTES

1. George B. Leonard, "Why Johnny Can't Write," *Look,* 20 June 1961, p. 103.
2. George Stade, "Hydrants into Elephants: The Theory and Practice of College Composition," *College English,* 31 (November 1969), 143.
3. Virginia M. Burke, "The Composition–Rhetoric Pyramid," *CCC,* 16 (February 1965), 5.
4. Malcolm G. Scully, "Crisis in English Writing," *The Chronicle of Higher Education,* 9 (September 23, 1974), 1, 6.
5. Warner G. Rice, "A Proposal for the Abolition of Freshman English, As It Is Now Commonly Taught, from the College Curriculum," *College English,* 21 (April 1960), 361–367.
6. Burke, p. 6.
7. James Moffett, "A Structural Curriculum in English," *Harvard Educational Review,* 36 (Winter 1966), 20, 21.
8. This division of composition or rhetoric into principles and forms is hinted at by Quintilian who argues that invention, arrangement and style belong to the "art" of rhetoric and that the "kinds" of oratory are part of the "material" of rhetoric. Each kind (i.e. mode) "requires invention, arrangement, expression, memory, and delivery," contends Quintilian. *The Institutio Oratoria of Marcus Fabius Quintilianus,* with an English Summary and Concordance by Charles Edgar Little (Nashville: George Peabody College for Teachers, 1951), p. 116.
9. It is not my purpose to argue how these principles are derived but to identify and place into a coherent system a few that I feel are self-evident. Clearly some of these principles (or laws)

are assumptions, some are self-evident, some are based on the observation of repeated events, and some are derived from theory.

10. See, for example, my discussion of rhetorical principles in *A Conceptual Theory of Rhetoric* (Cambridge, Mass.: Winthrop Publishers, Inc., 1975).

11. Alexander Bain, *English Composition and Rhetoric*, rev. American ed. (New York: D. Appleton and Co., 1890); George R. Bramer, "Like It Is: Discourse Analysis for a New Generation," *CCC*, 21 (December 1970), 347–355; James L. Kinneavy, *A Theory of Discourse* (Englewood Cliffs, N.J.: Prentice-Hall, Inc., 1971); Carol Kupendall, "Sequence Without Structure," *English Journal*, 61 (May 1972), 715–722; James Moffett, *A Student-Centered Language Arts Curriculum, Grades K–13: A Handbook for Teachers* (Boston: Houghton Mifflin, 1968); James Moffett, *Teaching the Universe of Discourse* (Boston: Houghton Mifflin, 1968); Leo Rockas, *Modes of Rhetoric* (New York: St. Martin's Press, 1964); Martin Stevens, "Modes of Utterance," *CCC*, 14 (May 1963), 65–72; Joshua Whatmough, *Poetic, Scientific, and Other Forms of Discourse* (Berkeley, Calif.: University of California Press, 1956).

WORKS CITED IN AFTERWORD

Booth, Wayne. "The Revival of Rhetoric." *Publications of the Modern Language Association* 80 (May 1965): 8–12.

Bruner, Jerome. *The Process of Education.* Cambridge: Harvard UP, 1960.

Burke, Kenneth. *Language as Symbolic Action: Essays on Life, Literature, and Method.* Berkeley: U of California P, 1966.

Burke, Virginia M. "The Composition-Rhetoric Pyramid." *College Composition and Communication* 16 (Feb. 1965): 3–7.

Christensen, Francis. *A New Rhetoric.* New York: Harper, 1976.

Corbett, Edward P. J. "The Usefulness of Classical Rhetoric." *College Composition and Communication* 14 (Oct. 1963): 162–64.

Frye, Northrop. *The Anatomy of Criticism.* Toronto: U of Toronto P, 1989.

Gorrell, Robert, M. "Not by Nature: Approaches to Rhetoric." *English Journal* 55 (April 1966): 409–14, 449.

———. "Rhetoric, Dickoric, Doc: Rhetoric as an Academic Discipline." *College Composition and Communication* 26 (Feb. 1975): 14–19.

———. "Very Like a Whale—A Report on Rhetoric." *College Composition and Communication* 16 (Oct. 1965): 133–44.

Kinneavy, James. "The Basic Aims of Discourse." *College Composition and Communication* 20 (Dec. 1969): 297–304.

Kitzhaber, Albert R. *Themes, Theories, and Therapy: The Teaching of Writing in College.* New York: McGraw-Hill, 1963.

Murphy, James. "The Four Faces of Rhetoric: A Progress Report." *College Composition and Communication* 17 (May 1966): 55–59.

Richards, I. A. *The Philosophy of Rhetoric.* London: Oxford UP, 1936.

Young, Richard E, Alton L. Becker, and Kenneth L. Pike. *Rhetoric: Discovery and Change.* New York: Harcourt, Brace & World, 1970.

In Search of a Philosophical Context for Teaching Composition
Glenn Matott

NOTES

1. Richard C. Gebhardt and Barbara G. Smith, "Writing as a Liberating Activity: A Position Statement," *WLA Newsletter,* the second issue (March, 1974), p. 3. (This issue of the *WLA* [writing as a liberating activity] *Newsletter* gives Findlay, Ohio, as the home address, lists Gebhardt and Smith as co-editors, and was handed to me—as it was to other selected persons—at the 1974 4C's convention in Anaheim.)

2. Martin Buber, *Between Man and Man,* trans. Ronald Gregor Smith (Boston: Beacon Press, 1955), p. 89.

3. Ibid., p. 87.

4. Ibid., p. 115.

5. Martin Buber, *The Knowledge of Man,* ed. and with an Introduction by Maurice Friedman (New York: Harper and Row, 1965), p. 79.

6. Ibid., p. 184.
7. Ibid., p. 29.
8. Leslie Farber, "Martin Buber and Psychotherapy," *The Philosophy of Martin Buber*, ed. by Paul Arthur Schilpp and Maurice Friedman (LaSalle, Illinois: Open Court, 1967), p. 587.
9. Buber, *Between Man and Man*, p. 88.
10. Ibid., p. 91.
11. Ibid., pp. 88–89.
12. Ibid., p. 88.
13. Ibid., p. 203.

WORKS CITED IN AFTERWORD

Zoellner, Robert. "Talk-Write: A Behavioral Pedagogy for Composition." *College English* 30 (Jan. 1969): 267–320.

Balancing Theory with Practice in the Training of Writing Teachers
Richard C. Gebhardt

NOTES

1. *College Composition and Communication*, 24 (May 1973), 166–167.
2. *College Composition and Communication*, 25 (February 1974), 47.
3. J. N. Hook, Paul Jacobs, and Raymond Crisp, *What Every English Teacher Should Know* (Urbana: NCTE, 1970), p. 18.
4. "A Special Course in Advanced Composition for Prospective Teachers," *Journal of Teacher Education*, 20 (Summer 1969), 173.
5. "Peak Experiences and the Skill of Writing," *How Porcupines Make Love*, ed. Alan Purves (Lexington, MA: Xerox, 1972), pp. 165–180.
6. Winston Weathers and Otis Winchester, *Copy and Compose* (Englewood Cliffs, NJ: Prentice Hall, 1969), p. 1.
7. "Tips for the Freshman," *Freshman English Shop Talk*, 1, No. 2, [p. 5].
8. "In Lieu of a New Rhetoric," *College English*, 26 (October 1964), 19.
9. "Toward Competence and Creativity in an Open Class," *College English*, 34 (February 1973), 646.
10. *Thoughts Into Themes*, 3rd ed. (New York: Holt, 1957), p. v.
11. (New York: Random House, 1970), p. 2.
12. (New York: Oxford, 1973), p. 15.
13. *College English*, 36 (October 1974), 219–220.
14. *Teaching the Universe of Discourse* (Boston: Houghton Mifflin, 1968), pp. 188–200.
15. It was this second limitation that led Larson to conclude that the prospective English teacher "needs a special course in advanced writing, in most cases different from the one open to all students in a university." "A Special Course," p. 168.
16. (Boston: Houghton Mifflin, 1968), p. 70.

WORKS CITED IN AFTERWORD

Bizzell, Patricia. "Cognition, Convention, and Certainty: What We Need to Know about Writing." *PreText* 3 (Fall 1982): 213–43.

Britton, James, Tony Burgess, Nancy Martin, Alex McLeod, and Harold Rosen. *The Development of Writing Abilities* (11–18). London: Macmillan, 1975.

Bruffee, Kenneth A. "Collaborative Learning and the 'Conversation of Mankind.'" *College English* 46 (Nov. 1984): 635–52.

Emig, Janet. "Writing as a Mode of Learning." *College Composition and Communication* 28 (May 1977): 122–28.

Flower, Linda S. "Writer-Based Prose: A Cognitive Basis for Problems in Writing." *College English* 41 (Sept. 1979): 19–37.

Gebhardt, Richard C., and Barbara Genelle Smith Gebhardt, eds. *Academic Advancement in Composition Studies: Scholarship, Publication, Promotion, Tenure*. Mahwah: Erlbaum, 1997.

———. "Training Basic Writing Teachers at a Liberal Arts College." *Journal of Basic Writing* 3 (Spring/Summer 1981): 46-63.

———. "Unifying Diversity in the Training of Writing Teachers." *Training the New Teacher of College Composition.* Ed. Charles W. Bridges. Urbana: NCTE, 1986. 1–12.

Hairston, Maxine. "The Winds of Change: Thomas Kuhn and the Revolution in the Teaching of Writing." *College Composition and Communication* 33 (Feb. 1982): 76–88.

Perl, Saundra. "The Composing Processes of Unskilled College Writers." *Research in the Teaching of English* 13 (Dec. 1979): 317–36.

Shaughnessy, Mina. *Errors and Expectations: A Guide for Teachers of Basic Writing.* New York: Oxford UP, 1977.

Sommers, Nancy. "Revision Strategies of Student Writers and Experienced Adult Writers." *College Composition and Communication* 31 (Dec. 1980): 378–88.

The Feminine Style: Theory and Fact
Mary P. Hiatt

NOTES

1. See Mary P. Hiatt, *The Way Women Write: Sex and Style in Contemporary Prose* (New York: Teachers College Press, Columbia University, 1977) for the complete report, including the list of the 100 authors forming the basis of the study.
2. A sentence is defined as any word or words beginning with a capital letter and ending with end punctuation. This is not a grammatical definition but one that accommodates the vagaries of dialogue and speech patterns.
3. The logical-sequence indicators were suggested by a system of eight logical relationships posited by Louis T. Milic, *Stylists on Style* (New York: Scribners, 1969), p. 21.

WORKS CITED IN AFTERWORD

Baym, Nina. *Women's Fiction: A Guide to Novels by and about Women in America, 1820–1870.* Ithaca: Cornell UP, 1978.

Hiatt, Mary P. *Style and "Scribbling Women": An Empirical Analysis of Nineteenth-Century American Fiction.* Westport: Greenwood P, 1993.

———. *The Way Women Write: Sex and Style in Contemporary Prose.* New York: Teachers College P of Columbia U, 1977.

Teachers of Composition and Needed Research in Discourse Theory
Lee Odell

NOTES

1. James L. Kinneavy, *A Theory of Discourse* (Englewood Cliffs, N.J.: Prentice Hall, 1971), p. 2.
2. Richard Beach, "Self-Evaluation Strategies of Extensive Revisers and Non-revisers," *CCC,* 27 (May, 1976), 160–164.
3. Charles R. Cooper and Lee Odell, "Considerations of Sound in the Composing Process of Published Writers," *Research in the Teaching of English,* 10 (Fall, 1976), 103–115.
4. Edward P. J. Corbett, *Classical Rhetoric for the Modern Student* (New York: Oxford University Press, 1965), pp. 408–409.
5. Charles R. Cooper and Barbara Rosenberg, "Indexes of Syntactic Maturity," Mimeograph. State University of New York at Buffalo, 1975. 25 pp.
6. W. Ross Winterowd, "Toward a Grammar of Coherence," in *Contemporary Rhetoric: Conceptual Background with Readings,* ed. W. Ross Winterowd (New York: Harcourt Brace Jovanovich, 1975).
7. Richard L. Larson, "Toward a Linear Rhetoric of the Essay," *CCC,* 22 (May, 1971), 140–146.
8. Richard Lloyd-Jones, "Primary Trait Scoring of Writing," in *Evaluating Writing: Describing, Measuring, Judging,* ed. Charles R. Cooper and Lee Odell (Urbana, Illinois: National Council of Teachers of English, 1977).
9. John A. Daly and Michael D. Miller, "The Empirical Development of an Instrument to Measure Writing Apprehension," *Research in the Teaching of English,* 9 (Winter, 1975), 242–249.

The Study of Error
David Bartholomae

NOTES

1. Mina Shaughnessy, "Some Needed Research on Writing," *CCC*, 28 (December, 1977), 317, 388.
2. Mina Shaughnessy, *Errors and Expectations: A Guide for the Teacher of Basic Writing* (New York: Oxford University Press, 1977).
3. The term "idiosyncratic dialect" is taken from S. P. Corder, "Idiosyncratic Dialects and Error Analysis," in Jack C. Richards, ed., *Error Analysis: Perspectives on Second Language Acquisition* (London: Longman, 1974), pp. 158–171.
4. Barry M. Kroll and John C. Schafer, "Error Analysis and the Teaching of Composition," *CCC*, 29 (October, 1978), 243–248. See also my review of *Errors and Expectations* in Donald McQuade, ed., *Linguistics, Stylistics and the Teaching of Composition* (Akron, Ohio: L & S Books, 1979), pp. 209–220.
5. George Steiner, *After Babel: Aspects of Language and Translation* (New York: Oxford University Press, 1975).
6. For the term "interlanguage," see L. Selinker, "Interlanguage," in Richards, ed., *Error Analysis*, pp. 31–55. For "approximate system," see William Nemser, "Approximate Systems of Foreign Language Learners," in Richards, ed., *Error Analysis*, pp. 55–64. These are more appropriate terms than "idiosyncratic dialect" for the study of error in written composition.
7. The term "stabilized variability" is quoted in Andrew D. Cohen and Margaret Robbins, "Toward Assessing Interlanguage Performance: The Relationship Between Selected Errors, Learner's Characteristics and Learner's Explanations," *Language Learning*, 26 (June, 1976), p. 59. Selinker uses the term "fossilization" to refer to single errors that recur across time, so that the interlanguage form is not evidence of a transitional stage. (See Selinker, "Interlanguage.") M. P. Jain distinguishes between "systematic," "asystematic" and "nonsystematic" errors. (See "Error Analysis: Source, Cause and Significance" in Richards, ed., *Error Analysis*, pp. 189–215.) Unsystematic errors are mistakes, "slips of the tongue." Systematic errors "seem to establish that in certain areas of language use the learner possesses construction rules." Asystematic errors lead one to the "inescapable conclusion" that "the learner's capacity to generalize must improve, for progress in learning a language is made by adopting generalizations and stretching them to match the facts of the language."
8. Donald C. Freeman, "Linguistics and Error Analysis: On Agency," in Donald McQuade, ed., *Linguistics, Stylistics and the Teaching of Composition* (Akron, Ohio: L & S Books, 1979), pp. 143–44.
9. Kroll and Schafer, "Error Analysis and the Teaching of Composition."
10. In the late 60's and early 70's, linguists began to study second language acquisition by systematically studying the actual performance of individual learners. What they studied, however, was the language a learner would speak. In the literature of error analysis, the reception and production of language is generally defined as the learner's ability to hear, learn, imitate, and independently produce *sounds*. Errors, then, are phonological substitutions, alterations, additions, and subtractions. Similarly, errors diagnosed as rooted in the mode of production (rather than, for example, in an idiosyncratic grammar or interference from the first language) are errors caused by the difficulty a learner has hearing or making foreign sounds. When we are studying written composition, we are studying a different mode of production, where a learner must see, remember, and produce marks on a page. There may be some similarity between the grammar-based errors in the two modes, speech and writing (it would be interesting to know to what degree this is true), but there should be marked differences in the nature and frequency of performance-based errors.
11. See Y. M. Goodman and C. L. Burke, *Reading Miscue Inventory: Procedure for Diagnosis and Evaluation* (New York: Macmillan, 1972).
12. Bruder and Hayden noticed a similar phenomenon. They assigned a group of students exercises in writing formal and informal dialogues. One student's informal dialogue contained the following:

What going on?
It been a long time . . .
I about through . . .
I be glad . . .

When the student read the dialogue aloud, however, these were spoken as

What's going on?
It's been a long time . . .
I'm about through . . .
I'll be glad . . .

See Mary Newton Bruder and Luddy Hayden, "Teaching Composition: A Report on a Bi-dialectal Approach," *Language Learning,* 23 (June, 1973), 1–15.

13. See Patricia Laurence, "Error's Endless Train: Why Students Don't Perceive Errors," *Journal of Basic Writing,* 1 (Spring, 1975), 23–43, for a different explanation of this phenomenon.

14. See, for example, J. R. Frederiksen, "Component Skills in Reading," in R. R. Snow, P. A. Fed-erico, and W. E. Montague, eds., *Aptitude, Learning, and Instruction* (Hillsdale, N.J.: Erlbaum, 1979); D. E. Rumelhart, "Toward an Interactive Model of Reading," in S. Dornic, ed., *Attention and Performance VI* (Hillsdale, N.J.: Erlbaum, 1977); and Joseph H. Denks and Gregory O. Hill, "Interactive Models of Lexical Assessment during Oral Reading," paper presented at Conference on Interactive Processes in Reading, Learning Research and Development Center, University of Pittsburgh, September 1979.

   Patrick Hartwell argued that "apparent dialect interference in writing reveals partial or imperfect mastery of a neural coding system that underlies both reading and writing" in a paper, "'Dialect Interference' in Writing: A Critical View," presented at CCCC, April 1979. This paper is available through ERIC. He predicts, in this paper, that "basic writing students, when asked to read their writing in a formal situation, . . . will make fewer errors in their reading than in their writing." I read Professor Hartwell's paper after this essay was completed, so I was unable to acknowledge his study as completely as I would have desired.

15. This example is taken from Shaughnessy, *Errors and Expectations,* p. 52.

16. Corder refers to "reconstructed sentences" in "Idiosyncratic Dialects and Error Analysis."

17. Shaughnessy, *Errors and Expectations,* pp. 51–72.

18. For a discussion of the role of the "print code" in writer's errors, see Patrick Hartwell, "'Dialect Interference' in Writing: A Critical View."

19. See Kenneth S. Goodman, "Miscues: Windows on the Reading Process," in Kenneth S. Goodman, ed., *Miscue Analysis: Applications to Reading Instruction* (Urbana, Illinois: ERIC, 1977), pp. 3–14.

20. This example was taken from Yetta M. Goodman, "Miscue Analysis for In-Service Reading Teachers," in K. S. Goodman, ed., *Miscue Analysis,* p. 55.

21. Nathalie Bailey, Carolyn Madden, and Stephen D. Krashen, "Is There a 'Natural Sequence' in Adult Second Language Learning?" *Language Learning,* 24 (June, 1974), 235–243.

22. This paper was originally presented at CCCC, April 1979. The research for this study was funded by a research grant from the National Council of Teachers of English.

WORKS CITED IN AFTERWORD

Bartholomae, David. "Inventing the University." *When a Writer Can't Write: Studies in Writer's Block and Other Composing-Process Problems.* Ed. Mike Rose. New York: Guilford, 1985. 134–65.

———. "Released Into Language: Errors, Expectations and the Legacy of Mina Shaughnessy." *The Territory of Language.* Ed. Donald McQuade. Carbondale: Southern Illinois UP, 1986. 65–89.

———. "Wanderings: Misreadings, Miswritings and Misunderstandings." *Only Connect: Uniting Reading and Writing.* Ed. Thomas Newkirk. Montclair: Boynton/Cook, 1986. 89–119.

Bartholomae, David, and Anthony Petrosky. *Facts, Artifacts, and Counterfacts: Theory and Method for a Reading and Writing Course.* Upper Montclair: Boynton/Cook, 1986.

Coles, Nick. "Empowering Revision." *Facts, Artifacts, and Counterfacts: Theory and Method for a Reading and Writing Course.* David Bartholomae and Anthony Petrosky. Upper Montclair: Boynton/Cook, 1986. 167–98.

Horner, Bruce. "Discoursing Basic Writing." *College Composition and Communication* 47 (May 1996): 199–222.

Hull, Glynda. "Constructing Taxonomies for Error (or Can Stray Dogs Be Mermaids?)." *A Sourcebook for Basic Writing Teachers.* Ed. Theresa Enos. New York: Random House. 231–44.

Labov, William. *Language in the Inner City: Studies in the Black English Vernacular.* Philadelphia: U of Pennsylvania P, 1972.

Lees, Elaine O. "Proofreading as Reading, Errors as Embarrassments." *A Sourcebook for Basic Writing Teachers.* Ed. Theresa Enos. New York: Random House. 216–30.

Lu, Min-zhan. "From Silence to Words: Writing as Struggle." *College English* 49 (Apr. 1987): 437–48.

Petrosky, Anthony. "Rural Poverty and Literacy in the Mississippi Delta: Dilemmas, Paradoxes, and Conundrums." *The Right to Literacy.* Ed. Andrea A. Lunsford, Helene Moglen, and James Slevin. New York: Modern Language Association. 61–73.

Salvatori, Mariolina. "Reading and Writing a Text: Correlations Between Reading and Writing Patterns." *A Sourcebook for Basic Writing Teachers.* Ed. Theresa Enos. New York: Random House. 176–186.

Shaughnessy, Mina. *Errors and Expectations: A Guide for Teachers of Basic Writing.* New York: Oxford UP, 1977.

Smitherman, Geneva. *Talkin' and Testifyin': The Language of Black America.* Boston: Houghton Mifflin, 1977.

Wall, Susan V. "Writing, Reading and Authority: A Case Study," *Facts, Artifacts, and Counterfacts: Theory and Method for a Reading and Writing Course.* David Bartholomae and Anthony Petrosky. Upper Montclair: Boynton/Cook, 1986.

The Rise and Fall of the Modes of Discourse
Robert J. Connors

NOTES

1. Albert R. Kitzhaber, *Rhetoric in American Colleges, 1850–1900,* Diss. University of Washington, 1953, pp. 191–196.
2. Samuel P. Newman, *A Practical System of Rhetoric* (New York: Mark H. Newman, 1827), pp. 28–29.
3. Alexander Bain, *English Composition and Rhetoric* (New York: D. Appleton and Co., 1866), p. 19.
4. Kitzhaber, p. 191.
5. John F. Genung, *The Practical Elements of Rhetoric* (Boston: Ginn and Co., 1887), Table of Contents.
6. It is interesting to note that Wendell, who mentions the modes only in passing, is the only one of the "Big Four" who admits any indebtedness to Bain. This is especially strange when we consider that Bain's paragraph model was also used in all these texts without direct citation. For more on Bain's paragraph theory—which undoubtedly helped spread the associated doctrine of the modes—see Paul C. Rodgers, Jr., "Alexander Bain and the Rise of the Organic Paragraph," *Quarterly Journal of Speech* 51 (December, 1965), 399–408.
7. Kitzhaber, p. 204.
8. This list is compiled from John S. Naylor, *Informative Writing* (New York: Macmillan, 1942); Joseph M. Bachelor and Harold L. Haley, *The Practice of Exposition* (New York: Appleton-Century, 1947); and Louise F. Rorabacher, *Assignments in Exposition* (New York: Harper and Bros., 1946).
9. Barrett Wendell, *English Composition* (New York: Scribners, 1891), pp. 18–19.
10. Norman Foerster and J. M. Steadman, Jr., *Writing and Thinking* (Boston: Houghton Mifflin, 1931), p. 3.
11. James M. McCrimmon, *Writing With a Purpose* (Boston: Houghton Mifflin, 1950), pp. viii–ix.
12. W. Ross Winterowd, *Writing and Rhetoric* (Boston: Allyn and Bacon, 1965), p. 199.
13. Kitzhaber, pp. 220–221.
14. James L. Kinneavy, *A Theory of Discourse* (Englewood Cliffs, NJ: Prentice-Hall, 1971), pp. 28–29.

WORKS CITED IN AFTERWORD

Altick, Richard. *The Art of Literary Research.* New York: Norton, 1963.

Berlin, James A. *Rhetoric and Reality: Writing Instruction in American Colleges, 1900–1985.* Carbondale: Southern Illinois UP, 1987.

Brereton, John C, ed. *The Origins of Composition Studies in the American College, 1875–1925.* Pittsburgh: U of Pittsburgh P, 1995.

Corbett, Edward P. J. *Classical Rhetoric for the Modern Student.* 3rd ed. New York: Oxford UP, 1990.

Crowley, Sharon. *Composition in the University: Historical and Polemical Essays.* Pittsburgh: U of Pittsburgh P, 1998.

Golden, James L., and Edward P. J. Corbett, *The Rhetoric of Blair, Campbell, and Whately*. New York: Holt, Rinehart and Winston, 1968.

Johnson, Nan. *Nineteenth-Century Rhetoric in North America*. Carbondale: Southern Illinois UP, 1991.

Woods, William F. "Nineteenth-Century Psychology and the Teaching of Writing." *College Composition and Communication* 36 (Feb. 1985): 20–41.

Responding to Student Writing
Nancy Sommers

NOTES

1. C. H. Knoblauch and Lil Brannon, "Teacher Commentary on Student Writing: The State of the Art," *Freshman English News*, 10 (Fall, 1981), 1–3.
2. For an extended discussion of revision strategies of student writers see Nancy Sommers, "Revision Strategies of Student Writers and Experienced Adult Writers," *College Composition and Communication*, 31 (December, 1980), 378–388.
3. Nancy Sommers and Ronald Schleifer, "Means and Ends: Some Assumptions of Student Writers," *Composition and Teaching*, 2 (December, 1980), 69–76.
4. Janet Emig and Robert P. Parker, Jr., "Responding to Student Writing: Building a Theory of the Evaluating Process," unpublished papers, Rutgers University.
5. For an extended discussion of this problem see Joseph Williams, "The Phenomenology of Error," *College Composition and Communication*, 32 (May, 1981), 152–168.
6. Ann Berthoff, *The Making of Meaning* (Montclair, NJ: Boynton/Cook Publishers, 1981).
7. W. U. McDonald, "The Revising Process and the Marking of Student Papers," *College Composition and Communication*, 24 (May, 1978), 167–170.

Topical Structure and Revision: An Exploratory Study
Stephen P. Witte

NOTES

1. The present essay has benefitted enormously from comments I have received on earlier drafts. In addition to Dick Larson's sage commentaries, I have found most helpful those of Roger Cherry, Lester Faigley, Linda Flower, Sarah Freedman, Roland Sodowsky, Keith Walters, and Joseph Williams. I am particularly grateful to Roger Cherry because he has suffered (sometimes willingly) through many drafts of the present essay.
2. D. Gordon Rohman and Albert O. Wlecke, *Pre-Writing: The Construction and Applications of Models for Concept Formation in Writing*, U.S. Office of Education, Cooperative Research Project No. 2174 (East Lansing, MI: Michigan State University, 1964); and Rohman, "Pre-Writing: The Stage of Discovery in the Writing Process," *College Composition and Communication*, 16 (May, 1965), 106–112.
3. Janet Emig was the first contemporary researcher to suggest the recursive nature of revision. See her *The Composing Processes of Twelfth Graders*, NCTE Research Report No. 13 (Urbana, IL: National Council of Teachers of English, 1971). Nancy Sommers' work supports Emig's suggestion by showing that writers revise at many points during the production of a text. See her *Revision in the Composing Process: A Case Study of College Freshmen and Experienced Adult Writers*, Diss. Boston University, 1978; "Response to Sharon Crowley," *College Composition and Communication*, 29 (May, 1978), 209–211; and "Revision Strategies of Student Writers and Experienced Adult Writers," *College Composition and Communication*, 31 (December, 1980), 378–388. The recursive nature of revision is also suggested by other studies cited elsewhere in the present essay.
4. Richard Beach, "Self-Evaluation Strategies of Extensive Revisers and Non-Revisers," *College Composition and Communication*, 27 (May, 1976), 160–164. Beach reports that writers who revise extensively often anticipate, in the comments they make on their own texts, the writing of subsequent drafts, while non-revisers seldom see beyond the text at hand. Daniel Dieterich, "Response to Richard Beach," *College Composition and Communication*, 27 (October, 1976), 301–302, challenges Beach's underlying assumption that revisers are better writers than non-revisers because they can better evaluate their own writing.

5. Lillian Bridwell, "Revising Strategies in Twelfth Grade Students' Transactional Writing," *Research in the Teaching of English,* 14 (October, 1980), 197–222. Bridwell reports that the most extensively revised papers in her sample received the complete range of possible quality scores (p. 216), thus suggesting the inadequacy of Beach's earlier conclusions.

6. Lester Faigley and Stephen Witte, "Analyzing Revision," *College Composition and Communication,* 32 (December, 1981), 400–414. Faigley and Witte report that the expert adults in their sample made fewer revisions than advanced college students (see pp. 407–410).

7. The idea that writers anticipate doing subsequent drafts is implicit in Linda Flower's representation of writers of "reader-based prose." See her "Writer-Based Prose: A Cognitive Basis for Problems in Writing," *College English,* 41 (September, 1979), 19–37. In this essay, Flower develops in an interesting way some of the same distinctions Wayne C. Booth, "The Rhetorical Stance," *College Composition and Communication,* 14 (October, 1963), 139–145, had previously made. Without any documentation whatsoever, Shirley M. Haley-Jones, "Revising Writing in the Upper Grades," *Language Arts,* 58 (May, 1981), 562–566, appears to have taken Flower's notion of "reader-based prose" as the basis for a scheme to teach revision to older secondary school children. According to Flower, writers of "reader-based prose" constantly make adjustments in their texts to accommodate the needs of an audience as well as their own goals for the text. Also relevant here is Flower and John R. Hayes, "Problem-Solving Strategies and the Writing Process," *College English,* 19 (December, 1977), 449–461, and "The Dynamics of Composing: Making Plans and Juggling Constraints," in *Cognitive Processes in Writing,* ed. Lee Gregg and Irwin Steinberg (Hillsdale, NJ: Lawrence Erlbaum, 1980), pp. 31–50.

8. Donald Murray contends that writers constantly revise "not to force the writing to what the writer hoped the text would say, but instead . . . to help the writing say what it intends to say." See his "Writing as Process: How Writing Finds Its Own Meaning," in *Eight Approaches to Teaching Composition,* ed. Timothy Donovan and Ben W. McClelland (Urbana, IL: National Council of Teachers of English, 1980), pp. 3–19 (p. 5 for quotation); and "Internal Revision: A Process of Discovery," in *Research on Composing: Points of Departure,* ed. Charles R. Cooper and Lee Odell (Urbana, IL: National Council of Teachers of English, 1978), pp. 85–103. Not enough has been made, I believe, of the important differences between Murray's view of composing and the theory articulated by Flower and Hayes, particularly their different notions of "revising."

9. Sommers—"Revision Strategies of Student Writers and Experienced Adult Writers"—classifies revisions in two ways: according to the amount of text affected by a revision and according to whether a revision added to, deleted, substituted for, or rearranged material in the original text, a taxonomy which reflects Chomsky's classes of grammatical transformations. Sommers' research led to the conclusion that revision, at least for experienced writers, includes more than cleaning up mechanical and stylistic flaws at the sentence level. Like Sommers, Sondra Perl also suggests that unskilled writers tend to be more concerned with local rather than global matters during revision, but that their revisions often have deleterious effects on their texts. See Perl's "The Composing Processes of Unskilled College Writers," *Research in the Teaching of English,* 13 (December, 1979), 317–336; "Understanding Composing," *College Composition and Communication,* 31 (December, 1980), 363–369; and "A Look at Basic Writers in the Process of Composing," in *Basic Writing: Essays for Teachers, Researchers, and Administrators,* ed. Lawrence N. Kasden and Daniel R. Hoeber (Urbana, IL: National Council of Teachers of English, 1980), pp. 13–32.

10. Bridwell—"Revising Strategies in Twelfth Grade Students' Transactional Writing"—employs a classification scheme similar to Sommers' and concludes that inexperienced writers tend to revise only at the sentence level.

11. In "Analyzing Revision," Faigley and Witte develop a system for distinguishing between revisions which alter the meaning of a text and those which do not, and apply their system to an analysis of within-draft and between-draft revisions in texts written by three groups of writers: inexperienced college writers, advanced college writers, and expert adult writers. The results of their study indicate that the revisions of the three groups differ substantially both within drafts and between drafts. For another application of their revision taxonomy, see Faigley and Witte, "Measuring the Effects of Revision on Text Structure," in *New Directions in Composition Research,* ed. Richard Beach and Lillian Bridwell (New York: Guilford Press, 1983).

12. The most detailed description of their use of protocols appears in their "Identifying the Organization of Writing Processes," in *Cognitive Processes in Writing,* pp. 3–30.

13. "The Dynamics of Composing: Making Plans and Juggling Constraints," and "The Cognition of Discovery: Defining a Rhetorical Problem," *College Composition and Communication,* 31 (February, 1980), 21–32.

14. For a brief review of some of these studies, see Bridwell, "Revising Strategies in Twelfth Grade Students' Transactional Writing," pp. 198–199.
15. As Paul C. Rodgers, Jr., points out, the modern notion of topic sentences derives from Alexander Bain, who was concerned that paragraphs be organized around a central "topic" expressed in a single sentence, usually at the beginning of the paragraph. On these matters, see Rodgers' "Alexander Bain and the Rise of the Organic Paragraph," *Quarterly Journal of Speech,* 51 (December, 1965), 399–408.
16. Perhaps the best known discussion of the nature of paragraphs is the one involving Alton Becker, Francis Christensen, Paul C. Rodgers, Jr., Josephine Miles, and David H. Karrfalt and published under the title "Symposium on the Paragraph," *College Composition and Communication,* 17 (May, 1966), 60–87.
17. The research of Willis Pitkin ("Hierarchies and the Discourse Hierarchy," *College English,* 38 [March, 1977], 649–659, and "X/Y: Some Basic Strategies of Discourse," *College English,* 38 [March, 1977], 660–672), Ellen W. Nold and Brent E. Davis ("The Discourse Matrix," *College Composition and Communication,* 31 [May, 1980], 141–152), and Joseph M. Williams ("Nuclear Structures in Discourse," in *Selected Papers from the 1981 Texas Writing Research Conference* [Austin: University of Texas, Department of English, 1981], pp. 165–189) is, I believe, moving in this direction. Particularly important is the work of Williams—in the article previously cited; in "Discourse Structure: The Prerequisites for a Useful Model," unpublished paper presented during the annual meeting of the Conference on College Composition and Communication, 1981; and in "From Style to Form," unpublished paper presented during the Penn State Conference on Rhetoric and Composition, 1982.
18. "On Linguistic Characterology with Illustrations from Modern English" (1928), reprinted in *A Prague School Reader in Linguistics,* ed. Josef Vachek (Bloomington, IN: Indiana University Press, 1964), pp. 59–67; "Zur Satzperspektiv im modernen Englisch," *Archiv für das Studium der neueren Sprachen und Literaturen,* 155 (1929), 202–210; and *A Functional Analysis of Present Day English on a General Linguistic Basis,* ed. Josef Vachek (Prague: Academia, 1975).
19. "On Defining the Theme in Functional Sentence Analysis," *Travaux Linguistiques de Prague,* 1 (1964), 267–280; and "Non-Thematic Subjects in Contemporary English," *Travaux Linguistiques de Prague,* 2 (1966), 239–254; and "Some Aspects of the Czechoslovak Approach to Problems in Functional Sentence Perspective," in *Papers on Functional Sentence Perspective,* ed. František Daneš (The Hague: Mouton, 1974), pp. 11–37.
20. "Functional Sentence Perspective in a Generative Description," *Prague Studies in Mathematical Linguistics,* 2 (1967), 203–225; "Zur Stellung der Thema-Rhema-Gliederung in der Sprachbeschreibung," in *Papers on Functional Sentence Perspective,* pp. 54–74; Sgall and Eva Hajičová, "Focus on Focus (Part 1)," *Prague Bulletin of Mathematical Linguistics,* 28 (1977), 5–54; Sgall and Hajičová, "Focus on Focus (Part II)," *Prague Bulletin of Mathematical Linguistics,* 29 (1978), 23–41; "Toward a Definition of Focus and Topic (Part I)," *Prague Bulletin of Mathematical Linguistics,* 31 (1979), 3–25; and "Toward a Definition of Focus and Topic," *Prague Bulletin of Mathematical Linguistics,* 32 (1979), 24–32.
21. "A Three-Level Approach to Syntax," *Travaux Linguistiques de Prague,* 1 (1964), 225–240; and "Functional Sentence Perspective and the Organization of the Text," in *Papers on Functional Sentence Perspective,* pp. 106–128.
22. William J. vande Kopple, "Functional Sentence Perspective, Composing, and Reading," *College Composition and Communication,* 33 (February, 1982), 50, calls attention to the influence of Henri Weil, *The Order of Words in the Ancient Languages Compared with That of the Modern Languages,* trans. C. W. Super (Boston: Ginn & Company, 1887), a work originally published in 1844 with the French title, *De L'Ordre des mots dans les langues anciennes comparées aux langues modernes.* Also important for his anticipation of Mathesius is A. Marty, "Über die schiedung von grammatischem, logischem und psychologischem Subjekt resp. Pradicat.," *Archiv für systematische Philosophie,* 3 (1897), 174–272, 294–333.
23. Leonard Bloomfield, *Language* (New York: Holt, Rinehart and Winston, 1933).
24. Halliday was first concerned with the notion of "information focus" in discourse. In "Notes on Transitivity and Theme in English, Part 2," *Journal of Linguistics,* 3 (October, 1967), 199–244, Halliday argues that in oral discourse in English, intonation or stress determines which sentence element the speaker wishes to call attention to, usually what the speaker regards as new information. See also his "The Place of 'Functional Sentence Perspective' in the System of Linguistic Description," in *Papers on Functional Sentence Perspective,* pp. 43–53. Later Halliday turned his attention to cohesion in a work he co-authored with Ruqaiya Hasan, *Cohesion in English* (London: Longman Group Limited, 1976). For treatments of Halliday's theory of cohesion in the context of modern composition instruction, see Dale W. Hal-

loway, "Semantic Grammars: How They Help Us Teach Writing," *College Composition and Communication,* 32 (May, 1981), 205–218; and Stephen P. Witte and Lester Faigley, "Cohesion, Coherence, and Writing Quality," *College Composition and Communication,* 32 (May, 1981), 189–204. For an interesting application of Halliday and Hasan's work on cohesion and an extension of Witte and Faigley's study of cohesion in the texts of college writers, see Ad Welschen, "Formuleervaardigheid en de cognitieve balans bij het schrijven," *Tijdschrift voor Taalbeheersing,* 4 (1982), 131–162.

25. Charles Hockett, *A Course in Modern Linguistics* (New York: Macmillan, 1959), p. 201, was apparently the first to use the term *topic* to refer to what the Prague School linguists called *theme.* Noam Chomsky, in *Aspects of the Theory of Syntax* (Cambridge, MA: MIT Press, 1965), also employs the term *topic* similarly. In later research, the two terms are often used interchangeably, as are the terms *comment* and *rheme.* See, for example, G. W. Turner, *Stylistics* (Harmondsworth, Middlesex: Penguin, 1975); Joseph E. Grimes, *The Thread of Discourse* (The Hague: Mouton, 1975); Teun A. van Dijk, *Text and Context: Explorations in the Semantics and Pragmatics of Discourse* (London: Longmans, 1977), and "Sentence Topic and Discourse Topic," *Papers in Slavic Philology,* 1 (1977), 49–61; Charles N. Li and Sandra A. Thompson, "Subject and Topic: A New Typology of Language," in *Subject and Topic,* ed. Charles N. Li (New York: Academic Press, 1976), pp. 457–489; and George Dillon, *Constructing Texts: Elements of a Theory of Composition and Style* (Bloomington, IN: Indiana University Press, 1981), pp. 100–125.

26. Following Daneš, this pattern may be represented graphically as

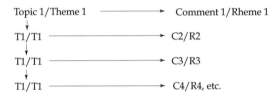

A similar graphic appears in Dillon (p. 106). Holloway (p. 209) would say such a text would have "an 'A-B. A-C. A-D.' construction."

27. Again following Daneš, we can graphically represent this pattern as

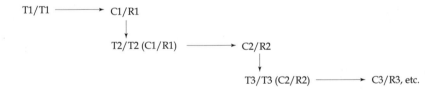

See also Dillon (p. 106) and Holloway (p. 208), who would represent the pattern as "A-B. B-C. C-D., etc."

28. Drawing again on Daneš, we can graphically represent this pattern as follows:

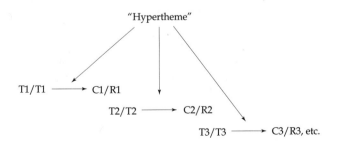

See also Dillon (p. 108). Holloway does not represent this pattern, but I assume she would offer something like this: "A. A/B–C. A/D–E., etc."

29. For accounts of some of the theoretical, and terminological, difficulties arising from a "topic" approach to text analysis, see Nils Erik Enkvist, "Theme Dynamics and Style: An Experiment," *Studia Anglia Posnaniensia*, 5 (1974), 127–135; Roberta Barry, "Topic in Chinese: An Overlap in Meaning, Grammar, and Discourse Function," in *Papers from the Parasession on Functionalism*, ed. Robin E. Grossman, L. James San, and Timothy J. Vance (Chicago: Chicago Linguistic Society, 1975), pp. 1–9; Joseph E. Grimes, "Topic Levels," in *Theoretical Issues in Natural Language Processing—2*, ed. David L. Waltz (New York: The Association for Computing Machinery and The Association for Computational Linguistics, 1978), pp. 104–108; Wallace Chafe, "Givenness, Contrastiveness, Definiteness, Subjects, Topics, and Point of View," in *Subject and Topic*, pp. 27–55; and Robert de Beaugrande, *Text, Discourse, and Process: Toward a Multidisciplinary Science of Texts* (Norwood, NJ: Ablex, 1980), pp. 118–126.

30. I am using the term "frame" in much the same way as it is used by Marvin Minsky, "A Framework for Representing Knowledge," in *The Psychology of Computer Vision*, ed. Patrick Winston (New York: McGraw-Hill, 1975), pp. 211–277, and by Terry Winograd, "Frame Representations and the Declarative-Procedural Controversy," in *Representations and Understanding: Studies in Cognitive Science*, ed. Daniel Bobrow and Allan Collins (New York: Academic Press, 1975), pp. 185–210.

31. On the importance of distinguishing between *discourse topics* and *sentence topics*, see van Dijk, particularly "Sentence Topic and Discourse Topic," and *Macrostructures: An Interdisciplinary Study of Global Structures in Discourse, Interaction, and Cognition* (Hillsdale, NJ: Lawrence Erlbaum, 1980), pp. 40–46 and 94–98. Also relevant here is Elinor Ochs Keenan and Bambi B. Schiefflin, "Topic as a Discourse Notion: A Study of Topic in the Conversations of Children and Adults," in *Subject and Topic*, pp. 336–384.

32. "Observations on the Development of the Topic in Simplified Discourse," in *Text Linguistics, Cognitive Learning and Language Teaching*, ed. Viljo Kohonen and Nils Erik Enkvist, Suomen Sovelletun Kielitieten Yhdistyksen (AFinLA) Julkaisuja, No. 22 (Turku, Finland: Åbo Akademi, 1978), pp. 71–104.

33. *The Thread of Discourse*, pp. 323–336; and "Signals of Discourse Structure in Koine," in *Society for Biblical Literature 1975 Seminar Papers*, vol. 1, ed. George MacRae (Missoula, MT: Scholars Press, 1975), pp. 151–164.

34. "The Effects of Staging on Recall from Prose," in *New Directions in Discourse Processing*, ed. Roy O. Freedle (Norwood, NJ: Ablex, 1979), pp. 287–330.

35. Dependency on orthographic boundaries is, I believe, one of the reasons Christensen's principles of "generative rhetoric" are of limited value in analyzing discourse. For a discussion of this limitation of Christensen's work, see Nils Erik Enkvist, "Some Aspects of Applications of Text Linguistics," in *Text Linguistics, Cognitive Learning and Language Teaching*, esp. pp. 14–17. For Christensen's work, see his "A Generative Rhetoric of the Sentence," *College Composition and Communication*, 14 (October, 1963), 155–161, and "A Generative Rhetoric of the Paragraph," *College Composition and Communication*, 16 (October, 1965), 144–156.

36. Such decisions are not necessarily conscious ones. Georgia M. Green, "Linguistics and the Pragmatics of Language Use," *Poetics*, 11 (March, 1982), 45–76, argues that decisions made during language production and comprehension are made "well below" the "level . . . of conscious deliberation" and are based on three kinds of linguistic knowledge—"knowledge of language" (grammar), "knowledge about the use of particular forms," and "knowledge about communicating."

37. Jerry R. Hobbes and D. Evans, "Conversation as Planned Behavior," SRI Technical Note 203 (Menlo Park, CA: SRI International, 1979); and Michael Agar and Hobbes, "Interpreting Discourse: Coherence and the Analysis of Ethnographic Interviews," *Discourse Processes*, 5 (January–March, 1982), 1–32. Agar and Hobbes explain the difference very succinctly as follows:

The requirements of global coherence say, "Given the overall goals I am trying to accomplish, what can I say next that will serve them?" Local coherence says, "Given what I just said, what can I say that is related to it?" For the most part, what is said next will satisfy both sets of requirements. (p. 7)

38. This passage is essentially the same as the one Lautamatti used in her study. It comes from Anne and Peter Doughty, *Language and Community* (London: Edward Arnold, 1974). Lautamatti gives no page reference for this passage.

39. The reader will note that the grammatical subject of a sentence is not always its *topical subject* (as in the case of this sentence). Once a "gist" for the following passage is constructed, iden-

tifying *topical subjects* or *sentence topics* is fairly straightforward, with the possible exception of (5-i) and (5-j). "Language" is the topical subject of (5-i) because "language" is what the sentence is about. The sentence is not about "biologists." In fact, "biologists" can be deleted without altering the "gist" of the passage, as when the sentence is transformed into a passive construction: "language is now considered species specific. . . ." In (5-j) "suggestion" is the grammatical subject but not the topical subject or sentence topic for two reasons: (1) "suggestion" seems not to be what (5-j) is about; and (2) "This suggestion implies that" can be replaced with "thus" without altering the "gist" of the text. Additional information about coding procedures appears in Footnote 50 below.

40. "Initial Mention as a Signal to Thematic Content in Technical Passages," *Memory & Cognition,* 8 (July, 1980), 345–553; and "How Readers Abstract Main Ideas from Technical Prose: Some Implications for Document Design," unpublished paper presented during a Document Design Center Colloquium, American Institutes for Research, Washington, D.C., 1980.

41. Given what I take to be the "gist" of the *Language and Community* passage, the sentence topics of (5-a), (5-b), (5-c), (5-d), (5-h), and (5-j) are referentially identical, even though apart from the context of the passage in which they appear some of the topics may seem to be superordinate lexical terms and others may seem to be subordinate lexical terms. In context, those six sentence topics, I contend, all have the same referent and thus function as synonyms or near-synonyms for each other.

42. The term *point* is used by Williams, "Nuclear Structures in Discourse," in a slightly different way from the way I use it here. According to Williams, the "point" of a paragraph is "the one sentence without which the paragraph would fail, the one sentence for whose sake the rest of the paragraph exists" (p. 166). My use of the term does not demand that the point be stated as a single clause or sentence in the text, whereas Williams' use does.

43. Walter D. Kintsch and Teun A. van Dijk, "Toward a Model of Text Comprehension and Production," *Psychological Review,* 85 (September, 1978), 363–394. Insofar as the *topical structure* approach I am advocating here is useful in explaining how readers comprehend texts, I would argue that the rules used to derive or construct *discourse topics* are theoretically consistent with those van Dijk delineates for deriving macropropositions (see van Dijk, *Macrostructures,* pp. 46–50).

44. The students were enrolled in four different courses at two state-supported universities: 18 were "provisional" students enrolled in a first course in freshman composition; 21 in a sophomore-level writing course; 19 in an upper-division course for prospective teachers of high school English; and 18 in a junior-level advanced expository writing course.

45. Lester Faigley, Thomas P. Miller, Paul R. Meyer, and Stephen P. Witte, *Writing After College: A Stratified Survey of the Writing of College-Trained People,* FIPSE Grant No. G008005896 Technical Report No. 1 (Austin: University of Texas, Writing Program Assessment Project, 1981, ERIC Document 210 708), p. 53.

46. Stephen P. Witte, Paul R. Meyer, Thomas P. Miller, and Lester Faigley, *A National Survey of College and University Writing Program Directors,* FIPSE Grant No. G008005896 Technical Report No. 2 (Austin: University of Texas, Writing Program Assessment Project, 1981, ERIC Document 210 709), pp. 67–71 and 96–104; Stephen P. Witte and Paul R. Meyer with Thomas P. Miller, *A National Survey of College and University Teachers of Writing,* FIPSE Grant No. G008005896 Technical Report No. 4 (Austin: University of Texas, Writing Program Assessment Project, 1982, ERIC Document 219 779), pp. 59–68.

47. None of the raters received formal training for the rating task; I did, however, give each rater a copy of the original text and the set of directions given to the students, and I did "suggest" that they read very quickly about 20 of the revisions to develop a sense of the range before beginning the actual rating process. No attempt was made to force an arbitrary number of revisions into each scoring category. These raters agreed with one another about 75% of the time even though no rater had knowledge of another's ratings. Interrater reliability was computed to be .748, according to the method outlined by R. L. Ebel, "Estimation of the Reliability of Ratings," *Psychometrika,* 16 (December, 1951), 407–424.

48. Studies using these indices are reviewed in Stephen P. Witte and Anne S. Davis, "The Stability of T-Unit Length: A Preliminary Investigation," *Research in the Teaching of English,* 14 (February, 1980), 5–17; "The Stability of T-Unit Length in the Written Discourse of College Freshmen: A Second Study," *Research in the Teaching of English,* 16 (February, 1982), 71–84; and S. Witte, "The Reliability of Mean T-Unit Length: Some Questions for Research in Written Composition," in *Learning to Write: First Language/Second Language,* ed. Aviva Freedman, Ian Pringle, and Janice Yalden (London: Longman, 1983), pp. 171–177.

49. The relevant statistical data appear in the following table:

Variable	Low-Score Texts (N = 20)		High-Score Texts (N = 24)		T Value
	Mean	SD	Mean	SD	
Text length (in words)	232.1	29.8	167.8	46.1	5.37***
Number of sentence topics	6.45	1.54	3.88	1.12	6.43***
Words per clause	11.69	1.45	10.57	1.13	2.88**
T-units per sentence topic	1.89	0.30	2.59	1.00	3.00**
% of t-units in sequential progressions	55.2	14.1	40.0	19.3	3.00**

***p < .001   **p < .01   df = 42

50. In coding the texts, I first read each in its entirety. This gave me a sense of what each text was about. With this sense (and I admit that texts which are not well-formed are often ambiguous and therefore susceptible to multiple interpretations), I then analyzed individual sentences for their topics, seeking an answer to the question, "What is this sentence about?" I moved from one noun phrase to the next until I found what I thought was a satisfactory answer for each sentence in the context of the whole discourse. Sometimes I located the topical NP in an introductory phrase or subordinate clause (as in 6-a and 6-f), sometimes in the grammatical subject of the main clause (as in 6-b, 6-d, and 6-e), sometimes in subordinate clauses following the verb of the main clause (as in 6-h and 6-k), and sometimes in the object (as in 6-g, 6-i, and 6-j). Sometimes "what the sentence is about" was expressed as old or given information (as in 6-e and 6-f). Sometimes it was not (as in 6-i and 6-j): in light of the whole text, neither 6-i nor 6-j is "about" "biologists."

51. The best known of these formulae is the one proposed by Rudolph Flesch, *The Art of Readable Writing* (New York: Harper & Row, 1949) and "A New Readability Yardstick," *Journal of Applied Psychology* 32 (June, 1948), 221–233. Other formulae have been proposed by Edgar Dale and Jeanne Chall, *Readability* (Columbus: Ohio State University Press, 1948), and by R. Gunning, *How to Take the Fog out of Writing* (Chicago: Dartnell, 1964). These formulae all associate reading difficulty with word length and sentence length, ignoring altogether semantic relationships which cross the boundaries of sentences. For critical appraisals of such formulae, see especially three reports produced by the Document Design Center of the American Institutes for Research in Washington, D.C.: Jennie C. Reddish, *Readability* (1979); Veda Charrow, *Let the Writer Beware* (1979); and V. Melissa Holland, *Psycholinguistic Alternatives to Readability Formulas* (1981).

52. Illustrations of *Type 1* sentences also appear in other example passages used in the present essay. See (l-a through -d), (2-a through -d), (3-b), (4-b and -c), (6-d and -e), (7-a, -b, -d, and -h).

53. In the other example passages, see (2-e), (3-a and -d), (4-a), (6-b), and (7-c, -f, and -g).

54. See also (3-c), (6-g, -i, -j, and -k), and (7-e).

55. See also (6-a and -f).

56. See also (6-c and -h) and (7-i).

57. The following table compares the frequency of sentence types in the original *Language and Community* passage with the frequencies in the two sets of revisions:

Sentence Types	No. in Original	Low-Score Revisions (N = 20)		High-Score Revisions (N = 24)	
		Mean	SD	Mean	SD
Type 1	1	3.60	2.30	2.79	2.04
Type 2	2	2.75	1.45	2.63	1.36
Type 3	3	1.85	1.66	1.08	1.28
Type 4	2	1.30	1.03	0.88	0.85
Type 5	2	2.25	1.86	2.00	1.59

Audience Addressed/Audience Invoked: The Role of Audience in Composition Theory and Pedagogy

Lisa Ede and Andrea Lunsford

NOTES

1. Ruth Mitchell and Mary Taylor, "The Integrating Perspective: An Audience-Response Model for Writing," *CE*, 41 (November, 1979), 267. Subsequent references to this article will be cited in the text.
2. Russell C. Long, "Writer-Audience Relationships: Analysis or Invention," *CCC*, 31 (May, 1980), 223 and 225. Subsequent references to this article will be cited in the text.
3. For these terms we are indebted to Henry W. Johnstone, Jr., who refers to them in his analysis of Chaim Perelman's universal audience in *Validity and Rhetoric in Philosophical Argument: An Outlook in Transition* (University Park, PA: The Dialogue Press of Man & World, 1978), p. 105.
4. Fred R. Pfister and Joanne F. Petrik, "A Heuristic Model for Creating a Writer's Audience," *CCC*, 31 (May, 1980), 213.
5. Pfister and Petrik, 214; our emphasis.
6. See, for example, Lisa S. Ede, "On Audience and Composition," *CCC*, 30 (October, 1979), 291–295.
7. See, for example, David Tedlock, "The Case Approach to Composition," *CCC*, 32 (October, 1981), 253–261.
8. See, for example, Linda Flower's *Problem-Solving Strategies for Writers* (New York: Harcourt Brace Jovanovich, 1981) and John P. Field and Robert H. Weiss' *Cases for Composition* (Boston: Little, Brown, 1979).
9. Richard E. Young, "Paradigms and Problems: Needed Research in Rhetorical Invention," in *Research on Composing: Points of Departure*, ed. Charles R. Cooper and Lee Odell (Urbana, IL: National Council of Teachers of English, 1978), p. 32 (footnote # 3).
10. Mitchell and Taylor do recognize that internal psychological needs ("unconscious challenges") may play a role in the writing process, but they cite such instances as an "extreme case (often that of the creative writer)" (p. 251). For a discussion of the importance of self-evaluation in the composing process see Susan Miller, "How Writers Evaluate Their Own Writing," *CCC*, 33 (May, 1982), 176–183.
11. Susan Wall, "In the Writer's Eye: Learning to Teach the Rereading/Revising Process," *English Education*, 14 (February, 1982), 12.
12. Wayne Booth, *Modern Dogma and the Rhetoric of Assent* (Chicago: The University of Chicago Press, 1974), p. xiv.
13. Paul Kameen, "Rewording the Rhetoric of Composition," *Pre/Text*, 1 (Spring–Fall, 1980), 82.
14. Mitchell and Taylor's arguments in favor of adjunct classes seem to indicate that they see writing instruction, wherever it occurs, as a skills course, one instructing students in the proper use of a tool.
15. Anthony R. Petrosky, "From Story to Essay: Reading and Writing," *CCC*, 33 (February, 1982), 20.
16. Walter J. Ong, S. J., "The Writer's Audience Is Always a Fiction," *PMLA*, 90 (January, 1975), 9–21. Subsequent references to this article will be cited in the text.
17. See, for example, William Irmscher, "Sense of Audience: An Intuitive Concept," unpublished paper delivered at the CCCC in 1981; Douglas B. Park, "The Meanings of Audience: Pedagogical Implications," unpublished paper delivered at the CCCC in 1981; and Luke M. Reinsma, "Writing to an Audience: Scheme or Strategy?" unpublished paper delivered at the CCCC in 1982.
18. Herbert W. Simons, *Persuasion: Understanding, Practice, and Analysis* (Reading, MA: Addison-Wesley, 1976).
19. Ong, p. 12. Ong recognizes that oral communication also involves role-playing, but he stresses that it "has within it a momentum that works for the removal of masks" (p. 20). This may be true in certain instances, such as dialogue, but does not, we believe, obtain broadly.
20. Walter S. Minot, "Response to Russell C. Long," *CCC*, 32 (October, 1981), 337.
21. We are aware that the student actually has two audiences, her neighbors and her teacher, and that this situation poses an extra constraint for the writer. Not all students can manage

such a complex series of audience constraints, but it is important to note that writers in a variety of situations often write for more than a single audience.

22. In their paper on "Student and Professional Syntax in Four Disciplines" (unpublished paper delivered at the CCCC in 1981), Ian Pringle and Aviva Freedman provide a good example of what can happen when a student creates an aberrant role for an academic reader. They cite an excerpt from a third-year history assignment, the tone of which "is essentially the tone of the opening of a television travelogue commentary" and which thus asks the reader, a history professor, to assume the role of the viewer of such a show. The result is as might be expected: "Although the content of the paper does not seem significantly more abysmal than other papers in the same set, this one was awarded a disproportionately low grade" (p. 2).

23. One danger which should be noted is a tendency to foster a questionable image of classical rhetoric. The agonistic speaker-audience relationship which Long cites as an essential characteristic of classical rhetoric is actually a central point of debate among those involved in historical and theoretical research in rhetoric. For further discussion, see: Lisa Ede and Andrea Lunsford, "On Distinctions Between Classical and Modern Rhetoric," in *Classical Rhetoric and Modern Discourse: Essays in Honor of Edward P. J. Corbett,* ed. Robert Connors, Lisa Ede, and Andrea Lunsford (Carbondale, IL: Southern Illinois University Press, 1984).

24. James Moffett, *Teaching the Universe of Discourse* (Boston: Houghton Mifflin, 1968), p. 47. Subsequent references will be mentioned in the text.

25. We have taken the title of this section from Scott Consigny's article of the same title, *Philosophy and Rhetoric,* 7 (Summer, 1974), 175–186. Consigny's effort to mediate between two opposing views of rhetoric provided a stimulating model for our own efforts.

26. Although we believe that the range of audience roles cited in our model covers the general spectrum of options, we do not claim to have specified all possibilities. This is particularly the case since, in certain instances, these roles may merge and blend—shifting subtly in character. We might also note that other terms for the same roles might be used. In a business setting, for instance, colleague might be better termed co-worker; critic, supervisor.

27. Douglas B. Park, "The Meanings of 'Audience,'" *CE,* 44 (March, 1982), 249.

28. Edward P. J. Corbett, *The Little Rhetoric and Handbook,* 2nd edition (Glenview, IL: Scott, Foresman, 1982), p. 5.

29. Donald M. Murray, "Teaching the Other Self: The Writer's First Reader," *CCC,* 33 (May, 1982), 142.

WORKS CITED IN AFTERWORD

Eberly, Rosa. *Citizen Critics: Public Deliberations on Literature, Censorship, and Democracy.* Urbana: U of Illinois P, forthcoming.

Elbow, Peter. "Closing My Eyes As I Speak: An Argument for Ignoring Audience." *College English* 49 (Jan. 1987): 50–69.

Kirsch, Gesa, and Duane H. Roen, eds. *A Sense of Audience in Written Communication.* Newbury Park: Sage, 1990.

Lunsford, Andrea A., and Lisa Ede. "Representing Audience: 'Successful' Discourse and Disciplinary Critique." *College Composition and Communication* 47 (May 1996): 167–79.

Park, Douglas. "Analyzing Audiences." *College Composition and Communication.* 37 (Dec. 1986): 478–88.

Porter, James. *Audience and Rhetoric: An Archaeological Composition of the Discourse Community.* Englewood Cliffs: Prentice Hall, 1992.

Rafoth, Bennett. "Discourse Community: Where Writers, Readers, and Texts Come Together." *The Social Construction of Written Communication.* Ed. Bennett A. Rafoth and Donald L. Rubin. Norwood: Ablex, 1988. 131–46.

Reiff, Mary Jo. "Rereading 'Invoked' and 'Addressed' Readers Through a Social Lens: Toward a Recognition of Multiple Audiences." *Journal of Advanced Composition* 16.3 (1996): 407–24.

Roth, Robert. "The Evolving Audience: Alternatives to Audience Accommodation." *College Composition and Communication* 38 (Feb. 1987): 47–55.

Selzer, Jack. "More Meanings of Audience." *A Rhetoric of Doing: Essays on Written Discourse in Honor of James L. Kinneavy.* Ed. Stephen P. Witte, Neil Nakadate, and Roger D. Cherry. Carbondale: Southern Illinois UP, 1992. 161–77.

The Shifting Relationships between Speech and Writing
Peter Elbow

NOTES

1. For quotations and references I give an abbreviated title and page number for works listed in the bibliography at the end. I am grateful for feedback by colleagues here at Stony Brook, the Breadloaf School of English, and the Penn State Conference on Rhetoric and Composition—where I read earlier drafts of this paper.

2. See Walter Ong, *Orality and Literacy,* 1982, for a powerful summary of his extensive work in this area and his wide-ranging citations to others working in it. For welcome warnings about stereotyping the mentalities associated with orality and literacy, see Cooper and Odell, "Sound in Composing"; Harste, "Assumptions"; Scribner and Cole, *Psychology of Literacy;* Heath, "Oral and Literate Traditions"; and Robinson, "Literacy." A number of the essays in Kroll and Vann, *Exploring Speaking-Writing Relationships,* e.g. O'Keefe, also warn against oversimplifying the contrast between speech and writing as media.

3. Ong focuses on the development of writing, but it is important to stand back and take a longer perspective. That is, the biggest boost to careful thinking came earlier with the birth of *language itself*—original spoken language. "As long as we carry intuitive belief without a symbolic representation, we are one with it and cannot criticize it. But once we have formulated it, we can look at it objectively and learn from it, even from its rejection." (Karl Popper, cited in Kroll and Vann, *Exploring Speaking-Writing Relationships,* p. 151.) See also Vygotsky, *Thought and Language,* on the effect of language itself as a "second signalling system."

4. It may be, however, that many of the effects we are tempted to ascribe to literacy are really effects of schooling. See Gere, "Cultural Perspectives"; Olson, "Languages of Instruction"; and Scribner and Cole, *Psychology of Literacy.*

5. Literate people like to complain that the telephone and other electronic media have almost destroyed writing by permitting people to do most of their business orally and refrain from writing unless there is some pressing need for "hard" (i.e. indelible) copy. But I suspect that more people write more now than ever before. Engineers are estimated to spend from a quarter to a third of their working time involved in some kind of writing. See Faigley et al., "Writing After College." The spread of radios and phonographs raised fears that people would no longer go to concerts or play musical instruments: the opposite has occurred.

6. This somatic perspective heightens the paradoxes. Writing is the external indelible medium—yet is the most easily changed. Thinking is the most internal and changeable medium—yet from another point of view it is the most intractable to change: try removing or changing a thought you don't like. Speech, chameleon-like, is in the middle.

7. In enumerating these characteristics of speech I am drawing on Tannen, "Oral and Literate"; see also Emig, "Writing as a Mode of Learning." In describing some ways to provide speech conditions in a writing class I am drawing on a discussion with members of the fall 1983 teaching practicum at Stony Brook—for whose help I am grateful.

8. I don't really grant this point, however. Though these procedures are particularly suitable for basic students, they are also the kinds of writing that occur in many workplace settings (for example with a research team, an investigative committee, or any other working group whose members communicate to each other in letters, queries, and rough position papers). Sometimes people who talk about the "inherent difference" between speaking and writing get carried away and ignore the brute fact that much of the writing in the world—perhaps even most of it—takes place in a strongly social or communal context: the writing is in response to an earlier discourse and gives rise to subsequent discourse and is asked for and read by particular people whom the writer knows—people who share a common context and set of assumptions with the writer.

9. See Lunsford, "Cognitive Development," and Shaughnessy, *Errors.* Instead of just talking about "oral interference" as a problem, I would also use the term in the positive sense: oral skills and habits can "run interference" for writing—knocking down some of the obstacles that make writing difficult.

10. This is particularly a problem in certain technical documents and reports, and it is interesting to see how canny readers of such genres have learned to accommodate to the bad treatment they receive: they "read" such documents as though they were looking at a diagram rather than reading a text—namely, by quickly scanning through it, perhaps more than once, trying to develop an overview and a sense of perspective which they know the writer does not provide. Being trained and consenting to read in this way, in a sense they perpetuate the problem.

11. Theorists of style in general and of cohesion and coherence in particular talk about this phenomenon at the sentence or syntactic level (see Joseph Williams, *Style*), but I'm not sure that there's enough recognition of it at the level of the whole. See, however, the reference to beginning work on the "macrotheme-rheme" problem in Witte and Faigley's "Coherence, Cohesion."

12. We should recognize how often good essays or books are actually held together by being stories: "here is the story of my thinking," or "here is a ride on the train of my thought," or even just, "this and this and this, and here is the moral."

WORKS CITED

Note: For two rich bibliographies on the relation between speech and writing, see the Kroll and Vann volume noted below, and the annotated bibliography by Sarah Liggett in the recent *CCC:* 35 (October, 1984), 334–44.

Auerbach, Erich. *Mimesis.* Tr. W. Traske, Berne, 1946.

Barthes, Roland. "Death of the Author." In *Image, Music, Text.* New York: Hill and Wang, 1977.

Bruner, Jerome. *Studies in Cognitive Growth.* Cambridge, MA: Harvard University Press, 1966.

————"Language, Mind, and Reading." In *Awakening Literacy.* Ed. Hillel Goelman, Antoinette Obeng, and Frank Smith. Exeter, NH: Heinemann Educational Books, 1984.

Calkins, Lucy. *Lessons from a Child on the Teaching and Learning of Writing.* Exeter, NH: Heinemann Educational Books, 1983.

Cooper, Charles, and Lee Odell. "Considerations of Sound in the Composing Process of Published Writers." *RTE,* 10 (Fall, 1976), 103–115.

Elbow, Peter. *Writing Without Teachers.* New York: Oxford University Press, 1973.

————*Writing With Power.* New York: Oxford University Press, 1981.

Emig, Janet. "Writing as a Mode of Learning." *CCC,* 28 (May , 1977), 122–128. Reprinted in *The Writing Teacher's Sourcebook.* Ed. Gary Tate and Edward P. J. Corbett. New York: Oxford University Press, 1981.

Faigley, L. et al. "Writing After College: A Stratified Survey of the Writing of College-Trained People," Writing Program Assessment Technical Report No. 1, University of Texas, Austin, 1981.

Gere, Anne Ruggles. "A Cultural Perspective on Talking and Writing." In Knoll and Vann, *Exploring Speaking-Writing Relationships.*

Goody, Jack. *The Domestication of the Savage Mind.* Cambridge, England: Cambridge University Press, 1977.

Graves, Donald. *Writing: Teachers and Children at Work.* Exeter, NH: Heinemann Educational Books, 1983.

Halpern, Jeanne. "Differences Between Speaking and Writing and Their Implications for Teaching." *CCC,* 35 (October, 1984), 345–357.

Harste, Jerome C., Virginia A. Woodward, and Carolyn L. Burke. "Examining Our Assumptions: A Transactional View of Literacy and Learning." *RTE,* 18 (February, 1984), 84–108.

Havelock, Eric A. *Preface to Plato.* Cambridge, MA: Belknap Press of Harvard University Press, 1963.

Heath, Shirley Brice. "Oral and Literate Traditions." *International Social Science Journal,* 36 (1984), 41–57.

Kroll, Barry M., and Roberta J. Vann (ed.) *Exploring Speaking-Writing Relationships.* Urbana, IL: National Council of Teachers of English, 1981.

Lunsford, Andrea. "Cognitive Development and the Basic Writer." *CE,* 41 (September, 1979), 38–46.

Meyer, Leonard B. *Emotion and Meaning in Music.* Chicago: University of Chicago Press, 1956.

Miller, George. "The Magical Number Seven Plus or Minus Two: Some Limits on Our Capacity for Processing Information." *Psychological Review,* 63 (March, 1956), 81–97.

Olson, D. R. "The Languages of Instruction: The Literate Bias of Schooling." In R. C. Anderson, R. J. Siro, and W. E. Montague (ed.), *Schooling and the Acquisition of Knowledge.* Hillsdale, NJ: Lawrence Erlbaum, 1977.

Ong, Walter J. *Orality and Literacy.* New York: Methuen, 1982.

Perl, Sondra. "Understanding Composing." *CCC,* 31 (December, 1980), 363–369.

Robinson, Jay L. "The Users and Uses of Literacy." In *Literacy of Life: The Demand for Reading and Writing.* Ed. Richard W. Bailey and Robin Melanie Fosheim. New York: Modern Language Association, 1983.

Schafer, John C. "The Linguistic Analysis of Spoken and Written Texts." In Kroll and Vann, *Exploring Speaking-Writing Relationships.*

Scribner, Sylvia, and Michael Cole. *The Psychology of Literacy.* Cambridge, MA: Harvard University Press, 1981.
—— "Unpackaging Literacy." In *Variations in Writing: Functional and Linguistic-Cultural Differences.* Ed. Marcia Farr Whiteman. Hillsdale, NJ: Lawrence Erlbaum Assocs., 1981, 71–87.
Searle, John. "The Word Turned Upside Down." *The New York Review of Books,* 27 October 1983, 74–79.
Shaughnessy, Mina P. *Errors and Expectations: A Guide for the Teacher of Basic Writing.* New York: Oxford University Press, 1977.
Tannen, Deborah. "Oral and Literate Strategies in Spoken and Written Discourse." In *Literacy for Life: The Demand for Reading and Writing.* Ed. Richard W. Bailey and Robin Melanie Fosheim. New York: Modern Language Association, 1983.
Vygotsky, Lev. *Thought and Language.* Cambridge, MA: MIT Press, 1962.
Williams, Joseph M. *Style: Ten Lessons in Clarity and Grace.* Glenview, IL: Scott Foresman and Co., 1981.
Williams, Joseph M., and Rosemary L. Hake. "Style and Its Consequences: Do as I Do, Not as I Say." *College English,* 43 (September, 1981), 433–451.
Witte, Stephen, and Lester Faigley. "Coherence, Cohesion, and Writing Quality." *CCC,* 32 (May, 1981), 189–204.
Zuckerkandl, Victor. *Sound and Symbol: Music and the External World.* New York: Pantheon Press, 1956, reprinted 1976.

Detection, Diagnosis, and the Strategies of Revision
Linda Flower, John R. Hayes, Linda Carey, Karen Schriver, and James Stratman

WORKS CITED

Atwell, Margaret. "The Evolution of Text: The Interrelationship of Reading and Writing in the Composing Process." Paper presented at the Annual Meeting of the National Council of Teachers of English, Boston, 21 November 1981.
Bartholomae, David. "The Study of Error." *College Composition and Communication,* 31 (October, 1980), 253–269.
Bartlett, Elsa Jaffe. *Learning to Write: Some Cognitive and Linguistic Components.* Washington, DC: Center for Applied Linguistics, 1981.
Beach, Richard. "The Pragmatics of Self-Assessing." In R. Sudol (Ed.), *Revising: New Essays for Teachers of Writing,* Urbana, IL: ERIC/National Council of Teachers of English, 1982.
Beach, Richard, and Sara Eaton. "Factors Influencing Self-Assessing and Revising by College Freshmen." In R. Beach and L. Bridwell (Ed.), *New Directions in Composition Research,* New York: Guilford Press, 1984.
Beach, Richard. "Self-Evaluation Strategies of Extensive Revisers and Non-Revisers." *College Composition and Communication,* 27 (May, 1976), 160–164.
Bean, John C. "Computerized Word-Processing as an Aid to Revision." *College Composition and Communication,* 34 (May, 1983), 146–148.
Bereiter, Carl, and Marlene Scardamalia. "From Conversation to Composition: The Role of Instruction in a Developmental Process." In R. Glaser (Ed.), *Advances in Instructional Psychology,* Vol. 2, Hillsdale, NJ: Lawrence Erlbaum, 1982.
Berkenkotter, Carol. "Decisions and Revisions: The Planning Strategies of a Publishing Writer." *College Composition and Communication,* 34 (May, 1983), 156–169.
Blau, Sheridan. "Invisible Writing: Investigating Cognitive Processes in Composition." *College Composition and Communication,* 34 (October, 1983), 297–313.
Bond, Sandra J., John R. Hayes, and Linda S. Flower. *Translating the Law into Common Language: A Protocol Study.* Document Design Project 1, Pittsburgh, PA: Carnegie-Mellon University, April, 1980.
Bracewell, Robert. "Investigating the Control of Writing Skills." In P. Mosenthal, L. Tamor, and S. Walmsley (Ed.), *Research on Writing,* New York: Longman, 1983.
Bracewell, Robert, Carl Bereiter, and Marlene Scardamalia. *A Test of Two Myths About Revision.* Technical Report, Paper presented at the Annual Meeting of the American Educational Research Association, San Francisco, April, 1979.
Bracewell, Robert J., Marlene Scardamalia, and Carl Bereiter. "The Development of Audience Awareness in Writing." *Resources in Education* (October, 1978), 154–433.

Bridwell, L. S. "Revising Strategies in Twelfth Grade Students' Transactional Writing." *Research in the Teaching of English,* 14 (October, 1980), 197–222.

Bruner, Jerome, Jacqueline Goodnow, and George Austin. *A Study of Thinking.* New York: Wiley, 1967.

Calkins, Lacy McCormick. "Notes and Comments: Children's Rewriting Strategies." *Research in the Teaching of English,* 14 (December, 1980), 331–341.

Collier, Richard M. "The Word Processor and Revision Strategies." *College Composition and Communication,* 34 (May, 1983), 149–155.

Daiute, Colette. "Performance Limits on Writers." In R. Beach and L. Bridwell (Ed.), *New Directions in Composition Research,* New York: Guilford Press, 1984.

de Beaugrande, Robert. *Critical Discourse: A Survey of Literary Theorists.* Norwood, NJ: Ablex, 1988.

Della-Piana, Gabriel. "Research Strategies for the Study of Revision Processes in Writing Poetry." In Charles R. Cooper and Lee Odell (Ed.), *Research on Composing: Points of Departure,* Urbana, IL: National Council of Teachers of English, 1978.

Elbow, Peter. *Writing Without Teachers.* London: Oxford, 1973.

Faigley, Lester, and Stephen Witte. "Analyzing Revision." *College Composition and Communication,* 32 (December, 1981), 400–414.

Flower, Linda. "Writer-Based Prose: A Cognitive Basis for Problems in Writing." *College English,* 41 (September, 1979), 19–37.

Flower, Linda, and John R. Hayes. "Images, Plans, and Prose: The Representation of Meaning in Writing." *Written Communication,* 1 (January, 1984), 120–160.

Flower, Linda, Linda Carey, and John R. Hayes. *Diagnosis in Revision: The Expert's Option.* Communications Design Center Technical Report, Carnegie-Mellon University, 1984.

Flower, Linda, and John R. Hayes. "A Cognitive Process Theory of Writing." *College Composition and Communication,* 32 (December, 1981), 365–387.

Flower, Linda, and John R. Hayes. "The Pregnant Pause: An Inquiry Into the Nature of Planning." *Research in the Teaching of English,* 15 (October, 1981), 229–243.

Freedman, Sarah. *Evaluation of and Response to Student Writing: A Review.* Technical Report, American Educational Research Association, New Orleans, April, 1984.

Gould, John D. "Experiments on Composing Letters: Some Facts, Some Myths, and Some Observations." In Lee W. Gregg and Erwin R. Steinberg (Ed.), *Cognitive Processes in Writing,* Hillsdale, NJ: Lawrence Erlbaum, 1980.

Halpern, Jean, and Sarah Liggett. *Computers & Composition: How the New Technologies Are Changing Writing,* Urbana, IL: National Council of Teachers of English, 1984.

Halpin, Jeanne A. *The Editing Process: Detecting Errors in Text.* Technical Report, Paper presented at the Annual Meeting of the American Educational Research Association, Montreal, Canada, April, 1983.

Hayes, John R. *Cognitive Psychology: Thinking and Creating.* Homewood, IL: Dorsey Press, 1978.

Hayes, John R., Linda Flower, Karen Schriver, James Stratman, and Linda Carey. "Cognitive Processes in Revision" (NSF Grant BNS 84-15367, Final Report). In Sheldon Rosenberg (Ed.), *Reading, Writing, and Language Processing,* Cambridge, England: Cambridge University Press, in press. (*Advances in Applied Psycholinguistics,* Vol. II.)

Hayes, John R., Karen Schriver, and Linda Flower. *Decisions in Revision.* Communications Design Center Technical Report, Carnegie-Mellon University, in preparation.

Hayes, John R., Karen Schriver, and Linda Flower. *Perceptual Processes in Revision: Seeing Problems in Text.* Communications Design Center Technical Report, Carnegie-Mellon University, in preparation.

Hays, Janice N. *The Effect of Audience Considerations upon the Revisions of a Group of Basic Writers and More Competent Junior and Senior Writers.* ERIC Document 204 802, Urbana, IL: Educational Resources Information Center, 1982.

Hillocks, G. Jr. "The Interaction of Instruction, Teacher Comment, and Revision in Teaching the Composing Process." *Research in the Teaching of English,* 16 (October, 1982), 261–278.

Hull, Glynda. *The Editing Process in Writing: A Performance Study of Experts and Novices.* Diss. University of Pittsburgh, 1983.

Knoblauch, C. H., and Lil Brannon. "Teacher Commentary on Student Writing: The State of the Art." *Freshman English News,* 10 (Fall, 1981), 1–3.

Langer, J. A. "Effects of Topic Knowledge on the Quality and Coherence of Informational Writing." In A. Applebee (Ed.), *Contexts for Learning to Write,* Norwood, NJ: Ablex, 1984.

Laurence, Patricia. "Error's Endless Train: Why Students Don't Perceive Errors." *Journal of Basic Writing,* 1 (Spring, 1975), 23–42.

Mann, William C., and James A. Moore. "Computer Generation of Multiparagraph English Text." *American Journal of Computational Linguistics,* 7 (January–March, 1981), 17–29.

Meyer, Bonnie J. F. "Reading Research and the Composition Teacher: The Importance of Plans." *College Composition and Communication,* 33 (February, 1982), 37–49.

Murray, Donald M. "Internal Revision: A Process of Discovery." In Charles R. Cooper and Lee Odell (Ed.), *Research on Composing: Points of Departure,* Urbana, IL: National Council of Teachers of English, 1978.

National Assessment of Educational Progress. *Write/Rewrite: An Assessment of Writing Skills.* Writing Report 05-W-04, Denver, CO: U. S. Government Printing Office, 1977.

Newkirk, Thomas. "Barriers to Revision." *Journal of Basic Writing,* 3 (Fall/Winter, 1981), 50–61.

Nold, Ellen. "Revising: Intentions and Conventions." In Ronald Sudol (Ed.), *Revising: New Essays for Teachers of Writing,* Urbana, IL: ERIC/National Council of Teachers of English, 1982.

Nold, Ellen. "Revising." In C. Frederiksen (Ed.), *Writing: The Nature, Development and Teaching of Written Communication,* Hillsdale, NJ: Lawrence Erlbaum, 1981.

Perl, Sondra. "The Composing Processes of Unskilled Writers." *Research in the Teaching of English,* 13 (December, 1979), 317–336.

Perl, Sondra. *Five Writers Writing: Case Studies of the Composing Process of Unskilled College Writers.* Diss. New York University, 1978.

Rose, Mike. "Rigid Rules, Inflexible Plans, and the Stifling of Language: A Cognitivist Analysis of Writer's Block." *College Composition and Communication,* 31 (December, 1980), 389–401.

Rubin, Lois. *An Investigation of Self-Evaluation: How Student Writers Judge Their Writing Process and Product.* Diss. Carnegie-Mellon University, 1984.

Scardamalia, Marlene, and Carl Bereiter. "The Development of Evaluative, Diagnostic, and Remedial Capabilities in Children's Composing." In M. Martlew (Ed.), *The Psychology of Written Language: A Developmental Approach,* London: John Wiley and Sons, 1983.

Schwartz, Mimi. "Two Journeys through the Writing Process." *College Composition and Communication,* 34 (May, 1983), 188–201.

Shaughnessy, Mina. *Errors and Expectations.* New York: Oxford, 1977.

Sommers, Nancy I. "Revision Strategies of Student Writers and Experienced Adult Writers." *College Composition and Communication,* 31 (December, 1980), 378–387.

Van Dyck, Barrie. "On-the-Job Writing of High-Level Business Executives." Paper presented at the Conference on College Composition and Communication, Washington, DC, 13–15 March 1980.

Witte, Stephen. "Topical Structure and Revision: An Exploratory Study." *College Composition and Communication,* 34 (October, 1983), 313–341.

Witte, Stephen. "Revising, Composing Theory, and Research Design." In S. W. Freedman (Ed.), *The Acquisition of Written Language: Response and Revision,* Norwood, NJ: Ablex, 1985. 250–284.

Young, Richard, Alton Becker, and Kenneth Pike. *Rhetoric: Discovery and Change.* New York: Harcourt, Brace and World, 1970.

WORKS CITED IN AFTERWORD

Hayes, John R. "A New Framework for Understanding Cognition and Affect in Writing." *The Science of Writing: Theories, Methods, Individual Differences, and Applications.* Ed. C. Michael Levy and Sarah Ransdell. Mahwah: Erlbaum, 1996. 1–27.

Hayes, John R., Linda Flower, Karen Schriver, James Stratman, and Linda Carey. "Cognitive Processes in Revision." *Reading, Writing, and Language Learning.* Ed. Sheldon Rosenberg. New York: Cambridge UP, 1987.

Underlife and Writing Instruction
Robert Brooke

WORKS CITED

Annas, Pamela. "Style as Politics." *College English* 47 (1985): 360–71.

Berthoff, Ann. *The Making of Meaning.* Upper Montclair, NJ: Boynton/Cook, 1983.

Dillard, Annie. "Lenses." *The Bedford Reader.* Ed. X. J. Kennedy and Dorothy Kennedy. 2nd ed. New York: St. Martin's Press, 1985. 101–05.

Elbow, Peter. *Writing Without Teachers.* New York: Oxford UP, 1973.

Emig, Janet. "Non-Magical Thinking: Presenting Writing Developmentally in Schools." *Writing: The Nature, Development, and Teaching of Written Communication, Vol. 2: Writing: Process, Development and Communication.* Ed. Carl Frederiksen and Joseph Dominic. Hillsdale, NJ: Erlbaum, 1981. 21–30.

———. *The Web of Meaning.* Upper Montclair, NJ: Boynton/Cook, 1983.

Goffman, Erving. *Asylums: Essays on the Social Situation of Mental Patients and Other Inmates.* New York: Anchor, 1961.

———. *Stigma: Notes on the Management of Spoiled Identity.* Englewood Cliffs, NJ: Prentice-Hall, 1963.

Knoblauch, C. H., and Lil Brannon. *Rhetorical Traditions and the Teaching of Writing.* Upper Montclair, NJ: Boynton/Cook, 1984.

Laurence, Margaret. *A Bird in the House.* Toronto: Seal, 1978.

Murray, Donald. *A Writer Teaches Writing.* 2nd ed. Boston: Houghton Mifflin, 1982.

Myers, Greg. "Reality, Consensus, and Reform in the Rhetoric of Composition Teaching." *College English* 48 (1986): 154–74.

Rich, Adrienne. "Teaching Language in Open Admissions." *On Lies, Secrets, and Silence: Selected Prose 1966–1978.* New York: Norton, 1979. 51–68.

Rose, Mike. "The Language of Exclusion." *College English* 47 (1985): 341–59.

Young, Richard, Alton Becker, and Kenneth Pike. *Rhetoric: Discovery and Change.* New York: Harcourt Brace Jovanovich, 1970.

Rhetorical Reading Strategies and the Construction of Meaning
Christina Haas and Linda Flower

WORKS CITED

Baker, Linda, and Ann L. Brown. "Metacognitive Skills and Reading." *Handbook of Reading Research.* Ed. R. Barr, Michael L. Kamil, and Peter Mosenthal. New York: Longman, 1984. 353–94.

Bereiter, Carl, and Marlene Scardamalia. "Cognitive Coping Strategies and the Problem of Inert Knowledge." *Learning and Thinking Skills: Research and Open Questions.* Ed. Susan Chipman, J. Segal, and Robert Glaser. Hillsdale, NJ: Lawrence Erlbaum Associates, 1985. 65–80.

Bransford, John. *Cognition: Learning, Understanding and Remembering.* Belmont, CA: Wadsworth Publishing Company, 1979.

Farnham-Diggory, Sylvia. *Cognitive Processes in Education: A Psychological Preparation for Teaching and Curriculum Development.* New York: Harper and Row, 1972.

Flower, Linda. "The Construction of Purpose in Writing and Reading." *College English* 50, 1988. 528–50.

Flower, Linda. "Interpretive Acts: Cognition and the Construction of Discourse." *Poetics* 16 (April 1987): 109–30.

Flower, Linda, and John R. Hayes. "Images, Plans, and Prose: The Representation of Meaning in Writing." *Written Communication* 1 (January 1984): 120–60.

Flower, Linda, John R. Hayes, Karen Shriver, Linda Carey, and Christina Haas. *Planning in Writing: A Theory of the Cognitive Process.* ONR Technical Report #1. Pittsburgh: Carnegie Mellon, 1987.

Haas, Christina, and John R. Hayes. "What Did I Just Say? Reading Problems in Writing with the Machine." *Research in the Teaching of English* 20 (February 1986): 22–35.

Scardamalia, Marlene. "How Children Cope with the Cognitive Demands of Writing." *Writing: The Nature, Development, and Teaching of Written Communication (Vol. 2).* Ed. Carl Frederiksen, M. F. Whiteman, and J. F. Dominic. Hillsdale, NJ: Lawrence Erlbaum Associates, 1981. 81–103.

Spivey, Nancy N. "Construing Constructivism: Reading Research in the United States." *Poetics* 16 (April 1987): 169–93.

Tierney, Robert, and P. David Pearson. "Toward a Composing Model of Reading." *Composing and Comprehending.* Ed. Julie M. Jensen. Urbana, IL: NCTE, 1984. 33–45.

Vipond, Douglas, and Russell Hunt. "Point-driven Understanding: Pragmatic and Cognitive Dimensions of Literary Reading." *Poetics* 13 (June 1984): 261–77.

WORKS CITED IN AFTERWORD

Bijker, Wiebe E. *Of Bicycles, Bakelites, and Bulbs: Toward a Theory of Sociotechnical Change.* Cambridge: Massachusetts Institute of Technology P, 1995.
Neustadt, Richard E., and Ernest R. May. *Thinking in Time: Uses of History for Decision Makers.* New York: Free Press, 1986.

The Idea of Community in the Study of Writing
Joseph Harris

NOTES

1. This essay began as part of a 1988 CCCC panel on "Raymond Williams and the Teaching of Composition." My thanks go to my colleagues on that panel, Nicholas Coles and Min-zhan Lu, for their help in conceiving and carrying through this project, as well as to David Bartholomae and Patricia Bizzell for their useful readings of many versions of this text.
2. One might argue that there never really is a "we" for whom the language of the university (or a particular discipline) is fully invented and accessible. Greg Myers, for instance, has shown how two biologists—presumably well-trained scholars long initiated into the practices of their discipline—had to reshape their writings extensively to make them fit in with "what might be said" in the journals of their own field. Like our students, we too must reinvent the university whenever we sit down to write.
3. A growing number of theorists have begun to call this vagueness of community into question. See, for instance: Bazerman on "Some Difficulties in Characterizing Social Phenomena in Writing," Bizzell on "What Is a Discourse Community?" Herzberg on "The Politics of Discourse Communities," and Swales on "Approaching the Concept of Discourse Community."
4. See, for instance, Dell Hymes in *Foundations in Sociolinguistics:* "For our purposes it appears most useful to reserve the notion of community for a local unit, characterized for its members by common locality and primary interaction, and to admit exceptions cautiously" (51).
5. See, for instance, Bizzell on the need for "emphasizing the crucial function of a collective project in unifying the group" ("What" 1), and Bruffee on the notion that "to learn is to work collaboratively . . . among a community of knowledgeable peers" (646).
6. Bruce Robbins makes much the same case in "Professionalism and Politics: Toward Productively Divided Loyalties," as does John Schilb in "When Bricolage Becomes Theory: The Hazards of Ignoring Ideology." Fish too seems recently to be moving towards this position, arguing that an interpretive community is an "engine of change" fueled by the interaction and conflict of the various beliefs and practices that make it up. As he puts it: "Beliefs are not all held at the same level or operative at the same time. Beliefs, if I may use a metaphor, are nested, and on occasion they may affect and even alter one another and so the entire system or network they comprise" ("Change" 429).

WORKS CITED

Barthes, Roland. *S/Z.* Trans. Richard Miller. New York: Hill, 1974.
Bartholomae, David. "Inventing the University." *When a Writer Can't Write.* Ed. Mike Rose. New York: Guilford, 1985. 134–65.
Bartholomae, David, and Anthony Petrosky. *Facts, Artifacts and Counterfacts: Theory and Method for a Reading and Writing Course.* Upper Montclair, NJ: Boynton/Cook, 1986.
Bazerman, Charles. "Some Difficulties in Characterizing Social Phenomena in Writing." Conference on College Composition and Communication. Atlanta, March 1987.
Bizzell, Patricia. "Foundationalism and Anti-Foundationalism in Composition Studies." *Pre/Text* 7 (Spring/Summer 1986): 37–57.
———. "What Is a Discourse Community?" Penn State Conference on Rhetoric and Composition. University Park, July 1987.
Brodkey, Linda. *Academic Writing as Social Practice.* Philadelphia: Temple UP, 1987.
Bruffee, Kenneth A. "Collaborative Learning and the 'Conversation of Mankind.'" *College English* 46 (November 1984): 635–52.
Coles, Nicholas. "Raymond Williams: Writing Across Borders." Conference on College Composition and Communication. St. Louis, March 1988.

Fish, Stanley. *Is There a Text in This Class?* Cambridge: Harvard UP, 1980.

———. "Change." *South Atlantic Quarterly* 86 (Fall 1987): 423–44.

Herzberg, Bruce. "The Politics of Discourse Communities." Conference on College Composition and Communication. New Orleans, March 1986.

Hirsch, E. D., Jr. *Cultural Literacy: What Every American Needs to Know.* Boston: Houghton, 1987.

Hymes, Dell. *Foundations in Sociolinguistics: An Ethnographic Approach.* Philadelphia: U of Pennsylvania P, 1974.

Lu, Min-zhan. "Teaching the Conventions of Academic Discourse: Structures of Feeling." Conference on College Composition and Communication. St. Louis, March 1988.

Myers, Greg. "The Social Construction of Two Biologists' Proposals." *Written Communication* 2 (July 1985): 219–45.

Porter, James. "Intertextuality and the Discourse Community." *Rhetoric Review* 5 (Fall 1986): 34–47.

Pratt, Mary Louise. "Interpretive Strategies/Strategic Interpretations: On Anglo-American Reader Response Criticism." *Boundary 2* 11.1–2 (Fall/Winter 1982–83): 201–31.

Robbins, Bruce. "Professionalism and Politics: Toward Productively Divided Loyalties." *Profession 85*: 1–9.

Rodriguez, Richard. *Hunger of Memory.* Boston: Godine, 1981.

Schilb, John. "When Bricolage Becomes Theory: The Hazards of Ignoring Ideology." Midwest Modern Language Association. Chicago, November 1986.

Swales, John. "Approaching the Concept of Discourse Community." Conference on College Composition and Communication. Atlanta, March 1987.

Williams, Raymond. *Second Generation.* New York: Horizon, 1964.

———. *The Country and the City.* New York: Oxford UP, 1973.

———. *Keywords: A Vocabulary of Culture and Society.* New York: Oxford UP, 1976.

———. *Marxism and Literature.* New York: Oxford UP, 1977.

WORKS CITED IN AFTERWORD

Sennet, Richard. *The Fall of Public Man.* New York: Knopf, 1997.

"This Wooden Shack Place": The Logic of an Unconventional Reading
Glynda Hull and Mike Rose

NOTES

1. In stimulated recall, a student's writing is videotaped and, upon completion, replayed to cue recall of mental processes occurring during composing. For further discussion of the procedure and its advantages and limitations, see Rose, *Writer's Block.*

2. Frankly, we had trouble arriving at a way to designate the readings we're calling conventional and unconventional. And we're not satisfied yet. Certain of Robert's responses seem to be influenced by class (e.g., his reaction to the wooden shacks and Sears), and we note that, but with reluctance. We don't want to imply that class is the primary determiner of Robert's reading (vs., say, socialization into an English department—which, we realize, would correlate with class). We also don't want to imply that middle-class readers would, by virtue of class, automatically see things in a certain way, would have no trouble understanding particular images and allusions. One of the people who read this paper for us, Dennis Lynch, suggested that we use Wayne Booth's notion of "intended audience"—that Robert is simply not a member of the audience for whom the poem was written, thus he offers a reading that differs from the reading we're calling conventional. The notion of intended audience makes sense here, and fits with our discussion of socialization. Hongo, like most younger American poets, honed his craft in an English department and an MFA program, places where one's work is influenced by particular audiences—fellow poets, faculty, journal editors, etc. But, finally, we decided not to use the notion of intended audience, for it carries with it a theoretical framework we're not sure does Robert or Hongo full justice here. We use words like "conventional" and "middle-class," then, with reserve and invite our readers to help us think through this problem.

3. For two different but compatible perspectives on this claim see Shor; Tharp and Gallimore.

4. We would like to thank Linda Flower, Kay Fraser, Marisa Garrett, Jonathan Lovell, Dennis Lynch, Sandra Mano, Cheryl Pfoff, Mariolina Salvatori, Melanie Sperling, and Susan

Thompson-Lowry for their comments on this paper. We benefited from a discussion at a meeting of the directors of the California Writing Project, and we would also like to acknowledge three anonymous *CCC* reviewers who gently guided us toward an understanding of the gaps and blunders in the essay. This work has been supported by grants from the McDonnell Foundation Program in Cognitive Studies for Educational Practice and the Research Foundation of the National Council of Teachers of English.

WORKS CITED

Bartholomae, David, and Anthony Petrosky, eds. *Facts, Artifacts, and Counterfacts: Theory and Method for a Reading and Writing Course.* Upper Montclair: Boynton, 1986.
Hongo, Garrett Kaoru. "And Your Soul Shall Dance." *Yellow Light.* Middletown: Wesleyan UP, 1982. 69.
Hull, Glynda, and Mike Rose. "Rethinking Remediation: Toward a Social-Cognitive Understanding of Problematic Reading and Writing." *Written Communication* 6 (Apr. 1989): 139–54.
Hull, Glynda, Mike Rose, Kay Losey Fraser, and Marisa Garrett. "The Social Construction of Remediation." The Tenth Annual Ethnography in Education Forum. University of Pennsylvania, Feb. 1989.
Mehan, Hugh. *Learning Lessons.* Cambridge: Harvard UP, 1979.
Rose, Mike. *Lives on the Boundary: The Struggles and Achievements of America's Underprepared.* New York: Free Press, 1989.
———. *Writer's Block: The Cognitive Dimension.* Carbondale: Southern Illinois UP, 1984.
Salvatori, Mariolina. "Pedagogy: From the Periphery to the Center." *Reclaiming Pedagogy: The Rhetoric of the Classroom.* Ed. Patricia Donahue and Ellen Quandahl. Carbondale: Southern Illinois UP, 1989. 17–34.
———. "Reading and Writing a Text: Correlations between Reading and Writing Patterns." *College English* 45 (Nov. 1983): 657–66.
Shor, Ira. *Empowering Education: Critical Teaching for Social Change.* Chicago: U of Chicago P, 1992.
Tharp, Roland G., and Ronald Gallimore. *Rousing Minds to Life.* New York: Oxford UP, 1989.

Remediation as Social Construct: Perspectives from an Analysis of Classroom Discourse
Glynda Hull, Mike Rose, Kay Losey Fraser, and Marisa Castellano

NOTES

1. The work reported here is part of a larger study, "Literacy, Underpreparation, and the Cognition of Composing." We gratefully acknowledge the support of the James S. McDonnell Foundation's Program in Cognitive Studies for Educational Practice, the Spencer Foundation, the National Center for the Study of Writing, and the National Council of Teachers of English Research Foundation.
2. For other discussions of interactional classroom competence and reviews of previous work in this area, see Mehan ("Competent") and Corno.
3. We should point out, however, that most of the research identifying the IRE sequence has been done with classrooms in the elementary grades. For an exception to this, and an example of how the IRE participant structure can be used to analyze writing conferences, see Freedman and Katz.
4. The transcription conventions were developed by John Gumperz, with help from Wallace Chafe and Noreen Barantz. Gumperz has stressed that the system is more interpretive than descriptive, and that the key to its proper usage is consistency.
5. In the interest of saving space, we haven't provided transcripts with contextualization cues for every stretch of classroom talk. Readers interested in seeing such transcripts can request a copy of Technical Report #44 from the National Center for the Study of Writing at the University of California, Berkeley.
6. For another account of this history, see Robert Sinclair and Ward Ghory's *Reaching Marginal Students.*
7. British researchers Michael Golby and John R. Gulliver make a related point in their critical review of remedial education in England and Wales: "In order to understand what exists, we must see remedial education firstly in its historical context, and secondly as a manifesta-

tion of ideologies obtaining not only within education but also having co-relative applications within wider social policy" (11). See also Michael Cole and Peg Griffin.

8. For a related argument, see Sandra Schecter and Tamara Lucas's position paper on "Literacy Education and Diversity."

9. A special issue of the *Journal of Basic Writing* (1981) was devoted to discussions of the kinds of programs that would best prepare basic writing teachers.

10. This explanation of Maria's interactional patterns is developed more fully by Kay Losey Fraser in a paper delivered at the 1989 Conference on College Composition and Communication.

11. To this end, with our colleague Cynthia Greenleaf, we are creating a set of cases and an interpretation of remedial education in America that we hope can be used to engage teachers in the kind of inquiry that leads one to trace the connections between the mind of the student and the classroom and the community beyond.

12. We aren't, however, offering student-led discussion, collaborative groups, or peer conferencing as a panacea. Thomas Fox has illustrated that conversation between peers can be dramatically and negatively affected by gender and race relations. See also Trimbur.

13. Martin Nystrand and Adam Gamoran at the University of Wisconsin–Madison are currently engaged in studies of classroom lessons aimed at characterizing high-quality instructional discourse.

14. We would like to thank Carmen Colon Montes de Oca for helpful conversation and Cynthia Greenleaf, Kris Gutierrez, Rebekah Kaplan, Jacqueline Jones Royster, and Gloria Zarabozo for reading and commenting on the manuscript. We also benefitted from the comments of three anonymous reviewers for *CCC*. We appreciate Susan Thompson's assistance throughout the research project.

WORKS CITED

Applebee, Arthur N. *Writing in the Secondary School: English and the Content Areas.* NCTE Research Report 21. Urbana: NCTE, 1981.

Au, K. "Participation Structures in a Reading Lesson with Hawaiian Children." *Anthropology and Education Quarterly* 11 (June 1980): 91–115.

Barnes, D. *From Communication to Curriculum.* London: Penguin, 1976.

Brodkey, Linda. "Transvaluing Difference." *College English* 51 (Oct. 1989): 597–601.

Brophy, Jere E. "Research on the Self-Fulfilling Prophecy." *Journal of Educational Psychology* 75 (Oct. 1983): 631–61.

Cazden, Courtney B. *Classroom Discourse: The Language of Teaching and Learning.* Portsmouth, NH: Heinemann, 1988.

Chase, Geoffrey. "Accommodation, Resistance and the Politics of Student Writing." *College Composition and Communication* 39 (Feb. 1988): 13–22.

Cole, Michael, and Peg Griffin. "A Sociohistorical Approach to Remediation." *Literacy, Society, and Schooling: A Reader.* Ed. S. de Castell, A. Luke, and K. Egan. Cambridge: Cambridge UP, 1986. 110–31.

Cook-Gumperz, Jenny. "Introduction: The Social Construction of Literacy." *The Social Construction of Literacy.* Ed. Jenny Cook-Gumperz. Cambridge: Cambridge UP, 1986. 1–15.

Corno, Lyn. "What It Means to Be Literate about Classrooms." *Classrooms and Literacy.* Ed. David Bloome. Norwood, NJ: Ablex, 1989. 29–52.

Corsaro, William A. "Communicative Processes in Studies of Social Organization: Sociological Approaches to Discourse Analysis." *Text* 1 (1981): 5–63.

Cuban, Larry, and David Tyack. " 'Dunces,' 'Shirkers,' and 'Forgotten Children': Historical Descriptions and Cures for Low Achievers." Conference for Accelerating the Education of At-Risk Students. Stanford U, 1988.

Dillon, J. T., ed. *Questioning and Discussion: A Multidisciplinary Study.* Norwood, NJ: Ablex, 1988.

Edmonds, Ronald. "Effective Schools for the Urban Poor." *Educational Leadership* 37 (Oct. 1979): 15–24.

Edwards, A. D., and V. J. Furlong. *The Language of Teaching: Meaning in Classroom Interaction.* London: Heinemann, 1978.

Erickson, Frederick. "Taught Cognitive Learning in Its Immediate Environments: A Neglected Topic in the Anthropology of Education." *Anthropology and Education Quarterly* 13 (1982): 149–80.

Everhart, R. B. *Reading, Writing, and Resistance: Adolescence and Labor in a Junior High School.* Boston: Routledge, 1983.

Fox, Thomas. "Collaborative Learning, Literacy, and Conversational Analysis." Unpublished paper. Chico State U, 1989.

Fraser, Kay Losey. "Classroom Discourse and Perceptions of Cognitive Ability: An Analysis of Interaction in a Basic Writing Class." Conference on College Composition and Communication Convention. Seattle, 1989.

Freedman, Sarah Warshauer, Anne Haas Dyson, Linda Flower, and Wallace Chafe. *Research in Writing: Past, Present, and Future.* Technical Report 1. Center for the Study of Writing, U of California, Berkeley, and Carnegie Mellon U, Pittsburgh, 1987.

Freedman, Sarah Warshauer, and Anne Marie Katz. "Pedagogical Interaction During the Composing Process: The Writing Conference." *Writing in Real Time: Modeling Production Processes.* Ed. Ann Matsuhashi. Norwood: Ablex, 1987. 58–107.

Giroux, Henry. *Theory and Resistance in Education.* South Hadley: Bergin, 1983.

Golby, Michael, and John R. Gulliver. "Whose Remedies, Whose Ills? A Critical Review of Remedial Education." *New Directions in Remedial Education.* Ed. Colin J. Smith. London: Falmer Press, 1985. 7–19.

Gould, Stephen Jay. *The Mismeasure of Man.* New York: Norton, 1981.

Gumperz, John. "Contextualization and Understanding." *Rethinking Context.* Ed. A. Duranti. Cambridge: Cambridge UP, 1992.

———. *Discourse Strategies.* Cambridge: Cambridge UP, 1982.

Heath, Shirley Brice. *Ways with Words: Language, Life, and Work in Communities and Classrooms.* Cambridge: Cambridge UP, 1983.

Hilliard, Asa G. "Teachers and Cultural Styles in a Pluralistic Society." *NEA Today* 7 (Jan. 1989): 65–69.

Hull, Glynda, and Mike Rose. "Rethinking Remediation: Toward a Social-Cognitive Understanding of Problematic Reading and Writing." *Written Communication* 8 (April 1989): 139–54.

———. "'This Wooden Shack Place': The Logic of an Unconventional Reading." *College Composition and Communication* 41 (Oct. 1990): 287–98.

McDermott, R. P. "The Explanation of Minority School Failure, Again." *Anthropology and Education Quarterly* 18 (Dec. 1987): 361–64.

Mehan, Hugh. "The Competent Student." *Anthropology and Education Quarterly* 11 (June 1980): 131–52.

———. *Learning Lessons: Social Organization in the Classroom.* Cambridge: Harvard UP, 1979.

Michaels, Sarah. *The Literacies Institute: Technical Proposal.* Newton, MA: Education Development Center, 1989.

Minick, Norris. *L. S. Vygotsky and Soviet Activity Theory: Perspectives on the Relationship between Mind and Society.* Technical Reports Special Monograph 1. Newton, MA: The Literacies Institute, 1989.

Mitchell, Jacquelyn. "Reflections of a Black Social Scientist: Some Struggles, Some Doubts, Some Hopes." *Harvard Educational Review* 52 (Feb. 1982): 27–44.

Moffett, James. *Teaching the Universe of Discourse.* Boston: Houghton, 1968.

Moll, Luis C., and Stephen Diaz. "Change as the Goal of Educational Research." *Anthropology and Education Quarterly* 18 (Dec. 1987): 300–11.

Nystrand, Martin, and Adam Gamoran. *Instructional Discourse and Student Engagement.* Madison: National Center on Effective Secondary Schools and the Wisconsin Center for Education Research, 1989.

———. *A Study of Instruction as Discourse.* Madison: National Center on Effective Secondary Schools and the Wisconsin Center for Education Research, 1988.

Obgu, John U., and Maria Eugenia Matute-Bianchi. "Understanding Sociocultural Factors: Knowledge, Identity, and School Adjustment." *Beyond Language: Social and Cultural Factors in Schooling Language Minority Students.* Los Angeles: Evaluation, Dissemination and Assessment Center of California State U, 1986. 73–142.

Philips, Susan U. *The Invisible Culture: Communication in Classroom and Community on the Warm Springs Indian Reservation.* New York: Longman, 1983.

Rose, Mike. "Complexity, Rigor, Evolving Method, and the Puzzle of Writer's Block: Thoughts on Composing Process Research." *When a Writer Can't Write: Studies in Writer's Block and Other Composing Process Problems.* Ed. Mike Rose. New York: Guilford, 1985. 227–60.

———. "The Language of Exclusion: Writing Instruction at the University." *College English* 47 (April 1985): 341–59.

———. "Narrowing the Mind and Page: Remedial Writers and Cognitive Reductionism." *College Composition and Communication* 39 (Oct. 1988): 267–302.

Sacks, H., E. A. Schegloff, and G. Jefferson. "A Simplest Systematics for the Organization of Turn-taking in Conversation." *Language* 50 (Dec. 1974): 696–735.

Schecter, Sandra R., and Tamara Lucas. "Literacy Education and Diversity. A Position Paper." Unpublished manuscript, U of California, Berkeley, 1989.

Shaughnessy, Mina. "Diving In: An Introduction to Basic Writing." *College Composition and Communication* 27 (Oct. 1976): 234–39.

———. *Errors and Expectations.* New York: Oxford UP, 1977.

Simon, Roger I. "But Who Will Let You Do It? Counter-Hegemonic Possibilities for Work Education." *Journal of Education* 165 (Summer 1983): 235–56.

Sinclair, J. M., and R. M. Coulthard. *Toward an Analysis of Discourse.* New York: Oxford UP, 1977.

Sinclair, Robert L., and Ward J. Ghory. *Reaching Marginal Students: A Primary Concern for School Renewal.* Berkeley: McCutchan, 1987.

Tannen, Deborah. *Conversational Style: Analyzing Talk among Friends.* Norwood: Ablex, 1984.

Tharp, Roland G., and Ronald Gallimore. *Rousing Minds to Life: Teaching, Learning, and Schooling in Social Context.* Cambridge: Cambridge UP, 1989.

Training Teachers of Basic Writing. Special Issue of the *Journal of Basic Writing* 3.2 (Spring/Summer 1981).

Trimbur, John. "Consensus and Difference in Collaborative Learning." *College English* 51 (Oct. 1989): 602–15.

Trueba, Henry T. "Culturally Based Explanations of Minority Students' Academic Achievement." *Anthropology and Education Quarterly* 19 (Dec. 1988): 270–87.

Wertsch, James V. *Vygotsky and the Social Formation of Mind.* Cambridge: Harvard UP, 1985.

Willis, Paul. *Learning to Labor: How Working Class Kids Get Working Class Jobs.* New York: Columbia UP, 1977.

Zehm, Stanley J. "Educational Misfits: A Study of Poor Performers in the English Class 1825–1925." Diss., Stanford U, 1973.

WORKS CITED IN AFTERWORD

Shaughnessy, Mina. *Errors and Expectations: A Guide for Teachers of Basic Writing.* New York: Oxford UP, 1977.

On Authority in the Study of Writing
Peter Mortensen and Gesa E. Kirsch

NOTES

1. Just as the critique of authority in composition studies continues to evolve, so does the critique of community (in addition to Harris, see Kent; Schiappa; Trimbur). Trimbur draws on the work of political philosopher Iris Marion Young for a rigorous discussion of the problems of theorizing difference within the construct of community. Young advances her analysis of community in the final chapter of *Justice and the Politics of Difference,* titled "City Life and Difference." Here Young examines the metaphor of the city, arguing that it, more aptly than community, represents the tensions and negotiations that characterize most heterogeneous social groupings.

2. To be sure, these two categories are interrelated in practice. For example, the power to enforce obedience is often presumed to derive from expertise. At the same time, the power to influence action, opinion, or belief may sometimes conceal the power to enforce obedience—the latter power only becoming apparent should influence fail.

3. Research identified with the expressive, cognitive, and social views of composing contributes to a necessary mosaic of knowledge about writing and its teaching. We are not here judging these contributions. We aim only to ascribe a mode of authority to each view that is *representative,* not *essential.*

4. Students often exercise authority in a variety of effective ways. They may use course evaluations to reject a teacher's classroom stance (Bauer, "The Other 'F' Word"); they may appropriate a networked computer classroom and engage in "nonacademic," sometimes hostile, conversation (Faigley, *Fragments* 185–99; Kremers; Sirc and Reynolds).

5. We wish to thank Janet Carey Eldred, Susan Jarratt, Barbara Tomlinson, and the anonymous consulting readers of *CCC* for their assistance in shaping this essay.

WORKS CITED

Arendt, Hannah. "What Was Authority?" *Authority.* Ed. Carl J. Friedrich. Cambridge: Harvard UP, 1958. 81–112. Vol. 1 of *Nomos.* 34 vols. to date. 1958– .

"Authority." *Oxford English Dictionary.* 2nd ed.

Bakhtin, M. M. "Discourse in the Novel." *The Dialogic Imagination.* Ed. Michael Holquist. Trans. Caryl Emerson and Michael Holquist. Austin: U of Texas P, 1981. 259–422.

Barthes, Roland. "The Death of the Author." *Image-Music-Text.* Trans. Stephen Heath. New York: Hill and Wang, 1977. 142–48.

Bartholomae, David. "Inventing the University." *When a Writer Can't Write: Studies in Writer's Block and Other Composing Process Problems.* Ed. Mike Rose. New York: Guilford, 1985. 134–65.

Bauer, Dale M. *Feminist Dialogics: A Theory of Failed Community.* Albany: State U of New York P, 1988.

———. "The Other 'F' Word: The Feminist in the Classroom." *College English* 52 (Apr. 1990): 385–96.

Berkenkotter, Carol. "Student Writers and Their Sense of Authority over Texts." *College Composition and Communication* 35 (Oct. 1984): 312–19.

Berlin, James A. *Writing Instruction in Nineteenth-Century American Colleges.* Carbondale: Southern Illinois UP, 1984.

Bizzell, Patricia. "Beyond Anti-Foundationalism to Rhetorical Authority: Problems Defining 'Cultural Literacy.'" *College English* 52 (Oct. 1990): 661–75.

———. "Classroom Authority and Critical Pedagogy." *American Literary History* 3 (Winter 1991): 847–63.

———. "Power, Authority, and Critical Pedagogy." *Journal of Basic Writing* 10 (Fall 1991): 54–70.

———. "What Happens When Basic Writers Come to College?" *College Composition and Communication* 37 (Oct. 1986): 294–301.

Chase, Geoffrey. "Accommodation, Resistance and the Politics of Student Writing." *College Composition and Communication* 39 (Feb. 1988): 13–22.

Cooper, Marilyn M. "Why Are We Talking about Discourse Communities? Or, Foundationalism Rears Its Ugly Head Once More." *Writing as Social Action.* Portsmouth: Boynton/Cook, 1989. 202–20.

Crowley, Sharon. *The Methodical Memory: Invention in Current-Traditional Rhetoric.* Carbondale: Southern Illinois UP, 1990.

Delpit, Lisa D. "Skills and Other Dilemmas of a Progressive Black Educator." *Harvard Educational Review* 56 (Nov. 1986): 379–85. Rpt. in *Teaching, Teachers, and Teacher Education.* Ed. Margo Okazawa-Rey, James Andersen, and Rob Traver. Cambridge: Harvard Educational Review, 1987. 50–56.

Elbow, Peter. *Writing with Power: Techniques for Mastering the Writing Process.* New York: Oxford UP, 1981.

Faigley, Lester. "Competing Theories of Process: A Critique and a Proposal." *College English* 48 (Oct. 1986): 527–42.

———. *Fragments of Rationality: Postmodernity and the Subject of Composition.* Pittsburgh: U of Pittsburgh P, 1992.

Fish, Stanley. "Anti-Foundationalism, Theory Hope, and the Teaching of Composition." *The Current in Criticism: Essays on the Present and Future of Literary Theory.* Ed. Clayton Koelb and Virgil Lokke. West Lafayette, IN: Purdue UP, 1987. 65–79. Rpt. in *Doing What Comes Naturally: Change, Rhetoric, and the Practice of Theory in Literary and Legal Studies.* Durham, NC: Duke UP, 1989. 342–55.

Flower, Linda, Victoria Stein, John Ackerman, Margaret J. Kantz, Kathleen McCormick, and Wayne C. Peck. *Reading-to-Write: Exploring a Cognitive and Social Process.* New York: Oxford UP, 1990.

Foucault, Michel. "The Eye of Power." *Power/Knowledge: Selected Interviews and Other Writings, 1972–1977.* Ed. Colin Gordon. Trans. Colin Gordon, Leo Marshall, John Mepham, and Kate Soper. New York: Pantheon, 1980. 146–65.

Frey, Olivia. "Beyond Literary Darwinism: Women's Voices and Critical Discourse." *College English* 52 (Sept. 1990): 507–26.

Giroux, Henry A. "Liberal Arts Education and the Struggle for Public Life: Dreaming about Democracy." *South Atlantic Quarterly* 89 (Winter 1990): 113–38. Rpt. in *The Politics of Liberal Education.* Ed. Darryl J. Gless and Barbara Herrnstein Smith. Durham, NC: Duke UP, 1992. 119–44.

———. *Schooling and the Struggle for Public Life: Critical Pedagogy in the Modern Age.* Minneapolis: U of Minnesota P, 1988.

Hamilton-Wieler, Sharon. "Empty Echoes of Dartmouth: Dissonance Between the Rhetoric and the Reality." *Writing Instructor* 8 (Fall 1988): 29–41.

Harris, Joseph. "The Idea of Community in the Study of Writing." *College Composition and Communication* 40 (Feb. 1989): 11–22.

Hoagland, Sarah Lucia. "Some Thoughts about 'Caring.'" *Feminist Ethics*. Ed. Claudia Card. Lawrence: UP of Kansas, 1991. 246–63.

Herzberg, Bruce. "Michel Foucault's Rhetorical Theory." *Contending with Words: Composition and Rhetoric in a Postmodern Age*. Ed. Patricia Harkin and John Schilb. New York: MLA, 1991. 69–81.

Jones, Kathleen B. "On Authority: Or, Why Women Are Not Entitled to Speak." *Authority Revisited*. Ed. J. Roland Pennock and John W. Chapman. New York: New York UP, 1987. 152–68. Vol. 29 of *Nomos*. 34 vols. to date. 1958–.

———. "The Trouble with Authority." *Differences* 3 (Spring 1991): 104–27.

Kent, Thomas. "On the Very Idea of a Discourse Community." *College Composition and Communication* 42 (Dec. 1991): 425–45.

Kremers, Marshall. "Sharing Authority on a Synchronous Network: The Case for Riding the Beast." *Papers from the Fifth Computers and Writing Conference*. Spec. issue of *Computers and Composition* 7 (Apr. 1990): 33–44.

Lamb, Catherine E. "Beyond Argument in Feminist Composition." *College Composition and Communication* 42 (Feb. 1991): 11–24.

Mandler, George. *Cognitive Psychology: An Essay in Cognitive Science*. Hillsdale, NJ: Erlbaum, 1985.

Miller, Susan. *Textual Carnivals: The Politics of Composition*. Carbondale: Southern Illinois UP, 1991.

Rosenblum, Nancy L. "Studying Authority: Keeping Pluralism in Mind." *Authority Revisited*. Ed. J. Roland Pennock and John W. Chapman. New York: New York UP, 1987. 102–30. Vol. 29 of *Nomos*. 34 vols. to date. 1958–.

Schiappa, Edward. Response to Thomas Kent. *College Composition and Communication* 43 (Dec. 1992): 522–23.

Schriver, Karen A. "Connecting Cognition and Context in Composition." *Methods and Methodology in Composition Research*. Ed. Gesa Kirsch and Patricia A. Sullivan. Carbondale: Southern Illinois UP, 1992. 190–216.

Schweickart, Patrocinio P. "Reading, Teaching, and the Ethic of Care." *Gender in the Classroom: Power and Pedagogy*. Ed. Susan L. Gabriel and Isaiah Smithson. Urbana: U of Illinois P, 1990. 78–95.

Sennett, Richard. *Authority*. New York: Vintage, 1980.

Sirc, Geoffrey, and Tom Reynolds. "The Face of Collaboration in the Networked Writing Classroom." *Papers from the Fifth Computers and Writing Conference*. Spec. issue of *Computers and Composition* 7 (Apr. 1990): 53–70.

Tompkins, Jane. "Fighting Words: Unlearning to Write the Critical Essay." *Georgia Review* 42 (Fall 1988): 585–90.

Trimbur, John. "Consensus and Difference in Collaborative Learning." *College English* 51 (Oct. 1989): 602–16.

Wall, Susan, and Nicholas Coles. "Reading Basic Writing: Alternatives to a Pedagogy of Accommodation." *The Politics of Writing Instruction: Postsecondary*. Ed. Richard Bullock and John Trimbur. Portsmouth, NH: Boynton/Cook, 1991. 227–46.

Weber, Max. *The Theory of Social and Economic Organization*. Ed. Talcott Parsons. Trans. A. M. Henderson and Talcott Parsons. New York: Oxford UP, 1947.

Young, Iris Marion. *Justice and the Politics of Difference*. Princeton: Princeton UP, 1990.

WORKS CITED IN AFTERWORD

Mortensen, Peter, and Gesa E. Kirsch, eds. *Ethics and Representation in Qualitative Studies of Literacy*. Urbana: NCTE, 1996.

sex, lies, and manuscript: Refiguring Aspasia in the History of Rhetoric
Cheryl Glenn

NOTES

1. I am grateful to Robert Connors for the print, to Cynthia Selfe for sharing her work on Aspasia, and to Jon Olson for his careful readings of this essay.
2. Bodily definition maps out class as well as gender: "Silence, the closed mouth, is made a sign of chastity. And silence and chastity are, in turn, homologous to women's enclosure within the house" (Stallybrass 127).

3. In general, feminist scholarship has helped create a space for reconceiving and thereby transforming the rhetorical tradition (Ballif, Biesecker, Bizzell and Herzberg, Blair and Kahl, Glenn, Jarratt and Ong, Lunsford, Peaden, Selfe, Swearingen). Edward P. J. Corbett anticipated women's rhetorical contributions: "Rhetoric is one of the most patriarchal of all the academic disciplines. But because of the active feminist movement, we may be on the verge of recovering the names of women who could lay claim to being rhetors" (577). Patricia Bizzell and Bruce Herzberg include for consideration the rhetorical discourse of a number of Renaissance and post-Renaissance women. Andrea Lunsford is editing a forthcoming collection of women's rhetorical endeavors, *Reclaiming Rhetorica.*

4. A regendered history does not reproduce traditional gendered categories of the "empowered" and "other," nor does it reduce them, but rather imagines gender as an inclusive and nonhierarchical category. In *Rhetoric Retold* I locate women's contributions to and participation within the rhetorical tradition and write them into an expanded, inclusive tradition.

5. Joan Kelly tells us that "women's history has a dual goal: to restore women to history and to restore our history to women. . . . In seeking to add women to the fund of historical knowledge, women's history has revitalized theory, for it has shaken the conceptual foundations of historical study" ("Social Relation" 1). Carole Blair contests the histories of rhetoric both when she interrogates the politics of preservation as well as when, together with Mary L. Kahl, she argues for revising the history of rhetorical theory. And Barbara Herrnstein Smith's "Contingencies of Value" eloquently demonstrates how such inclusions do and must problematize genres.

6. Miletus had relatively large numbers of literate citizens, among them the philosophers Anaximander, Anaximenes, and Thales (Harris 63; Vernant, *Origins* 127, *Myth and Thought* 343 ff.; Kirk and Raven 73 ff.). In *Myth and Society in Ancient Greece,* Jean-Pierre Vernant writes that alongside moral thought, "a philosophy of nature starts to develop . . . in the Greek cities of Asia Minor. The theories of these first 'physicists' of Ionia have been hailed as the beginning of rational thought as it is understood in the West" (96).

7. Most scholars (Bloedow, Flaceliere, Halperin, Just, Keuls, Licht, Ober, for instance) have labeled Aspasia a courtesan, schooled in intellectual and social arts. But both Eva Cantarella and William Courtney argue that the Athenian suspicion and misunderstanding of such a powerful, political, non-Athenian, unmarriageable woman living with their controversial leader, Pericles, led automatically to the sexualized and undeserved label of *hetaera;* Nicole Loraux refers to Aspasia as a foreigner and as a nonpolitician; Mary Ellen Waithe calls her "a rhetorician and a member of the Periclean Philosophic Circle" (*History* 75); and Susan Cole writes only of Aspasia's intellectual influence and measure of literacy (225).

8. Cantarella clearly describes the *hetaera* as "more than a casual companion," "more educated than a woman destined for marriage, and intended 'professionally' to accompany men where wives and concubines could not go [namely social activities and discussions]" (30). "This relationship was meant to be somehow gratifying for the man, even on the intellectual level, and was thus completely different from men's relationships with either wives or prostitutes" (31). Robert Flaceliere agrees that "in practice, if not in law, they [hetaerae] enjoyed considerable freedom" (130). He goes on to quote Athenaeus' *Deipnosophists* (XIII) that the *hetaerae* "applied themselves to study and the knowledge of the sciences" (131).

9. H. D. F. Kitto places Athenian women in Oriental seclusion: "In this pre-eminently masculine society women moved in so restricted a sphere that we may reasonably regard them as a 'depressed area'" (222). He accepts such restrictions as sensible.

10. Keuls suggests that a female educational underground might have been the source of male anxiety, for the philosopher Democritus wrote, "Let a woman not develop her reason, for that would be a terrible thing" (Fr. 110, qtd. in Keuls 104). And a character in a lost play by Menander pronounced that "he who teaches letters to his wife is ill-advised: He's giving additional poison to a horrible snake" (Fr. 702 K, ibid.).

11. Roger Just reminds us that "Aspasia's notoriety and the popular resentment her supposed influence aroused should . . . be remembered—a resentment transmuted into mockery by comedy" (21). In the *Acharnians,* Aristophanes writes that the Megarians "abducted *two* whores from Aspasia's stable in Athens" (523); Plutarch writes that Cratinus, "in downright terms, calls her a harlot": "To find him a Juno the goddess of lust/Bore that harlot past shame,/ Aspasia by name" (201). Flaceliere assures us that "the Athenian comic poets never tired of repeating that Aspasia led a life of debauchery, though apparently she was as well behaved as she was well informed, and even a scholar" (131). And Cantarella writes, "It is not surprising that many Athenians hated Aspasia. She was not like other women; she was an intellectual" (54–55).

12. Pomeroy, *Goddesses* 89; Just 144. But Hans Licht (a pseudonym for Paul Brandt) explains that "the preference for Aspasia shown by Pericles afforded a welcome excuse for his opponents to attack him; people would not hear of a woman having anything to say in political life, especially one who was not an Athenian but was brought from abroad, and even from Ionia . . . , which was notorious for the immorality of its women. . . . Hence she was severely criticized by the comic poets. . . . [A]ccording to a statement in Athenaeus . . . she was said to have maintained a regular brothel. . . . When she was accused of *asebeia* (impiety) and procuring, Pericles defended her and secured her acquittal" (352–53).

13. Pierre Vidal-Naquet writes that "the sole civic function of women was to give birth to citizens. The conditions imposed upon them by Pericles' law of 451 was to be the daughter of a citizen and a citizen's daughter" (145). Women of low reputation could be spoken of publicly and freely; for some, Aspasia fit such a category. For others, Aspasia's intellectual and political gifts earned her a measure of public distinction. David Schaps asserts that there were three categories of women whose "names could be mentioned freely: disreputable women, opposing women, and dead women" (329).

14. *Areté* is variously referred to as various manifestations of human excellence: as virtue (the prerequisite of a good human life; cf. Democritus' "On *Areté* or Manly Virtue"), as a combination of self-control, courage, and justice, as moral nobility, or as valor. See Gutherie III: 253 ff.

15. The tautology of Jean Bethke Elshtain's argument rightly encompasses Aspasia: "I am not impressed with the claims made for powerful women who influenced men through their private activities—in Athenian society this claim is frequently made for the *hetaera*. . . . Were such 'women-behind-the-men' to have attempted to enter the public arena to speak with their own voices, they would have been roundly jeered, satirized, and condemned" (14–15 n. 11).

16. Taylor quotes from the fragments of the *Aspasia* collated in H. Dittmar's *Aeschines von Sphettos*.

17. In her epistolary arguments with Abelard, Heloise relies on ancient authorities. In one particular case, her crown *auctoritas* is Aspasia. Quoting from the now-missing text of Aeschines, Heloise argues for the excellence of a good wife and a good husband (Moncrieff 58). In her reading of Heloise's letters, Andrea Nye challenges the philosophical community to be "informed by Heloise's and Aspasia's wisdom, their subtle, sensitive, mobile, flexible women's tongues." She also wants us to admit that "a woman can be the teacher of a man" (17).

18. Thucydides writes, "Everyone who wishes to, both citizens and foreigners, can join in the procession, and the women who are related to the dead are there to make their laments at the tomb" (II.34).

19. For example, recent issues of both *CCC* (October 1992) and *Rhetoric Society Quarterly* (Winter 1992) center on feminist readings of rhetoric and composition, theories and practices. Also see notes 3, 4, 5.

WORKS CITED

Aristophanes. *The Acharnians.* Trans. Douglass Parker. *Four Comedies.* Ed. William Arrowsmith. Ann Arbor: U of Michigan P, 1969. 99–112.
Aristotle. *Politics.* Trans. H. Rackman. Cambridge: Loeb-Harvard UP, 1977.
———. *The Rhetoric and Poetics of Aristotle.* Trans. W. Rhys Roberts and Ingram Bywater. New York: Modern Library, 1984.
Athenaeus. *The Deipnosophists.* Trans. Charles Burton Gulick. Cambridge: Harvard UP, 1967.
Ballif, Michelle. "Re/Dressing Histories: Or, On Re/Covering Figures Who Have Been Laid Bare by Our Gaze." *Rhetoric Society Quarterly* 22 (1992): 91–98.
Biesecker, Barbara. "Coming to Terms with Recent Attempts to Write Women into the History of Rhetoric." *Philosophy and Rhetoric* 25 (1992): 140–61.
Bizzell, Patricia. "Opportunities for Feminist Research in the History of Rhetoric." *Rhetoric Review* 11 (1992): 50–58.
———. "*The Praise of Folly,* the Woman Rhetor, and Post-Modern Skepticism." *Rhetoric Society Quarterly* 22 (1992): 7–17.
Bizzell, Patricia, and Bruce Herzberg. *The Rhetorical Tradition: Readings from Classical Times to the Present.* Boston: Bedford-St. Martin's, 1990.
Blair, Carole. "Contested Histories of Rhetoric: The Politics of Preservation, Progress, and Change." *Quarterly Journal of Speech* 78 (1992): 403–28.
———, and Mary L. Kahl. "Introduction: Revising the History of Rhetorical Theory." *Western Journal of Speech Communication* 54 (1990): 148–59.

Bloedow, Edmund F. "Aspasia and the 'Mystery' of the Menexenos." *Wiener Studien (Zeitschrift fur Klassiche Philologie und Patristic)* Neu Folge 9 (1975): 32–48.

Cantarella, Eva. *Pandora's Daughters.* 1981. Baltimore: Johns Hopkins UP, 1987.

Cicero. *De Inventione, De Optimo Genere, Oratorum, Topica.* Trans. H. M. Hubbell. Cambridge: Harvard UP, 1976. 1–348.

———. *De Oratore.* 2 vols. Trans. E. W. Sutton. Cambridge: Harvard UP, 1979.

Cole, Susan Guettel. "Could Greek Women Read and Write?" Foley 219–45.

Corbett, Edward P. J. *Classical Rhetoric for the Modern Student.* 3rd ed. New York: Oxford UP, 1990.

Courtney, William. "Sappho and Aspasia." *Fortnightly Review* 97 (1912): 488–95.

Delcourt, Marie. *Pericles.* N.p.: Gallemard, 1939.

Elshtain, Jean Bethke. *Public Man, Private Woman.* Princeton: Princeton UP, 1987.

Ferguson, Margaret W., Maureen Quilligan, and Nancy J. Vickers, eds. *Rewriting the Renaissance.* Chicago: U of Chicago P, 1986.

Flaceliere, Robert. *Love in Ancient Greece.* 1960. Trans. James Cleugh. London: Frederick Muller, 1962.

Foley, Helene P. *Reflections of Women in Antiquity.* New York: Gordon, 1981.

Glenn, Cheryl. "Author, Audience, and Autobiography: Rhetorical Technique in *The Book of Margery Kempe.*" *College English* 53 (1992): 540–53.

———. *Rhetoric Retold: Regendering the Tradition from Antiquity Through the Renaissance.* Carbondale: Southern Illinois UP, 1998.

Gutherie, W. K. C. *A History of Greek Philosophy.* 6 vols. Cambridge: Cambridge UP, 1969.

Halperin, David M. *One Hundred Years of Homosexuality.* New York: Routledge, 1990.

Harris, William V. *Ancient Literacy.* Cambridge: Harvard UP, 1989.

Jarratt, Susan C. "The First Sophists and Feminism: Discourses of the 'Other.'" *Hypatia* 5 (1990): 27–41.

———. "Performing Feminisms, Histories, Rhetorics." *Rhetoric Society Quarterly* 22 (1992): 1–6.

———. *Rereading the Sophists: Classical Rhetoric Refigured.* Carbondale: Southern Illinois UP, 1991.

Jarratt, Susan L., and Rory Ong. "Aspasia: Rhetoric, Gender, and Colonial Ideology." Lunsford, *Reclaiming Rhetorica,* 1995.

Jehlen, Myra. "Archimedes and the Paradox of Feminist Criticism." Warhol and Herndl. 75–96.

Just, Roger. *Women in Athenian Law and Life.* London: Routledge, 1989.

Kelly, Joan. "The Social Relation of the Sexes." Kelly 1–18.

———. *Women, History, and Theory: The Essays of Joan Kelly.* Chicago: U of Chicago P, 1984.

Keuls, Eva C. *The Reign of the Phallus.* New York: Harper, 1985.

Kirk, G. S., and J. E. Raven. *The Presocratic Philosophers.* Cambridge: Cambridge UP, 1962.

Kitto, H. D. F. *The Greeks.* Middlesex: Penguin, 1951.

Kneupper, Charles, ed. *Rhetoric and Ideology: Compositions and Criticisms of Power.* Arlington: Rhetoric Society of America, 1989.

Laqueur, Thomas. *Making Sex.* Cambridge: Harvard UP, 1990.

Licht, Hans [Paul Brandt]. *Sexual Life in Ancient Greece.* London: Abbey Library, 1932.

Loraux, Nicole. *The Invention of Athens.* Trans. Alan Sheridan. Cambridge: Harvard UP, 1986.

Lunsford, Andrea A., ed. *Reclaiming Rhetorica.* Pittsburgh: U of Pittsburgh P, 1995.

Mackin, James A., Jr. "Schismogenesis and Community: Pericles' Funeral Oration." *Quarterly Journal of Speech* 77 (1991): 251–62.

Moncrieff, C. K. *The Letters of Abelard and Heloise.* New York: Knopf, 1942.

Nye, Andrea. "A Woman's Thought or a Man's Discipline? The Letters of Abelard and Heloise." *Hypatia* 7 (1992): 1–22.

Ober, Josiah. *Mass and Elite in Democratic Athens.* Princeton: Princeton UP, 1989.

Peaden, Catherine. "Feminist Theories, Historiographies, and Histories of Rhetoric: The Role of Feminism in Historical Studies." Kneupper 116–26.

Plato. *Euthyphro, Apology, Crito, Phaedo, Phaedrus.* Trans. H. N. Fowler. Cambridge: Harvard UP, 1977. 405–579.

———. *Gorgias.* Trans. W. C. Helmbold. Indianapolis: Bobbs-Merrill, 1952.

———. *Republic.* Trans. Paul Shorey. 2 vols. Cambridge: Harvard UP, 1982.

———. *Timaeus, Critias, Cleitophon, Menexenus, Epistles.* Trans. R. G. Bury. 1929. London: Heinemann-Loeb, 1981.

Plutarch. *The Lives of the Noble Grecians and Romans.* Trans. John Dryden. Rev. Arthur Hugh Clough. New York: Modern Library, 1932.

Pomeroy, Sarah. *Goddesses, Whores, Wives, and Slaves.* New York: Schocken, 1975.

———. *Women's History and Ancient History.* Chapel Hill: U of North Carolina P, 1991.

Quintilian. *Institutio Oratoria.* Trans. H. E. Butler. 1920. 4 vols. London: Heinemann, 1969.

Schaps, David M. "The Woman Least Mentioned: Etiquette and Women's Names." *Classical Quarterly* 27 (1977): 323–31.

Scott, Joan Wallach. *Gender and the Politics of History.* New York: Columbia UP, 1988.

Selfe, Cynthia. "Aspasia: The First Woman Rhetorician." Unpublished essay.

Smith, Barbara Herrnstein. "Contingencies of Value." *Contingencies of Value.* Cambridge: Harvard UP, 1988. 30–53.

Sprague, Rosamond Kent, ed. *The Older Sophists.* Columbia: U of South Carolina P, 1972.

Stallybrass, Peter. "Patriarchal Territories: The Body Enclosed." Ferguson et al. 123–44.

Swearingen, C. Jan. *Rhetoric and Irony.* New York: Oxford UP, 1991.

Taylor, A. E. *Plato, the Man and his Work.* 7th ed. London: Methuen, 1960.

Thucydides. *History of the Peloponnesian War.* Trans. Rex Warner. London: Penguin, 1954.

Vernant, Jean-Pierre. *Myth and Society in Ancient Greece.* 1974. New York: Zone, 1980.

———. *Myth and Thought Among the Greeks.* 1965. London: Routledge, 1983.

———. *The Origins of Greek Thought.* 1962. Ithaca: Cornell UP, 1982.

Vidal-Naquet, Pierre. *The Black Hunter.* Trans. Andrew Szegedy-Maszak. Baltimore: Johns Hopkins UP, 1986.

Waithe, Mary Ellen, ed. *A History of Women Philosophers, Vol. I/600 BC–500 AD.* Dordrecht: Martinus Nijhoff, 1987. 4 vols.

Warhol, Robyn R., and Diane Price Herndl. *Feminisms.* New Brunswick: Rutgers UP, 1991.

Xenophon. *Memorabilia and Oeconomicus.* Trans. E. C. Marchant. Cambridge: Harvard UP, 1988.

WORKS CITED IN AFTERWORD

Campbell, JoAnn. *Towards a Feminist Rhetoric: The Writings of Gertrude Buck.* Pittsburgh: U of Pittsburgh P, 1996.

Garratt, Mary. "How Far We've Come; How Far We Have to Go." *Making and Unmaking the Prospects for Rhetoric.* Ed. Theresa Enos. Mahwah: Erlbaum, 1997. 43–48.

Glenn, Cheryl. *Rhetoric Retold: Regendering the Tradition from Antiquity Through the Renaissance.* Carbondale: Southern Illinois UP, 1997.

Hobbs, Catherine, ed. *Nineteenth-Century Women Learn to Write.* Charlottesville: U of Virginia P, 1994.

Kates, Susan. "The Embodied Rhetoric of Hallie Quinn Brown." *College English* 59 (Jan. 1997): 59–71.

Logan, Shirley Wilson. *With Pen and Voice: A Critical Anthology of Nineteenth-Century African-American Women.* Carbondale: Southern Illinois UP, 1995.

Ratcliffe, Krista. *Anglo-American Feminist Challenges to the Rhetorical Traditions: Virginia Woolf, Mary Daly, Adrienne Rich.* Carbondale: Southern Illinois UP, 1996.

Wertheimer, Molly Meijer, ed. *Listening to Their Voices: The Rhetorical Activities of Rhetorical Women.* Columbia: U of South Carolina P, 1997.

Wu, Hui. "The Enthymeme Examined from the Chinese Value System." *Making and Unmaking the Prospects for Rhetoric.* Ed. Theresa Enos. Mahwah: Erlbaum, 1997. 115–222.

Importing Composition: Teaching and Researching Academic Writing Beyond North America
Mary N. Muchiri, Nshindi G. Mulamba, Greg Myers, and Deoscorous B. Ndoloi

NOTES

1. For some examples of this process of transformation across cultures, see Edward Said, "Travelling Theory,"; Tzvetan Todorov; Cantor, *Inventing the Middle Ages;* and Ngugi wa Thiongo, *Moving the Centre.*

2. Mary, Mulamba, Greg, Ndoloi. Teachers who puzzle over class lists with names from many nations will recognize our problem here. University forms require a Christian name and a surname; teachers use one for informal address, and the other for formal address, alphabetization, and official documents. But for many people, African or Asian, the names do not work this way. We finally just used the names we use with each other, even if that means two Christian names and two family names. What counts as informality is, of course, culture-specific.

3. These studies are often supported in Britain by such agencies as the British Council, which funds research studentships and conferences as part of its mission to spread British language and culture (and thus trade and political links). Thus they are part of an explicit program of promoting the national interest.

4. To take some examples, our various projects at Lancaster have drawn on papers on disciplinary differences in texts (MacDonald; Kaufer and Geisler); on discourse communities (Harris; Raforth); on collaborative writing (Bruffee); on genre (Miller); on theories of composing (Faigley); and on textual construction of knowledge (Bazerman). This is not meant as a list of Greatest Hits, but as an indication of the eclectic range of studies that, for one reason or another, cross the Atlantic.

5. We are particularly indebted to Brigid Ballard in Australia, Hywel Coleman at Leeds, John Swales's appendix to *Genre Analysis,* Jin and Cortazzi, and to our colleagues Roz Ivanic and Romy Clark.

6. *Matatus* (in Nairobi) and *daladalas* (in Dar) are the mainstays of local transportation; minibuses that run out to the suburbs or to outlying towns, they are typically cheap, crowded, fast, and (to the uninitiated) terrifying.

7. This is not counting colleges of education in these countries or the new private universities in Kenya or Zaire, which serve different functions.

8. Ngugi wa Thiongo comments bitterly on this break in discussing African writers' use of European languages: "The writers who emerged after the Second World War were nearly all the products of universities at home or abroad. Some of these universities like Ibidan in Nigeria, Makerere in Uganda, Achimota in Ghana had been set up to manufacture an elite that could later make a good partnership with the British ruling circles. The curricula reflected little or nothing of the local surroundings. The situation was quite ironic. Many of the educated Africans had been sent to the higher seats of learning by their peasant communities so they could come back and help in the collective survival. But at the end of the educational pipeline, these select few had more in common with the very forces which kept the communities down in the first place" (106). We may disagree with Ngugi's socialist evaluation of this movement, but the sense of being sent out as a lifeline is recognized by many university students in highly selective systems.

9. Mulamba was taking the phrase from MacDonald.

10. For a good introduction to the issues of multilingualism in literacy research, see David Barton, *Literacy: An Introduction to the Ecology of Written Language,* Ch. 5. On the relation of English to Neo-colonialism, see any of Ngugi's non-fiction collections; on linguistic imperialism from the point of view of critical English language teaching, see Phillipson.

11. For background on English in Africa, see Schmied; Rubagumya; Mulamba; and Bloor and Bloor.

12. On Critical Language Awareness and Knowledge About Language in the LJK, see Clark and Ivanic.

13. Now Kenya has embarked on a new system called 8-4-4, with two years less of secondary school and one more year of university, that does include a foundation year for everyone. It is partly in response to these changes, and a huge influx of new, less prepared students, that Mary is studying the examination system.

14. This word was "fascinating" in an earlier draft, but Mary revised it. Let's not overdo the enthusiasm.

15. Students resisting the changes were taken away from the university by troops, and three lecturers who supported the students were summarily transferred within 24 hours.

16. Latest reports are that all holders of doctorates in the department, not being Shaba, have had to leave.

17. See Hairston, "Diversity," and responses in later issues.

18. Ngugi wa Thiongo comments on his teaching in exile: "The kind of issues we are raising in classrooms of Yale would land all of us in prison for anything between one and ten years" (157). There is in his comment thankfulness for the real academic freedoms in the US, but also a kind of astonishment at the innocence of the US students, who do not realize that these issues (in this case, the relation of literature to society) could be (and in his view, *should* be) explosive and threatening to those in power.

WORKS CITED

Anderson, Benedict. *Imagined Communities: Reflections on the Origin and Spread of Nationalism.* Revised ed. London: Verso, 1991.

Ballard, Brigid. "Improving Students' Writing: An Integrated Approach to Cultural Adjustment." *Common Ground: Shared Interests in ESP and Communication Studies.* Ed. H. Swales, R. Williams and Kirkman. Oxford: Pergamon, 1984.

Bartholomae, David. "Inventing the University." *When a Writer Can't Write: Studies in Writer's Block and Other Composing-Process Problems.* Ed. Mike Rose. New York: Guilford, 1985. 134–135.

Barton, David. *Literacy: An Introduction to the Ecology of Written Language.* Oxford: Blackwell, 1994.

Bazerman, Charles. *The Informed Writer.* 2nd ed. Boston: Houghton, 1985.

———. *Shaping Written Knowledge: The Genre and Activity of the Experimental Article in Science.* Madison, WI: U of Wisconsin P, 1988.

Bizzell, Patricia. "College Composition: Initiation into the Academic Discourse Community." *Curriculum Inquiry* 12 (1982): 191–207.

———. *Academic Discourse and Critical Consciousness.* Pittsburgh: U of Pittsburgh P, 1992.

Bloor, Tom, and Meriel Bloor. "English in Post-colonial Africa." *Language and Power.* Ed. Romy Clark, et al. London: BAAL and CILT, 1991.

Bruffee, Kenneth. "Social Construction, Language, and the Authority of Knowledge." *College English* 48 (1986): 773–90.

Cantor, Norman F. *Inventing the Middle Ages: The Lives, Works, and Ideas of the Great Mediaevalists of the Twentieth Century.* New York: Morrow, 1991.

Clark, Romy. "Principles and Practice of CLA in the Classroom." *Critical Language Awareness.* Ed. Norman Fairclough. Harlow: Longman, 1992. 117–40.

Elbow, Peter. "Reflections on Academic Discourse: How It Relates to Freshmen and Colleagues." *College English* 53 (1991): 135–55.

Faigley, Lester. "Competing Theories of Process: A Critique and a Proposal." *College English* 48 (1986): 527–42.

———. *Fragments of Rationality: Postmodernity and the Subject of Composition.* Pittsburgh: U of Pittsburgh P, 1992.

Hairston, Maxine. "Diversity, Ideology, and Teaching Writing." *CCC* 43 (1992): 179–93.

Harris, Joseph. "The Idea of Community in the Study of Writing." *CCC* 40 (1989): 11–22.

Irvine, Patricia, and Nan Elsasser. "The Ecology of Literacy: Negotiating Writing Standards in a Caribbean Setting." *The Social Construction of Written Communication.* Ed. Bennett A. Raforth and Donald L. Rubin. Norwood, NJ: Ablex, 1988. 304–20.

Ivanic, Roz. "Critical Language Awareness in Action." *Knowledge About Language.* Ed. Ronald Carter. London: Hodder, 1990. 122–32.

Ivanic, Roz, and John Simpson. "Who's Who in Academic Writing." *Critical Language Awareness.* Ed. Norman Fairclough. Harlow: Longman, 1992. 141–73.

Jin, Lixian, and Martin Cortazzi. "Cultural Orientation and Academic Language Use." *Language and Culture: Papers from the Annual Meeting of the British Association for Applied Linguistics.* Ed. David Graddol, Linda Thompson, and Mike Byram. Clevedon: Multilingual Matters, 1993. 84–97.

Kaufer, David S., and Cheryl Geisler. "Novelty in Academic Writing." *Written Communication* 6 (1989): 286–311.

Labov, William. *The Logic of Nonstandard English.* Urbana, IL: NCTE, 1967.

MacDonald, Susan Peck. "A Method for Analyzing Sentence Level Differences in Disciplinary Knowledge Making." *Written Communication* 9 (1992): 533–69.

Muchiri, Mary N. "The Effect of Institutional and National Cultures on Examinations: The University in Kenya." *Society and the Language Classroom.* Ed. Hywell Coleman. Cambridge: Cambridge UP, 1997.

Muhlhauser, Peter, and Rom Harré. *Pronouns and People: The Linguistic Construction of Social and Personal Identity.* Oxford: Blackwell, 1990.

Mulamba, Nshindi G. "English Teaching in Zaire: Objectives and Users' Needs." *Teaching and Researching Language in African Classrooms.* Ed. C. M. Rubagumya. Clevedon, UK: Multilingual Matters, 1994.

Ngugi wa Thiongo. *Moving the Centre.* London: Heinemann, 1993.

Phillipson, Roger. *Linguistic Imperialism.* New York: Oxford UP, 1992.

Raforth, Bennett A. "Discourse Community: Where Writers, Readers, and Text Come Together." *The Social Construction of Written Communication.* Ed. Bennett A. Raforth and Donald L. Rubin. Norwood, NJ: Ablex, 1988. 131–46.

Rose, Mike. *Lives on the Boundary.* New York: Free Press, 1989.

Rubagumya, Casmir M., ed. *Teaching and Researching Language in African Classrooms.* Clevedon: Multilingual Matters, 1994.

Said, Edward. "Travelling Theory." *The World, the Text, and the Critic.* Cambridge, MA: Harvard UP, 1983. 226–47.

Sampson, Gloria Paulik. "Exporting Language Teaching Methods from Canada to China." *TESL Canada Journal/Revue TESL du Canada* 1 (1984): 19–31.

Schmied, Josef. *English in Africa: An Introduction.* Harlow: Longman, 1991.

Shaughnessy, Mina. *Errors and Expectations: A Guide for the Teacher of Basic Writing.* New York: Oxford UP, 1977.

Swales, John. *Genre Analysis: English in Academic and Research Settings.* Cambridge: Cambridge UP, 1990.

Todorov, Tzvetan. *Literature and Its Theorists: A Personal View of Twentieth Century Criticism.* London: Routledge, 1988.

WORKS CITED IN AFTERWORD

Canarajah, A. Suresh. "'Nondiscursive' Requirements in Academic Publishing, Material Resources of Periphery Scholars, and the Politics of Knowledge Production." *Written Communication* 13 (Oct. 1996): 435–72.

Mulamba, Nshindi G. "Deconstructing Student Viva: A Master-Apprentice Perspective." *Les Annales de L'Université de Mbujimayi,* forthcoming.

Pennycook, Alistair. "Borrowing Others' Words: Text, Ownership, Memory, and Plagiarism." *TESOL Quarterly* 30 (Summer 1996): 201–30.

Silva, Tony, Ilona Leki, and Joan Carson. "Broadening the Perspective of Mainstream Composition Studies: Some Thoughts from the Disciplinary Margins." *Written Communication* 14 (1997): 398–428.

The Rhetorician as an Agent of Social Change
Ellen Cushman

NOTES

1. While this idea of the physical surroundings having significance isn't novel, it is often overlooked as a tool to critique our own context, the university setting. Bakhtin, for example, finds that "everything ideological possesses semiotic value" (929). In other words, "any physical body may be perceived as an image. . . . Any such artistic-symbol image to which a particular physical object gives rise is already an ideological product. The physical object is converted into a sign" (928). This allows us to critique how even the construction and setting of the Approach can take on significance. Thus, "a sign does not simply exist as a part of a reality—it reflects and refracts another reality" (929). The stairway is a sign of the connection between the city and university, a connection that needs maintenance.

2. Cheryl Geisler offers a cogent summary of these ideas in the second chapter of her recent book on expertise in the academy. Further, Bowles and Gintis present a Marxist analysis of the ways in which schooling serves to perpetuate the class hierarchies necessary for modern capitalism to flourish.

3. Mike Rose's latest work reveals the rich and complicated ways in which primary and secondary school teachers still move toward this democratic principle. His book challenges the country's impoverished discourse used to describe education, and takes steps toward envisioning a discourse of possibility centered on a fundamental belief in the strong ties between education and democracy.

4. Activist research expands upon notions of *praxis.* Originally developed by Aristotle, praxis resembles "phronesis, action adhering to certain ideal standards of good (ethical) or effective (political) behavior" (Warry 157). Marx embellished this political agenda for participation in his "Eleventh Thesis," and some applied anthropologists have since adopted praxis as a term describing, loosely, ethical action in the research paradigm geared toward social change. For example, Johannsen brings postmodern critiques to ethnography and finds that research as praxis demands that we actively participate in the community under study. While expanding the participant side of social science research is necessary in order to achieve praxis, examinations of praxis in social sciences are for the most part "wholly theoretical and with only occasional reference to methodological or pragmatic concerns associated with planned change, intervention, or action research" (Warry 156). Even though applied anthropology, a subfield of anthropology, provides theoretical models for how praxis

enters into the research paradigm (see Lather), many scholars still need to do the work of intervention at the community level.

5. Some may question the potency of such activism and the extent to which these literacy events really did challenge the status quo. In his classic social scientific study entitled *Black Families in White America,* Andrew Billingsley depicts some of the historically rooted everyday struggles of African-Americans in achieving social and geographic mobility. Education "is a most reliable index and a potent means of gaining social mobility and family stability in our society. The absence of systematic training and education during slavery and reconstruction depressed the social structure of the Negro people most, just as the presence of education in small and scattered doses proved such a powerful source of achievement" (79). Raejone's application essay for college suggests one way we worked against this historically rooted absence of education that Billingsley mentions in an effort to create the presence of higher education in her family. Similarly, the literacy which contributed to Lucy's relocation to a suburban area loosens "the tight white noose around the central cities [that] has kept Negro families from being able to penetrate suburbia in any appreciable numbers" (74).

6. Different types of discourses constitute different contexts, an idea Bakhtin described well as the difference between "everyday genre" ("what ordinary people live, and their means for communicating with each other") (*Dialogic* 428) and "social languages" ("the discourse peculiar to a specific system of society (professional, age group, etc.)") (430). Thus, "heteroglossia" allows us to understand how "language is stratified, not only into linguistic dialects . . . but also—and for us this is the essential point—into languages that are socioideological: languages of social groups" (272).

7. I found Pauline Uchmanowicz' recent article particularly disturbing. She describes her "dog years" as a part-time college writing instructor at two institutions where she teaches "between twelve and sixteen scheduled classes per week" and is paid "a little over half the salary of a full-time teacher for teaching double the course load" (427). Add to this burden her commute of five hundred miles every week and lack of job security, and I begin to worry that the luxury needed for activism is out of reach for many composition teachers.

8. Jennifer Gore insightfully critiques "some shortcomings in the construction of 'empowerment' by critical and feminist educational discourses which create problems internal to their discourses" (54). For example, she identifies how the agency of empowerment stems from the teacher, while the subject of empowerment is usually the student. As the center of activity in these discourses, the teacher is more important than the students—a practice that contradicts the theoretical emphasis on the student.

9. I think many of us work so closely from Freire's model of pedagogy we believe the impact his literacy projects have will be in equal kind and type to the impact our classes may have. However, Freire cautions "it is impossible to export pedagogical practices without reinventing them. Please, tell your fellow American educators not to import me. Ask them to recreate and rewrite my ideas" (Macedo xiv).

10. James Scott, a political scientist, makes a convincing argument against the label of "false consciousness." His ethnographic fieldwork in Malaysia depicts not only the social forces which daily influence Malay peasants, but also reveals their unseen defiance and hidden ideology used to challenge these forces. He differentiates between those public and private behaviors that relate to power struggles. The peasants appear to cordially accept the authority of landlords in their public encounters with them; however, they actually fought this oppressive ideology in private spheres. This resistance Scott terms as the difference between "public and hidden transcripts," and reveals how these peasants have devised a number of ways to challenge their subordination. These forms of often "low profile, undisclosed resistance" create the infrapolitics of larger society (198), but also suggest the limitation of the notion of false consciousness. Since most researchers and teachers aren't privy to the hidden ideologies of their informants/students, we miss the ways in which resistance and critical consciousness are constructed in subtle, often unnoticed ways.

11. For example, Keith Basso found that Western Apaches have clever, elaborate systems of mocking "the Whiteman." Luis Moll immersed himself in a Mexican-American community in Tucson, Arizona, and characterized complex systems of knowledge and strategies shared by households in order to "enhance survival within harsh social conditions" (225). Carol Stack in *All Our Kin* found African-Americans devised many strategies to undermine the welfare institution's influence in their fund allocation, including withholding information, foot dragging, and misrepresenting census data. Perhaps with more access to their students' communities, critical scholars would not be so quick in their dismissal of their students' critical abilities.

12. Fundamental to activism, I believe, is not only a basic trust in the potential and abilities of people, but also a basic mistrust of assessments that diminish and dismiss others. Brian Fay, a philosopher of social science, describes the ontological values of critical social science this way: "An active creature . . . is intelligent, curious, reflective, and willful" (50). All people have these qualities regardless of their socio-cultural circumstances. Activism has roots in a genuine care and respect for all people. Anything short of this and our work quickly takes on a paternalistic, patronizing, and ingenuine flavor.
13. Pierre Bourdieu's sociological model of the *habitus* describes dispositions as patterns of behavior, such as language behaviors, which then combine to make the "acquired system of generative schemes, the habitus" (54).
14. As Giroux points out, "though Freire provides the broad theoretical framework needed to help bridge the gaps that plague radical education in North America, his analysis in key places warrants further substantiation and depth" (136). For the sake of this argument, I believe that in North America, teaching is different from activism. Teaching is institutionalized because a certain social status is constructed around the knowledge used in this role (see Berger and Luckmann). Yet, activism in the politics of the community is not institutionalized, per se, rather, it's a civic duty that all people can potentially fulfill without needing specialized knowledge related to schooling (Geisler; Bowles and Gintis). So activism is more closely related to civic duty and teaching related to an institution. I see these two activities on the same continuum of the democratic process, as potentially mutually informative, but not interchangeable projects of democracy.

WORKS CITED

Bakhtin, Mikhail. *The Dialogic Imagination.* Ed. Michael Holquist. Austin: U of Texas P, 1981.
———. "Marxism and the Philosophy of Language." *The Rhetorical Tradition.* Ed. Patricia Bizzell and Bruce Herzberg. Boston: St. Martin's, 1990. 924–63.
Basso, Keith. *Portraits of "The Whiteman."* Cambridge: Cambridge UP, 1979.
Beach, Richard, et al., eds. *Multidisciplinary Perspectives on Literacy Research.* Urbana: NCTE, 1992.
Berger, Peter, and Thomas Luckmann. *The Social Construction of Reality.* New York: Anchor, 1966.
Billingsley, Andrew. *Black Families in White America.* New York: Simon, 1968.
Bourdieu, Pierre. *The Logic of Practice.* Stanford: Stanford UP, 1990.
Bowles, S., and H. Gintis. *Schooling in Capitalist America.* New York: Basic, 1976.
Fay, Brian. *Critical Social Science.* Ithaca: Cornell UP, 1987.
Freire, Paulo. *Pedagogy of the Oppressed.* New York: Herder, 1971.
Geisler, Cheryl. *Academic Literacy and the Nature of Expertise.* Hillsdale: Erlbaum, 1994.
Gere, Anne Ruggles. "The Extracurriculum of Composition." *CCC* 45 (1994): 75–92.
Giddens, Anthony. *The Constitution of Society.* Berkeley: U of California P, 1981.
Giroux, Henry. *Ideology, Culture, and the Process of Schooling.* Philadelphia: Temple UP, 1981.
Gore, Jennifer. "What We Can Do for You! What *Can* 'We' Do for 'You'?" *Feminisms and Critical Pedagogy.* Ed. Jennifer Gore and Carmen Luke. London: Routledge, 1992. 54–73.
Halloran, S. Michael. "Afterthoughts on Rhetoric and Public Discourse." *Pre/Text: The First Decade.* Ed. Victor Vitanza. Pittsburgh: U of Pittsburgh P, 1993. 52–68.
Herzberg, Bruce. "Community Service and Critical Teaching." *CCC* 45 (1994): 307–19.
Johannsen, Agneta. "Applied Anthropology and Post-Modernist Ethnography." *Human Organization* 51 (1992): 71–81.
Lather, Patti. "Research as Praxis." *Harvard Educational Review* 56 (1986): 257–77.
Macedo, Donald. Preface. *Politics of Liberation.* Ed. Peter McLaren and Colin Lankshear. Routledge: London, 1994. xiii–xix.
Moll, L. "Literacy Research in Community and Classrooms: A Sociocultural Approach." Beach et al. 211–244.
Moll, L., and Stephen Diaz. "Change as the Goal of Educational Research." *Anthropology and Education Quarterly* 18 (1987): 300–11.
Powell, Malea. "Custer's Very Last Stand: Rhetoric, the Academy, and the Un-Seeing of the American Indian." Unpublished essay. 1995.
Rose, Mike. *Lives on the Boundary.* Boston: Penguin, 1989.
———. *Possible Lives: The Promise of Public Education in America.* New York: Houghton, 1995.
Schiappa, Edward. "Intellectuals and the Place of Cultural Critique." *Rhetoric, Cultural Studies, and Literacy.* Ed. Frederick Reynolds. Hillsdale: Erlbaum, 1995. 26–32.
Scott, James C. *Domination and the Arts of Resistance.* New Haven: Yale UP, 1990.
———. *Weapons of the Weak.* New Haven: Yale UP, 1985.

Stack, Carol. *All Our Kin: Strategies for Survival in a Black Community.* New York: Harper, 1974.

Uchmanowicz, Pauline. "The $5,000–$25,000 Exchange." *College English* 57 (1995): 426–47.

Warry, Wayne. "The Eleventh Thesis: Applied Anthropology as Praxis." *Human Organization* 51 (1992): 155–63.

Moments of Argument: Agonistic Inquiry and Confrontational Cooperation
Dennis A. Lynch, Diana George, and Marilyn M. Cooper

AUTHORS' NOTE

The citation for Andy Rooney's column, as it originally appeared in *CCC*, is incorrect. Readers can find this column in the *Chicago Tribune,* March 14, 1992, or in the *Sacramento Union,* March 10, 1992, p. A7.

WORKS CITED

Bauer, Dale M. "The Other 'F' Word: The Feminist in the Classroom." *College English* 52 (1990): 385–97.

Berlin, James. *Rhetorics, Poetics, and Cultures.* Urbana: NCTE, 1996.

Bizzell, Patricia. *Academic Discourse and Critical Consciousness.* Pittsburgh: U of Pittsburgh P, 1992.

———. "Power, Authority, and Critical Pedagogy." *Journal of Basic Writing* 10 (1991): 54–70.

Buker, Eloise A. "Rhetoric in Postmodern Feminism: Put-Offs, Put-Ons, and Political Plays." *The Interpretive Turn: Philosophy, Science, Culture.* Ed. David R. Hiley, James F. Bohman, and Richard Shusterman. Ithaca: Cornell UP, 1991. 218–45.

Churchill, Ward. "Crimes Against Humanity." *Z Magazine* March 1993: 43–48.

Elbow, Peter. "The Doubting Game and the Believing Game." *Writing Without Teachers.* New York: Oxford UP, 1973. 147–91.

Faigley, Lester. *Fragments of Rationality: Postmodernity and the Subject of Composition.* Pittsburgh: U of Pittsburgh P, 1992.

Fitts, Karen, and Alan W. France, eds. *Left Margins: Cultural Studies and Composition Pedagogy.* New York: State U of New York P, 1995.

Gage, John. "John Gage's Assignment." *What Makes Writing Good: A Multiperspective.* Ed. William E. Coles, Jr., and James Vopat. Lexington: Heath, 1985. 98–105.

———. "An Adequate Epistemology for Composition: Classical and Modern Perspectives." *Essays on Classical Rhetoric and Modern Discourse.* Ed. Robert J. Connors, Lisa S. Ede, and Andrea A. Lunsford. Carbondale: Southern Illinois UP, 1984. 152–70.

Graff, Gerald. *Beyond the Culture Wars: How Teaching the Conflicts Can Revitalize American Education.* New York: Norton, 1993.

Hanson, Jeffery R., and Linda P. Rouse. "Dimensions of Native American Stereotyping." *American Indian Culture and Research Journal* 11 (1987): 33–58.

hooks, bell. *Talking Back: Thinking Feminist, Thinking Black.* Boston: South End, 1989.

———. *Teaching to Transgress: Education as the Practice of Freedom.* New York: Routledge, 1994.

Jarratt, Susan C. *Rereading the Sophists: Classical Rhetoric Refigured.* Carbondale: Southern Illinois UP, 1991.

———. "Feminism and Composition: The Case for Conflict." *Contending With Words: Composition and Rhetoric in a Postmodern Age.* Ed. Patricia Harkin and John Schilb. New York: MLA, 1991. 105–24.

Lunsford, Andrea A., and Lisa S. Ede. "On Distinctions between Classical and Modern Rhetoric." *Essays on Classical Rhetoric and Modern Discourse.* Ed. Robert J. Connors, Lisa S. Ede, and Andrea A. Lunsford. Carbondale: Southern Illinois UP, 1984. 37–50.

MacLean, Norman. *A River Runs Through It.* New York: Pocket, 1992.

Menand, Louis. "The War of All against All." *The New Yorker* 14 March 1994: 74–85.

Pratt, Richard H. "Remarks on Indian Education." *Americanizing the American Indians: Writings by the "Friends of the Indian" 1880–1900.* Ed. Francis Paul Prucha. Cambridge: Harvard UP, 1973. 277–80.

Reisner, Marc. *Cadillac Desert.* New York: Viking, 1986.

Rooney, Andy. "Indians Have Worse Problems." *Chicago Tribune* 14 March 1991: 14, 92.

Rouse, Linda P., and Jeffery R. Hanson. "American Indian Stereotyping, Resource Competition, and Status-based Prejudice." *American Indian Culture and Research Journal* 15 (1991): 1–17.

Young, Iris Marion. *Justice and the Politics of Difference.* Princeton: Princeton UP, 1990.

Dispositions toward Language: Teacher Constructs of Knowledge and the Ann Arbor Black English Case
Arnetha Ball and Ted Lardner

ACKNOWLEDGMENTS

We would like to thank Ralph Stevens, Margaret Marshall, and Thomas Fox for their careful reading and suggestions on this article.

WORKS CITED

Abrahams, Roger. *Deep Down in the Jungle.* Chicago: Aldine, 1970.
Balester, Valerie. *Cultural Divide.* Portsmouth: Boynton, 1993.
Ball, Arnetha. "Community-Based Learning in Urban Settings as a Model for Educational Reform." *Applied Behavioral Science Review* 3 (1995): 127–46.
———. "Cultural Preference and the Expository Writing of African-American Adolescents." *Written Communication* 9 (1992): 501–32.
———. "Expository Writing Patterns of African-American Students." *English Journal* 85 (1996): 27–36.
Ball, Arnetha F., Kimberley C. Broussard and Delvin M. Dinkins. "Investigating Interactive Discourse Patterns of African American Females in Community-Based Organizations." American Educational Research Association. New Orleans, 1994.
Bowie, R., and C. Bond. "Influencing Future Teachers' Attitudes Toward Black English: Are We Making a Difference?" *Journal of Teacher Education* 45 (1994): 112–18.
Brannon, Lil. "Toward a Theory of Composition." *Perspectives on Research and Scholarship in Composition.* Ed. Ben McLelland and Timothy R. Donovan. New York: MLA, 1985. 6–25.
"Commentary." *Black Caucus Notes.* Urbana: NCTE. March, 1997.
Delpit, Lisa. "Education in a Multicultural Society: Our Future's Greatest Challenge." *Journal of Negro Education* 61(1992): 237–49.
Dyson, A. H., and S. W. Freedman. *Critical Challenges for Research on Writing and Literacy: 1990–1995.* Technical Report No. 1–B. Berkeley, CA: Center for the Study of Writing, 1991.
Fulkerson, Richard. "Composition Theory in the Eighties: Axiological Consensus and Paradigmatic Diversity." *CCC* 41 (1990): 409–29.
Foster, Michelle. "Educating for Competence in Community and Culture: Exploring the Views of Exemplary African-American Teachers." *Urban Education* 27 (1993): 370–94.
———."Effective Black Teachers: A Literature Review." *Teaching Diverse Populations Formulating a Knowledge Base.* Ed. Etta Hollins, Joyce King, and W. Hayman. Albany: State U of New York P, 1994. 225–42.
Gilyard, Keith. *Voices of the Self.* Detroit: Wayne State UP, 1992.
Giroux, Henry. *Teachers as Intellectuals: Toward a Critical Pedagogy of Learning.* New York: Bergin, 1988.
Harkin, Patricia. "The Postdisciplinary Politics of Lore." *Contending With Words.* Ed. Patricia Harkin and John Schilb. New York: MLA, 1991. 124–38.
Howard, Harry, Lee H. Hansen and Thomas Pietras. *Final Evaluation: King Elementary School Vernacular Black English Inservice Program.* Ann Arbor: Ann Arbor Public Schools, 1980.
Knoblauch, C. H. "Rhetorical Constructions: Dialogue and Commitment." *College English* 50 (1988): 125–40.
Labov, William. "Recognizing Black English in the Classroom." *Black English Educational Equity and the Law.* Ed. John W. Chambers. Ann Arbor: Karoma, 1983. 29–55.
Lu, Min-zhan. "Conflict and Struggle: The Enemies or Preconditions of Basic Writing?" *College English* 54 (1992): 887–913.
McLeod, Susan H. "Pygmalion or Golem? Teacher Affect and Efficacy." *CCC* 46 (1995): 369–86.
Memorandum Opinion and Order. Martin Luther King Elementary School Children v. Ann Arbor School District Board. Civil Action No. 7–71861. 473 F. Supp. 1371 (1979).
Morgan, Marcyliena. "Indirectness and Interpretation in African American Women's Discourse." *Pragmatics* 1 (1991): 421–51.
North, Stephen. *The Making of Knowledge in Composition.* Portsmouth: Boynton, 1987.
Pang, Valerie O., and Velma Sablan. "Teacher Efficacy: Do Teachers Believe They Can Be Effective with African American Students?" American Educational Research Association. San Francisco: 1995.
Phelps, Louise Wetherbee. "Practical Wisdom and the Geography of Knowledge in Composition." *College English* 47 (1992): 338–56.

Quality Education for Minorities Project. *Education That Works: An Action Plan for the Education of Minorities.* Cambridge: MIT P, 1990.

Richardson, Elaine. *Where Did That Come From? Black Talk for Black Student Talking Texts.* MA Thesis. Cleveland State U, 1993.

Schilb, John. *Between the Lines: Relating Composition Theory and Literary Theory.* Portsmouth: Boynton, 1996.

———. "Cultural Studies, Postmodernism, and Composition." *Contending With Words.* Ed. Patricia Harkin and John Schilb. New York: MLA, 1991. 173–88.

Shaughnessy, Mina. *Errors and Expectations.* New York: Oxford UP, 1977.

Smitherman, Geneva. *Talkin and Testifyin.* Detroit: Wayne State UP, 1977.

———. "'What Go Round Come Round': *King* in Perspective." *Harvard Educational Review* 51 (1981): 40–56.

Spears, A. K. "Are Black and White Vernaculars Diverging?" *American Speech* 62 (1987): 48–55, 71–72.

West, Cornel. *Race Matters.* Boston: Beacon, 1993.

Williams, Patricia J. *The Alchemy of Race and Rights.* Cambridge, MA: Harvard UP, 1991.

Zeichner, Kenneth M. "Alternative Paradigms in Teacher Education." *Journal of Teacher Education* 34 (1983): 3–9.

Zeichner, Kenneth, and Daniel Liston. "Teaching Student Teachers to Reflect." *Harvard Educational Review* 57 (1987): 23–48.

Zemelman, Steven, and Harvey Daniels. *A Community of Writers.* Portsmouth: Boynton, 1988.

NOTES ON CONTRIBUTORS

Arnetha Ball is an associate professor in the Language, Literacy, and Learning program in the School of Education at the University of Michigan. Her research interests focus on linking sociocultural and linguistic theory concerning the oral and written literacy patterns of marginalized, vernacular English speakers and the practices of teachers in urban and inner-city schools in the United States, in community-based organizations, and in the cross-national contexts of classrooms and community-based organizations in South Africa and the United States.

David Bartholomae is professor and chair in the Department of English at the University of Pittsburgh. He was an assistant professor there when he wrote "The Study of Error." Bartholomae is coeditor of the University of Pittsburgh Press series "Composition, Literacy, and Culture." He is the author (with Anthony Petrosky) of *Ways of Reading; The Teaching of Writing;* and *Facts, Artifacts, and Counterfacts.*

Richard Braddock served as chair of the first-year rhetoric program at the University of Iowa during the 1960s and 1970s. Although he is known for such scholarly efforts as "The Frequency and Placement of Topic Sentences in Expository Prose" and *Research in Written Composition,* he was primarily a facilitator. Braddock founded the journal *Research in the Teaching of English,* chaired the Conference on College Composition and Communication in the crucial years of the early 1960s, organized a program for training teachers of writing in high schools, and served on countless committees of the National Council of Teachers of English. In these and other ways, he influenced many in the field of composition studies.

Robert Brooke is professor of English at the University of Nebraska–Lincoln, where he has taught since 1984. He currently edits the Studies in Writing and Rhetoric monograph series, directs the Nebraska Writing Project, and continues to write about the negotiation of identity, especially in rural and academic settings.

Linda Carey was a Ph.D. student at Carnegie Mellon University at the time that she coauthored "Detection, Diagnosis, and the Strategies of Revision." Carey currently lives in Ireland.

Marisa Castellano is a research associate in the Graduate School of Education at the University of California, Berkeley. At the time when she and her coauthors wrote "Remediation as Social Construct: Perspectives from an Analysis of Classroom Discourse," she was a graduate student in that program. Recent publications include "'It's Not Your Skills, It's the Test': Gatekeepers for Women in Skilled Trades" and "Teaching and Learning in a Job Training Program: An Interactional Sociolinguistic Perspective." Her current research interests include adult education, vocational education, and the educational implications of welfare reform.

Robert J. Connors is professor of English and director of the University Writing Center at the University of New Hampshire, Durham. At the time he wrote "The Rise and Fall of the Modes of Discourse," he was teaching at Louisiana State University. His most recent publication is *Composition-Rhetoric: Backgrounds, Theory, and Pedagogy.* Currently, he is working on the rhetoric of citation structures and the history of process pedagogy in writing.

Marilyn M. Cooper is associate professor of humanities at Michigan Technological University. Cooper works in an interdisciplinary way in composition studies, focusing particularly on interactions of writing and society. She is currently working on a book on postmodern subjects in writing classrooms.

Jim W. Corder had a long and rich history at Texas Christian University. He earned his B.A. and M.A. degrees at TCU, then received his Ph.D. at the University of Oklahoma. He returned to TCU in 1958 and taught there until his death in August 1998. Corder was a passionate and committed teacher with interests in many subjects, including writing and the relationship between literature and rhetoric. He published many works, including textbooks, scholarly works, and creative nonfiction. He helped to establish the rhetoric program at TCU and directed the dissertations of many graduate students in the program. Corder served as chair of the English department, and later as dean of the College of Arts and Sciences. He wrote and edited numerous books and articles and was active in the Conference on College Composition and Communication and in other professional associations. Those who knew Corder remember him for his self-deprecating wit and generous nature.

Ellen Cushman is a lecturer in the college writing programs at the University of California, Berkeley. When she wrote "The Rhetorician as an Agent of Social Change," she was a Ph.D. student at Rensselaer Polytechnic Institute. Recent publications include *The Struggle and the Tools: Oral and Literate Strategies in an Inner City Community,* the ethnography upon which her *CCC* article was based. Cushman's current research interests include a service learning course she has developed in which undergraduates read literacy scholarship and act as participant observers in a YMCA afterschool program.

Frank D'Angelo is professor emeritus of English at Arizona State University. At the time that he wrote his Braddock essay, he was an assistant professor of English at that same institution. Recent publications include "The Rhetoric of Ekphrasis," "Professing Rhetoric and Composition," and "In Search of the American Dream." He is currently revising the manuscript of his forthcoming text, *From Narrative to Argument*, which is based on the *Progymnasmata*, a series of exercises in late antiquity designed to introduce students to the study of persuasion.

Lisa Ede is professor of English and director of the Center for Writing and Learning at Oregon State University, where she has taught since 1980. She has published a number of articles and books collaboratively with Andrea A. Lunsford, including *Singular Texts/Plural Authors: Perspectives on Collaborative Writing*. Other publications include *Essays on Classical Rhetoric and Modern Discourse* (with Andrea A. Lunsford and Robert J. Connors) and *Work in Progress: A Guide to Writing and Revising*, now in its fourth edition.

Peter Elbow is professor of English and director of the writing program at the University of Massachusetts at Amherst. At the time that he wrote "The Shifting Relationships between Speech and Writing," he was teaching at the State University of New York at Stony Brook, where he also directed the writing program. Elbow has continued to remain interested in various aspects of voice and writing—but he has also embarked on substantial research on issues of assessment and grading. A collection of Elbow's essays from the last decade is being published by Oxford University Press.

Linda Flower is professor of rhetoric and director of the Center for University Outreach at Carnegie Mellon University. Her current research focuses on how writers construct negotiated meaning in the midst of conflicting internal and social voices in school and inner-city community settings. Flower's recent publications include *Problem Solving Strategies for Writing in College and Community; The Construction of Negotiated Meaning: A Social Cognitive Theory of Writing;* and *Making Thinking Visible: Writing, Collaborative Planning, and Classroom Inquiry.*

Richard C. Gebhardt, now professor of English at Bowling Green State University, was an associate professor of English and the humanities division chair at Findlay College when his article was published in 1977. In the 1980s, Gebhardt published articles on writing processes, collaboration, and other subjects in a number of journals; and from 1987 to 1993 he edited *College Composition and Communication*. His most recent book is *Academic Advancement in Composition Studies: Scholarship, Publication, Promotion, Tenure.*

Diana George is associate professor of cultural theory and composition studies in the humanities department at Michigan Technological University. With John Trimbur, she has just completed the third edition of *Reading Culture: Contexts for Critical Reading and Writing*. She and Trimbur also have two forthcoming pieces: "The Communication Battle: Or, Whatever Happened to the Fourth C?" and "Cultural Studies and Composition: A Bibliographic Essay."

Cheryl Glenn is associate professor of English at Pennsylvania State University. At present, she is working on *Rhetorics of Silence,* a book-length project that interrogates silence as delivery. She wrote "sex, lies, and manuscript: Refiguring Aspasia in the History of Rhetoric" while she was teaching at Oregon State University.

Christina Haas is associate professor of English and an associate in the Center for Research in Workplace Literacy at Kent State University. When "Rhetorical Reading Strategies and the Construction of Meaning" was published, she was finishing her Ph.D. in rhetoric at Carnegie Mellon University and writing a dissertation under the direction of John R. Hayes and Christine Neuwirth. Her current research projects examine the practices of situated literacy in a city government, engineering workgroups, and a medical facility.

Joseph Harris is associate professor of English at the University of Pittsburgh, where he also directs the composition program. He was an assistant professor there when he wrote and published "The Idea of Community in the Study of Writing." Harris is the current editor of *College Composition and Communication* and the author of *A Teaching Subject: Composition Since 1966* and *Media Journal: Reading and Writing about Popular Culture.*

John R. Hayes is professor of psychology and director of the Center for Innovation in Learning at Carnegie Mellon University. He was teaching at CMU at the time he coauthored "Detection, Diagnosis, and the Strategies of Revision." Hayes's current research explores aspects of writing processes through a combination of methodologies including thinking aloud protocols, expert-novice comparisons, experimental studies of comprehension and perception, and naturalistic observation. Recent publications include *The Complete Problem Solver* and (with R. Young, M. Matchett, M. McCaffrey, C. Cochran, and T. Hajduc) *Empirical Research in Literacy: The Emerging Rhetorical Tradition.*

Mary P. Hiatt is professor emerita of the Department of English at Baruch College of the City University of New York; she was teaching at Baruch when she wrote "The Feminine Style: Theory and Fact." Now retired from academe, Hiatt is currently writing mystery fiction—in a terse, feminine style, of course.

Glynda Hull is associate professor of education at the University of California, Berkeley; she was teaching at Berkeley when she wrote her two Braddock essays. As in the past, Hull's research focuses on issues related to students who are labeled "underprepared" as writers, but she has recently broadened the context of her research to include literacy and education programs in the workplace. Recent publications include *Changing Work, Changing Workers: Critical Perspectives on Language, Literacy, and Skills* and *The New Work Order* (with James Gee and Colin Lankshear).

Gesa E. Kirsch is associate executive director at the National Council of Teachers of English and visiting associate professor at the University of Illinois, Urbana–Champaign. When Kirsch and coauthor Peter Mortensen wrote "On Authority in the Study of Writing," she was teaching at Wayne State University. Kirsch's current research interests include feminist critical pedagogy and research methodology; ethics and representation in qualitative research; and theories of audience, authority, and identity. Recent publications include *Ethical Dilemmas in Feminist Research, Ethics and Representation in Qualitative Studies of Literacy* (coedited with Peter Mortensen), and *Women Writing the Academy: Audience, Authority, and Transformation.*

Ted Lardner is associate professor of English at Cleveland State University. His research interests include pedagogical theory in writing studies broadly conceived, especially the relationships between composition and creative writing and between theater arts and performance techniques and the language arts classroom.

Richard Lloyd-Jones is professor emeritus of English at the University of Iowa, where he taught from 1950 to 1997. Lloyd-Jones and Richard Braddock were colleagues in the 1960s and 1970s. Lloyd-Jones served as the chair of the English department from 1976 to 1986. He is a former chair of the Conference on College Composition and Communication and a former president of the National Council of Teachers of English. In 1991 Lloyd-Jones was honored with the CCCC Exemplar Award.

Kay M. Losey is associate professor of English and director of the writing program at the State University of New York at Stony Brook. She was a Ph.D. candidate at the University of California at Berkeley at the time she coauthored "Remediation as Social Construct." Recent publications include *Listen to the Silences: Mexican American Interaction in the Composition Classroom and the Community* and *Generation 1.5 Meets College Composition: Issues in the Teaching of Writing to U.S.-Educated Learners of English as a Second Language.*

Andrea Lunsford has been writing collaboratively with Lisa Ede since the early 1980s, when she taught at the University of British Columbia and they began zooming up and down I–5 to work and play together. Lunsford now teaches at the Ohio State University, where she is interim director of the Center for the Study and Teaching of Writing and Distinguished Professor of English. Lunsford has written and edited a number of books, including *Singular Texts/Plural Authors: Perspectives on Collaborative Writing* (with Lisa Ede), *Reclaiming Rhetorica: Women in the History of Rhetoric, The New St. Martin's Handbook, The Everyday Writer,* and *EasyWriter* (all with Robert J. Connors), and *Everything's an Argument* (with John Ruszkiewicz).

Dennis A. Lynch is assistant professor of English and director of writing programs in the humanities department of Michigan Technological University. Lynch's research interests include student-teacher relations as relations of power, the nature and extent of student autonomy in the writing classroom, and the conditions that make argumentation possible. Recent publications include "Beyond Master and Slave: Themes of Power in the Composition Classroom" and "Rhetorics of Proximity: Empathy in Temple Grandin and Cornel West."

Glenn Matott is professor emeritus of English at Colorado State University, where he taught from 1955 to 1986. In lieu of information about research interests and publications, Matott writes of his current life: "As Martin Buber said of religion, I have abandoned scholarship or scholarship has abandoned me; like Whitman, I loaf and invite my soul."

Keith D. Miller is associate professor of English at Arizona State University, where he served as director of composition between 1993 and 1995. He became interested in rhetoric when, as a senior at Texas Christian University, he took a course from Jim Corder called Rhetoric and Literature. Later, he earned a Ph.D. at Texas Christian University, where he studied with Gary Tate and again with Corder. Miller is the author of the recently reissued *Voice of Deliverance: The Language of Martin Luther King, Jr., and Its Sources.* He and Elizabeth Vander Lei are now working on a book about King's "I Have a Dream."

Peter Mortensen is associate professor of English and director of the writing program at the University of Kentucky. He was an assistant professor at the University of Kentucky when he and Gesa E. Kirsch wrote their CCCC Braddock essay. Mortensen's current research interests include the history of rhetoric and of literacy in the United States. With Janet Carey Eldred, he is completing *Imagining Rhetoric: Women's Civic Rhetoric in Postrevolutionary America.*

Mary N. Muchiri is head of the Department of English at Daystar University, Nairobi. Previously, Muchiri taught in the communication skills Department of Kenyatta University. "Importing Composition: Teaching and Researching Academic Writing Beyond North America" was written while Muchiri held a technical co-operation training fellowship in the Department of Linguistics and Modern English Language at Lancaster University, United Kingdom. Muchiri's current research interests include learning and teaching English in a multilingual situation, computers in linguistic research, the role of women in church and society, and critical thinking and rationality from an African perspective.

Nshindi G. Mulamba teaches at Mbuji-Maya in what is now the Democratic Republic of the Congo. Previously, Mulamba was a lecturer in linguistics at Lubumbashi University, in what was then Zaire. "Importing Composition: Teaching and Researching Academic Writing Beyond North America" was written while Mulamba held a technical co-operation training fellowship in the Department of Linguistics and Modern English Language at Lancaster University, United Kingdom.

Grey Myers is senior lecturer in the Department of Linguistics and Modern English Language at Lancaster University, United Kingdom. Myers's recent publications include *Writing Biology, Words in Ads,* and *Ad Worlds,* as well as a number of articles on aspects of scientific texts. He is currently working on the dynamics of group discussions, as part of a collaborative interdisciplinary research project on "Global Citizenship and the Environment."

Deoscorous B. Ndoloi lectures in the Department of Foreign Languages at the University of Dar es Salaam, Tanzania. "Importing Composition: Teaching and Researching Academic Writing Beyond North America" was written while Ndoloi held a technical co-operation training fellowship in the Department of Linguistics and Modern English Language at Lancaster University, United Kingdom.

Lee Odell is a professor of English and the writing program director at Rensselaer Polytechnic Institute. When he wrote "Teachers of Composition and Needed Research in Discourse Theory," he was teaching in the English department at the State University of New York at Albany. Odell's current research interest is in the integration of visual and verbal elements in "composing." NCTE recently published a new edition of his 1977 collection *Evaluating Writing.*

Mike Rose is professor in the Graduate School of Education and Information Studies and in the writing program at the University of California, Los Angeles. Over the last year or so, he has been studying the cognition involved in doing skilled work.

Karen Schriver is a teacher, researcher, and consultant in document design. She studies how organizations can improve their communications through excellence in writing and visual design. She has held academic positions at Carnegie Mellon University and at the University of Utrecht in the Netherlands (the Belle van Zuylen Chair of Language and Communication). She is currently president of KSA, Document Design and Research. She is winner of five national awards. Her book, *Dynamics in Document Design: Creating Text for Readers,* has been praised by reviewers around the world. She is currently exploring the nature of expertise in document design—asking what it takes to excel in developing communications that orchestrate text, graphics, audio, and video. This research will suggest new ways to help nurture students' developing expertise.

Nancy Sommers is Sosland Director of Writing at Harvard University, where she directs both the expository writing program and the Harvard writing project. At the time that she wrote "Responding to Student Writing," she was not teaching but was "in service of the species" raising her daughters; she was teaching at Harvard when she wrote "Between the Drafts." Currently, Sommers is conducting a longitudinal study of the role of writing in undergraduate education, following the Harvard Class of 2001 through all four years.

James Stratman is associate professor of communication and director of the technical communication program at the University of Colorado at Denver. He was an adjunct assistant professor in the Graduate School of Industrial Administration at Carnegie Mellon University when he coauthored "Detection, Diagnosis, and the Strategies of Revision" with Linda Flower, John R. Hayes, Linda Carey, and Karen Schriver. Stratman's research interests include lay and professional readers' comprehension of legal arguments and legal documents, health risk communications, issues in the courtroom presentation of empirical language and communication studies. His current work focuses on readers' comprehension of citizen-initiated ballot texts. His most recent research appeared in *Forensic Linguistics.*

Stephen P. Witte is currently Knight Professor of composition theory and professor of English at Kent State University where he directs the Center for Research on Workplace Literacy and chairs the program committee for Kent's new doctoral major on Literacy, Rhetoric, and Social Practice. At the time that he wrote "Topical Structure and Revision: An Exploratory Study," Witte was assistant professor of English at the University of Texas at Austin. Cofounder of *Written Communication* in 1984, Witte was recently honored during a reception at CCCC for his fifteen years as editor or coeditor of the journal. Witte's recent publications build on his 1992 "Context, Text, Intertext: Toward a Constructivist Semiotic of Writing," and his current research extends that work even as it seeks—through multiple case studies of workplaces entered by college graduates—to develop an integrated perspective on literacy in advanced workplaces, a perspective that combines elements from non-Saussurean semiotic theory, cognitive theory, and activity theory to understand the roles, uses, and functions of literacy in a variety of professions and occupations.

INDEX